Barbara Reynolds

Thursday July 8th Rather more pleasant. I went into town rather late but nevertheless went to the Sem and got a very comfortable seat. had a little talk with Mr. P. Hobbs. told him he had changed and he said I had changed too. he is not near so handsome Friday 9th I came home at noon but went in again in the evening and went up to Houck's went with them Mrs Boyd & Dr. Schaeffer were along Dr. Lelasmuth was there also after we returned. I remained over night but slept very little as night started home about 5 O'clock Friday 9th and soon father and mother went to town to bring Miss Kester and instead of which Mrs. P. Karit came and we were extremely busy all day but succeeded pretty well so somewhat atoned for the worry. Mag & Ed came out about seven and soon Fred & Mary and then John & Lizzie Koch and our aunt & cousin Misses Kenney 3 Schleys, 3 Houck & Dr. Schaeffer. Lou Lew Mary Len Ella B & Lizzie H. Gin Boyd & Len Jones. Harr Boyd & Mr. Brooks of Balt. & Messrs Geo Birely, Ned Sambill & Lychingno Hodges & Dr. Lelasmuth All seemed to enjoy themselves and remained till after twelve till the last left.
Saturday July 10th Still warm was up early and got the dishes out of the way. Father & mother went into town with Mrs. Karit in the morning and Jane was busy sweeping &c. so I did not get to take my nap till after dinner and I slept nearly all afternoon and did not feel a great deal refreshed so went to bed early at night.

The Diaries of Margaret Scholl Hood
1851-1861

Edited by:

Rose Barquist,

Mary Frear Keeler and Ann Lebherz

PICTON PRESS
CAMDEN, MAINE

The end papers of this book are taken from entries in September 1856 and July 1858. The original diaries of Margaret Scholl Hood are owned by The Historical Society of Frederick County, Inc. and are transcribed and published here with their kind permission. The copyright remains vested in The Historical Society of Frederick County, Inc.

All rights reserved
Copyright © 1992 The Historical Society of Frederick County, Inc.
International Standard Book Number 0-929539-91-5
Library of Congress Catalog Card Number: 91-68231

No part of this publication may be reproduced or transmitted in any form or by any means, electronic or mechanical, including photocopying, recording, or any information storage or retrieval system, without permission in writing from the copyright holder, except for the inclusion of brief quotations in a review.

First printing July 1992

Available from:

Margaret Scholl Hood Diaries
Hood College
Frederick, MD 21701-9988
(301) 696-3480

also available from:

Picton Press
PO Box 1111
Camden, ME 04843-111
Visa/MasterCard (207) 236-6565

Manufactured in the United States of America
Set in 10 point Times Roman type
printed on 60# acid-free paper

CONTENTS

SPECIAL CONTRIBUTORS iv
ACKNOWLEDGEMENTS v
INTRODUCTION vii

THE DIARY

1851 1
1853 53
1854 119
1855 159
1856 211
1857 261
1858 309
1859 355
1860 371
1861 423

ILLUSTRATIONS

Margaret Scholl Hood xii
Dearbought 52
Ceresville Mill 118
Edward A. Shriner 260
Rev. D. Zacharias 370
Evangelical Reformed Church & Chapel, Frederick 370
Manchester Farm 422
Margaret Derr Shriner 427
John Derr, Sr. 427
The Graduating Class of 1868 428
Frederick in about 1850 429
Conewago Chapel 1787 468

BIBLIOGRAPHY 430

APPENDIXES

Appendix I.   Scholl Genealogy Chart 435
Appendix II.   Thomas Genealogy Chart 436
Appendix III.   Derr Genealogy Chart 437
Appendix IV.   1858 Map: south of Frederick 438
Appendix V.   1858 Map: north of Frederick 439
Appendix VI.   1858 Map: Frederick City 440

INDEX OF PLACES 441

INDEX OF PERSONS 445

SPECIAL CONTRIBUTORS

The cost of publishing *The Diaries of Margaret Scholl Hood* has been largely borne by The Historical Society of Frederick County, Inc., Hood College, and the following contributors:

Louise Beachley
Diane Beers
Elizabeth Boyce
Martha E. Church
Joy Derr
Frederick Art Club
Frederick Arts Council
Frederick Hood College Club
Friends of the Hood College Library
Harrisburg Hood College Club
Jacqueline Heatherington
Virginia Hendrickson
Mary Hoffman
Ann and John Holtzinger, Jr.
Mary Frear Keeler
Margaret Larsen
Ann Lebherz
Elizabeth Eckhardt May
Margaret Myers
Eleanor Nelson
Nancy Nolf
George and Muriel Paterson
Douglas and Gordette Ramsburg
Martha Reynolds
Barbara Rickman
Lewis Bunker Rohrbach
Karen Shue
Marie Stauffer
Mary Townley
Lisa Tumpa
Lloyd Wagner
Margaret Weaver
Kathleen Wickman
Elizabeth Wiegand

ACKNOWLEDGMENTS

We are deeply indebted to The Historical Society of Frederick County, Inc., owner of the manuscript, and three successive Presidents, Mr. Hunt Hendrickson, Mr. David Maloney, and Mr. James Singleton, as well as Vice President Col. William Willman and Judith Proffitt, all of whom have warmly supported this project. Mr. William Failor, Chairman of the Publications Committee of the Society, secured the copyright of the microfilmed diary, with the assent of Mrs. Nancy Anderson, one of Margaret Hood's legal heirs. We are grateful to Dr. Edward Papenfuse, State Archivist, who arranged to have the diaries microfilmed. We are grateful also to Martha Reynolds, Director of C. Burr Artz Library, who procured photocopies of the microfilm. The Joseph Henry Apple Library of Hood College, under the direction of Lloyd Wagner and subsequently Charles Kuhn, has generously provided facilities and resources to the editors. The library staff has been steadily helpful. Nancy Nolf, Joy Derr, and Gordette Ramsburg of the Development and College Relations Division at Hood College have enthusiastically assisted in preparing the typescript for publication. Martha E. Church, President of Hood College, has been consistently supportive of the project.

We appreciate permission of the Historical Society to quote from the *Diary of Jacob Engelbrecht*. We also appreciate permission of Melinda Derr Cecil (Mrs. William) to use the manuscript diary of Mary and Alice Derr.

Several organizations have contributed funds for transforming the manuscript pages into typescript. These include the Frederick Arts Council, Frederick Art Club, Frederick Hood Club, The Historical Society of Frederick County, Inc., and Hood College. Supplementing these grants was the Holdcraft-Delaplaine Award given also by the Historical Society. The formidable task of typing from manuscript was accomplished by Polly Sliger and Patricia Lufkin.

Many volunteers from the community have made invaluable contributions to this project. Dr. Adrienne R. Mindel, Professor of History at Hood College, assessed the diaries and recommended publication. For genealogical information we are grateful to Frank Hedges Lewis, Margaret Myers, and George and Donna Russell. Also helpful on various local details were Walter Williams, Dr. James Hammond, Carol Stoel, Angie Brosius, Dr. Sidney Silverman, and Mrs. Peter Dyer. We thank Samuel E. Householder and R. Amelia Moore-Eubinag of the Frederick Planning and Zoning Commission for help in the preparation of maps. Mira Stancioff, Lisa Mangiafica, Eileen Conklin, Cathy Mizell, Charlotte Kessinger, Mary Hargis, Lib Rhoads, and Karen Haje also helped with the typing. We thank them.

Active members of the *Ad Hoc* Committee for the Preservation and Publication of the Margaret Scholl Hood Diaries are:

Rose Barquist, Chairman and Editor
Edward Campbell, Frederick Community College
Joy Derr, Hood College Office of Communications
William Failor, The Historical Society of Frederick County, Inc.
Dr. Mary Frear Keeler, Editor
Charles Kuhn, Hood College Library
Ann Lebherz, Treasurer, Researcher, and Editor
Nancy Nolf, Hood College Office of Centennial
Planning and Programs
Martha Reynolds, C. Burr Artz Library
Helen Smith, The Frederick Art Club
Lloyd Wagner, Hood College Library

INTRODUCTION

The Diaries Come to Light

While working in The Historical Society of Frederick County, Inc., one hot August day in 1983, Judy Proffitt, who was then the curator, made a startling discovery. She found six notebooks with marbleized paper covers that were the diaries of Margaret Scholl, later Mrs. James Mifflin Hood. The year before, in connection with researching a monograph on Margaret Scholl Hood, a search for manuscript material had been made, and nothing was found in Frederick libraries. No one knows when, how or from where the notebooks came, but there they were! The news spread rapidly, and soon Lloyd Wagner of Hood College Library, Martha Reynolds of C. Burr Artz County Library, Ann Lebherz and Rose Barquist, who had written the aforementioned monograph, were spending many hours reading the faded writing on the brownish yellow pages of the old notebooks.

There are six of them. The two earliest were written when she was 14, 15, and 16 years old. They are filled with verses, most of them by friends from her years at Frederick Female Seminary. The remaining four notebooks contain a true diary, with daily entries, recording her life from 1851 until the beginning of the Civil War. She had begun in 1850, although that volume is missing. The first of the four begins, "Margaret Scholl's Journal, Jan. 1st, 1851. Continuation from 1850." The entries for 1851 end with September, and the entire year of 1852 is missing. In 1859 the entries also end in September. Those for 1860 and 1861 become increasingly more intermittent until the dramatic final entry, "There was a battle at Bull's Run."

It was obvious to those of us interested in documentary history that we had stumbled upon a window into Frederick's past. So, together with representatives from The Historical Society and local organizations that had benefitted from Mrs. Hood's support, we held a meeting. And, although we hadn't the slightest idea of how it would be done we called ourselves "The *Ad Hoc* Committee for the Preservation and Publication of the Margaret Scholl Hood Diaries."

In October, 1983, Dr. Adrienne Mindel, a professor in the Department of History at Hood College, assessed the diaries for the committee. She spelled out in detail the value of publishing them for the insights into local history as well as for the view they provide of women's life in the mid-nineteenth century. Consequently, the committee began investigating the long-term possibilities of editing and publishing in addition to addressing the more immediate problems of preservation of the contents of the notebooks.

The preservation problems were solved for us in the spring of 1984 by the State of Maryland and the C. Burr Artz Library. Dr. Edward Papenfuse, of the Hall of Records in Annapolis, had the diaries microfilmed and made a permanent part of Maryland's history. Two copies of the microfilm and the notebooks from which they were made were brought back to Frederick. The notebooks have been returned to the library at The Historical Society of Frederick County, Inc., where they are now under the supervision of the librarian, Angie Brosius. The microfilm was photocopied and bound in two copies by the C. Burr Artz Library in the summer of 1984. One microfilm and a bound photocopy remain there and are available to the public. The other microfilm and photocopy are at the Hood College Library, where the photocopy has been used in the editing process.

Upon reaching the goals of preservation and accessibility, the committee turned its attention to editing, the next step on the road to publication. For editing, a typescript was needed, and typing from a manuscript is slow, expensive work. One hundred fifty dollars from the Frederick Art Club, of which Mrs. Hood was a charter member, started the ball rolling. Polly Sliger began the typing, with Patricia Lufkin later assisting with the use of her word processor. The Frederick Arts Council, the Frederick Hood Club, a further gift from the Frederick Art Club, as well as the money won in the Historical Society of Frederick County sponsored Holdcraft-Delaplaine competition contributed to the cost of typing. As the pages of the typescript became available, the committee began to consider plans for editing the manuscript for eventual publication.

In August, 1985, the long-sought professional editor appeared in the person of Dr. Mary Frear Keeler, a retired professor of history and Dean *Emerita* from Hood College and experienced editor of historical documents. The process began with proofreading the typescript against the manuscript, undertaken by Rose Barquist, and preparing the footnotes, which Ann Lebherz researched.

The Nature of the Diary

The diary is a reflection of the life of a young woman between her 18th and 28th years, living on a farm on the outskirts of Frederick in the mid-nineteenth century. One of the values of Margaret Scholl Hood's diary, besides the mention of many persons, is the frequent reference to events and customs of the region, ranging from women's fashions to household or farm management, to community occurrences such as lectures, concerts, parades, fairs, means of travel, and occasional historical events. Because many of such references are very general or casual, we have provided some annotation to assist the reader to see more clearly the life and the interests of the Frederick community in the 1850s. To a limited extent, we have been able to provide notes pertaining to Baltimore and several other places which Margaret visited. Some of them fill in more of the historical context for her relatively few observations on national trends. For example, although she once attended a performance in Baltimore of *Uncle Tom's Cabin*, her diary did not note a reaction, and her references to "the darkies" were very casual. We have turned for a deeper understanding of some of the political events she mentions to parallel comments by the older Jacob Engelbrecht, whose diary has been printed under the auspices of the Historical Society of Frederick County. Another diary of the same period, kept by Margaret's close friends Mary and Alice Derr, has recently been found. This diary has been graciously lent to us by its present owners, Mr. and Mrs. William Cecil, and provides some other observations on local events. With supplements from such contemporary sources, the Scholl diary gives a picture of life in an agricultural region and thriving small town, as well as the interests and activities of a young woman, fairly well educated for her time, and of her warm friendships and local interests.

Margaret Scholl Hood, 1833-1913

Born on July 7, 1833, Margaret Scholl [Hood] was the only child of Daniel Scholl and Margaret Thomas Scholl. She began her formal education with Hiram Winchester in his school on North Market Street, then was sent to Thorndale, a boarding school in Carroll County. She returned to Frederick to attend the newly established Frederick Female Seminary, where she spent the years 1847 to 1849.

Thereafter, she lived with her parents on Manchester Farm where she helped with household affairs and farm activities, and carried on an active social life with her many friends. She had many suitors, but did not marry until 1873, following her parents' deaths. That year she married James Mifflin Hood, a carriage-maker on South Market Street. Their residence continued to be at Manchester Farm, although they spent parts of the winter at the City Hotel (now Homewood Retirement Center). Margaret had no children, but was very fond of her husband's three children from a previous marriage. After James's death in 1894, Margaret spent her last years at the newly established Woman's College of Frederick (now Winchester Hall) at the invitation of Joseph Henry Apple, President. She died on January 13, 1913, and is buried in Mount Olivet Cemetery.

During her life, Mrs. Hood maintained an active interest in her church and other institutions of Frederick. When she died, this modest little woman showed her tremendous influence in the community; her will, with her personal touches, is a study in itself. Her bequests included gifts to the Evangelical Reformed Church of Frederick, the Home for the Aged, the Frederick Hospital Association, C. Burr Artz Library, Mercersburg Academy, and Franklin and Marshall College. Especially important were her donations to the Woman's College of Frederick, which resulted in the purchase of the land where the College, now given her name, is located. Her support, in the form of matching funds, was an innovation and inspiration to other donors.

Editorial Policies

Because Margaret kept her diary for no eyes but her own, she often wrote as if she were hurrying to get the record of a day's activities on paper. She dutifully listed the dates, but, although her handwriting is quite readable, her words are often crowded together at the margins or the bottom of a page, and she frequently inserted between lines some added detail that had been overlooked. She seems to have noted her comments daily, perhaps in the morning after a busy social evening, and followed an almost customary routine when she was at home on Manchester Farm or in Frederick with friends. Some of her accounts of long visits with out-of-town friends and other travels appear to have been written after she had returned to her home, although retaining her system of dates. To assist the reader we have modified the dates of her entries, including not only the day of the week, but inserting, for the first day of each new month, the year; such as, Sunday, June 1st [1851]. In the manuscript, the number of the year appears only at its start in January, accompanied by some comment about a new year's beginning.

We have included almost all of the entries for the whole period of the diary. At times, however, when a series of entries for consecutive days contains merely notes on the weather or family routine, or with an occasional comment about "no company," we have deleted such series, indicating the omission by a group of asterisks (*****). Nothing of significance has been omitted. Otherwise, the only omissions occur when, because of crowded pages, an occasional word or phrase has been impossible to decipher; in such cases, we have either suggested a word that seems probable, or have noted the passage as illegible. Words that are interlined on a page have been inserted into the text, if the meaning is clear, or have been printed at the end of a sentence, enclosed within slashes (//). Any words inserted by the editors to fill in for the diarist's own omissions, to bring a sentence into correct form, have been included in square brackets [ ].

It has been our goal to preserve the diarist's own style as much as possible. This has meant the retaining of such frequent misspellings as <u>staid</u> for <u>stayed</u>, and often colloquialisms such as omission of <u>the</u> before family names, as Derrs or Houcks. It has been necessary, however, to modernize some spelling when the meaning is not obvious, and especially to provide punctuation for many of the long, run-on sentences in which Margaret listed details of visits to town. We have corrected her unusual habit of using semicolons when apostrophes are called for, have standardized her capitalization, and have corrected such gross grammatical errors as misuse of singular and plural verbs. Perhaps she used such verbs in conversation, as did many country people of the period, but she surely had been taught the correct usage at her schools.

The reader of the diary becomes accustomed to Margaret's abbreviating names of persons and places, such as M. (for Mary), Mag (for Margaret), and B. or Balt. (for Baltimore). These forms we have retained, but for the benefit of the reader we have, in various places in the earlier part of the diary, extended in square brackets an abbreviation or an initial to its full form; for example, E[llen] B[runner]. In our index of names, we have tried to indicate the various abbreviations the diarist has used.

We have not attempted to establish the identity of every one of the many persons the diarist has mentioned, especially visitors from outside of Frederick or acquaintances of the families that she visited in other towns. It has been possible, however, thanks to several local sources in print, to identify many of the relatives, friends, and neighbors of the Scholl family, and in numerous cases to determine, at least approximately, the locations of their homes. We have provided such information about them in our footnotes, and have included also an index for such names and places. In the Appendix there are genealogical charts for the extended Scholl family, and for the Derrs; maps showing the locations in Frederick and in the region of the homes and other places mentioned in the diary; and other materials.

(Photo courtesy Frederick Memorial Hospital)

Margaret Scholl Hood

1851

"May I spend it better and be more useful to mankind and perform better the part assigned to me in the great drama of life."

January 1st, 1851, Wednesday. Still in Baltimore staying with my friend Mary Sauerwein[1], No. 68 Park St. I have passed a Merry Christmas and a happy New Year's day. Today was bright and clear. I have again seen the end of an other year and time has borne on its wings this commencement of an other one. May I spend it better and be more useful to mankind and perform better the part assigned to me in the great drama of life. Neither Mag Derr[2], Coz Ed Shriner[3] or I can have any reason for regretting our visit here commenced last 23rd December. We dressed for the street when we got up but were prevented by company from going out before dinner. Charlie Sadtler was here three times this morning, measured us. I am 5 feet 3 inches.

---

[1] The Sauerwein family of Baltimore was connected with the Scholl and Shriner families through the flour milling business. J. Thomas Scharf, *History of Western Maryland* (2 vols., Philadelphia, 1882), I, 624-625; hereafter cited as Scharf, *Western Maryland*. Another branch of the Sauerweins, Mr. P. Sauerwein's family, lived on a different street. There were daughters Mary and Kate in each household. See also note 9, 1855.

[2] Margaret (Mag) Derr was Margaret Scholl's closest Frederick friend. The Derr family was a very old Frederick family. They lived at "Dearbought" on the Liberty Road just before the Monocacy River crossing. The first house on this plantation was built by Sebastian Derr in 1755, the second built for John Derr, Sebastian's son, in 1776 closer to the Monocacy. T. J. C. Williams, *History of Frederick County Maryland...* (2 vols., Frederick, 1910), II, 1246-1247; hereafter cited as Williams, *History*. See Appendix III; and Roy H. Wampler, *The Derr Family 1750-1986* (Baltimore, 1987), pp. 436-438.

[3] "Coz Ed" was Edward Shriner, son of Cornelius Shriner and Rebecca Scholl, sister of Daniel Scholl. Their residence and their mill are located on the Liberty Road (Route 26) at Ceresville. Scharf, *Western Maryland*, I, 624-625. See Appendix I.

1851

Lizzie Sadtler was here also, remained but a few moments. Katie B[4] & Miss Metzger were here. Kate just came from Fred'k yesterday morning; Miss Fanny Jenks was here also when they were here. After dinner we went out and met Mary and Eliza Jamison; they said they were coming here but E said she would go in and see Fanny Jenks while we were gone, so Mary went shopping with us. We were also at Mr. Wilson's, where Mr. P. B. Rau stays, and were weighed. I weighed 123 lbs with my bonnet & sacque[5]. And as we came home we found there was church at the Dutch Catholic Church, so we came over and remained a few moments and then we all came home. Eliza & Miss Fanny Jenks also came over. We had a mile long talk, and then they left and we were all busy when Mary Bosely and Miss Bausman called; they remained but a short time; then we dressed. Miss Fanny Jenks came over and took tea with us. Mr. Rau came after tea and we all got ready and just as we got to the door we met Charlie Sadtler and we all went out to Mr. Sadtler's and there met beside our own party two Miss Browns, Miss Morris, her friend Miss Gilbert, Miss Morris again, Dr. Mound, Mr. John Morris and Mr. & Mrs. Sadtler. Spent a pleasant evening. There was a bridal scene[6], Kate Sauerwein was the groom, Dr. Mound the bride, and Lizzie J. the bridesmaid. We did not leave Mr. Sadtler's till about half-past eleven o'clock. Mr. Sadtler came home in company with us. The gentleman did not come in but left us at the door. After we came home Mary and I went up and fixed George's and Edward's bed and, Oh, the fun we had about it.

January 2nd, Thursday. A very pretty morning but it clouded over before dinner. Mary and Kate Sauerwein, Mag Derr, Coz Edward and I got ready and took a walk. First we called to see K. Bantz at her Mother's, No. 25 N. Bea St. Staid there a few moments, then proceeded down to Fells Point[7], went around there to see all that was to be seen, and then we got in a

---

[4]Kate was the daughter of Gideon Bantz, who ran a tannery in Frederick. They lived in a house adjoining the Central Hotel on Patrick and Court Streets. C. S. Williams, *Williams' Frederick Directory...* (Silver Spring, MD, 1985), I (1859-1860), 2, 7; hereafter cited as *Williams' Directory*. Kate married Henry G. Davis on February 22, 1853 (see note 13, 1853).

[5]A sacque was a wool wrap, or short coat. Sometimes additional warmth was provided by a quilted silk lining filled with wool wadding. Claudia B. Kidwell, *Suiting Everyone* (Smithsonian Institution Press, Washington, D.C., 1974), p. 63.

[6]The bridal scene was a mock wedding.

[7]Fells Point is an area east of the Baltimore harbor which was largely settled by Quakers. Its fine harbor provided an area for shipping and shipbuilding. Sherry H. Olson, *Baltimore, The Building of an American City* (Baltimore, 1980), pp. 8, 9, 20.

Omnibus[8] and rode up to corner of Market and Howard Sts. and from there walked home; stopped at Mr. Wilson's store and caught Mr. Rau Philopoena[9], and then came on home, and when we arrived there found Capt. Steiner, Sallie Moon and Mrs. John Rau had been here to see us. I was very sorry we were not at home as I am very anxious to see her. I wrote a letter to Mother to send by Coz E. this evening but he did not go to-day, as something prevented and he did not go. Mrs. John Bayfield was here immediately after dinner. I think [her] a pleasant lady; she gave us a very polite invitation for us to visit her. Charlie Sadtler was here a little; Lizzie & her nephew Willie were here also. While we were at tea Mr. P. Rau came and he, George & Edward went out some where. While [here] Mr. Rau handed Miss Derr & I each a package and said he was going to try woman's curiosity and that we must not open it till he went, and we did not. We found it to be a beautiful China inkstand intended for a Philopoena from him. Charlie was here a short time after tea.

January 3rd, Friday. Mary S[auerwein] and I went to market and from there up to see Kate Bantz a few moments and, as we were coming away we met Sarah Moon at the door who said she was coming round to see us and we went on home. Very soon Sarah came round and remained a right long time. After dinner Eveline Ware and Mely Sauerwein called to see us. Coz Ed left this evening for home. We were quite sorry he went. M[ag] Derr had some idea of going home with him but she abandoned the plan. Mary Sauerwein, Mag Derr and I went out to Mrs. Steiner's on W. Lombard St., 225, and we met Miss Birely, old Mr. V. B. & Mr. L. Birely, Mr. Beard & Gorman I. Roach, Mr. & Mrs. Steiner; spent a delightful evening & about 9 o'clock Geo. Sauerwein (the writer) came for us. In consequence of the noise inside he had to pull the bell, rap at the door & window some ten times, before he was able to enter into the play of jogging along, which was in progress. Mr. Beard & G[orman] accompanied Mary & Mag & led the way so fast that I & Mr. S[auerwein] had difficulty in keeping with them. The girls invited them in but they had only half a notion and deferred it to another time when they would be able to stay longer.

---

[8]An omnibus was a four wheeled vehicle with seats along the sides and sometimes on the roof. At this time it was pulled by a horse. *Webster's Dictionary.*

[9]Philopoena is a game in which each of two persons, who have shared twin halves of a nut, tries to draw the other into paying a penalty or giving a present as a penalty when certain conditions have been fulfilled. *Webster's Dictionary.*

1851

January 4th, Saturday. When we got up we found it had snowed just a little, scarce enough to cover the ground, but it cleared away towards dinner, and after dinner we dressed ourselves and went out. Called at Mr. P. Sauerwein's to see the girls and from there we went to Mr. John Rau's store and afterwards out to old Mr. Rau's, Penn. Avenue, and as we came back met old Mr. Rau and Charlie Sadtler, who came home with Mag D[err] & Kate & I, and we stopped at Mr. R[au]'s store and Mr. J[ohn] R[au] came home with Mary & I. Afterwards we all went to market and Charlie too; he treated us to candies and he left us at the door, and after supper Lizzie Jenks came round and spent the evening.

Sunday [January] 5th. It is very cold today. Sarah Moon called according to promise and Mag D[err], Mary S. & myself went with her for Kate B[antz] and from there went to Charles St. Church and heard a very good sermon from Rev. Mr. Hurst. We came home from church to dinner. After dinner a short time Mr. P. Rau came down here and soon Capt. Steiner & Lady, and when they left we got ready and called K[ate] B[antz] and all went to St. Paul's Church; heard a very [good] sermon from Rev. Mr. Baker and from there we took a long walk out Charles St. & Madison and from there came home very cold. At night we all went to hear Dr. Plummer and when we came home found Mr. Charlie Sadtler and Mr. D[err] here but they left very soon.

Monday [January] 6th. It was warmer a good deal to-day than it has been. Sarah Moon called here early and I went out with her; she called at Mr. Rau['s] so of course [I] had an introduction and a lump of sugar in the bargain and from there we went up to see K[ate] Bantz and from there we met Mary Phelps & Mrs. W. Boyd. Mary P[helps], S[arah] Moon and I took a walk down Market St. and I bought myself a fluting iron[10] and then came on home. After dinner Kate B[antz] called for us and we all called to see Miss S. Metzger and thence down to Mrs. Strohn's where Mr. Sauerwein stays & were weighed; 122 1/2 lbs, lost 1/2 lb. Kate B. stopped at Miss Metzger's and all the rest of us came on home and found Miss Jenks here and also that Mr. Rau had been down here and left an invitation for us for Tuesday evening. Mr. Sauerwein walked home with us from the store and down to Capt. Steiner's door but there left us. We then met Mr. Birely, Miss Bausman, Mrs. Munder, Messrs. Munder, Gorman, Beard & Birely. Mr.

---

[10]A fluting iron is especially shaped for pressing material into pleated or grooved forms. *Webster's Dictionary.*

1851

Sauerwein came for us. Messrs. Gorman & Beard came home with Mag & Mary & I; spent a pleasant evening. Came home about 1/2 past 11.

Tuesday Jan. 7th. A very pretty day, much warmer. Kate B[antz] was around here and said her sister would like us to come to dine with her so we told her we would avail ourselves of her kind invitation. Mary then went to market & when she came home we three went into Mrs. J. Sadtler's to see Miss Jenks and while there Mr. P. Rau and Mrs. P. Sauerwein called to see us but we saw Mrs. P. S. at Mrs. J. Sadtler's. We went round to Mrs. T. Bantz['s] about twelve o'clock and there met Miss Wechebeger, and Mrs. Drakely & little son were there to dine. Kate B. and all of us got ready & came round home and Miss Jenks & us all went to Mr. Rau's and there met Misses C. & K. Sadtler but they left immediately and we staid to tea. Mr. Shipley, Mrs. Sauerwein, Mrs. Shipley came with Mary & I. Mr. P. R. constant attendant with M Derr & Miss Jenks. Mr. Rau went home with Kate B.

Wednesday Jan. 8th. Pretty day. Mr. P. Rau was here a little this morning and also in the evening. When Mr. P. Rau went away we dressed ourselves and went round and made a call at Mr. Sadtler's and also at Mrs. James Bayfield's. After dinner Charley called but did not stay long. Mr. John Rau called for a few moments. After tea, Lizzie Sadtler and Charlie came to stay with Kate while Mag D[err], Mary & Mrs. Sauerwein & I went out to S. Moon's to a large company. We called at Misses Metzgers; but they were going up to Mr. T. Bantz's and from there Kate, Misses S & B Metzger went to Mr. J. Endsor's store to wait for an omnibus, but were disappointed. Mr. Johns and Mr. Endsor joined our agreeable party. I had the agreeable company of Mr. E[ndsor]. We were quite a large company contrary to our expectation and I spent a very pleasant evening. We all came home in company. We got home about quarter of two o'clock.

Thursday [January] 9th. We got up this morning about nine o'clock and were very sleepy even then on account of the dissipation of last night. A very damp & disagreeable day. Mr. P. Rau called here a little this morning on his way to the bank, first to see how we came on after last night's walk and also to see who came home with M[ag] D[err]. Kate Bantz spent the day with us today and Charley called a little while after dinner, brought a rabbit with him to show us or Miss M. Mag D., Mary S. & I went up to Mrs. James Bayfield's to tea and then met Miss Annie Harwood and the family, Mr. and Mrs. B., Miss M. Lavins & Mr. Gregg. We spent a very pleasant evening. Mr. Sauerwein and Mr. Rau came up for us about 8 o'clock; we left about half-

1851

past ten. Mrs. J. Bayfield came with M[ag] D[err], Mr. Rau [with] Mary S[auerwein], and Mr. Sauerwein with me. I wrote a letter home to-day.

Friday January 10th. A very pretty day, the sun shone beautifully and it is much warmer. Mrs. J. Sadtler, Mrs. Fitzgerald & Miss Fanny Jenks came and about one o'clock, to our exceeding surprise, who should come but John Derr from Fred'k. I was delighted to see him. After dinner we dressed ourselves, Mary, Kate, Mag and myself, and went out, first to Mr. Bayfield's store according with our invitation the night before, and were treated to pound cake and perfectly lovely Anise Cordials and had a long talk with him, and from there we went to see K. B. but she was out, and from there we went out Lombard St. and I met Mrs. Dunham, Annie E[*illegible*] and then went in the house to see Ginnie; I had not intended going till the next day. Mary & Mag called for me on their way back from Mrs. Hughes's. The family appeared to be so glad to see me and G upbraided me for not answering her letter, whereas I had never received it. Mr. P. B. Rau, John Derr, Kate B and her nephew O. Ebbert [came]. We spent a very pleasant evening. We got to retire about twelve.

Saturday [January] 11th. A very warm day for winter. Mag & John D., Mary & Kate S. and I went up and called for K. B. and then we all went to the Jewish Synagogue[11]. J[ohn] D[err] took dinner here today. While we were at dinner Ginnie Dunham and her friend Miss May from Philadelphia called to see us. After dinner, M[ag] and J. D., Mr. Rau and Kate went out to Green Mount[12]. Mary S and I went out first to Mrs. Bayfield's and from there we went with Mrs. B & Miss M. to Mr. B[ayfield]'s store and had some more pound cake. Called to see K. B. who was not at home, saw Mary B. and Miss Bausman at Mr. Warner's [and] invited them to tea on Monday, also Mr. & Mrs. B. & Miss M. From there [we went] to Mrs. Stover's; did not see her as she is sick but left word for her to come also, called at Coz J. Bierley. Mr. and Mrs. R were not at home, so I left my card. Mr. J. D. took tea here, Mr. Rau spent the evening here.

---

[11]The Jewish Synagogue known as the Madison Avenue Temple was founded in 1830. Francis F. Beirne, *The Amiable Baltimoreans* (New York, 1951), p. 212; hereafter cited as Beirne, *Baltimoreans*.

[12]Greenmont Cemetery at Greenmont Avenue and Oliver Street was established in 1839. It was considered Baltimore's most fashionable burial ground. *Ibid.*, p. 181.

1851

Sunday January 12th. Charley Sadtler and J. Derr came to go to church with us. George, Mary & I went together [with] Kate and John D. and Mag D. and Charley and heard an excellent sermon from Dr. Morris from Job 22, Chapter 16th Verse. Mr. Rau came with Mr. D. from [church] and the rest came as they went. J. D. took dinner here. Mr. Rau and C[harlie] S[adtler] came round. I went to Sunday School with Emma. G. went up for K. B. to bring her down and we waited for them till half-past four and then Mr. Rau, Charley, Mag D, Mary S. and Miss Carter, next door neighbor who was in here at the time, and I all took a long walk out by Franklin Square. Kate S[auerwein] and J[ohn] D[err] went to the Cathedral and it was late till we all got home. After tea we all went to Mr. Webster's church to hear the Rev. Mr. Stockton preach from Ps. 22, 6. It was a very pleasant day all day to-day; so very warm, just like a summer's day.

Monday Jan. 13th. A beautiful day. /I had a letter from Mother to-day./ John D. came round here and Mary S., Mag D and I all went up and called for Kate Bantz [and] from there we all went out to Sallie Moon's and there staid a little while and came home just in time for dinner. Charlie was here a little at dinner. After dinner we all dressed and went out shopping. Mrs. Wm. Sadtler was here while we were out. Mrs. J. Bayfield, Mrs. John Rau, Mary Bierley, Miss S. Bausman, Kate B. & Fanny Jenks were here to tea, Mrs. Bayfield, Mr. J. & P. Rau, Messrs. Bierley, Gorman, Beard, J. Derr & Charlie [came]. We spent a very pleasant evening. The company left at half-past eleven.

Tuesday January 14th. A beautiful day. Mary S. and I went to market in the morning and then we went to see K[ate] Bantz and as we were coming home Mr. Bausman joined us at Mr. J. B.'s door and walked home with us. We met Mr. P. B. Rau at the door, who remained here to entertain Mag D[err] till we came back. Kate B. called here a little. When I came home I told Mag D. that if she could not wait till Wednesday, why, I would remain as I was enjoying myself and did not feel that <u>duty</u> called so loud to me; so Mag D., Mary, and I went out to make last calls. We went to Mrs. Bayfield's, Mrs. Rau's, to Messrs. Rau's & Bayfield's store, to Mrs. Hughes's, Mrs. Steiner's, Capt. Steiner's, Misses Metzgers, Mrs. Sauerwein's, old Mrs. P. B. Sadtler's. After dinner Mr. P. B. R[au] and Charlie were here a little. Mary Sauerwein and two Misses Horns also called. Mag D. and John D. left about four o'clock. Miss Kate & Eliza Dorney called. After Mr. P. Rau called and Mary S., George and I all went down to Misses Metzger's according to invitation and then met a pleasant party of about 38 -- I spent a pleasant evening. Eliza Sauerwein invited us there for Thursday evening to a company. While we

1851

were at Miss Metzger's there were four gentlemen called to see Mary and left their names as Mr. Hammond. We got home at about half-past one o'clock. I came home with Mr. Rau.

Wednesday Jan. 15th. A very beautiful day like a summer's day. Sarah & Hester Moon called here this morning according to promise but we did not take our walk, for Kate Bantz was not ready to go when they called, so we concluded to go that evening. After they left Mary S. and I went up to Mrs. Trump's to see Mrs. Tucker & Miss Beatson, but they were not in, so we only saw Mrs. Trump. Met Dr. Morris, the Lutheran minister there. He seemed to know a good deal more concerning me than I expected to hear from a stranger. We also called to see Miss Annie Harwood; then came on home. After dinner, Mary & I went up to Mrs. T. Bantz's and there [saw] Sallie Moon, Misses S. & B. Metzger. We then all took a walk. Sallie M. and I were together, Kate and Mary and K. B. and Misses M[etzger]. We had a very pleasant walk. Kate B[antz] came home with us to tea and after tea Mr. P. B. Rau came and we all went to the museum[13] together, Kate & George together, Mary & I were with Mr. Rau. We saw "Romeo and Juliet". Mrs. Mouss, of late Mrs. Hunt, personated Romeo. Charlie & Lizzie Sadtler were here while we were gone.

Thursday Jan. 16th. A beautiful day but we did not avail ourselves of the pleasure of going out. Mr. P. B. Rau was here only for a few moments and Miss M. Horn and Mr. Kerchner were also here, and Miss Beatson and Tilyard called here late in the evening. Mr. P. B. R. called after tea and Miss Fannie Jenks came in and we all went down in company with Mary S. & Mr. Rau. I spent a very pleasant evening, had an introduction to a great many strangers and also saw Kate B., Charlotte Trail and Mr. C. Markell. There were about fifty or sixty persons there. We came home about half-past twelve o'clock; I came with Mr. P. B. R., Mary with Mr. A. George, Kate B. with George S., Miss Fannie Jenks with Mrs. Silk. Kate B. went to market with us. Charlie came round this evening for Kate S. to go round and spend the evening. Wrote to Coz Aaron Ogle to-day a long letter.

---

[13]The museum started by Raphael and Rembrant Peale in 1813 housed at Holiday and Lexington Streets was taken over by P. T. Barnum in 1845 and moved to Baltimore and Calvert Streets. J. Thomas Scharf, *The Chronicles of Baltimore*... (Baltimore, 1874), pp. 90-91; hereafter cited as Scharf, *Baltimore*.

1851

Friday Jan. 17th. A rather cloudy [day] and little colder this morning. Kate B. went as far as Misses Metzger's with us and there left us and we went on to market. When we returned we dressed ourselves and called to see Miss Dorney and from there to see the Misses Horn and from there we went down on Market St. to Mr. Kretzer to get some braid for a pair of slippers; came home to dinner. After dinner we went to Mr. P. S. to see if Uncle S. had come but he had not. We went into next door Mrs. Carter's a little and also to Miss Haines. We went down Market St. with Mary to make some purchases. We spent a pleasant evening at home.

Saturday Jan. 18th. It is clear and cold. We all received a letter from Mag D. and Kate one from Mary D. by Uncle [Cornelius] Shriner, who came down last night. Mary and I went out, went to Mr. P. S. to see Aunt S[hriner] and heard from home saying I could stay as long as they did. We also went to see Miss Alice Tilyard & Mrs. Tucker & Miss Beatson; were all very pleasant & agreeable. When we came home found Miss Mary Lavin had been here. Mr. Rau was here for a few minutes. After dinner we were in all day. Miss Bausman & M. Birely called here a little. After tea Uncle & Aunt Shriner and Mrs. P. Sauerwein were here till nearly nine o'clock.

Sunday Jan. 19th. Mrs. Rau came down here this morning and went with Mary & I to church to hear an excellent sermon from Dr. John Morris. I was surprised to find it so clear and cold but it clouded over before night. Mr. Rau and Mrs. Bayfield were here this evening; the former stayed to tea and we all went to Dr. Wolfe's church, corner of Paca & Saratoga Sts. After we got home, Mrs. Wm. Sadtler, Lizzie, Lum and Charlie came round here. Mrs. W. S. and Lum did not remain long but Lizzie & Charlie staid till nearly ten o'clock.

Monday Jan. 20th. Arose this morning to find it very disagreeable. It had snowed but little then turned to rain and had frozen and made it very sleety. Mr. P. Rau was here a little this morning. I had a letter from Vallie this morning saying they were all well & that C. Taylor was going to St. Louis to remain till June. There was no one till after tea when Mr. & Mrs. J. P. Sadtler & Miss F. Jenks came and spent the evening. Mr. A. George was here and asked Mary & I to accompany [him] to the Holyday [sic] St.

1851

Theater[14] on Wednesday evening to the opera of "Ernani"[15]. We were not out all day. Commenced a pair of slippers. We all had a note in conjunction from Coz Ed S. through G. S.'s letter.

Tuesday Jan. 21st. A very pretty day, so bright. When I came down in the morning I found some gentleman had called to see me at 7 o'clock, but he would not leave his name when asked but said he would call again in the afternoon but he did not come. Mary & I dressed ourselves and took a walk and I made several purchases. Went to market too, called Mr. P. Sauerwein's to invite them to tea. Mrs. Bayfield was here a little after dinner. Mr. Bavie was here a little but I did not have the pleasure of seeing him. Uncle & Aunt Shriner, Mr. & Mrs. P. S. were to tea; they told us Mr. J. A. J[ohnson][16] was in B[altimore]. Mr. Kerchner called and Mary invited him to go with us down to Mr. J. Horn's to spend the evening. G. accompanied us to the door then returned. We called for Mary S. Met Messrs R. Trail, J. Harvey, A. Henderson there; spent a pleasant evening. Mr. A. Henderson came home with me, Mr. J. Harvey with M. S.

Wednesday Jan. 22nd. Found it raining when we got up this morning. Had a note from Mr. A. George concerning the postponement of the "Opera". Mary answered, saying we should be happy to accompany him the next evening according with his wishes. Ed Sauerwein came up soon saying his Ma wanted us to spend the day there. We promised we would, so we dressed ourselves and went down about eleven o'clock. Mr. & Mrs. P. Sauerwein, Jr., Mrs. Clarke & Dot were there to dine. Our Kate came down about three o'clock and told us K. Bantz was there and wanted to see us, also that Mr. J. A. J. had been there and was coming again at night. We got ready and went

---

[14]The Holiday Street Theater was located in the present location of Baltimore's City Hall. It was built in 1813, replacing an earlier wooden structure. It was destroyed by fire in 1873. Scharf, *Baltimore*, pp. 679-680. *Baltimore: A Picture History 1858-1968* (Maryland Historical Society, Baltimore, 1968), p. 15.

[15]The opera *Ernani* was written by Verdi in 1843. John W. Freeman, *Stories of Great Operas* (New York, 1984), p. 454.

[16]Mr. J. A. Johnson, one of the main characters in these diaries, was the son of Dr. Thomas Johnson and Miss Dorsey whose father built their home. Here he lived with his brother Clint on the farm called "Auburn" which was on Stauffer Road one-half mile from the Woodsboro Pike. J. A. J. and his brother not only ran the farm, but ran a distillery as well. He was a member of the Maryland House of Delegates in 1860. Scharf, *Western Maryland*, p. 623; Isaac Bond, *Map of Frederick County, MD...* (Baltimore, 1858); hereafter cited as *Bond Map*, 1858.

1851

home. Kate soon left. We were in at Mr. J. Sadtler's a little time before tea. After tea Messrs. Bavie & Rau came, then Mr. J. A. Johnson. They all spent the evening. It passed quickly and very pleasantly.

Thursday [January] 23rd. Cloudy in the morning but it cleared off very prettily. Mary & I dressed ourselves and went down to Mr. P. S. and went out shopping with Aunt Shriner. Called to see the Misses Metzger & Misses Sadtler and bid them good-bye. I wrote a letter home saying I would be home on to-morrow evening. I was in the house all the evening. Mr. J. A. J. called here and talked an hour or two, invited us to attend the opera in company with him but of course we could not on account of previous engagement with Mr. A. George. Mr. A. G[eorge] called for us, also Mr. Bausman & K[ate] Bantz and we all went in company together. We spent a very pleasant evening. The Opera was Italian but there were books of translation. They had excellent music, such tunes I never heard. I saw a good many persons I know. As we came home stopped in at Childes' for oysters and then had a nice long sociable talk. I regretted very much to learn that Coz. Harrison Smith had been to see me while we were away. I should like so much to see [him].

Friday Jan. 24th. A beautiful day, so warm and bright. My last day in Baltimore of this visit. Mary & I went to market, called to see K. B. but she was not at home; saw Mr. Bausman there who walked home with us. Mary & I dressed ourselves to bid my friends good-bye. Went to Mrs. Bayfield's, Mr. Rau's store, Mr. Bayfield's store, to Mr. Dorney's, ladies not at home, Mrs. Rau's, Mrs. Dunham's, Ginnie & her friend out, Mrs. Steiner's, Mary B not there, Mrs. Trump's, Kate B.'s, Mr. Horn's & old Mr. P. Sauerwein's, when we got home found Sallie Moon & Mr. J. A. J. had been there. I was very sorry we were not at home. While we were at dinner some one came and asked for me. I ran in the parlor expecting to find J. H. Smith but I was -- I cannot [say] disappointed -- for how glad was I to see Coz Will Dean who had just come from Fred'k. and very kindly wanted me to go with him over to Washington, Alexandria and Georgetown to see our relatives there. I told him I did not think I could. However, he said he would return at half-past three to find out my decision. Mr. J. A. J. was here a little to bid the family good-bye. I was in a little to Mr. J. P. Sadtler's to bid them farewell. Coz Will came again at the appointed time. I told [him] I should be very happy to go, but that I hope he would not be angry and excuse me for not going as

1851

I was not prepared. Mary S., Miss Fannie Jenks, Lizzie Sadtler & George went to the cars[17] with me. Wm. went as far as Market St. with us and left on business, [but] came to cars again to bid me good-bye. I was then stowed away in the cars with Uncle & Aunt S[hriner] and swiftly carried away from the many kind friends I found and scenes where I had been enjoying myself so much lately. Mr. J. A. J. was with us all the time after we left Ellicott's Mills[18]. Pa met me in town with the carriage and brought me home. I shall always remember the kindness shown to me in Baltimore this visit.

Saturday Jan. 25th. A lovely morning, almost like a summer's day. I dressed myself and went in town to Mrs. B. F. Winchester's[19] for the express purpose of seeing P. Mering[20] but she had gone home on the Friday morning previous. I had a nice long talk with Mrs. W., then did some shopping and came on home. There was no company to-day.

---

[17]The Baltimore and Ohio Railroad, started July 4, 1828, was extended to Frederick in 1831. Leaving Baltimore on December 1, 1831, at 7 a.m. the first train of the Baltimore and Ohio Railroad arrived in Frederick at 2 p.m. to the accompaniment of artillery fire and church bells. Steam locomotives were introduced in 1832, eliminating the 12 stops for exchanging horses. A freight station was built in 1834 on the corner of South and Carroll Streets. A later station was built in 1854 on Market and East All Saints Streets. However, most passengers boarded at Frederick Junction until the 1920's, when new gas and electric lines took over the passenger runs. Then the passenger station on Market and All Saints became the terminal. By 1850 regular service between Baltimore and Frederick took about two hours. A telegraph line was strung along the track line in 1855 to help transmit orders to the crews. Herbert H. Harwood, Jr., *Impossible Challenge: The Baltimore-Ohio Railroad in Maryland* (Baltimore, 1979), pp. 26-53, 164-165.

[18]Ellicott Mills, west of Baltimore, were started by the Ellicott brothers from Pennsylvania, who were encouraged to come to Maryland by Charles Carroll of Carrollton. M. P. Andrews, *History of Maryland: Province and State* (New York, 1929), p. 270.

[19]B. F. Winchester was a relative of Hiram Winchester, founder of the Frederick Female Seminary. Both Mr. and Mrs. B. F. Winchester taught there. They lived on the west side of North Market Street between 4th and 5th Streets. *Williams' Directory*, p. 41.

[20]Penelope (Nellie or "Pench") Mehring [Mering] was a schoolmate of Margaret's at Thorndale. She lived in Bruceville, a one-street town on Rt. 194 near Keymar in Carroll County. The Mehring house which is still in use, was the home and jail of Sheriff Narmand Bruce in 1769. Scharf, *Western Maryland*, I, 480.

1851

Sunday [January] 26th. Joe[21] drove the carriage into town to-day. I went to church, saw several of my friends. Had a nice long talk with Mr. Powell at the hotel. Saw Abram [Adams] and he said he was coming up this evening; he came up about half-past three o'clock and staid till after tea.

* * * * *

Tuesday [January] 28th. At home in the morning, Ma & Pa went into town. John[22] took me into town after dinner and stopped for Mother and then went out to Grandmother's[23] and staid till after tea and as we came home stopped for Father and brough[t] him home with us. It was cloudy and damp in the morning and commenced raining after dinner.

Wednesday [January] 29th. A very cold day & occasional snow squalls. At home in the morning but after Mother, Father & I all went out and spent the afternoon at Mr. Derr's. I spent a very pleasant day talking about B[altimore] and our friends.

* * * * *

Friday, Jan. 31st 1851. A very cold, stormy day. There was some company here and I was at home all day.

Saturday February 1st [1851]. Much warmer to-day and very clear. I was at home in the morning but after dinner I rode to town on horseback and John brought my horse home. I stopped in at Mrs. L[ewis] Markell's[24] and there

---

[21] Joe and John were servants, possibly slaves, belonging to Daniel Scholl according to the 1850 census. The listing reads "1 female age 57, 1 female age 11, 1 male age 12, 1 male age 7, one laborer named Samual Haller age 17." Mary Fitzhugh Hitselberger and John Dern, *Bridge in Time: The Complete 1850 Census of Frederick County, Maryland* (Monocacy Book Co., Redwood City, CA, 1978), pp. 70, 459; hereafter cited as Hitselberger, *Bridge in Time*.

[22] See note 21 above.

[23] Margaret's maternal grandmother was Margaret Ogle Thomas (born 1776; died 1854). She lived with her daughter Mrs. C. Burr Artz on North Market Street extended. G. L. Thomas, *Thomas Genealogy* (Adamstown, MD, 1954), p. 27; hereafter cited as *Thomas Genealogy*; and *Bond Map*, 1858. See Appendix II.

[24] Mrs. Lewis Markell was a daughter of John Brunner (son of Jacob Brunner of the Schifferstadt family) and his first wife, Maria Stickle. A younger half-sister was Ellen Brunner (see note 33, 1851). Williams, *History*, II, 917. The Markells' home and store were

1851

saw the procession of the different fire companies of Fred'k[25] pass and afterwards Nellie B. dressed herself and we went out to the Sem[inary][26] to see Mr. J. Hammond, K. [*illegible*], & K. Brady and from there to Dr Zack's[27] to see Lucretia Brewer, saw Mrs. S. Brengle & Mrs. R. Macgill, & also to see Mrs. John Loats & Miss S. Reich, and then came on home as John had brought my horse.

Sunday Feb. 2nd. When I arose this morning I found it snowing and in consequence did not get in to church. Cousin L. Hedges[28] came about twelve o'clock and brought the sad intelligence that Aunt C. Gittinger[29] was dead, died at six o'clock that morning, and was to be buried at two the next

---

on South Market Street in Frederick. *Williams' Directory*, p. 26. See also Hitselberger, *Bridge in Time*, p. 14.

[25]"The United Hose (or Swampers) got a new engine this week. Today paraded through the streets and tried its Power--the Company was escorted through the town by the Juniors and Independent Fire Companies." Jacob Engelbrecht, *The Diary of Jacob Engelbrecht, 1818-1878* (3 vols. Edited by William R. Quynn, published by The Historical Society of Frederick County, Inc., Frederick, MD, 1976), II, 523; hereafter cited as Engelbrecht, *Diary*.

[26]Frederick Female Seminary was opened by Hiram Winchester in 1839. The school and residence were leased by the Woman's College of Frederick in 1893. In 1913 the name of the college was changed to Hood College. These buildings, called Winchester Hall, are now the Frederick County government offices, 12 East Church Street. Some of the windowpanes in the Hiram Winchester room on the second floor have the names and dates of students of the Woman's College incised in them. Mary Derr, one of the seminary's graduates, commented in her diary (April 18, 1854), on the school's progress.

[27]Dr. Daniel Zacharias was the minister for the German Reformed Church (now known as The Evangelical Reformed Church, United Church of Christ) for 38 years, 1835-1873. During his ministry the present church at 15 West Church Street and Kemp Hall on the southeast corner of Market Street were built. James B. and Dorothy S. Ranck, *"Unto Us,"* A *History of the Evangelical Reformed Church* (Frederick, MD, 1964), pp. 89, 113; hereafter cited as J. & D. Ranck, *History of Evangelical Reformed Church*. Dr. Zacharias had a home on the east side of Market Street between Patrick and Church Streets. *Williams' Directory*, p. 42.

[28]Daniel Scholl's sister Catherine married Andrew Hedges. Their second son was Lycurgus Hedges. John J. Scholl, *The Colonial Branches, Scholl, Sholl, Shull Genealogy* (Grafton Press, New York, 1930), p. 784; hereafter cited as *Scholl Genealogy*. See also Appendix I; note 39, 1851; and notes supplied by Frank H. Lewis.

[29]Daniel Scholl's sister Charlotta (1801-1851) married George Gittinger. *Scholl Genealogy*, p. 784.

day. Uncle Adams[30] was up a little in the evening. Mrs. I. Jamison came out about three o'clock and staid till after tea. Mr. J. A. Johnson came about five o'clock and sat the evening.

Monday [February] 3rd. It still snowed this morning but stopped before dinner. We went out to the funeral; it was [a] very large one for the weather; there was a funeral address in the lecture room of the New Church by the Rev. Dr. Zack, from Ecc. 3 -- "A time to mourn."

Tuesday Feb. 4th. A damp and rather disagreeable day. I wrote a polite little note to Mr. P. Kunkel requesting the return of my Daguerreotype[31] likeness taken from our house July 13th/50. I received a note from Vallie[32] requesting Ma & my company down there to-day to help her sew. I went down directly and Ma came after dinner. Mrs. I. Howard, Misses H & C Keefer, Mrs. Chandler, Mrs. & Miss Clingan, Miss B. Fout & Miss James who is with Vallie helping to sew. When I came home found a letter from G. Dunham who was well and in fine spirits.

Wednesday [February] 5th. A very pleasant day. I was at home in the morning very busy while Mother and Father were in town. After dinner John took me into town in the carriage. I stopped at E[llen] Brunner's[33] and E.

---

[30]Valentine Adams mentioned in the diary as "Uncle Adams," was a very active man, president of the Agricultural Society and an elder in his church. On May 6, 1851 (see note 54, 1851), he married Sarah Jacob Mehrling. See Appendix II; and *Thomas Genealogy*, p. 28. The Adams farm was about a mile south of Manchester Farm on the New Design Road. *Bond Map*, 1858.

[31]Daguerreotyping was a photographic process used in Frederick by Charles Byerly as early as 1848. Williams, *History*, p. 927. By 1859 there were three daguerreotype saloons in Frederick: William Smallwood, J. E. Riddlemoser, and Jacob Byerly, whose collection can be seen at the Smithsonian Institution, and the Historical Society of Frederick County. *Williams' Directory*, pp. 48, 927.

[32]Vallie was Valietta S. T. Adams, third daughter of Valentine Adams and Sybilla Thomas Adams, a sister of Margaret Scholl's mother. She married (1) James Weagly (1853) and (2) Charles Keller (1884). A brother was Abraham Adams, and younger sisters were Jeannette M. (Jenny, Ginny, Mrs. Henry Nelson), and Fanny, all of whom are mentioned later by the diarist. Adams-Nelson Family Bible (pr. 1859).

[33]Ellen Brunner, close friend and distant cousin of Margaret Scholl, was a direct descendant of the Brunners of Schifferstadt, being a daughter of John Brunner (son of Jacob) by his second wife, Miss Doll. Williams, *History*, II, 917. See also Appendix I. In the 1850s, Ellen was living with her older half-sister, Mrs. Lewis Markell on South Market Street

1851

and I went down street and did some shopping and then called at the F. F. Sem. to see if K. Brady could come home with me but she had an engagement and could not go. Ellen and I then came on home. After tea Coz Ed & Mr. J. A. Johnson came and spent the evening and made themselves very agreeable and as pleasant as usual.

* * * * *

Friday [February] 7th. Nellie and I staid at home in the morning while Mother went into town for Kate B. & old Mrs. Fessler but neither of them came; the former had an engagement, the latter was not at home, but Cousin M. Beer & Mrs. A. Feller came out. E[llen] & I went over to Mrs. I. Howard's[34] after dinner to spend a very pleasant evening with the family & E. Keefer[35]. When I came home found a package containing my likeness and note from Mr. P. Kunkel apologizing for keeping it so long.

Saturday Feb. 8th. A rather cloudy day but not cold. I was at home in the morning busy. Mother went into town with E. B. this morning as she wished to go home now but I wanted her to stay longer but she seemed to think she could not. I wrote a letter to Genie K. and a note to Mr. P. Kunkel telling he was mistaken as regards Pa & I having any objections his visiting our house and that he had been wrongly informed. After dinner I walked down to Mrs. J. Keefer's to spend the afternoon. Saw the family & Mrs. I. Howard. We came home soon after tea.

Sunday [February] 9th. It rained and in consequence I was at home all day. Mr. Jameson came out about half-past one o'clock and remained till about four o'clock. He seemed to be in excellent spirits and had a good deal to say.

* * * * *

---

in Frederick. *Williams' Directory*, p. 26; and note 24, 1851). In 1859, she married Martin N. Rohrback. L. B. Rohrbaugh, *Rohrbach Genealogy* (Philadelphia, 1970), p. 377.

[34]The Isaac Howards and the J. Keefers lived close to Manchester Farm on the New Design Road. *Bond Map*, 1858.

[35]See note 34 above.

1851

Tuesday [February] 11th. Much colder and quite windy. Mother was out to Grandma's & Pa was in town so I had the house all to myself to-day; there was no company. Mrs. Killian sent for me and I went over about sundown and soon came home; found a note from P. Brunner saying her sister and she wanted me to come in on tomorrow evening and stay over night with [them] and also an invitation to a Cotillion Party to be given to Mr. & Mrs. Jones to be given at the Herald Buildings[36] on next Tuesday evening.

Wednesday Feb. 12th. At home in the morning. After dinner I rode to town on horseback and went to Mrs. L[ewis] Markell's and staid. Kate Houck soon came & spent the evening. Mrs. D. Shafer, Mrs. G. Tyler, Mrs. Myers, the widow, Misses A. Campbell, Tilly Jackson & A. Late called there. Tilly J. staid to tea, Cally B. also came over to tea. Mr. & Mrs. D. Markey & M. Ellen were over a little after tea. Messrs. W. Reich & B. Brown spent the evening with us. We spent a very pleasant evening [and] invited the girls to go with us to Mrs. P. Reich's and they said they would. Mr. W. Reich kindly offered to send us out. We girls accepted his offer.

Thursday [February] 13th. A very pretty day. Nellie [Ellen] & I went to market. Kate H. & Tilly J. came over about half-past nine o'clock. The hack came for us about half-past ten at our desire. Mr. W. Reich put us in. We spent a delightful day, it seemed so short. The family are always so kind. We left Mr. R. about half-past seven o'clock. Mr. P. Reich & Raymond went with us till we met Messrs. W. Reich, C. Page & F. Webster. We were to come up [to Frederick] in the cars, but we were too soon, so we walked on till they over took us and then got in. Mr. Brown is very obliging. Nellie & I went up to Mrs. Houck's and staid till about half-past nine o'clock.

Friday [February] 14th. When we got up found it raining. Nellie received a Valentine at breakfast. They sent for me about nine o'clock and I rode out on horseback. At home the rest of the day and no company. To-day is St. Valentine's Day but I was quite disappointed to find when Pa came home that none of my friends had remembered me so much as to send me a valentine.

Saturday Feb. 15th. It rained till about noon then cleared off and got colder. I was at home all day and there was no company. Father was in town in the evening and when he came home brought me a Valentine that had been left

---

[36]The *Herald* building was on the west side of Market Street, the second door north of Patrick Street. *Williams' Directory*, p. 18.

1851

at Uncle H[enry] Thomas'[37] store for me. It's a "Pledge of Friendship" from an unknown friend.

Sunday [February] 16th. A very pretty day, clear & tolerably cold. I had a note from Vallie and the papers containing the "Baymonts". Vallie expects to go to Washington City on next Tuesday. Mother & I went into church and heard a sermon from Dr. Zack on Ps. 11-36[38]. Messrs. S. B. Jamison & J. A. Johnson were out this evening and spent the evening. They had a good deal to say. Mr. J. A. J. expects to go to Philadelphia very soon, perhaps this week.

Monday [February] 17th. A cold & clear day. At home all day & no company, read the "Baymonts" tonight.

Tuesday [February] 18th. At home all day. Right pleasant, warmer. I had a note from Marion H[oward] saying some of the ladies of the neighborhood would come and see us if we would be at home. I wrote a note in return saying we would be very happy to see them. I had such a nice long letter from M[ary] Sauerwein, I was so glad to have it & hear all the news from B[altimore].

Wednesday [February] 19th. A pretty day, clear & tolerably warm. At home all day. After dinner pretty soon Mrs. I. Howard, Mrs. J. A. Taylor, Marion & Emily H[oward] came and soon Sarah Miller, Isa & Mary Buckey & Mr. R. Cromwell. They all spent the afternoon. They were very pleasant & agreeable. I wrote a note to E[llen] Brunner. Mrs. Howard invited Ma & I to come the next day & meet the ladies there.

Thursday [February] 20th. A damp day with occasional showers. At home in the morning. After dinner Ma & I went over to Mrs. I. Howard's and spent the afternoon. [We] saw the family, Mrs. J. A. Taylor, Mr. & Mrs. Louis Kemp & three children, Mr. & Mrs. J. Buckey & Mary Buckey.

* * * * *

---

[37]Henry Thomas had a Dry Goods Store on the north side of Patrick between Market and Court Streets. *Ibid.*, p. 38. He was an uncle of Mrs. Daniel Scholl. *Thomas Genealogy*, p. 29.

[38]Both of these psalms refer to the punishment of the wicked.

1851

Saturday Feb. 22nd. A beautiful day. I was at home all day, no company came. To-day the anniversary of the birth of the greatest man that ever lived.

Sunday [February] 23rd. Mother and I were into church and heard an excellent sermon from Dr. Zack. After dinner Jennie, Fannie & Nellie Adams were up, left after tea, and Mr. S. B. Jamison came out directly and sat till about nine o'clock. A lovely day.

* * * * *

Tuesday [February] 25th. I awoke to find it had cleared off. Father & Mother went away to spend the day so I had to keep house. I had a note from Mrs. I. Howard to know if Ma & I would go with her & Mrs. J. Taylor to see Mrs. Louis Kemp. I wrote her one in return saying I could not go. Vallie spent the afternoon with me and she had a great deal to say about her late visit to Washington.

Wednesday [February] 26th. A beautiful day. I rode to town on horseback; called at Mrs. Markell's and Ellen & I went to see Mary Kunkel, who gave us a glowing account of her visit to Lancaster, Philadelphia, Balt[imore]; also to see K. Houck [and] promised to spend Friday afternoon with her. Abram walked part the way up the street with us and Mr. S. B. J[amison] walked down with us. Took dinner with Mrs. Markell and then rode out home, changed my dress, and went down to Mrs. M. C. Claybaugh's and spent the evening. Mrs. Clingham, Miss M. Clingham from Balt[imore], Vallie & Frances Eagle. We were all weighed; I weighed 132 1/2 lbs. Have such a nice long letter of Genie Kephart.

Thursday Feb. 27th. At home all day. Rather cloudy but it did not rain. Mr. Jamison came out this evening according with our engagement and we went into town to attend the concert. Met Mr. J. A. Johnson on our way who turned and went back with us and we all went down to K. Bantz who just came home last night, but she could not go with us in consequence of wanting to go see Ally Sharp who is going away to-morrow. We left then and went. There was quite an audience, very fashionable and I was very much pleased with Mr. and Mrs. A. Hall and Mrs. Gosden. We got home about ten o'clock. Kate B. gave me a letter from Kate S.

Friday [February] 28th. A tolerable early morning but a little of every kind of weather during the day. I was at home in the morning but after dinner rode to town on horseback and called at Mrs. Markell's, and Ellen B[runner]

1851

and I went up according to invitation and spent the afternoon. Tillie Jackson was there also. After tea, Messrs. Pavel & Endsors, B. Brown, conductors on cars, A. Adams, S. B. Jamison, Messrs. Thomas & John Lewis came and spent the evening. We had quite a pleasant time. Ellen and I came over to Mrs. Markell's about ten o'clock. H. Adams and Mr. Jamison came with us. Wrote a letter to L. Garrott.

Saturday March 1st [1851]. A beautiful day. Nellie & I went to market. Abram went part the way up with us; met Tillie Jackson there who came home with us. Saw Mr. Jamison, also gave him a package for O. Garrott which he so kindly offered to take her. Came home about twelve o'clock & remained at home all evening.

Sunday, March 2nd. Mother and I went to church in the morning and heard a very good sermon from Dr. Zack. About five o'clock Mr. S. Jamison came and staid till about half-past five, brought a sweet little note from Coz Harrison Smith. Mr. J. A. J. was out also and spent the evening, left about ten.

Monday March 3rd. A clear but windy day; at home in the morning but after dinner Ma & I went down to Mrs. Clingan's to spend the evening but found her just getting ready to go to Mrs. Fout's, so we proposed to going too; so we all went over, saw the family and Mrs. Bushey & Mrs. Mary Clingan of B[altimore]. We came home that evening rather early.

Tuesday [March] 4th. Pa & I went up to Cousin D. Hedges['s][39] and spent the day. Mr. & Mrs. D. Devilbiss spent the day also. Messrs. John Fulton, G. Cockey, C. Scholl took dinner there. I spent a very pleasant day, came home about sundown. Saw Mr. Greg & Dr. Nelson on the road, <u>polite bows</u>. A delightful day.

Wednesday [March] 5th. Cloudy & smokey like Indian Summer all day. I rode in town on horseback this morning, went to see Nellie Brunner & Kate Bantz; took dinner at the latter's place. Came home and Mother & I went down & spent the evening with Mrs. S. Clingan, saw Miss Mary Clingan & Mrs. Clingan; got home early.

---

[39]Daniel Hedges lived above Biggs Ford on the Emmitsburg Pike (Route 15) south of Lewistown. *Bond Map*, 1858. See also note 28, 1851.

1851

Thursday [March] 6th. It was cloudy and sprinkled a little of rain in the morning; cleared off colder about twelve o'clock. Pa, Ma & I got ready and went up and spent the day at Uncle Elias Scholl's[40], saw most of the family and Mr. P. H[ines]. Saw Mr. J. A. J. very busy in his field beside the road ploughing. We saw Mr. & Mrs. J. Dutrow & Miss Francina D[utrow] pass through the yard. Got home about sundown.

Friday [March] 7th. Arose to find it snowing quite fast; it continued so through the day.

* * * * *

Sunday [March] 9th. At home all day; tolerably clear. Mr. Jamison came out after tea and spent the evening. He had left the note with Lenie Garrott which he so kindly offered to take. He was up on Thursday but did not [go in] on account of it being too late to stop.

Monday March 10th. I was at home in the morning. Mrs. Albaugh was here a little, begging for something connected with the church; after dinner I went down and spent the evening with Vallie; found that Judge Cooper[41] was there. He came from town just before I left; he walked up home with me and sat about an hour and left again for Uncle Adams's. A beautiful day.

* * * * *

Wednesday [March] 12th. A beautiful day, so warm; went into town in the morning, called at Mr. L. Markell's & did some shopping. Nellie B[runner] told [me] that she, Tilly Jackson, Kate & Georgia Houck[42] were coming out

---

[40]Uncle Elias Scholl was a brother of Daniel Scholl, Margaret's father. He was born in 1804, married twice, and died in 1856. His farm was located on the west side of the Woodsboro Pike (Route 194) south of Walkersville. *Scholl Genealogy*, p. 786; *Bond Map*, 1858.

[41]Judge Cooper was a relative of David Cooper who married Eleanore Adams in 1848. *Thomas Genealogy*, p. 27.

[42]The large family of Ezra Houck included Kate and Georgia. Their mansion on the east side of Market between Second and Third Streets is thought to have been built originally by Upton Sheriden, a Revolutionary war hero. It was rebuilt in 1889. Mr. E. Houck was the president of the Farmers and Mechanics Bank, the Mutual Insurance Co., the Junior Fire Co., the Woodsboro and Frederick Turnpike Co., as well as an elder in the German Reformed Church. Scharf, *Western Maryland*, I, 456, 538, 539.

1851

the next evening to spend the afternoon. Did some shopping & came home with a note to Vallie and had one from her at night and wrote one in return.

Thursday [March] 13th. Quite as a pretty day. Busy in the morning. About two o'clock Nellie B., Kate & G. Houck & Tilly Jackson came, and about four Vallie came; they all spent the evening. Messrs. Adams, Eader & Rice came out after tea to go home with the girls. They left about nine to have a beautiful walk by moonlight. Vallie remained over night. I wrote a note to Coz E. Shriner for him and Annie to come out but they did not come.

Friday [March] 14th. Still beautiful weather. I was busy in the front yard in the morning. Wrote a note to K. Bantz about some flowers; she was not at home. However Mrs. B[antz] sent on some different kinds; sent Vallie a rose bush and she sent me a privet and flowering locust.

Saturday [March] 15th. At home all day, very busy in the front yard. Joe, John & Jane were assisting me. A very pleasant day. Mr. J. A. Johnson came out about half-past six and spent the evening; he was in quite fine spirits & looked so nicely this evening. Uncle Adams was up a little this evening.

Sunday March 16th. It rained last night but in the morning it looked like clearing off, so Ma & I went into church & heard a very good sermon from the Rev. Mr. Hoffmeyer from Matthew, Chapter 3, Verse 7,.. "Flee from the wrath to come", but it was raining when we came home & continued raining through the day. Mr. Rice was to preach at the school house but none of us went down.

Monday [March] 17th. It snowed all day but Pa went into town, and when he came home brought me a letter from P. Mering saying she was going to B[altimore] but that she would be home the first of May, the time I had appointed to visit, and looking for me.

* * * * *

Thursday [March] 20th. Still blowing out but I went over to Mrs. I. Howard's and staid till nearly twelve; then came home, dressed myself and went into town to see Aunt Kemp & Aunt M. Scholl and Mrs. L. Markell.

Friday [March] 21st. A tolerably pleasant day; at home in the morning; after dinner went down to Mrs. Green[berry] Fout's [on New Design Rd.] and spent

1851

a very pleasant evening; met Mrs. I. Howard & Miss R. Keefer. Then when we came home found Mr. J. Shanks had been here.

Saturday [March] 22nd. It looked rather cloudy all day. I was at home all morning but [after] dinner I rode to town on horseback, called at Mrs. L. Markell's and intended going from there to catechism[43] but was prevented by seeing G[enie] Kephart. We went to the Sem[inary] to see the girls and down to Mrs. Fout's and from there we both started for home. Met Messrs. Stone & Pickens at the latter place.

* * * * *

Monday [March] 24th. A very pretty day. Sarah Ann Shank with her two children were up and spent the day. I did not feel at all well, having a very bad cold. J. A. J. is staying down at his father's for a few days.

Tuesday [March] 25th. Quite pleasant again to-day; got up about six but soon went to bed again as I felt so badly from the effects of my cold; but I got up about nine again. Maggie, Mary & Tommie Derr came out and spent the day. They were all pleasant as usual and we had as much to talk, laugh, etc. about as ever. I wrote a note to Mrs. I. Howard saying I would not be able to go with her to Mrs. L. Kemp's according to previous engagement, on account of the girls.

Wednesday [March] 26th. A pleasant day, little windy. Wrote a letter to P. Mering. Ma & I went out in the carriage to see Grand-ma in the evening. Aunt M. Artz[44] was not at home; Uncle Adams was there a few moments.

Thursday [March] 27th. Was at home in the morning. Miss Elsie Hoffman was here. It was so pleasant and warm that I rode down to see Vallie after

---

[43]The Heidelberg Catechism, published in Germany in 1563, contains the creed of the Reformed Church in question and answer form. J. D. Dubb, D.D., *The Reformed Church in the United States* (Lancaster, PA, 1885), p. 256. Catechism classes were held in the 1850s at certain seasons of the church year, often in preparation for Easter.

[44]Aunt Margaret Artz was a sister of Mrs. Daniel Scholl. She was born in 1815, married C. B. Artz in 1845 and died in Chicago in 1887. Their daughter was Victorine. They left the funds that were used to incorporate the C. Burr Artz Library in Frederick. *Thomas Genealogy*, p. 28.

1851

dinner; met Uncle D[avid] O[gle] Thomas[45] & wife & Laura T. there. Coz Ed came down after I got home & spent the evening. He was in fine spirits, laughing & talking about Valentines, etc.

Friday [March] 28th. Still so warm. Went over to Mrs. Killion's in the morning & told her she could go to town with us in the carriage after dinner. She came over & after dinner we went. Ma & I were to see Aunt C. Scholl[46], cousin Kitty Myers & family, Mrs. Dr. Shields, Mrs. Reese[47]. I was to see Mrs. Markell & Ellen at K. Bantz's; her friend, Miss A. Coblentz, has come. Saw Annie & O. G. Ogle[48] in town, who said they were out to see us but we were not at home. We had not returned [*illegible*].

Saturday March 29[th.] A beautiful day, the sun shone so bright and clear. At home all day. Old Mr. Alco was here for his paper and staid till after supper. Mr. J. A. J. came out between seven & eight o'clock and staid till ten; he has such a nice little <u>Moss-rose</u> bush. Cousin L. Hedges came out about half-past eight & staid over night. Mrs. Margaret Claybaugh had a daughter to-day.

Sunday [March] 30th. A rather pleasant day. At home all day. Mr. Jamison came out after tea & spent the evening. Cousin L. Hedges left in time to go to church. When the colored people came home, what can express my surprise when I heard that Cousin Mary Nicodemus[49] was dead and buried. She died yesterday evening at two o'clock and was buried this evening at four. I knew she was sick, for we met Uncle Elias & Aunt Mary on last Wednesday & they told us that she had a babe on the Saturday before but that it was

---

[45]Uncle David Ogle Thomas was a brother of Mrs. Daniel Scholl. *Ibid.*, p. 28. See also January 6, 1853; and note 16, 1853.

[46]Aunt Christina Scholl lived on the corner of Third and Court Streets. *Williams' Directory*, p. 34. See *Scholl Genealogy*, pp. 782-789.

[47]Mrs. Jacob Reese was John Derr, Sr.'s sister, Catherine. Wampler, *The Derr Family*, p. 436. The Reeses lived on the east side of North Market Street between 4th and 5th Streets. *Williams' Directory*, p. 31.

[48]Margaret's maternal grandmother was an Ogle. See note 23, 1851.

[49]Cousin Mary Nicodemus lived in Walkersville. She was a member of the Glade Reformed Church on Devilbiss Bridge Road near Walkersville (J. M. Holdcraft, *Names in Stone, 75,000 Cemetery Inscriptions from Frederick County, Maryland* (2 vols., Ann Arbor, MI, 1966), II, 846; hereafter cited as Holdcraft, *Names in Stone*.

dead, and Mr. J. A. J. told that he had seen old Mr. N. and that he had said he was waiting for the mail, that he did not know whether she was dead or alive as she was so ill when they heard of her.

Monday [March] 31st. A quite warm day. At home all day. Vallie sent me a paper and wrote me a note and I wrote one to her in return. Mrs. I. Howard & R. Keefer spent the evening with us. Mother was down to Mrs. Clingan's and she said what we had heard respecting Cousin Mary's death was correct and said that she and her babe were buried in the same coffin & grave; at her request, that the babe had been taken up and she was brought to Fred'k and buried at her own request. It was but two years January 16th since she was married. I stood beside her at the bridal but not at her grave for I knew nothing of her death.

Tuesday April 1st [1851]. Quite warm, at home all day. Had a note from Vallie & wrote her one in return and sent her some <u>bittersweet</u> in return, & wrote her a note saying it was flower seed & that she must sow it directly. I sent it for an <u>April Fool</u>. Wrote a letter to G. Kephart.

Wednesday [April] 2nd. A rainy disagreeable day. Had a note from Mrs. G. Taylor saying she and M. Gardiner would spend the next day with us. Wrote her one in return, saying we should be happy to see them.

Thursday [April] 3rd. Beautiful day; about nine o'clock Mrs. Taylor, Mrs. Chandler, Miss Lottie Leigh & M. Gardiner came up and spent the day. Had a note from V[allie]. Wrote one in return.

Friday [April] 4th. A pleasant but cool day; rode into town after dinner and called at Mrs. L. Markell's & soon Vallie came. Then she & I went down to the Sem[inary] and spent the evening with the teachers, Mrs. Pearson, Misses C. Wright, Coleman, H. Halbert & Evie Winchester, Kate Matthew & Mary J. Hammond. Two of the girls were in, too. Mrs. F. Winchester, Mrs. Delaplaine, G. Vernon, came after tea. Spent quite a pleasant evening and went with Vallie and staid over night.

Saturday [April] 5th. Came home quite early and was at home all day. It rained in the night. Had a letter from Mary & Kate Sauerwein & a note enclosed from George.

Sunday [April] 6th. I went in the carriage into town and heard an excellent sermon from Dr. Zack; came home, got my dinner and went over to Mrs. I.

1851

Howard's and from there Mrs. H., Marion & I went down to the school house[50] and heard a very good sermon from Mr. Rice. I saw the neighbors there & Mr. Jamison who had been to our house & returned. Mr. French walked home with me & I found Mr. J. A. Johnson there when I got home. /Mr. J. A. J. was here yesterday./ Mr. Jamison told me he was going to Phila. on Tuesday & that I should write by him.

Monday April 7th. A beautiful day. Wrote a note to Harry to send by Mr. S. B. J[amison] but had not an opportunity of sending it to town, or rather was disappointed in the opportunity I expected to have. A pretty day. Went over to Mrs. I. Howard's directly after dinner and she & I went over to spend the evening with Mrs. Lewis Kemp for the first time; spent quite a pleasant evening. Sarah Miller & Isa Buckey were there to tea & invited [me] to spend the next day with them as Mrs. G. Taylor, Mrs. L. Kemp and others were expected. We left Mrs. L. K[emp]'s directly after tea and came home by Mrs. Howard's. Marion came home with me and staid over night.

Tuesday [April] 8th. Awoke to find it raining, continued in showers all day. Marion wished to go home to school, so we sent her on horseback. Did not go to Mrs. B[uckey]'s to-day.

Wednesday [April] 9th. A beautiful day. Ma & I rode to town on horseback and did some shopping; got my spring bonnet, etc. & when I came home found Mrs. I. Howard's servant boy waiting for us saying Mrs. H. wanted me to go to Mr[s]. J. Buckey's with her, so I instantly ate my dinner & went. Mrs. H. was nearly ready when I got there. We stopped at Mr. Keefer's for the girls but they could not [go]. We spent a very pleasant evening with Mrs. J. Buckey, J. Miller & I. Buckey; Mr. & Mrs. L. Kemp were over to tea. When I got home found a note from Vallie saying she would go into town to-morrow & expect[s] me to come home with them.

Thursday [April] 10th. At home busy till about three o'clock, when I walked into town and spent the evening at Mrs. L. Markell's. Lucretia Brunner & Vallie were there & spent a very pleasant evening. Went home with Vallie & Uncle A. and staid over night.

---

[50]The schoolhouse was located about one-half mile south of Manchester Farm on the New Design Road. *Bond Map*, 1858.

Friday [April] 11th. It rained in the morning but cleared after dinner; Uncle Adams brought me home behind him. I was quite sick in the evening. Had a dispatch from Coz H. Smith & Mr. Jamison from Phil[adelphia].

Saturday April 12th. Quite clear to-day; up & down all the morning but after dinner I felt much better. Mr. J. A. Johnson came when we were at tea & spent the evening; he was here to-day one year. He was in excellent spirits.

* * * * *

Monday [April] 14th. A tolerably pleasant day. I rode down to Miss B. Fout's[51] took my dress down to have it plaited; it was.

* * * * *

Wednesday [April] 16th. I was at home all day & not well; had a note from Vallie saying Minnie was not so well or she would have been up and that she would be up to-morrow if Minnie's health would permit. I wrote her she should.

Thursday [April] 17th. Still blustery; had a note from Vallie saying Minnie was not well enough for her to leave & wrote her one in return. Bettie L. Johnson was married one year to-day. I was quite sick to-day.

Friday [April] 18th. To-day is Good Friday, right pleasant day though I was not well enough to enjoy its pleasures. Jenny & Fanny Adams were up and said Minnie was still sick.

Saturday [April] 19th. Unpleasant day, rained very hard part of the day. I felt much better this evening & was up most of the evening.

Sunday [April] 20th. Rather pleasant day. I of course was at home all day, not being well enough to go out. Mr. S. B. Jamison was out and took tea. He was quite talkative.

Monday [April] 21st. Easter Monday. The anniversary of my acquaintance with Mr. J. A. Johnson. I thought a great deal of him to-day, perhaps more

---

[51]Miss B. Fout lived about a third of a mile south of Manchester Farm on the New Design Road. *Ibid.*

1851

than I should for we are only friends <u>as yet</u> and not engaged as report says. I feel much better to-day. Very clear but cold & windy.

Tuesday April 22nd. At home all day, much better; indeed, so well that I got ready to go to town, but was prevented from going by Mrs. I. Howard's & Marion coming who spent the evening with us.

Wednesday [April] 23rd. A beautiful day; about nine o'clock Mr. & Mrs. Reese & Martin & Mrs. Winchester came. Mrs. Reese & Mrs. W. spent the day. Mr. R. & Martin went back but came out to tea. Uncle & Aunt Elias Scholl & Mrs. L. Kemp spent the day here too.

Thursday [April] 24th. A pretty day. Rode to town on horseback & stopped at Mrs. Markell's and Ellie & Callie Brunner went with me to see Kate Bantz, Mr. & Mrs. Doub, Kate Houck & Tilly Jackson. I then came home.

Friday [April] 25th. A very clear & warm day. Rode down to Miss B. Fout's on horseback & got my dress, called over to see Vallie & then came home. Was at home the rest of the day.

Saturday [April] 26th. Clear. Was at home in the morning, but after dinner Father took us into town and we did some shopping & was to see Mrs. Dr. Shields, Miss Sallie Reich a little while.

Sunday [April] 27th. Ma & I went into town in the carriage this morning and heard a very good sermon from Dr. Zack. There was all kinds of weather almost to-day. Mrs. Jamison came out about three o'clock and remained till about four. Mr. Johnson came out and spent the evening.

Monday April 28th. Much cooler. Went down to Miss B. Fout's and had my dress fit, came home, ate my dinner, & went into town to get some trimmings. Was to see K. Bantz, and came down to Mrs. L. Markells & took tea [and] then came home.

Tuesday [April] 29th. Went down to Miss B. Fout's & took her the trimmings this morning. Mrs. Jamison was out & spent the evening. Pleasant day.

Wednesday [April] 30th. Rainy & cloudy all day. Vallie came up after dinner and spent the evening. Mother went out to Aunt M. Artz & brought Vic[torine][52] home with her to stay.

Thursday May 1st [1851]. Clear & somewhat cooler. V[ictorine] is still here.

Friday [May] 2nd. A clear though rather cool day. Ma took Victorine home to-day and when she and Pa came home they brought me a letter from Lou Hersh[53], saying she would pay me a visit in the early part of the third week in May if convenient, and also a letter form P[enelope] Mering saying she was expecting me down, and an invitation to the May party. I went down to Miss B. Fout's and got my dress and came home. Pa took me into town to K. Bantz's and I met Annie Coblentz & Lucretia Eberts there. We all dressed and went to the May Party. Met numerous acquaintances there & saw Mollie J. Hammond crowned Queen of May. I spent a delightful evening. Mr. J. A. Johnson accompanied us at twelve o'clock to Mrs. Bantz.

Saturday [May] 3rd. Wrote a letter to Lou Hersh saying I should be delighted to see her. Came out home about twelve o'clock. Called to see Nellie Brunner's letter. Went into town again to see Miss Fannie Burrier at Mrs. Reynold's and then came home.

* * * * *

Tuesday [May] 6th. It was somewhat cooler. Uncle Adams was up a little in the morning but did not give the news of his wedding.[54] Mr. Jamison spent the evening here.

Wednesday [May] 7th. A very pretty day. Mrs. J. A. Taylor & Annie Howard spent the evening and I had a note and some papers from Vallie. Wrote a letter to Mary & Kate Sauerwein.

* * * * *

---

[52]Victorine Artz was a cousin of Margaret Scholl, since their mothers were sisters.

[53]Lou or Louise Hersh was a friend from New Oxford, Pennsylvania, a town located between Gettysburg and York on Route 30.

[54]On the remarriage of Valentine Adams, whose first wife was Mrs. Daniel Scholl's sister, see note 30, 1851.

1851

Saturday [May] 10th. Warm like the middle of summer. We were very busy white washing & house cleaning to-day.

Sunday [May] 11th. Very warm. Mother & I went into church and heard a sermon from Dr. Shaff. Came [home], found Uncle Artz here; and while we were at dinner Mr. Jamison came out and we walked over to the schoolhouse to preaching. Saw most of the neighbors there. Sarah Miller told me William Miller & Mary Buckey were to be married on Tuesday at seven o'clock and that they would be pleased to see me. Had a note from Carey Hamm.

Monday [May] 12th. Still so warm. Father took me into town in the evening and I went to see Aunty Kemp & Mrs. L. Markell and did some shopping.

Tuesday [May] 13th. Quite as warm as it has been; was down at Mrs. Fout's to pay Miss B. this morning. It rained this evening & was cloudy.

* * * * *

Friday [May] 16th. A beautiful day. I had a letter from Lou to-day saying she would start for Fred'k next Monday or Tuesday and also one from P. Mering saying how sorry she was that I could not visit her but inviting Lou & I both down; she says she will take no excuse.

Saturday [May] 17th. Much warmer and looked like rain almost all this evening but did not till after night. Mrs. C. Markell brought Mrs. L. Markell out after tea and made a fashionable call of about an hour.

Sunday [May] 18th. Rained in showers during the day. Ma & I went into church. Mr. Jamison was out after tea and spent the evening.

Monday [May] 19th. Rainy disagreeable day. I commenced a letter to G. K. but did not finish it. Vallie, Lucretia Brunner & Kate Zacharias came about three o'clock and spent the evening. Lou Hersh and her brother Charles came about six o'clock. I was quite delighted to see her and she looks quite like herself.

Tuesday [May] 20th. Still rainy. Mr. Hersh left this morning for Gettysburg. Lou & I went over and spent the evening with Vallie & her company.

Wednesday [May] 21st. Cleared off beautifully when we arose this morning. Lou, Ma & I went into town this morning and made some purchases and then came home. Mrs. Jamison brought Mr. C. Kunkel out after tea. Mr. J. A. Johnson was out also.

Thursday May 22nd. A pretty day. Wrote a note to Mrs. I. Howard's telling her Lou had come. She sent me word she would be over. She came over about four o'clock and remained till after tea.

Friday [May] 23rd. As we wished to show Lou the sights, Father took Lou an I out to the reservoir[55]; stopped in town for Ella Brunner and brought her out home with us. Ella, Lou & I all went over & spent a very pleasant evening with our new neighbor Miss C. Smith. Lou's friend Mrs. Pugenet and Abram came out and spent the evening. Rained during the night.

Saturday [May] 24th. Somewhat cooler. Father took us into town and we took Lou round to see the sights.

Sunday [May] 25th. Lou & I went to church in the morning and heard a sermon from Dr. Z; went home and walked over to the schoolhouse and heard a sermon from Mr. Rice. Mr. Jamison was out after tea.

Monday [May] 26th. Father, Lou & I started for Harper's Ferry very early this morning; enjoyed the scenery on the road and arrived there about ten o'clock. Lizzie Keller was boarding at the hotel and that made it very pleasant. Father, Lou & I were out after dinner visiting the armory[56], etc. When we came, Lizzie with us, to call on Mrs. A. Herr, formerly Miss N. Hoffman, who insisted upon our staying with her over night. We did so [and] found her husband a very pleasant agreeable man. Mrs. Burton was there to tea. Narciss' two sisters were there after tea and also the Presbyterian minister Mr. _____.

---

[55]The Frederick Water Company was established in 1825. Water was pumped from a spring two and one-half miles northwest of the city limits to a reservoir. Wooden pipes delivered the water to several pumps on the city streets, from which the water was distributed to homes. In recent years the reservoir has become a park known as Max Kehne Park on Seventh Street. Scharf, *Western Maryland*, I, 557.

[56]The armory at Harpers Ferry was an important Federal arsenal. It became the focal point of John Brown's attack in 1859. Works Progress Administration, *West Virginia, A Guide to the Mountain State* (New York, 1941), p. 224.

1851

Tuesday [May] 27th. Awoke to find the sun shining brightly & quite warm. Lizzie Keller was already there to take a break-fast. We bid farewell to Narciss about nine o'clock. Lizzie, Lou & I went up on Jefferson Rock[57] to take a view and returned to the Hotel; told Father we were ready to start but he thought better to wait till after dinner. We got home about 7 o'clock. Met Ed & Annie Shriner short distance from the house and got them to return with us. Maggie, T[om] Derr, Uncle Adams, Sarah A. & Vallie had been up to see us.

Wednesday [May] 28th. A pleasant day. Gusty in the evening. I went into town early, did some shopping & called to see Mrs. Markell. Had a letter from Gene Kephart. We were very busy till about three o'clock, when we went over to Uncle Adams. Took tea, and then Vallie, S. Adams, Lou, Abram & I proceeded on our way to Mr. Eagle's to attend a wedding day party given to Francis Delashmutt. They danced all night till broad daylight.

Thursday [May] 29th. Spent most the day after we got home in the arms of Morpheus, all except to get our meals and a short time in the evening to see company. Annie Buckey & Kate Bantz were out to see us to make a call.

Friday [May] 30th. Rather rainy. Mrs. I. Howard, Mary & Annie Keefer were over after dinner.

Saturday [May] 31st. Lou & I spent the evening with Mrs. I. Howard; saw Mrs. French, Mary, Ellen & Ann Keefer there. We walked out to Uncle Adams' after tea and returned about ten o'clock.

Sunday June 1st [1851]. Pa's birthday, 63 years old. We were not into church in the morning. After dinner we went into town. Met Mr. Jamison on his way out but he returned with us. He & Mr. G. Rice came up to Mrs. Markell's to meet us; Ellen went with us to Catholic Vespers, then returned home; found Mr. Johnson here. Mr. Jamison came out after tea, also Mrs. Smith & Mrs. Pugenet spent the evening.

---

[57] Jefferson Rock on the hillside overlooking the Potomac and Shenandoah Rivers was named for Thomas Jefferson who visited Harpers Ferry in 1801. He stated that the view here was worth a trip across the Atlantic. *Ibid.*, p. 225.

1851

Monday [June] 2nd. A pleasant day. We were at home all day. Ellen Keefer, Marion, Virginia & Emily Howard, C. Smith & Jennie Adams spent the afternoon.

Tuesday [June] 3rd. A pretty day, so clear, so soft, so cool. Father took us into town early; stopped at Mrs. L. Markell's and got Ellen and went out and spent the day with Maggie & Mary Derr. We were out to Uncle Shriner's a short time. Mr. J. & Coz Ed were over in the evening & took tea there.

Wednesday [June] 4th. We went up and spent the morning at Mrs. C. Howard's & after dinner went down to Mr. J. Keefer's. A. R. Late, Mr. & Mrs. Wm. Fout, Sarah Miller, Isa Buckey, & Dick Cromwell were all there to tea. Sarah, Isa & Dick stopped on their way from our house. When we got home found Mr. G. Birely & sister, Vallie & Willie Adams there. Vallie & Willie left pretty soon. Mr. & Miss B. spent the evening.

Thursday [June] 5th. Ellen Brunner's birthday. We went into town after dinner. Saw Mr. Sam Hersh[58] pass and go out to our house, but he soon returned and we met him as we went out. We were to see Kate Bantz & Annie Zacharias. We spent the evening at Mrs. L. Markell's; Mr. Hersh was there to tea. Messrs. Johnson, Shriner, F. Markell, Mr. Rice & Jamison came after tea & spent the evening. M[ess]r[s]. H., Jamison, Shriner & Johnson brought us out home in buggies, including Maggie Derr & Nellie B. Mr. Hersh staid with us.

Friday June 6th. The long looked-for day of our Pic-nic[59] came at last. A beautiful morning. Messrs. Jamison, Johnson & Shriner came out in buggies to take Lou, Nellie & Maggie down. Mr. E. Creager brought Kate Bantz out & Mr. Hersh took me. We went over to the ground about half-past two o'clock in [sic] the evening about sundown, spent the day in dancing, riding, eating, drinking & the various ways in which such days are spent. I enjoyed the day very much indeed. There was a shower came up in the evening which made a great scattering, some to the schoolhouse, some to carriages and some under the table. Lou & I retired as soon as all the company left as she was to start for home to-morrow morning early.

---

[58]Mr. Sam Hersh was a brother of Lou from New Oxford, Pennsylvania.

[59]One of the social pleasures of the out of doors which was very popular with young couples was the "Pic-nic." The men usually provided the transportation while the women brought the food. Carle Bode, *American Life in the 1840's* (Berkeley, CA, 1959), p. 267.

1851

Saturday June 7th. Today is fair. Lou & her brother Sam left immediately after our early breakfast and I was so lonely & had so much to think of as regards to-day one year. I went down to Miss B. Fout's & had a dress fit; was to see Vallie a few moments. Her new mother had not come home yet, but would that evening.

Sunday June 8th. Warm & sultry in the morning & quite a heavy rain in the evening. I was in to church in the morning and heard a sermon from Dr. Zacharias. Mr. Jamison was out after tea.

BRUCEVILLE

Monday [June] 9th. Quite pleasant this morning, wrote a letter to P[enelope] Mering saying I would be down [to Bruceville] to see her to-morrow, but soon Father told me he would take me down that evening. We started after dinner and arrived there about six o'clock [and] found them home with the addition of some company. Lou Finckel, a young lady from Washington, was spending some time with her. Mr. Milton and I spent the evening there. Mr. D. Landis was there too; he is Mrs. Mering's clerk. I met with a very warm reception. They are such a kind family.

Tuesday [June] 10th. Father left for home this morning. We spent the day with the family till after tea when Penelope, Lou F. & I walked over to Mr. Scott's to see Genie & Miss Wolse. Charlie came home with us.

Wednesday [June] 11th. Lou, Penelope & I went over to Mrs. Wm. Mering and spent a very pleasant day. Saw the family. I like Grannie Mering very much indeed.

Thursday [June] 12th. A very pretty day. We had early tea and then Nellie, Lou, and I took a long ride on horseback; we went through Middleburg & nearly up to Ladiesburg. Mrs. Abington Slick & Charlie Scott spent the evening with us. We stopped to see Miss Krantz in Middleburg.

Friday June 13th. We were at home all day till after tea, when we went to see Mrs. Slick & Miss Joanne Mering a little.

Saturday [June] 14th. A beautiful morning. Mr. Landis took Penelope & I down to the Misses Birnies. Leon went so far as Taneytown and staid there.

We got to Thorndale[60] about ten o'clock and were very pleasantly entertained till about three o'clock by the ladies & Sallie Reisman, Fanny Jarboe, Kate Sauerwein & Nannie Waters. About three o'clock Miss Ellen, Sallie R., Penelope, Mr. Landis & I went up to Mrs. R. Birnies and took tea. They were all very kind and appeared very glad to see us. We got home a little before eight o'clock. Mr. T. F. Cover was to see us till about half-past eleven o'clock. Wrote a letter home.

Sunday [June] 15th. Mr. Mering took Penelope & I into church to Taneytown. Annie Mering came out home with us after dinner. Dixon Mering, Mrs. D. Landis, Penelope, Annie & I all rode on horseback over to Key's schoolhouse to preaching; we went first to Hawk's [sic] Church[61] but there was no preaching. Mrs. Milton Cover came home with us and took tea & spent the evening.

Monday [June] 16th. A beautiful day. Miss H. Koontz took dinner with us. Joanne Mering was here a little this morning. Mr. Landis took Annie & I over to his father's that evening and we spent a very pleasant evening with Miss Sarah and three Miss Carmacks. Miss E. Carmack was there a short time. When we came back to Mr. Mering's found Eugenia Scott and Miss Wolse had been to see us.

Tuesday June 17th. Mr. Dixon Mering came over this morning and took Penelope, Annie & I down to see Caroline Haines. We spent a very pleasant day; directly after dinner Mr. Ensor took his carriage, Mr. Mering and we all went into New Windsor. Stopped at Mr. Haines's and saw his daughter and Miss Cox. We went to the springs and then up to the College[62]; on our way

---

[60]Thorndale was a boarding school located near Taneytown in Carroll County. It was run by Misses Birnies who claimed that pupils had the advantage of daily association with a family and were under constant care and supervision. The school year cost $200, with an extra charge for piano ($25) and 50 cents for the use of the library. Nancy M. Warren, *Carroll County, Maryland* (Westminster, MD, 1976), pp. 57-58.

[61]Haughs German Reformed Church is located on Haughs Church Road west of Ladiesburg which is located on Route 194, the Woodsboro Pike.

[62]The New Windsor College was erected in 1849 as a Presbyterian School. Later it became a Roman Catholic College. In the early twentieth century it became Blue Ridge College. In 1937 it became the Brethren Service Center which now houses an International Gift Shop and other facilities of the New Windsor Service Center. Historical Society of Carroll County, *The First 150 Years, A Pictorial History of Carroll County, MD, 1837-1987* (Westminster, MD, 1986), p. 88.

1851

up, Misses Kate, Lucretia & Maggie Pool, Miss H. Shriner, another Miss Cox & Mr. Pool joined us; we all went through the College. Had a great deal of sport. We came back to Mrs. E's, took tea and started for home. We got home about ten o'clock; found we had had company. I was very much pleased with the county and with Uniontown. It is such a neat little village.

Wednesday [June] 18th. A very warm day. Expected Drs. C. and Martin this evening but they did not come. They told Miss H. Koontz they were coming. We were at Mrs. Slick a few moments this evening to look at a trunk.

Thursday June 19th. Still clear; we dressed ourselves as usual but no company came. We took a nice long walk and when we came back home found Annie Mering's brother had come for her and she went home; had a letter from home this morning saying Father would either come for me on Friday evening or Monday.

Friday [June] 20th. At home in the morning but after dinner Penelope and I rode over on horseback to her uncle W. M. Mering's to tea and afterwards Annie rode with us as far as Mrs. Snook's where we called a few hours. They are quite a pleasant family, I think. When we got home in the evening found Father there. He had a letter for me from M & K Sauerwein & card of invitation from Mr. Sam Hersh. I had my clothes to pack as yet.

Saturday [June] 21st. We started for home pretty soon and got home about one o'clock. Stopped to see Aunt M. Artz a while and also to give a letter to Mrs. B. F. W[inchester]. Father went to the post office and I had a letter from Lou Hersh.

Sunday [June] 22nd. Mother & I went into church and heard a sermon from Dr. Z. It rained a little this evening. Mr. J. A. Johnson was out and spent the evening.

Monday June 23rd. I went into town this morning with Mother, and Father was to see Mrs. B. F. Winchester & her sister Miss Fanny Dunham who is staying with her. I went round to see Kate Bantz & Annie Coblentz; took dinner with them and staid till about four o'clock, when I came over to see Ellen Brunner a few moments and then came out home. It rained a little this evening.

Tuesday [June] 24th. Commenced harvesting this morning. I was down at Miss B. Fout's, got my dress, and was over to see Miss V. Adams & family.

1851

Wednesday [June] 25th. A very warm day. Mr. Bantz brought Kate B[antz] & Annie C[oblentz] out this morning and left them; they remained over night.

Thursday [June] 26th. Mr. Bantz came out for the girls this morning and I wrote a letter and sent it by them. I wrote to Penelope [Mering]. I was over to Mrs. I. Howard's and spent the evening. After tea, Mrs. Pugenet & Miss Jenkins walked out and spent the evening.

* * * * *

Saturday [June] 28th. Still pleasant. I went into town this evening, did some shopping, was to see Sue Thomas and girls at the FF Sem, Mary, Emily and Ellen Brunner. After supper I wrote to Eugenie Kephart[63] and Lou Hersh.

Sunday June 29th. I went into church this morning. Stopped for Ellen B and went to church with her; heard a sermon from Dr. Zack; it was excessively warm. We had quite a fine shower after night.

* * * * *

Tuesday July 1st [1851]. Rained last night and still a little in the morning. Annie and Oliver Ogle came out about twelve o'clock and left about half-past four o'clock. O. was as entertaining as usual.

Wednesday July 2nd. I was down at Miss B. Fout's to-day about my dress, went over to Uncle Adams and remained to dinner. Lucretia Brunner and Kate Zack to dinner there. They were out spending the day. Mrs. I. Howard, Mrs. Chandler, Mrs. Finney, Ann F. Keefer were there to spend the evening too. I left about four. When I was at tea I heard a Rap-Rap at the door. I went out and what was my astonishment to find it was Messrs. E. Creager and J. A. Johnson. They made themselves very agreeable and I enjoyed the evening very much.

Thursday [July] 3rd. A beautiful day. I was sorry I was not able to go spend the evening with Kate Bantz as I promised but it was impossible, for I had [*illegible*] offered so kindly to bring me home.

---

[63]Eugenia Kephart was a schoolmate of the diarist at the Frederick Female Seminary.

1851

Friday July 4th. The anniversary of our independence. I had an invitation to two pic-nic parties but remained at home, preferring [it] to all other places. I was down to Miss B. Fout's on business.

Saturday [July] 5th. Was in town a short time this morning shopping; when I came home went down to Miss B's and had my dress fit. Mrs. Sally Adams and Vallie spent the evening here. I had a letter from Lou Hersh this morning.

Sunday [July] 6th. Ma and I were in town to church this morning and heard a sermon from Dr. Zack. Mr. Jamison came out after tea and spent the evening.

Monday [July] 7th. To-day so bright, so clear. 'Tis my 18th birthday. Mr. Taylor was to see me; he is much changed and I think would be improved were it not for the moustache. Vallie and Jennie and I spent the evening with Caroline Smith; met Mrs. I. Howard & C. Keefer there.

Tuesday [July] 8th. I was in town this morning to see Mrs. B. F. W[inchester]; saw Penelope [Mering], Lou Finckle, & Mrs. Dunham, Ophelia D. and Mary Shope. P. and I went shopping. Saw G. Kephart was into town. Went to see Mrs. L. Markell.

Wednesday [July] 9th. Went into town after dinner; stopped at Mrs. Markell's. E. Brunner, C. Doll of Martinsburg and I went up to the examination; was pleased with the exercises, especially Gregg Brady's composition. I went up to Mrs. B. F. W.'s and took tea. We all went down to the F F Seminary to the soiree; there were a good many persons there. We left between ten & eleven. Mr. J. A. J. went home with me; Mr. D. Hunt with O., GP., Martin with Lou. Mr. J. A. J. had been out to see us.

Thursday [July] 10th. Quite a pleasant day but a little shower during the day. We all went down to the F. F. Seminary at ten o'clock and heard the Senior Class read their compositions; was very much gratified they did very well. Dined and took tea at the F. F. Sem. Went with the ladies to see K. B. and as I was going, met Cousin Harrie Smith [and] took him along. Was quite surprised to see him, he had just arrived. Went over to E. Brunner's and came with the girls to the church; saw the diplomas and testimonials given and

1851

afterwards came to Mrs. L. Markell's. Dr. Magill[64] came with Ellen, Lottie A. Campbell and I were together. Shortly after we got home we took a walk. Mr. C. Hoffman and Cousin Ed Shriner joined [us] and staid till nearly eleven o'clock.

Friday [July] 11th. It rained this morning but cleared off soon. Was to see Mrs. B. F. Winchester; then came out home.

Saturday July 12th. Quite clear and pleasant. At home till about three o'clock, when I went into town for E. Kephart. She was not at her Aunt's. Went up to Mrs. B. F. W.'s and invited Ophelia, Penelope & Gene to come out home with me, which they did. I was to see E. B. a few moments. The girls staid overnight.

Sunday [July] 13th. We all got ready and went into church. They remained in town; I came out home after church. Uncle Ed & Annie Shriner came out from church. Cousin J. Harrie Smith & Mr. Jamison came out about four o'clock. Mr. J. A. Johnson came out about six.

Monday [July] 14th. Clear & pleasant. I went in town with Mother & went to Mrs. Winchester's. Penelope expected to leave, but was disappointed. Was to see E. B. a little; met her on the street and went home with her and Lottie. Got a letter from M. Sauerwein & a circular from Mercersburg[65] farm C[ollege].

Tuesday [July] 15th. Went into town this morning; called for Lottie Doll and we went to the Distribution at the Seminary. Penelope & Ophelia were along; had quite a pleasant time, met a good many acquaintances there. I staid in town. Went up to Mrs. B. F. Winchester's and staid. Harrie, P., Mr. J. A. J. & I went over to see E. B. a little. We all went to the concert that evening

---

[64]Dr. McGill had his office and residence on the north side of Patrick west of Bentz Street. Later he moved to Record Street to Dr. William Tyler's house. *Williams' Directory*, p. 26.

[65]Mercersburg College began as Marshall College or Seminary in 1836. When the Seminary merged with Franklin College in Lancaster, Pennsylvania, the Evangelical Synod decided to separate the girls' section of the Mercersburg school from the boys'. In 1893 the Synod took over the building of what had been the Frederick Female Seminary and opened the Woman's College of Frederick, Maryland. J. & D. Ranck, *History of Evangelical Reformed Church*, pp. 131-132.

and had quite a pleasant time. Mrs. W. invited me. It was a free concert given by the Amateur Society assisted by gentlemen from B.

Wednesday July 16th. Penelope really left this morning; Harrie and I went as far as the bridge. There was quite a merry party to & from the bridge. C. Taylor was with us. I went to the boy's distribution of premiums at St. John's College[66] of Fred'k. I came home after tea with Ma & Pa. Dick Cromwell & Mr. Jamison came out soon after I got home. Wrote to Mary Sauerwein by Penelope.

Thursday [July] 17th. At home all day. Mother went to Grandma's in the evening. Coz H. arrived & Mr. Jamison came out and took tea with me. They said I did the honors of the table gracefully. Harrie leaves tomorrow.

* * * * *

Sunday [July] 20th. Ma & I went into church; heard a very good sermon from Dr. Zack. Kate B came up to Ma & I, and persuaded her to let me go home with her; she did so. Lydia Moore was not well, had toothache. We went to church at night. Mr. Jamison was out.

Monday [July] 21st. A pleasant day. Had a note from Marion [Howard] saying Huldah was with her and that she & her Ma would be very glad to see Mother and I. We went over & spent the evening. Charlotte & Ellen Keefer were there.

Tuesday [July] 22nd. Pleasant day. Marion & Huldah Howard spent the evening with me. What was my surprise to see Cousin Harrie about four o'clock. He had a friend, Mr. Clark of Emmitsburg with him; they only made a call. Mr. Jamison was out after tea and spent the evening.

Wednesday [July] 23rd. According to engagement I went over to Mrs. Howard's and went blackberrying with Marion & H. Got back about twelve o'clock.

---

[66]St. John's College was incorporated in 1828 as St. John's Literary Institute. It became the rival of Georgetown until 1852, when a large number of students were dismissed at one time. Thomas R. Bevan, *220 Years, A History of the Catholic Community of the Frederick Valley* (Frederick, MD, 1977), p. 16.

Thursday [July] 24th. At home all day. It rained this evening. Mr. J. A. Johnson was out & spent evening.

Friday [July] 25th. I rode in town on horseback. Was to see Kate Bantz, K. Kunkle[67] & E. Brunner; they have a pic-nic in contemplation, to which I am invited and they are very anxious I shall attend. Got home about twelve. Mrs. Lewis Kemp, Jr. & Ann Keefer were up and spent the evening.

Saturday [July] 26th. About twelve o'clock Cousin Annie Serena & John Scholl, Cousin Bob & Mary E. Wood from Alexandria came and took dinner. After dinner we went in to the menagery[68] [*sic*] & out to the reservoir. Mr. Jamison joined us and went to the reservoir. We had a very severe gust at night.

Sunday [July] 27th. We all went in to church; it rained very hard this morning. They all left after dinner. Mr. Jamison spent the evening with me.

Monday July 28th. Went into town this morning; was to see Kate Bantz and did some shopping, then came home.

Tuesday [July] 29th. I was in town this morning; was to see Kate Kunkel; did some shopping & then came home.

Wednesday [July] 30th. I woke expecting to go to the pic-nic but, what was my disappointment, when I found it was raining; it continued raining all day.

Thursday [July] 31st. Still raining part of the day; however I ventured out and went to Miss B. Fout's. Was caught in the rain and stopped at Mrs. Heiner's till it ceased raining. When I got home found a note from Marion Howard saying her Uncle Isaac Hall of Washington City was up and would

---

[67] Kate Kunkle was a daughter of John Kunkle who lived on the south side of Patrick between Carroll and East Streets. *Williams' Directory*, p. 26. Another Kunkle family lived on West Church Street (*Ibid.*, p. 23).

[68] Menagerie is a collection of wild or strange animals, especially for exhibition; a place where they are kept or exhibited. *Webster's Dictionary.* "The Menagerie took place at the Barracks on South Market Street. It was blown down but no one was injured, but hats and bonnets were thrown about in style. The awning was torn in several places." Engelbrecht, *Diary*, II, 523.

1851

come and see me if we would be home. I wrote I would, and so he and Mary Keefer rode over about four o'clock to make a fashionable call.[69] He is quite handsome though rather large, very agreeable; had a letter from G. Kephart.

Friday August 1st [1851]. Ma & I went out to Grandmother's in the evening and spent the evening.

Saturday [August] 2nd. After dinner I rode over to Mrs. I. Howard's and spent the evening. Mrs. Kemp, Deatrick, Mrs. Thomas & Howard, Misses Hall, Buckey, Tillie & Howard were all there. When I got home found Mr. J. A. J. there. He invited me to a pic-nic on next Saturday.

Sunday August 3rd. Ma & I went to town to church and heard an excellent sermon from Dr. Zack. Mr. Jamison came out after dinner and remained till after tea.

Monday [August] 4th. Wrote a letter to M. Sauerwein and sent her an invitation to the pic-nic. Had a note from Ginnie Adams and wrote her one in return, also one from M. Howard. I was quite surprised about two o'clock when Mr. P. Rau of Balt. came out to see me. He was as agreeable as usual.

Tuesday [August] 5th. Quite a pleasant day. Went over to Mrs. I. Howard's this evening and went with her and sisters over to Mrs. L. Kemp's. Met Mary & Ellen Keefer, Ginnie & Emily H., S. Miller, Mrs. Thomas and Mrs. Deatrick & others. I think Alice Tylard is very much improved. When I got home found Chett Taylor had been there to invite me to a pic-nic.

Wednesday [August] 6th. At home in the morning; had a letter from M. Sauerwein saying she would be here on Friday. Went down to Mrs. Keefer's to spend the evening; met Mrs. H[oward], sisters & Marion, Isy Buckey & S Miller, Mrs. Kemp, Alice Tylard, John & Irene Orndorff, Tommy Kemp & Juliet Buckey.

Thursday [August] 7th. I had given up all idea of going to the pic-nic when Mr. Jamison came and said I must come. I had quite a pleasant time. It

---

[69]It was fashionable to pay a formal call between two and four in the summer and two and five in the winter. Many ladies had regular days when they received callers. Everett B. Willson, *America's Vanishing Folkways* (South Brunswick, NJ, 1965), p. 184.

1851

rained and then we went over to Mr. G[*illegible*] and danced till sundown. Mr. J. & Ginnie Brengle brought me home.

Friday August 8th. I was busy in the morning and after dinner I went into town in the carriage and met & brought Mary Sauerwein out home. She looks quite well and pretty. Had a letter from Lou Hersh by Vallie, who is quite well and happy, and also a note from Vallie saying she was so pleased I wrote her one in return. It was rainy this evening.

Saturday [August] 9th. Awoke to find the weather had much the appearance of clearing. Mr. Johnson was here by eight o'clock for us to go to the pic-nic. Ed Shriner came and then we started, went to Uncle S's and walked from there over; there were quite a number there. Saw Kate Sauerwein there & enjoyed the pic-nic very much; had an introduction to several gentlemen. Brother C. was all attention. We came home after sundown, stopped in town to get ice cream, got home about nine; the gentlemen left about ten or eleven. Invited us to go to camp and we excepted [*sic*]. Met a great many strangers today. Had a letter from P[enelope] Mering.

Sunday [August] 10th. Quite a pleasant day, much cooler. The gentlemen were out here between 7 & 8 o'clock and we soon started for camp[70]. Spent a very pleasant day. Saw Mr. DeFord from B. and got acquainted with some other gentlemen. Came home between 8 & 9 o'clock.

Monday August 11th. We were at home all day. Somewhat cloudy. Vallie & Fannie Adams spent the evening with us.

Tuesday [August] 12th. Quite a pleasant day. Uncle L. Scholl was here a few moments in the morning, took Father to the sale. Mr. Bantz brought Kate and Miss R. Metzger out to call on us this evening. Mr. Jamison was out after tea and spent the evening.

Wednesday [August] 13th. A pretty day. Maggie & John Derr and Kate Sauerwein came out at eleven o'clock and remained till we left. Messrs. Jamison & Shriner came out according to engagement and took us down to

---

[70] The day of the camp meeting reached a peak of religious revivalist spirit in the mid-nineteenth century. People gathered as though for a carnival. Isabel Ross, *Taste in America* (New York, 1967), p. 38.

1851

Cousin H. Scholl's, but what was our disappointment to find them not at home. We came on home and the gentlemen spent the evening with us.

Thursday [August] 14th. Mr. Jamison called out for us to attend Mary Kunkel's & Mrs. Loates's Pic-nic. We spent the day very pleasantly in the usual way in which such days are passed. As we returned home we stopped at Mrs. Leigh's and were treated to ice cream. When we got home found Mr. & Mrs. Dutrow, Mr. & Mrs. L. Scholl and Miss C. Brunner had spent the day here.

Friday [August] 15th. Mary & I went down & spent the evening with Vallie, Mrs. Howard & Marion, & Mrs. H's sisters, Kate Bantz [and] Annie Coblentz, Miss Metzger and Mr. Wm. Bantz were there to tea. We returned home after tea.

Saturday August 16th. Mrs. I. Howard & sisters, Emily & Virginia Howard and Eveline Smith were here and spent the evening here; they all left after tea.

Sunday [August] 17th. Mary and I went to church. Mother went with us as far as town; that is, she went out to Grandmother's and we stopped at Mrs. L. Markell's and [saw] the family and Ellen's friends staying with her, the Miss Daughertys of Balt. We all went to church together. Saw Mr. Bassemer in church. Mr. Jamison had [for] us a note from cousins Mr. E. W. and A. E. Scholl. We came home. Cousins Ed & Annie Shriner, Mary, Annie, Ed & I went into town; Mr. Jamison joined us and we went to Catholic church. Mary received three letters and in George's [letter] there was a note for me.

Monday [August] 18th. A rainy drizzling day. Mr. Bansemer of B. and Mr. Schaeffer of Frederick were out and made a call of about two hours. We went out to take a walk in the evening and in our way met Mr. J. A. J. & Cousins F. Adams, who spent the evening with us; also Cousin Ed Shriner was out.

Tuesday [August] 19th. We were invited to a pic-nic but did not attend. Mary & I walked into town and made some purchases, and called to see Mrs. Markell; they were not at home. Saw Kate B & saw Lizzie Keller.

Wednesday 20th. August. A rainy cool day but, as we did not know when we would get an opportunity to go to Mrs. Derr's again, we, that is Mary & myself, went out and found Maggie [Derr] keeping house. Upon Maggie &

1851

Tommie offering so kindly to bring us home we consented to stay overnight. Ed Shriner was over that evening; we went riding on horseback.

Thursday [August] 21st. Still damp and drizzling. Mr. & Mrs. Derr came home after dinner. Mr. Johnson called here, and when we started to come home Maggie D. rode out to our house with him. Mary & Kate Sauerwein, Tommy and I came in Mr. D's carriage. They all took tea with us, Maggie & Tommy left after tea; Mr. J. left about nine o'clock. /I had a note from G. Kephart telling me of the pic-nic and saying I was invited. Had a (paper) of Sam Hersh./

Friday [August] 22nd. Drizzly morning but clear in the afternoon. We were at home all day and no company. Took a walk after tea.

Saturday [August] 23rd. Were disappointed at the ladies not coming; had a note from Vallie and wrote one in return. Edward Shriner & Mr. Jamison were out to tea, left pretty soon after. Ed took Kate S. out to Mr. Derr's as she had no Sunday rigging with her. Very pleasant day.

Sunday [August] 24th. Mother, Mary & I went into town in the carriage and went to the Lutheran Church and heard an excellent sermon from Mr. Deihl. Wrote a note to Vallie inviting her to dinner and then to go with us to Mrs. E. Howard's after dinner.

Monday August 25th. Clear & warm in the morning, but after dinner very sultry and drizzly. I had a note from Vallie saying she could not come to dinner, wrote one in return & I had one from her saying she could not go. Wrote a note to Evie Smith & had a verbal reply. Wrote a note to M. Howard and had one in return. Mary & I went up to Mr. E. Howard's after dinner; saw the family & Marion Howard there; spent the afternoon and returned after tea. Cousin Ed Shriner came out and staid over night.

Tuesday [August] 26th. A beautiful morning so clear so cool. Mr. Jamison was out about seven o'clock. We started for the pic-nic about eight o'clock. Mr. Jamison took me, Ed took Mary. There was quite a large gathering, about five hundred. A plank floor to dance on and very good music. We spent the day in much the usual manner in which such days are spent. I was introduced [to] a good many persons all of whom I do not remember. In the evening, Louise Garrott, Misses Hardy & Lindsay, Messrs. H. Garrott, & R. Garrott of Balt., Bladen of Phila., & E. Willard of Burkittsville, Drs. Hardy & J. Garrott, our party, & Mr. Johnson went into town; took tea at Rice's,

1851

then went to Kate B.'s to the Sem. & to Dr. Zack's; when we returned home [found] Mrs. W. Schaeffer had been out.

Wednesday August 27th. We were at home all day. We expected Mr. Johnson and Cousin Ed out to tea but they did not come till after tea. We got ready and went out to Mr. Derr's soon after tea. They told us Mr. Sauerwein had come. Met Mr. Irving & Uncle Shriner at Mr. Derr's & Miss Bausman. Maggie Derr told us she could not go as her mother & Mary were not at home. We were very much surprised.

Thursday [August] 28th. I rose to find it a lovely morning. Messrs. Creager, Johnson, Sauerwein & Shriner & Annie S. came over about ten o'clock and we started for the mountain. Mary with Mr. C., I with Mr. J., Mr. S., Kate, Ed & Annie in the two-horse carriage. On our way we stopped at the reservoir. We stopped on the mountain at a spring, and then Mary and I arranged the table on the rocks while the gentlemen attended their horses and made the lemonade. We ate our dinner, all of us in hearty good earnest. We enjoyed the mountain water very much. After we had eaten & drunk we prepared to ascend the mountain on foot, had a great deal of sport, one downfall, Annie S., going up. We enjoyed the view very much; saw good old Fred'k; could even distinguish the houses with a glass. Mr. C. saw his house, Mr. <u>Staufer's</u>, the bridge, Mr. D's & other <u>noted</u> places; could not distinguish our house as it was hid by the woods. We had a good deal of trouble in getting to the "White Rock"[71] after we were on the mountain, although we could see it, as the path was much impeded by trees there having been felled across the road. The Rock consists of a range of rocks about 30 or 40 perhaps 60 feet long and about 70 or 80 in height. They tower one above the other. Mr. S. wrote our names and left them under a stone on the rock. In descending we ran almost all the way. Mary and Ed fell running but were not hurt much. When we arrived we got supper about 6 o'clock, and then prepared to return home. We went back to Uncle S and remained over night. Messrs. J & C. remained till after ten o'clock. We spent a delightful day; all parties appeared charmed [and] declared the most delightful day of their lives.

---

[71]White Rock is still a favorite place for picnics and excursions. It is located on the eastern slope of the Catoctin Range a few miles north of High Knob. Here one can secure a sublime view of Frederick valley. According to legend it was here that an Indian maiden, her lover, and a discarded suitor tumbled off the cliff to their deaths. Scharf, *Western Maryland*, I, 570.

1851

Friday [August] 29th. Still as clear; Maggie D. came soon after breakfast and invited us to dinner with her; we all went [and] took dinner with her. Mr. J. & Mr. S. came over to take us in to take tea with Kate B., but we concluded it was too late, so the gentlemen remained to tea. The horse laid on the shaft and broke it. So we had to wait till Ed came over in the carriage. We went into town and staid with K. Bantz till about ten. Evie Winchester & Mr. S. Mort were there. Mr. Johnson & I went up to E. Brunner's a few moments, saw the family; Cally B., Lizzie, Melia Hoffman [were] there; we then came out home. Ma then handed me a note from Vallie and an invitation from C. Hersh to the commencement at Gettysburg. Vallie, Ann & E. Keefer were up and spent the afternoon here this evening.

Saturday [August] 30th. We found it a lovely day. We were at home till late in the evening, when we went into town in the cart, did some shopping and then came home. Mr. J. A. Johnson came out at half-past eight and remained over night. Wrote to Lou Hersh.

Sunday [August] 31st. A beautiful morning cool and clear. Mr. Jamison came out and we went to camp meeting at Urbana. There was a great crowd there; saw a great many acquaintances there; had a introduction to a cousin of Alexandria, E. Koones. Saw Em. Pearce there. Cousins Ed, Abram, Vallie, our party, Messrs. Brunner, Sauerwein. We spent a pleasant day and got home about half-past seven. When Mr. Jamison went to leave, found his horse and buggy gone.

Monday September 1st [1851]. Rather cloudy in the morning and very warm. Mary, Mother and I went over to Mr. I. Howard's and spent the evening. Misses Taneyhill of Baltimore were there.

Tuesday [September] 2nd. We arose early and as they could not send us in we walked in town to see Kate & George S.[auerwein] leave; but just as we arrived the cars left and we did not get to see them. We saw Misses Derr, John D. & Kate B., Georgianne Houck and Ed Shriner. Mary and I went to Kate B's and changed our shoes and then went out and did some shopping. Was to see Mrs. B. F. W. She was not at home, and to see Mary Kunkle and from there up to Aunty Kemp's to dinner. Saw Aunt Mary Scholl and Davy there. After dinner, we went to see Aunt M. Scholl, to Nussbaum's to see Mrs. L. E. Brunner, and back to Kate B's to tea; then came up to M. Derr's and got in the carriage and came out home. Mr. G. Birely, Mary B. and Miss Bausman were here and staid till about ten.

1851

Wednesday [September] 3rd. We were at home till about six o'clock when Father, Mother, Mary and I went out. Mary and I stopped at M. Derr's; Father and Mother went over to Uncle S. We went with M. Derr's family to singing school. Cousin Ed and Mr. Johnson returned with us to Mr. Derr's. We came home about ten o'clock.

Thursday Sept. 4th. We were at home all day. Messrs. Johnson and Creager came soon after tea. Mr. Jamison brought Misses Mary Byre and Miss Donohue of Georgetown; they remained till about ten o'clock, Messrs. J & C till nearly eleven; we spent a very pleasant evening.

Friday [September] 5th. A damp, drizzling day. Father took Mary an[d] I out to Mrs. Derr's, Mary to stay; but I expected to return immediately with Father, but the girls were anxious for me to stay, so I did till evening when John Derr brought me home.

* * * * *

Wednesday [September] 10th. At home in the morning. After dinner, I went into town and spent the evening with Mary Kunkle. Maggie Derr and Mary Sauerwein were spending the day there. Mr. Jamison and Ed soon came and sat about an hour. Mr. Jamison invited us to attend the concert at night; we concluded we would. We were over to see Mr. Birely and Miss Bausman. Misses Gallagher were over to see us. We went to the concert, Mary S. and Mr. Derr, Mary K & I with Mr. Jamison. On our way home stopped for ice cream at Mrs. Leigh's. Was invited to a pic-nic to-day. /Letter from Lou Hersh./

Thursday Sept. 11th. Excessively warm to-day. Mother sent in for Mary and [*illegible*]. Mr. Kunkle came up for us about eleven to go down to the White Oak Springs to attend the pic-nic. Spent as pleasant a day as possible for the warm weather. Mr. Johnson brought me home; found John and Maggie Derr at our house, who left very soon. Mr. J. left about nine.

Friday [September] 12th. Still so very warm. I went into town this morning; stopped at Mrs. Markell's and what was my astonishment to see Laura Mainster there. Ellen and Laura got ready and we went to see Misses Houck, [and] Callie B. and then came over to Mrs. M's and remained the rest of the day. Callie B. was there too. Messrs. Johnson, Creager and Jamison were there, also Maggie D., Mary Sauerwein, Georgia Houck. Mary had a letter

1851

from home to come home Monday or Tuesday. /The Red Men[72] turned out to-day and town was quite lively, with strangers. The Independent and Grays were here from Washington./

Saturday [September] 13th. Still so very warm. I wrote a letter to Kate S. to let Mary stay a week longer. Had a note from Vallie; wrote one in return. Cousin Sarah Ann, Vallie & Ginnie, Lucy Kunkel and father spent the afternoon with us. I left immediately after tea; went into Kate B's and then she, Mary and I took a stroll round town and when we returned to Mr. B's found Mr. J. A. J. there. John & Maggie D. soon came & we left for Mr. Derr's. I went with Mr. J.; he left Mr. D's about ten.

Sunday [September] 14th. What a change in the weather. I was awakened by the wind blowing and the rain pattering and <u>Mary up shutting the windows down</u>. We were disappointed and did not get to country church. Uncle Shriner and Mr. Sering, Mr. Hammond of Anne Arundel County were there to tea. Messrs. Johnson and Creager came out about seven, and Ed Shriner about half-past nine; remained till after ten.

Monday Sept. 15th. Still cool. Maggie D., Mary S. and I went out to Uncle S's to the Mill[73] and to old Mrs. Derr's, and then returned to Mr. J. Derr's to dinner. After dinner we all went up to Mr. and Mrs. Worman's and sat there awhile; returned home, dressed ourselves and ate supper and then John D., Mary S., Maggie D. and myself started for Uncle Lewis Scholl's but when we got to the mill they showed us the utter folly of starting as it was late and the roads bad; so Ed jumped in and we went up to Uncle Elias'[s] and sat awhile.

Tuesday [September] 16th. A lovely day. We were busy in the morning preparing cake for the wedding. After dinner, Mary D. and I took a walk to old Mrs. D[errs]. Mary S and Maggie took a walk in a different way. After

---

[72]"Red Men Chipawa Lodge of our town had their first procession this day--there were lodges from Washington, D.C. Weaverton, Baltimore and Hagerstown there was a military Co. from Washington and part of a marine band at the Naval Yard--the whole cavalcade was about two squares in length. Bradley T. Johnson, Esquire delivered the address to the Red Men." Engelbrecht, *Diary*, II, 529.

[73]Shriner's Mill or the Ceresville Mill was established in 1812 by Gen. Williams. Cornelius Shriner leased the four storied mill in 1826, purchasing it the next year. Scharf, *Western Maryland*, p. 624. See note 3, 1851. It was in continuous operation until 1988, when it was put on the market by R. L. Kelley.

1851

tea Ed S and Annie arrived, the former all <u>trigged</u> to be groomsman, the latter in white. Mrs. Fries was there too. The groom arrived not knowing he was to be married, of course not in wedding gear. Mary S. was bride; she looked quite well with her bridal habiliments, white dress, veil and wreath. I was bridesmaid in white. They were married by the Rt. Rev. John Autobinen in the name of <u>Pope</u>, quite solemn, we laughed all times. Maggie D was dressed as mother, Tommie [Derr] as beggar woman and came in as the ceremony was being performed. Everything passed in sport. The company retired at a reasonable hour but the bride could not be persuaded to take a seat behind the groom on a sheepskin.

Wednesday [September] 17th. A cool & clear day. We were at old Mrs. Derr's after Coz Ed left; came home to dinner & got ready for our trip to New Windsor. Just as we were about starting, Mother came out in the carriage to take me home, but at the entreaties of all, she at last consented to let me go. So away we all went merry and happy. We passed through Liberty and went about 8 miles below to Mr. Devilbiss's, Mag D's cousin. We, that is, Mary and Mag D., Mary S and John D. and myself were very kindly received by Mr. & Mrs. D[evilbiss] & four daughters. We remained over night with them. We were quite surprised when one of the ladies told us her brother C[asper] was to be married next day. We had supper, chatted awhile, retired.

Thursday 18th Sept. We rose early, set our room in order, repaired down stairs, had our breakfast. Got ready and went into New Windsor to attend the commencement at Calvert College[74] (Mr. Baker's). Saw Mr. C. Devilbiss this morning; he took Maggie to the commencement and his sister went in the carriage with us. We were pleased with exercises, some good orations, & excellent music. We returned to Mr. Devilbiss's to dinner and we found Mr. Nauss there, the groomsman. We saw them off to the wedding, then left ourselves for Mr. Derr's. Got there, took tea and went over to Uncle Shriner's. Ed gave me a letter from O. Garrott. Mr. J. A. J. and Ed were on their way to Mr. D's but turned back after they met us. They walked over to Mr. D's with us but soon left.

Friday [September] 19th. Mary bid farewell to Mr. D's family this morning. Tommie took Maggie D., Mary S. and myself into town; took dinner with

---

[74]Calvert College was the New Windsor College. See note 62, 1851.

Kate Bantz and tea with Mary Birely. Saw the firemen's procession[75] and thought it excellent. Mary had a letter from home saying she must come tomorrow; we were disappointed. We were at Houcks', Ellen Brunner, Mary Kunkle too. Ma came in the carriage for us about dark and took Maggie D., Mary S. & I out home, found Messrs. Johnson, Jamison & Shriner there; they spent the evening; they were very agreeable. Got a letter from P. Mering this evening. We did not retire till after twelve o'clock.

Saturday [September] 20th. We got our breakfast early and went into town, [and] bid Mary "good-bye" at the depot[76]. Mr. Jamison was there. He walked up street with Maggie D and I to Mrs. Reese's and left. We were to see K. B. a few moments; left Maggie in town, then came home.

Sunday [September] 21st. Ma and I went into town to church. Came home to dinner and after dinner went over to Mrs. I. Howard's to go to the school house to church. She did not go. Marion and I came home as far as her house. Mr. Jamison came out after tea.

Monday Sept. 22nd. At home in the morning. After dinner John drove the carriage and we went out to Aunt M. Artz, but did not remain long, and then down to [*illegible*] and took tea; returned soon after. Damp and cool day.

Tuesday [September] 23rd. Still damp and cool. Ma and I went over to Mrs. I. Howard's to help her quilt; found her sisters, Misses Hall and V & E. Howard.

Wednesday [September] 24th. Was at home in the morning; after dinner went down to see Miss B. Fout on business about my dress. Quite clear and pretty.

Thursday [September] 25th. Was in town this morning; had a letter from M. Sauerwein. Did some shopping and was to see Kate B. & Mrs. Dr. Sheilds; came home to dinner. Cousin E. Shriner came here this evening about four & remained till some time after tea. Wrote a note to Maggie D. and sent her Mary's letter to read.

---

[75]"Firemans Parade. The Hagerstown 'Independent Junior' fire company paid our town a visit yesterday and today we have a General Firemans parade the numbers amount to 290 which is a very large appearance." Engelbrecht, *Diary*, II, 530.

[76]See note 17, 1851.

1851

Friday [September] 26th. Lovely day. I went down to Miss B. Fout's & had a dress fit, then went over to Uncle Adams' and spent the evening. Mother was there; Vallie was not home.

Saturday [September] 27th. Disappointed in not having Uncle Shriner's to spend the day with us; it rained in the evening and at night. Wrote a letter to G. Kephart and Ginnie Garrott.

* * * * *

Tuesday [September] 30th. I was at home all day; kept house in the evening as Mother was gone to Grandma's after tea. Mr. J. A. J. came out and spent the evening; he was quite agreeable; he is going to leave for Somerset Co. tomorrow. I wrote a little note to Mary Sauerwein by him.

(Photo from Williams *History of Frederick County, Maryland*)

DEARBOUGHT

Home of John Derr family, Frederick, Maryland

1853

"Home is so dear, I feel as if I never want to leave it again. I wonder if I shall ever consent to leave it forever...marrying is a lottery and if I ever do, and who, O God, may it know a prize; but we know not our future destiny."

SYLVAN RETREAT [MANCHESTER FARM], 1853

January 1st 1853. Showery in the morning, but cleared off in the afternoon, and Mother went out and spent the afternoon with Grand-ma; but Pa and I remained at home and at night I wrote a letter to Gene Kephart.

Sunday [January] 2nd. Very pleasant day. I rode to town on horseback and as I was going down street was joined by Vallie Weagley[1], having sent Mr. W. back to look for her velvet cape which she had lost, and we proceeded to the City Hotel[2] together; and as Mr. W. had not arrived I went alone to church and heard an excellent sermon from Dr. Zacharias on New Year & its responsibilities. Mr. Ham. Boyd[3] joined Maggie Derr & I and walked with me to the edge of town and helped me on the horse; and then old Mr. Worthington Johnson[4] joined me and rode to his gate with me. He is a very agreeable old gentleman, I think.

* * * * *

---

[1]This was Vallie Adams, see note 32, 1851.

[2]City Hotel was located on the north side of West Patrick Street between Market and Court Streets. *Williams' Directory*, p. 47. The building was expanded to become the Francis Scott Key Hotel, which is now Homewood Retirement Center.

[3]Hamilton Boyd lived on a farm near Manchester Farm on New Design Road. *Bond Map*, 1858.

[4]Worthington Johnson had a farm near Manchester Farm on New Design Road. *Bond Map*, 1858.

1853

Thursday [January] 6th. At home in the morning, but after dinner Ma and I went up and spent the evening at Uncle D. Thomas's. Aunt Lizzie has quite a fine young daughter.

Jan. 7th, Friday. Weather like summer. Uncle Lewis Scholl came about twelve o'clock and remained till after dinner sometime.

Saturday [January] 8th. I rode into town on horseback this afternoon and called for E. Brunner, and we called to see Kate Bantz and did some shopping. I had a long letter from Fannie Koones wanting me to come down there by the twenty-fourth of next month as somebody is to be married then. I would like very much to know who but she leaves all in mystery there, just says <u>some</u>body.

Sunday [January] 9th. Beautiful day, almost too warm to be pleasant. Ma & I rode to town on horseback and heard a sermon from Dr. Zacharias from 2 Eph[esians] and then came out home. Cousin L. Hedges & Mr. Glaize came out about three o'clock and remained till after tea and then left. Mr. J. A. J. came out about half-past four and remained till eight; was given [*sic*] me an account of the manner he had been spending his time and, as I was not in a very good humor, I suppose he left sooner. I own I did feel a little pettish and to my shame I let it be displayed, but shall I say I don't care, for perhaps I do and I should not like to write an untruth.

Jan. 10th, Monday. I was up before the sun and from my window saw it rise while I was writing to Fannie Koones, in answer to a letter I received from her on Saturday. After dinner rode to town on horseback and met Maggie D in town and went with her to call and see Mary Birely, Kate Bantz, Misses Houck & Mrs. B. F. Winchester & Mary Barthelow, who is staying there, and Mrs. Mary Brown of Columbia, Pa.; the latter three were not home. Saw Mr. J. A. J. in town. He certainly must have a very kind brother, or his affairs are woefully neglected. I left Maggie D. about 20 minutes after four and rode out home.

Tuesday [January] 11th. Beautiful day, like summer. There was a gentleman here with goods from China and Pa bought me a brocade satin, and [he] remained till after dinner; and then Ma & I walked down to Mr. Finney's[5] &

---

[5]The Finneys lived near Manchester Farm on New Design Road. *Bond Map*, 1858.

spent a very pleasant but short afternoon with the family & Mrs. Nellie Keefer. We returned home about dark.

Wednesday [January] 12th. Found it had been raining when I arose, and we had wind and rain & snow all day. I received a nice long letter of Harrie Smith when Pa came home this evening. His partly elucidates Fannie's, as he says it is a cousin that['s] to be married but don't know which one.[6]

Jan. 13th, Thursday. Snowing a little all day. I was busy sewing all day, and had my curiosity satisfied when Pa came home by receiving a letter from Fannie explaining her last, saying Mary E. Wood was to be married and wanted me to serve as bridesmaid and that I would receive a letter from her very soon.

* * * * *

Saturday [January] 15th. Still cold weather unsettled. I rode to town on horseback and did some shopping, and relieved my mind considerably by returning some letters that I have had in my possession for some time; but I fear I may have given offense perhaps. If so, I did not intend it.

* * * * *

Monday [January] 17th. Still cold. Immediately after dinner I took my sewing and went over and spent the afternoon with Evie Smith[7], and soon Messrs. L. Boyd & J. Hoffman of Baltimore came out and took tea with us. I returned home immediately [after] supper, Mr. Wm. Smith accompanying me.

Tuesday [January] 18th. Clear in the morning, but snowed very fast for a short time about dusk. I was in town for a short time this morning; called to see Kate Bantz & her company, Miss E. Davis, a sister of Capt. D. I left my watch in town to have a crystal put in it. I received a very nice long letter of Mary Sauerwein and also one of Mary Lizzie Wood wishing me to serve as bridesmaid for her, but which office I fear I will not be able to fulfill.

---

[6]The reference is to the letter Margaret received on January 8th from Fannie Koones.

[7]Evie Smith lived on a farm north of Manchester Farm on New Design Road. *Bond Map,* 1858.

1853

* * * * *

Thursday [January] 20th. We were all up very early this morning so as to start from home early. I went into town in the cart; did some shopping and called to see Mrs. B. F. Winchester who has Miss McCann and her brother; Mr. Dunham of Richmond is also with her. I had a long letter of Vallie and I mailed a letter to Mary Lizzie Wood. I saw Maggie Derr in town and took her out with me to Mrs. Derr's, where I remained till after three o'clock, and then went to Aunt Margaret and there remained to tea; and then we started for home, where we arrived by sun-down.

Friday [January] 21st. I was at home all day and felt I had taken cold.

Saturday [January] 22nd. I was lying down almost all day. Mr. J. A. J. was out after tea and I went down stairs to see him; he left about nine o'clock.

Sunday [January] 23rd. Not any better; lying down or sitting on a rocking chair all day.

Monday, Jan. 24th. Clear part of the day and very damp in the afternoon; still have this cold.

Tuesday [January] 25th. Much better; however, Father is going to tell the Dr. to come out. Snowed very fast for a few moments about three o'clock. Dr. Waters arrived in the snow; said I wasn't much sick but prescribed a dose of Calomel, foot bath, etc.

Wednesday [January] 26th. Very cold. I felt badly from the effects of the medicines and was in bed all day. Mr. Perry B. McCleary and Miss Jane Doud were married today.

Thursday [January] 27th. Better again, made my appearance down stairs this morning. Had a long letter from Gene Kephart when Father came home.

Friday [January] 28th. Pa and Ma were in town. When they came home I received a letter of invitation to the Independent Fireman's[8] ball for Friday

---

[8]The Independent Fire Company was established in Frederick in 1818. It is the oldest existing company in Maryland. Scharf, *Western Maryland*, p. 493. It was located on the south side of West Church Street between Market and Court Streets. *Williams' Directory*, p. 20.

one week. Saw by the paper Mr. Jones and E. Beatson were married yesterday.

Saturday [January] 29th. Beautiful day. Sent Mrs. Taylor's pattern home and she accompanied Jane[9] back and spent this afternoon here.

Sunday [January] 30th. Clear warm day. Mr. J. A. J. was out after tea and spent the evening. I gave Mr. J. a hurriedly written note for Penelope M. He's to go up tomorrow to wait on Mr. S. B. J.

Monday, Jan. 31st. Still clear and pleasant weather. I had a long letter from Lou Hersh; she expects to return home in three or four weeks; she appears to be spending her time so pleasantly. I wrote letters to Lizzie and Fannie R. Koones this evening.

Tuesday February 1st [1853]. Bright, clear day. Mr. Jamison is to be married to Miss Lizzie Bentz of Martinsburg, so one by one my friends are taking partners to themselves for better or worse. Ma was in town and came home; said she saw the bridesmaids and groomsmen arrive, talked with Penelope and Mrs. I. H. Johnson. Mr. and Mrs. Jamison have gone to Baltimore.

Wednesday [February] 2nd. Cloudy, damp day; heard Mr. and Mrs. Jamison are to return this evening. Mrs. Shields sent me a jar of sweet pickled peaches and a glass of quince jelly for my cold, for which I am very much obliged. She's very kind.

Thursday [February] 3rd. Foggy in the morning, but cleared off by noon. I thought of going to town, but Pa did not arrive soon enough to know whether I could go in the carriage; however, when he came he said the roads were very muddy. Ma was out to Grandma's and got the news.

* * * * *

Monday, February 7th. Cloudy early in the morning but cleared off cooler at or about noon. What was my surprise about eleven o'clock to see cousin E. Shriner and George Sauerwein, the latter of whom had arrived last Thursday. In answer to my inquiry why he had not been to see me before, said on account of the weather and then they explained to me that they had

---

[9]Jane was one of the servants owned by Daniel Scholl. Hitselberger, *Bridge in Time*, p. 459.

1853

started yesterday evening, as also [had] Mr. J. A. J., to come out but that their gears[10] had broken and [they] were obliged to retrace their steps even in the rain, so why or how could I scold! George does not look very well. I don't think he is going to leave today and insists upon my coming down to the wedding. I should like to go. I think it strange Mr. J. A. J. did not come out to see if I was going to the party to be given to Mr. and Mrs. S. B. Jamison.

* * * * *

Thursday [February] 10th. I walked into town; stopped at Mrs. Markell's and had a long talk with her about Mr. Jamison's marriage, and then went down to Kate B's for her to make some calls with me, but was prevented from doing so by hearing the Miss Derrs had walked out to our house, so I came on home. Saw Nellie Mering on the street and also Mr. Creager, with whom I had a talk. Found Miss Ds at our house when I arrived and they remained until about four o'clock and then walked to town.

Friday Feb. 11th. I went into town early according to my engagement with Maggie D. and we went round to look for a dress but was very undecided between two opinions, so she went home and I to Aunty Kemp's[11] to dine without getting a dress. About two o'clock I went round for Kate Bantz, so she and I called to see the Misses Houck and Nellie Mering, who is staying there, and on our way up to see Mrs. S. B. Jamison met Mr. Jamison, who returned with us. I think she looked beautiful, I was very much pleased with her. We also called to see Evie Winchester[12] and B. Late, and was going to see Annie Schley, but found she was out. I wrote a long letter to Mary Sauerwein about her coming to Kate B's wedding, also a letter to Harry Smith.

---

[10]The mishap of the gears was mentioned also in the diary kept at this time by Mary Derr. Derr diary, p. 3. This diary is now in the possession of Mr. and Mrs. Robert Cecil of Dearbought, Mrs. Cecil being a descendent of the Derr family. Mary Derr's notes often confirm and clarify Margaret Scholl's account of events.

[11]Mr. and Mrs. Abraham Kemp lived on the north side of Second Street between Court and Record Streets. *Williams' Directory*, p. 22. Mrs. Kemp (née Ann Mary Brunner) was an aunt of Daniel Scholl. See *Scholl Genealogy* and note 21, 1855.

[12]Evie Winchester was the twenty year old daughter of Hiram Winchester, the founder of the Frederick Female Seminary. Hitselberger, *Bridge in Time*, p. 65.

1853

Saturday [February] 12th. Rode to town on horseback; got my watch and endeavored to succeed in deciding what dress to get, or have mother decide, but she could not, so we came home again without a dress. I rode down to Uncle Adams' and spent the afternoon with Vallie, Fannie and Abram. J. A. J. is down but had gone to town with Sally.

Sunday [February] 13th. Raining when I arose, but it cleared off cool and windy. I received a pamphlet from J. Derr today. Mr. J. A. J. came out about five and remained till eight. Reckon he won't want to hear me lecture about distillery again. I think it a pity for him.

Monday Feb. 14th. A clear, bright St. Valentine's day, and when Father came home from town brought me one of St. V's love missive[s] which had been sent from Lancaster; however, it must have originated from some other place as I <u>know no one</u> there, but I do in York and I have a slight inclination to believe it was a return of the compliment from last year, and so in my haste I opened another envelope Pa handed me and found it to contain a <u>comic Valentine</u> for Mrs. Margaret Scholl which the Postmaster had given to Pa through mistake. Vallie sent word up she & Sarah H. would not be up <u>this</u> afternoon but tomorrow, if S. did not go home.

Tuesday [February] 15th. Quite cold. Vallie & Sarah did not come up, so suppose S. went home. Pa did not call at the P. O., or suppose I would have got the invitations to K[ate] B[antz]'s wedding which were to make their appearance today.

Wednesday [February] 16th. Rained in showers all day; however Ma went into town and procured my dress, and when Pa and she came home brought me my invitation to Kate Bantz's marriage, and also a long letter from Mary Sauerwein saying she would not be up but insisted upon my coming down. Just about <u>tea</u> time, I heard someone rap and on proceeding to the door I found a tall and handsome gent who introduced himself as Mary H. Smith's brother, Lewis Motter S[mith]. He remained over night and I found him agreeable. He brought me a letter from M. H.

Thursday Feb. 17th. I was at home all day sewing on my dress for Kate B's wedding. Cousin L. Smith left about nine o'clock, intending to take the half-past nine train of cars for Cumberland, where he is engaged in mercantile business with his brother-in-law under the firm of Hollins & S. I like him quite much. He is very trusting and I hope this cold fleeting world may not teach him to be otherwise, for I think it incompatible with his disposition. I wrote a long note to Maggie Derr and enclosed Mary Sauerwein's letter.

* * * * *

Saturday [February] 19th. I was at home all day. It was damp [and] cold afternoon, so I did not go into town to go out to Mrs. Derr's with Coz. E. S. as I intended. When Father and Mother came home [they] brought me, that is the family, an invitation to Mary E. Wood's marriage which is to take place the 23rd of Feb.

Sunday [February] 20th. As it was so cold Mother and I walked into town and were joined by cousin A. Adams, who accompanied us to church, where we heard a good and very long sermon from Dr. Zacharias. The Misses D's were in church and insisted upon me accompanying them home. Soon after dinner, we went over to Uncle Shriner's and sat an hour or two, and Ed. S. came home with us, where we found Mr. Daniel Getz and missus and they both remained till about ten and indeed Ed till eleven.

Monday Feb. 21st. Well, although it snows slightly, Tommy Derr bring[s] Maggie D. and myself into town and we call[ed] to see Mrs. B. F. Winchester, who gave me a very pressing invitation to come stay with her tomorrow night. We also called at Houck's to see all the girls & Nellie Mering, and did some shopping, and on our way met Judge Cooper, who told us the ladies were at our house, so we walked briskly out home and found Mrs. Sharpstein & Vallie here. Judge C. came out about two o'clock and remained till after tea, when they all left. Maggie D., however, rode into town about four o'clock after having assisted me with my dress (she is so kind). At the supper table Pa handed me a letter, which proved to be an invitation to [from] Cousin C. Koones to a party for next Friday night.

Tuesday [February] 22nd. Was very sorry to see it rain all day; however, Father took me in the buggy up to Mrs. Winchester's. I then went down to Houcks' to see if Mrs. Harmon was there, but she was not. Misses D's were over a short time. We got ready and went down to Mr. Bantz's by eight o'clock. We were ushered in the front parlor, and soon some fifty or sixty persons arrived, and suddenly the folding doors were thrown open and we beheld the bride and groom[13], attended by their three maids, Misses O. Garrott, E. Davis & M. J. Hammond and three groomsmen, Messrs. P. Roman, [*illegible*] and Brown. After the ceremony was performed the usual congratulations were given, and then every one seemed to be trying to see who could be the "gayest of the gay," and at nine she received her other company who were not allowed the pleasure of seeing her married, and till eleven chit-chat, promenade, and perhaps a little slandering occupied the company, when we were invited out to the tables, which were supplied with both the substantials and delicacies that any one could wish, from thence to promenade, etc. till about twelve, [when] everyone seemed to have been leaving as if by common consent. I went up in the hack with Mr. Johnson, who had brought the Misses D's, who remained at Mrs. Winchester's over night.

Wednesday [February] 23rd. Raining still when I arose. We were down to breakfast about half-past eight. We put everything together, and even had our bonnets on when Mr. J. A. J. arrived, so he walked over to Mrs. L. Markell's with me, not telling me what he promised yet, and left me at the door. I had a long talk with Mrs. Markel[l] when John[14] arrived with my horse. When I rode out home found Father quite sick in bed, but is better by night time. Mary E. Wood is to be married to Mr. D. Hartman tonight; would like to be present.

Thursday Feb. 24th. Found it very windy but not so cold as I expected as I went to town this morning. I called at Mrs. L. Markel's and had a long talk. I then went up street, did some shopping, and on my return saw Mrs. B. Brown at her door, who would have me come in; we had a long talk about the party, etc. I got my invitation from Uncle H. T.'s store to Dr. Hammond's[15]

---

[13]Kate Bantz was marrying Henry Gassaway Davis, whose career with the B&O Railroad had already gained him the post of station agent at Piedmont, West Virginia (Henry Decker, "Bantz Fortune Influenced History," *The Frederick News*, November 28, 1990). Davis's continuing success with railroad, land, and mining development in West Virginia and western Maryland led not only to wealth but to political activities, U.S. Senator (1871-1883), and was the Democratic nomination for vice president in the 1904 national election. *Dictionary of American Biography*.

[14]See note 21, 1851.

[15]Dr. Richard Hammond of Woodsboro (born 1815, died 1896) married Mary Ann Cramer. Williams, *History*, II, 1212.

1853

party. I then came on out home, eat my dinner, and went over to Mrs. I. Howard's and spent the afternoon with her.

Friday [February] 25th. Still cold and windy. Mother went out to spend the day with grandmother. I wrote a long letter to Mary Sauerwein to send by Ed. S., also a note to Ed. and one to Maggie Derr. Fanny Koones gave Mary E. W[ood] a party; wish I was there tonight.

Saturday [February] 26th. Much milder. I finished my apron and then did up collars, etc.

Sunday [February] 27th. Felt sick in the morning and did not go to church; rained at night.

Monday [February] 28th. Maggie Derr was to go to Balt.; hope the rain did not prevent her. Cleared off beautiful, just like spring.

Tuesday March 1st [1853]. Raining again all day. Charlotte Trail and Mr. Charles Markell are to be married this afternoon, and Kate Sadtler to Mr. I. Sadtler of Chicago tonight; and Dr. Hammond is to give Kate Davis a party to the two latter. I am invited but cannot attend either.

* * * * *

Friday [March] 4th. Today the nation is to witness the out-going of President ever to be praised Millard Fillmore, and today Washington is thronged with friends of Gen. Frank[lin] Pierce who are to witness his inauguration. It snowed more today than anytime this winter.

* * * * *

Sunday [March] 6th. Clear and warm, just like spring in the morning, but got cold till night. I walked into town, stopped at Mrs. L. Markell's and went to church with Ella B., Messrs. M. & V. Brunner, and returned; and they insisted upon my remaining to dinner and I did so; then came out home on horseback, and by my yielding I kept John from Sabbath School.

* * * * *

Tuesday [March] 8th. Cloudy and warm. Wonder I have not heard from Mag Derr & Mary S. Saw a notice of Emily B. Pearce's marriage to Mr. Wm. A. Brown on the 17 Ult.

Wednesday [March] 9th. Witnessed all the vicissitudes of an April day. Received a note from Mrs. I. Howard, and wrote one in return about going to Mrs. J. Buckey's to-morrow afternoon.

Thursday March 10th. Awoke this morning to find the sun shining brightly and very pleasant. What was my surprise to find, on opening the *Herald* this morning, an announcement of Mr. V. Brunner & Miss Mag. M. Pypher, although he told me Sunday he was going to be married soon, in April I think he said. After an early dinner I went over to Mrs. I. Howard's and she, Marion and I went to Mr. Keefers and were joined by Mary & Harriet, and then went up to Mrs. J. Buckey's and spent the afternoon. Sarah Miller and Isy Buckey had started for our house and hearing I was there, returned. Spent the evening pleasantly and returned to Mrs. H[oward]'s and remained over night.

Friday [March] 11th. Found it snowing fast, so Pa and Ma sent for me soon after a very nice dinner. Mrs. Chandler, Ann Keefer & Mary E. Finney arrived and spent the afternoon. John came for me while at supper, and I left immediately after.

* * * * *

Sunday [March] 13th. I rode to town on horseback this morning and called at Mrs. L. Markell's; found Mr. and Mrs. V. Brunner there. I went to church with Nellie & Mr. & Mrs. M[arkell]. Cousin Ed came down street with us and handed me a letter from Mary E. which was written last Monday. Mr. J. A. Johnson came here on his road from Mr. Richardson's and took tea. It is a pity so nice and agreeable a gent should take to distilling liquor. I fear he will have cause to regret it but hope not; it would be a mercy were something to happen to prevent its creation[?].

* * * * *

Thursday [March] 17th. St. Patrick's Day. Erin's sons rejoice today. Warmer today.

1853

* * * * *

Saturday [March] 19th. Clear. I intended going to town but was intimidated by the wind that rose about eleven o'clock. Father & Mother went to town, and when they came home told me that Uncle D. Thomas had sold his farm back to <u>old Mr. Johnson</u> & had bought <u>Rose Hill</u>[16] and was going to move immediately.

* * * * *

Tuesday [March] 22nd. Clear, warm morning. I walked into town; stopped for E. Brunner and we then went to see Mary H. Kunkle, L. Brewer & Mrs. Luther Schaeffer, but could make no one hear the bell, so we merely left a card. Walked out home.

* * * * *

Friday [March] 25th. Being <u>Good Friday</u>. After an early dinner I took John and went out to Aunt M. Artz's, and from thence she & I went down to see grandma a short time, and I then returned home. Wrote a letter to M. E. Sauerwein.

Saturday March 26th. I was busy at home all day. Mr. J. A. Johnson was out after tea and spent the evening.

Sunday [March] 27th. I went into town, called at Mr. L. Markell's and [went] up street to church with them; and after church they would have me stay to dinner. Kate Houck told me of Mrs. J. Hammond's death. I was very much surprised and feel so sorry for her little children.

Monday [March] 28th. Well, Easter Monday has arrived again; and five years ago on Easter M[onday] I met Mr. J. A. Johnson for the first time and thought him an <u>ugly red faced man</u>; but now think him agreeable, at least as

---

[16]Rose Hill, built in 1793 by Mr. and Mrs. John Graham, the son-in-law and daughter of Governor Thomas Johnson, was occupied by them until 1819. It was one of the finest plantations in Frederick County. David Ogle Thomas, uncle of Margaret Scholl (see note 45, 1851), purchased the farm in 1853 and lived there until his death in 1876. The Thomas family continued to own Rose Hill until 1906. Glen L. Little, *A Brief History of Rose Hill Manor* (Frederick County Parks and Recreation, Frederick, MD, 1971), pp. 80, 81, 88, 89, 90; *Thomas Genealogy*, p. 28.

tolerable as the other men; indeed he makes himself quite agreeable. I was making ready for an early dinner when John came from town and said the ladies were coming and soon John, Maggie & Mary Derr, Georgie Houck & Ella Brunner arrived and we all spent the day agreeably. They left about four o'clock.

Tuesday [March] 29th. Pleasant day. I walked over to Evie Smith's this afternoon but found she had gone over to Mrs. C. Howard's about five o'clock. G. Sauerwein & Ed S[hriner] arrived. G. came down from Martinsburg yesterday; leaves for B[altimore] tomorrow morning.

* * * * *

Thursday March 31st. Eat breakfast very early and went to town in the cart; and just as I was starting received a note from Evie Smith saying Mrs. E. Howard & daughters & herself would spend the afternoon with us. I hurried home and about half-past one o'clock Mrs. H., Ginny H. & Evie Smith arrived and all appeared to spent a pleasant afternoon.

Friday April 1st [1853]. All-fool's day, but friends must think me wise, as not one wrote me an A. P. F. I was busy in the yard this morning, when Uncle E. Scholl, Aunt M. & Annabelle & Louis arrived, and very soon Uncle Lewis Scholl came; so they all spent the day; that is, left about three o'clock. Rained in the evening.

Saturday [April] 2nd. Cleared away beautifully. Father took me into town and I called to see Mrs. B. Fout and show her Gene K[ephart]'s letter; and from thence went to Mrs. L. Markell's; saw Callie B. there, and Ella & I went and took a long walk and called to see Mrs. Mag Brunner and then came home.

Sunday [April] 3rd. A little cloudy in the morning and rained before noon. Ella & I had quite a run (almost) from church; then John called for me & I came home.

Monday [April] 4th. A rainy disagreeable day. I was very busy making pants for servants all day.

* * * * *

1853

Wednesday [April] 6th. Went into town very early this morning; called at Ella Brunner's and then did some shopping and came out home; and was busy, and wrote to Mr. H. Smith a long letter.

* * * * *

Friday [April] 8th. Ma was in town in the morning; and when she came home we went over to Mrs. I. H[oward]'s and spent the afternoon. Marion came home with us.

Saturday [April] 9th. Very windy most of the day; about one o'clock Marion & I went into town in the carriage and Pa & Ma in the buggy to try "Billy." We did some shopping and a good deal of walking and then returned home. Mr. J. A. J. came out after tea and spent the evening; I had a letter from M. E. Sauerwein.

Sunday [April] 10th. Ma, Marion, and I went into town and all went to the Methodist Church, and after church returned; and just after we had fixed for a very nice nap, Mr. P. Kunkel arrived, having on hand his vast amount of fun and wit, "being so very dry." "J. A. J." [sic]. M[arion] left after tea, so did Mr. P. K.

Monday [April] 11th. Quite cool this morning, there being a thin skin of ice. Pa & I went out and spent the day at Mr. John Derr's; and after dinner we went over to Uncle L[ewis]'s. Saw Aunt L, who told us G. Lewis had that day opened a warehouse in Balt[imore]. I was weighed 122 lbs.

Tuesday April 12th. Pleasant day, having a tolerable wind. After dinner I went over to Mrs. I. H.'s and Marion and I went to look for Alder berries or blossoms but found they had not yet put out and then I came home.

Wednesday [April] 13th. Rained in showers all the morning but not in the afternoon. Mrs. B. Kunkel, according to engagement, walked and went over with me to Evie Smith's and spent a very pleasant afternoon; came home about six, and Mrs. K. left about dusk, brought me some candy, to be sure.

Thursday [April] 14th. Rained in showers all day till about two o'clock, when it cleared off beautifully and somewhat colder. I received a nice long letter of Nelly Mering to-day; insists upon my coming down next month and I mean to go if I can.

1853

Friday [April] 15th. Beautiful day. About eight or half-past, Eva K. Winchester arrived and I was surprised to see Mr. H. Smith of Emmitsburg with her. She arrived from Georgetown last night. They insisted, so I went into town with them and, as E. was engaged (assisting about the music), Mr. S. and I went out and walked. Taylor Motter came for her, so she left about one or half-past, and I went round to meet Mother, promising perhaps that I would return to hear composition's end and to be present at the soiree; but after seeing Ma I concluded to go home. We went to see Aunty Kemp a little while then for my bonnet, and came out home.

Saturday April 16th. At home all day making linen bosom[17] for Father; it rained hard in showers in the afternoon.

Sunday [April] 17th. Looked very threatening all day but very little rain. Mr. J. A. Johnson came out in his buggy about half-past three and left about half-past six. I do not know whether it's my or his fault but methinks he is not as agreeable as he "used to was," seeming quite low spirited but of course I attribute it [to] distillery.

* * * * *

Tuesday [April] 19th. Clear in the morning but soon after dinner, as we were ready to start to town, it commenced raining and rained hard all evening; however, I did some shopping.

Wednesday [April] 20th. Clear, bright day. Pa took me into town this afternoon and I did some shopping with Mother and then went round to see Mrs. Kate Davis, and there met Mr. D. too, and had a very long talk with them both, after which I came down to Mrs. L. Markell's, where Pa called for and brought me home.

Thursday [April] 21st. Very warm and clear. Mother and I rode to town on horseback this morning, did some shopping and then returned home; and after dinner I walked over to Mrs. I. Howard's; returned their paper and got the other one. I remained an hour or so, as Evie Smith was there.

---

[17]A bosom shirt was a man's formal white shirt with a starched bib front. Usually the collar and bib part were made of linen, the rest of inferior fabric. Charlotte Calasbetta, *Fairchild's Dictionary of Fashion* (New York, 1975), p. 52.

1853

Friday [April] 22nd. Day of the great Temperance Jubilee[18]. However, I did not go in as it looked like rain & not feeling well.

Saturday April 23rd. Very pleasant day. I rode into town in the carriage but on meeting Mother afoot I turned and took her home. Received a Godey's Lady's Book[19] & letter of G. Kephart.

Sunday [April] 24th. Raining & windy all day; wrote, received, & wrote a note again to Vallie.

* * * * *

Tuesday [April] 26th. Found it had cleared off beautifully; soon after dinner I rode down to Uncle Adams' and found only Vallie at home; however they all arrived from town before I left. I had a letter from Lizzie A. Koones.

Wednesday [April] 27th. Still clear and warm; after an early dinner, I went over to Evie Smith, and we two went over and spent a very pleasant afternoon at Mrs. E. Howard's with the family and Mrs. A. Taylor. They seemed to think me uncommonly lively to-day; perhaps I was. Dr. Zacharias & Uncle J. H. Brunner were here.

Thursday [April] 28th. One of the <u>loveliest spring days</u>. Vallie, Miss C. Keefer, & Mrs. Chandler spent the afternoon here and all seemed to enjoy themselves.

Friday [April] 29th. So very warm in the morning, but there was considerable blowing before night and of course it got cooler. I rode to town on horseback after dinner, called to see Mrs. Frank Winchester, the Misses Houcks, & told them I was going to visit Nellie Mering to-morrow; did some shopping and

---

[18]The "Temperance Movement" began in England to combat the effects of alcoholism. In the United States the movement became very strong in the 1850's. A. E. Martin, *History of the United States* (2 vols., New York, 1928), I, 680-681. "Procession in our town. They will have a feast at the barricks [sic] and speeches at the Court House. Now they are marching through town." Engelbrecht, *Diary*, II, 581. Mary Derr decided to miss the procession and refreshments but saw a number of people on their way. Derr diary, p. 19.

[19]Godey's magazine, begun in 1830 by Mr. Louis A. Godey, became known as *Godey's Lady's Book*, one of the most successful women's magazines. It was edited by Mrs. Sarah Josepha Hale, one of America's first women editors and authors, from 1837 almost until her death in 1879.

then returned home to find Coz E. Shriner there. He staid so late, and I had my trunk to pack, so that I did not get to bed till nearly twelve o'clock. [I] received a letter from Nellie Mering to-day.

BRUCEVILLE, CARROLL COUNTY, MARYLAND

Saturday April 30th. Rose early and started immediately after breakfast for Nellie Mering's. We stopped for a few moments at Mr. Derr's. We arrived about half-past ten o'clock after a right rough ride. Found the family well and appeared very glad to see me. Father left about two o'clock.

Sunday May 1st [1853]. Tolerably cool. Mr. F. Troxell was over soon this morning, and it was proposed he should take us to church, so we got ready -- that is Nellie & I -- and then [were] joined by Misses Mary Crooks & Mrs. F. T[roxell]. We went into Taneytown to church and there saw Misses Hester, Fannie, Ellen & Rose & Mr. Roger Birnie; we heard a very excellent sermon from Rev. Mr. Williamson. Soon after dinner Barney was hitched and we went up to Hawk's [Haugh's] Church and heard Mr. Fritchey preach. We got home sometime near four o'clock. Mr. and Mrs. Zacharias were in, in the course of the evening, and Mr. T. F. Cover came and spent the evening with us. Mr. Troxell got home about nine and came in and sat till nearly eleven.

Monday May 2nd. Pleasant day again. At home in the morning; soon after dinner Nellie and I walked over to Middleburg[20] and got her bonnet, and afterwards came home and was in the store two or three times giving orders to be sent to Balto. Took a walk & were weighed; weighed 128 lbs. Joan Mering was to see me in the morning. Mr. Troxel was in for a short time.

Tuesday [May] 3rd. Very pretty day. After tea Gene Scott, Miss May Crooks & Dr. Wm. Martin were here and sat an hour or so.

Wednesday May 4th. Very warm and sultry day. After an early tea Nellie and I went over and sat the evening with Mrs. F. and Miss M. Crooks.

Thursday [May] 5th. Showery all day and very sultry. After tea, thinking it would not rain, Nellie, Miss Mary C. and I walked over to see Gene Scott and after sitting a while started for home, not thinking it would rain; but Lo! we had but just arrived at the bridge when it commenced raining very fast, so off

---

[20]Middleburg is a town about one mile east of Bruceville in Carroll County.

1853

we started to run, but were hailed very kindly & lustily too by Mr. Roy George Mering by, "You had better stop! Do stop!" & the like; so in we ran for a few moments. But, lo and behold, it rained, thundered & lightened at such a dreadful rate that we were detained till nearly nine o'clock, when one Mr. M. arrived with a horse and took me home behind him, and Misses M. & P. walked. We were perfectly drenched, and P. nearly green from her green silk. After a thorough change of dress we chatted a while and then retired, the storm not abated.

Friday [May] 6th. Raining all day. Mr. Troxell arrived from Balto. this evening. As he is the only beau of the place, his appearance & non-appearance of course creates some or rather considerable interest. As I felt badly, Nelly and I took a very short walk between the showers up "Nigger Holler." Charles Scott & Charlie Boyle of Westminster joined [us] and came in and spent the evening. I found C. B. a very pleasant little fellow.

Saturday [May] 7th. Although it looked a good deal like rain, Nelly and I got ready to go with Mr. Mering as far as Mrs. Caroline Shriver's, as he was going to Westminster on business. We arrived about half-past ten, found Caroline alone with baby (Catherine Frise) & servants. We were perfectly delighted with her home and think her an excellent housekeeper. Says she is perfectly happy and advises every one to marry. Her baby Kate is a sweet little pet, so very good. Mr. Augustus Shriver arrived with Keener, his little son; Cally and he seem perfectly devoted to each other. Her mother-in-law is not with her now, but considers it her home. Carrie entertained us with music on piano and Mr. A. S. with music on the "Glasses."[21] Mr. Mering arrived about four o'clock and we left about six, having partaken of a very delightful repast, well pleased with our day's pleasure; it had rained in showers during the day but ceased till we arrived at home. We came a new road home and had a great deal to attract our attention as we came home, Mr. Mering leading the horse through "Nigger Holler." Commenced writing a letter home to Mother.

Sunday [May] 8th. Raining till after night fall. Finished my letter home. Mr. Troxel was in a couple of times to-day.

---

[21]The "glasses" was a musical instrument also called a Harmonium. It consisted of a set of glasses arranged in a box. They were filled with varying amounts of water so as to provide differing musical tones when rubbed around the rims by hand. *Webster's Dictionary.*

1853

Monday [May] 9th. Arose to find it a beautiful clear day. We were busy till after tea; however, we went in the store so early as to find Mr. Troxel just performing his daily [chores]. After tea Nelly was busy, and I entertained Gene Scott and Miss Mary Crooks till she came; and when Gene left, we walked part way home with her, and as we were returning, we had quite an adventure running from a horse that appeared unmanageable. When we got home, found Dr. Martin had been there, and very soon Dr. Martin returned, bringing Mr. Tom Cover with him. They sat till about half-past ten o'clock, not being late.

Tuesday [May] 10th. Thorndale. Nellie wrote Gene Scott to go with us to Miss Birnie's but she sent an apology saying she could not possibly go. So, about nine we started, having "Swan" for the driver. We were met at the door very kindly by Miss Margaret, and one by one all the six sisters were gathered in (except Miss Rose). Mrs. Roger Birnie was down in the afternoon. There was a shower about three o'clock and we left as soon as possible after it, and arrived at home in very good season.

Wednesday May 11th. Mr. Mering, Nellie and I went over to a neighbor's to hear a funeral preached of a small child; and when we returned home found a note for us from Gene Scott inviting [us] to come over and spend a sociable afternoon. We concluded we would go and Nelly wrote her a note to that effect. We went over about three o'clock and spent a very pleasant evening with the family. Found old Mrs. Scott very agreeable; she played for us on the piano. Little Annie is a very interesting child, about the age of M. Cooper, and she lost her mother about that same time. Gene walked home with us.

Thursday [May] 12th. Pleasant morning, and we availed ourselves of the opportunity to loll about during the morning. While we were at dinner, a buggy arrived containing Mrs. J. Bentz and Mrs. Jamison & little Lewis Bentz. They left for Uniontown after dinner, and while they were gone we had fun redding up[22]. I received a letter from home [from] Mother this evening; she seems to be getting along remarkably well without me. Mrs. B., L. B., & Mrs. S. B. J. arrived about 8 o'clock.

Friday [May] 13th. Pretty day. After dinner Nelly and I took a ride on horseback over to her Uncle Wm's. [and] saw the family; all well except

---

[22]"Redding up" is a colloquial Pennsylvania German expression meaning to put in order.

1853

Dickson, who is quite ill with inflamatory rheumatism. When we returned, found Miss Lizzie Cover had been here; so we sent down to Mrs. Slick's for her and she came up to tea. Mr. Tom Cover came after tea and sat the evening. I like him very much.

Saturday May 14th. Very pleasant day. We were busy preparing to go to Taneytown to church about eleven o'clock when a carriage drove up, and who should it be but Georgie & Lizzie Houck. They gave a deplorable account of the state of the roads. Immediately after dinner we all got ready to go to town to Mrs. Lentman's preparatory exercises before communion season. Nellie and I had a nice ride on horseback into town, while Mr. and Mrs. Mering, G & L Houck went in the carriage. We arrived at home about five o'clock and, just as we were dressing for tea, we were surprised to see a buggy drive up containing Messrs. P. Kunkel and Simmons. They appeared very much surprised to see Lizzie & G. We spent the evening pleasantly together and retired to rest about ten o'clock; forgot to mention that Gene & Charles Scott, Kate & Mr. Troxel & Miss M. Crooks [were also here].

Sunday [May] 15th. We rose very early, eat our breakfast and dressed for church. As there were so many of us to go, it fell to Nelly's lot to ride on horseback, accompanied by Messrs. Troxel and Kunkel. Mr. & Mrs. Mering, Georgie & Lizzie started in the carriage, and I had to go with Mr. Simmons. But, lo and behold, <u>Lark</u> took a fit and would not go, as Mr. Mering tried, but to no use. So Mr. S & I got in the carriage, and Mr. M. borrowed 2 horses to go to town. We did not get back to dinner till 3 o'clock on account of communion. We took a long walk. Dr. Martin was here after tea.

[Monday] May 16th. Quite warm. We were ready between eight and nine o'clock and started for Dunkard[23] Meeting. Mr. Troxel took his sister Kate and Georgie Houck. Mr. Simmons drove Mr. M's carriage containing Nellie & Lizzie H., and I went with Mr. Kunkel. We arrived about ten o'clock. Lew E. Shriner [arrived] immediately also. [I] was introduced to Mr. E. Henry, Mr. Cox, Dr. Roberts, and saw Messrs. Wilt, & Lou Cover, Dr. Martin and L. Hedges. We spent the day pleasantly, considering we got no dinner; we returned home about six o'clock and all appeared to enjoy their supper. After tea our party [was] joined by Mr. Troxel and sister, took a walk to see Gene

---

[23]The Dunkards were a Baptist sect which was started in Germany by Alexander Mack in 1708. Now referred to as the Church of the Brethren, their first congregation in Frederick County was established in 1750 in Middletown. Williams, *History*, I, 459.

Scott, and sat an hour or two, and then stopped at Mr. Zacharias' a while too, then came home, and soon Georgie and Mr. K. and I started for a walk and was joined by Mr. T., and in all, enjoyed it very much. We came home, wrote dream tickets for all.

May 17th. Tuesday. Still very warm. Messrs. Simmons and K[unkel] left this morning. A couple of showers in the afternoon. Charlie Scott came, [and] soon Kate Troxel & Miss Mary Crooks and then Dr. Martin. We had Quaker Meeting[24] a part of the time; then Dr. left about nine o'clock, and then the rest of us took a nice moonlight walk up the hollow; and we came home, amused ourselves for some time, then retired. I wrote a hurried note to Ma and sent it by Mr. Kunkel.

May 18th. Wednesday. Clear but very warm. After dinner we all got ready and went down to Mr. John Cover's to spend the afternoon with Lizzie. Nellie drove the carriage and had Misses Kate Troxel, Georgia & I in, and Lizzie Houck and Mr. F. J. Troxel rode on horseback. We spent a very delightful afternoon and returned home about ten o'clock. We saw the family and Dr. White & lady; also Dr. Martin spent the evening with us.

May 19th. Thursday. Very warm in the morning, but about ten o'clock it turned quite cold. Soon after dinner, as Georgia and I were sleeping, Nellie came bolting in and hurrying us up, saying there was company downstairs; so we dressed ourselves and went down to see Miss Becky White, who proved to be a very agreeable lady. After tea we called with Miss W. to see Miss Kate Troxel and Miss Mary C[rooks], and when we returned, the ladies returned with us and all, except Lizzie and I, walked part home with her. Very soon after they returned Dr. Wm. Martin & Dr. Roberts of Uniontown arrived and spent the evening, that is till 12 o'clock. I think Dr. R. a very intelligent, agreeable gentleman. We played Dominoes for a long time and all seemed to enjoy themselves, although Miss Mary was anxious to get Miss Kate home long before she went. I had a long letter from Mother saying she did [not] care; I could stay till Cousin Ed came for me.

---

[24]Because Quakers would sit in silence waiting for the Spirit to move them, as a parlor game all persons sat with solemn faces until the first person unable to maintain that pose, burst into laughter. It might begin with the incantation: "Quaker meeting has begun. No more laughing, no more fun, no more chewing chewing gum."

1853

May 20th. Friday. Much more pleasant today. We had an early tea and then, joined by Misses K. Troxel & M. Crooks and Mr. Troxel, took a walk up to Middleburg, leaving Lizzie H. at home for fear she would take cold. I attempted to do some shopping but could procure no satin ribbon; we then called at Mr. Delaplaine's, found Mr. & Mrs. D. at home and found them very pleasant. Mrs. D. showed us her garden and selected rose-buds for us. Misses Kate & Caroline Delaplaine soon arrived accompanied by the Rev. Mr. Wyatt; they proved to be very agreeable ladies. Dr. Martin came in very soon. We all left about ten o'clock. Dr. M. accompanied G. home, Mr. T. with me.

Saturday [May] 21st. Very pleasant day. We commenced dressing about three o'clock and by four o'clock we were ready to start, but when we called for Miss Mary C. and Kate T. they were not ready but by dint of great hurrying they were ready by five o'clock, and we ladies, accompanied by Mr. Troxel, proceeded over to Gene Scott's to tea; saw the family after tea. Mr. T. came home and, when he returned, brought Dr. Martin and cousin E. Shriner whom we had been expecting all afternoon. We amused ourselves with courting and Gambling Cards. G. calls music till nearly ten o'clock, when we returned home well pleased with everything.

May 22nd. Sunday. Sun rose so bright and by eight o'clock we were ready to start to Quaker Meeting. Coz E. Shriner took Nellie and Mr. Mering took Georgie, Lizzie and me. We had a delightful ride through a beautiful country and when we arrived at the Quaker Meeting[25], we found it very much crowded and were satisfied to have a stand at the door. We found numerous there and had a nice long time of talk. We came home quite a different route from which we went. After dinner Kate T. & Mary C. came over, and were over [for] the afternoon, and then after tea Annie Mering, and her brother Thomas came about three, and Mr. T. Cover about five, and all took tea. Mr. Troxel was over after tea and we all spent the evening pleasantly. Gene Scott was here too and, with a great deal of persuasion, they got me promise to remain till Friday. They promised a pic-nic and many other inducements.

---

[25]The Pipe Creek Friends' Meeting House in Union Bridge, a few miles from Bruceville, was built in 1771. It has been in continuous use since then. Historical Society of Carroll County, *The First 150 Years, A Pictorial History of Carroll County, MD, 1837-1987* (Westminster, MD, 1987), p. 69.

1853

Monday [May] 23rd. Clear till about one o'clock when there was a gust, and continued raining all day. Cousin E. Shriner left about eight o'clock, taking a letter to Mother and a note to Maggie Derr. He seemed anxious for me to remain. Mr. Troxel was here too. Kate was over this evening and we were in the store after tea.

Tuesday [May] 24th. Rained all day. We were in the store hearing about the pic-nic, etc. Mr. Cover, Mr. Troxel, Gene Scott & Dr. Martin were here during the day.

May 25th. Wednesday. Raining [to]day, sometimes fast and sometimes in light showers. Mr. Cover was here this morning. Mr. Troxel and Kate were to see us during the day and we were over there. I wrote a note to Cousin E and a letter home concerning the Pic-nic. We waited to see Mr. T. but he did not come till ten. We girls were to have taken a ride (buggy) with Messrs. Cover and Troxel and Dr. Martin to Uniontown but were prevented by the rain; busy preparing for pic-nic.

Thursday [May] 26th. Rained quite hard in the morning but stopped after dinner. I got the materials for a bonnet and commenced making it. Lizzie Houck and I were over and sat nearly all afternoon with Kate Troxel.

Friday [May] 27th. Clear, pretty day. We were busy for the pic-nic again. Joanna Mering was up in the afternoon and, after [she] left, we went over to see Kate Troxel and then Georgia Houck. Kate T. and I took a long walk up on Laurel Hill and the Big Rock.

Saturday [May] 28th. Beautiful, bright morning. Well everything [was ready] for the pic-nic this morning and about ten we all started. Mr. T. Cover drove Mr. M's carriage with Kate Troxel, Georgia H. and me. Mr. T. took Lizzie H. and Gene Scott; Nellie and Joanna went in J's father's carriage. We were there all of us in time to see the company, and indeed it was necessary as we had the committee with us; however, the company consisting of about 60 or 70 persons. Dr. Wm. Pifer and band were there and used every exertion to make the day pass pleasantly. Every one seemed to enjoy themselves very much. I had an introduction to many persons and among the gents, physicians predominated. We amused ourselves dancing, playing cards, and angling. I was very much disappointed at not seeing Cousin Ed. Shriner. Mr. J. A. J. had an invitation. Mr. Cover made an arrangement with me to go [to] church tomorrow. I can scarce tell of the enjoyment, mixed with some pain on account of sad disappointment. We left the ground about 8 o'clock. I came home in Mr. Troxel's carriage and Gene Scott in the buggy with Dr. Martin. Mr. Cover, Kate Troxel and Mr. T. and Dr. M. were here during the evening. I bid adieu to many friends before we left. We retired about ten.

Sunday [May] 29th. So bright shines the sun. We were in no hurry to dress, so I had a [note] from Mr. Troxel and then hurried myself and went down to see him. We dressed by nine o'clock; then the carriages were ready, Mr. C. with his new buggy and pretty horse. We all enjoyed our ride into town and heard a very good sermon from Mr. Williamson and then returned home. Mr. Cover took dinner with us. Mr. Troxel and Kate T. were here after dinner. Mr. T. took tea with us. Mr. A. Clabaugh came about three and remained till about eight o'clock. Gene Scott was here to bid us good bye. Clay Mering came home with Mr. and Mrs. Mering when they came home. Mr. D. Mering is much better. The company all left and we retired about eleven o'clock.

Monday [May] 30th. Very pleasant morning. We, Lizzie & I, were over to see Kate and she was over to see us. The colored man came for Georgia and Lizzie about ten o'clock and they started about 2 o'clock, and after a little fussing were ready to go over to Mr. Wm. Mering's through the rain. Mr. Troxel took Kate, Nellie, and myself over; we spent the evening very pleasantly and got home about nine o'clock, after very near upsetting once. Found a letter from Mother, saying Father would come for me tomorrow. We had quite a time bidding good-bye. Dr. Martin called to say the hated word adieu and also Mrs. Ada Clabaugh of Sykesville, Md. We had quite a time, seemed sad, wrote a letter home.

31st May. Tuesday. Although Nellie wished it might rain, sky is perfectly clear and no clouds to mar the atmosphere. We were amused, from our window observing Dr. Martin admiring and examining a buggy, and Mr. Troxel a Sulky which he finally bought for five dollars. Dr. M. has I suppose purchased the buggy that he is going to bring Nellie to Fred'k in, that is not ordered yet. I'll have some fun yet. Father arrived about ten o'clock, and soon afterward it was proposed that we should take a walk, so off we started, Kate Troxel and Nellie and I and were then joined by Mr. T. I think he is an excellent young man; worth lay there, enshrined by purity, no self-conceit; Nellie says not enough self-confidence. However, modest, retiring persons are to be preferred to forward ones; so, he is a medium in my standard; he seems so candid and frank. We were about 15 minutes behind the rest. I then prepared him a large bouquet and took it over, and as I was returning he

1853

called me in [and] showed me he had displaced Gene S's for mine. We started about one and, after bidding them good-bye, I forgot the seal ring and called back; Mr. T. brought it to me. We found the road bad; stopped at Mr. D's a few minutes and then came on home. Home is so dear, I feel as if I never want to leave it again. I wonder if I shall ever consent to leave it forever. I sometimes think perhaps, but if ever I will, how? I believe all were intended to marry, at least the greater portion, but marrying is a lottery and if I ever do, and who, O God, may it know a prize; but we know not our future destiny.

SYLVAN RETREAT, FRED'K CO., MD.

June 1st [1853]. Lovely, mild and balmy the air. I was very busy in the Front Yard and dusting in the house nearly all morning. After dinner I went into town and called to see Mary C. Kunkel, Georgia & Lizzie Houck, who told me Dr. Martin had just left town. I then stopped a few minutes with Mrs. L. Markell to talk about Call Brunner's intended marriage to Mr. Wm. Bantz. She is to be married to-night at eight o'clock at church and then go round to Mr. B's to receive company. I am sorry I cannot get in to see them married but circumstances unavoidably prevent [it]. If that I had a kind brother! I used to have a kind friend, but I suppose there is too much monotony in visiting and being so very attentive to a lady for so long a time, and this is like the Young Man's Love (plant) [that] requires to be moved every couple of years in order to have it flourish. I have thought seriously and often, too, and feel that I ought either to discard him altogether or engage myself positively, but oh! I like not long engagements and do not wish to marry for at least a year -- say next fall one year. However, when that time arrives I may want to wait longer. I have thought often and long, too, of it of late and maybe I have thought too much of it. I shall act honestly with him and may very soon make myself unutterably, miserably or perfectly happy (worldly happiness). Oh! that I may seek direction from the proper source and let not self influence me too much; but oh! may I be prevented from sacrificing my own proper self respect and never place my affections where they never can be returned. It would be unmaidenly and in the end perhaps make more than two people utterly miserable. I feel so sad this evening, perhaps for not having my wish complied with but also I must learn to bear up against disappointments, for there may be many severe ones in store for me yet. I think and feel of every thing that tends to make me sad this evening. I think of how sad it is to know of Mr. J. A. J. having anything to do with a distillery. May he never have cause to regret, but some thing points me to a darkened future if he continues on with it. But oh! heavens, he can never have me to reproach for

1853

encourag[ing] him in it, for I know I did all I could, when I knew of it, but it was too late. I feel my love is too strong and too fervent for my better judgment; the spirit is willing but the flesh is weak. I could write much more but I feel I have said enough. The seventh of June will be three years since he first told his love in words, or rather proposed, but since it has not been spoken by words, but do not eyes reveal secrets sometimes? I made a promise, and I have kept it, never to tell any person but perhaps I ought to have consulted my parents. I think if I had it to do over, I would tell him I never could receive a proposition of the kind without first consulting them, one I mean that I regarded any way favorably. Would it not have been better? But it is too late now and I must keep it now till I consult him now, which I may perhaps have soon [sic]. I suppose he is now enjoying himself and oh! does he ever think of me? My heart whispers often, very often, and the crimson that mantles my cheek tells of my interest in his welfare. I must cease this strain and write and think of something else. I had yesterday when I arrived at home put into my possession three letters, one from Cousin A. B. Ogle, a very kind letter from Harry [Smith] inviting me to accompany him to Alexandria, and also a long one from Lou Hersh giving me an account of how she had been spending her time since she had been home, etc. Lou has such a happy manner of writing description of every thing without any effort. I commenced a letter to Nelly [Mering] and wrote three pages without stopping, told her of her Cousin Eli C's being down; she will wonder how I got the news, I reckon. I received a letter of Fanny Koones this evening. She had been sick and is still so, so much that she has not been able to go out at night.

June 2nd, Thursday. Very warm day. Ma went to Grand-ma's, Father down to the creek, and as my friends do not appear to know I am at home, I have plenty of time for meditation, reading, etc. Although I take an active part in household affairs for I know not when I may be called upon to be in that responsibility.

June 3rd, Friday. Very warm in the morning with a refreshing shower in the afternoon. I was busy sewing and had gone down stairs in <u>deshaible</u> [sic] and had a long talk with Father on the back porch, and was going forthwith into the front yard to see my roses when Lo! my progress was averted at the front door by a gent in a <u>tall white hat</u>; but I heeded it not, but <u>slammed the door in his face and ran out right</u>, and when Mother went down I ascertained it was Harry S. I assure you it was an unexpected pleasure to me, although I expected from his letter that he would be here this month. He sat and chatted of <u>olden & good</u> times till near ten o'clock and then left. He leaves for Hagerstown to-morrow.

June 4th, Saturday. Very pleasant pretty day. Early in the morning Father, Mother and I got ready and went over to Uncle E. Scholl's and spent the day, enjoyed <u>Fried Chicken</u> for the first time this season. We came home between seven and eight o'clock.

June 5th, Sunday. Cloudy in the morning but cleared off to be a beautiful day. Ma and I went into church to-day and heard a sermon from Dr. Zack. I had a good long nap in the afternoon and then got up and refreshed myself and had supper. Mr. J. A. J. came out after tea and spent the evening. He is in an usual good humour, seemed glad to see an old friend, told me of the various disappointments with regard to getting down to Mr. M[ering]'s while I was there, did not hear I was home till Friday. Seems to be very busy. <u>Distillery comes on finely</u>.

June 6th, Monday. Cloudy all day but no rain. Father started very early on business below Woodsboro and I went with him as far as Aunt M. Artz's. Aunt M and I went over to Uncle D. O. Thomas's and took dinner and remained till about three o'clock. Went all through the fine house and garden, was well pleased with every thing, but think I know a prettier place.

Tuesday [June] 7th. Very warm day. Father took Mother and I into town very early; did our shopping and then I went up street to meet Maggie & Mary Derr according to previous engagement, and we then went to see Mrs. Wm. L. Bantz, who seems very happy in her new home and is very much pleased with the children. We then called at Dr. Zack's to see Liza J. Brewer and saw Mrs. Z of Wash. and Mrs. Spear of Balt. Eliza looks so very badly. We also called to see Mrs. Calvin Page; saw them both. Lucretia advises every one to marry at a <u>suitable age</u> (various opinions) if they can get as kind a husband as hers. We called to see Mary Birely and Mary Marken of Va., and then a few minutes at Kunkel's to see Kate K. Father came in for me about one o'clock. I came home and was very busy sewing and writing a long letter to Lou Hersh.

Wednesday 8th [June]. Clear, bright. Father, Mother & I all started in the buggy for Uncle Lewis Scholl's and had a delightful ride, and met him just below New Market on his way to the depot to see if Aunt Jemima has come home from King & Queen Co., Va.; he went his way and we towards the

1853

house. We stopped on the way at the Copper Mines[26] and had some explanation from the miners; I procured a small piece of ore, and then we left and went our way, wondering why Aunt J was always away when we went down. We had not been there long before Uncle & Aunt Elias Scholl and Lewis came, according to arrangement. Old Mrs. Maynard[27] was over also to spend the day; told me she came expressly to become acquainted with me. I think her a very pleasant old lady. Uncle Lewis arrived about twelve without Aunt J. but accompanied by Mr. Wm. Hobbs, a very talkative old gentleman. We had a very nice dinner and after spending the afternoon had supper, when we all left. I went with Uncle L. as far as New Market. We arrived at home in good season.

Thursday, June 9th. Very warm day. Mary Birely & friend, M. Markell and Mary Kunkel were out to spend the day. Phil K. came about five, and Ed Shriner brought Georgia & Lizzie Houck about half-past, and Oliver Ogle came as we were at tea, and Mr. George Birely about eight o'clock. All seemed to enjoy themselves; the girls, Mr. K & Ed left about nine, Mr. B about half-past ten and, Oliver staid over night. Phil Kunkel is real mean, has got my daueggertype [*sic*] again, and says he won't give it to me. I'll steal it if I can. I think they all seemed to enjoy themselves and I like them all. Was over very early this morning to see about the pic-nic. I shall not invite my Carroll Co. friends up to it, I know.

Friday, June 10th. Another pleasant day. Oliver Ogle left soon this morning and then Pa, Ma & I started again in the buggy. We went in fine style till we came to Uncle Elias S's lane, where Ma & I got out and walked down to the house, and very soon we all jumped into the wagon and took a ride to Mr. J. Dutrow's. There was a Miss Dixon & Miss Crumbaugh there. We spent a pleasant day, had a very nice dinner and supper and then we left again all in company, but Mr. A. Shriner & Mrs. Julia Dutrow soon turned off. We got home about eight o'clock and found Harry Smith waiting our return; he had been here since six o'clock. I invited him to attend the pic-nic but did not insist upon it and so, after talking matters and things in general, he concluded he would go to Georgetown to-morrow.

---

[26]There were copper mines at New London north of New Market. The Lewis Scholls had a house on Georgetown Road below Walkersville. D. J. Lake, C.E., *Titus Atlas of Frederick County Maryland* (Philadelphia, 1873), p. 73. See also note 8, 1858.

[27]Mrs. Maynard was the mother of Aunt Jemima (Mrs. Lewis Scholl).

1853

Saturday, [June] 11th. Very early Mother and I started for Mrs. Howard's, and about ten o'clock Marion and I started for the pic-nic grounds. Found Misses Keefers, Howard's, Fouts, etc. and one or two gents, but soon an omnibus of ladies and gents arrived from town, and we all spent the day pleasantly. The ladies of the neighborhood came during the day. We had a game of "Fox & Geese" during the day and all seemed to enjoy it. We all left about seven o'clock for home, and afterwards I betook myself to writing to Mary Sauerwein but did not succeed in finishing the letter.

Sunday, June 12th. Although it's very warm yet, I went into town to church and heard a very good sermon from Dr. Zack. Mr. Kunkel accompanied me to the Hotel and made an engagement to walk over and see Evie Smith; so about half-past one o'clock and I had just left the room to attend to early tea (about four), when Mr. J. A. Johnson arrived, but said he would return tomorrow as long as we were going away, but I would not leave him, so he remained without much persuasion and later on after tea we all walked over to see E. Smith and company. We returned [home] soon after eight and, after treating the gents to some fine cherries sent from Mrs. Mines; they left, Mr. J. first and then Mr. K. Sent in for Miss Dihoff and she came out to help me sew.

Monday, [June] 13th. We were very busy sewing all day and finished my pink gingham. I finished my letter to Mary Sauerwein.

Tuesday, [June] 14th. Very warm indeed, and so hard to sew.

Wednesday, [June] 15th. I went into [town] very early and did some shopping and returned by nine o'clock, and was busy, part housekeeping and part sewing. About three o'clock, here came Isa Buckey, Lizzie Cromwell and Sarah and Lou Miller and spent the afternoon. We had a very fine shower while they were here. They left soon after tea; Sarah Miller drove the carriage.

Thursday, [June] 16th. We were very busy with the silk dress, so that I had not time to write to Nellie Mering as I intended.

Friday, June 17th. Very warm, but had a refreshing shower between 12 & 1 o'clock which seemed to revive everything. Silk still busy at.

Saturday, June 18th. Very warm, and we were very busy sewing and had to see about dinner, too, as Mother had gone to grandmother's. Just after we

1853

had some dinner Mrs. I. Howard and Mrs. Taylor arrived and spent the afternoon. We had a very early supper, and John took Miss Annie in immediately after; and when he came home gave me the news that Mr. J. A. J. was in town and asked if Miss M was in town, but he did not come out (strange). I wrote a long letter to Nellie Mering.

Sunday, [June] 19th. Very warm. I went into town early with Mother as she was going out to Grand-ma's, and stopped at Mrs. Markel[l]'s till church time; had Mr. M. and Mr. Val B for escorts to church, and Mr. M. from church. I slept most of the afternoon.

Monday, [June] 20th. Quite warm. I find my ring-worm has turned out to be Erysipelas; it is all over my face. C[hett] Taylor called here about four, and remained till nearly seven. I wanted him to remain to tea but he had an engagement; he has a wretched cough; was talking over the usual theme. I think my single friends must be anxious to get me off their list.

Tuesday, [June] 21st. Very warm and I felt very uncomfortable on account of my face.

Wednesday, [June] 22nd. So hot. At home sewing, although not well yet, but better.

Thursday, [June] 23rd. So warm, but we had a couple of showers that cooled the air somewhat.

Friday, June 24th. Much cooler to-day. Finished my white dress to-day.

Saturday, [June] 25th. Quite pleasant today; immediately after dinner Father and I went into town in the buggy. I called to see Mrs. Frank Winchester, Georgia Houck, and to see Mary Kunkel, expecting to see Miss Kate Kern of Phila[delphia], but she had left that morning. I did some little shopping and returned home about seven o'clock. Mr. J. A. J. came out for me to go into the <u>Museum</u>. I said "<u>NO</u>" at first but, after talking it over & concluding I would take no cold, I went. We were delighted, although I had to hold my fan to my face all evening for fear of taking cold. Lew Arnold and Mrs. Phillips perform[ed] "Ingomar." I think they exceeded the general acting at the Balt. Museum.

Sunday, [June] 26th. Still pleasant. I did not go to church. However after dinner Mother and I took John and went out to Aunt Margaret's, and had such nice cherries. We went down to Grand-ma's for a while and then returned home.

Monday, [June] 27th. Good air stirring. I was asleep about ten o'clock and was awakened by a buggy turning and when I went down found it to be Maggie Derr & Mr. & Mrs. Stern, Lizzy Steiner that was; she looks remarkably well now, younger than when she went to school.

Tuesday, [June] 28th. I went into town this morning and did some shopping and called to see Jane Ramsburg got her Cape pattern and then came out home. I do think it's so warm. Had a letter of Nellie Mering.

Wednesday, June 29th. So very warm. I was busy at my Cape. Marion H. was over a few minutes after dinner and I walked part way home with her; stopped in the woods to get raspberries.

Thursday, [June] 30th. To-day one year we four, Kate Bantz, Harry S., Mr. J. A. J. and I started for Emmitsburg and did not arrive till half-past eleven, P.M.; was stopped on the way by the storm. We went up to attend the Distribution at Mt. St. Mary's and St. Joseph's[28].

Friday, July 1st [1853]. I was in town this morning to do some shopping, and was at M. Houck's to have Georgia pierce my ears. I got home about nine o'clock. Cousin I. Harry Smith came out about sundown and remained over night; he told me how much he had enjoyed himself, and of Fanny having such a very bad cough.

Saturday, July 2nd. Quite pleasant. Harry and I went into town this morning in the buggy. I was to draw a check but forgot it; however, got the money by writing my name on one. After a very early tea, Harry and I went into town for Ellen Brunner and we all went out to M. Derr's; we hailed E. Shriner and he came in and remained till we left for home; arrived at home about 9 o'clock. I took Mary S's letter for Mag Derr to read. I also had one from Lou Hersh. I forgot, Harry and I called to see Mary Kunkel, Mary Birely,

---

[28]Mt. St. Mary's College, the oldest Catholic college in continuous operation in the United States, was founded in 1808 in northern Frederick County near Emmitsburg by Father John DuBois. Nearby, the Sisters of Charity and St. Joseph's Academy were founded by Mother Elizabeth Seton in 1809. The distribution of diplomas was part of the commencement ceremonies. Williams, *History*, I, 511-518.

1853

Miss Marmaduke and Georgia Houck. I thought Mary K. would be better; said she felt badly that all night.

Sunday, July 3rd. A small shower this morning but it cleared off by eight o'clock, so Harry and I got ready and went to church. Saw Vallie & Mr. W. at the hotel. I was very sick in church, and don't know that I was even more so immediately after I got home. I laid down and did not get up till three o'clock when Mr. Johnson arrived. I still had a severe headache but it wore off in the course of the evening. Mr. J. and Harry both made me a basket of a cherry seed which I am to wear for charms. Mr. J. left about 9 o'clock and I fear he was caught in the rain, as it rained in torrents in less than an hour after he left, and I think I can say truly I never heard it thunder so loud.

Monday [July] 4th. Wrote letters to Mary Sauerwein & Nellie Mering. Harry left about 10 o'clock for Fred'k, intending to go to Hagerstown. I had an invitation to attend M. Winchester's pic-nic but did not go on account of the inclemency of the weather and suppose they did not go out either. Cousin Wm. A. Dean of Balt. was out this afternoon to tea; told me of Cousins Neal Gorden and Annie Gwynn of Alex[andria] being in town. Mr. & Mrs. John Loats were out this evening to make a call.

Tuesday [July] 5th. I went into town early this morning to make a call on Neal & Annie; found them at Mrs. Lehman's. Cousin Wm. soon came and we took a walk and had ice cream & oranges. We finished harvesting to-day and I am so glad. Marion Howard was here for a short time this morning.

Wednesday, July 6th. Quite warm in the morning. Georgia Houck arrived about ten o'clock, sent the carriage home again, and also Ella. We spent the day sewing, talking, etc.

Thursday [July] 7th. As G[eorgia] wanted to go home, Ma & I went into town and took her; and as G. and I were walking up the street, who should we meet but Mrs. Mering taking Nelly and Miss Jenny Troxel going out to our house. So I turned and went home with them. Mrs. Mering left soon after arriving, and of course the girls remained. Received an invitation to a pic-nic near Lisbon. My birthday.

Fri. [July] 8th. Quite warm. Uncle Lewis Scholl was here to dinner. About four o'clock John took Nellie, Miss Jenny T. & I into town. We called to see Mrs. B. F. Winchester, Mrs. Jamison, did some shopping and returned home. Cousin E. Shriner came out soon after tea and sat till about ten o'clock.

Saturday [July] 9th. I was very busy in the morning and in the afternoon till about four o'clock. Mrs. S. B. Jamison, Lizzie Houck, Messrs. Price and Brooks from Prince Georges Co. [came]. They remained till about nine o'clock. They were all remarkably quiet.

Sunday [July] 10th. Very warm; nevertheless, Nelly, Ginny & I went into town to church. We took a good long nap and then dressed ourselves for supper.

Monday [July] 11th. Rained awhile in the morning, in showers. Harry & I took Nelly & Jenny into town and left them at Mrs. B. F. Winchester's. I went out to Aunt M. Artz's for rose cuttings. Mr. J. A. J. was here after tea.

Tuesday [July] 12th. I got ready early in the morning and went into Mrs. Houck's to remain a few days. Miss Webb of Balt. is there too. Miss W, Lizzie, Georgia, & I went up to the Old Catholic Church to attend the boys' commencement[29]; cannot say that I was infinitely pleased. We returned to Mrs. H's to dinner, and after dinner and after Lewis Trail left, we went up stairs to lay down but not to sleep. We took a walk after tea and brought Tilly Jackson back with us, and soon after eight o'clock Dr. Fleming of Fred'k Co. arrived, and very soon Dr. MacGill & Messrs. Trail, Kunkle, Simmons, Johnston, Byrne & Eader, and we started and had a nice moonlight walk to the Reservoir[30] which all appeared to enjoy. /Nellie Mering & Jennie Troxel came about 7 o'clock down from Mrs. Winchester's./ The gentlemen only remained a few minutes after we returned. We retired between 11 & 12.

Wednesday [July] 13th. Still cool enough to make it pleasant. We all went to the Examination this morning, though we were out about an hour and went to see Kate Davis but only saw Mrs. Bantz, Kate having gone to see Lou Garrott. Dr. Fleming went to the examination with us this evening, also Mag Derr. After tea Drs. Fleming & MacGill and Messrs. Johnston, Eader, Trail, Boyd & others were in and spent the evening; we were quite sleepy till they left. Sarah Kemp was in to spend the day and went with us too, but she left immediately after tea.

---

[29]St. John's Academy had its commencement at St. John's Church on East Second Street. It was attended by Frederick residents as a social event.

[30]See note 55, 1851.

1853

Thursday July 14th. Still cool and pleasant. This is the day Mary Sauerwein is to arrive. We all went to the examination[31], and just after eleven Georgia H., Mag Derr and myself went down to the cars to greet Mary S. She came and Father sent her bandbox up to Mrs. H's and we went up and she dressed and we all went to the Sem. Most did not go in the room as it was crowded. I forgot, Mr. Troxel came up in the morning and went to the examination with me, and he and Dr. MacGill returned with me. Tilly Jackson was round after tea. Georgia, Mary S, Mag Derr & I went to the commencement at night. Dr. Fleming, Mr. Ken Boyd and Dr. MacGill went with us and Mr. J. A. Johnson joined us as we returned. Found Lewis Trail, Mr. C. Johnston & Eader there when we returned; the gentlemen all left some time after eleven, and after eating some we retired. Mary Derr left about ten o'clock. I forgot, Nellie, Mr. & Mrs. Troxel left between six & seven o'clock.

Friday [July] 15th. Quite cool this morning. Dr. MacGill called to see us this morning before we left town. Father came in for us about nine o'clock. Mrs. Taylor, Miss Isaces, Marion, Emily & Ginny Howard spent the afternoon with us, and Mary & I went as far as Evie Smith's with them. Evie is better, expects to leave home next Wednesday. When we got home found Mr. J. A. J. brought us some apricots. Johnny D. came to tell us he would take one of us to the pic-nic, so we got ready and Mr. J. took us out to Mr. Derr's to-night.

Saturday [July] 16th. Found it had rained when we got up but it proved to be a beautiful day. Georgia Houck and Gussie Webb were out before we ate breakfast and Mr. J. A. J. soon came, so about eight o'clock we all started, spent a pleasant day and had a very nice ride. Annie & May Schley were there, and Nelly Mering, Gene Scott, Cally Delaplaine, Messrs. Troxell, Covers & Dr. Martin, all seemed lively. Nelly insisted upon our going home with her and we should have done so if we would have followed our own inclinations. Mr. J. and I turned once to return with them, but I reminded Mr. J. that Mr. Derr had placed them all under his care. We arrived at home soon after ten o'clock and after eating a very hearty supper, retired. Mr. J. A. J. remained over night. Mr. Ken Boyd had brought Ginny & Miss A. Stonebreaker out, but left before we returned.

---

[31]The examination at the Frederick Female Seminary included the reading of four compositions and a Valedictory. It was really commencement. Derr diary, p. 82.

1853

Sunday [July] 17th. Quite cool and clear. We all got ready for church and Mr. J. A. J. took me as far as town but did not return with us as he feared the ladies would wish to take a nap. Cousin L. G. was here after tea and spent the day.

* * * * *

Tuesday [July] 19th. Rained in the morning but we concluded to go to town as soon as it cleared. We were delighted with the seats we procured or rather that Mr. Jamison had for us; we were able to see all that was going on. We left about sundown. /Mary & Mag Derr took dinner with Mrs. H's. Today at Houck's Ginny B. and A. Stonebreaker were there too./

Wednesday [July] 20th. Raining in showers all morning. I wrote a long letter to Lou Hersh and in the afternoon, Mary and I being so much interested [in] "Miss Theresa's Spinning Wheel," we sent down to Ginny for the rest of the papers; she kindly sent them.

* * * * *

Friday [July] 22nd. Mary, Mother and I went to town in the buggy; we did some shopping and then called to see Kate Davis and some others. We returned home to dinner and soon after Ginny Adams came up and spent the afternoon. /I had a long letter of Nelly Mering./ We were disappointed the girls did not come out.

Saturday [July] 23rd. We were at home all day; about seven o'clock Mag, Mary & Tom Derr, Lizzie Houck & Ham Boyd came out on horseback. They remained till after nine o'clock.

Sunday [July] 24th. Quite warm, but nevertheless Mary, Mother & I got ready and went to church and heard Dr. Zach's harvest sermon. Mag Derr came home with us. Mr. J. A. J. and Ed Shriner came to the hotel with us. We laid down after dinner and about half-past eight o'clock as we were sitting on the porch in dishibilli [sic], we were aroused by the sound of carriage wheels, and we were dressed and repaired to the parlour; found it to be Misses Boyd, Stonebreaker, & Story and Messrs. H. Boyd, Hunt & Slifford. They only remained a short time after nine o'clock.

Monday [July] 25th. I wrote a note to Uncle Lewis Scholl saying we would go down, provided he would come up for us on Friday. I wrote a P. S. in

1853

Mary's letter to Kate. Mr. Derr & Kate are out for an hour or so and Mag Derr went into town with them.

Tuesday [July] 26th. Found it raining when we got up, but it cleared away for a short time and we were ready and started for the Derrs'. We stopped according to promise to see Ginny Boyd and Alice Stonebreaker; they leave for Balt. to-morrow morning. We then went on to Mr. D's. and were caught in a heavy shower. After dinner, the sun came out and Mr. & Mrs. B. F. Winchester, Mrs. Belvin and [Messrs.] B., Mrs. C. Steiner, Mrs. Max Schley and Mr. & Mrs. Reese came out and spent the afternoon. We were over to the Ceresville Mill[32] and got weighed. When we started for Mr. D's it had the appearance of a very heavy gust, but it proved to be only a little sprinkle.

Wednesday [July] 27th. We were looking for company all morning, but as they did not arrive by twelve we sat down to dinner, and as we were about desert I heard a rap and then it proved to be Mr. & Mrs. B. F. Winchester, Madam Pearson, Mrs. Belvin, Miss Annie B; so dinner must be got in a hurry and so it was. Mag, Mary & Eugene Derr arrived about four o'clock and staid till after tea. Harry Smith was here an hour or so this afternoon, goes to Phila. to-night.

Thursday [July] 28th. Quite pleasant. Mary & I went for blackberries this morning. Ginny arrived and after an early dinner Mary L., Jenny Adams and I went up to Mr. E. Howard's and spent the afternoon. Had a letter from Lou Hersh. Mr. J. A. J. was here and spent the evening; goes to Montgomery to-morrow.

Friday [July] 29th. Rainy, damp, but cleared by three o'clock. Uncle Lewis Scholl arrived and took us by way of New Market to his house; found Aunt Jemima well and expecting us. Mary had a letter from Kate with a note for me.

Saturday [July] 30th. Drizzling & foggy in the morning but soon cleared off. We were on the eve of taking a walk of the hills when Mr. Nathan Maynard arrived and sat till bedtime with us.

---

[32]See note 3, 1851.

Sunday [July] 31st. We had quite a time deciding whether we should accept Mrs. Maynard's invitation to spend the day with her or go over to New Market to church, but finally concluded on the former. We went over and spent a very pleasant day with Mrs. M. and her sons, Howard, Nathan & Tom. Ed Shriner arrived about dinner time. Mr. Thomas M. left after an early tea for Liberty. He gave us a very pressing invitation to attend a pic-nic on Tuesday. Ed S. and Mr Nathan M. accompanied us home and remained till bedtime.

Monday August 1st [1853]. So very warm and sultry. We were busy making and baking a sponge cake, which was spoiled in baking; so after dinner we baked an excellent pound cake. We [were] sitting about when, just about five and I went to look after the tea, here arrives Misses H. Stevenson, J. Angle & Clara Hobbs & Messrs. T. Maynard & Rod. Hobbs. They staid till after tea. I am glad they came for we will know someone at the pic-nic.

Tuesday August 2nd. Day awakened us earlier than usual this morning as the sun was shining so bright. We hurried to prepare for breakfast and then for the pic-nic. Soon cousin E. Shriner & then Mr. Nathan M. [came]. Mary went with Ed in the buggy to the pic-nic and Mr. M. took Aunt J[emima] and I in the carriage and Uncle L rode on horseback. We arrived about half-past ten o'clock and were welcomed by the managers and our four acquaintances and introduced to most every body on the ground. I danced the first set with Mr. E. Poole and danced every successive set till tea time; was introduced to many persons whom I had heard a great deal of but had never seen. Most prominent one, [was] Mr. Basil Warfield. Every one seemed to enjoy themselves. We returned about dusk and Ed and Mr. M. left about ten o'clock. Rod Hobbs rode beside of the carriage home.

Wednesday [August] 3rd. After breakfast we busied ourselves packing for going home. Mr. Howard Maynard was over to see us this morning. We arrived home about twelve o'clock and Uncle Lewis left about two. Mary and I went for blackberries and got quite a quantity, but not so sweet as the hill berries.

Thursday [August] 4th. We went into town and went to see Mrs. L. B. Jamison, Misses Kunkels; got pears and plumbs at Mrs. Myers. Mailed a letter to Nellie Mering. Called to see Call Loats and did some shopping and returned home.

1853

Friday [August] 5th. I took Mary out to Mrs. Derr's this morning and left her there. I found Madam Pearson there. We went to M. Derr's for a short time. I returned home to dinner.

Saturday [August] 6th. I was at home alone. Anna Scholl arrived about six o'clock staid over night. Mr. J. A. J. was there too.

Sunday [August] 7th. Annie and I went to church. /Saw Mrs. Sauerwein & Emma in church./ She left after early tea.

* * * * *

Wednesday [August] 10th. Ma was in to see Mrs. S[auerwein] and invited her out.

Thursday [August] 11th. Still so very warm. Had a note from E. Shriner saying his father and Jno. Derr's family would be out to-morrow. Had a letter of M. H. [*illegible*] of Emmitsburg.

Friday [August] 12th. I was very busy helping to prepare dinner. Uncle & Mrs. Shriner, Mrs. Sauerwein, and George S arrived about eleven, and Mrs. Derr, Mary [and] Emma Sauerwein, Mag, Alice & Tommy Derr [came] about twelve. They all appeared to enjoy the day and we held "sweet converse" of friends that were dear.

Saturday [August] 13th. Very warm. Mr. J. A. J. arrived about seven and he first accosted me with, "Miss M. how have you spent this warm week?" He brought me some delicious pears and I in turn treated him to some peaches. He wanted me to go out to Mr. D[err]'s with him and I should have enjoyed the moonlight ride, but I only made an engagement for the morrow.

Sunday [August] 14th. Mr. Johnson arrived in time and we went out to the "Woods meeting" and went over to Mr. Derr's and remained till evening; met Messrs. Poole, <u>Cookson</u> and Todd there and others too.

* * * * *

Tuesday [August] 16th. Still at home. Wednesday 17th, Thursday 18th Still at home and busy.

1853

Friday [August] 19th. Quite cold. Mother and I were in town to do some shopping and then came home.

Saturday [August] 20th. I was quite busy, and who should arrive about five o'clock but Mr. Sam Preston. I sent Mother in the parlor and very soon Mr. J. A. J. and cousin Ed S. [came,] so I had to make my appearance. Father, Mother and Mr. P. went to camp meeting and the other gents remained with me till about 9 o'clock.

Sunday [August] 21st. I staid at home and prepared dinner. Father, Mother, Mr. P. Davis and Randolf Scholl came up to dinner and, as the Misses D[err], did not call, I went down with Mr. P. after dinner; saw numerous friends and acquaintances there, Mary Sauerwein, Mag & Mary Derr & Georgia Houck. We returned to tea about five or six. Dr. Kerchner & Will Boyd of Balt, Mr. P., [and] Uncle & Aunt E. Scholl took tea with us, and we all together with Ham Boyd and M. Stonebreaker of Washington Co. went to camp at night. We all returned about half-past eleven, but time was told by small numbers when they left. Bert Ritchie came along.

Monday [August] 22nd. Very pleasant day. We preferred remaining at home to going in the day [to the camp meeting], so we were at home all day. We intended going at night, but as I felt badly I said I would remain at home and let Mother go with the girls, but after some disputing they concluded they would all remain. Mr. Geo. Birely and Tommy Derr called about eight and then went down to the camp. Girls thought they would go with them but changed their minds. About eleven o'clock Dr. Kerchner and Will Boyd called to bid us adieu, and soon Mr. Preston and then Mr. Davis brought Melinda Shafer of Middletown, Md. and Hal Hoke of Mercersburg, Pa. down. With the exception of the first two [they] spent the day.

Tuesday [August] 23rd. Well, a very pretty day, and after Mag Derr's suggestion we all went in the cart to camp meeting; saw numerous friends there and some nice beaux there. We had fun about our cart ride; some were amused, others astonished, and we pleased. We concluded we would go again in the cart but there were so many beaux about that we went in buggy: G. Houck with Dr. Fleming, Mary Derr with Mr. Preston (who made his appearance again the eve), Mag Derr with Mr. Todd, Mary Sauerwein with E. Shriner, and I with Mr. J. A. Johnson. We had a very pleasant drive and it was even two o'clock I believe till we got shut of all the beaux. Mr. P. staid over night.

1853

Wednesday [Aug.] 24th. Quite pleasant day. As the girls were expecting to be sent for, none of us went to camp. Ed Shriner came out about four o'clock and after conversing awhile told us of a dispatch[33] he had received relative to Mary's coming home; that Kate was worse. So we had early tea and then cousin Ed took the girls all home. George Birely called after tea but the girls had left and I did not feel like going to camp. I had a paper from Lou Hersh.

Thursday [Aug.] 25th. Father took me into town and I saw Mary Sauerwein off. There was hurry and bustle to get her off as she was rather late. I walked out home and took my dress off as I had a boil under my arm. I feel very uneasy about Kate.

Friday Aug. 26th. I was at home all day busy and complaining with my arm.

Saturday [Aug.] 27th. I wanted to go to town but my arm was not well enough.

Sunday [Aug.] 28th. Mother rode to town this morning to church but I did not go as my arm is still sore.

Monday [Aug.] 29th. First sounds that accosted my ears this morning were when Father said, "If Margaret was ready I would take her over[34] this morning," so I threw open the blinds and said I would be ready. But he concluded twas too late. However, just after breakfast I got ready and started; we stopped for a few minutes at Mrs. Mering's and they insisted and we remained to dinner. Nellie is in Balt. Co. Jenny Troxel was in to dinner and Mr. T. was in to see us. We then went on our way rejoicing. We had a good deal of inquiring to do after we left Littlestown, but we finally arrived at Mrs. Hersh's about dusk. There seemed to be a general rejoicing over me. I certainly could not help being gratified. I was met by Mrs. Geo. Hersh, Mrs. Wm. Hersh of Pittsburg, John & Lou Hersh, and then, one by one, Messrs. Geo Hersh, Frank, James, Allen & Paul were introduced. I think from first impression I shall be delight[ed] in Penn. They had supper soon prepared for

---

[33]The dispatch from the Baltimore Sauerweins to Ed Shriner is mentioned also in the Derr diary, p. 37. It had evidently come through their telegraph business connection. Subscriptions for Morse's invention (1844) had been offered in Frederick in 1850. Williams, *History*, I, 241-245.

[34]The trip was for Margaret's visit with the Hersh family in New Oxford, Pennsylvania, going on Route 194 by way of Bruceville and Littlestown.

us. Sam [Hersh] says Lou wrote him t'was no use deferring his visit home any longer for she did not believe I was coming but he happened then just in the nick of time. I think I like to surprise people; it shows how you are appreciated. Lou and I went up stairs about 9 but did not sleep till I am sure it was two o'clock, as we had so much to talk about and were so glad to meet each other once more.

Tuesday Aug. 30th. A lovely morning. Father left this morning for home and left me with the family. I think Oxford[35] a very quaint little village. So far, every one seems to attend to their own business. I took a long nap this afternoon as we were awake so long last night and then we dressed ourselves in White Swiss for tea. Lou went over for Miss Ciders of Chambersburg who is staying at old Miss Heim's, and we then took a long walk, and she came over and sat till nearly bed time with us and family. Col. Leiby called tonight.

Wednesday [Aug.] 31st. Very bright morning. I wrote a long letter to Mary Sauerwein, telling her of my whereabouts and inquiring for Kate. When the stage[36] arrived, Mrs. Bolles of Cleveland O[hio] and Mag McClelland of Gettysburg were added to our number -- quite an acquisition. After dinner we, that is, Mrs. B., Mag McC., Lou, Sam, Col. Leiby, and myself went fishing. Mrs. B. caught several and Sam and I caught one. We had quite a pleasant walk & to vary it a ride on a wagon. Col. Leiby spent the evening with us, the family. After tea Mag McC, Lou, Sam and I took a walk, met the stage and rode in town.

Thursday Sept. 1st [1853]. Col. Leiby was of course to see us several times today. I wrote a long letter to Mag Derr. After tea, Lou, Mag McC & myself, Sam & Frank & Col. Leiby were just sauntering forth when Mr. Gates Myers arrived, and so we had a beau to spare, Lou had two up the road and Mag two in town. We used our best efforts and detained Col. L. till eight and Mr. M. till about half-past nine from Mrs. Miley's party. Lou & brothers F & S were invited [too], but of course did not attend in consequence of company not being invited. We were going to have some sport with playing Post Office but feared Mag would tell on us.

---

[35]New Oxford, Pennsylvania, is on Route 30 between Gettysburg and York.

[36]The stagecoach traveled on the main east-west road (Route 30) between Philadelphia and Western Pennsylvania.

1853

Friday Sept. 2nd. Yet another very warm day. As we were disappointed with our trip to Conawaga [sic] Chapel[37] yesterday, being Mr. Hersh would not let us go with Col. L's horse, so Mrs. H. had two horses hitched to the little wagon and Mrs. Bolles, Mag Mc, Lou, Col. Leiby, Sam and myself jumped into the wagon and took a jolly ride over to the chapel. The scenery round is similar to Fred'k Co. and the land about the same quality I believe. The Chapel certainly has some of the most life like pictures I ever beheld. After we had been through the Chapel and grounds we were invited in by the Superior and treated to some very fine wine and cakes. We then went off home, <u>Sam</u> making a fuss about my sitting beside him. After tea, Lou, Mag, Sam and myself took a walk out in the country and were treated to pears and grapes. Col. Leiby was here of course after tea. Mag made an engagement with Col. L. and I with Sam to take a walk before breakfast next morning. He left about nine.

Saturday Sept. 3rd. Pleasant in the morning but cloudy and rain during day and night. According to promise, Mag, Col. L., Sam and I took our walk, went down to Myers Mill and was weighed. I weighed 120, Sam 138, and don't remember the rest. Mag, Lou and I had some fun trying to catch peaches that were thrown to the window. Charley arrived this afternoon, he had changed considerable since I saw him last, quite <u>preacher-like</u> now. Mag Mc would leave this morning in spite of rain or shine. After she left we were all seated around in the parlor when I was handed a letter and it was from Mollie Sauerwein. Kate is much better now, able to eat something.

Sunday Sept. 4th. When we awoke this morning found it cloudy and raining in showers. Lou, Frank and I went to Sabbath School and we returned about ten and then read and talked till time to dress for dinner. After dinner we all got ready and went to church to hear Charley [Hersh] preach. Sam went with Lou & me. And after tea Sam, Lou, Mrs. Bolles & I went to hear Charley preach in the Methodist Church. Sam came with Lou and I, Frank with Mrs. B.

Monday [Sept.] 5th. Well, soon after breakfast the stage arrived and Sam waited till the last moment and then left. Charley is still left but he is not so

---

[37]Father William Wappiler established a Jesuit Mission of the Sacred Heart at Conewago (near Hanover) in 1730. This chapel is one of the oldest in continuous use in the United States and is a major shrine with the status of a basilica. It is now known as Sacred Heart Basilica. Sylvester K. Stevens, *Pennsylvania, Birthplace of a Nation* (New York, 1964), p. 93.

much company. Old Mrs. Leiby is very ill; [we] won't get to see the Col. often now. We miss Sam very much. Mrs. Cornelia Himes not at all well. Col. Leiby was here this evening.

Tuesday [Sept.] 6th. Very warm day again. I wrote a long letter home. Well, if some has left, there comes Mrs. Wm. Hersh of Pittsburg and Mr. Ed Hersh of Wash. to-night. Mrs. H. is not very well and fears she cannot leave in the morning. I like them both very well. Every one seemed impressed with the idea that there is to be a general breaking in the morning. Charley and I took a nice long moonlight walk and he told me of "his Missy".

Wednesday [Sept.] 7th. Beautiful but very warm morning. The carriage was at the door at 7 o'clock and into it was stowed Mrs. Wm. Hersh, Georgie H. and nurse, John Denniston, Messrs. Ed & Wm. Hersh and they were carried away to York and from thence to be transported to Pittsburg, with the exception of Mr. E. Hersh. I find our plan for York is spoiled, and we do not go to-morrow. The house seems "like some hall deserted". Charley leaves too this evening after tea. Misses L. Karl, C. Ciders & Mr. Al Heims were over to spend the evening with us, told fortunes, etc.

Thursday Sept. 8th. Much cooler this morning. Our quiet house was thrown into quite a state of excitement this morning by the arrival of Mr. G. Harper of Gettysburg and his taking Mrs. Bolles over to Hanover[38]. Mrs. Ellis sent for us to take tea with her and we excepted [sic]; we had quite a time getting Mrs. B. dressed and off. They returned just as we were dressing to go down to Mrs. E's, so we all went down; and I tell [sic] we did an ample justice to her broiled chicken and toasted bread, etc. Mrs. E., Mrs. B., Lou and I took a walk and met the stage containing Miss Maria McClelland, so we all got in and rode to town. Miss M. had a great deal to say about Mr. H. and Mrs. B., did not know he had taken her to Hanover. Frank, Lou, Mrs. B. and I took a ride about a mile up to the pike and walked down. Lou had a letter from Sam saying we should come, he would meet us at the depot in the morning.

Friday [Sept.] 9th. Pleasant early in the morning but commenced raining by dinner. Mrs. John Hersh sent up for us to come down to tea that afternoon. Misses Karl, Ciders, Lou and I took a walk to the mill and were weighed, I have gained 4 lbs. We rode home in a wagon. We went down about three and spent a delightful evening. They had another letter of Sam, wants to

---

[38]Hanover is between New Oxford and Littlestown, Pennsylvania, on Route 94.

1853

know if I have captivated Mr. Heims, also sent the dispatch from Will H. [that he] got home safely.

Saturday [Sept.] 10th. Rained till about two then cleared off beautifully. Frank took me out in the buggy with his new horse. Mr. Edward Slagle was with us most of the time we were in Hanover. I wrote a long letter to Harry Smith. Frank took Lou and I into Hanover, we spent the afternoon with Miss Rosenmiller. We were on the streets a great deal. John Hersh & wife and Mrs. Ellis were here to-day but they are most every day. There are no strangers.

Sunday Sept. 11th. Beautiful morn. James H. took Mrs. Bolles, Lou & I up to Hunterstown to church and we heard an excellent sermon from Mr. [*illegible*] a Presbyterian. I think it the prettiest and neatest country church I ever was in and such a nice congregation. I was delighted. Lou said we were dressed so fine the reason none of the beaux came up to talk to us. We saw Miss Karl leave for home just as we arrived. We all went to hear the Reform minister in the afternoon; he preached on "Hypocrisy" and at night of "Predestinananism" [*sic*].

Monday [Sept.] 12th. Morning very bright, and little when I awoke this morning did I think I would have such a subject [to] consider at night. Sam arrived from York about ten o'clock. Lou and I were busy doing up collars so I just met him in the dining room. He asked me to go with him to take a ride as he was going out on business. So about two o'clock we started and went to Irishtown on business and then took a long ride. When we were about a mile from home he startled me from a revery by "Miss M., I love you". I gave him no answer for [I] believed it merely a quiz, but soon I found from his protestations and confessions that he was in earnest and had cherished a love for me unknown to me since I knew him. I was taken so by surprise I was unable to give him an answer. I studied long at night and till late and felt that I could not conscientiously say it was returned, and I know Sam hates delays, so I determined to dream on it but did not. They all teased us about not eating at tea; I felt little like it. I wrote to Nellie Mering this morning.

Tuesday Sept. 13th. Rather a gloomy morning, but cleared off during the day. I was awake early this morning studying how I could tell Sam of my conclusion. I scarcely can tell him how I felt when I met him, for I wanted to meet him as I always did and wanted to convince him of my friendship. There seemed to be no opportunity for us being alone so he took the seat just vacated by Lou in the door beside me and wanted to know if I had come to any conclusions. I said let's be the <u>Friends</u> we've always been; he seemed hurt and disappointed and I pitied him (but pity will not express the mending). He wanted to know if I loved another or if I rejected his love because of my parents or doubting his love. I told him I knew not their opinion but simply because I feared I did not love him. He wished to know if it was a final answer or if he might hope. He finally told [me] whatever might happen he should never feel as great respect for any other lady. I told him I would do any thing to convince him of my friendship for him or the family, told him I would correspond if he wished it, but we concluded under present circumstances it would not be so pleasant. He left about nine and I never shall forget his last look when I saw him from the window or his tones when he said "Good-bye." I felt in rather a sad humour or rather sorrowful, but it was off soon when I got to conversing with Mr. John Hersh on religion. I wrote a letter home to-day. Mrs. Edward Slagle of Hanover called to see us to-day. We were to see some folks after tea and then Lou & I went down to Mrs. Ellis['s] and had plenty of peaches. I did not think this would be my last evening of O[xford], but I think so. I think of S. today tho' as a friend.

Wednesday Sept. 14th. Beautiful morning. Miss Lou M. McClelland of Gettysburg arrived in the stage and she was joined by Mrs. Bolles & Mrs. John Hersh and they proceeded on their way to Lancaster Co. Mr. James Hersh took his mother over to attend old Mrs. Leiby's funeral while Mr. Frank Hersh took Lou and me to Gettysburg. We stopped at Mrs. McClelland['s] and were welcomed by Mrs. McC., Mag McC, Ella McC. Soon after dinner we got ourselves ready and went into town and met Mary M.; we all took a walk and by three o'clock we were all in church, for this being commencement week[39] there is to be exercises this afternoon and night. We heard an address from Rev. Mr. Passivant of Pittsburg and Rev. Dr. Morris of Balt. When we were going home found it raining, but very fortunately, Mrs. C. Hersh had an umbrella so we got out very well. We would not let Mr. C. Hersh go out with us as he had no umbrella. It rained very hard till about ten o'clock; nevertheless Mr. Stevenson (a young lawyer, I think Lou Mc.'s beau) and Mr. C. Hersh were out. They proved themselves very agreeable.

---

[39] Gettysburg College was founded in 1832; Gettysburg Seminary was founded in 1826. *Profile of American Colleges*, New York, 1984.

1853

Thursday Sept. 15th. We were all so glad to find how beautifully it had cleared off. C. Hersh was out very early. We all got ready and went into town to hear the Graduating Class addresses and were very much gratified both with the essays and music. Dr. Dealman was there. When we returned Mr. S[tevenson] accompanied us. We found Allen Hersh had been up, and when I saw him he handed me a letter from home saying Father would come for me to-day. There is some mistake. I am sorry, for I want to remain till Saturday; but then Lou & I packed our trunk and off we sent it to Oxford, reserving ourselves for the next opportunity. We went into town thinking we might see Father pass and go down with him, but we did not. We took a walk out to the college and went through the Halls, Libraries, etc. We remained to tea at Mrs. John McClelland's and after tea walked out to the seminary and all round. We returned to Mrs. McC's, and Mr. S. and Mr. David Swope spent the evening with us.

Friday Sept. 16th. We took a walk into town with Mary McC. and I was joined by Mr. Stevenson, who is quite a nice escort. Soon after we returned to Mrs. McC's, Charley & James Hersh came out, and we got ready for our start to Oxford, & when we arrived found Father waiting for me. So Mrs. Hersh, Lou & I packed my trunk and I ate my dinner and Father and I were ready to start by one o'clock. We stopped a few minutes at Nellie Mering's and then arrived home by ten o'clock. We had a breakdown, but with the assistance of some withes[40] and a <u>gentleman</u> it was soon remedied. I felt fatigued by my ride. Found a package of music marked "Island of Hope", so of course it must be from Rod Hobbs. It arrived soon after I left.

Saturday Sept. 17th. Unpacked my trunk and put things in their place and after dinner as Father was going into town I accompanied him. I did some shopping and called to see Nelly B. on my return.

Sunday [Sept.] 18th. Mother and I were in church. Capt. H. Davis came down street with me. I slept most of the afternoon.

Monday Sept. 19th. I wrote a long letter to Lou Hersh but did not send it off.

Tuesday [Sept.] 20th. Mother and I went out to Grandmother's. I was down at Uncle L's and got rose cuttings.

---

[40]Withes are flexible twigs or branches.

Wednesday [Sept.] 21st. Father, Mother and I went into town in the cart and I put Lou's letter in the office, and had one from Harry which had been sent to Oxford, and Lou sent it on; she had written considerably on it. I went to see Mrs. Winchester and told her if she would be ready, Mother would take her down to Merings' on Friday. Met Evie there, so we came down street together and I went and called to see Kate Davis, and then came on down street to go out with Father and Mother, but they had gone, so I walked out.

Thursday [Sept.] 22nd. Beautiful morning. Mother and I walked up to see Mrs. Maria Johnson and sat about an hour and then went home; after dinner I went over to Mrs. I. Howard's and found Linden quite sick, so I volunteered my services to sit up at night. Mary & Harriet Keefer soon arrived and H remained. Mr. Barney Taylor of Va. came and remained over night.

Friday [Sept.] 23rd. I left Mrs. H's pretty early and came home. We had a note from Mrs. W. that she could go, so Mother got ready and started off and [left] me to keep house.

Saturday [Sept.] 24th. Very busy all day. I sent John to town for the papers and to the P. O. and when he returned brought me a letter from Lou H. and one from Nelly Mering, so I prepared for company as she said she was coming, but she did not arrive. I answered Lou's letter this evening. Mr. J. A. Johnson was out after tea. He had started to Lou's last Saturday but when he arrived at Nell Mering's found I had come home. Had a note from Ed Shriner telling us of his sister. She is dead.

Sunday Sept. 25th. Beautiful day. I went over to see Linden Howard and found the baby sick too. We had dinner about eleven o'clock and then started out to Uncle Shriner's to attend the funeral; we stopped and took Aunt Margaret Artz & Vic along. It was nearly sundown till we got home. It was quite large.

Monday [Sept.] 26th. Beautiful morning. I dressed myself, expecting Nellie Mering and cousins to arrive with Mother, but they did not come. Wrote to Harry Smith. I went over to Mrs. H's after tea and remained over night.

Tuesday [Sept.] 27th. When I got home found Father and Mother had gone to town but they soon returned.

* * * * *

1853

Saturday Oct. 1st [1853]. Very pleasant in the morning but cloudy before night. I wrote to Lou Hersh. Mr. J. A. Johnson was out after tea and spent the evening. He was [as] usual lively.

Sunday [Oct.] 2nd. Quite pretty day. John drove me into town to church.

* * * * *

Tuesday [Oct.] 4th. I received a letter from Cousin A. Ogle.

Wednesday [Oct.] 5th. Ma & I were in town. Bought my pink dress.

* * * * *

Saturday October 8th. Mother and I were in town this evening; we did some shopping and called at Houcks' a few minutes. I bought my pick[41].

Sunday [Oct.] 9th. Mother and I were in church to-day. Just as I was leaving church Mr. C. Steiner stepped up and handed me a letter from Mag Derr; she is in Balt. now.

Monday [Oct.] 10th. I staid at home and made my dress while Mother went to town to purchase me a shawl, but it did not please.

Tuesday [Oct.] 11th. Ma & I were in town early this morning, called to see Mrs. Howard, and then stopped till nearly noon. Town all business and stir.

Wednesday [Oct.] 12th. Delightful day for the commencement of the Agriculture Fair[42]. I was at home busy all morning preparing for and expecting Nellie Mering but as she did not arrive by three o'clock; so I got myself ready and John took me into town & Father came in and met me and took me into the [fair] ground. I was gratified by the display of stock,

---

[41]Picks were used to tease strands of hair for making hair wreaths and jewelry.

[42]This was the first Fair to be held in Frederick in a number of years. It took place on the hill where the Hessian Barracks stand and was very successful. "I am told all the stalls are full and more have to be made." Engelbrecht, *Diary*, II, 597. "I believe there was one on a small scale a good while ago. They had everything arranged in good order." Derr diary, p. 38.

vegetables, fancy & useful needle work, etc. I soon found lots of friends there, amongst the rest Nelly Mering & Miss Choate & Mary Chapman. I was delighted. Mrs. B. F. Winchester gave me a very pressing invitation to take tea with the ladies, so I consented. Mary Chapman & I went up and took tea with Mrs. W., and Nellie, Miss Choate & Lizzie Houck took tea with Mrs. Jamison. Miss Mary Daniels was there to tea. As Mrs. Houck's was appointed our Rendezvous when Mrs. W. went to the fair, Mary C. and I stopped there and found Mr. J. A. Johnson and Messrs. Slingluff & Weaver of Carroll Co. there. As the girls staid so long we sent Mr. Johnson after them and when we all got to-gether started for the Fireman's Fair. Georgia H. & Nellie went with Mr. S., Lizzie H. & Miss Choate with Mr. J. & Mary E. and I with Mrs. W., Lewis Trail, & Miss A. Pifer called during the evening. The Fair-room was very much crowded and few persons I knew. We left about ten o'clock. Mr. J handed me a work basket saying Mrs. W. sent it to me, but it proved to be Mr. J. gave it.

Thursday Oct. 13th. Very pleasant day. We sat on the steps a long time looking at the country people coming in and then got ready and went down to H's and met Mother on the street. We went shopping awhile and then, joined by Mr. & Mrs. Winchester, we all went up to the ground. There was lots of people there. The grounds crowded; every one says there was never so great a crowd in Fred'k since LaFayette came to town.[43] About one o'clock we all went up to Mrs. W's to dinner and did not return to the grounds any more. Nellie M. & I took a long walk. I saw Chett Taylor; he looks wretchedly badly. I came up to see Mrs. Chandler a few minutes. Father handed me a nice long letter from Lou Hersh and a magazine from A. J. H., an unknown friend or from Al Heims, I think. We all came home then amidst the crowd and dust.

Friday Oct. 14th. Very pleasant day. Well, I want[ed] to go to town and as the cart was going I determined to go in that way. I dressed to feel comfortable. I met a number of friends and soon fell in with Mary Derr & Houck's, Nell & others. We had Mr. Johnson and others all morning. I went down to Rices to dinner. I went up and went down to the table with Mr. & Mrs. Page. Soon after dinner, Mrs. P and I went up to the ground but could

---

[43]LaFayette arrived in Frederick in 1824 and was royally entertained with processions, dinners, and a ball. Williams, *History*, I, 182, 184.

not get close enough to hear the awards of Premiums[44], so we took a seat on the "Chicken Coop" and we soon joined Mr. J. A. J. Soon saw Aunt Jemima and about four o'clock we got ready to turn our head homewards. Mother and Bill Kiel came in for us. As we were passing the Cemetery we passed a horse that appeared unruly and jumped against the carriage and very much alarmed us; and as we were hurrying down a hill old Barney fell and we all jumped from the carriage and tried to get him up, and soon Mrs. H's Aaron[45] was there and he drove us home. Aunt J. was very much frightened.

Saturday [Oct.] 15th. Beautiful morning. After dinner Aunt J. and I walked into town and called at Rev. Mr. Jones' and then she, Miss Lizzie and I went out to do some shopping for her. Mother came in for me. I called to see Aunt Betsy Scholl & Mrs. Lizzie Machly. Aunt J. did not return with me.

Sunday [Oct.] 16th. Pleasant morning. I went to church this morning and heard a good sermon from Dr. Zack.

Monday Oct. 17th. Right pleasant day. Soon after dinner Mother and I started for Mrs. Michael Keefer's, stopped at Mrs. Finey's for her, but she could not accompany us. We met Miss A. R. Keefer there, and Miss Kitty Warfield and sister are there too, living. We spent a very pleasant afternoon indeed. Soon after we came home Mr. Geo. Birely came out and sat the evening with me; he made himself very agreeable and I treated him to some cake and cordial.

Tuesday [Oct.] 18th. Weather continues pleasant. Mother started for Aunt M. Artz's & Grandmother's but found Aunt M. was not at home, so we went down and took tea with Grandmother.

Wednesday [Oct.] 19th. We had some difficulty about the carriage harness but finally got it fixed and started for Uncle Elias Scholl's. We spent a very pleasant day. The family all home but David.

---

[44]"The people flocked into town from every direction. The street and pavements full. I counted 80 carriages, Barrouches, carryalls. What a gathering of human beings." Engelbrecht, *Diary*, II, 589.

[45]Aaron was a slave belonging to Isaac Howard who lived near Manchester Farm. Hitselberger, *Bridge in Time*, p. 459.

Thursday [Oct.] 20th. I concluded as Father was going into town I would go along. I called to see Kate Davis and then down to Capt. Ed Schley's to see Clara Hobbs & the girls, and to see Mary Birely, and then went up street to go home, but found Father gone; so I called to see Mrs. Salman, Kate Kunkel and finally it was raining before I started home. I was sorry.

Friday [Oct.] 21st. Still raining. While at the dinner table Father proposed, if we were ready, starting for the World's Fair[46], so up I took and ordered the carriage, to go see if I could hear of Nell M. or whether G. H. would go. Sent a message to cousin Ed Shriner by Mr. J. A. J. to come go with us. Called to see Mrs. W. but she knew nothing of Nell. I came home & was busy. I received a note from Lizzie Houck this evening that G. would go.

FREDERICK CO. & BALTIMORE

Saturday Oct. 22nd. Cloudy in the morning but cleared off about noon. Father took me into town and I did some shopping and then went up to Mrs. Houck's to see if they had heard from Georgia, but they knew not what to make of it, and so I had to content myself to wait till the dispatch arrived saying she would go. I then went down street and told Father, and we hurried out home, packed my trunk, eat my dinner and hurried back to town; and we were carried to Bal.[timore], intending to leave for Phila. at the half-past seven train, but we were too late. George Sauerwein had Georgia H[ouck] at the depot to meet us but it was of no avail, so we all went back to Mrs. Sauerwein's who was surprised to see us. Mr. John Sadtler & Rev. M. of Frostburg and Mr. Camel of Manchester [were there]. We spent the evening together and retired early for City, about ten o'clock. I feel very much disappointed in not getting to Phil'd to-night.

Sunday [Oct.] 23rd. We all went to church this morning and heard a sermon from Mr. Diehl of Fred'k. Saw Nell Mering at the cathedral and wanted her to go along. We took a walk out Madison and out Charles St.; I wrote a letter to cousin Harry telling him we would pass through Phil'd to-morrow. Mr. Perry walked and went to church with us also. Mr. Rau took tea with us.

---

[46]The first American World's Fair was opened by President Pierce in New York. It was held in the "Crystal Palace" which was a glass and iron exhibition hall erected in 1852 between 41st and 42nd Streets, on the site now occupied by the New York Public Library. John Kouwenhoven, *The Columbia Historical Portrait of New York* (New York, n.d.), pp. 201, 207.

1853

Mother thinks us in P. We went to hear Mr. Duncan preach to-night, Mary's favorite.

FROM BALT ON OUR WAY TO NEW YORK DIRECT THROUGH PHIL'D

Monday [Oct.] 24th. We were awake early, and what was my surprise when Mary said it was raining; but we did not stop for weather and about eight we were nicely fixed in a hack for the Phila depot on President St. We were started for Phila. by half-past eight o'clock, Georgia & I occupying one seat and Father another. We had not a view of the country for it was raining, snowing, hailing & blowing all day; we passed safely over the Gunpowders and all other dangerous places. On the boat crossing the Susquehanna Georgia espied a friend, which proved to be Mr. Locke of Shepherdstown and his sister and we had their company to Phila. Cousin Harry met us at the depot and went with us over to Camden, and I was very glad he did for it was raining so hard and we had only one umbrella in [our] company, and from thence we made no acquaintances till we were safely landed in New York. We took a hack for the St. Nicholas[47] [hotel] but could not get accommodations, nor at the Metropolitan, and then tried at the Prescott and found we could be very comfortably situated. I think we are very fortunate, and so say friends. We might almost imagine we were in some palace of olden times when we are handed from the hack into the parlours. I see groups seated around, but all strangers and strange faces. We took the cars from Camden to Amboy and then steam boat to New York. The city at a distance looked beautiful, as it had cleared cool and the sea was calm. Every one seemed to be anxious about rooms and none had them engaged. What a variety of persons and characters we met in travelling but I think we are particularly fortunate in meeting people with so genteel appearance.

NEW YORK

When we arrived at the Hotel, after being shown to our rooms and our baggage arrived, we were informed that we had supper from 9 till 12 o'clock, and so we dressed for supper and after retired to the parlour. The supper table presented the delicacies of the season and was set elegantly and the

---

[47]St. Nicholas Hotel, Broadway at Broome and Spring Streets, was noted for its fine decorations. The Metropolitan, at Broadway and Prince Street, could accommodate 1000 guests. Leslie Dorsey and Janice Devine, *Fare Thee Well* (New York, 1964), pp. 50-65.

White Waiters are so attentive and polite. The parlours are very handsomely furnished and the ceiling and walls are handsomely gilded, chairs of painted cloth and every thing in proportion, and maids and waiters stationed on every landing. We retired to our rooms between ten and eleven and I soon forgot I was in a large hotel and slept very soundly.

Tuesday [Oct.] 25th. Awoke and dressed for breakfast and when Father came for us the gong had not sounded, so we went up to have a view from the Housetop; we found it clear and cold. I find New York much colder than Fred'k. The city spread for miles around and we see immense ships and different sorts in its port. We meet at table a number of bo[a]rders but no doubt not half or quarter at these meals. We fixed ourselves immediately for the street and now to-day we are to realize my long expectation of the "Crystal Palace." When we were first out met Mr. John Wilson and had a long talk with him, and then took a walk down Broadway and was in several of the stores, and down near to the Battery; sorry did not go in. We then returned and went into Stewart's[48] and I purchased a pair of gloves, and from thence we went up to the St. Nicholas and were shown through the parlours, dining, and breakfast rooms, and the Bridal Chamber. It exceeds all description I have seen of it. Walls of fluted satin and chairs of cloth of gold, etc. After leaving the St. Nicholas we proceeded to an omnibus and went out to the palace. The splendor on entering did not strike me at first, but every instant something new attracted my attention and really I felt my incapability to retain the half I saw. The pictures are so life like and such great variety of subjects and the sculpture is unexceptionable. I feel my incapability even to give a faint idea of how much I was gratified; our attention was attracted first from one thing to another. We were wandering round all the time till almost four when I sat down to rest awhile, when Lo! who should I espy but Dr. Mort Anderson of Montgomery Co., Md. He joined us and we had a very pleasant time afterwards; he assisted us in admiring some things and we discussed the different departments together. I saw the mineralogical departments, saw the immense lump of pure gold. The policemen are stationed in all the different departments of the building. To say I was delighted will give no idea of how I was pleased. Well, we wanted to see the Palace lighted with Gas at night but we had another object in view. We wanted to take dinner at the hotel for today, then we want to be here to-morrow to dinner. We got home and soon

---

[48]Stewart's marble department store on the east side of Broadway between Reade and Chamber Streets became the prototype for the modern department store. Jay E. Cantor, *Winterthur Portfolio* (New York, 1985), pp. 1-5.

1853

dinner was commenced at 5 o'clock. Father, G & I proceeded to the table and was met by the usher and handed to our seats, and the Bill of Fare was very inviting with soups, fowls, roasts, boils, pastry, nuts, fruits, custards, ice cream, etc. We had the cloth removed for the fruits. I love to see the drill of the servants. I wonder how it is possible for the servants to walk with so much ease and precision without falling over each other or in the least interfering with an other. We remained in the parlour about a half hour with Mr. Johnathan Wilson and then got ready to go with Father to the Hippodrome[49]. We were very much gratified there. I never saw such riding and driving. Saw monkeys ride and drive. A man walk[ed] up an inclined plain [sic] on an ivory globe; saw an elephant harnessed and drove, and an ostrich harnessed; few things will soon seem impossible soon. We were on our way home about ten o'clock and just after we left the omnibus and were attempting to cross the street, Father was knocked down and had his knuckles bruised, etc. I felt thankful he received no worse injury. After getting to the hotel, I wrote to Harry and soon retired. I have a severe headache and feel badly; suppose it's from fatigue and fright.

NEW YORK AND PHILADELPHIA

Wednesday Oct. 26th. Still cold and clear. We were out early this morning and did some shopping and some walking and then came home, packed our trunks and had lunch in our traveling attire and prepared to bid adieu to New York. We were soon carried to the steam boat landing, and looking around after starting had an excellent or beautiful view. I think if I ever go to New York again I will go by sea or another route, as we have come and gone the same way. The little Islands look beautiful and the Houses along the beach look so Quiet and picturesque. We arrived in Phil. between six and seven and, as we did not find Harry there, Father procured a hack and we were driven to the Union Hotel, High Street and ushered into the parlour. And what was my cousin H's surprise. His reception was "Well, you are a pretty one not to let me know of your coming". I thought he could not have received my letter or he would have met us. We did not get our trunks to dress for supper so we went in our traveling attire. After supper we retired to our

---

[49]Franconi's Hippodrome, built in 1853 on Madison Square at 23rd Street and Broadway, had brick walls with a wood and canvas roof which was supported by outside pillars. It seated 10,000 people. John Kouwenhoven, *The Columbia Historical Portrait of New York* (New York, n.d.), p. 201.

rooms and soon retire[d]. Harry had an engagement and I would not let him break it.

Thursday Oct. 27th. Well, it seems we are doomed to rainy weather while away, for now it looks so threatening. G. was not well enough to go to breakfast so I went without her but about 9 o'clock she got up and was ready to go out. Father, Harry, Georgia and I just went to Fairmount[50], Waterworks, to see the Wire Bridge and from thence took the steamboat to Laurel Hill[51]. I was particularly gratified out there but was very sorry to find it rained so hard; however we walked all round. We intended to stop at Fairmount as we returned, but as it rained so, we got directly in a carriage and returned to the Union. We had dinner immediately and as it rained so hard we were obliged to remain in the house till after tea when we went /Georgia, Harry & I/ to the Arch St. Theatre[52]. There was quite a large audience notwith-standing the unfavorable weather, and all appeared delighted with the Lewis Family. I feel sorry Georgia is so much indisposed and I hope she will be better. We sat and talked in the parlour till after twelve o'clock, then bid each other good night. I made to-day my first travelling acquaintance. We met two gentlemen on the boat going to Laurel Hill and [one] of them proved very loquacious and I concluded he was a Southerner or had been once. We were discussing Mrs. Stowe, her writings, etc. and as we were standing under the portico of the old station house his discourse served to pass away time as the rain was pouring down. This was our first ride through town and every thing attracted our attention; we passed Logan Square[53], two Houses of Refuge[54] and the Cathedral[55] that has been

---

[50]Fairmont Park was the first large urban park in America. On its grounds were the waterworks designed by Benjamin Latrobe. Sam Bass Warner, Jr., *The Private City, Philadelphia in Three Periods of Its Growth* (Philadelphia, 1968), pp. 105, 106.

[51]Laurel Hill was a cemetery and park of about 350 acres four miles north of the State House on the banks of the Schuylkill River. John Hope Franklin, *A Southern Odyssey* (Baton Rouge, 1976), p. 120.

[52]The Arch Theater was opened in 1828. Pennsylvania's Writers Project, *Pennsylvania* (New York, 1940), p. 147.

[53]Logan Square is one of five parks included in William Penn's original plan of Philadelphia. *Ibid.*, p. 278.

[54]The House of Refuge at Fairmont and 15th Street was built in 1828, its main purpose being to house juvenile delinquents. Russell S. Weagley and Nicholas B. Wainwright, *Philadelphia - A 300 Year History* (n.p., n.d.).

1853

building five years and is expected to be completed in five more. It's a massive building of Brown Stone Columns are immense. Philadelphia attracted our attention as it does all others by the very handsome and neat appearance of the houses and the cleanliness and regularity of its streets. I am very much pleased here now and do not know what it would be in fair weather.

Friday October 28th. Found it still rained when we awoke. I dressed for an early breakfast this morning and we went in at the first table, as Father intends leaving for Balt. He left immediately [after] breakfast and left Georgia & I under Harry's charge. As Georgia felt badly and Harry went to the store, I sat down and wrote a long letter to Fanny Koones and by the time I had finished Harry returned and we got ready and went up to the U. S. Mint. It is perfect curiosity and I wonder why money is so plentiful there but it is distributed from there to the World. We had dinner very soon after we returned and then, as it is still so disagreeable, H. started out for Miss Emma Haslet, his particular friend, but she had some friends with her so did not come to tea. Mr. Paul Keller called to see us, H's particular male friend, and about four o'clock, as it was just misting, Harry, Georgia & I took a promenade on Chestnut Street. I did not see the crowd I expect[ed] to see but Fourth was quite crowded with ladies out shopping. I met but one familiar, Anna Petit of Frederick, MD. I think it must be a delightful promenade on a fair day. I saw the State House in its Old Grandeur. I could [comment] lots but as this is intended for only my eye, why write any more on that subject. We dressed for tea soon after we returned and then H. went round for Miss Haslet, and very soon Mr. Keller arrived, and about seven G. & I got our bonnets and we all, Mr. Keller with me and G. & Miss H with Harry, [went] to hear Jack Owings' account of his ascent to Mt. Blanc. The scenery was very fine, the painting well executed and his description so amusing and yet so concise. We all were well pleased and on our return stopped in at Parkinson's Saloon and had oysters. It is the most elegant saloon in P. The garden is all lighted with gas in summer and there are numerous summer arbours & etc. They all were anxious for us to stay and to-morrow morning we would go to Gerard [sic] College, but I concluded if I had to go to-morrow I had rather go in the morning, and so it rested. We sat and talked till nearly twelve. It had cleared off now. Packed our trunks.

---

[55]The cathedral at the northeast corner of 18th and Race Streets was not completed until 1864. *Ibid*, p. 278.

Saturday Oct. 29th. When we arose this morning found it a beautiful clear day. I felt glad to have such a pleasant day to travel but very sorry it had rained for the last two days. We had eaten our breakfast and were seated in the carriage to go to the Depot on Broad Street at half-past seven.

ON OUR WAY TO BALT. FROM PHILADELPHIA

Harry accompanied us and got our tickets & checks and us seats in the cars and then bid us adieu till next month, when he is coming. We had a delightful ride to Balt., no difficulty in changing [to] the boat; we concluded we could get along as well without as with Father. We were on deck crossing the Susquehanna and admired the scenery so much, but then I looked for <u>ducks</u> on the Gunpowders but saw none. When we arrived [in Baltimore] what was our surprise at not finding Father at the depot. We engaged a carriage and were in [it], when I espied G. Sauerwein coming and we talked with him a few minutes; he seemed mortified that [he] did not get down [in] time enough. Said he had seen Father, who said I could remain till Monday. We invited him to take a seat with him [us] but he had business in the neighborhood and preferred walking up. We were received very kindly by all the family and had lots of questions to answer. After dinner as I heard no more of Father, Mary Sauerwein, Georgia and I started to see Kate H. [and] Till Jackson, who are staying on Fayette Street but they were not in, so we walked down Market St. [and] met them there. Miss Margaret Fox joined us and staid to tea with us. Ken Boyd walked home with us. Lem Stadtler was there a few minutes. We had a fine game of Blindman's Bluff and Miss F. left about ten o'clock; and Oh! I was glad to get to bed as I was very tired.

Sunday October 30th. Rather cloudy. We all got ready and went to church; heard a sermon from Rev. Dr. Morris. Mr. Rau came home with us. After dinner, G., Kate S. & I went round to see Kate H & Tilly J. and then took a walk after they returned. Lem Sadtler was here a short time about four. Mary & Mr. Rau & George & I took a walk out Charles St. There was quite a number out but not near so many as a week ago. Soon after supper Messrs. M. & K. Boyd & Tom Schaeffer arrived and went with us to Charles St. Methodist Church and heard an excellent sermon from Rev. Mr. Morgan. They remained only a short time after our return. M. Boyd told me of Chett Taylor's death.

Monday [Oct] 31st. Beautiful day. Georgia went for her sister's immediately after breakfast, and about then Mary and I went out to do some shopping. When we returned found Mary Sauerwein had been to see us and very soon

1853

Kate & Eliza Downey came and sat about an hour, then we went to dinner. Found Georgia had arrived immediately after dinner. Mr. Rau & Lem came to bid me good-bye, and then the Miss Bayfield called, so I had very little time to pack my trunk in. Mary, Georgia H. & George S. went to the depot with me. I bid them adieu and then took my place in the ladies' saloon[56] with Mr. & Mrs. Levening of Harpers Ferry and Kate H. & Till J. where we remained all the way. There was a very large train and we were detained on the road very long. However, Father awaited me and it was eleven o'clock till I got home. I had many things to tell Mother so it was nearly one till we retired.

Tuesday Nov. 1st. [1853]. Father took Mother and I out to Aunt Margaret's and from there Aunt M., Mother and I went down and took tea with Grandmother.

Wednesday [Nov.] 2nd. I did not go to town as intended but wrote a letter to cousin Aaron Ogle in answer to his three last ones.

Thursday [Nov.] 3rd. Cloudy in the morning. However, I had some shopping to do and I rode to town on horseback [and] hitched my horse at the end of town. I did my shopping, then called at Houck's and Lizzie showed me Kate H's cloak. Met Till Jackson and she went with me to Mrs. Winchester's and the stores and I then left her and came out home.

Friday [Nov.] 4th. Quite cold. Mother and I started about ten o'clock and went over and took dinner with Mrs. Col. Taylor. She is truly grieved by Chett's death. Met Miss Caroline Millet there; she told me how it had pleased C. when she told him I intended to go see him. I wish I would have done so. Mrs. Taylor never mentioned his name.

Saturday November 5th. It is clear and I was very busy preparing my cloak. I sent for Kate Houck's and she kindly loaned it. When Father came home he brought me a note from Mag Derr; she wants me to go home with them from church to-morrow.

Sunday [Nov.] 6th. Quite cool. Mother & I went to church and every thing seemed familiar. After church [she] and I went up street to Mrs. Reese's[57]

---

[56]The "saloon" was a separate compartment or parlor for women travelers where they could avoid tobacco smoke.

[57]Catherine Reese was Margaret Derr's aunt. See also note 47, 1851.

with Mag and Mary Derr, and soon the carriage called for us and we went out to Mrs. D's. After dinner Mag, Mary, John Derr & I went to Sabbath [School]; it was very small, few teachers & scholars. We went down to Uncle Shriner's for a few minutes. Aunt wants us to come to tea to-morrow. Mr. Johnson and Cousin E were over after tea and staid till after ten o'clock. We had plenty to tell of our trip, but Mr. J., being to see Mother & Father twice since I had been gone, had some of the points.

Monday [Nov.] 7th. We were very busy sewing in the morning and in the afternoon till after three, when we went over and took tea with Aunt S and family. Mr. Johnson came down after tea. Mr. J. & Ed went over to Mr. D[err]'s with us about eight and remained till about ten.

Tuesday Nov. 8th. Rather cloudy. Mag Derr and I went into town about ten o'clock, stopped at Mrs. R[eese]'s for a few minutes. We then called at Houck's and to see Mrs. Kate Davis and did some shopping and then parted. I came out home and Mag [went] to Aunt Kitty's; found Mrs. B. Fout here. Father took her home after tea. I wrote a letter to Harry at night.

* * * * *

Saturday [Nov.] 12th. Quite sultry. I finished my cloak and did various other things. I have felt so happy all week but felt a warning of something to happen. And sure enough, when Father came home, what was my surprise at receiving a letter from Sam Hersh wishing me to correspond with him or rather to allow him to correspond. I thought it had been decided at our last interview exactly two months to-day. The 12th of Sept. it was. How liable persons' minds are to change. I hardly know how to act for I wish to preserve my friendship with the family. I reckon I'll try it. Wonder how soon I ought to answer it. It shall be trying.

* * * * *

Monday [Nov.] 14th. Bright clear day. I wrote a long letter to Nelly Mering this morning. After dinner Father took Mother and I to town and I did some shopping; called to see Mary Eichelberger, but she was not at the Seminary, had just gone out. I also called to see Ellen Brunner and Mrs. Markel. I had a note from Mag Derr inclosing a letter she had received from Mary Sauerwein. She wishes my opinion but I don't like to give it.

1853

Tuesday [Nov.] 15th. Very warm this season and rather sultry. After dinner I started over to Evie Smith's to spend the afternoon, but I found her all ready to go to town, so I could not be persuaded to remain. She spoke to me of her intended marriage and her brother's too. I then went down to Mrs. I. Howard's and spent the afternoon with the family and Sarah Miller, Isie Buckey & Lottie Hauer of Manchester, Md. Father had brought me a letter from Lou Hersh chiding me for not writing; 'twas written before she could receive my last one.

Wednesday [Nov.] 16th. Pretty morning but clouded over in the afternoon and rained some too. Mrs. P. Fout, Miss Clabaugh & Mary Fout & Miss [*illegible*] were down to spend the afternoon, and just as they came Father & I were starting to town, so I excused myself and was gone only about an hour. I wrote a note to Mag Derr last night & took it to Mrs. Reese's to-day; also put a note in the P. O. for Mr. S. H. saying I would correspond. I wish the circumstances would have permitted me to have consulted a friend but I dare not. I hope 'tis well answered not too willing, for I fear it will be a task before I can drop it.

Thursday [Nov.] 17th. Found it raining when I arose this morning and it continued off and on all day, preventing me from going to town.

Friday [Nov.] 18th. Mother was in town on business; still very warm and foggy.

Saturday [Nov.] 19th. Fog cleared off by noon. Mother and Father went to town this evening but I staid at home. Finished the shaving case that I was making for Harry Smith; somewhat disappointed he did not arrive today. I had a pamphlet from Mrs. A. Himes of Oxford this evening. Mr. J. A. Johnson was out this evening, gave me the news, etc.; brought me a bouquet.

Sunday [Nov.] 20th. Very warm and I think sultry. Mother and I were into town and heard a sermon of Dr. Zacharias. After dinner as I felt so like a nap I concluded I would walk over to the Killions' for a few minutes; and when I had not been there longer than an hour or so, over came Mother saying I must come home as there was company. I dressed myself and spent the evening very pleasantly with cousin Ed Shriner and Mr. Nathan Maynard. I think Mary S. and I were very much mistaken in our opinion for I never met a more sensible and agreeable young gent. He reasons so very well.

1853

Monday [Nov.] 21st. Drizzling all day, still so warm. Cousin Lewis Smith came out about two o'clock and remained till after tea. He is going to Cumberland to-night. How much he improves on acquaintance.

* * * * *

Wednesday [Nov.] 23rd. Cleared off very warm to-day. Father was in town this morning and purchased two lots in the Mt. Olivet Cemetery. After dinner he took Mother and me to look at them; [we] were very much pleased with situation. We went into town to do some shopping and afterwards out to Aunt M. Artz' a little while. Met Vallie & M & Jenny Adams there. I had a letter from Lou Hersh.

Thursday [Nov.] 24th. The day set apart by the Governor of the State and various of the states as a day of Thanksgiving[58]. Mother went into church and I was at home all day. I think if very strange indeed if Harry Smith is in town that he does not come out. I wrote a long letter to Gene Kephart in answer to one received April 23rd. Clear and cold.

Friday [Nov.] 25th. Cold, windy day. Received a note from Mary Kunkel inviting me to come in and remain over Sunday. Sarah Miller came up in the afternoon and took tea. I walked part way home with her. When I returned Father handed me a letter which proved to be a very friendly & interesting letter from Sam Hersh.

Saturday [Nov.] 26th. Much warmer but still clear. Father took me into town after dinner. I stopped at Kunkels' & Melia & I went to [catechism]. Afterwards we took a walk, had a long talk with M. Jamison, saw Mrs. Page a few minutes. Met cousin Harry S., Mr. M. S. Peiper, of Phild at the depot on their return from Harper's Ferry, and had them for an escort down to Mr. Kunkel's but they did not remain for tea. Mr. Johnson was there a few minutes before tea and they all three were there after tea. Melia & I had quite a romp with Harry about our watches; we got 'em too. I sent Evie Smith's books home this evening and wrote her a short note.

---

[58]"Yesterday was set apart by the Governor of Maryland as a day of Thanksgiving and Prayer and it was generally observed in our town also by 7 or 8 other states in our Nation." Engelbrecht, *Diary*, II, 489.

1853

Sunday Nov. 27th. Cloudy this morning. Nevertheless we were ready for church by ten o'clock and the beaux [were] there, so off we strung in church and up to our pew, Mr. P. Kunkel with me, Mr. P. with Mary, and Harry with Melia. We created quite an excitement. Mother handed me a note she had received for me from Evie Smith in which she invited me up to see her married on Tuesday. The gents remained for dinner at Mr. K's and only left about half-past three o'clock. Mr. J. A. Johnson returned with them after tea to go to church. Mr. J. left about nine o'clock but H. & Mr. P. staid till nearly twelve.

Monday [Nov.] 28th. Cloudy. Mary Birely called and so Mary, Melia K and I all went out & met Harry on the street and had a walk, and before we returned met Mr. Peiper in the street and [they] returned home with us remained till eleven o'clock and then bid us adieu. After dinner Mary and I went to Catechism, & when we were taking a walk up street met Father, so we took a ride with him out to the lot. Took Mary home and then we came home. Cousin A. Adams was up to give Mother the news of his marriage.[59]

Tuesday [Nov.] 29th. Raining & damp all day. Evie Smith is married today to Mr. J. L. Nicodemus.

Wednesday [Nov.] 30th. Quite pretty day. Mrs. I. Howard came over this morning; brought the babe along and spent the day.

Thursday December 1st [1853]. Cold, damp day. Wrote to Lou Hersh.

Friday [Dec.] 2nd. Clear to-day. When Father came home this evening I got a letter from cousin A. Ogle who says he'll be here by 20th.

Saturday [Dec.] 3rd. Damp and cold again.

Sunday [Dec.] 4th. Very cold. I went into town to church and heard a sermon to young people by Dr. Zacharias. After church when I came to the hotel saw cousin L. Hedges, and he came out home with me and remained until after tea. Mr. J. A. Johnson came out about half-past two and staid till about eight o'clock.

---

[59]Cousin Abraham F. Adams married (December 14, 1853) Sarah Ann Kemp, daughter of David Kemp who lived on a farm on Yellow Springs Road. Williams, *History*, II, 1251. They went to live in Cincinnati, Ohio. Derr diary, p. 39.

1853

Monday [Dec.] 5th. Quite a pleasant day and Father took me into town after dinner. I did some shopping and then went to Catechism, and afterwards went to see Mrs. Annie Middleton of Phil'd (A. Zacharias that was). Mary Kunkel walked up street with me and I came out home. I had a long letter from Nelly Mering; she has been very ill.

Tuesday [Dec.] 6th. Foggy, damp, clear and cold to-day. Emily & Marion Howard came over after dinner and it was late when tea was finished; staid over night.

Wednesday [Dec.] 7th. The girls left about 9 or 10 o'clock. Walked part way home with them. Fixed mince meat when I returned and was busy the rest of the day.

Thursday [Dec.] 8th. Quite cold. Father and Mother were in town this morning and after dinner Father and I went out to see Aunt M. Artz; she is well, but how badly Uncle A looks.

Friday [Dec.] 9th. All at home today.

Saturday [Dec.] 10th. Delightful day, much warmer; had early dinner and then John took me nearly to town in the cart. I called to see Nelly B. a few minutes [and] saw her friend Miss Hoffman; they just came from Balt. this morning. Went to Catechism and afterwards Lizzie Baugher and I went to the Seminary to see Mary Daniels & Almira Stonebreaker. I then came on up street and Father and I walked out home. He handed me a letter from Lou Hersh and a paper from Mr. Sam Hersh dated Oct. 19th.

Sunday [Dec.] 11th. Mother and John took me into town, and I went to church while they went out to Aunt M. Artz's and Uncle D. Thomas'. They brought me home on their return.

Monday [Dec.] 12th. Another summer day in wintertime. I wrote letters to Mag. McClellan, Lizzie Koones, & Mr. H. Smith; commenced one in reply to Sam Hersh's of 23rd Nov. but did not finish it. Father and Mother returned about 7 o'clock from Uncle Shriner's.

1853

Tuesday [Dec.] 13th. Delightful weather as yet. I was busy with my <u>carpet strips</u>[60]. What was my surprise when about four o'clock Louise Hersh and brother Frank arrived. My feeling so happy all day must have been a presentment of their arrival. We had much to talk of. Cousin E. Shriner was out to tea and I wrote a note and sent [it] by him to the Misses Derr.

Wednesday Dec. 14th. Was up early this morning and assisted Mother in getting off to attend the marriage of Coz. A. F. Adams to Sarah A. Kemp. We (the rest of us) had breakfast about eight o'clock and then we were in town by half-past nine o'clock. Saw the two wedding parties off. Kate Houck was married to Mr. B. L. Jacobs of Martinsburg this morning and left in company with Mr. and Mrs. Adams for Cincinnati, who intend living there, while Mr. & Mrs. J will return by way of New York. Mr. Johnson sent up for us, but we thought it was Mr. H and that he might wait, so we merely saw Mr. J. from Mrs. Page's window, but when we went down stairs found Mr. Bob Hickley with Mr. H. He sat and talked a while and then left. Lou and I walked [Mr.] H over town to see various <u>Lions</u>, and then left him return to the hotel while we went to see Mrs. Davis [and] Ellen Brunner & did some shopping. We returned home to dinner. Mag, Mary & John Derr came out after about four o'clock and staid till about eight o'clock. I was busy baking cake part of the afternoon. We retired between ten & eleven o'clock.

Thursday [Dec.] 15th. Very foggy early. Lou still persists in going home as they fear the weather may change. However, it cleared off soon after they started. I sent a bottle of my currant wine and a pound cake to old Mrs. Hersh. I was in town in the afternoon; did some shopping, called at Kunkel's, and Mary & I took a long walk.

* * * * *

Sunday [Dec.] 18th. Weather has changed. Windy and clear. I had such a cold that mother went to church alone. Mr. J. A. Johnson came out about two o'clock and sat till eight; seems in very good spirits.

Monday [Dec.] 19th. All busy as 'tis butchering day, an important day in the <u>Farmer's life</u>. I wrote a letter to Sam Hersh in answer to one from him on the 23rd [ult] but won't send it till to-morrow. /Snowed a little to-day./

---

[60]Margaret was preparing strips of material for making either hooked, braided, or crocheted rugs.

1853

Tuesday [Dec.] 20th. Very cold but clear. Just as I was in the midst of cleaning cupboards Marion Howard arrived and brought a dress with her she wants me to fit; she remained till after tea.

Wednesday [Dec.] 21st. Another clear day. Mother was in town in the afternoon.

Thursday [Dec.] 22nd. Mother was at Mrs. I. Howard's this morning, and when she came home wrote a note to Ed Shriner for him to go with me to Mrs. H.'s on Saturday night. I had a long letter from Mary Sauerwein in which she told me lots but not plainly.

* * * * *

Saturday [Dec.] 24th. Cold and windy again. I was in town this afternoon went to Catechism and as we were returning Mr. J. A. Johnson joined me and walked to the buggy with me. Soon after dinner I walked over to Mr. I. Howard's and soon Cousin Ed came. He had written me a note but I did not receive it. Charlotte & Harriet Keefer, Emily, Charlie & William Houck, Miss & Mrs. Getzandanner, Martha Rice, Mr. & Mrs. Wm. Smith & Frank Clingan were there; we all remained till about eleven o'clock. Passed the evening talking, playing, etc. Everyone seemed to enjoy themselves.

Sunday [Dec.] 25th. Clear and not so windy. Cousin Ed and I went to church and afterwards we went out to Mr. E. Howard's to dinner. We left there between four and five o'clock. Ed then went out home. Dr. Zack had a sermon to suit Christmas.

Monday [Dec.] 26th. To-day is generally celebrated as Christmas. Cold and windy. I wrote a long letter to Nellie Mering to-day.

Tuesday [Dec.] 27th. Clear but pretty cold. After an early dinner I walked down to Uncle Adams and was [in] time enough to dine with them [for] a duck dinner. Mr. Wagely and Vallie are down.

Wednesday [Dec.] 28th. Warm and damp in the morning and commenced snowing after dinner and continued till night.

Thursday [Dec.] 29th. At home all. Wind very high and cold.

Friday [Dec.] 30th. What was our surprise to find it snowing, and it continued all day. I had a letter from Lou Hersh.

1853

Saturday [Dec.] 31st. Warm, and the snow melts very fast. Father took me into town but there was no Catechism, so I went up to Houck's for awhile. Mrs. Kate Jacobs has returned to Martinsburg. This is the last day of the year and the question should be, Have I spent the year profitably to myself?

(Photo from Williams *History of Frederick County Maryland)*

Ceresville Mill, Frederick, Maryland
Home of Cornelius Shriner and family

1854

"...when he wanted to know my reasons for rejecting his suit, and I told him I could not give <u>my hand where my heart</u> was not..."

Sunday January 1st, 1854. Many have been the changes amongst friends and relatives, and there may be many more this coming year, for who can tell what a day may bring fourth. I did not go to church as I did not feel very well, and I feared the pavements would not be cleared off as the snow fell last night. About three o'clock Mr. J. A. Johnson came out and staid till nearly ten. A good beginning for him and a fine prospect for plenty of beaux. He handed me a <u>gold</u> <u>thimble</u>, saying it was a New Year's gift and, as I hesitated somewhat, he said he did not see why I should not take it from a friend, so of course that explained our position. He came out in the sleigh.

Monday [Jan.] 2nd. Quite cold today. After dinner Father took me into town and I went down to Kunkels'. Meallie and I were out together some on the street. When we returned Mary fixed a cap in my bonnet. About seven o'clock the merry sleigh bells jingled and we were warned company was coming, and it proved to be Mr. & Mrs. Page and Capt. Doub and Lizzie Hagge and they sat till bed time.

Tuesday [Jan.] 3rd. Pleasant day. Father and Mother went into town in the sleigh this afternoon. Ella Brunner and Miss Ada Hoffman came out about one and sat a couple of hours and, soon after they left, Mr. & Mrs. Ross Johnson and Mrs. Dr. B. P. Johnson came and made a call, but not so very fashionable one as they sat till nearly five. After tea John Derr brought Mag and Mary out and staid till nearly ten o'clock. Mag brought my letter home that I had got from Mary S.

Wednesday [Jan.] 4th. Much warmer today; however, Father took me to town in the sleigh. I went up to Miss B. F. Winchester's to meet Mag D. according to engagement. Saw Mary Eichelberger there; she is on her way to Mary Barthelow's, who is to be married next Tuesday to Mr. Buckingham, and she is to officiate as bridesmaid. Mag and I called to see Mag Brown (Wolfe

1854

that was), Mrs. C. Steiner, and Kate Davis. Kate is ever so proud of her babe; 'tis a fine large girl; and [we stopped] at Houcks' a few minutes.

Thursday [Jan.] 5th. Warm and sultry to-day.

Friday [Jan.] 6th. I sent Mrs. I. Howard word to meet me at Mrs. Wm. L's this afternoon and so she did, and I never had such a muddy tramp. Spent a very pleasant afternoon and think Ginny is very pleasantly situated.

Saturday [Jan.] 7th. Quite cold. Father took me into town and as it was too soon for (Catechism) I went to see Aunty Kemp[1] a little while, and after (Catechism) I went to see Tilly Jackson. I had a letter from Fanny Koons.

Sunday Jan. 8th. Cold, raw day. I went into town to church. Capt. Davis accompanied me down street. Dr. Shields was at the hotel and we had a sociable chat.

Monday [Jan.] 9th. I finished a muffler for Father to-day.

Tuesday [Jan.] 10th. I commenced knitting a muffler of white worsted for Mr. J. A. J. Wanted to go to Mrs. I. Howard but feared I would soil it.

Wednesday [Jan.] 11th. Rained to-day and very sultry. Wrote letters to Mary Sauerwein and Lou Hersh. Will send them by to-morrow's mail.

* * * * *

Sunday [Jan.] 15th. Clear and I think cold, though every one saluted your ears with, "What a pleasant day". Mother and I were into town and heard a very good sermon from Dr. Zacharias. Mr. J. A. Johnson was in church and accompanied me to the hotel. He has been sick with a bad cold this last week but I think looks very well. Told me he was coming out after dinner and he arrived about three and remained till about six o'clock.

Monday [Jan.] 16th. Very warm and [it] drizzled after night. Mrs. Sophia Osborne and Mrs. J. Clingan and Annie spent the day here.

* * * * *

---

[1] See note 11, 1853.

1854

Saturday [Jan.] 21st. Cleared off cold and windy. When Father came home [he] brought me a letter from Lou and Sam Hersh, both long ones. Sam seems to have an idea of seeing me soon if agreeable to me; as a friend it will be.

Sunday Jan. 22nd. Cold and, as Mother's neck is still stiff, neither of us went to church.

* * * * *

Wednesday [Jan.] 25th. Much more pleasant. Father and I were in town this afternoon. I called at Mrs. Salmon's to see Neal Gordon but she had not arrived from Winchester. Was also to see Mrs. Kate Davis and her little one. It grows very finely & she has had several presents sent her. One [was] from Judge Isaac Anderson, a servant girl fourteen years old. Father gave me a letter from G. Kephart, four pages. She is in Balt.

Thursday [Jan.] 26th. At home, all drizzling; had a note from Neal saying she arrived yesterday.

* * * * *

Saturday [Jan.] 28th. Cold and windy. I walked into town, did some shopping and called at Mrs. Salmon's to see Neal Gordon, but she was out.

Sunday [Jan.] 29th. Cold and cloudy; nevertheless John took me into town and I went up to Mrs. S. for Neal to go to church. Henrietta Beauman went with us. Also Neal told me cousin Wm. Dean was here, and he joined us as we were coming from church and came out home with me and remained till nearly five o'clock. Mr. J. A. Johnson was here also (anxious about my Report).

Monday [Jan.] 30th. Much warmer. Mrs. P. Fout was here in the afternoon and John Derr at night. He's in high glee about going to Balt., starts Thursday.

Tuesday [Jan.] 31st. Beautiful day, so warm and pleasant.

Wednesday February 1st [1854]. Summer's day, so warm and clear. To-day Lou Hersh and I have set about to burn our letters, so I burnt hers at half-

1854

past nine and then wrote her a long letter. I received a nice long one of Mary Sauerwein.

Thursday Feb. 2nd. This weather certainly cannot last for I found my shawl quite a burden in town this morning. I did some shopping and called at Mrs. Salmon's but Neal had left with Will on Monday. So I came out home. [I] met Mr. Bushey, who said Mrs. B. was coming up this afternoon, so I kept on my silk dress; and about twelve o'clock she arrived accompanied by her two little daughters; and soon Miss Jennie Smith and E. Howard arrived and all spent the afternoon.

Friday [Feb.] 3rd. Found it had snowed a little this morning and quite cold.

Saturday [Feb.] 4th. Cold and windy. I went to look for my breast pin and then [went] to Mrs. Killion's a few minutes.

Sunday [Feb.] 5th. Cold; nevertheless I went into church and heard Mr. Miller preach from 2nd Peter 3:11th verse, a very good, practical sermon. Mr. Davis accompanied me to the hotel. Mr. Johnson was out after tea. He is in an excellent humour, is going to Balt. to-morrow and from thence to Washington Tuesday or Wednesday.

Monday [Feb.] 6th. Quite a pleasant day; I was at home all day.

Tuesday [Feb.] 7th. Cold, raw day; nevertheless Father took Mother and I into town and she bought me a black silk dress and some other things.

Wednesday [Feb.] 8th. Busy all day at my dress; it has snowed and is raining and freezing all day.

* * * * *

Sunday [Feb.] 12th. At home in the morning, but after four I went with John to town to bring Miss Scholl[2] out.

Monday [Feb.] 13th. Annie & I were busy all day sewing. Rainy [and] drizzling.

---

[2]Annie Scholl, a cousin of Margaret's, was the daughter of the widowed Henry Scholl who lived on a farm in New Market. Hitselberger, *Bridge in Time*, p. 27.

* * * * *

Thursday Feb. 16th. Found it snowing this morning but cleared off soon. Mrs. Shields sent me such a nice jar of pickled peaches to-day.

Friday [Feb.] 17th. Very pretty day. I walked into town with Father this morning and Ellen and I called to see Mary Kunkle & Callie Bantz, and I also stopped to see Mrs. Chandler on my way out. When Father came out he brought me a nice long letter from Lou Hersh and a number of Godey's Magazines sent from Annapolis. Suppose Mr. Johnson is there. I wrote a letter to Sam Hersh in answer to his of last month but did not send it.

Saturday [Feb.] 18th. Very pleasant day.

Sunday [Feb.] 19th. Damp but warm. I stopped for Ella B. as I went up to church. Mr. J. A. Johnson accompanied us down from church. He just returned from Washington [and] has a bad cold.

Monday [Feb.] 20th. Snowed and stormed all day and night.

Tuesday [Feb.] 21st. Found snow very much drifted and about two feet deep on a level. Father & I went to town in the sleigh. I put my letters to Sam H. in the office. I was to see Kate Davis also and told her of Harry Smith's wishes concerning her and Miss D.

Wednesday & Thursday [Feb.] 22nd & 23rd. First very warm, second very cold.

Friday [Feb.] 24th. Father when he came home from town brought me a long letter from Mag McClelland, also a Valentine from Columbia [from] Sam, I reckon.

* * * * *

Saturday March 4th [1854]. Pleasant day. Mr. John A. Johnson came out after tea and spent a pleasant sociable evening; told me of his visit to Balt., Washington & Annapolis.

Sunday [March] 5th. So very pleasant this morning. I stopped for E. Brunner and we went to church together. I asked Mag Derr and she came

1854

on home with me. John Derr came down street with me, Will Boyd with Mag, & Ed S. with E. Brunner. Soon after dinner Mr. Nathan Maynard arrived and sat till after seven o'clock and Ed S. staid till nearly eleven. 'Twas a beautiful night.

Monday [March] 6th. Beautiful morning. Mag D. and I rode down to Uncle Adams' on horseback to see Miss Annie Weagely and sat a couple of hours. Took a nap in the afternoon and just as we were sewing carpet strings John D arrived for Mag. They left about six o'clock.

* * * * *

Saturday [March] 11th. Was busy in the morning about the house and wrote a note to Lou telling her I should not be able to meet her in Balt. next week. Called for E. Brunner and we called to see Houcks, Kunkels, Birelys, Mrs. Cal Bantz, & friend Miss Entler, Miss Loats and Mrs. Page & Liza Brewer; the latter two were out.

Sunday [March] 12th. Very bright beautiful day. Mother & I were into town to church. Wils Boyd came down from church.

Monday [March] 13th. Very pleasant & bright day. Mother and I spent the afternoon with Mrs. Peter Fout. Olivia Fout and brother were there.

Tuesday March 14th. Still beautiful weather. At home all day, when Father came home and said George Sauerwein and Ed Shriner were coming out. They came out to tea and remained some time. G. looks so well. Gave me all the Balt. news.

Wednesday [March] 15th. Clear & warm. Miss C. Olney Schley was married to Mr. F. R. Wilson to-day.

Thursday [March] 16th. Quite windy. I was in town this morning for a short time and after dinner I went over to Mrs. Smith's expecting Ginny would go in to her father's with me, but found her quite unwell and her mother & Annie here with her. However, after conversing some time Annie went with me up home, and soon Mrs. H. came and I spent a very pleasant afternoon. Emily accompanied me as far as Mrs. Smith's.

Friday [March] 17th. Pleasant in the morning but very windy in the afternoon and night.

1854

Saturday [March] 18th. Clear, windy & cold. Mother & Father were away all day. Mother and Aunt Margaret Artz were up to spend the day at Uncle E. Scholl's.

Sunday [March] 19th. Mother and I went into church and stopped at Tablers [Talbotts] Hotel[3]. Mr. J. A. Johnson came out about two o'clock and staid till nine o'clock and Mr. Wilson Boyd & Tommy Derr came about four and sat till ten o'clock.

Monday [March] 20th. Cold and windy. I wrote a letter to Mary E. Sauerwein and enclosed a note to Lou Hersh, who is staying with Maria Morris in Balt. Cousin Aaron Ogle of Tiffin, O[hio], surprised us this morning as we had not been expecting him. He remained over night and entertained us about the West.

Tuesday [March] 21st. Still windy. Mother went down to Mrs. Clingan's to help her quilt and Cousin Aaron went to Uncle Adams'. Ann & Margaret Gittinger were out to spend the day. I had a letter from Lou Hersh.

Wednesday March 22nd. Snowing & raining all day.

Thursday [March] 23rd. An April day, a little sunshine and a little shower all day long. Emily & Huldah Howard came over about four o'clock and remained over night. Cousin A. Ogle came out about dusk and remained over night with us, and I introduced him as Dr. Magruder.

Friday [March] 24th. Still windy but clear. Cousin A, Em & H. Howard, and myself went over and spent the day and took dinner with Mrs. I. Howard. Found Mr. Howard very much indisposed. We returned about four and the girls remained only a short time. Cousin A went with them as far as Mrs. Smith's, then returned to supper & left immediately. I had a letter from Sam Hersh saying he would be here this week or next.

Saturday [March] 25th. Cold and very windy. I awoke with a bad cold.

Sunday [March] 26th. So very cold, and as not feeling well I did not go to church. I was lying down about three o'clock when Mr. Sam Hersh came. He

---

[3]Talbotts Hotel, which afterwards became Drills Hotel, was on the southeast corner of Court and Church Streets. Scharf, *Western Maryland*, p. 555.

1854

looks so very well and is in excellent spirits. We sat conversing till near eleven of what we had been doing, seeing, etc. since we had seen each other. Sam looks so very handsome and is so agreeable. I can appreciate friendship such as his, for he never even mentioned the past, and our friendship is likely to continue on, if he never does aught to interrupt it by speaking of his sentiments toward me; and for the family's sake I hope he may not unless my sentiments change.

Monday [March] 27th. More pleasant. I wrote a long letter to Fannie Koones. Ella B. and I went to Catechism, and from thence to see Call a few minutes, and then called to see Mrs. Shields and had a long talk with her and Dr. Shields.

* * * * *

Saturday April 1st [1854]. Cold & clearer. Cousin A. Ogle came out & remained over night.

Sunday [April] 2nd. Mother, Cousin A & I went to town to church and all returned to dinner. About three o'clock Mr. J. A. J. came out and remained till about seven or eight. Cousin A. left about dusk for Uncle Adams'. He is going to start home to-morrow night.

* * * * *

Saturday [April] 8th. Very pleasant day. Mother went out to Grandmother's and I stopped for E. Brunner, and after we were dressed, we called to see Huldah Howard (met Mrs. I. Howard there) and then walked the rest of the afternoon. I had a long letter (on commercial note) from Mr. S. Hersh and also two York papers. Mr. J. A. J. joined us and walked down street with us.

Sunday [April] 9th. Another beautiful day. I went in the afternoon and called for E. Brunner and we went to hear Rev. Mr. Jones.

Monday [April] 10th. Very warm in the morning, but we had a very heavy shower in the afternoon and it was much cooler afterwards.

Tuesday April 11th. I was busy this morning when Uncle Elias, Aunt Mary, Lewis & Annabelle Scholl arrived. They had lots to say and all appeared to enjoy the day. So very pleasant.

1854

Wednesday [April] 12th. I enjoyed a cart ride to town to-day and went and sat an hour or two with Mrs. Kate Davis. Wrote letters to Gene Kephart, Nelly Mering and Miss L. Hersh.

Thursday [April] 13th. Beautiful day. Father, Mother and I got ready early this morning and stopped in town and for Aunt M. Artz, and they all went to Mr. P. Kemp's[4] to spend the day while I stopped at Mrs. Derr's. After dinner, Mag, Mary D., Miss Moffat & I went over to Mr. P. Kemp's and, joined by our family, Uncle & Aunt E. Scholl, Mrs. Kemp, Miss Powers, etc., all went to the mill and were weighed. I weighed 132 lbs. Lidye Wenner was married to Mr. Henry Johnson to-day and goes to [*illegible*].

* * * * *

Wednesday [April] 19th. Very pleasant day. I received a letter of Fanny Koones; says they are all anxious for me to pay them a visit.

Thursday [April] 20th. Wrote to Lou Hersh.

Friday [April] 21st. Beautiful day. Just after dinner Father said, as he was going to the mill, he would take me behind him to Mrs. Jacob Buckey's to spend the afternoon. They gave me a full account of their Balt. visit. I rode home on horseback.

Saturday [April] 22nd. Very pleasant all day with a heavy shower about four o'clock. I had letters from Cousin A. Ogle and Mary Sauerwein.

Sunday [April] 23rd. A true April day. Very clear & pleasant; in the morning quite cloudy and afterwards very pleasant. Mr. J. A. Johnson came out at four and sat til nearly ten o'clock. Last day of our first six years' acquaintance.

Monday [April] 24th. Beautiful day. To-day six years I saw Mr. J. A. J. for the first time. It was Easter Monday, too. This morning Mother went over to see our new neighbors. Dr. Rau's family was very well pleased, etc. After

---

[4]Mr. Peter Kemp, whose mill was in the Woodsboro district (Hitselberger, *Bridge in Time*, p. 281), was the tenth child of Reverend Peter Kemp, the founder of the United Brethren Church in 1800. C.E.S. Schildknecht, *Monocacy and Catoctin*, (n.p., 1985), pp. 395-404. (The church is on Rocky Springs Road off of Fourth Street near Fort Detrick.)

1854

dinner Mother and I went up and sat the afternoon with Mrs. Ross Johnson[5]. Little Mary Potts is a very fine child and of course the pet of the household. Mrs. Goldsborough and Mary and old Mrs. Johnson were there during the afternoon.

Tuesday [April] 25th. Pleasant with a shower in the afternoon.

Wednesday [April] 26th. Pleasant day with a very heavy hailstorm. I had such a very nice long letter of Sam H. to-day. Wrote a note to Harry Smith to send by Mary Kunkel.

Thursday [April] 27th. Showery all afternoon, but in the morning I was in town; called and sat sometime with Mary Kunkel and then did some shopping and came out home.

Friday [April] 28th. True sample of an April day. When Father came home he brought me such a <u>very nice long letter</u> from Nelly Mering and four papers from Mr. Sam Hersh. Two should have arrived a week ago.

* * * * *

[May] 4th. Thursday. [1854] Clear still and warmer. About ten o'clock what was my surprise to see Mrs. B. F. Winchester & Mrs. Mering. Mr. Frank W. & Missouri Belvin came out to tea also. Mr. Preston was here. They all left except Mrs. M. after tea. <u>Mr. French was married to-day to Lottie Hauer.</u>

Friday [May] 5th. We all passed the day at home. I had a long letter of Mr. Sam Hersh.

Saturday [May] 6th. According to appointment Mrs. B. F. Winchester, accompanied by old Mrs. Vernon, came out for Mrs. Mering. I rode to town on horseback and called for Ella Brunner, did some shopping then came out home. Mr. J. A. Johnson came out after tea and we had such a nice long chat.

---

[5]Ross Johnson (son of Worthington) was a lawyer who lived near the Scholls on New Design Road (Hitselberger, *Bridge in Time*, p. 70). Mrs. Goldsboro was the wife of Edward Y. Goldsboro. They lived on the south side of Patrick between Market and Court Streets. *Williams' Directory*, p. 15.

Sunday [May] 7th. Pleasant day. Mother left me in town as she went out to grandmother's and Ella B. & I went to Lutheran Church and heard a good practical sermon from Mr. Diehl. When Mother came I told her I would remain, so I went with E. to Sunday School; and we were going to Baptist Church but there was none. Mr. Frank Markel[l] was there. John came for me soon after tea.

Monday [May] 8th. Very pleasant day. Marion Howard came over about nine o'clock and after dinner we walked over to Ed Howard's[6] and took tea. Huldah is there. Marion remained with me over night.

Tuesday [May] 9th. Pretty day. Marion left about ten o'clock. Wrote a note to Nelly Mering to send by her mother. Betsy Hoffman was here.

Wednesday [May] 10th. Rode into town on horseback, called at Houck's, saw the family, Mrs. Kate Jacobs; intended going to see Mrs. Mering but Houcks told me she had gone. Very heavy rain this afternoon.

May 11th. Thursday. Pa took me to town in the buggy to see the consecration of Mt. Olivet Cemetery but it was deferred on account of the weather.[7] I was at Mrs. Markell's a long time. /Received three papers from Mr. Sam Hersh./ Went shopping with Mary Derr & Mother & I came home to dinner.

* * * * *

Monday [May] 15th. Beautiful day. Mag Derr was out about seven and sat till nearly ten o'clock. John [Derr] came up Saturday night and left this morning. Mrs Fout & Miss Ann Matilda Wilson spent the afternoon here. Wrote to Lou Hersh.

* * * * *

---

[6]Edward Howard's farm was on the Ballenger Creek Road, about one mile west of Manchester Farm. *Bond Map,* 1858.

[7]"Tremendous storm accompanied by rain and hail. Dedication of Mt. Olivet Cemetery. Different Protestant Clergymen of our town are to conduct the Ceremonies, together with instrumental Music - a Goodly Number of Natives went out." Engelbrecht, *Diary,* II, 615. The Derr family went to the consecration. Mary describes the keeper's cottage as beautiful, and some lots enclosed with iron railings. Derr Diary, p. 70.

1854

Sunday [May] 21st. Showery in the morning but cleared off by noon. John took me into town & came for me again, and I heard an excellent sermon from Rev. Mr. Hammond[8]. Soon after tea, Mr. Marsh of Balt. came out to see Father, and just as he was leaving Mr. J. A. Johnson came and brought me such a handsome bouquet. He is right lively.

Monday [May] 22nd. Wrote to Mary Sauerwein [that] I would be with her on Wednesday.

Tuesday [May] 23rd. Cloudy and cool. I was busy fluting collars when cousin Harry arrived. /Dr. Wilson was married to-day./ I was quite surprised to see him. He went into town with us and accompanied Ella B. and I to the Cemetery[9] and staid with us till nearly eleven o'clock. (Ed accompanied us down street from the cemetery). I did some shopping and went home. Mother and I went out to Aunt Margaret's and grandmother's.

BALTIMORE

Wednesday May 24th. Quite pleasant. I was in town very early, did some shopping and called to see Ella B. and Mrs. Markel[l], and then was carried off to Balt. in a hurry. George [Sauerwein] met me at the depot and took me up to the house. Mrs. Fanny Dix was to see us during [the] afternoon. John Derr and Charlie Sadtler were here at night.

Thursday [May] 25th. Rose Abell was here to dinner. The Misses Bayfields were here and just as they were leaving there came up a shower; and immediately we started down to Metzer's and engaged our bonnets. It rained very hard while we were there. Charlie & Lem Sadtler were here at night.

Friday [May] 26th. Pleasant day but owing to Poison making its appearance on my face I was kept in the house all day. At night Miss Fox & Rosa Abell, John Derr, & George Beam & Mr. Rau were here. Wrote to Harry Smith to-day, told him I could not accompany him.

Saturday [May] 27th. Pleasant day. Mrs. S[auerwein] sent for Dr. Chatard and he gave me a prescription and I took the powders about five. I was very

---

[8]"Rev. William Hammond of the Methodist Church preached in the German Reformed Church yesterday morning and evening." Engelbrecht, *Diary*, II, 615.

[9]See May 11, 1854, and note 7.

sick after taking it. Mrs. Rau and Johnny were here. Miss Fox, Rosa Abell & Miss Nicholson were here at night.

Sunday [May] 28th. Very warm. Old Mrs. Rau & Messr. John & Philip Rau were here before church. Emma, George & I staid home. Mr. Rau was here after dinner. Miss Seville called for Kate, so Mary and I went with them out Charles St. We returned about half-past seven. John Derr & Philip Rau & George went with us to church.

Monday [May] 29th. Very warm. Mary and I were out shopping this morning and evening, and at night we were round at Abells'. George Beam was here while we were gone.

Tuesday [May] 30th. Miss Fox & Kate and I took a walk to the office and deposited the letter which I wrote home. Charlie Sadtler was here to tea. Geo. Beam was here after tea.

Wednesday [May] 31st. Cloudy and cool all day. Mary & Kate & I were busy this morning for the pic-nic. Mary & I were out in the afternoon to do some shopping and were at Abells'. Miss Fox, John Derr & Wm. Derr were here at night.

Thursday June 1st [1854]. The morning was bright and beautiful. Charley was here "betimes" and we went round with him to Abells' and [were] joined by Miss Fox [and] started for Rider's Grove in the cars. As soon as we reached our destination [we] met Rev. Dr. Morris, who insisted upon our accompanying him up to Lutherville[10], and we spent a very pleasant day. We had the whole house at our command, Mr. Charles Morris of York was with the Dr. We returned to Rider's Grove [with] time enough to see the Balt. train arrive and some of our friends were in. Misses Herman, Nicholson, McGowan & Messrs. Sauerwein, Nicholson, Herman & Richardson came out, but only had a few minutes to stay as we were to return by the down train. We returned home well pleased. Miss Chrissy House of Fred'k City was here when we returned. She had seen Mother just before she left. They were all well. /Mrs. Alice Powell, Lillian was here to-day./ Kate Sauerwein was here at night.

---

[10]Lutherville is a suburb north of Baltimore on the York Road. It was named for the Lutherville Female Seminary. Edward C. Papenfuse. *A New Guide to the Old Line State* (Baltimore, MD, 1976), p. 299.

1854

Friday [June] 2nd. Very pretty day. Got our new bonnets. Miss Chrissy left to-day. Mary and I went out about four or five o'clock and went to Biers' and to see Lizzie Jamison but as she stayed so long we merely left our cards. Kate and I went out shopping this morning. John Derr, (old) Mr. P. Rau, Mrs. Rau and Miss Fox were here.

Saturday [June] 3rd. Beautiful day. I wrote a letter to Mother and enclosed a note to Ella B. I received one from Miss Fox. Mrs. Sauerwein received a box from our house and there was a letter for me from Lou Hersh. Cousin Harry S. arrived about half-past twelve and remained an hour or so. He is going to Alexandria. He gave me a letter from Gene Kephart which Fannie K. had sent to Fred'k for me. Mary & I went out to Mrs. Rau['s] and then called for Miss Fox & Kate and we took a walk out Charles Street. Hester Moon [and] Louisa Tell were here to see us. I had the toothache very bad. George said he caused it.

Sunday [June] 4th. Messrs. John & Philip Rau were here. Mr. P. accompanied us to church to [hear] Dr. Morris. Mary & I went to Grace Church. Philip was here to tea. Lum Sadtler & Jack Brady were here after tea. About half-past nine Mary, Philip, George & I took a long walk out Charles Street. George talked a great deal of Kochs and his not speaking.

Monday [June] 5th. Rather warm. Marguerite Nicholson was here to invite us to a pic-nic this morning. About half-past five Mary & I started out. We were to see Mrs. Fanny Dix and Mag Brown [and] Lottie Wolfdale. When we returned [we] found Maria Mochis had been here. I was very sorry I did not get to see her as she is going to the country to-morrow. Mrs. Urhlaub, Charlie Sadtler were here to tea; and after tea, Misses Nicholson, McGowan, Hearne & Abell, Messrs. Nicholson, Waight, Dean, Koones, Schaffer.

Tuesday [June] 6th. Warm day. Mary & I were at market. Mr. & Mrs. Disney were in from the country. I wrote a letter to Fannie Koones. Mr. P. Rau called in the morning and in the afternoon Mary, Kate & I got ready and went out to Mrs. Rau's to tea. George and Mr. Shipley came after tea. We spent a very pleasant evening and returned home about eleven o'clock, Mr. Rau with Kate, G. with me and Mr. Shipley with Mary. We had ice cream and cake etc, at just about ten o'clock.

Wednesday June 7th. Sultry damp morning. The anniversary of <u>something long to be remembered</u>. I wrote a long letter to Lou Hersh. The Misses

Bayfields were here to tea. Will Dean and Mr. Eichelberger were here after tea. Mrs. S., Kate, and I were out shopping.

Thursday June 8th. Quite pretty morning but at night it rained; nevertheless Rod Hobbs was up to see me and brought me a beautiful bouquet. Kate and I were in to see Mrs. John Sadtler when they sent for us. I had a letter from home, and Mrs. Charles Hausey was there to bid us adieu. /Mary, Mrs. S and I were out for a few things./

Friday June 9th. Cool and clear. Kate and I took a long walk down Sharp St. and then returned home and, after changing shoes, etc., went out to Green Mount about nine and remained till two o'clock. Spent a very pleasant morning. After dinner, Mary, Mrs. S. and I went out to do some shopping and then called at Mrs. Harman's to see them and then to see Mrs. Tucker and she was not at home and to see Emma Lowes and we could get no one to come to the door. At night, Mr. David Gordon & Will Dean were to see me. Misses Fox & Rose Abell were round also.

Saturday [June] 10th. Quite pleasant. Mary & I went early and had our daguerreotypes taken for each other, and then did some shopping [and] called at Abell's a few minutes. Mr. Rau called after dinner to bid us adieu. Mrs. James H. Bayfield had been here the day before and was very sorry she did not get to see us. Miss Fox called to accompany us to the cars. Wils Boyd met us and went to the cars also. Came down this morning. Father met me at the cars and took me out home. All seemed glad to see me and even Claude knew me.

FREDERICK CO.

Sunday [June] 11th. Found it drizzling this morning. John took me into church and I heard the Union Sabbath school[11] agent preach. After dinner, Father and I rode over to see Uncle Jake Scholl[12]. He seemed to be

---

[11] The American Sunday-school Union, formed in 1824 among various churches of the East coast, aimed to establish Sunday Schools as widely and as quickly as possible. The project met with considerable success. William H. Harris and Judith S. Levey, *The New Columbia Encyclopedia* (Columbia University Press, New York, 1975); hereafter cited as *The New Columbia Encyclopedia*.

[12] Jacob Scholl, 79 years old, uncle of Daniel Scholl was a farmer in the New Market area. Hitselberger, *Bridge in Time*, p. 272.

1854

satisfied, but to see him I think would convince bachelors of their folly. When we returned found Mr. Johnson here.

Monday [June] 12th. Cloudy, drizzling. Wrote to Nellie M[ering][13] telling her Mr. J. and I would be down next Saturday, winds and weather permitting. After dinner I went out to Mr. Derr's and spent the afternoon. Maggie Derr returned with us and I brought Mother home too in the buggy.

Tuesday [June] 13th. Beautiful day. Mag D. & I went into town early; called to see Kate Davis and bid her farewell. She is going to Piedmont[14] [sic] today. Mr. Ogburn[15] was here putting up our reaping machine.

Wednesday [June] 14th. Another pleasant day. After dinner, Father took me into town and I called at Mrs. Markel[l]'s, at Mrs. Winchester's and at Houcks'. Lizzie Jamison, Kate Jacobs & Mrs. Stipes of Martinsburg were there. Mother came in town and I returned home with her. Mag Derr, Tom Derr, Miss Moffatt & Ed Shriner were out after tea; returned home soon after nine o'clock.

Thursday [June] 15th. Busy to-day. Soon after dinner Allen Brunner and Mr. Jarrett arrived and sat an hour or so.

Friday [June] 16th. Very pleasant day. Blanche & Aunt Shriner & Aunt C. Scholl spent the day with us. I went into town did some shopping & walked home. I wrote to Mr. Sam Hersh.

Saturday [June] 17th. Very pleasant morning. Mr. J. A. Johnson was here by about nine and we then hurried out to Mrs. Derr's and, joined by Mag D & Ed S, proceeded down to Mr. M[ering's at Bruceville] and met the family & Misses Annie O'Dell & Kate Travers & Lizzie Fite. We spent the evening pleasantly and after tea, Gene Scott & Dr. Wagner were to see us; we walked

---

[13]"Nellie Merring is pleasant girl, we went to school together at the seminary, she boarded there." Derr Diary (June 15, 1854). See also note 20, 1851.

[14]Kate Bantz Davis, who had continued to live in Frederick after her marriage in February 1853, now was joining her husband in their new home in Piedmont, West Virginia (see note 13, 1853). The diarist visited Piedmont in 1860.

[15]Mr. Ogburn was the representative of an Illinois firm from which Daniel Scholl had ordered a new reaper. See also June 26 and 29 below.

1854

home with Gene. I am so very sorry to see Nellie have such a wretched cough.

Sunday [June] 18th. Pleasant day. We all, joined by Mr. Troxell & Kate & Mr. Wagner, went up to Hawkes [Haughs] Church. After dinner, Dr. Martin, Mr. John Galt, Mr. Troxell, Kate Troxell & Dixon Mering were to see us. We talked of going home but to no effect. About dusk we started to Middleburg to church. Heard Rev. Mr. Mathias [?] preach. Kate & Nellie Delaplaine [were] there. We met Swan with a lantern for us to go through Niger Holler [*sic*], but it was of very little service to us as we were in the last buggy. After we came home the company disappeared one by one and we retired about eleven o'clock, to be awakened by four as Mr. J. said.

Monday [June] 19th. Another warm day. Mr. Johnson came and called us at five o'clock and we hurried through breakfast by six o'clock and on our way home by quarter of seven. They all seemed glad we had come and sorry we were going to leave. We were home by ten o'clock. Gave Mr. J. A. Johnson some potatoes to take home with him. He is always so obliging.

Tuesday [June] 20th. Mother went into town and brought Annie Scholl out home with her. We were ever so busy sewing all day. Mr. March was out to see us at night.

* * * * *

Friday [June] 23rd. Early in the morning, Ma & I went out to spend the day at Uncle Shriner's. Mag & Mary Derr were there in the afternoon. Aunt C. Scholl had been spending some time there. We took Annie home.

Saturday [June] 24th. Rode into town on horseback and did some shopping & returned home again. Mary Marsh was out after tea.

Sunday [June] 25th. Quite cool & pleasant. I stopped for E. Brunner and we went to church together. I was at home all afternoon.

Monday [June] 26th. Quite a pleasant day. Sarah Ann Shank and two children & Fanny Adams were here to spend the afternoon. Mr. Ogburn & his assistant from Illinois were here over night. Mr. Marsh was here after tea & we are busy white washing, too.

Tuesday [June] 27th. Very warm. Mr. O. left this morning. I went into town with Father and on the street met E. Shriner coming out, so I merely did my

1854

shopping and came out home with him. I wrote a letter by Ed Shriner and sent money & my breastpin to Mary Sauerwein for a <u>pearl</u> <u>one</u>.

Wednesday [June] 28th. Very warm. I was busy sewing, etc. all day. Mr. Marsh was out after tea.

Thursday June 29th. Very warm. Mr. Hand was out to see the reaper in operation.

Friday June 30th. I walked up to Mr. Howard's and engaged his hands [for harvesting] when he had finished. Aunt M. Artz, Victorine A. & Laura Horman were out to spend the day.

Saturday July 1st [1854]. Pretty warm day. Mother was in town and when she came home brought me letters from Lou Hersh & Mary Sauerwein.

Sunday July 2nd. John took Mother and I into town and we went to church. Mr. J. A. Johnson accompanied us down to the hotel. Saw Messrs. Marsh & Reed at the hotel. Old Mr. Creager died yesterday. Messrs. Clingan & Keefer were here. <u>Uncle Lewis Scholl took dinner here.</u>

Monday [July] 3rd. Very warm. John took me into town in the cart and I did some shopping and returned home again.

Tuesday [July] 4th. Excessively warm. A great many harvest hands & very busy.

Wednesday [July] 5th. Excessively warm again, all very busy. A storm about four o'clock.

Thursday [July] 6th. I wrote a hurried note to Mary Sauerwein, rode down to Uncle Adams, and on my return found Uncle & Aunt Elias Scholl, Annabelle & Louis Scholl. I went into town at twelve o'clock to transact some bank business[16], and then returned and was busy baking cake, etc. Company left about six o'clock. <u>I am so very glad we have finished</u> harvesting.

---

[16]Margaret's father was on the board of the Mutual Insurance Co. and owned shares in various local banks. The Farmers and Mechanics Bank calculates that 134 shares of Margaret's F&M stock, if still held today, would amount to 2213 shares worth $107,330.50.

1854

Friday [July] 7th. Still so very warm. My birthday [21st], but I was sick all day.

Saturday [July] 8th. Felt much better; a good shower but no cooler.

Sunday [July] 9th. Mother went out to Grandmother's and left me in town at Mrs. Markell's. I called for Ellen and we went to church together. I thought I would melt almost. Mr. Johnson came out about five o'clock and it commenced raining about eight and continued I know till twelve. He remained over night.

Monday [July] 10th. So very much cooler. Mr. J. A. J. left between seven & eight o'clock and I was busy the rest of the day. Had a letter from Mary H. Smith.

Tuesday [July] 11th. I was quite sick all day with cholic [*sic*].

Wednesday [July] 12th. Very pleasant day. I feel so much better but did not go to town.

Thursday [July] 13th. Very pleasant day. Mother took me into town and I stopped at Houcks' and soon the Misses Derrs & Moffat arrived, and we all went to Mr. W[inchester]'s commencement and were very much pleased. Dr. Shields & Ham Boyd came home with us. Messrs. Stonebrakers & H. Boyd were there in the afternoon. Georgia had a letter from Mary saying she was coming at night. Mag D. & I were out in the afternoon & saw Gene Kephart. Mary & Kate both came at night. Dr. Shields, Mac Gary & Wm. Rice went with us at night to the Seminary & Wils Boyd and Dan Getzandanner returned with us.

Friday July 14th. Pleasant day. Mother came in for me and I went out home about ten o'clock.

Saturday [July] 15th. I went into town for a short time and did some shopping and stopped at Houcks' a few minutes. Dr. Shields came out for me about five o'clock and we went out to see Uncle & Aunt Artz awhile, and when we returned, found Mr. J. A. Johnson here. They both left about half-past nine o'clock. I returned the letter I received from S. S. today.

1854

Sunday [July] 16th. Very warm. Mother went out to grandmother's and I stopped at Mrs. B. F. W[inchester]'s and went to church with them. Ed Shriner went up street with me. He got back last night.

Monday [July] 17th. I was very busy this morning when Georgia H., Mary & Kate S. & Jenine Hall arrived on two horses. They sat an hour or so and, as they were leaving and Kate did not fancy her riding behind, so she waited and I went with her in the cart and returned directly.

Tuesday [July] 18th. The day of the distribution [of prizes at the school]. I went into town and called at H's & Mary S., Emma, Georgia and I went. It was very crowded and there were a great many strangers. Nellie Mering was at H's to tea. I started to walk home, but I was overtaken by Mr. Finey before I left the pike, & rode to our gate.

Wednesday [July] 19th. Sent a paper to Mr. Sam Hersh containing an account of the examination. I had a note from Nellie Mering saying she and Mrs. W. would not be out.

Thursday [July] 20th. I wrote a long note to Nellie and in return [she] sent me word Mrs. W. & she would be out to spend the day with us. They arrived about eleven o'clock and staid till after tea.

Friday [July] 21st. Mrs. Howard & Emily were here very early and I went with them to spend the day at Mrs. Isaac Howard's. Miss Ann Hall from Anne Rundal[17] [sic] is there. Ginnie Howard was over after tea. Emily & I got back about dusk.

Saturday [July] 22nd. Emily & I went out to Aunt Margaret's and sat an hour or so, and then on our way back stopped at Mrs. W's to see Nellie Mering. Emily left after an early tea.

Sunday [July] 23rd. Mother & I were into church. Mr. Diehl preached in our church.

* * * * *

---

[17]The reference is to Anne Arundel County, Maryland.

1854

Wednesday [July] 26th. Bright day. About eight o'clock Aunt & Uncle Kemp and Annie Bentz arrived; and very soon Mrs. Harry Taylor, Misses Isaac & Marion H. arrived and all spent the day. Mrs. Howard came about three and staid till after tea.

Thursday [July] 27th. Father took me into town. I called to see Ellen B. & did some shopping and then returned home.

Friday [July] 28th. Felt very badly all day.

Saturday [July] 29th. About eight o'clock Livie Garrott, Miss Gidings & Mr. Preston arrived, and after an early dinner we all went in to attend Mr. Barnum's Menagerie[18] and there came up a drenching rain and we were all uneasy about our new bonnets. After the menagerie we, accompanied by Dr. Magill, took a ride round town and saw the Misses Houcks & Mrs. B. F. Winchester. Ed Shriner brought Mary S. and Mag Derr out to tea. The "Least Folks" [left] soon after tea but the others staid till about nine. I had a letter from Mr. S. Hersh.

Sunday [July] 30th. I was into town and found it quite warm.

Monday [July] 31st. Very warm. Mother & I drove Billy down to Mrs. Bushey's and spent the afternoon.

Tuesday August 1st [1854]. I was very sick all day.

Wednesday [Aug.] 2nd. Much better. I wrote a letter to Lou Hersh.

Thursday [Aug.] 3rd. Uncle Lewis Scholl & Mr. Roderick were here this morning to look at the place. Cousin Ed Shriner came out for me about 6 o'clock and took me over to Mrs. Derr's. Wils Boyd & Mr. Dan

---

[18]"Today Barnum Exhibits his animals etc. about 8 Elephants and 1 Baby Elephant one year old and 3 1/2 feet high, General Tom Thum[b] 22 years old & weighs 15 pounds, Mr. Nellis without arms, Mr. Lengal the Lion King, Wax Statuary; the people have been flocking into Town from all quarters." Engelbrecht, *Diary*, II, 622. "I was scarcely in the tent before I wanted to come out. Twas a perfect crowd of Negroes and people of the lowest order, with a few of the better class. There were some animals and other curiosities worth seeing, but on the whole 'twas a perfect piece of humbug'." Derr Diary, July 29, 1854.

1854

Getzandanner were there. We had a wedding in fun[19] -- Tom [Derr] & Kate S[auerwein]. Miss Moffatt was there too.

Friday August 4th. Cool & pleasant. Ed Shriner was there at night.

Saturday [Aug.] 5th. Day of the Sabbath School Celebration. Georgia & Tillie Houck came out early. Mag D., Miss Moffatt and I went over to the school house and went with the Scholls to the Island[20] and the other girls came afterwards. George Sauerwein was there too, came up last night. After spending a pleasant day the girls together with Misses Miller & Byer, Messrs. Johnson, Shriner & Sauerwein & Boyd went over to Mrs. Derr's to tea. They all left about ten o'clock.

Sunday [Aug.] 6th. We all came into church and each had a beau from church, Mr. Ken Boyd with Georgia, Wils with Mary, Geo S with Mag D & Ed with Kate S, Mr. Johnson with me. The buggy came for me and I came out home.

Monday [Aug.] 7th. Cool & pleasant. Had quite a nice shower about noon. Geo. Sauerwein & Ed Shriner came out about six and remained till after ten. Mr. Sam Preston was here for a few minutes this morning.

Tuesday [Aug.] 8th. Cool, pleasant day. Father took me into town and I called to see Ellen B & friend and also at Mrs. French's, but could get no answer, so merely left my card and did some shopping and returned home. Had a nice long letter from Lou Hersh.

* * * * *

Thursday [Aug.] 10th. Pleasant day. Ma and I went out to Mr. Kemp's to see Mrs. S. H. Adams and contrary to expectations, took tea. Mary, Mag & Tommy Derr, Mary & Kate Sauerwein, G. Houck, Aunt Liz Thomas &

---

[19]"Tom Derr and Kate Sauerwein were married. Dan Getzendanner and I were the attendants. Lizzie Moffatt came over. Had a very nice time." Derr Diary, August 3, 1854.

[20]The school house was very close to the Derr house but on the north side of the Route 26 across the Monocacy River bridge. *Bond Map*, 1858. The island is in the Monocacy River below the Derr house. Mary Derr called it "Queens Island" in her diary. See also Grace L. Tracey and John P. Dern, *Pioneers of Old Monocacy: The Early Settlements of Frederick County, MD, 1721-1743* (Baltimore, 1987), pp. 285, 288.

1854

[*illegible*] were all there. Mr. Johnson was here when I got home; he brought me such nice pears.

Friday August 11th. Father went down to Uncle Lewis Scholl's but I did not accompany him. I wrote a long letter to Lou Hersh.

Saturday [Aug.] 12th. It looked like rain but was only very sultry with a slight shower in the afternoon. Mr. Johnson came out for me about ten o'clock and we went out to Mr. Derr's. About one o'clock, accompanied by Mr. Johnson, Ed S. and Tom Derr, we all went over to the Island and spent the day. Messrs. D. Getzandanner & Frank Steiner were there at Mr. D's to tea. Mary S. came out home for a ride with me. I had some papers from Mr. S. Hersh.

Sunday [Aug.] 13th. I was in town to church.

Monday [Aug.] 14th. Very warm day again. Busy in the morning. About four o'clock Tom Derr brought Mary S., Kate S., Mary Derr and Miss Moffatt out to tea & <u>Mary S. moved to-day</u>. George Birely was out to spend the evening.

Tuesday [Aug.] 15th. Mary & I were in town in the morning. At Houses and did some shopping also and called at E. Brunner's to see them.

Wednesday [Aug.] 16th. We were surprised about four o'clock by the arrival of Mrs. S. A. Adams, H. Kemp & G. Houck. They remained to tea but left immediately after.

Thursday [Aug.] 17th. To-day our places were rented[21] away. Had a letter from Nellie Mering.

Friday [Aug.] 18th. Mary & I were in town at Houck's awhile, Kunkels & Mrs. Winchester, and then came out home.

Saturday [Aug.] 19th. We were very busy all day. Mr. Johnson & Ed S. came out after tea and staid till nearly eleven o'clock.

---

[21]Daniel Scholl owned several farms which he rented.

1854

Sunday [Aug.] 20th. Very pleasant day. Mother went out to see Victorine Artz and left Mary & I in town to go to church.

Monday [Aug.] 21st. We were in town early this morning and left with the train for Monrovia[22]. Old Mr. Cronise & Louis D. met us at the cars. Mr. C. went to Balt. We saw Miss Kate Cronise, Mrs. C. and two Miss Abbotts from Georgetown. We took a long nap in the afternoon. After tea, Mr. Miller and Dr. Geyer came and we took a nice long walk. Saw Rod Hobbs; he was on his way to Balt.

Tuesday [Aug.] 22nd. We spent another pleasant day at Monrovia & left in the evening train for Fred'k. Met Lewis Wolfe & Mr. Kay from Balt., who accompanied us up to Mr. Houck's with Mary. Tilly Jackson, Georgia & I took a long walk and when we returned found Messrs. Wils Boyd, John Gifford & Wolfe.

Wednesday [Aug.] 23rd. After doing some shopping Mary & I returned home. Soon after dinner, Mother went to town and very soon Aunt Lizzie Thomas, Lewis & Mary Ball came out and remained till after tea.

Thursday [Aug.] 24th. Mary & Melia Kunkel were out to spend the day and after tea Mr. Johnson & Ed came out. They brought us a watermelon.

Friday [Aug.] 25th. Very warm day. Messrs. Body & Birely were out after tea.

Saturday [Aug.] 26th. Very warm day. Mary & I went into town and went up to Houcks' and accompanied by Lizzie H. went down to see the cornerstone[23] laid, and returned to H's to tea. Just before we came home saw Mary & Tom Derr & Kate Sauerwein come out. Mr. Johnson was out after tea. Heard of Uncle Shriner's[24] sad accident falling from his horse. Tom left about eight o'clock.

---

[22]Monrovia, named for President James Monroe, is nine miles east of Frederick, south of New Market. Scharf, *Western Maryland*, p. 611.

[23]"The cornerstone of the New German Reformed Church at the Glade, near Walkersville in this County was laid this forenoon Saturday 5 o'clock p.m." Engelbrecht, *Diary*, II, 627.

[24]Cornelius Shriner, according to Williams (*History*, pp. 1352-1353), was an officer of the Frederick County National Bank, an old line Whig, and a great supporter of the Reformed Church in Frederick. He died September 13 and was buried September 14. See below.

1854

Sunday August 27th. Quite warm. Mary S. & Mary D, Kate S and I all went into town to church, and found Mr. Roderick here when I returned. Mother was away all day.

* * * * *

Tuesday [Aug.] 29th. Cloudy morning but cleared soon. Eugene came out for Mary, so we all got ready and went out to Mrs. D's and then got into the buggy, and we had a merry ride to Uncle L's, Elias' and stopped at Mrs. D's [a] little while on our return. Kate & I practiced all evening.

Wednesday [Aug.] 30th. We went into town this morning to spend the day with Mary Kunkel. Mag D. was in too. Miss L. Miller & Mother were there too. Ed S. to tea, very little difference in Uncle Shriner. I had a nice long letter from Lou and a note from Rod H. telling me he had selected me for his best friend ever since he knew me. I wrote a note to Sam Hersh.

Thursday [Aug.] 31st. Warm day. Lizzie H. came out this morning; also the Dr. was [out] to see Father. Tilly H, Annie Bentz, & George H rode out with T. but returned home immediately.

Friday Sept. 1st [1854]. Very warm day. So Lizzie H. was anxious to go home and the cart was going. Kate and I went to town with her, did some shopping, was at Houses' & Kunkels' and just stopped to get my breastpin & money of H. Daugherty. Kate and I had a nice long talk on the horseblock till after ten o'clock.

Saturday [Sept.] 2nd. Very warm. I was busy almost all day. Mr. Johnson came out after tea and remained over night; brought us some pears.

Sunday [Sept.] 3rd. An excessively warm day. Tom Derr & Wils Boyd were here and we were ready for camp by eight o'clock. We had a warm & dusty drive to the campground near Urbana. There were a great many persons there but not a great many of my acquaintances. We had a shower about four o'clock which cooled the atmosphere and made it considerably more pleasant; we started for home about seven o'clock and arrived about ten. We had another light supper and then the gentlemen left. And after a very great washing we retired about twelve.

Monday [Sept.] 4th. Still warm. Kate, Mary S. & I all took the buggy and went out to Mrs. Derr's to spend the day. Stopped [at] several places in town,

1854

Hauses', Kunkels', Houcks', Mrs. Reese', Mrs. B. F. W., to see Nellie Mering, and was at Mrs. Derr's by half-past ten. Kunkels came out after dinner. Mary D., Mrs. K. & I all went over to see Aunt S. Uncle is worse, I think, from the statements. Immediately after dinner we all started for home. Mary S & Mag D. came with K's as far as town and then we four came out home in the buggy. Mother was very uneasy about us as it was sometime after eight. Father much better.

Tuesday [Sept.] 5th. Still quite warm. We were busy talking, arranging, etc. all day. Father and Mother were away this afternoon. After tea we were very much afraid the rest of our company would not come, however just about seven as the wind was blowing hardest, Tom, Mary D. & Lizzie K. arrived and when it cleared away, Will Boyd came. We appeared in character[25]; Mary S., Fortune Teller; Kate, Flower Girl (Lucille); Lizzie H., Highlander; Mary D., Fae; Mag Derr, Indian Girl (Winona); & myself as a Spanish Senorita. The evening passed pleasantly and the company left between ten & eleven o'clock. We had quite a time righting things.

Wednesday Sept. 6th. As the girls are going to-day, we are ready by half-past seven to start to town - Mag D., Mary S. & I in the carriage with John & trunks, Kate S. with Father. We had a nice long talk with the girls, and after the last whistle blew we bid adieu. I returned home to spend the day in trying to keep cool & amuse myself. Dr. Rau & Mr. Bealle were here to tea.

Thursday [Sept.] 7th. At home in the morning and after dinner, as it appeared cooler, Mother & I walked over to Mrs. Howard's and spend the afternoon. Ann Hall looks miserably. Her sister Julie has been with her for two weeks and her brother Joe came to-day. They are going to take her home to-morrow. Miss Pattie Hall is there. Mrs. Taylor, also Ginnie & Fannie Adams, came as we were at tea.

Friday [Sept.] 8th. Another warm day. When Father came home [he] brought me a couple of papers from Mr. S. Hersh, also a letter from Mary S. from Charleston S. C., which I must send her directly.

Saturday [Sept.] 9th. Did not rest well last night and feel badly all morning and am lying about. Raining in showers, raining day and night.

---

[25]This is a parlor game, a form of charades in which the players try to guess the character being represented.

1854

Sunday [Sept.] 10th. Mother and I went into town; weather like rain but none however; very cool, I think. Mag D gave me a letter she received from K. S.

Monday [Sept.] 11th. Cool all day. Mother & Father have gone to see Uncle Shriner & from there to Uncle Elias Scholl's to spend the day. Evie Winchester & her Pa were out to see us this morning. Uncle S. is no better and they have all given up all hope. I had a letter from Mary & Kate Sauerwein and wrote an answer; also wrote a letter to Lou Hersh.

Tuesday Sept. 12th. Cloudy in the day and showery at night. Mother and I went over to Mrs. E. Howard's to spent the afternoon. Mrs. H. was not at home. Charles H. came home with us.

Wednesday [Sept.] 13th. I was in town early this morning and at Houcks' to borrow a pattern. When Father came home at noon told us Uncle Shriner was dead, died at seven o'clock. George Sauerwein came up to see us this morning. Light showers through the day.

Thursday [Sept.] 14th. Got ready early this morning and started out to attend Uncle Shriner's funeral. There was a very large concourse of friends gathered and about nine o'clock they started for town. The funeral services were held in the church. It rained all the time till we went to the graveyard.

Friday [Sept.] 15th. Very much cooler to-day. Mrs. Taylor, Miss Patty Hall & Marion H were here to spend afternoon. Geo. Sauerwein was here to tea, told me he had expected to see me alone. They all left after tea except Mrs. T., who staid over night.

Saturday [Sept.] 16th. Quite cool. Mrs. Taylor left early this morning. I had a note from Lou H. wanting me to come over to attend the "Saims"[26] [*sic*].

Sunday [Sept.] 17th. Still Cool. Mother & I were in to church, I stopped at Mrs. Chandler's a few minutes. Mr. Marsh came out about three o'clock & staid till eight.

Monday [Sept.] 18th. Cool. I wrote a letter to Nellie Mering and a note to Lou H. in answer to one received August 30th. Father took me into town and

---

[26] We have been unable to discover the meaning of "Saims."

1854

I did some shopping and was out to Aunt Kemp's & Uncle Dennis L's. Mary & George Birely & <u>Mrs.</u> Lottie <u>French</u> were out about and sat an hour after tea.

Tuesday [Sept.] 19th. Mother and Father were away all day and I was busy commencing my collar.

Wednesday [Sept.] 20th. Mother & Father were away again in the evening and I [was] still engaged with collar.

* * * * *

Saturday [Sept.] 23rd. Finished what little I had to do at my collar and did it together with some others up [*sic*].

Sunday [Sept.] 24th. Quite pleasant. I was in town to church and heard a very able sermon from a strange minister. About three o'clock Messrs. J. Bealle & Bane arrived and sat an hour or so. Then Mr. J. A. J. came to tea, [and] brought me a package from Mary & a note, and as Mr. J. A. J. was leaving about seven o'clock, Messrs. Wils Boyd & Ulysses Hobbs arrived and sat till about nine.

Monday [Sept.] 25th. Very pleasant day. Wrote a long letter to Mary Sauerwein.

* * * * *

Wednesday [Sept.] 27th. Very warm. I was at home all day and when Mother came home brought me a letter from Mr. Sam Hersh offering me his hand, a whole generous heart, an honest name, and an untarnished character. I believe Sam sincere, at least [he] thinks, but the vacuum will soon be filled by some fairer face and he will learn to think of me as a true friend. /Heard of Dr. John Sheild's death to-day./

Thursday Sept. 28th. At home all day, I was busy racking off currant wine after dinner till about three o'clock when I saw a carriage coming, and it proved to be Kate Jacobs, Georgia & Emma Houck. They left after an early supper.

Friday [Sept.] 29th. At home all day and busy. George Sauerwein & Ed S were here to tea and I had a nice long talk with George.

Saturday [Sept.] 30th. Very pleasant day. I went into town with Father and went to see Mrs. Winchester and to see Tilly Jackson & Miss Gittings but [they] were not in; also to see Mag Derr & I called to see Mary Kunkel, Mary Birely & Mary Marmaduke, Mrs. Phillip Kunkel & Mrs. Ellen Webster, who was out, and to see Mrs. Markel[l] beside some shopping. I received a long letter from Rod Hobbs.

Sunday October 1st [1854]. John took me into town and came for me again. Mr. Ball was here to tea. I got so tired of him. Guess he won't see me again. Rained all night.

Monday [Oct.] 2nd. Pleasant day. Mr. Barr was here after tea and sat till after nine. He's decidedly intellectual and deigns scarcely to converse on ordinary topics. He wanted to know if Mr. J. A. J. stood in any other light than a friend. I told him not. Commenced raining soon after he left.

Tuesday [Oct.] 3rd. I sent a long letter to Lou Hersh. Mrs. Peter Fout was here a short time this afternoon. We had a shower at night.

Wednesday [Oct.] 4th. Much like April or March day. Busy ripping dresses & fixing a collar.

Thursday [Oct.] 5th. Pleasant day. Mother & I were in town this morning; did some shopping and was at Mrs. Reese's the rest of the morning. Soon after we had dinner Mrs. E. Howard, Mrs. Taylor & Emily H. arrived. E & I went over and took tea with Mrs. I. Howard. Miss Patty Hall still there. Em remained [with us] over night.

Friday [Oct.] 6th. Very pleasant. E. left early this morning. Mother & I went to town and met Mag Derr & we went shopping together and bought a shawl apiece, was at Houck's a short time. Had a nice long letter from Lou Hersh and one from Mr. Bell telling of his love.

Saturday [Oct.] 7th. Quite warm. I was busy all day. Mrs. Phleeger[27] died to-day. Mother went down and remained over night. Mr. J. A. J. came out after tea and sat till nearly eleven o'clock.

---

[27] The Phleegers lived near Manchester Farm on the Ballenger Creek Road. *Bond Map*, 1858.

1854

Sunday Oct. 8th. Very pleasant day, indeed quite warm. I was in church and heard a very fine sermon from Dr. Zack. I was seated writing a note to Mr. S. Hersh when Messrs. Hobbs and Boyd arrived. They had plenty of news and brought me a bottle of such nice "Grape Wine". We had some fun testing it & my currrant wine. They left about five or half past. I finished my letter before I retired. I am so sorry but I fear we will not be such good friends.

Monday [Oct.] 9th. Mother & I walked into town this morning, put my letter to Mr. H in the office and also returned the one I received from Mr. Bell. Mr. Barr and Dr. Rowe were over after tea and I spent a very pleasant evening and they seemed to enjoy it very much.

Tuesday [Oct.] 10th. I was at home all day. Mrs. Rhoderick was here to dinner. [I] sent a bottle of my currant wine to the cattle show.

Wednesday [Oct.] 11th. Home busy in the morning but after dinner Father and I went in to the Cattle Show. There was quite a fine display of vegetables, stock, needle & fancy work, etc. I saw a number of friends but I feel so very sad this evening, perhaps thinking of Mr. S. Hersh. Maybe I think some of my intimate friends forgot me when others were present.

Thursday [Oct.] 12th. Foggy early but cleared off warm. Father, Mother & I went into town about nine o'clock and already barracks hills[28] were covered. I met a large number of friends there; took dinner at Mr. H's. We went up in the afternoon again and still saw large crowds. The ladies riding attracted a great deal of attention. Messrs. Johnson & Cox accompanied Lizzie H & me down street. Mr. J. A. J. made an engagement to go with us to the Fair and accordingly came up about half-past six to go. We went about eight and spent a very pleasant evening; there were a great many friends and acquaintances there. We returned about ten. Ed Shriner accompanied Lizzie home; found it had rained.

Friday [Oct.] 13th. Gideon Bantz, Senior died to-day. Rain had settled the dust and, as the sun did not shine, by far the most pleasant day of the Cattle Show. There were five ladies entered for competition in equestrian exercises.

---

[28]"Today the Fred. Co. Cattle Show takes place on the Barricks hill - I am told that all the stalls are full & more have to be made - Also the two Candidates for Governor of Md. Messrs Ligon and Bowie are to address the Public at the Court House." Engelbrecht, *Diary*, II, 597.

There were quite a large number of persons collected. The address was delivered by Dr. Higgins and the premiums read by Mr. O. Horsey. I received a discretionary[29] for Currant Wine. There were a great number of premiums. Mr. J. A. J. accompanied me to Mrs. L. Markel's and sat a few minutes. He presented my bottle of wine for me. When I got home, [I] found a nice long letter from Lou Hersh.

* * * * *

Sunday [Oct.] 15th. Cold, windy & clear; nevertheless I went into town. Old Mr. Bantz was buried this morning and Dr. Z's discourse was to the afflicted of the family and friends.

Monday [Oct.] 16th. Somewhat warmer and not so windy. Mr. Barr was over after tea and sat till ten o'clock. He brought a set of chess men with him and wanted me to honor him as to accept, but I politely declined, saying I wouldn't use them.

Tuesday [Oct.] 17th. Busy at various pieces of sewing. Miss Betsy Hoffman here. [I] had letters from Mary Sauerwein and Nellie Mering.

* * * * *

Saturday [Oct.] 21st. Pleasant day. Father took me into town and I called to see Ella B., [who] got home Wednesday. I called for Mary K. and together we called to see Mrs. French, [and] Mrs. B. F. W. & then took a walk and came home. Mr. J. A. J. came out after tea and was in a very excellent humor.

Sunday [Oct.] 22nd. Mother & I went to church and as Mary Derr insisted upon my going home, I went with her. We went to Sunday School and to Aunt Shriner's a few minutes. Mr. Wm. Lee Morris was at Mr. D's to tea.

Monday [Oct.] 23rd. Very pleasant day. Mag Derr, Eugene, Alice & I came into town in the morning in the buggy. I did some shopping with Mag and at Mr. C. Steiner's and to see Kate Jacobs. Mother met me in town and we called to see Mrs. Shields; poor woman, she is sorely distressed.

---

[29]A discretionary was a type of premium given as an award.

1854

Tuesday [Oct.] 24th. Pleasant day. I wrote to Lou Hersh. I walked into town to-day.

Wednesday [Oct.] 25th. Quite a pleasant day. Mrs. Killion & two children were out this afternoon.

Thursday [Oct.] 26th. After dinner I went into town in the buggy, did some shopping. After tea, Mr. J. A. J. & Ella B. came out and staid till nine o'clock, both in very good spirits.

Friday [Oct.] 27th. Still pleasant. Father took me out to Aunt Margaret's & sat an hour or so. Mrs. Ritman was there.

* * * * *

Tuesday [Oct.] 31st. Delightful day. After dinner Father took me into town and I called for Nellie B. and we took a long walk. [We] called to see Huldah Howard; she is to be married to-morrow morning; met her beau there. Mr. Barr here at night.

Wednesday Nov. 1st [1854]. Much cooler. Mother and I were down to spend the day at Mr. I. Clinghan's to spend the day. [sic] Misses M. Clingan & G. Wilhelm of Balt are there. Stopped a few moments at Mrs. Chandler's. /Mrs. I. Howard and Mrs. Taylor were here while we were gone./

Thursday [Nov.] 2nd. Beautiful, and one of the loveliest nights I ever saw.

Friday [Nov.] 3rd. Cloudy & Damp

Saturday [Nov.] 4th. Cold & windy. I had such a nice letter of Lou H, and also Mother & I were out to see Grand-ma after dinner. She is quite poorly. Fannie & Mrs. Adams were there & Aunt M.

Sunday Nov. 5th. Cold & windy. Mother went out to grandmother's and sat all day, and I stopped in town and went to church with Ella B and walked out home after church. Mr. J. A. J. came out about half-past three and sat till nine o'clock.

Monday Nov. 6th. Still very cold. Mr. Barr was over after tea.

1854

Tuesday [Nov.] 7th. Much warmer & also on <u>Wednesday 8th</u> & <u>Thursday 9th</u>.

Friday [Nov.] 10th. I was in town this morning, did some shopping. Sophia Gaither and Sam Wilson of Rockville were here about an hour or two in the afternoon.

Saturday [Nov.] 11th. Rained last night and at intervals during the day.

Sunday [Nov.] 12th. Still raining in showers during afternoon.

Monday [Nov.] 13th. I was shopping again to-day and was at Houcks' a short time and met Mary Birely and Mary Marmaduke there.

Tuesday [Nov.] 14th. Was in town this afternoon and called to see Miss Styles at Kunkels' and was to see Ella Brunner too. Mary invited me to her company for Thursday.

Wednesday [Nov.] 15th. Went into town again to do some shopping; met Mary Birely and Mary M. on the street and had a long talk with them. Heard grandmother's worse, so I hurried home and Mother went out. About three o'clock Dr. & Mrs. Rowe came over and sat till about five o'clock. I found her very talkative & quite agreeable.

Thursday [Nov.] 16th. Pleasant day. Mother came home about noon and said I could go to Mary K's company, so I got ready and about half-past six Cousin Ed S. came out for me; and while I was upstairs fixing, Mr. J. A. J. came. When I came down we could hardly decide who I should go with. However, Mr. J. decided and we proceeded into town. Stopped a few minutes at Ella Brunner's and then Mr. J. took me to Kunkels', and [he] went up to the hotel and came some time after without Ed S., and I sent him up but he would not come. There was some beauty and much wit and plenty of dancing; everything seemed to pass off pleasantly. The party generally left about half-past twelve o'clock. Several of the girls insisted upon my going home with them but I politely refused.

Friday [Nov.] 17th. Pleasant day. I took Mother out to grand-mother's, and came home by myself. Found Mrs. Taylor, Emily & sister had been here.

Saturday [Nov.] 18th. Rained most of the day.

1854

Sunday [Nov.] 19th. Very pleasant day. John took me out to grandmother's but as she was so very ill, Mother did not come home with us.

Monday [Nov.] 20th. Quite cold. Mrs. Doll, Mrs. Keller & daughter came out and staid till after dinner and they, Mrs. D. & Mrs. K., left about two o'clock; and about three, John took me out to grand-mother's and I took Miss K. as far as town, but still Mother did not come home. Wrote letters to Mary E. Sauerwein & Lou Hersh.

Tuesday [Nov.] 21st. Mother came home this morning and told us of grandmother's death[30]. She died last night about eight o'clock. John & I took her out after dinner and then returned.

Wednesday [Nov.] 22nd. Father and I got ready and went out to attend the funeral. The funeral started from the house at one o'clock. Mr. Barr and Mr. Bell were here at night.

Thursday [Nov.] 23rd. Thanksgiving Day. I went into town and called for Ella B. to go to church. Ed S accompanied us down street and afterwards I went up to Killions' a few minutes.

Friday Nov. 24th. Rained most of the day.

Saturday [Nov.] 25th. I went into town this morning in the cart. Ella B called for me and we did some shopping together and on my way down street, Mr. Finney saw me and invited [me] to take a seat in his carriage and I accepted. About half-past eight o'clock, just after I had retired, I heard the stones rattling, and when all things [were] arranged I went down to see Mr. J. A. J. and Harry Smith. H. arrived last night, looks so very well.

Sunday [Nov.] 26th. I went into church and stopped for Ella B, but she did not go to church and so, as H[arry] was not in time, I started with Mr. & Mrs. Markell and met H & Mr. J. A. J. on the road down there; so they retraced their steps with me. Harry came out home with me and remained over night. Messrs. Hobbs and Boyd were out to tea and sat till after eight o'clock. I received a note from Mary Sauerwein.

---

[30]Grandmother, Margaret Ogle Thomas, died November 20, 1854, and was buried in Mt. Olivet Cemetery. *Thomas Genealogy*, p. 27.

1854

Monday [Nov.] 27th. I went in with Harry and bid him adieu at the square, and went to see Kunkels', and afterwards did some shopping and came out home. Mr. Barr came out after tea and sat the evening. Shut of the carpenters.

Tuesday [Nov.] 28th. Butchering day, everyone busy.

Wednesday [Nov.] 29th. Still so very busy. Had a note from G. Houck & wrote one in return and a note from Fanny Koones.

Thursday [Nov.] 30th. Mary K. & Miss Styles of Phil'a were here to dinner; and Meallie K and Ed Shriner, & Ella B & Mr. J. A. J. came out to tea. They all seemed to enjoy themselves and left between nine and ten o'clock.

Friday Dec. 1st [1854]. Pleasant day. Mrs. Griffin Taylor, [and] Dr. & Mrs. Johnson were here about ten o'clock but would not stay on account of Mother's not being at home. Mr. U. Hobbs came out about three o'clock and staid till after tea; we had a nice game of chess & a nice long talk.

Saturday Dec. 2nd. Cloudy most of the day. Jimmy Houck was out this morning.

Sunday Dec. 3rd. Snowed quite fast till about four o'clock.

Monday [Dec.] 4th. Clear but blowing all last night and to-day. About seven o'clock Mr. Barr arrived and sat the evening. In course of conversation he stopped short by saying "he believed me to be a candid young lady & he was very candid, and wanted to know if it would be worth while his visiting here in the hope of sometime obtaining my hand." I told him we would be pleased to see him as a friend and neighbor but anything more would be useless; and he thanked me for my candor and delicate manner of telling him, and said he would be pleased to accept my invitation and visit here occasionally as a friend, etc. He left with as good will and feeling towards me and all of us as ever, at least apparently so.

Tuesday [Dec.] 5th. Very cold. At home all day. I wrote a long letter to Nellie Mering.

Wednesday [Dec.] 6th. Somewhat warmer. After dinner, Mother and I went out to see Aunt Margaret A. On our way home met Mr. J. A. J., and after I got home found from tracks, etc. that he had been to our house and could

1854

not get in. I had quite a sweet letter from Mr. U. Hobbs asking me to correspond with him. I wrote Mag D. a note to meet me to-morrow.

Thursday [Dec.] 7th. Cold and snow squalls to-day, so I did not go to town. Cousin Harry Smith was out at night; is going to Balt. to-morrow evening, wants me to go with him.

Friday [Dec.] 8th. Still so cold so I could not go to town to meet H.

Saturday [Dec.] 9th. Much more pleasant. John took me into town & I called to see Kunkels, but they were not home, and to see E. Brunner a few minutes, and called to see the neighbors Misses Smith but [they] were not home.

Sunday [Dec.] 10th. Somewhat damp and cold. I called for Ella B to go to church and immediately after church came out home.

Monday [Dec.] 11th. Much more pleasant. Mr. Barr was here after tea and we had numerous games of chess but all the same fate - he beat.

Tuesday [Dec.] 12th. Quite comfortable to-day. John took Mother & me over to Uncle E. Scholl's; called a short time to see Aunt Shriner, and also to see Derrs a few minutes as we returned and also in town.

Wednesday [Dec.] 13th. Very pretty day; to-day one year, Lou came over. After dinner Mother and I went over and spent the afternoon with Mrs. I. Howard.

Thursday [Dec.] 14th. Rather a pleasant day, at least not so cold. About eight o'clock there was a tremendous rap and what was my surprise to see Nellie Mering accompanied by G. Houck & Mr. John A. Johnson. She came up this morning and leaves to-morrow. She is going to wait on Mary Shobe who is to be married the 26th Inst. When Father came home he brought me another note from Mr. U. Hobbs wanting to know why I had not answered his first, etc. and urging me to a correspondence.

Friday [Dec.] 15th. Still quite damp and not clear.

Saturday [Dec.] 16th. Quite damp to-day. I was busy to-day. After Mother & Father retired I wrote an answer to Mr. U. Hobbs' notes.

1854

Sunday [Dec.] 17th. Damp, dreary day.

Monday [Dec.] 18th. Snowing in the morning but cleared off cold. After tea, Mr. Barr came over and we played chess till nearly ten, when he wanted to know my reasons for rejecting his suit, and I told him I could not give <u>my hand where my heart</u> was not, and then he went into quite ardent terms telling of his education, fine society friends in power, etc. told me his visits had been received with favor when he first visited here but would not tell me why.

Tuesday [Dec.] 19th. Pleasant day so late in Dec. When Mother came from town she handed me a letter which proved to be from Mr. U. Hobbs in answer to [my] few lines in answer to his two other notes. He still urges me to correspondence.

Wednesday [Dec.] 20th. Quite a pleasant day. Mr. Bell arrived about three o'clock and staid over night.

Thursday [Dec.] 21st. Somewhat colder. Mr. Bell left about nine o'clock and after Mother and Father retired, I wrote a note to Mr. Hobbs. Perhaps I ought not but hope I have done nothing wrong and only answered it as I should. He speaks of giving vent to tenderer expressions than mere courtesy; and as I am not easy to think any one loves me, of course it is only friendship, and I have therefore merely answered it in that light. He is too pleasant a friend to lose or even be converted into a lover, for there never can be that intimacy of friendship after one's proposed and been refused. Had I been a vain girl I would have read his notes different.

Friday [Dec.] 22nd. A very pretty day. About eleven o'clock Mr. Marsh came and staid till next morning. Ed Shriner gave me a nice long letter from Mary Sauerwein. About two o'clock Mother and I went into town; we did some little shopping together. I called to see Houcks and Miss Reynolds who is staying there; they gave me lots of news. I deposited my note to Mr. Hobbs in the P. O. As I came down street Ella B. stopped me and begged Mother and me for me to stay in over night to attend the Irving Association[31]; so I

---

[31]"The Irving Society, to which Washington Irving granted permission for the use of his name, was a literary society whose aim was to promote - 'correct literary taste'." D. Hein, *A Student's View of the College of St. James on the Eve of the Civil War: The Letters of W. Wilkens Davis (1842-1866). Studies in American Religion*, vol. 30 (The Edwin Mellen Press,

1854

consented and we engaged Dr. Sanderson to accompany us. There were a great many persons there and we were well pleased. Dr. S. left about eleven and we retired at twelve.

Saturday [Dec.] 23rd. A cold morning and very damp afternoon. Ella & I got up and went to market[32]. There were a great many persons on market. Soon after breakfast I started to walk out home but I met Father coming in for me, and he had brought Mr. Marsh to town with him. I went out home and was very busy till three o'clock, when I started to town again and did some shopping and called to see Mrs. Markell & Ella B. About seven o'clock Mr. J. A. Johnson came out and sat till nearly ten o'clock; he was right talkative and when he was going away he gave me an invitation to come out to his house next Thursday evening "as we are going to have some company and I will be pleased to see you". It was sleeting when he left.

Sunday [Dec.] 24th. Too slippery to leave the house to-day; however, as it is getting warm, the ice is thawing a great deal.

Monday [Dec.] 25th. Bright, warm, yes too warm for Christmas day. About half-past eleven Maggie, Mary and Thomas Derr arrived and half-past twelve Mr. J. A. J. arrived. We spent a merry day; all seemed to enjoy it. Mr Robinson from Balt. & Mr. H[iram]. Winchester were out on business with Father. They all left between six and seven o'clock. He gave them an invitation to his house for Thursday night.

Tuesday [Dec.] 26th. Rained all day to-day.

Wednesday [Dec.] 27th. Rather more pleasant this afternoon so I went in town to meet Mag Derr as by our appointment, and we met at Ellen Brunner's. We then called to see Mrs. Page & Eliza Brewer and from there went to Mrs. Markell's store, where we were joined by Mr. J. A. J. and we went up to Houcks' and afterwards did some shopping and was down at the

---

Lewistown, NY, 1988), p. 67. See also note 2, 1855.

[32]"The Frederick Market House, on the east side of Market Street between Church and Second Streets, was erected on this site over 200 years ago. It was replaced by the building used as the old City Hall and the Opera House Theatre. During the process of change the city market eventually found itself in the square in the rear of the municipal property. It functioned as a market until 1948 when the last stall was abandoned." *Frederick News Post* (n.d.).

warehouse and made an engagement for Ed Shriner to take us out to Derr's to-morrow evening. I had a nice long letter from Lou Hersh and a note from Mr. U. H. thanking me for the manner in which I had answered his two notes. [He] thinks and feels it will be useless for him to entertain any hopes and commence to love the one I [sic] do with my whole heart etc. I little need that advice be given me, for when I do love any one I know and feel that I shall love devotedly. Mr. J. escorted me to the buggy and bid me good evening, he treated Ella and I to candy at Fisher's.

Thursday [Dec.] 28th. Not raining, neither clear. I was busy this morning and immediately after dinner got ready and went into town; saw Ella and did some shopping and returned for her and we two went out together and called to see Ginny Brengle when, Lo, I saw a written invitation to Mr. D. C. [Clint] Johnson's party to-night. I had decided to go, but now I was decided to stay [away]. However, Ella and I determined to go out to Lou's, and it was about five when we got there and from that time till nearly half-past eight we were deciding to go or stay and finally Mary, Mag & Tommy Derr & Ella went up to Mr. Johnson's and I went with Ed over to see his little brother and staid there till about half-past ten. We did not retire till nearly twelve and the girls came home [at] half-past four o'clock. They had lots to tell about the things that were said and done and spent a very pleasant evening. The reason I did not attend was simply because I did not think my invitation sufficient, as I thought, if Mr. J. A. J. desired me and it was his brother's party, he should have desired his brother to give me a written invitation and I would have attended with pleasure, but under existing circumstances I think I acted right and indeed I cannot entertain the same high opinion of him till I have matters explained, and it must be very satisfactorily, too. It has given me a great deal of trouble but I am supported by the confidence that I have acted right and so as to support my own proper self respect.

Friday Dec. 29th. Much cooler and quite clear. We got up at eight o'clock for breakfast and about ten Cousin Ed stopped for us, we talked, etc., the girls giving Ed the particulars of the party till about eleven, when we started for town. Mother met me at Mrs. Markell's and took me home. Mother approved of my not going and Mrs. M. said Mr. M. hoped the girls would not go, and when I came home and told Father he was glad I did not go. Mr. Marsh came about three o'clock and sat till dusk.

Saturday [Dec.] 30th. Pretty day so very seasonable. I finished some sewing to-day, etc. I really am surprised at Mr. J. A. J's. non-arrival to-night, but suppose he thinks he has not acted wrong and has nothing to explain and I am sorry to think to contrary; perhaps he thinks he will wait awhile and give me time for reflection. I fear if I am deceived in him I never can find another gentleman with whom I can be as intimate.

Sunday Dec. 31st. A beautiful day and lovely night. I was home all day, did not go to church for fear of taking cold and [sic]. To-day brings the year 1854 to a close; how very many changes have taken place and very different do I now feel towards some of my friends than I did at the commencement of the year. I now feel in particular as if I had been treated very badly by a very particular friend or his brother and as if I should call for redress; but may be they feel as if they are justified in acting so, and if they can explain all we may still be friends, but according to my ideas we never will be again exactly as we have been and I may feel the necessity of forbidding him visiting me again, but time alone will show and no one can tell what a day will bring forth. This year has been one of singular import to me. I have had plenty of things to have flattered me very much, and with all it has only tended to make me feel more sad, for most if not all that have proposed to me I would rather have had as friends than lovers and it only makes me more suspicious of the world and feel afraid to treat gentleman as kindly as I might, for once I thought I could teach them by my frankness that it would be unavailing to attempt to approach me [as] more than a friend but then the question only rises, have I been less frank? I hope not.

1855

"About eight Mr. J. A. J. & Ed S came for us and we went down to the court house to see the fire works & hear the speeches. We were very much pleased...stopped at Mrs. Luman's and got ice cream..."

January 1st, 1855. A beautiful day. Eventful as was the past year it has passed away and I now am one year older, and fruitful [as] may the future be in rather sad or joyful events, even now I feel as if I had lost a dear friend. Little thinks he how a little slight, be it only imaginary, affects me, but may I only strive to do my duty better and by my efforts accomplish more good for the greatest number if it be my Father's will. As regards domestic operations, I have made a new beginning, as I roasted a turkey to-day, etc. After dinner I went to town with Father; called for Ella B and we went to Kunkels' and had a long talk with the girls and were to see Mrs. Wm. Bantz and were walking the rest of the afternoon. As we were going into town met Mr. & Mrs. P. Kunkel on their way out to see me but they would not allow me to return for them. I really enjoyed going into town so much to-day.

Tuesday [Jan.] 2nd. Pleasant day. Mr. Barr was over to-night first time for about two weeks. I beat him two games at chess. Cousin Ed Shriner was here a short time this afternoon.

Wednesday Jan. 3rd. Cloudy, unpleasant day. Heard of Mrs. Shriner's babe's death.[1]

Thursday [Jan.] 4th. Still cloudy. I was at home all day. Mother has gone to the funeral and Father went to town and I am all alone.

Friday [Jan.] 5th. Clear, beautiful morning but cloudy again before night. Miss A. B. Keefer & Mrs. Ellen Jarboe were here to spend the afternoon and Mr. Barr at night.

---

[1] Mary Derr noted in her diary on this date that the doctor said the baby had dropsy.

1855

* * * * *

Sunday [Jan.] 7th. Although very cloudy I went into town, as I expected Mag Derr to come home with me and she did so. We were talking very earnestly when about four o'clock Mr. J. A. Johnson arrived, and as it rained at night he remained over night. I had no opportunity of giving my views and asking his explanation relative to the party at Auburn. We retired about half-past eleven.

Monday [Jan.] 8th. Beautiful day. Mr. J. A. J. left about nine o'clock. Mag and I were busy all day. Mr. Barr came about seven and sat till ten.

Tuesday [Jan.] 9th. Found it raining this morning but [it] ceased before dinner. Father took Mag in town and I rode in on horseback and we called to see Ella B. Mrs. Frank Wand [was] at Mrs. Bantz's. Kate D. had gone but we saw Mrs. Eberts & Lucretia E. and did some shopping and returned home. Had a note from Mr. B. sending the umbrella home.

Wednesday Jan. 10th. Very pleasant day. After an early dinner, Mother and I went up and spent the afternoon at Mr. E. Howards. They were all excessively polite and very newsy.

* * * * *

Saturday [Jan.] 13th. We had quite a variety of weather to-day ending in cold and blowing. In consequence of rain I did not start into town till nearly three o'clock, and I only had time to call and see Miss Prissy Giddings at the F. F. Sem. and [do] a little shopping and return home. Cousin L. Hedges came out after tea and remained over night. Had a note and patterns from Mag Derr.

Sunday [Jan.] 14th. Very cold. Cousin L. H. rode to town with [me] on horseback but did not return again. I heard a very good discourse from Dr. Zack.

Monday [Jan.] 15th. Quite cold to-day. Mr. Barr was here at night.

Tuesday [Jan.] 16th. Surprised to find how the weather has changed, like a spring day. I had started for town but met Mrs. I. Howard and returned with her. She had plenty of news on hand.

1855

Wednesday Jan. 17th. Very pleasant day. It seems as if I am not to get to town, for about nine o'clock Mrs. Clingan, Osburn Shearer came to spend the day, also Lewis Clingan. Wrote letters to M. E. Sauerwein & Lou Hersh.

Thursday [Jan.] 18th. Much cooler this afternoon. Just as we were finishing dinner Uncle Artz arrived, so John took me into town. Ella & Mrs. M. were just going down street and I went as far as Mrs. L. Ramsburg's, but she was not home, so we parted then and I went on to see Kunkels, but they were not home. Saw Ed S. who is going to Balt.; [he] promised to come out and give me the news when he gets back. I then was to see Sophia Gaither; she & Sam had lots to say. Was at Aunty Kemp's a short time but she was not home.

Friday [Jan.] 19th. Quite cold. I rode to town on horseback in the afternoon, stopped at Mrs. M's, and she went with me to Mrs. B. F. Winchester's; saw Mrs. D. & Annie Schley there. We came on down street and I remained with them over night. Soon after tea Billy Price called for us, as Tommy Derr was engaged, & Ella says Mr. Hobbs was coming too and we started for the Irving Association.[2] The question was whether Utah should be admitted into the Union or not. It was argued very ably, in the affirmation, Messrs. Hobbs & Lynch & negative, Mr. Hoffman besides several volunteers. Mr. Hoffman offered his services to see anyone home but I declined. /Mr. Barr was here, but found me out & did not come in./

Saturday Jan. 20th. I feel very badly this morning and was glad that they sent for me. I was lying down all day. Mr. John Smith was down in the afternoon but I was not well enough to see him.

* * * * *

Tuesday [Jan.] 23rd. Quite cold but not quite so windy. Mr. Barr was here after tea but as Mother told him at the door that I was not well, he did not come in.

---

[2]"Irving Association was formed by several young lawyers of Frederick in order to debate on different and interesting subjects for their own improvement. The '22nd' is always honorably celebrated." Derr diary. Also see note 31, 1854. Utah was admitted to the Union in 1896, though it became a territory in 1848 at the end of the Mexican War. Statehood was denied for a long time because of the practice of polygamy there. *The New Columbia Encyclopedia.*

1855

* * * * *

Friday [Jan.] 26th. Still snowing when we got up but cleared away about twelve o'clock. Mr. Barr was over at night.

Saturday [Jan.] 27th. After dinner, Father took me into town and I called for Ella B. and we went up street, and as she was going to church I accompanied her. Called for my watch and after church we did some shopping and called to see Mrs. Callie Bantz.

Sunday [Jan.] 28th. Joe took me in town in the sleigh and I stopped for Ella B. and we went to church together; it was Communion Sunday but we got out in very good season.

Monday Jan. 29th. Quite warm nevertheless, after the snowstorm. Father and I went into town. I stopped at Kunkels', had a long chat with Mary and afterwards was up to see Aunt Kemp; and on my way down street Mr. Johnson joined me and walked with me to Mrs. Markell's. Mr. Barr here after tea.

Tuesday [Jan.] 30th. Not feeling very well. I staid at home while Father and Mother were out to see Aunt M. Soon after six o'clock Mr. Johnson arrived to take me to M. Derr's, but I did not feel well enough; and soon after we had eaten supper, Messrs. Wils & Ken & Ginny Boyd and Mary Birely arrived and they all staid till after ten o'clock. Ken Boyd just came last night from Balt.

Wednesday [Jan.] 31st. Very cold this morning. Father, Mother, and I were ready about nine o'clock and started for Uncle Elias'. I stopped at Derrs'. Old Mrs. Derr is very ill. I spent a very pleasant day.

Thursday Feb. 1st [1855]. Quite a variety of weather to-day. I intended going to town to-day but was disappointed. About three o'clock Mr. Bell arrived and just after he left, Mr. J. Smith & his sister Kate and very soon Ed Shriner came and sat till about ten o'clock. They all had plenty to say.

Friday Feb. 2nd. Quite cold. There was quite a panic this morning. The roost had been disturbed, two turkeys' heads cut off, and many chickens stolen. Mother went into town and brought Ella B[runner] out with her and I returned with her again. Dr. Sanderson was at the house but soon left. Ed Shriner arrived some time before seven and when Ella was ready about half-past seven we three started for the Lyceum[3]. Met Mr. J. A. J. About Bickenbaugh's, and he went off with Ella as they had an engagement & I with Ed. Mr. J. said there was a crowd of strange gentlemen gone out to our house. We heard the debate and saw the people but I was not as well pleased as before. Messrs. Hobbs & Hinson, aff[irmative], Messr. Sanders & Bert Ritchie neg[ative]. Ken Boyd walked part way down street with Ed & me. We returned to Mrs. Markell's about half-past nine; gentlemen left about ten, and we retired at twelve o'clock.

Saturday [Feb.] 3rd. Father came in and I went out in the sleigh. Mr. Barr was here last night but no other gentlemen. Very cold.

Sunday [Feb.] 4th. John took me into town, met Eliza Brewer and we went up to church; heard a pretty sermon on Love of Jesus. After dinner Mother & I & John went over to Mr. I. Howard's and took tea. Quite cold in the morning, but changed very much. /Saw John Derr; [he] came up last night./

* * * * *

Wednesday [Feb.] 7th. Still snowing, raining & sleeting all day and night. Nevertheless, about eight o'clock Messrs. Ken & Wils Boyd, Geo. Sauerwein & Ed Shriner arrived, bringing with them Mary Birely, Lizzie & Georgia Houck & Ella Brunner. They remained till after eleven o'clock and then I returned to Mrs. Houck's with them.

Thursday [Feb.] 8th. Still snowing till about noon. They did not send for me. Ed S. & Geo. S. came up about four and invited us to go out to Mr. Derr's to-night and we concluded we would accept. Georgia, Lizzie & I were over to see Ella B. a short time. About half-past seven we all, Messrs. K & W Boyd, Ed S, Geo. S, Ella B., Ginny Boyd, Lizzie, Georgia H. & Mary Kunkel and myself started for Derrs', [and] had a very pleasant evening; staid till nearly eleven o'clock.[4]

Friday [Feb.] 9th. Much warmer. Ed S. called for me and took me out home. Geo. Sauerwein left for Balt. this morning.

---

[3]The Lyceum was a hall where there were debates or lectures.

[4]Mary Derr concurs that they all had a pleasant time. She also states that, "We generally have cake and other refreshments in readiness in sleighing time." Derr diary, February 8.

1855

Saturday [Feb.] 10th. Very bright pleasant day.

Sunday [Feb.] 11th. Mother and I went into town & Ella & I went to hear Mr. Gibson preach and were very much pleased.

Monday Feb. 12th. Bright morning and quite pleasant. Mother was in town this morning, and about two o'clock Mrs. Wm. Bantz and Mrs. L. Markell arrived and staid till after tea.

Tuesday [Feb.] 13th. Rather a dull morning. Nevertheless, Father and I went into town and stopped for Ella B and we went down to see Mary Kunkel, and Ed S joined us. I had a nice long letter from Nellie Mering. Rained all afternoon & night.

Wednesday [Feb.] 14th. Foggy all day and drizzling part the time but notwithstanding Mr. Barr had to come traipsing over here. <u>I wish he would stay at home.</u> Entertained him in the dining room. I wrote a letter to Fannie Koones.

Thursday [Feb.] 15th. Much of an April day, so changeable. Lewis Clingan was here to tell of Mrs. Susan Sheares' child's death; [to be] buried tomorrow.

Friday [Feb.] 16th. Warm, damp day. I was busy at home. I had a valentine to-day signed B. Suppose someone did it to tease me.

Saturday [Feb.] 17th. Very pretty day. Father took me into town after dinner, and I stopped for Ella B and we together were at Houcks' and to see Mrs. Callie Bantz, & did a little shopping and went down to Mrs. Markell's and Ella made up her mind to accompany me out home. About eight o'clock Mr. Barr arrived and sat till after ten. We had a nice long talk after he arrived and did not retire until after half-past eleven o'clock.

Feb. 18th Sunday. Pleasant morning. Ella & I started before nine for town and we went to our church. Thomas Derr came part way down street, Mr. J. A. J. all the way. We had a strange minister to preach for us. Mr. J. A. J. came out about five and sat till after nine o'clock.

1855

Monday [Feb.] 19th. Very pleasant day. We were very busy all day fixing for the sale[5].

Tuesday [Feb.] 20th. Bright morning but with it wind and cold; nevertheless by nine o'clock, persons commenced coming and by ten there was quite a crowd collected. Everything passed off well. Aunt Mary & Annabelle came with Uncle Elias & Davie and they together with Ed S were here to supper; but the generality, after partaking of a bite at 1 o'clock, left & everything had been disposed of.

Wednesday [Feb.] 21st. Father was kept busy delivering the articles sold today. /Messrs. J. A. J. & Ed Smith were here a few minutes./ Mr. Barr was here at night, but in no condition to leave home.

Thursday [Feb.] 22nd. Beautiful warm, bright day. Dr. Rowe & Mr. Barr were here but I did not see them. /I laid <u>Mr. B's chess men</u> by his hat & he took them with him./ I was lying down most of the morning. Mr. J. A. J. came about twelve o'clock, & his wagon soon arrived & he sent his hogs home but [he] remained till about four.

Friday [Feb.] 23rd. Not so bright, & colder again. Ed Brunner came about ten & sat till one. Mr. John A. Smith and his brother Dr. F. Smith from Bal. were down for a short time on business, besides numerous others. I had a nice long letter from Mary Sauerwein.

* * * * *

Wednesday [Feb.] 28th. Beautiful day, bright but cold. I went into town about four o'clock, called for Ella B and we went up to Houcks' for a few minutes, and then came out home.

---

[5]Daniel Scholl was giving up farming for himself. See note 6 below. "Some of the grain sacks that were sold at this sale bore the initials of Mr. Scholl's father and the year 1778. They were made of flax and stenciled by his father. Mr. Scholl was a methodical old man. He always kept the best of everything he raised, and saved all he made." William Jarboe Grove, *History of Carroll Manor, Frederick County, Maryland* (Lime Kiln, MD, n.p. 1928), p. 355.

1855

Thursday March 1st [1855]. Very bright, and warmer. Mother and I were in town shopping all morning and after dinner we were out to see Aunt M. Artz a short time.

Friday [March] 2nd. So very tempting, too pleasant to be in the house. Father took me into town this afternoon. I was to see Ella B, also did some shopping & called to see Mary K at her brother's; how very handsomely his house is furnished, but he can have very little domestic pleasure. Had a very pleasant visit.

Saturday [March] 3rd. Not so very clear but still warm. I wrote a note to Ed S to go to church with Mary K & I tomorrow night.

Sunday [March] 4th. Very pleasant day. Mother & I were in town & heard a very excellent sermon from Dr. Zack, and about five Mother & John took me in town to old Mr. K's. Very soon Mary K. & I got ready & went to hear Mr. Gibson preach his last sermon. Ed S came home with me & Wils Boyd with Mary. They remained till half-past ten o'clock.

Monday March 5th. Spring morning--bright morning. Mary K & I were out shopping, and then I came out home and was busy all the remainder of the day.

Tuesday [March] 6th. Another very beautiful day. <u>Victorine Artz came out to stay to-day</u>.

Wednesday [March] 7th. Very pretty, somewhat cooler. Mother was in town and brought Annie Nihoff out and we were very busy sewing all day. Mr. Johnson was out after tea and was very commendable. /I spoke to him of the party at Auburn and he gave his explanations./ Geo. Sauerwein is coming to-night.

Thursday [March] 8th. Still a pretty weather. Just as A[nnie] & I were very busy after dinner, Geo. & Ed arrived and sat till nearly six o'clock but would not remain to tea.

Friday [March] 9th. Sent Annie home this morning. And after dinner Victorine Artz and I walked over to see Marion Howard [and] found them at home; spent a very pleasant evening but found it very windy coming home. Wrote a note & sent to borrow Ginny Brengle's Collar pattern & when I got home found it waiting for me.

Saturday [March] 10th. Very windy. Nevertheless, as I wanted to commence my collar, I started to town, did my shopping, & was to see Ella M. for a minute or two and then came out home.

Sunday [March] 11th. Cloudy. Mother & I were in to church this morning.

Monday [March] 12th. Cloudy & raining part of the day. Mrs. I. Howard did not arrive & I was very sorry I did not go to town to meet Derrs. Had a note from E. Howard & some roses; wrote one in return.

Tuesday [March] 13th. Cloudy day. I took Vic [Artz] & we went to town and then out to their house to see them, but I could not persuade her to return with me. /[I] was at Houcks' a few minutes./

* * * * *

Saturday [March] 17th. Not raining in the afternoon. I went into town about half-past three o'clock, and Ella & Mrs. Markell were going up street & we met Mag Derr coming down. We all went to Mrs. Wm. Bantz', for a few minutes, & then did some shopping & went our respective ways, "home again." I had such a nice long letter from Lou Hersh; her letters always do me so much good.

Sunday [March] 18th. Rather windy & threatening. Nevertheless, after church I went out with Derrs. Mr. & Mrs. Reese, Mr. & Mrs. Dan Getzandanner were there to dinner & tea, and about eight o'clock Ed Shriner came out and sat till half-past ten o'clock.

Monday [March] 19th. Much more pleasant day. We had a pleasant morning to ourselves and after dinner Mag & I walked over to see Aunt Shriner, and she came with us as far as Mrs. Kemp's.

Tuesday [March] 20th. Cold & windy. Our new tenant[6] came up to-day and we are to commence a new life. I hope everything will pass off well. After dinner Mag, Mary & I started and went up to take tea with Mary Worman.

---

[6]"Mr. Scholl will no longer farm himself at Manchester Farm. There is still a tenant house on the property. Mr. Roderick and family were the tenants." Derr diary. See note 5 above.

1855

We were out to see the old folks & then Billy took us home. Ed S. came out after tea and sat the evening.

Wednesday [March] 21st. Pleasant day. Ed S. called early for me and took me to town. I stopped to see Ella B a few minutes and then walked out home.

Thursday [March] 22nd. Cold, windy day. Mr. P. S. Fout's sale.

Friday [March] 23rd. Very cold. Ed S[hriner's] sale at Linganore Mills of personal Estate.

Saturday [March] 24th. Mild in the morning but very windy & cold till night. I was in town, attended catechism, and then went with Mag & Mary Derr to see Mrs. Phil Kunkel. Amelia K [is] at [her] father's, & Mary at Brother Jacob's. Finished my collar to-day. Wrote a letter to Mary E. Sauerwein

Sunday [March] 25th. Very windy. I was in town to church, stopped for Ella to go up street with me. Ed Shriner came down with us and Tommy Derr part way. Lum Sadtler of Balt. was in church too. After dinner I went over to the other house and sat about two hours with Mr. Roderick & family.

Monday [March] 26th. Very windy and cold. About two o'clock Lum Sadtler of Balt. came out and made a call. He looks well, has been travelling all winter.

Tuesday [March] 27th. Cold and windy. Nevertheless, I went into town after tea and stopped at Ella B's, and after her tea we walked up to Mrs. Reese['s] to see if Derrs were in, but they had not fulfilled their engagement. About half-past seven o'clock Ed Shriner arrived and we started for the Lyceum. The exercises consisted of a very pleasant debate from B. F. Semmes and a debate by U. Hobbs and Geo. Harbough--aff[irmative] & B. F. Ritchie--neg[ative]. Afterwards Tom Derr joined us and walked down street with us. We [Margaret and Ella] then slept together as Mrs. Markell did not return tonight.

Wednesday [March] 28th. It had snowed last night and snowed in squalls during the day. While we were at breakfast they came for me about ten o'clock. Emma Howard & Mrs. Hulda Johnson arrived and staid to tea.

1855

Thursday [March] 29th. Much warmer and not so much wind. In the afternoon John took me down to Mrs. Cromwell's and I spent a very pleasant afternoon; met the family & Mrs. D. Getzandanner; Isie Buckey & Sallie Miller [were] there. Left about sundown and was very much pleased.

Friday [March] 30th. Very pleasant day. I was at home all day. Mr. Johnson came out and spent the evening; he has been complaining with his sprained ankle again. He was rather low-spirited.

Saturday [March] 31st. Still warm and rather cloudy in the afternoon. I went into town after dinner and went to Catechism, and then went down for Ella B, and we together were to see Amelia Kunkel and Miss Myers & Mrs. French. At the latter two places, [we] merely left cards. Met M. Barr on the street, but I believe he did not speak to me, so Ella says.

* * * * *

Monday [April] 2nd. Cold & windy. Mag Derr came at about five o'clock and only sat a few minutes; she came to see me about going to Balt. We determined to go to-morrow one week. /Wrote to Nelly Mering./

* * * * *

Wednesday [April] 4th. Very pleasant day. After an early dinner, John took me out to Aunt M. Artz' where I remained about an hour, and then came on home, & afterwards went up to see the Misses Smiths where I spent an hour very pleasantly. /Rained some at night./

Thursday [April] 5th. Busy to-day. Cloudy & damp in the morning, but clear by noon. I had such a nice letter from Lou Hersh. Her brother Ned is married.

Friday April 6th. Clear, bright morning, but rained in slight showers at night. About three o'clock Mag & Mary Derr arrived and while we were at tea Cousin Ed S. came. The ladies left about six o'clock, E. about nine. He brought me some linen to make him collars.

Saturday [April] 7th. Quite pleasant all day, no company and I was very busy baking, sewing, etc.

1855

Sunday [April] 8th. Beautiful morning. I went into [town], called for Ella B & we went to church together and heard a very excellent sermon from Rev. Mr. Davis. There was communion. About two o'clock Tommy Haines came and sat some time. About four Ed Shriner and Mr. J. A. J. came and staid till after tea, & about or nearly eight, Messrs. Wils Boyd & U. Hobbs came & staid till after ten; and after I had retired they came back again and told of their break down, but I did not <u>see</u> them but <u>heard</u> them.

Monday [April] 9th. Drizzling & damp in the morning but somewhat clearer in the afternoon. About two I went into town to meet Mag Derr and very soon Mag & Mary Derr joined me at Houcks' and we called together at Miss House's & at Kunkels' and did some shopping; met Ed S [on] the street & he was with [us] part of the time. I stopped to see Ella B and then went out home.

BALTIMORE

Tuesday April 10th. Although rainy in the morning I got ready to go to Balt. & John took Mother & me into town and I met Mag Derr, & we bid Mother, Mary & Thomas Derr adieu and started for B[altimore]. Mollie Davis & Father were on the cars. George [Sauerwein] met us and took us up to the house and we were welcomed very kindly by all the family. Well, after talking & eating dinner we fixed to go out to look for spring bonnets & we were not out long till it commenced raining, so we hurried home again.

Wednesday [April] 11th. Cold, windy day. Miss Fox was here in the morning and just as we finished dinner, Dr. Johnson, Mrs. Huldah Johnson & Emma Howard were here for a right long time. Mrs. S., Mary & Kate S., Mag Derr & I were out shopping all afternoon and Lum Sadtler was here for a short time, and John Derr[7] was here for a short time at night. We took our bonnets to Miss Metzger's to be trimmed till to-morrow noon.

Thursday [April] 12th. Very pleasant day. Received our bonnets, so of course we got ready to go. Old Mrs. Rau arrived just as we were ready to go out, so we sat a few minutes and afterwards we were down to Dr. Kinneman's to see Lizzie Schell & saw Mrs. Harriet Shields there too. I accompanied

---

[7]Mary Derr notes in her diary about this time that her brother John is working as a salesman.

them to see Belle Bailey & Mary Birely at Warners'. Mr. Phil Rau was here and staid till after ten o'clock.

Friday 13th April. Pleasant day but not clear all day. Belle Bailey & Miss Abrahams were here in the morning, and after dinner Miss Lizzie Dickey and Kate & Eliza Dawney, and at night Miss Fox, Mrs. Rau & John Derr. /Mrs. Nash here in the morning./

Saturday [April] 14th. Bright early, rain at noon and ceased soon after dinner. About four o'clock we dressed ourselves and were out to see Mrs. Johnson & Emma Howard & also to see Mrs. Wolfe. Fred Steiner was here for a few minutes.

Sunday [April] 15th. Raining all day. Mag D., Mary & Mrs. S. went to church. Mr. Rau called, went with Mag. Kate, Geo & I staid at home. Soon after dinner Mr. Rau returned and Lum Sadtler was here to tea. We all went to church to hear Dr. Morris. John Derr was here a short time in the afternoon.

Monday [April] 16th. A bright, beautiful day. Mag D., Mrs. S & Mary & I were out shopping this morning and on our way home paid Miss Fox a visit; found Mary Birely & Miss Warner had been to see us. Fanny Dix was here after dinner. I wrote a letter home. Lizzie Schell was here to tea and afterwards Mr. Rau came and every one seemed to enjoy themselves. And some time during the evening we proposed a bet and I bet with Mr. Rau a set of decanters that he would be married in five years, and with Geo a Castor[8]. I do wonder who will gain.

Tuesday April 17th. Cloudy in the morning, rained very hard with thunder, and towards evening cleared off. Kate and I were out for a while late in the evening shopping. After tea we all went round to Abells' and sat till eleven o'clock. I enjoyed it very much.

Wednesday [April] 18th. Clear and very warm. About twelve o'clock Mary S, Mag Derr and I went out together and were to see Mrs. Thos. Sadtler, who we found in bed with chills and fever. We then called out at Mr. Rau's and Mrs. Rau gave us an invitation to tea for next Friday afternoon. Found when

---

[8] A caster/castor is a cruet for oil or vinegar often used as part of a table setting.

1855

we got home that Mary & Kate Sauerwein[9], Margrette Nicholson & Eliza M. Gowen had been here and left an invitation for either Thursday or Friday evening after tea. About five o'clock we started again and were at Dawney's and Mrs. Dix's but found them both out, so we proceeded down Market St. for a promenade. When we got back found Mary Birely, Miss Bausman, & Miss Webb had been here. As we were returning home met Marianne Gardner. They are living here now. Mr. Rau was here for a few minutes at night. We failed to see the occultation of the planet Venus & the moon.

Thursday 19th April. Very warm to-day. The thermometer stood as high as 88 1/2 in the shade. Lum Sadtler was here for a while about two. I had a nice letter from Mother this morning. We went out about six o'clock. We were at Sadtlers' saw Lizzie Dickey only. We were at Warners' but Mary Birely was not well enough to see us. Mr. Bausman joined us and walked a short distance with us. Messrs. Shipley & Rau were here and soon John Derr arrived to accompany us. The Misses Bayfield & Miss Fox was [sic] here for a few minutes. Just as we were ready to go, Mr. Perry arrived, but did not stop long as he found out we were going out; so immediately after they left John Derr, Mary & Kate S., Mag D & I went to Miss Nicholson's and spent a very pleasant [time] with her, Miss McGowen & Ike Nicholson. She had invited other friends but they disappointed her.

Friday [April] 20th. Very warm in the morning, blowing at noon and continued till night. Mary & Mag, and very soon Kate & I followed, went out to Mrs. Rau's and took tea. Mrs. Mason was there to tea and after tea Mr. Shipley came. /Wm. Dean was here at night./ We spent a very pleasant evening, had such a nice supper. George came very soon after tea. About half-past ten o'clock we started for home, Mary bearing off Mr. Shipley, Mag D & Kate S with Mr. Rau, & Geo with me. We were kind of afraid, so we [girls] slept four in a bed.

Saturday April 21st. A beautiful day. We were busy sewing till about ten o'clock, when Kate started out and had a nice walk and made some purchases. I had a letter from Mother this morning saying probably she would be down on Monday or Tuesday next. We had dinner about twelve o'clock and by one o'clock we, that is Geo., Mary, Mag D. and I, were out seated in a carriage

---

[9]The visitors, Mary and Kate Sauerwein, were daughters of Mr. P. Sauerwein of Howard Street. See note 1, 1851, and April 23, below.

on our way to Lutherville. We all enjoyed the ride very much and the scenery too. We passed numberless country seats, some very handsome and possessing such an air of elegance. We were unfortunate enough to lose a screw, and by so doing had the pleasure of seeing Miss Ware for a few minutes. We arrived at Lutherville about three o'clock and remained about an hour & a half and were home again by six o'clock, all delighted with our ride. Found Mrs. Jamison had been here, and at night Wm. A. Dean was here for a short time.

Sunday [April] 22nd. Pleasant day. Messrs. John & Philip Rau [came] before church; the latter accompanied Mag Derr, Mary S., Mrs. S. & me to church. Mr. Butler of Washington City preached the sermon; had communion at Mr. Morris'. We all went out to hear Mr. Seiss in the afternoon; took a walk, Geo with me, Mr. Rau with Mag, John D with Kate, and Mr. Fox with Mary. We had a very pleasant walk out Charles Street. At night we all went to Robinson's church, Wm. Dean with Mary, Geo with me, Mr. R with Mag.

Monday [April] 23rd. Lovely day. Mrs. Fred Steiner was to see us this morning and wants us to spend the afternoon with her. About three o'clock John Derr called for Mag, & K & Mag went with him down to Blakes', while Mary and I stopped to see Miss Randall; but she was out, so we went down and joined the girls at Blakes', and John proposed we should go down to the wharf to go see a steamboat, so we consented; had quite a time passing through boxes & bales down South St. [We had a] very pleasant drink of ice water at Ball's & Clarke's store, and then proceeded on board the Gladiator[10], a steamboat that plies between Balt & Yorktown. The clerk, Mr. Lou Robbins, was very polite in showing and explaining all things. On our way up Market Street [we] saw Mrs. Cal Loats, Isie Buckey & Annie Schley. After shopping, we were at Mr. P. Sauerwein's, saw Mary, Kate S. & her mother. Soon after eight o'clock Rose Abell, Belle Bailey & Beverly Buck were here to spend the evening. Belle wants us to take tea with her on Friday.

---

[10]The *Gladiator* was part of the fleet of The Old Bay Line, Baltimore Steam Packet Company, founded in 1840, which continued to operate between Baltimore and Yorktown, Virginia, until 1958. Baltimore became a great sea port first through its clipper ships. Later steam ships and railroad connections sent Maryland products (flour and iron) around the world. Francis F. Beirne, *Baltimore, A Picture History* (Maryland Historical Society, NY, 1967), pp. 124, 125.

1855

Tuesday [April] 24th. Rather cloudy all day. Mother arrived with the cars at twelve. Immediately after dinner, Mother, Mag D., Mary, Kate, and I all went out shopping and were out till nearly seven. Mother, Mary & I were at Cousin I. Biers' for a while. I made a purchase of a silver cake basket. When we came home found Misses McGowen, Mr. E. Harmon, & Miss Fox had been here, the latter of whom wanted us to spend to-morrow evening with her. Billy Schaffer & Mr. Bausman were here to spend the evening.

Wednesday April 25th. Very warm. Mag D., Kate S., Mother & I went out to Green Mount and had a very pleasant time viewing the grounds and returned by eleven o'clock. About four o'clock Mother, Mary, Kate & I went out to shop & were out till we were caught in a rain at Cortlan's; so Mr. S. loaned us umbrellas and we proceeded on our way home. Met Geo on the way. Soon after tea, Messrs. John D. [and] Philip R. arrived and we were soon on our way to the Charles St. Theatre to see "Uncle Tom's Cabin" performed. Mr. Howard was St. Clair, Mrs. H. as Topsy, Cordelia H. as Eva[11]. We were very much pleased. Kate with John D, Mary S & Mag D with Mr. R., & George with me, we were at home about eleven.

Thursday [April] 26th. Cloudy and warm. Mother, Mag D, Kate S & I were out all morning. I was with Mother to Mr. McEldowneys & she bought me a dress, mitts, etc. Mother did a good [deal] of shopping and we returned to Mrs. S about half-past twelve o'clock. [We] found Miss M. Nicholson here; she is going to the country to-day to live. Mrs. Helena Urhlaub was to see us about two o'clock. Kate, Geo & I went down to the cars with Mother; and on our way up it rained a little. Nevertheless Mag D & Mary S. went down to Dr. Deffenderfer's to tea. Lum Sadtler was to see us; also John Derr, Messrs. Rau & Shipley were at door for a few minutes.

Friday [April] 27th. A lovely day. Mrs. Uhrlaub's little daughter was here with her nurse; she is a sweet little creature. At eleven o'clock Mary, Mag D & I started; we were at Gladhill's dagueration saloon [sic] and Mary & I had a 50 ct. one taken for Mag D; and at Pollock's Mary S & Mag had a good one taken. We returned to dinner at half-past two o'clock. Mrs. Louisa Sadtler was here and sat a long time this afternoon. Just after she left Mag D, Mary, Kate S & I started over to Belle Bailey's to tea, Miss Holton, Abrams & Williams. We spent a very pleasant evening, found Belle's sister Mary very

---

[11]Harriet Beecher Stowe's anti-slavery novel *Uncle Tom's Cabin* was published in 1852. Stage companies quickly adapted it for performances in many theatres.

pleasant and the company disposed to be very sociable. A Mr. Johnson stopped in and spent the evening. George S & John came at about half-past nine, and we started for home about eleven. It was a beautiful night and we had a delightful walk.

Saturday [April] 28th. A bright, beautiful day. Mary Bier and Sophie Bantz were to see me and want me to spend an evening with them next week, and I have promised if I stay longer than Tuesday I will do so. After they left Mary, Mag D & I fixed to go out, and was to see old Mrs. Steiner, Mrs. Fred Steiner; and when we returned found Miss Fox had been here and waited nearly an hour. Lizzie Dickey was to see us and staid about an hour. After she left we started again and was to see Lizzie Jamison, the Misses Bayfield, and Mrs. Stonebreaker. [*Illegible*]. Mr. Rau weighed us and I weighed 126 lbs.

Sunday [April] 29th. Rather warmer. Mary, George & I went to Emanuel Church[12]; heard a very good sermon from Dr. Johns. Mag D, Katy, P. Rau & I went to Heiner's Church. After dinner, Wm. Dean was here for a short time and Mrs. Rau and Mrs. Uhrlaub were here to tea. Mr. Perry came to go to church. We all went to hear Rev. Mr. Hayne, Mr. P. with Mary, Mr. R. with Mag, & Geo with me.

Monday April 30th. Rather warmer to-day. Mary, Mag D & I started to go to Moons', but met Hester on the street and promised her to go out tomorrow. We then went to see Mrs. Rau & saw young Mrs. R, too, [to] bid them adieu. We were also to see Mrs. E. Harmon and her cousin Em. H., quite pleasant young ladies. Misses Sophia Bausman, Mary & Kate Sauerwein were to see us this afternoon. Mag D, Mary & Kate S, Geo & I all went round to Abells' and spent the evening with Misses F. & Rose and were joined by John Derr & Messrs. Abells, Jr.

Tuesday May 1st [1855]. I had a nice long letter from Mother enclosing me ten dollars. Immediately after breakfast we went to see Miss E. I. Taylor married. She was married in La Mours Church. There was quite a collection of friends. About ten o'clock we started for Moons' and spent an hour very pleasantly with them; and on our way home stopped at Mrs. Wolfe's and saw Mrs. Steiner of Fred'k also. Called to see Mrs. Houcks (Amelia Sauerwein)

---

[12]Emmanuel Church, located on Reed and Cathedral Streets, was opened for services in 1854 as an Episcopal Church. Scharf, *Baltimore*, pp. 523, 524.

1855

but she was out. Mr. & Mrs. Dix, Mr. & Mrs. John Sadtler were here to tea; & Rose Abell, Miss Fox & Messers. Len Pillbury & Reynolds all came after tea and, although I had such an awful toothache, I spent a very pleasant evening.

Wednesday May 2nd. Very pleasant day. Kate and I started out about 9 o'clock and were at various places shopping; in at McEldowney's shopping a long time, and then at Mr. Sadtler's and some other places. Geo S joined us at Sadtler's and accompanied us till we were home again. Found Will Dean there; he sat a while, and then Mary, Mag D & I started out visiting. We were to see Mrs. Bayfield, Mrs. Gregg, Mrs. Uhrlaub & Sadtlers, saw Lizzie Dickey's wedding finery and how nicely she is fixed in her room. After we returned and got our dinner, there was quite a time packing my trunk, and everything was hurry with me till we started for the cars. Mr. Rau was at the house to bid us adieu. Met John D at the cars, who accompanied us up to Frederick. Saw Annie S at the cars; she is not coming home for a couple weeks. Mr. Johnson & Geo Sadtler were both at the cars; brought my spoons and knives. Bid Mary, Kate & George good-bye at the cars and were carried rapidly away to good old Fred'k. Father met me at the cars and I stopped a minute or so at Mrs. Markell's and then hurried out home, found the family well and quite small consisting of Father & Mother, John & Jane. Everything looks pitiful.

Thursday May 3rd. It rained, most all day, in showers and all vegetation seems to improve from its influence.

Friday [May] 4th. Much cooler and windy. I wrote a few hasty lines to Mary & Kate this morning about a cape and my forks, and Father got in too late for the mail. I was in a short time to see Annie Knifroof about sewing. She was at Mrs. Hart's. [She] promised to have my dress ready to fit on me till Tuesday morning at six o'clock. I heard such a noise at Mrs. Markell's, and Sarah told me that Miss Mary Kunkel was there, so I stopped in for a short time.

Saturday [May] 5th. Very pleasant day. About three o'clock I was over to see Mrs. Roderick and sat a short time; took the baby a dress. After tea, Mr. Johnson brought Ella B. out and they sat till nearly ten o'clock. We had a nice time talking over all old things. I showed E. all the new fixings.

Sunday [May] 6th. Very pleasant day. Mother and I went into town and I stopped for Ella B. and we went to church with Mr. Markell. Had quite a nice talk with Lizzie B. coming from church. Mr. Cramer was here to see Father and about three o'clock, Messrs. Hobbs & Boyd came out and <u>sat right down</u> a whole couple of hours.

Monday May 7th. Very warm day. I wrote a long letter to Lou Hersh this morning and after dinner went into town and stopped for Ella B and we went together out to see Em. Howard, but she had not yet arrived from Balt. And after we came in, we were sitting on the porch steps when who should come up but cousin Harry Smith. I was very much surprised as well as delighted. He staid with us till Father arrived for me and then we bid Ella adieu for a short time, as E & H are to come out yet this evening, and I had only time to take till they arrived. And Ella & H insisted upon my accompanying them, so I got ready and we all took a ride to town. Harry staid with us till nearly eleven. It rained hard and for a couple of hours I believe, after H left us.

Tuesday [May] 8th. Cloudy day. Mrs. M awakened us, by the sounds Mr. & Mrs. M. I went to Annie's immediately after breakfast to be fit, and then came down and saw Harry at Mrs. Markell's for a while, then came out home. About three o'clock Em. Howard & Dr. A. J. Johnson of Balt. arrived, just came up this morning. E. brought me a note from Mary, and my forks for which I was very much obliged. Cleared off cooler about noon.

Wednesday May 9th. Very much colder again. I was in town for a short time this afternoon to do a little shopping.

Thursday [May] 10th. Found a very severe frost has fallen last night. I was busy in the morning and about two o'clock Em. Howard, Dr. Johnson and Charley D. came for me to go see Marian [Howard], so I fixed myself and went with them. [We] found Mr. Riser in the parlour when we went down but did not stop for him. Met Annie Clingan and Mr. & Miss Lewis at Mrs. Howard's. Spent a very pleasant evening and returned about half-past eight. I was very much pleased with Miss Lewis and intend to go see her very soon.

Friday [May] 11th. Another frost this morning but the weather quite pleasant through the day. Ed Shriner was out to tea and we were talking of Baltimore, etc. and he sat till nearly ten; and after he left I wrote a long letter to Mary Sauerwein.

Saturday [May] 12th. Very pleasant day. I was at home all day, finished my silk dress to-day.

1855

Sunday [May] 13th. Quite warm. Mother & I went into church and I stopped at Mrs. Markell's but found Ella had gone to be with Mr. Rhoback. /I had a nice note from Kate Sauerwein to-day sent in Derr's letter./ Mrs. Markell went to church with me. Mary Derr came out home with us. Mr. J. A. Johnson came out about three o'clock and staid till after tea. Mary & I rode up past the way as far as Smith's gate. We talked till nearly ten o'clock.

Monday May 14th. Still warm to-day. Anne Keefer was here for a few minutes this morning about eight o'clock. Mary D & I started for town and did some shopping and called at Houcks' a few minutes. We bid each other adieu at H's. Georgia walked down street with me to Mr. Derr's store, where John was with the buggy. I was in town twice more, once took Father in & called for him again.

* * * * *

Wednesday [May] 16th. Very warm day. I was in town for a short time. Had a note from Harry Smith which I ought to have received several days ago. I saw him on the street and he called down at Mrs. Markell's to see me, and after having a nice long talk we parted.

Thursday [May] 17th. Quite pleasant after last night's rain. I was just ready to go to town when Marian and Mrs. Howard & Clara arrived; so Marian & I went in for a short time. Marian remained over night. /I saw Ella & Mrs. M for a short time./

Friday [May] 18th. Notwithstanding the general appearance of rain, Marian and I started over to her Uncle Edward's and took dinner. E. was expecting Dr. A. J. Johnson but he had not arrived when we left at four o'clock. Marian only stopped for a few minutes at our house on her way home.

Saturday [May] 19th. Found it had been raining all night last night. I had a note from Ed Shriner saying the party would go to see Miss Lewis on Tuesday next.

Sunday [May] 20th. Delightful day. I went into town about nine o'clock and stopped for Ella B and we went to church to-gether to the Presbyterian Church, as we had no church in consequence of Dr. Z's absence.

* * * * *

Tuesday [May] 22nd. Very pleasant day. Mag, Mary & Thomas Derr and cousin Ed Shriner came out to our house to tea on horseback, and after tea we all went over to see Miss Lewis; found her at home and spent an hour or more very pleasantly. They all came home with me, but afterwards rode out home.

Wednesday [May] 23rd. Did not feel so well to-day as I took salts last night. About half-past four o'clock Emily & Charlie Howard, Dr. Johnson & Mr. Shaw arrived and staid to tea but left soon after, as they were going to see Miss Lewis, too.

Thursday [May] 24th. Very warm day. I was in town early; called to [see] Ella B whom I found sick in bed, and did some shopping; on my way to Aunt M. Artz saw Mary Kunkel and took her along. Mary K, Mrs. Kunkel and little John were out to tea.

Friday May 25th. Very pleasant day. After dinner went into town and met Maggie Derr at Mrs. L. Markell's and we went together to see the Misses Houses. Mary Kunkel (Ed S went there with us) to Miss Houck's and met a very pleasant young lady, Miss Lefevre of Martinsburg, and to see Mrs. Frank Winchester, and to see Mary Jane Hammond at the Seminary. Mary is going to leave tomorrow for Lewistown. /Ella Brunner is up again, sewing./

* * * * *

Sunday [May] 27th. Quite pleasant day. I went into town and called for Ella B but she was not going to church as she was not well enough, so Mr. Markell walked to the church door with me. I heard a very fine sermon from Mr. Heiner and church was rather late coming out as it was communion sermon. About two o'clock I saw Marian Howard going along the field, so I started to meet her; she was on her way to her Uncle Edward's to go to Jefferson with E. to attend the Fair. Mr. U. Hobbs came out about three o'clock and sat till after tea.

Monday [May] 28th. Very pleasant day. We had but just finished breakfast when a message arrived telling us of Aunt Betsy Scholl's death, and wanting to borrow our horse or let Cousin Henry and Mr. Cronise's family know about the funeral. So Father concluded I should go down and I was soon on

1855

our [*sic*] way. Mother was going to Uncle Jake's[13], going with us as far as the bridge, but just at the bridge met cousin H. Scholl, so we only gave him the news and left Mother out and returned. We stopped for a few minutes at Mrs. I. Howard's; saw Mrs. Rice there. In town, Ella B would have me come over so I went and talked till nearly twelve o'clock. There was no one at home but me this afternoon, and about four o'clock Mr. Riser arrived and staid till eleven o'clock. When Mother and Father came home, [they] told me of Uncle Jake's death and that he would be buried tomorrow at 2 o'clock.

Tuesday [May] 29th. Quite warm. We went into town early this morning and went up to Aunt Betsy's and attended with the rest of the friends the funeral at 10 o'clock, and returned and took dinner at the house; and there the hack called for us to go to Uncle Jake's funeral; Lycurgus Hedges went in the hack with us. We got home about four o'clock.

Wednesday May 30th. Quite pleasant day. I was at home in the morning, but after dinner rode to town on horseback and called for Ella B, but she was too busy so I went by myself to see Aunt Kemp, and from there to see Aunt Jemima Scholl, and then to Kunkels', and Mary joined me and we went to Houcks' to call a few minutes. They are coming out Friday afternoon. I left Mary K. at the square and I came on up to Mr. Derr's to come out home.

Thursday [May] 31st. Rather pleasant day.

Friday June 1st [1855]. Was busy in the morning but by noon it commenced raining and of course I gave Houcks' up for today.

* * * * *

Sunday [June] 3rd. Cloudy most of the day but quite windy at night. Mr. Haines was over all afternoon and to tea, and just after tea, Mr. Johnson arrived and sat till after ten o'clock. He is in better spirits again.

Monday [June] 4th. I went into town early and was Kunkels'. Lizzie K stole my daguerreotype for me. I called for Kate Jacobs and we went together to

---

[13]Aunt Betsy Scholl, aged 72, née Elizabeth Stroup, was the second wife of Johannes, the brother of Margaret's grandfather, Christian. Uncle Jake (George Jacob Scholl, aged 80 when he died), also a brother of Christian, was unmarried. He farmed in the New Market area. His property all went to his collateral heirs. *Scholl Genealogy*, pp. 782, 784. See also note 12, 1854.

1855

see Kate Davis. When I got [home] found Marian and Emily Howard had been here and wanted to see me badly; so after dinner I walked over to Mrs. I. Howard's and remained to tea. Miss Plummer and Mrs. Harwood were there during the afternoon.

Tuesday [June] 5th. Rather pleasant. Had the appearance of rain about noon but cleared away again. Marian & Emily H were here to spend the afternoon. Ed Shriner came to tea and we walked home part way with both girls and left about ten o'clock.

* * * * *

Thursday [June] 7th. Very warm & sultry. After dinner Father took me into town & I stopped at Mrs. Markell's for E. to go up street with me. We were amusing ourselves looking at the people going to see the Balloon Ascension[14], when Mr. J. A. J. came along and stopped at Mr. M's and insisted on Ella & I going up with him. When we had given our partial consent but found people returning as we were ready to start. Mag, Mary & Thomas Derr had stopped, & Mary Markey, mother & sisters, & Kate Jacobs were there. We all left after the very heavy shower & E & I were caught in one on the street, but Father sent the buggy for us. I well remember five years ago.

Friday June 8th. Quite a pleasant day. After dinner I walked out to Uncle Adams' to spend the afternoon. About six o'clock Mr. & Mrs. James Weagly & Mr. & Mrs. Wm. W. & their three children arrived. Vallie boy is a very fine child. Mother sent for me and I returned home about seven o'clock. Mr. D. C. Johnson & Mary Schley had been to see me.

Saturday [June] 9th. Very pleasant day; was at home all day. I had such a nice letter of Mary Sauerwein & one of Nellie Mering.

Sunday [June] 10th. I was just making my mind up whether to go to church or not when about eight o'clock Miss Hannah Haines & Mr. Henry Nelson arrived and staid till nearly twelve o'clock. There was quite a heavy shower in the afternoon. Mr. R. was here this afternoon.

---

[14]"Balloon ascension--Professor Pusey intends to make an ascent in a Balloon this afternoon from the Barricks Hill--so says his Handbills--P.S. 5 p.m. the Balloon ascension did Not Come off--wind too high--and rained very hard." Engelbrecht, *Diary*, II, 652.

1855

Monday [June] 11th. I was in town a short time this morning and was to see Tilly Jackson, who had a very great deal to say. I had a note from Mary Kunkel & answered it that I would go out to Derrs' Wednesday.

Tuesday [June] 12th. Quite pleasant. Mother & I went to Elias Scholl's and spent the day. Miss Rinehart was there. Mr. Richard Marlow was down in the afternoon & I found him very pleasant. I got home about dusk.

Wednesday June 13th. Quite warm. I went into town early in the morning, called at Ella Brunner's till after nine o'clock, then went down to Mary Kunkel's and waited till Mr. Jacob Kunkel's carriage called for us, and Mary, Meallie & I went out to spend the day with the Misses Derrs. Misses Dutrow & Perry arrived as we were at tea, & Ed Shriner was there to tea, also. Kunkels' colored man came out for us after tea and we returned about nine o'clock.

Thursday [June] 14th. Very pleasant day. Mary Kunkel came out home with me; we stopped at Mrs. Markells' till Father came up street and then came out home with him. [We] wanted Ellen to go out with us but she would not. After tea Mother, Mary & I walked up to see the Misses Smith, found both them & their mother there with company, Mr. & Mrs. Clity & son. We staid till dusk. Mr. John Smith accompanied us home & sat till nearly nine o'clock.

Friday [June] 15th. Rather pleasant day. Mother was in town in the morning, and after dinner we were busy baking cakes, pies, etc. About half-past five o'clock Mary & I went into town, did some shopping, [and] stopped at their house & Mrs. Markell's. Ed Shriner was to see us at her father's a while.

Saturday June 16th. Rather warm but otherwise very pleasant. Cousin Ed S. came out about nine o'clock, but we did not go till about half-past ten o'clock. When we arrived on the ground where the pic-nic was held I thought it was going to be very dull, but about one o'clock a fiddler arrived and some gentlemen from Fred'k and indeed both Mary & I enjoyed a very pleasant day. We stopped and took tea with Miss Lewis and remained till nearly nine o'clock. [We] found there was a gust coming up. Cousin Ed & Mr. Hobbs (who had accompanied us home) both remained over night. I was introduced to several gentleman, and among the rest an oddity Haze Saunders. The ladies were generally of the neighborhood, Misses Keefers, E & M Howard, F Adams, H & L Reich, Louis[e] Wagely, Mary and myself and Mrs. Howard and Mrs. Taylor, and gentlemen two Messrs. Gambrels, Huff, Marlow, Hobbs,

Saunders, Hoffman, Lewis, two Reichs, C. Howard, Ritchie, Shriner, Schaffer, Cronise, Dr. MacGill, Willie Adams and Wagely, & some few other boys and old Mr. Taylor, & Castle. Everything appeared to pass off well.

Sunday June 17th. Found it raining hard when we arose and [it] continued raining in showers all day. About five o'clock the gentlemen made a movement to leave as it had ceased for a while, and E had an engagement at twelve to take Mr. J. A. J. out home. We undressed ourselves for a quiet [*illegible*], as soon as they left, and after tea Mary kept me talking till nearly or quite eleven o'clock.

Monday [June] 18th. We were busy all day, finished Mother's dress, etc. It continued raining all day.

Tuesday [June] 19th. It ceased raining about 8 & [was] merely drizzling, & Mary insisted upon accompanying Father as he had to go on business, and Mother went along to Aunt Margaret Artz's and brought some rose cuttings with her.

Wednesday [June] 20th. Cleared off bright and warm before noon. I finished reading The Lamplighter[15] this evening.

Thursday [June] 21st. Suppose it rained a little but do not remember.

Friday [June] 22nd. Warm morning. A very heavy shower just after dinner but cleared away again. I rode on horseback, stopped at Mrs. Smith's for Miss Kate, but she was in town. I then returned The Lamplighter and stopped and talked a while with Tommy & Fanny Adams, & afterwards went over & took tea at Mrs. I. Howard's. We returned to M. Adams.

Saturday June 23rd. Rather warm. I was busy all day. About six o'clock I went into town for Father, & Ella B sent me word she wanted to see me, so I went over there a few minutes. Mary & Melia Kunkle were there while I was there. Uncle Elias Scholl's Jane & little Lewis Scholl were here over night.

---

[15]*The Lamplighter* was a popular novel, by Maria S. Commins (1854). William Rose Benét, *The Readers' Encyclopedia* (New York, 1948).

1855

Sunday [June] 24th. Very warm. Joe took Mother & I into town and I stopped and went to church with Ella B., Mr. & Mrs. Waske. Ed Shriner came down street with us, & Haze Saunders joined me at the hotel and walked up to Mrs. Markel[l]'s with us and they both sat a few minutes. Ella insisted so much on my staying that I concluded I would till after noon, as Mother was coming in to Mr. French's funeral. After the gents left, E & I made ourselves comfortable, and about four o'clock dressed in our silks and started for church again; but as we were warned by several friends that it was going to rain, we returned. Mother came in for me after tea, but I was again prevailed on to stay. Dr. Sanderson, Mr. Frank Markel[l], Messrs. Landis & Hobbs were there after tea; the latter two remained till after ten o'clock.

Monday June 25th. Cloudy & a little showery early, but it cleared off by noon. Ella & I were up to see A. Nihoff a short time about my visit. We were all busy quilting [until] about eleven o'clock, when Mother arrived for me to take me home. Mrs. I. Howard & Taylor were here to tea. Wm. Riser was here a while also this afternoon.

Tuesday [June] 26th. Went into town immediately after dinner and stopped at Mrs. M['s], and about four o'clock Ella & I started out visiting. [We] were to see Eliza Brewer, Hoggs, Kunkels, Jane Ramsburg & Ginny Boyd. Hear[d] much of the usual report relative to Mag D & myself going to get married. Ella B came out home with me. I had a real love epistle from Mr. U. Hobbs. I do wish he only wished to be a friend.

Wednesday [June] 27th. Ella & I spent the day very quietly, with ourselves. I took her into town about seven and remained about an hour. Saw Ed Shriner on his way out but, as he saw us both in town, he remained there.

Thursday [June] 28th. Finished stitching my quilts to-day.

Friday [June] 29th. Mother and I were in town in the morning and did some shopping, and after tea, Father & I rode in for a short time. It's very warm.

Saturday June 30th. Still very warm. Father and I were into town about four and remained a couple hours. Mrs. Markel told me Ellen was sick so I stopped a few minutes to see her. Ed Shriner was on the street with me.

Sunday July 1st [1855]. Still quite warm. I did not feel well, so did not go to church but went out to Aunt M. Artz's & left Mother in town to go to church. Aunt M. was not well & I was very near fainting, and Uncle Felty

1855

Thomas & David O. Thomas were there. I brought Uncle F into town with me. I was lying down all afternoon till Mr. & Mrs. Roderick came about six o'clock; and very soon Mr. Johnson came, and about seven Mr. John A. Smith dropped in but he did not remain long. Mr. J. A. J. left about ten; he was giving me the news & an account of his Hagerstown trip.

Monday [July] 2nd. Right pleasant. I was in town, stopped for Ella B. /Ed S went with us./ We went together to see Mary Kunkel's cape but she had gone to Hagerstown, so we only talked to Amelia a few minutes & went up to Mr. Markel's[16] and ordered our lace capes and I came out home.

Tuesday July 3rd. Commenced harvesting to-day, but not as many hands as other years as we are using the reaper[17]. At night, Wills Boyd brought Ginny & her friend, Miss Sally King, out and sat the evening.

Wednesday [July] 4th. The anniversary of our National Independence. There was quite a heavy shower about ten o'clock but it cleared away soon after 12 o'clock.

Thursday [July] 5th. Rather warm all day. Immediately after dinner I rode into town on horseback called at Ellen's, but our cape[s] had not come, so I went on up street and went to see Aunt C. Scholl and Mrs. Salmon; & on my way down, Mr. Markel told me the goods for our capes had come, so I went on over and found E had sent for Mele Kunkel's cape but did not get it, so I went for it and got it immediately, and when I told her of Sally King's we went for it too, but finally decided on a scarf cape the shape of Maggie Derr's. I saw Lizzie Cromwell on the street & had a nice long talk with her and also Mary Smith. I walked out home after tea, & after cutting out my cape I wrote to Mary Sauerwein --- a good deal in a short space and time.

* * * * *

Saturday [July] 7th. My birthday. Raining in the morning but cleared off about 3 o'clock. Was over at Mrs. Roderick['s] this morning, finished my <u>lace cape</u>.

---

[16] Mr. Markel had a dry goods, book and stationery store on the south side of Patrick Street between Market and Court Streets. *Williams' Directory*, p. 26.

[17] Daniel Scholl purchased and used his reaper for the first time in 1854. See June 13, 26, and 29, 1854.

1855

Sunday [July] 8th. Most delightful day. Mother & I went to church this morning & heard an excellent sermon from Dr. Zack. Stopped & went up street with Ella B & Mrs. Markel. Derrs were in church & insisted upon my going out home with them, so I was prevailed on. After tea, Thomas Derr brought me out home in the buggy, & had a very pleasant ride after spending a very pleasant afternoon.

Monday [July] 9th. Still harvesting, quite busy to-day. Uncle Artz was here this morning.

Tuesday [July] 10th. Sprinkled rain this morning, but not sufficient to prevent harvesting. Hannah Haines was over a couple of hours this morning. I rode to town on business for a short time; finished with cradles[18] to-day.

Wednesday [July] 11th. Quite warm; we finished harvesting to-day.

Thursday July 12th. Still warm. I went into town early this morning and called for Ella B., but she was not going to the examination so I went on up to Houcks' and went with them. Mag & Mary Derr were there also. We were much gratified by the compositions and everything passed off well. We all stopped at Boyds' on our way up from the examination and met lots of company there. Immediately after tea Mag & Mary Derr, Georgia Houck & I went up to see Kate Davis. She has a fine little daughter and seems very well indeed. We sat there about an hour, and on our return Mr. Hobbs arrived and before we were ready to start Mr. Schaeffer, both of whom accompanied [us] up to the Methodist Church to see the Diplomas delivered[19]. Thomas Derr came for the girls after we got back, & Georgia, Mr. S & Mr. Hobbs & I accompanied them as far as Mrs. Reese['s] and as a variety G & I rode from Miller's store to Mrs. R in the wagon. Messrs. H & S left about eleven o'clock. I had a note from Annie Scholl which ought to have been received 2 weeks ago, wanting me to spend the 4th with her. I wrote to Nellie Mering to-day.

---

[18] A cradle was attached to a scythe to lay the grain in a swath. *Webster's Dictionary.*

[19] Mary Derr wrote in her diary, "This is commencement and closes school until September. The graduating class read their compositions, there were only four this year, all very good. Ellen Doub's Valedictory was very much liked. She read it very well.... The Methodist church was where the testimonials were awarded to the introductory and junior class and diplomas to the senior." The Methodist Church was in the first block of East Church Street, on the north side. Scharf, *Western Maryland*, p. 514.

1855

Friday July 13th. Pleasant day. I was just getting ready to start home when there arrived from the Misses Derrs a letter they had received from Mary Sauerwein containing a note for me. Poor girl, I fear her health is very bad just now from the way she writes, and hope her visit to the country may be of service to her. Georgia H walked down street with me even to the edge of town, and I walked on but had the good fortune to meet E. Shriner coming for me, and when I got home found Aunt Scholl, Aunt Shriner, Mary & George S. there. E returned to town and came on for them in the evening & took tea & all left.

Saturday [July] 14th. Quite warm all day. About three o'clock Miss Hannah Lewis & a Mr. Hersh arrived and sat an hour or two; made themselves very agreeable.

Sunday [July] 15th. Rather warm. John took me into town and I stopped for Ella B and we went to church together. Haze Saunders was up for a few minutes. After dinner I went out home & Mr. Jeremiah Cramer was here.

Monday July 16th. Very warm all day. After an early tea I went into town and staid over night with Ella B. I was over at Mrs. I. Howard's a short time this morning. About eight Mr. J. A. J. & Ed S came for us and we went down to the court house to see the fire works[20] & hear the speeches. We were very much pleased, and on our way up to Mrs. Markell's stopped at Mrs. Luman's and got ice cream, and then went back and took another look at the court house, and then back to Mrs. M and sat on the steps till half-past eleven, when the gents left, and we went up stairs and retired in about an hour after we had a nice long talk.

Tuesday [July] 17th. A very warm day. They sent for me about eleven and I had quite a warm ride out in the cart. I wrote to Mary E. Sauerwein.

---

[20]"Has been an excitement in town today: there was a mass meeting of the 'No Nothings' or 'Native Americans'; a distinctive and separate party from the Whig and Democrat, and has been formed within the last couple of years. If this party continues as it has been in this country they will in a short time completely counterbalance the other. Their principle object is to prevent foreigners from voting until they have been in this country 21 years, also, I believe, to abolish the right of Catholic holding office at all. The Courthouse and yard was brilliantly illuminated, and a grand display of fireworks also exhibited." Derr diary. Also see Engelbrecht, *Diary*, II, 655.

1855

Wednesday [July] 18th. Quite warm. Early in the morning John took me into town and I stopped for Ella B and we went out to Mr. E. Howard's to see Emma H & Huldah Johnson, but we knocked & got no answer and went all through the house and found none of the family. We stopped in town a few minutes and then came on out home, and after an early tea I took Ella into town & went up to Houck's for a few minutes, and then I came out home about half-past eight o'clock.

* * * * *

Friday [July] 20th. Very warm. After an early tea I went into town and stopped [at] the P. O. and had a letter from Mary saying she was coming on Tuesday. I then went down to Mrs. Markell's and Ella & I got ready and waited till Messrs. Johnson & Shriner arrived for us to go out to see Miss Lewis. We had a very pleasant ride and a very pleasant evening. We left about nine o'clock and Mr. Johnson brought me out home.

Saturday [July] 21st. I was quite busy in the morning. Uncle Dennis Scholl came out & surprised us with telling us of the death of Aunty Kemp[21]. Mother went into town with Uncle & Father went in after dinner. It rained very hard during the afternoon.

Sunday [July] 22nd. Cloudy all day & some rain. Mother, Father & I went in about one o'clock to attend the funeral. There was service in the church & then laid the corpse in a vault.

Monday July 23rd. Pleasant morning but a very heavy thunder gust about six o'clock. Uncle Artz was here to dinner.

Tuesday [July] 24th. Very warm day and rain about six again but cleared off afterwards. Annie Scholl & Ellen Gittinger spent the day, and after tea we three went into town in the buggy and sent the wagon in for baggage, and Ella B, Maggie Derr, & Mealie Markel joined us and went to the cars to meet Mary & Kate Sauerwein, and we three went out together. Mary does not look badly I think. Kate very pretty.

---

[21]Ann Mary, wife of Abraham Kemp, died July 1855. Holdcraft, *Names in Stone*, I, 648. She was the daughter of John Brunner and a sister of Margaret's paternal grandmother. *Scholl Genealogy*, p. 782. Also see note 11, 1853.

1855

Wednesday [July] 25th. Very warm shower in the afternoon. Keefers sent me word that they & Buckeys would spend tomorrow with us. We took a walk after tea.

Thursday [July] 26th. Very warm with a gust of thunder and lightning. Mary & Ann Keefer were here but Buckeys could not come. Father quite unwell. I had a letter from Lou Hersh.

Friday [July] 27th. Very warm & heavy gust at night. Mag Derr & Thomas were out in the morning, & we went to town when they left & were at Houses' and Houcks'.

Saturday July 28th. Very pleasant day. After tea Mr. & Mrs. Christian Steiner, Mrs. Fairfax Schley & two children were out for a short time, & very soon Ed Shriner & Meallie Kunkel & Mr. Johnson came out & spent the evening. Mr. J. A. J. staid till eleven & the others till 10 1/2 o'clock.

Sunday [July] 29th. Quite a pleasant day. We went into town & Ed Shriner met us at the hotel and went to church with us. Ed & Thomas Derr came down street with us. Ginny Gambrill came in to see us awhile.

Monday [July] 30th. Warm morning but it rained in the afternoon. Mag & Mary & Eugene Derr came and remained to tea & Mary remained over night. Kate & Mary Derr took a ride with Thomas & Mag. Mary S. & I walked over to Mrs. Roderick & remained a few minutes; when we got back found Ed S at our house, who spent the evening with us.

Tuesday [July] 31st. Quite warm. Aunt Margaret A[rtz] & Mr. Hinkel of Ill. were here to dinner. Mary & I were out on horseback. Lizzie & Georgia Houck & Kate Jacobs were out for about any hour. Mr. Johnson came out & sat till eleven o'clock.

Wednesday August 1st [1855]. Warm & very heavy gust at night. We were reading the "Two Guardians".

Thursday [August] 2nd. Showery after 11 o'clock but, notwith-standing the cloudy [day], we went into town. Mary S, Mother & I went shopping and at Houcks' & Aunt Jemima Scholl's a few minutes.

Friday [August] 3rd. Cloudy morning but cleared off beautifully about three o'clock. Eugene & Willy came out for Mary Derr & she left. I wrote a letter to Harry Smith. Hannah Haines came over after tea, and about seven o'clock

1855

we girls started for town and stopped at Ella Brunner's. About eight o'clock we saw three buggies and thought they were going to our house, so we started home & over took them and found it to be Misses Ginny Boyd & Sally King, & Messrs. Wils & Dan Boyd, John Gifford & James Higgins of Balt. They remained till nearly twelve o'clock. Mr. Higgins was a source of a great deal of amusement to us & everything passed off pleasantly. We went in to see the fire works[22].

Saturday August 4th. Delightful morning but rained very hard about six o'clock. About 9 o'clock Mary & Kate S & I started for Mr. Derr's to spend the day. After dinner Mary & Kate, Mag D & I went over to see Mrs. Shriner and sat an hour or so; heard Ed & Mr. J. A. J. had gone out to our house. When we got back to Mr. Derr's, found Mr. Hershey there and he said he had seen Father at home, & he had told him where we were and that he had come to take one of us home. After tea and the worst shower we started home, I with Mr. Hershey & Mary & Kate with Thomas [Derr] as far as town, and afterwards in our buggy home. Mr. H. remained overnight and we were all sleepy and soon retired.

Sunday [August] 5th. Mr. H. left about eight o'clock. [We] found [it] very bright in the morning but [it] rained in the afternoon & night in showers. We went to church and had Ed S, Thomas & John Derr down street with us to the hotel. Ed S. brought Kate home & staid till about eight o'clock. John & Thomas Derr were here to tea but left soon after.

Sunday Aug. 6th. Rather pleasant day. Mag Derr arrived about ten o'clock. We had written a note to her & sent it town. Mr. Sam Preston arrived between four & five o'clock and we had early tea and went into [town] immediately after. Mr. P. took Mag D into town in his 2 horse buggy & Mary, Kate & I went in the carriage. We stopped at Kunkels' awhile & then went up to Boyds' & made a call; saw Mr. Higgins there. We then came out home well pleased with our visit.

Tuesday [August] 7th. Very pleasant day, no shower I believe. The girls had a letter from home saying Geo would be up to-night. We did not dress till after tea; consequently [we] had no time to take our walk to the woods as intended.

---

[22]"I believe a great display of fireworks is to come off tonight. They have been disappointed several times on account of rain." Derr diary.

1855

Wednesday [August] 8th. Very warm with showers after five o'clock. Mary, Meallie & John Kunkel & Geo Sauerwein came out about ten o'clock & spent the day with us. Tommy Derr came out & took tea with [us] & took Mag away with him. The rest left about seven or half past. /We sent Aunt Lewis Scholl word we would spend to-morrow with her./

Thursday August 9th. It was showery till nearly twelve o'clock but nevertheless as we had sent Aunt Jemima word, we determined to go in; met Geo Sauerwein, who also spent the day with us. We had a very pleasant time. Misses Jones & Riggs spent the afternoon there & after tea Mary & Meallie Kunkel & Ed S. were there. We enjoyed the day very much. We were at Uncle Kemps' a few minutes & at the Misses Houses'. I had a letter from Cedar Rapids, Iowa to-day.

Friday [August] 10th. Quite a pleasant day. I was busy all morning doing up collars. After, I was sewing, etc. till five, when we had tea and afterwards went into town & stopped [at] Boyds' a few minutes, & met Geo. S[auerwein] & Ed S. by appointment & also Harry Smith. Mary, Kate S., Geo S, Ed S, Harry S & I all went round to Mr. C. Steiner's for a few minutes & then up to Houcks', and then returned to Boyds' & sat till nearly nine o'clock. Geo S. went out & staid over night with us. We had a nice talk after we got back.

Saturday August 11th. Delightful day. As we did not have breakfast till eight o'clock, Geo S walked into town and we got ready & started for town and met Geo S., and all went out to Mr. Derrs' woods to attend the Sabbath School celebration. There were Kunkels, Houcks, Derrs, Boyds in this afternoon; Mr. J. A. J., Ed S., Mr. Cox of Carroll Co. [and] Messrs. Ham Boyd & James Higgins [were] among our immediate acquaintances in our party. We remained after all had left & amused our party with playing Fox & Geese. Messrs. Abe Shriner & Ham Dutrow [also there]. We had everything plentiful & very nice and spent a very pleasant day. /Cousin Fred Koones & lady of Washington were here while we were gone. Babe quite sick./ We returned home about six o'clock. Geo S remained in town & called to see Ella B.

Sunday [August] 12th. Cloudy but no rain. We went to church in the morning & heard a very good sermon from Rev. Mr. Philips. Geo S met us at the hotel & met Ed S & Tom Derr on the way down, so we had a beau apiece to & from church. I asked for Mr. & Mrs. Koones at the hotel, but she did not wish to see company as her child was so ill, but I saw cousin Fred for a few minutes after church. /Messrs. John & Ed Smith were down after tea & made themselves very agreeable./

Monday August 13th. Very pleasant day with a slight shower about five o'clock. I was up at about half-past four o'clock & busy getting ready for our mountain party till about eight, and then dressed ourselves and waited till about ten o'clock. Mr. J. A. J. & Ed S arrived and very soon Wils Boyd and we soon started. Mary with Wils, Mr. J. A. J. took me & Ed S., K[ate], and we went on to Mrs. Reese's and was joined by Geo S. with Mag D & Johnny with Mary D. We found the road very rough but every thing passed off pleasantly. We arrived at the spring about half-past one o'clock & prepared dinner, & the gentlemen attended to their horses & really every one seemed to enjoy their dinners so much. After dinner was cleared away & gentlemen had got some Fox Grapes, we started for the "White Rock"[23] & Mary S. & I had quite a blowing time till we arrived there. We recognized many familiar spots & sat on the rock till it commenced raining, when we started for the buggies. We fixed ourselves some cake and prepared to go home and had a very slow ride home till about nine o'clock. Derrs went out with us but all only remained a few minutes. /<u>Everyone seemed to enjoy it so much.</u>/

Tuesday Aug. 14th. Very pleasant day. We were all quite stiff this morning but had the trunks packed & sent into town by eight o'clock. We got ready when John came back and went into town, & I left the girls at Houcks', as they are going to stay there next. We were very much surprised to see Geo S again as he bid us good-bye last night, but Ed S was too slow in getting him to town. I felt strange to bid the girls good-bye in Frederick. Geo S walked down street with me to Mr. Derr's store. I slept a part of the afternoon & fixed some Fox Grapes to preserve & put some in salt water for pickle.

Wednesday [August] 15th. Rather cloudy all day with a few showers. About half-past five o'clock Miss Kate & Mr. J. Smith came down & took tea with us but left soon on account of the weather.

---

[23]"We went to a place called 'White Rock' from 4 to 6 miles from town. Some of the country through which we passed is certainly the most wild and romantic I ever beheld. Climbed to the top and were well repaid for our trouble. There lay the whole valley of Frederick exposed to our view. We could distinguish places 10 to 12 miles around, and perhaps further. A huge bed of stone as large as an enormous house was growing from the side of an exceedingly high mountain. Looking down from the top to an immense depth, it presented a fearful aspect." Derr diary.

1855

Thursday [August] 16th. Very warm morning. I went into town, called to see Ella B & friend Miss Annie D. Ella went with me to Mr. Houck's, & I called for Mary S and we went to Kunkels' & did some shopping; had a letter of Nellie Mering. Spent evening [at] Mrs. I. Howard's and found a letter from Mr. H. Smith when I returned.

* * * * *

Wednesday [August] 22nd. Cloudy day, tho' early I thought it would be clear. So I sent Mary Kunkel word I would be in to-night and after the shower about six o'clock I went in to town and remained over night with her. Ed S dropped in soon after and very soon Dr. Delasmuths & Mr. Nevins Dorsey, but the latter gentleman left very soon; & then Mary, Coz Ed & I went up & spent the evening at Houcks'. Mag & Mary & Tom Derr, Mary E. Mackey & Messrs. Ken & Ham Boyd, Dr. McGill, J. Clifford & James LeFevre & saw Miss Lizzie Lefevre, too. She came yesterday. Dr. McGill came home with me.

Thursday [August] 23rd. Very warm with showers in the afternoon but clear again at night. In the morning Mary Kunkel & I were at Dr. Dorsey's & Houcks' at Baughers' to see Miss Greiner of Phil'd & Lizzie. The ladies made themselves very agreeable indeed. After we had been at the P.O. I received letters from Annie Scholl & John Derr, the latter telling me he had sent my order and directed [it] to care of Henry Thomas, Esqr. I expected Mary S. down but it rained about time appointed. After tea, Melia K. and I went up street to Mrs. Markell's for a few minutes, and then to Mr. H's; saw Annie Trail & Annie Campbell there. As we passed Boyds' my name was called, so I stopped & saw Ginny, Wils & J Cann, Miss King & Mag Derr, [and] Dr. McGill, and while standing Thomas Derr & Ham B joined us. We returned home about 9 o'clock and Dr. Mc with me & Ham with Melia. Dr. staid till after 10 o'clock.

Friday [August] 24th. Sultry & warm. About eight o'clock Mary S. called for me and went down to see Aunt Jemima S. and at Houses', and out walking. I returned with her to Houcks' and sat about an hour & then returned to Mr. Kunkel's about three o'clock. Mary K. & I went down to go with Aunt Jemima and we went with her to D. Dorsey's & Mrs. Solman's and we sat a long time at each place. Ed S came in as soon as we got back & took tea with us; and after, I fixed myself and Ed & I went to Aunt Jem. S, and went over to call & see Mrs. P. Kunkel, but she was out so we only left our names. When we returned we all went over and sat about an hour with Ellen &

1855

Annie D., and then went up to Houcks' and Mary & I were joined by Mr. J. A. J. at <u>Cad I's</u> corner. We were the only company for a while & then Dr. McGill came in and [he] had been to see us. We spent the time very pleasantly till after ten o'clock and then left, Ed with Ellen, Dr. Mc with Mary & Mr. J. with me.

Saturday [August] 25th. Quite warm. About eight o'clock this morning, Melia Kunkel & I started up street. I went shopping with her and she went as far as Ellen B's with me & there I remained till twelve o'clock with them & came out home with John in the cart. When Father came home, I had a note from Geo Sauerwein saying one of the baskets of peaches were for me & hoped the cream would make them palatable. I wrote a reply to John Derr's note.

* * * * *

Tuesday [August] 28th. I was very busy all day, made <u>Tomato Catsup</u>, etc. I was at Mrs. Roderick['s] [a] few minutes. Father brought me a note of Georgia Houck saying they would be out to-morrow.

Wednesday [August] 29th. Cloudy till about eleven and then very pleasant. Georgia & Ella H., Mary S, & Lizzie LeFevre arrived about ten, and about eleven Mr. LeF brought Kate S & Lizzie H, and they all remained till about seven. Mag & Mary Derr arrived about 3 o'clock & Ed S came as we were at tea. Every thing passed off pleasantly. Thomas Derr came for the girls about seven and the Misses K & Mary S & Ed S remained till about nine and then bid me "Good Night".

Thursday [August] 30th. A delightful day; busy all day at Mother's cape. I answered Geo Sauerwein's note to-night & a letter to Lou Hersh.

Friday [August] 31st. Rather cloudy & dull all day. About five o'clock I went into town, called to see Annie Bentz if she would go to her Mother's on Tuesday. School pic-nic to-morrow. Was at Houcks' and saw Tom & Mary Derr there; took a ride with Tom & was at Kunkels' and saw Ed S. He called up & took me out to Derr's as per engagement. /I had a written invitation from Mrs. B. C. Marlow to the Sabbath School picnic tomorrow./

Saturday Sept. 1st [1855]. Cloudy in the morning but cleared off to be a beautiful day. Cousin Ed S came about half-past 9 o'clock & we started about ten, Mag with Ed & Mary & I with Thomas. We had a close ride to Mr.

1855

Winebrenner's woods and were there welcomed by the members, etc. Misses Rachel Norris & Erner were very attentive, Mr. Norris also & Mrs. Wm. Cox in particular. We all spent the day very pleasantly & had plenty of good things, etc. There were numerous different parties there. After the most of the folks had left we amused ourselves with several games and then left. Mr. B. C. Marlow took Mary Derr home. Messrs. Marlow & Shriner remained till nearly ten o'clock. Maggie & I both received a letter from John P. Derr.

Sunday [Sept.] 2nd. Very warm day with quite a heavy shower in the afternoon. Cousin Ed called for me about half-past eight & soon we started for town, Ed & I together in buggy. Mary, Maggie, Tommy & Mr. Derr in the carriage, we all stopped at Houcks'. After church they insisted upon my remaining so I told Mother she should send for me in the morning. /Mr. S with me, Geo with Mary D, M with Georgie & Mr. Eader with Kate./ When we were about starting for church Miss Schaeffer & Dr. McGill arrived, & Mr. Eader & Mr. Geo Birely accompanied us back & remained till after ten o'clock.

Monday Sept. 3rd. Mother sent for me before six o'clock. Cloudy all day, showery in afternoon.

Tuesday [Sept.] 4th. Cloudy & threatening all day. Notwithstanding, Father & I started into town & called for Annie Bentz & went out to her mother's. Uncles Kemp & Hedges came with Father & Uncle John from the sale & took dinner. We were over at Aunt Kitty Brunner's for a few minutes. We were weighed. I weigh 126 lbs. We started for town about half-past two o'clock. I stopped at Houcks' about an hour. Mary & I had just gone to M. Derr's. Heard of Mr. Jacob Keefer's death, died this morning at four o'clock.

Wednesday [Sept.] 5th. Rather cloudy. Emily Howard arrived about 9 o'clock and staid with me till after dinner. She is just on her way home from a visit to Montgomery. Saw Mr. Keefer's funeral pass.

Thursday [Sept.] 6th. Still cloudy. Uncle Elias Scholl & Aunt Mary & Davis, & Mr. & Mrs. Randolph Dutrow & two children spent the day here to-day.

Friday [Sept.] 7th. Cloudy all day, busy in the morning putting up tomatoes, and immediately after dinner I started for town and went to Aunt Jemima's to go to Linganore, but she was otherwise engaged and gave me the strawberry plants from her own garden. Mary Kunkel sent for me & I went up to see her & she wanted me to go out to Derrs', so off we started. Mary

1855

D & Mary S were just getting ready to take a ride on horseback, so we were entertained by Mag D & Kate S. We remained only about an hour & half. I stopped a few minutes at Aunt M. Artz & saw Mrs. John Cooper, Mary Cooper & Little Minnie. She has grown very much & improved, too. We saw Mr. Johnson on the road; said he was coming to see me at night, so he arrived about half-past seven & sat till about ten.

Saturday [Sept.] 8th. Clear & rather warm. After dinner I went in to go to catechism and afterwards Mary Kunkel, Mag Derr, & I went to Houcks' to wait for Mary & Kate S., & then we all went down to Kunkels' & afterwards to the warehouse. Mary S. went out with Ed S and we left her with Mary K. & Mag D. Kate S. & I went on up street. Mr. Clint Johnson walked part way up street with us. I called again at Houcks' for Lizzie and we went together to see Tilly Schoolfield at Mrs. McGill['s]. I was very much pleased with her.

Sunday [Sept.] 9th. Very warm day. Mother & I went into church, found Ed Brunner here when we got back. He remained till after tea. Mr. Jerry Cramer arrived after tea & sat till ten. I was so sleepy.

Monday [Sept.] 10th. Very warm day. Fanny Adams, Mrs. John Cooper, two children & nurse & Mary & Minnie Cooper all arrived about 9 o'clock. Willie Adams was here for a short time about six o'clock & Fannie Adams accompanied him home. Minnie, Bobbie & I were over at Mrs. Roderick['s] for a short time.

Tuesday [Sept.] 11th. Another very warm day. About seven o'clock I started into town & called for Aunt Jemima & we went out to Uncle Hedge's; stopped at Mary Horman's for a short time. Mrs. Solman was at Uncle H's & she went with us down to Daniel's after dinner; everything was very nice. Uncle Elias, Aunt Mary & Annabel & Ed S & Uncle Lewis Scholl came to Daniel's also. Immediately after tea we started home. Ed S brought me to town & Uncle & Aunt came in our buggy. They got out at the edge of town & walked down home; found the ladies had left when I got home.

Wednesday [Sept.] 12th. Very warm. I was very busy all day putting up tomatoes. About four o'clock I went into town to Kunkels' to meet the girls. Mary & Kate S. & Mag Derr were there. We all remained all night. Mary S & I slept together, Kate & Mag. After tea Dr. Delasmuth was there for a few minutes. And about eight o'clock Ed Shriner arrived & very soon Mr. Schaeffer & Georgia & Lizzie Houck. About nine we were invited out to very nice table. Messrs. Hobbs & Henderson came ten o'clock and remained nearly an hour. We all appeared to enjoy the evening very much. Mary S & I were up street a few minutes, called for Tilly Schoolfield but she was out, & Kate S & I were down at Uncle Lewis' for a few minutes.

Thursday [Sept.] 13th. Shower in the morning and cleared off very warm. Mary Kunkel & I were up to see Tilly S about an hour and then went home to dinner. We slept in the afternoon and I had a nice letter of Lou Hersh. Shower again in the afternoon. Derrs went home about seven & we eat & drank & retired soon after 9 o'clock.

Friday [Sept.] 14th. Sent for me about seven o'clock, and I went up and brought Tilly S. out with me to spend the day. It rained nearly all afternoon, but she seemed anxious to be in town so I went in with her.

* * * * *

Sunday [Sept.] 16th. Rather dull day but I went into town and Ella B & I went to the Methodist church & heard the Rev. M. preach in favor of the Sunday School Union. Saw Hannah Lewis & her two friends in church.

Monday [Sept.] 17th. Very pretty day. Mag Derr, Mary & Kate S, Ed S., Messrs. J. A. J. & Wils Boyd were out after tea and sat the evening. We had such excellent peaches for them. They all seemed to enjoy them very much.

Tuesday [Sept.] 18th. I was very busy all day till about four o'clock, when I got ready and went into town to meet Cousin Ed S, notwithstanding Mrs. E. Howard, Emma H., Mrs. Taylor & Mrs. Clingan & Herman were all here, but as I had made an engagement of course they excused me. I stopped at Kunkels' and Mary & I went up street for a few minutes, & I stopped at Mrs. Boyd['s] a few minutes to see Tilly Schoolfield, & then Cousin Ed & I went on out to Mr. Derr's. Messrs. Eader & Geo Birely were there also to spend the evening, & also old Mr. Lewis, John Lewis, Mr. Lee of Phil'd., Misses Lewis, Lee & Davis. We had quite a merry time & after Lewis left we had a dance. Turned very cold about half-past ten.

Wednesday Sept. 19th. Quite cold & damp, & I had quite a time trying to get a thicker dress to fit me. About two o'clock Mag Derr, Mary & Kate S. & I all started in the wagon for Mr. Schell's. We had a merry ride over there and had spent an hour or so very pleasantly with Lizzie, had grapes & peaches, and from there we went to Noonans' awhile. Was introduced to Mr. & Mrs.

1855

Noonan, Miss McCartney & Mr. O'Brien of Balt. Then we left there, we went on to Mr. Derr's and spent the evening very quietly till we were going to bed, when we had some few words.

Thursday [Sept.] 20th. Quite a cold, damp day. Lizzie Houck arrived about 9 o'clock, and about eleven o'clock Mary D., Mary & Kate S., Lizzie Houck & I went out to see to spend the day at Aunt Shriner's. Dr. & Mrs. Cockey of Balt., Mrs. McCannon, & Mrs. Dutrow were there also to spend the day. Lizzie H brought me a note from Tilly Schoolfield. Mr. J. A. J. came down after tea. We had a time playing thimble, and after about 9 we all went back to Mr. Derr's. The gentlemen left about ten or eleven.

Friday [Sept.] 21st. Very pretty day. After dinner Cousin Ed stopped & we were ready. We were all to spend the evening with Mrs. F. Winchester, but I had a letter of Nellie Mering saying she would be up to-morrow, so after going to see Ginny Boyd & Ella Brunner I walked out home. Ginny Boyd wants us to come there Monday afternoon.

Saturday Sept. 22nd. Very pleasant day and I was very busy all morning. Nellie did not arrive by noon, so I gave her up till night, but about three o'clock Emma Houck & Ginny came out & took tea. Mary S., Kate, Mag Derr, Thomas & Ed were out after tea.

* * * * *

Monday [Sept.] 24th. Very pleasant day. After dinner Father took me into town and I went to Catechism, and Mag Derr & I went up to Mrs. Reese's and met Mary D & Mary & Kate S., who had just got in from Lizzie Schell's. Mary & Kate S & I went down to Houcks' and from there to Boyds'. I had no idea of staying but Wils very kindly offered to take me home, so I concluded I would stay & I enjoyed the evening very much. Besides us Mrs. Martz & Misses Appold of Balt. & Miss Clifford took tea with us, & after tea Mary & Meal Kunkel, Dr. McGill, Messrs. Tom Morgan, Ed Shriner, U. Hobbs, B. McCleary, Rev. Mr. Busey, Dave & Wils Boyd [came]. It was quite a merry party and we did not leave till about half-past ten. Wils Boyd brought me out home & Mrs. Hobbs accompanied us. /I had a note from Nellie Mering saying Dr. Martin would bring her up on Wednesday./

Tuesday [Sept.] 25th. Very pleasant day. Mary & Meallie Kunkel were here by nine o'clock and about ten Maggie D, Mary, & Kate S came, and all took dinner with us, & about two o'clock we all started in Kunkels' carryall for town. Met Eugene with the buggy, so Mag Derr & Mary S. got in with him and Kate & I went on to Kunkels' and met Ed S, who took us out to Mr. Derr's. Mr. Johnson arrived first and Mary & I walked down to the bridge with him and met Ed S who came on back with us. About 8, Mary & Meallie K, Messrs Hobbs & Boyd arrived and we spent a very pleasant evening.

Wednesday [Sept.] 26th. Bright beautiful morning. Ed S came about half-past seven & very soon we all started for town, Kate & Ed in buggy & [the] rest of us with Thomas in the carriage. We all saw the girls off. Mag & Lizzie H went to the bridge, and Coz Ed brought me out home and went on to the mill & returned about eleven, and by that time, Dr. Martin & Nellie had arrived. We spent the evening talking, playing cards, etc. It rained hard all afternoon & night. Ed started to go home, but [it] commenced raining, so they both remained over night.

Thursday Sept. 27th. We were up early and had an early breakfast and the gentlemen left very soon. After dinner Nellie & I went into town with Father and called to see Mrs. Winchester & Houcks & found all well; stopped to see Ella B. a few minutes. When we had come home, found Mrs. I. Howard & Marion there. They had spent the afternoon.

Friday [Sept.] 28th. Very pretty. Nellie & I were home all day, took a long walk in the afternoon. I had a note from Mr. Hobbs to-day requesting me to destroy all his notes and excusing himself for trying to order my affections.

Saturday [Sept.] 29th. Very pretty day. I was very busy in the morning baking, etc. Mrs. Denham, Mrs. F. Winchester & Evie were out to tea but left immediately after.

* * * * *

Monday Oct. 1st [1855]. Very pretty day. Nellie & I walked over to Mrs. I. Howard's after dinner and spent the afternoon there. Jenny Adams was there. Mr. J. A. J. arrived soon after we returned and sat till about eleven.

Tuesday [Oct.] 2nd. Nellie & I went in about eleven and spent a very pleasant day with Evie Winchester, & returned home through the rain.

Wednesday Oct. 3rd. Quite clear and very bright. Nellie and I started in good time to go out to Mr. Derr's. Stopped awhile in town. I was to see Mary Kunkel a few minutes. We arrived out there about eleven. Mrs.

1855

Dunham and Evie came about twelve. We spent a delightful day. Soon after dinner we all jumped into the wagon and went on the island and gathered pawpaws and afterwards went over and got weighed at Ed's. Ed S came to Mr. Derr's as we were eating supper, and he and Tommy accompanied us home and sat till nearly ten.

Thursday, Oct. 4th. Very pleasant day. After dinner Nellie, Mother and I went over & spent the afternoon with Emma Howard. Mary Kunkel arrived soon after we left and John came with her over to Mrs. Howard['s]. We returned about dusk. I wrote a letter to Lou Hersh.

Friday [Oct.] 5th. Quite [a] pleasant day. Just as we were ready to start to Uncle Adams', Lizzie & Emma Houck arrived, so Nellie took them in the buggy & Mary Kunkel & I walked over. We spent a very pleasant afternoon. Lizzie & Emma H. went home. Dr. McGill & Mr. Schaffer spent the evening with us.

* * * * *

Sunday [Oct.] 7th. Quite cold again. Nellie, Mary K & I went into church and stopped at Mr. Kunkel's a short time, & after church went down to the hotel to tea & Cousin Ed & Wils Boyd [came] after tea. Cousin Ed walked down street with us. Mr. J. A. J. was here.

Monday [Oct.] 8th. Quite a pleasant day. Nellie & I went into town and spent the day with Mrs. Frank Winchester. I was at catechism and from thence, Mag went with me to Mrs. W's for a few minutes. When we left Mrs. W's and came down street to meet Father [but he] had gone out home, so I borrowed shoes of Ella Brunner and Marty W walked out with us. He returned immediately to town.

Tuesday Oct. 9th. Nellie and I went in town early, called at Ella B's a few minutes, then went down to Mrs. Kunkel's to spend the day. Nellie and I were out shopping a while in the after-noon. At night Cle Gifford & Ginny Boyd, Tom Derr, Cousin Ed, Dr. Delasmuth, [and] Dr. McGill were in to spend the evening. Time passed so pleasantly that we did not leave till half-past ten. [We] found Mary H. Smith & D. Horman at home. Ed staid till about 11 1/2, & we all soon retired.

Wednesday Oct. 10th. Very pleasant day. Dr. Horman took Mary H & Nellie into town and I was very busy till about twelve, when Mary & Mag

Derr arrived. Very soon the girls came home and we had dinner. Dr. Harmon returned in the evening, and soon after tea Tom Derr came, & the girls left about 9 o'clock. I had such a nice long letter from Mary & Kate S.

Thursday [Oct.] 11th. Very pleasant morning. Mary H & Dr. Harmon started for home about 9 o'clock, and after dinner Nellie and I were over to Mrs. Roderick's a few minutes.

Friday [Oct.] 12th. Cloudy damp day. After dinner I took Nellie into town and left her at Mr. Houck's.

* * * * *

Monday [Oct.] 15th. Was very busy all day helping Jane to wash paint. After Hannah & John Lewis came and spent the evening with me.

Tuesday [Oct.] 16th. Wednesday 17th. Very pleasant days and very busy whitewashing & cleaning up. Received an invitation to Mrs. Fout's party.

Thursday Oct. 18th. Very pleasant day. After dinner Mother & I walked to Mrs. Clingan's and spent the afternoon. Annie C. & I were over to Mrs. M. Keefer's a little time but only Miss Caroline was at home.

Friday [Oct.] 19th. Very pleasant morning. I went into town early with Father. I was at Kunkels' a short time and then went up and took dinner with Mrs. Winchester. I sent a paper to Lou Hersh so she could see about the cattle show. About three o'clock Nellie walked down street with me and I came on out home.

Saturday [Oct.] 20th. Foggy but we thought it would clear away, so Mother & I went over to Uncle E. Scholl's, and from thence Annabelle, Miss Hughes & I went with Randolf in the carriage, & Mother & Aunt Mary went in our buggy, up to see the Buckey Meeting cornerstone laid. Met Mr. Marlow & Mr. Crampton there; they were very attentive. We returned home although raining slightly. /I was at Mr. Grafton Fouts party tonight returning home by eleven o'clock. Nice eatings./

Sunday [Oct.] 21st. Beautiful day. Mother & I were in to church. About two o'clock I walked over to Mr. Roderick's & remained till after four. Found Mr. Riser & Jeremiah Cramer there.

1855

Monday Oct. 22nd. Pleasant all day. N. Mering returned with Father in the evening from town and remained over night. John Derr was out after tea and brought me a pair of corsets[24] and a note from Mary S. He had a great deal to talk about and left before ten or about. Mary's note was "short but sweet".

Tuesday [Oct.] 23rd. Rained all day hard. Notwithstanding, Mother went into town and deposited her knit shirt and brought me a package from M. H. Smith containing the pattern of her basque body & sleeves, and some boots and a note from cousin B saying it had been delayed a week.

Wednesday [Oct.] 24th. Still raining till late in the evening, so I got myself to work and commenced making my black silk body.

Thursday [Oct.] 25th. Very clear but cold. Indeed, some said there were some flakes of snow fell. Father took me into town and I stopped for Ella B. and about eleven o'clock we started for the grounds of the Agricultural Fair. It was thronged with visitors and every one seemed to be interested in the one great affair. I met numerous friends and, amongst strangers, Gene Kephart. Dr. McGill met Ella & I at the gate and was our escort all morning. As Ella complained of being cold we returned to Mr. Markel's about twelve, & I went to Mrs. Fout's a short time to see Gene. Mr. J. A. J. saw me and joined, and we went together over to Mr. M's. He told us the ladies would not ride that day so we did not go till after dinner. Mr. J. A. J. took dinner with us and [ac]companied us. We remained till tolerably late then went up street. Had Mr. Baslan for a beau a short distance. After tea Ella & I started for the Ladies' fair and met a friend of E's, Mr. Rohrback, who accompanied us to see the <u>Democratic</u>[25] <u>speaking</u> and from there to the fair. We had some fun behind Gin[ny] Boyd's table and returned home by ten o'clock, well pleased with day's performance.

Friday 26 Oct. Another bright [day] & not quite so cold. Mary Kunkel came about ten, & about eleven Mrs. Markel, Mary K & I started for the

---

[24]"In the 1830's and 1840's the corset emphasized the long waist, but by 1855 the waist was quite small because the upper bust was meant to be visible amid the voluminous folds of the dresses." Carl Kohler, *A History of Costume* (New York, 1963), p. 431.

[25]"The anti-Americans have political Speaking to day at the Court House. The Frederick Cattle Show is Now in full operation crowded with Natives from the County." Engelbrecht, *Diary*, II, 663. The Democrats were speaking against the Know Nothings, the "American" Party.

[fair]grounds. We soon came across Ed & had him the rest of the day. He took dinner with us. There was a large crowd & the ladies rode today[26] & the address was delivered by Mr. Colbert, Pres. of State Fair. Mr. J. made numerous apologies for leaving us so suddenly yesterday. Dr. McGill was my escort again. Ella, Ed S, Tom Derr, & I were all up at Houcks' a few minutes to see Nellie & all. Mary & Mag Derr were there also. Cousin Ed called for us after tea and we were at the Fair again and spent a pleasant evening. Mr. Hobbs had told E. we were to have a serenade & we heard a very sweet one.

Saturday [Oct.] 27th. Another cold day. I was up at Houcks' about an hour this morning. After I returned Ella & I got ready & started, met Maggie Derr just before I went in the gate and soon with Houck's [sic]. Nellie & I had a seat very high up to see them ride. We had an excellent place to hear the premiums read, but the wind blew in an opposite direction, and I comforted myself with a nice chat with Dr. McGill & some other friends. Our unknown friends were as usual very nice and wanted to know of Dr. Mc why we had not noticed their serenade, when we were informed [sic] them on account of our having no acquaintance. When the performances were all ended we went down to Mr. Markel's, Dr. McG with me & Wils Boyd with Ella B. After dinner E & I started for Houcks', met Mr. J. A. J. coming down to see us, & took him up to Houcks' with us & sat an hour or so. Bid Nellie good bye & left. Mr. J. A. J. sat about an hour with us & went home & I came too. I had a nice letter of Lou Hersh.

Sunday Oct. 28th. Very windy. I was all ready in the buggy to go to church when it commenced blowing so hard I gave up the idea of going. Thomas Derr & Beverly Buck were here after tea and were very agreeable & time passed quickly away.

Monday [Oct.] 29th. Pleasant day. Mr. Mering came out from town and remained all night; said Nelly & he arrived safe at home Saturday night. I wrote letter to Mary Sauerwein & note to Kate.

Tuesday [Oct.] 30th. Pleasant day. Father started to Balt. before I was up. I feel my bad cold very much. Mr. M. left about nine.

---

[26]"There were six ladies in the female equisterianism. Some of them acquitted themselves very well. The ladies department was also very good. They had fine assortments of sweetmeats, jellies, some beautiful specimens of fancy needlework. The ladies who rode each received $10." Derr diary.

1855

Wednesday [Oct.] 31st. A very warm day for the season. Dr. McGill & Mr. Schaeffer were out & spent the evening with me. They were very agreeable.

* * * * *

Friday Nov. 2nd [1855]. Very warm day again but very dark at night with few drops of rain. Mother & John went into meet Father, who is to come from Balt. tonight. They got home about nine o'clock & he was very pleased with his trip.

Saturday [Nov.] 3rd. Raining in hard showers all day but nevertheless Father found a short time to go in for the Sofa & Rocking Chair.

Sunday Nov. 4th. Very bright & clear in the morning but clouded over before noon. I went into church, stopped for Ella B and we went up to church together. Mother called & brought us home.

Monday [Nov.] 5th. I awoke this morning with dreadful pain in my eye.

Tuesday [Nov.] 6th. Still my eye pains. I had a note from Ginny Adams wanting some dahlia roots.

Wednesday [Nov.] 7th. Election day[27], rather clear weather, no rain anyway. My pain in my eye.

Thursday [Nov.] 8th. Pretty day. Mother insisted on it, so we got ready & went out to Uncle Chas. S's; stopped awhile [at] Aunt Artz['s]. When we got to uncle's found all the family away, so we followed & found them in Walkersville at Rhineharts'; took tea & returned to Uncle's. Mrs. Biser is

---

[27]"The election in Frederick County Md. Terminated in the Complete Triumph of the American or Know Nothing Ticket by an average Majority of 732." Engelbrecht, *Diary*, II, 664.

"It is unsafe for ladies to be alone on the street at nights, for the last couple of weeks such as a constant bustle of shooting cossacks, firing of pistols, ascending rockets, burning tar barrels, and everything which tends to excite, and attract a multitude of rowdies and men of every class and order. All this is caused by politics. The great contest between the Native Americans and Democrats, filling the offices for Congress. I believe the American ticket has been entirely successful." Derr diary.

1855

staying there also. Mr. Slifer was there after night. /Found my neck all broken out with Erysipelas./

Friday [Nov.] 9th. About 9 o'clock Uncle & Aunt May, Mother & I started for Mrs. Duderar. We took dinner & started for home about half-past three and got home all safe. Found Miss Buckey & Mrs. L. Fout had been here this afternoon and also Mr. J. A. Johnson at night.

Saturday [Nov.] 10th. Very pleasant day. When Father came home at dinner he had letter from Nellie Mering and one of Harry Smith containing cards of invitation for Kunkels & me to Mr. & Mrs. G. Reiper's Reception. Father sent Dr. Dorsey out to see me; he made very light of it and left some pills & Davis powders for me.

Sunday [Nov.] 11th. Not a very bright day. About 2 o'clock Ed S & Wils Boyd were out to see me & very soon Annabelle Scholl & Mrs. B. C. Marlow came out. Mrs. M. & A staid till after tea but the others left before. Ginny Adams was up for a few minutes.

Monday [Nov.] 12th. Found my eye entirely swollen shut on getting up, so we sent in for the doctor he gave me other medicine and said I had taken cold. I had a nice long letter of Mary & Kate Sauerwein.

Tuesday [Nov.] 13th. Beautiful day. Dr. was out to see me again but thinks there is no necessity to come again. Marion Howard was here for a couple of hours this morning and [after] dinner Mrs. Rhoderick, & soon after she left Mrs. Peter Fout & Mrs. Margaret Clabaugh were here for a short time.

Wednesday Nov. 14th. Very pleasant day. Mrs. I. Howard was over and spent the afternoon and also Ginny Adams for an hour or so. Mr. Riser was here also.

Thursday [Nov.] 15th. Thanksgiving Day.[28] Maggie & Mary Derr came about two o'clock and spent the afternoon. Thomas came for them about five and took tea with us. They left about seven o'clock. Hannah Haines was here for a few minutes too.

---

[28]"Thanksgiving. This is a day appointed by the government to be kept as a holy-day to show our gratitude to the Almightily Provider for all his kindness during the year. But this day is not generally kept as it should be." Derr diary.

1855

Friday [Nov.] 16th. Ever a memorable day to many for the Grand Know Nothing Barbecue, and to me also, for Bill running off with the buggy & breaking so much and endangering Mother & John's lives, though they came off nearly unhurt. I went into town about 2 o'clock and stopped for Ella, and we went up street first to see Mary Kunkel to hear the news and then round town some and at Mr. Wm. Bantz'. Cousin Ed was with us some on the street and then we were joined by Mr. J. A. J., who came up to Mr. Markel's with us and sat some time. Mr. John Lewis was in too. Mary Derr came to stay all night. Old Mr. Lewis & Hannah were there too. I can give no account of the illumination or any thing else after I saw Billy running so.

* * * * *

Sunday [Nov.] 18th. Quite a pleasant day but we were all at home. About half-past four o'clock, Ed S. & Geo. Sauerwein came. G. came up Friday night. He looks badly, I think, but seems in excellent spirits. Mr. J. A. J. arrived just as we were at tea. G & Ed left about 8, and Mr. J. about half-past nine. They all had lots to say.

Monday [Nov.] 19th. Quite cool day. Mrs. Buckey & Annie, Mary & Mrs. Lewis Fout were up & spent the afternoon.

Tuesday [Nov.] 20th. Very much colder. No company except the gentleman who is surveying the co. with reference to making a map of the co.[29] Wrote to Mary H. Smith.

* * * * *

Friday [Nov.] 23rd. Rather cold, but nevertheless Mother & I went into town to spend the afternoon at Kunkels'. I stopped awhile at Ella B's. Cousin Ed S. was at Kunkels' for a few minutes. We came home soon after six o'clock & very soon Mr. J. Lewis came and brought me a note from Hannah to spend to-morrow evening with her.

Saturday [Nov.] 24th. Very pretty day. I wrote Cousin Ed S a note to meet me at Mrs. Markel's, also a note to E. that I would start from there. I got

---

[29]Isaac Bond published in 1858 a large map of Frederick County, using a subscription method for payment. (If one paid him $10 his name would be listed where his farm or business existed.) A copy hangs in the C. Burr Artz Library.

into town about dusk, and about seven Mr. J. A. Johnson & Cousin Ed both arrived to take me to Mr. Lewis'[s] but as the Old Gent had been too attentive Ella did not go. I went with Ed. Mr. J. followed us. There was quite a large party to celebrate Hannah's birth night. Everything passed off well and we all dispersed about eleven. I was introduced to Mr. Dod Gambril and a Mr. O'Neal & I believe I knew the generality of the others.

Sunday [Nov.] 25th. Rained part of the day but I went into church; stopped for Ella, [and] gave her the orange apple cake Mrs. L. had sent her. We went to church and Derrs insisted upon my going home with them, so I went. Cousin Ed was over & spent the evening with us. We did not retire till nearly twelve.

Monday [Nov.] 26th. Very pretty morning but windy in the afternoon. Maggie Derr came into town with me and we went together to Houcks' and Mrs. Markel's and then I came out home.

Tuesday [Nov.] 27th. Very pleasant day. Mother & I went into town and were shopping awhile, and then Mother went on home and I stopped for Ella B, who came out home with me. Mr. Hobbs & Dr. McGill were out at night and spent a very agreeable evening, left about eleven.

Wednesday [Nov.] 28th. Rather cloudy day. Lizzie Nickle was here during the afternoon. I wrote a letter to Mary Sauerwein this morning. Ella went home in the evening. I was to stay all night but fell out of the cart so came home again. Mr. John Lewis was over at night.

Thursday [Nov.] 29th. Very windy day. Ginny & Fanny Adams & Marion Howard were over to spend the afternoon. They expected to see Ella B. here.

Friday [Nov.] 30th. Pleasant afternoon, so, notwithstanding my black eye, I went in to town to meet Mag & Mary Derr but they were so long in coming, so Mrs. Markel & I started up street alone, met them about half-way down. So [we] went to look for bonnets and afterwards called to see Callie Bantz. [We] met Ella B. & Mrs. M. there [and] intended to see Jane Ramsburg but too late, so Derrs & E went to Mrs. M, & I came on down street & I came out home.

Saturday Dec. 1st [1855]. Very pleasant day. I went into town in the afternoon to see Annie Bentz [a] short time, also to see Mary Kunkel, &

1855

stopped at Mrs. M's a few minutes. Had the patterns & a letter from Mary Sauerwein.

Sunday Dec. 2nd. Very pleasant day. I went into church, stopped for Ella B. and went to church with them. Maggie Derr came home with me. Cousin Ed & Tom Derr escorted us to the hotel. Cousin Ed was out in the afternoon.

Monday [Dec.] 3rd. Rather windy. Mother, Mag D & I went into town, called for Ella B. & then all went up to Houcks' and from there to the store and made some purchases.

Tuesday [Dec.] 4th. Pleasant day. Mother was gone to town. Mrs. I. Howard was here for a short time. Mrs. McClain & Har[r]iet Fleming were here to spend day; Mag Derr and I went into town. We were shopping & to see Houcks, Mrs. Markel's, Mrs. Reese's. [We] saw Ed & asked him to take us home.

Wednesday Dec. 5th. Cut out the lining to my cloak and was busy with it all day. Mrs. Clabaugh & two children & Mrs. P. Fout were here to dinner; left soon after for Mr. Lewis Fout's. Ella B & Dr. McGill were out after tea and spent the evening.

Thursday [Dec.] 6th. I was very busy all day with my cloak. I had a note from Ginny for a pattern and she sent me The Watchtower.[30]

Friday [Dec.] 7th. Pleasant day. Still at my cloak & at night read The Watchtower.

* * * * *

Wednesday [Dec.] 12th. Quite cold yet, but not so windy. After dinner Mother & I went over to Mrs. I. Howard's and spent the afternoon. Kate & Mary Smith were there for a few minutes. Dr. McGill was here after tea and

---

[30] *The Watchtower* was a religious family magazine printed in Portland, Maine from 1852 to 1895. This is not to be confused with later publication of the same name. *National Union Catalog* (Library of Congress, 1956).

spent the evening. When he left [he] handed me Tupper's Practical Philosophy[31] very handsomely bound for a Philepoena.

Thursday Dec. 13th. Very pleasant day. Butchering day, very, very, busy.

* * * * *

Monday [Dec.] 17th. Very pleasant day. Quilted my skirt to-day.

Tuesday [Dec.] 18th. Lovely day. After tea Ella B. & Dr. McGill were out and sat till about 9 o'clock, and Mr. J. A. J. was out and staid till half-past ten.

Wednesday [Dec.] 19th. Rather pretty day. Mother and I went down to Reichs and spent the afternoon. Mrs. I. Howard was there also. They seem in pretty good spirits.

Thursday [Dec.] 20th. Very pleasant day. I wrote to Mary S. for my dress bonnet, etc.

Friday [Dec.] 21st. I was in town a short time this morning and saw Ella B and did some shopping.

Saturday [Dec.] 22nd. Rained all day long

Sunday [Dec.] 23rd. Delightful day but I did not go to town. About one o'clock Mr. J. Kramer arrived, and soon after dinner Mr. K and I walked over to Mr. Roderick['s] and about three looked over home & found two buggies hitched, and then we went home and found Messrs. W. Boyd, J. A. J., & Mr. Hobbs, also Dr. McGill. Messrs. K., B. & J. left after tea, & Houcks about eight, but the Dr. & Mr. Hobbs remained till ten o'clock. They were all in excellent spirits.

Monday [Dec.] 24th. Rather cloudy, but nevertheless I went into town & remained over night with Ella B. We were up street a shor[t] time & Cousin Ed S. came down with us. Dr. McGill was to see us at night. He was in admirable spirits and beat us at cards.

---

[31]*Tupper's Practical Philosophy* by Martin Farquhar was a book of theories and arguments and some poetry, published by C. H. Pierce, Boston, 1848. *Ibid.*

1855

Tuesday [Dec.] 25th. Christmas day. Raining all day, but [it] did not prevent some of our friends from calling and children from getting their Christmas gift of Mrs. M. Mr. Robach was there through the day and at night. Dr. McGill called at four and remained till eleven. Mr. Boyd [came] at nine & staid till eleven.

Wednesday [Dec.] 26th. Very windy, but clear. Ella and I were out at Cal Bantz['s], Houcks', & new Episcopal Church[32], and after dinner, Houcks were in to see us. Derrs are staying there. We were at express office and Mrs. Val Brunner's. /I walked home with Father./

Thursday [Dec.] 27th. Still cold and windy. I walked into town & met Mary Derr and I went shopping with her.

Friday [Dec.] 28th. More pleasant. Mother went into town after dinner, and when she came home I received my long looked for bandbox, everything safe & sound. Mr. Cox came out about two and sat till some time after four. Letter from Mary.

Saturday [Dec.] 29th. Snowed all day. I wrote to Mary Sauerwein.

Sunday [Dec.] 30th. Very pretty but I did not go to town, but about seven Mr. J. A. J. came and sat till half-past ten o'clock. He was in such excellent spirits.

Monday [Dec.] 31st. Rather a pleasant day. I went into town for a short time; saw Ella and was up street a short time. [I was] at Boyds' a short time and returned home and spent the evening with the family, and so ends 1855. How many things to regret.

---

[32]See note 9, 1856.

1856

"So ends July, and many pleasant reminiscences of the past are connected with this <u>Volume</u> of my journals, and also some regrets..."

Tuesday Jan 1st. [1856]. A very cold [day] but nevertheless spent it delightfully. Quite early I started for Derrs; took Ella along. Found the family all well and John at home too; very soon Mr. J. A. J. arrived and cousin Ed stopped, too, for a while. We had a very fine dinner and all seemed to enjoy it. Henry and Tench Schley brought Annie Bentz, Sis Haskins & Miss Carmack out and sat an hour or so. After an early tea we started home and Mag, John & Thomas came with us. I made a delightful beginning for the New Year.

Wednesday [Jan.] 2nd. Rather cloudy. I was in town a few minutes to see Houcks & Annie Scholl.

* * * * *

Monday [Jan.] 7th. Still so cold. I went into town & stopped for Mrs. Markell, and we went out to see Aunt M. Artz for an hour or so. E. came home & staid over night with me.

Tuesday [Jan.] 8th. Very pleasant day. I went into town with Ella & we went together to see Kunkels, and as usual got news. Old Mr. Lewis was here in the afternoon and invited me there, & cousin Ed came to take me but it proved too cold.

Wednesday Jan. 9th. I think coldest day yet. After dinner I went into town and stopped at Kunkels' and cousin Ed joined us and we all went out to old Mr. Lewis's for a short time. I stopped at Mrs. M.['s] for a short time before I came home.

* * * * *

1856

Sunday [Jan.] 13th. Very pretty day. About two o'clock Mr. J. Cramer arrived and wanted [me] to go to singing Association[1] with him, so I concluded I would go if he would take another girl, so we called for Mary Kunkel and went on out to Mr. Derr's. Mr. Ed Birely soon came, and after tea we all got ready and went over to Ceresville and heard a few tunes, and returned to Mr. Derr's for a short time, then on to town. Dr. McGill was down at Kunkels' for us and waited till we came home, and Mr. C. & Dr. remained till eleven o'clock.

Monday [Jan.] 14th. Rather pleasant day. Meallie Kunkel and I were out shopping awhile, then I went over to Mrs. Markel's and waited for Father, who came about noon.

Tuesday [Jan.] 15th. Quite pleasant day. At night Dr. McGill and Mr. Schaeffer were out and spent the evening.

Wednesday [Jan.] 16th. Lovely day. I went into [town] about twelve and stopped for Ella B. till after their dinner hour, when we got ready and went out to shop & visit. We were at Houcks', Mrs. Brunner's, etc. I enjoyed the walk very much. Mrs. Johnson was to see us a while, an hour or so. I had a letter from Gene Kephart.

* * * * *

Friday [Jan.] 18th. Quite pleasant day. Father took me into town and I went up to Mrs. Winchester's to wait for Maggie & Mary Derr. Saw Miss Cramer there. When Mag & Mary came we went to see Mrs. D. Schley, Kunkels' and to old Mrs. Bantz's. [We] saw Mr. J. A. J. on the street and told him that I would not stay in town tonight, but he should bring Ella out. Said he would. After leaving the girls down street I went to Mrs. M's. Mrs. Derr called to me saying Father was sick, so I hurried over & found he had one of his old attacks. I saw Ella a minute or so & Mr. J. was there. Mr. Derr brought me out home and Mother & John went in the sleigh & brought Father; he was much better. Mr. J. arrived about seven & wanted me to sleigh with him, so we took a ride to meet them, and then came on home all together, Mag D. & Ed S., Thomas D., Mary D., & G. Houck. All seemed to enjoy themselves & left about half-past ten o'clock. Ella did not come on account of sister's indisposition.

---

[1]Singing school was near the Derrs' on Route 26 across the Monocacy Bridge at Ceresville. According to Mary Derr's diary, the Derrs often went there. Derr diary.

1856

Saturday [Jan.] 19th. Very pleasant day. I was in town a few minutes; saw Mrs. M. & Ella. They insisted on my coming in for Monday, and Uncle John Ogle & Catherine spent the day with us. Willie Adams was here to see how Father was.

* * * * *

Monday [Jan.] 21st. Blowing & snowing till late in the evening but, as I was anxious to hear Prof. Howard & Dr. McGill play, I went in & remained over night, but, Lo, the gentlemen did not make their appearance.

Tuesday [Jan.] 22nd. Mother sent in for me early as we expected Uncle Elias's family but I was disappointed again by their non-appearance. A very unagreeable day.

Wednesday [Jan.] 23rd. Quite cold. I was in town a short time late in the evening; did some shopping and received a nice letter of Mary Sauerwein.

Thursday [Jan.] 24th. A clear, cold day. Mother & I went out to spend the day at Ed S's; found them butchering but they would have us remain. Mr. & Mrs. Bierly & son from Westminster were there also. We left about three o'clock & stopped a while at Derrs'; Mag was not home. Soon after I got home saw a sleigh coming and found it to contain Lou & Sam Hersh. I was delighted to see them. They had come from [New Oxford] to-day. After warming nicely and a little firing we were ready to receive Ella & Dr. McGill, who arrived pretty soon. Dr. McGill brought me candy, & Lou Hersh a bottle of perfume. We all spent the evening very pleasantly and E & Dr. left about ten, and Sam retired about eleven. We remained downstairs till after twelve, talking of the past and of our future, particularly Lou's.

Friday [Jan.] 25th. Quite cold, so we did not go to town as we thought of, but I wrote Maggie a note saying they should come out. Mr. H. looks so well, so handsome, as he used to be, & Lou is the same she always was. We were upstairs a couple of hours, and while there a couple of gentlemen arrived, Mr. Hobbs and Mr. Dorsey of Howard Co. They left before tea, and we three spent our time pleasantly together till about eight o'clock, when Mag, Mary & Thomas D. arrived and staid till after ten o'clock. About eleven, Mr. H. retired & we staid up an hour or so longer and talked on various subjects and Lou's friend, Mr. C. L. Clippinger. I hope he is every way deserving of her.

1856

Saturday [Jan.] 26th. We were up rather early, as Lou & Sam were in a hurry to start, and they bid us adieu shortly after eight o'clock. Mr. H had asked me yesterday to exchange our letters and I gave my ready consent of course, and this morning we had an opportunity and exchanged but after he left I found there was one of mine wanting, but I do not know whether it was detained designedly or not, but I have copies of all. I was in town a short time this evening. I had a paper from Mr. Cox to-day. Wrote to Cousin I. Harry Smith to-night.

* * * * *

Monday [Jan.] 28th. Rather pleasant day. About noon I had a note from J. H. Gambrill, saying some of my friends from town would be out at night. Father had another sick spell so I went to town to shop. About eight o'clock Dr. McGill & Ella B arrived, and very soon Messrs. J. & L. Gambrill, Hobbs, & Prof. Howard, bringing Annie, Mary & Ella Schley; they remained till nearly eleven o'clock and all left apparently well pleased. I enjoyed the music very much. Prof. H. had his violin along & he & Annie S. played some very brilliant pieces together.

Tuesday [Jan.] 29th. Rather cloudy but no ways cold for the season. I stopped for Ella B & we together went to see Kunkels and did some shopping, and we came on together down street & very soon Mother stopped for me.

Wednesday [Jan.] 30th. I took Jane as far as town, then went to Mrs. I. Howard's and sat a couple of hours. Found Misses Maggie H. and Martha Rice there. I returned home by five o'clock. Commenced reading <u>Miss Brinkley's Book</u>[2].

Thursday [Jan.] 31st. Very pleasant day. After an early dinner I went in & stopped for Ella & found she had an invitation to accompany Mr. Wils Boyd out to Mrs. Derr's to-night. I went up street and found that Mr. Hobbs was coming out for me, so I told them I would meet them at Mrs. M's. Ella & I then went out to Uncle Adams' and paid a visit of a couple hours. Met with J's friend, Miss Pool & some other company, and then came home for a few minutes, and into town again. Mrs. M. had a headache again, but she got better & insisted on E's going. Mrs. Hobbs came about a quarter before

---

[2] Miss Brinkley's book has not been identified.

seven and we waited till Wils came about half-past seven and then started and joined part[y] at K's, then on we went to Mrs. Derr's. Tilly Jackson was with H. Boyd, G. H. with J. Sifford, & Allen Lail with Lizzie & Emma H. All seemed to enjoy themselves. Mr. H rendered himself very agreeable. We returned home after eleven & E & I talked till after twelve down stairs, & I did not sleep till after 2 o'clock. I was very sorry to find that I had lost my cameo earring.

Feb. 1st. Friday [1856]. Very pretty day. Mrs. M. better. They did not come for me till nearly twelve o'clock, when we came out home, and we started off again. I stopped in town, and was to see Mary Kunkel a short time, and Aunt J. Scholl, & at Mrs. M's. She is still better.

Feb. 2nd. Saturday. Beautiful day. I went in town after dinner, did a little shopping & came up street & stopped Ella's awhile; met Mr. J. A. J. there, who wanted her to come out with him. She could not. I came home with him and he remained till after ten.

Sunday Feb. 3rd. Very cold. Mother & I went into town. I stopped for Ella B and we went to church together. Cousin Ed came down street with us. Mrs. M. is up to-day.

Monday [Feb.] 4th. So very cold that I did not go out to sleigh.

Tuesday [Feb.] 5th. Somewhat warmer. Mother was in town to-day and when she came home she brought me a package from the P O containing a handsome book from Mr. Hobb, *Great Truths by Great Authors*[3]. Wrote to Gene Kephart.

Wednesday [Feb.] 6th. Cloudy most of the day. I wrote a long letter to Mary Sauerwein. At night Dr. McGill, Messrs. Schaeffer & Howard were out & spent the evening. Dr. had his violin and we were favored with some very fine music.

Thursday [Feb.] 7th. Not very pleasant day, but as I had a note from Ginny A. to meet her in town to-day, I concluded I would go but did not find her at

---

[3]This was a collection of quotations, maxims, and proverbs of writers of all ages. It was published by Lippincott, Philadelphia, 1853.

1856

Mrs. W's, so came on down to Mrs. Markel's, where they made me remain over night. Dr. McGill was there at night.

Friday [Feb.] 8th. Rather cloudy & damp. Ella & I came out home with Father about noon. There was no company at night.

Saturday [Feb.] 9th. No company all day. Mother went over to Uncle E. Scholl's and I took Ella in town when they came back.

Sunday [Feb.] 10th. Mother and I were in town & I went back to remain over night, and went to hear the Rev. M. Busey preach with Dr. McGill.

Monday Feb. 11th. Warm and damp. Mother sent in for me early, and after dinner Mother and I went over to Uncle E. Scholl's[4] and found him dying; and as Aunt Mary wished me to stay, Mother said I could. There were plenty to do everything and every one seemed so kind. I was up till after two o'clock & then slept till about five.

Tuesday [Feb.] 12th. Windy and snow squalls & very cold. There seemed to be a constant run of company coming and going. There were numerous gentlemen to sit up and I staid up only till after one, as there were many others to attend to things.

Wednesday [Feb.] 13th. We were up early to have everything ready, and persons generally were collected by nine o'clock and the funeral left about [sic]. It was very long, and my uncle seemed to be lamented & kindly remembered by every one. His remains were deposited in a vault after services in the church. We then came on home.

Thursday [Feb.] 14th. Mother & I were at Mrs. Clingan's to tea and I remained in town over night with E. Dr. McGill was there and we expected D. S., but he was not well enough.

Friday [Feb.] 15th. Pretty day. Ella & I were up street [a] short time. I received two valentines and letters from Lou Hersh & Mary Sauerwein. I came on home & brought Mrs. Markel & Mrs. Derr out with me to spend the day. Frank & Annie Clingan & Marion Howard were here to tea and left about five.

---

[4]Elias Scholl, see note 40, 1851.

Saturday [Feb.] 16th. Very warm for the season. About 2 or three o'clock Cousin Harry S. arrived. We took a sleigh ride and came to an end in the road, where H. had to lift the sleigh some and I had to sit on the fence. I received another valentine from Middletown. Cousin Ed Shriner & Hannah Lewis were here to tea and left about seven o'clock.

Sunday [Feb.] 17th. Very cold day. John took me into town and I went to church. Mr. Johnson came down with Ella & me and they would have me to stay, so Mr. Johnson came down for us, but as it was so cold he said something about not staying, so we went without him. We were pleased at Presbyterian Church[5]. We remained till after seven o'clock and then Mr. J. A. J. brought me out home. We found they had retired at home but we [had] made Mother lie awake. Mr. J. sat till about 9 1/2 o'clock.

Monday [Feb.] 18th. Cloudy day. I wrote to Mary Sauerwein. Wrote to Lou Hersh.

Tuesday [Feb.] 19th. I was in town and Ella & I were at Houcks' and with Call at several places.

Wednesday [Feb.] 20th. Cloudy day. I was in town & went with Ella B to have a tooth filled at Dr. Jenks[6]. We were at Houcks' a short time and then met Dr. McGill on the street, [who] said he would be out at night. About seven o'clock, Dr. McGill & Mr. Schaeffer arrived and remained till after eleven. Ella & I both received invitations to go to Mrs. Derr's tomorrow.

Thursday [Feb.] 21st. Clear & very warm. E & I were troubled for fear the snow would all go. About five o'clock Mr. Wm. Cox arrived, and very soon Dr. McGill & Mr. Schaeffer arrived with their sleighs to take us to Derrs'. About seven o'clock we all started. Mr. Cox would not accompany us. It was a very pleasant evening & [we] returned by eleven o'clock.

---

[5]Established in 1780 as the "English" Presbyterian Church at the corner of Fourth and Bentz Streets, a new building was completed in 1825 on West Second Street, where it is still being used today. The pastor from 1855-1857 was Rev. Jacob W. B. Kerr. Mary Frear Keeler *et al*, *The Frederick United Presbyterian Church: Chapters in Its History 1780-1980* (Frederick, 1980), p. 95.

[6]The office of Dr. Jenks, Margaret's dentist, was located on the upper floor of a building on the north side of Patrick Street, west of Market Street. *Williams' Directory*, p. 20.

1856

Friday Feb. 22nd. Another very warm day. Ella went in with Mother early and I went in after dinner. Stopped at Mrs. M's [and] found Miss Entler spending the day there. Very soon Mrs. M & I went out visiting & were very agreeably entertained by Aunt J. Scholl, Mrs. B. F. Winchester & Mad[am] Pearson, and then returned to Mrs. M's. About seven o'clock Dr. McGill & Mr. Schaeffer arrived, and very soon we started for the Irving Association and spent [a] very pleasant evening there in hearing <u>good</u> music, an oration by Mr. Hoffman Roen, [and] by Mr. Seabrook[7]. Dr. McGill rendered himself very agreeable & treated us to candy. Maggie, Mary, John & Thomas Derr went over & sat a while with us; gents left half-past eleven o'clock.

Saturday [Feb.] 23rd. Pleasant morning. Ella & I were out nearly all morning together at Call's to see them, & the rest was shopping. Saw Mr. Sam Preston at M. Markel's store. We were at Kunkel's [a] short time to tell them to let Schleys know we would be down at night. I went out home about twelve and immediately after dinner slept till nearly four, when [I] dressed myself to go to town. I received a package & letter of Mary Sauerwein, also [a] letter of Gene Kephart. I stopped at Mrs. Markel's a few minutes then went on to Kunkels'. Soon after six o'clock Dennis Dorsey arrived and very soon Dr. McGill & Schaeffer and quite shortly Maggie & John Derr, and then we all went down to Schleys'[8] and spent a very pleasant evening. They are a very pleasant family and seem to entertain so well. All returned before eleven o'clock.

Sunday Feb. 24th. Very pleasant day. Mary K & I started early and went over to Mrs. M's to get my cloak and then went to church. Mag, Mary & John Derr went down to K's with us but I did not remain to dinner. Tom & John Derr were both to tea. After tea, at church time Dr. McGill & Messrs. Schaeffer, J. A. Johnson, E. Shriner & T. Derr arrived and we had a beau apiece to accompany us to Episcopal Church[9]. John Derr & John Gifford

---

[7]"First meeting this winter. Oration and reading of Washington's 'farewell address' by W. D. Willis, poem by Seabrook. Excellent music by Proffs Howard and Ide." Derr diary.

[8]Dr. F. Schley a druggist, sold jewelry and fancy goods and had his store and residence on the south side of Patrick Street between Market and Court Streets. *Williams' Directory*, p. 34.

[9]All Saints Parish was founded in 1742. The first Episcopal Church was located on East All Saints Street. In 1814 a new church was built on South Court Street using a design by Henry McCleery. The present church on West Church Street facing City Hall was opened in 1856. Ernest Helfenstein, *History of All Saints Parish* (Frederick, MD, 1932), pp. 7, 32, 91, 102.

were down also. The Messrs. D left soon after tea but the others remained till after eleven.

Monday [Feb.] 25th. Tom Derr came for Mag about seven & John was [there] to see us about eight o'clock. I came up street to come home about five, stopped to see Ellen few minutes.

* * * * *

Thursday [Feb.] 28th. Rather cloudy. After dinner Father and I went into town and I found it very bad walking. I was to see Annie Bentz, Kunkels', and at Mrs. Markel's. Dr. McG came to Mrs. M's while I was there, saying he wanted to see Miss Ella as he was just going out for Miss Derr, and wanted me to come in & go, and I promised if I could I would return, and so I did. Dr. & M. Schaeffer came about seven and we got ready and we all went up to the Junior Hall[10]. [We] found a crowded audience so much so that our gentlemen could not be seated by us. The gents left about eleven o'clock. We retired about twelve.

Friday [Feb.] 29th. Came out home about nine o'clock. I had a letter of Lou Hersh.

Saturday March 1st [1856]. Snowing hard all day.

Sunday [March] 2nd. Warm, pretty day. Mother and I went to town in the sleigh and road [sic] up to church; had a very good sermon from Dr. Zack. John Derr came down to the hotel with me & Mr. Schaeffer part way, but I know Dr. McG & Mr. Johnson were both cut out. Mr. J. A. J. was out, hired a sleigh, in the afternoon for [a] couple hours.

Monday [March] 3rd. John & me [sic] went to town with Father then over to Mrs. Howard's for a couple of hours. Miss M. Plummer was there. Pleasant, cold day.

* * * * *

---

[10]The Junior Fire Hall was located over the Junior Company's Engine House on the east side of Market Street between the Market House and Second Street. *Williams' Directory*, p. 21.

1856

Wednesday [March] 5th. I wrote to Lou Hersh. Mrs. Griffon Fout & her sister Miss Joan Grove were up & spent the afternoon. Rather pleasant day.

Thursday [March] 6th. Very windy in the afternoon. I went into town with Father but did not go up street, as Mrs. M. was sick and Ella could not go out. <u>Dr. McGill</u> & <u>Mr. Schaeffer</u> were here at night.

Friday [March] 7th. Very pretty day. I went into town after dinner and stopped for Ella and we went to Kunkels', saw Meal Giffords but Clea was in Balt., & spent time at Cal Bentz's. Mag Derr & Fanny Entler stopped at Mrs. Markel's to see if I was in town. They were going out but I was in town.

* * * * *

Sunday March 9th. Very cold & windy, but I wanted to go to church so Mother and I walked in, & I stopped for Ella and she, Mrs. M, & I went to Lutheran Church[11] and heard sermon from Mr. Diehl. No church at ours. When we came out [we] found it snowing so they persuaded me to stay in. It continued snowing all afternoon so we did not get to go to church at night to hear Rev. Mr. Gibson. Mr. F. Markel was over during afternoon.

Monday [March] 10th. Very cold but Mother sent for me, & I rode out on horseback. I wrote to Mary Sauerwein.

Tuesday [March] 11th. Still cold. When John came from town I received a letter from Lou telling me of her expected marriage, also a couple pieces of music marked M. from Balt, so [I] suppose Dr. is there. /I feel I cannot tell how, when I think of Lou's marriage, I ought not to feel sorry; and I suppose like I one day may marry too. I think all are better satisfied with marriage./

* * * * *

Thursday [March] 13th. At home all day. I wrote note to Lou Hersh saying I would be with her at the time of her marriage unless providentially prevented.

---

[11]The Evangelical Lutheran Church, located at 35 East Church Street, is the oldest church in Frederick, having been established in 1737. Dr. George Diehl was the pastor of this church from 1851 to 1887. Abdel Ross Wentz, *The Lutheran Church of Frederick Maryland 1738-1938* (Harrisburg, PA, 1938), pp. 47, 225, 245.

1856

Friday [March] 14th. A beautiful day and, as I had made an engagement to meet Mag Derr in town this afternoon [and] Father had gone with the buggy, I walked into town. I had a paper from Johnsville, Mr. Cox, I suppose. She came to Mrs. Markel's about three and we went together to see Kunkels, Mrs. Page & Eliza Brewer, Houcks, also Maria Johnson but she was out. Mr. Hobbs came out about half-past seven and staid till half-past ten. His horse went off to the barn with the buggy.

Saturday [March] 15th. I was at home all day. Mother was taken very sick today.

Sunday [March] 16th. Snowing all day. After dinner sent for Dr. Dorsey[12] to see Mother.

Monday [March] 17th. Beautiful day. I was in Mother's room all day & night except a couple of hours when Messrs. J. A. Johnson [and] Wils Boyd called. The latter had a note to me enclosing a note to Lizzie Brengle[13] from Till Schoolfield.

Tuesday [March] 18th. Pretty morning, but snowed before night. Dr. Ritchie[14] was out to see Mother as Dr. D. has been called from home. Aunt M. Artz was out and remained till about four o'clock. I sent John in town and had a note from Lizzie Brengle saying she wanted me to call [the] next time I am to town.

Wednesday [March] 19th. Snowed most all day. Dr. Ritchie was out to see Mother late in the evening and bled her.

Thursday [March] 20th. Very pretty day. Fannie Adams was up in the morning, and about 11 o'clock Mrs. I. Howard came and remained till after dinner. Dr. Ritchie was to see Mother twice today & bled her again. Dr.

---

[12]Dr. Lloyd Dorsey was a graduate of the University of Maryland Medical School, who died in 1857. Williams, *History*, I, 588.

[13]On this Brengle-Scholl family relationship see note 25, 1858.

[14]Dr. Albert Ritchie was a graduate of the University of Tennessee Medical School in 1826, and practiced in Frederick until he died in 1858. He lived on Birmingham farm, part of which he sold to Mt. Olivet Cemetery. His grandson Albert was the Governor of Maryland, 1920-1925. G. L. Tracey and J. P. Dern, *Pioneers of Old Monocacy* (Baltimore, 1987), p. 123.

1856

McGill was out at night, brought me a beautiful pair of gauntlets <u>as a</u> present. I had a note from Ella B. by Father.

Friday [March] 21st. Pleasant day. Aunt Margaret was out to-day. I wrote a note to Ella B. & had one in return. Dr. Dorsey was out to see Mother.

Saturday [March] 22nd. Aunt M. & Uncle D. Thomas were out in the morning. Aunt M. remained and sat up at night. Ginny Adams & Mrs. Borsley were here in the afternoon.

Sunday March 23rd. Mother's fever is much better, so [sic] she was yesterday, & the Dr. prescribes Opium Pills[15] as she needs rest so much. Mrs. I. Howard was up after dinner but I could not invite her in the room as the Dr. wished Mother kept quiet. Alfred Thomas came for Aunt M. and she went home, notwithstanding her high fever.

Monday [March] 24th. Easter Monday. Rained several times through the day. Dr. was out and considered Mother better again. I had a note from Tilly Schoolfield. Uncle Artz again in the afternoon. Dr. out again.

Tuesday [March] 25th. Very windy day. Fanny Adams was up a while in the morning to see Mother.

Wednesday [March] 26th. Still windy. The Dr. was out today & says he will not be out again unless sent for. I had a note from Fanny Adams & wrote one in return.

Thursday [March] 27th. So very windy. Mrs. Lewis Fout was up to see Mother awhile this morning.

Friday [March] 28th. Windy again. Jenny Adams was up to see Mother in the afternoon.

Saturday [March] 29th. Windy in the morning but not as much so in the afternoon. Father & I went into town after dinner. I stopped for Ella & she went out shopping with me. <u>Dr. MacGill</u> brought her out after tea and sat an hour or so. He bro't [sic] me <u>a package of candy for my cold</u>.

---

[15]Opium, despite its addictive properties, was used to relieve pain. *Webster's Dictionary.*

Sunday [March] 30th. Very pretty day. John took me into town. I stopped for Ella and we went to church together. Dr. MacGill joined us & soon cousin Ed Shriner came down to Mrs. Markel's with us. I soon came out home. Jerry Cramer was here to tea & staid till about ten o'clock. He invited me to go to a consecration with him.

* * * * *

Thursday [April] 3rd [1856]. Very pleasant day. I went into town after dinner, stopped for Ella and we did some shopping together. Dr. McGill was out at night and proposed, etc., that is, a trip to the South, etc. and invited me to accompany him as his bride, but of course I declined; but he was not willing to take it as a positive answer. I wrote to Lou tonight.

* * * * *

Sunday [April] 6th. I went into town, stopped for Ella, and we went together to church. Mr. J. A. J. accompanied me down street; & Mr. Snyder, Ella, [and] Mr. J. A. J. came out about two and staid till seven or after. Tea saw me preside.

Monday [April] 7th. Pretty day. Mrs. I. Howard & Marion were over and spent the afternoon. Had a note from Tilly Schoolfield.

* * * * *

Saturday [April] 12th. I was busy housecleaning in the morning, but after dinner stopped for Ella & we were shopping again. Cousin Ed walked down street with us. I had a short note from Lou saying she would be with us the last of next week.

Sunday [April] 13th. Pretty day. E & I went to church together. Mrs. Schaeffer accompanied us down street. I went into town after dinner and we went together to hear Ham Davis preach.

Monday [April] 14th. Changeable all day. I went in town about four o'clock and Ella & I went up to pay for my bonnet.

* * * * *

1856

Wednesday [April] 16th. Had couple notes from Ella. I went out to Derr's in the afternoon, stopped to see Aunt M. Artz, & also we girls went to see Aunt Shriner. I intended to stop to see Nellie Mering but it rained too hard.

Thursday [April] 17th. The weather changeable. I was very busy housecleaning when, about three o'clock, Lou Hersh and her brother Frank arrived. I soon finished & dressed myself & went down. We were all sleepy & therefore retired about nine o'clock.

Friday [April] 18th. I went in with Mr. Frank Hersh & Lou with Father. We stopped at Houcks' a few minutes, & spent the rest of the day till one shopping, [and] then sat till about five at Mrs. Markel's till Father came through town. Mr. Schaeffer & Dr. McGill were out at night.

Saturday April 19th. Showery. Lou, Mother & I were in town in the morning and [in the] afternoon Lou and I were in. Saw Mr. J. A. J. at Mrs. Markell's and he walked up street with us. [He] told us Ed S. & he were coming out, but [I] suppose the rain prevented him [*sic*].

* * * * *

Monday [April] 21st. Rainy, damp day. I went into town soon after 5 o'clock expecting Annie Nihoff to return with me, but she disappointed [me] but recommended Lizzie Butler to me, and I took her with me & Lou set her to sewing, etc.

Tuesday [April] 22nd. Pleasant morning. Lou & I were in town doing some shopping & to see Miss Reding to fit Lou a dress. Dr. McGill & Mr. Schaeffer were out again & spent the evening. So cold today.

Wednesday [April] 23rd. At home all day sewing. Rainy; nevertheless Mr. J. A. J. was out to tea but left before nine o'clock.

* * * * *

Saturday [April] 26th. I was very much complaining, so Lou & Mother went into town together. Mr. Hobbs & Dr. McGill were out & spent the evening. Very agreeable.

Sunday April 27th. Very pleasant day. We went into church and stopped at Mrs. Markel[l]'s. Mrs. M. went up with us, but Mr. S. came down with me,

Dr. McG. with Ella, [and] Cousin Ed with Lou. We took a nap after dinner and about three or half-past Messrs. Hobbs & Jimmy Gambril arrived and sat till six. Mr. J. A. J. & Ed S. came about five & staid till sometime after ten o'clock. Wils & Jenny Boyd came about seven and left at ten o'clock.

Monday [April] 28th. Very warm. Lou & I stopped in town while Mother went to Aunt M. Artz's. We did some shopping. We stopped & asked Ella to come with us, then told her that Dr. McGill would call for her at half-past six. Soon after six o'clock Cousin Ed & G. Houck arrived, and very soon Dr. McGill & Ella. They all seemed to enjoy the evening and left about or near ten o'clock. /Marian Howard was here a while in the morning./

Tuesday [April] 29th. We were in town a while about noon. Jenny Adams was here about an hour.

Wednesday [April] 30th. Very pleasant day. Lou & I were in town a while in the afternoon but saw John & Mag Derr and they were coming out, so we soon came too. They left [at] nine o'clock.

Thursday, May 1st, 1856. When we arose found it raining, but about ten o'clock we started for town. [We] stopped at the door, and Ella B. jumped in the carriage and went up to the hotel and waited with me till I saw Lou off. We then went down to Mrs. Markel[l]'s. It was a rainy, disagreeable day. At night Messrs. Johnson & Wils Boyd came and spent the evening. Mr. J. just returned from Baltimore.

* * * * *

Sunday [May] 4th. A lovely morning. I went into town & stopped for Ella & we went to church together. Mr. Schaeffer joined us at the church door & Tom Derr very soon joined me, & I went down street with him. Mr. Rizer was here in the afternoon.

Monday [May] 5th. Another lovely spring day. Mother & I were in town shopping all morning. <u>Maggie Kilion brought me a letter</u>.

Tuesday [May] 6th. Lovely morning but rained hard by night. Lou's trimmings arrived from Mrs. Kuster, also a letter to me from Mrs. K. & a note from Maggie D. to meet her tomorrow afternoon. I wrote an answer to Mrs. Kuster, to Lou, & a note to <u>Jenny</u>.

1856

Wednesday [May] 7th. Rained in showers all day; nevertheless I took Lou's trimmings, [and] did a little shopping. Called to see Ella & Mrs. M.

* * * * *

Sunday [May] 11th. I went into town, stopped for Ella & went to church. I went out home with Derrs. Mr. Johnson was there in [the] evening; [he] was going to our house but heard I was not at home.

Monday [May] 12th. Beautiful day. Mary, Mag & Tom Derr & I all went up to Israel's Creek Church[16] and heard a sermon for Elder Monroe. We returned to dinner, & soon after Mr. J. A. J. stopped with his buggy & pair of horses & brought me out home. He remained only a few minutes & left.

Tuesday [May] 13th. At home in the morning, but after dinner went to town & stopped for E. Brunner, but she had gone to Baltimore that morning, so [I] just came home with Father.

Wednesday [May] 14th. I went into [town] and went to Mrs. Winchester's & met Derrs, and from there we went shopping. I had letters from Mr. H. Smith & Mr. C. L. Clippinger[17]. E. Howard & Mrs. Taylor were here.

* * * * *

Friday May 16th. Showery in afternoon. Mag D. & Tom were out awhile. I was in town to meet Mr. H. Smith & Sue Holland & children, all pleasant.

* * * * *

Sunday [May] 18th. Very pleasant day. I wrote a hurried letter to Lou. I was in town to church, stopped at Mrs. M's & went to church with them. Mr. Rizer was at our house a while. I was over to Mr. Roderick's a while after tea and sat the evening.

---

[16]Israel's Creek Church is no longer in existence. *Frederick News Post*, June 19, 1988.

[17]Mr. C. L. Clippinger from Pittsburgh is Lou Hersh's fiance.

1856

Monday [May] 19th. Pretty day. I was very busy all day. Dr. McGill was out after tea and sat the evening. He brought me a piece of poetry dedicated to "Amis Maggie" by Rod Hobbs. Letter of Mary Sauerwein.

Tuesday [May] 20th. I started into [town] early to meet Mag Derr and met at Houck's and went shopping and to see Lizzie Brengle, & I also called to see Mrs. Markell. I had a letter from Cousin Oliver Ogle.

Wednesday [May] 21st. I had intended starting to Lou's but concluded to defer till tomorrow.

Thursday [May] 22nd. Delightful day. Father & I started for Lou's by half-past five o'clock and had a delightful ride. [We] arrived at Emmitsburg by half-past ten o'clock. [I] sent my card to Mary Eichelberger, and she staid all the time with me till I left and from there we proceeded on through to Gettysburg [and] to New Oxford, where we were met by Lou, Mrs. H[ersh], and soon saw all the family and also Mrs. Nellie Gillen. After tea Mrs. Frank Hersh & Mrs. G. left for Gettysburg. About 7 1/2 o'clock Mrs. Nelson Hersh of Pittsburg arrived and we very soon became acquainted; and very soon Mr. C. L. Clippinger arrived, and I liked him very much, and we all spent a very pleasant evening together. We retired about eleven. Mr. John Hersh was up also during the evening.

NEW OXFORD

Friday May 23rd. Another pretty day. Mr. C. L. Clippinger was over and spent the morning and took dinner with us; and after dinner Lou and Mrs. Nels[on] Hersh went to Gettysburg and we did not see them till after tea. Mr. F. Hersh & Mrs. Reily arrived about ten o'clock. After tea Lou, Paul & I went over to Mrs. Ellis' for a while, & Mr. F. Hersh came for us in the buggy & we took a ride around town. We spent the evening very pleasantly & Mr. C. left about ten. Mr. & Mrs. John Hersh, Mrs. Ellis & Lucy were all [in] to see us. I do think it such a delightful family; all conversed so kindly.

Saturday [May] 24th. Very warm day. Mr. C. took breakfast with us and Mr. C., Nels, Lou & I all started for York and had a delightful ride and arrived by ten o'clock. [We] stopped at the "Washington House" and all walked down to Mr. Geo. E. Hersh's house. [We] met Mr. H. on the street & he accompanied us up to the house. I was introduced to Mrs. Ellen Hersh and formed a very favorable opinion of her and thought Ledda a very sweet little child. We passed the morning very pleasantly together. Allen Hersh took dinner with us. After dinner Lou & I went up street with Mr. C., Nels & Allen and stopped at the Misses Hersh's store and saw Mr. Sam Hersh and Lou. Nels & I went down to Dr. Fisher's and saw Mrs. [*illegible*] & Miss Jane Fisher and returned to Mr. E. H's to tea. Lucy Gardiner also took [tea] with us. We left about six o'clock for Oxford, found Mr. Sam Hersh there when we arrived.

Sunday May 25th. Much cooler. Mrs. Hersh, Mrs. Riley, Sam, Frank & Nels Hersh & I all went to Methodist church and heard a sermon from Rev. Mr. Anderson. After[wards] we all talked till about three o'clock when Rev. Mr. Mahon arrived, and Mrs. Hersh, Mrs. Riley, Sam, Frank & Nels H and I all went to church and heard a very good practical sermon from Rev. Mr. M. Tanent. I went with Nels by prior arrangement. Messrs. King & Mahon took tea with us but left directly after. At night Mrs. Hersh & Mrs. Riley went with Frank & I with Sam to the Methodist church at night. Mr. C. remained with Lou.

Monday [May] 26th. Pleasant day. I wrote a letter early to Mary Sauerwein and sent for some ribbon. We were busy sewing all morning and had all the gentlemen to entertain us by turns. After dinner Nels invited me to take a ride with him, so we started about two o'clock and went to Conawinga Chapel[18] and through McSherry's town to Hanover, stopped at the Hotel awhile, and then we called to see Misses Rosenmiller; spent an hour very pleasantly and then Mr. Myers' store awhile, and then we started for home and had a delightful ride home; found them all expecting us. Lou & I were up at Mrs. Sherman's a while, and afterwards we went to the P. O., and afterwards Nels, James, Lou & I all went up street & were treated to pop & cake. Afterwards we all spent the time together in the dining room. Mr. and Mrs. John Hersh spent the morning with us.

Tuesday May 27th. Very pleasant day. Lou & I were busy. Sam & Nels went fishing. Mrs. H. was sick all day in bed. Mrs. Ellis spent the day with us and each one seemed sad at times, but every one did the most to hide their feelings but our dinner was eaten somewhat in silence. Each one seemed to think of it's being Lou's last dinner [at home]. We were busy all evening packing her trunk, etc. Mr. C. arrived after tea and we all spent the evening together -- the family, Mr. C., Mr. & Mrs. John Hersh, Mrs. Ellis & children, Mrs. Riley & Miss Maria McClelland & Will Riley who arrived this evening.

---

[18]See note 37, 1853.

We left the parlour about ten & gave Lou an opportunity of talking to Mr. C. for the last time as Miss Hersh.

Wednesday [May] 28th. A bright morning but we were up early in the morning and busy fixing matters & things in general till about 9 1/2 o'clock, when Lou & I retired to our room to dress for the bridal. We met Mr. C. & Sam at the head of the steps and proceeded to the parlor, where Lou & Mr. C. were married in the presence of Mr. & Mrs. Hersh, Mr. & Mrs. John Hersh & 2 children, Mr. & Mrs. Ellis & four children, Mrs. Riley & Wm., Miss Maria McClelland & Messrs. Frank, Nels, James & Paul Hersh & Rev. Mr. Gerhart[19], [his] lady & two children. Every thing passed off well. We had a sett table and everything nice. We were ready to leave Oxford before two o'clock, and Lou, Mr. C., Mr. [Sam] H. & I were stowed away in a carriage & proceeded thus to Hanover, where we were to take the cars[20] [to Baltimore]. Nels H. & Wm. Riley went in a buggy to see us off. We were early, so Mr. Sam & I took a walk & went to Mr. Myer's store awhile, and when we returned found the company enlarged by the two Miss Rosenmillers, Miss Grace Darling, Dr. Hay, Mr. King & sisters. They all remained till it was time for the cars to leave. Lou shed a few tears in saying adieus but we all did every thing in our power to be cheerful.

BALTIMORE, GILMORE HOUSE

We arrived at Baltimore by about seven o'clock. Mr. Geo. S[auerwein] met me but they would not consent to my leaving & I proceeded with the party to the Gilmore House[21], where we were all assigned very pleasant rooms. But very soon Mr. C. came for me and said Lou wanted me, so I went down and staid with her that night. We all went to tea and, immediately after, Mr.

---

[19]Rev. Mr. Gerhart was the Reverend Isaac Gerhart (father of Dr. Emmanuel V. Gerhart, the President of Franklin and Marshall College in 1897 and later President of The Theological Seminary). Rev. Isaac Gerhart led the German part of the Reformed congregation of Frederick from 1844 until 1849. J. and D. Ranck, *History of the Evangelical Reformed Church*, pp. 93, 113.

[20]The "cars" refers to the Northern Central Rail Road which ran from Hanover Junction to Baltimore 46.4 miles away. Scharf, *Baltimore*, pp. 245-247.

[21]The Gilmore House was remodeled from the Gilmore residence into a hotel in the 1850s. It was located on the southwest corner of Calvert Street and Old Court Lane until it was torn down in 1895. The new city court house is now located there. Lois B. McCauley, *Maryland Historical Prints 1752-1889* (Baltimore: Maryland Historical Society), pp. 100, 129, 207.

1856

S[am] H[ersh] and I went up to Mrs. S[auerwein's] where we met the family, Miss Lefevre & her Rev. brother, Mr. Webster & Mr. Gregg. We only staid a few minutes and then took a walk & returned to the hotel, but not before Mr. H. renewed an old subject which I think had better [have] been dropped. I felt somewhat sad & Mr. H. seemed to have lost some <u>of his old love for me</u>.

Thursday May 29th. Very pleasant morning but showery in the afternoon. I was up by five o'clock & busy on my dress till breakfast & afterwards till nearly ten, and then we all went out & stopped for Mrs. Kuster and she went shopping with us. Mr. H & I had something to attend to ourselves, so [we] left Mr. & Mrs. C to get rid of Mrs. K. We returned to dinner & had a nice talk before & at dinner. After dinner we were all out again and did some shopping. Mr. Clippinger gave me a very handsome <u>ring</u>. We had several showers. We went to supper rather late and, after being in the parlor a few minutes, Mr. S. H. & I had [a talk] on the <u>veranda</u>, and <u>Oh!</u> <u>the</u> <u>conversation</u>. John Derr called & Sam & I bid each other adieu in the room. George S[auerwein] was to see us but, [I] did not see him. Sam left tonight. I slept alone.

May 30th Friday. Clear but much cooler. We went shopping awhile and then we came back again and arranged our trunks and bid the Gilmore adieu perhaps for ever. I went down in the carriage with Mr. & Mrs. C. & bid them adieu at the Philad[elphia] depot, and then proceeded to Mrs. Sauerwein's and settled myself down as being at home. John Derr came immediately. He was just five minutes too late at the hotel for me, so came to let me know. Neal Dean was to see me to-day. We were not out all day. Miss Fox was here & spent the evening. Mr. Rau [was here] for a short time. <u>I wrote home</u>. Misses Bayfield [called] but we did not see them.

Saturday [May] 31st. Clear & quite cool. Mrs. John Rau was to see us in the morning. I had a letter of <u>Maggie Derr</u>. Mary & I were out in shopping and at Dr. Jamet's.

Sunday June 1st [1856]. Very pleasant day. Mrs. S., Mary & I went to church and heard a very sermon [*sic*] from Rev. Mr. Morris. Afternoon Mary, Kate & I went to St. Paul's to church. While we were gone Mr. & Mrs. Peter Sauerwein, Sr. & two children, also John Derr, were here. Mr. Rau was here afternoon & at night. We did not go to church [in the evening].

Monday [June] 2nd. Very warm day. Margretta & Lizzie Nicholson were here in afternoon. Mrs. S., Mary, Kate & I were out [in the] afternoon. Rose Abell & Rev. and Miss Lefevre were here at night. Phil Rau [was] here a while at night.

Tuesday June 3rd. A warm day. Mercury stood 85, later evening 92. Kate & I were out in the morning and procured my dress and some other articles. I had a letter from Mr. Sam Hersh, rather unexpected, though from his professions I might have expected. I cut out my dress & commenced sewing. Mrs. Urhlaub was here nearly all morning. Catherine Sadtler & her little boy were here in the afternoon. I wrote a letter to Mrs. Hersh tonight.

Wednesday [June] 4th. Cooler in the evening. Rose Abell's compliments for a ride this evening. I accepted and went round about five and to my surprise found I was to go with Mr. Gregg, Rose, Mrs. Fox & I. We had a very pleasant drive out to Franklin[22], stopped for a few minutes and then returned home again. I took tea with Rose & Mrs. Fox and then came round, found G[eorge] S[auerwein] had been here for me also that Mr. Perry had been to see us.

Thursday [June] 5th. Very warm in morning. Kate & Mary were out to see <u>Mr. & Mrs. John Harmon</u>, the bride also. I wrote letters to Mag Derr; Charley Sadtler [was] here awhile. I had a letter from Lou & wrote one in return. [It] rained in the afternoon, so Mr. & Mrs. Harmon did not leave till after tea. Mr. Lefevre & Miss Martha Savage during the morning and after Mr. & Mrs. H. left, Mr. A. Gregg was here and staid till 10 1/2 o'clock.

Friday June 6th. Rained in showers all day. I was down at Miss Metzer's in the morning, also in the afternoon to be fit. Rose Abell was here & sat more than an hour. Cousin Ed Shriner took tea with [us] and John Derr [came] after tea. They left between 10 & 11 o'clock.

Saturday [June] 7th. Another cloudy & showery day. I wrote a note home to send by cousin Ed. Cousins Neal Dean & Harry Smith were here & sat [a] couple hours. Cousin Ed took dinner here & then bid us good bye & left for Fred'ck. I then wrote a note to Mr. Sam Hersh, and Mary & I went out & I deposited it in P.O., & then went to cousin Jacob Bier's and saw cousin

---

[22]Franklintown or Franklinville, a picturesque village, is about five miles distance from the city on the Franklin Road or Street. Scharf, *Baltimore*, p. 828.

1856

Mary, Sophie & Tilly Schoolfield, & stopped shopping a little & dentist [sic]. I got my dress. Miss Fox & Rose Abell were here & spent the evening.

Sunday [June] 8th. Rainy all day. Mrs. S., Kate went to church. Mr. Rau was here in the afternoon and after tea Mr. Wilson Boyd came. Mrs. S., Kate and Em S. & Mr. Rau went to Dr. Morris['s church] & Mary, Mr. B., Geo & I went to Mr. Robinson's. Mr. Rau left about ten, Mr. B. [at] half-past ten. Mr. B. just came from Fred'k.

Monday [June] 9th. Very bright day. Cousins Sophie Mantz, Mary Bier & Tilly S[choolfield] were here, also Mary Sauerwein; and after they left Kate & I went and got weighed. I weighed 128 lbs. We were at Miss Metzger's too. After noon we were down street shopping & afterwards to old Mrs. Rau's and Misses Bayfields'. [We] had an invitation for Wednesday evening at Mrs. John Rau's. Geo. took Mary & I to the theatre. *Abu Ben Ezra* performed. Mr. Lefevre was here. /Biers want us to take tea with them Thursday evening./

Tuesday [June] 10th. Sultry morning. I had a note from Nellie Dean this morning wanting me to come there this evening. Mrs. Urhlaub & Rose Abell were here. Mary & I were out to see Mrs. James Bayfield & Margretta Nicholson, and at Abells'. When we got home found Mr. Webster here, but he soon left & immediately after tea Mary, Geo. & I got ready to go down to cousin Will's to spend the evening. Mr. Rau was here when we left. We spent the evening very pleasantly with Mr. & Mrs. Dean, Coz Fred Koones, Charles Gordon & Rev. Mr. Hitchcock. Mr. H. came home with me and we found Mr. A. Gregg here, who invited us to go riding with him, first for Wednesday [or] Thursday & finally, when he found we had no engagement for Friday, we accepted for that evening.

Wednesday [June] 11th. Much warmer. Mrs. Wm. Sadtler & son were here before we had finished breakfast. I had a letter from Mr. Sam Hersh. Kate & I were out shopping this morning & did not return till after eleven. Mary, Kate, Em & I were out to Mr. John Rau's to tea. Mr. P. Rau, George & Mr. W. Boyd & Louisa Bowie came after tea. We all enjoyed the evening very much, returned home about eleven o'clock.

Thursday [June] 12th. Rather cloudy in the evening. Rev. Mr. Hitchcock & Nellie Dean were here about an hour. Miss Fox was here a long time this morning. Mary and I went down & took tea at cousin Jacob Bier's with the family & Sophie & Maria Cockrel, Natta Burke & Belle Burke of Washington

1856

and after tea Clinton Welles, Geo Burke, Messrs. Hall & Sauerwein. We all enjoyed the evening. I wrote a letter to Mr. S. Hersh telling him I did not expect to return on Saturday.

Friday June 13th. Quite pretty day. I was sick all night and felt very badly still this morning. Cousin Sophie Mantz & Mary Bier were to see me, also Tilly Schoolfield twice in the morning and after dinner Rev. Mr. Hitchcock called and invited us to go out to Ft. McHenry[23] with him tomorrow; we accepted as I had written home I would not return tomorrow. Rev. Mr. LeFevre came soon after Mr. H. left, but soon Mr. A. Gregg arrived with his carriage, so Mary, Kate & I had to excuse ourselves, and we went out to enjoy a delightful ride down to Canton. We stopped awhile at Canton House[24] & had something to drink and returned very much refreshed. While at tea John Derr called but [he] had an engagement so could not accompany us to Margretta Nicholson's; but Wils Boyd came very soon to go with us. /Mr. Rau was here for a few minutes./ Miss Fox, Rose Abell, Miss Denison & brother, Mr. Gregg, & George, Kate, Mary & I, & Mr. Boyd all spent the evening very pleasantly with the family. Note from Mag & Mary Derr today.

Saturday [June] 14th. Very pleasant day. When I awoke found I had a visitation from an old enemy erysipelas, so commenced packing my trunk and told Mary of my resolution of returning home tonight. After breakfast Mary & I started out and stopped first & [saw] Dr. Chatard's, who pronounced the eruption "Nettle Rash" and gave me a prescription to be procured at the McKenzie drug store. We attended to that and some other little shopping, and then to Mrs. S's and afterwards down street again and procured a dress; and was [sic] to see Nellie Gordon Dean and got her to present our regrets to Rev. Mr. Hitchcock, and say that we could not accept of his kind offer to go to the Fort. Found Mr. LeFevre at Mrs. S's when we returned but he soon left. I packed my trunk & bid them good bye &, accompanied by Geo., Mary & Kate [were] soon on our road to the depot, where I saw Dr. Anderson, Ken

---

[23]This Fort figured prominently in the War of 1812. It was named for one of the original owners of the land, Dr. James McHenry, who was Secretary of War in the cabinets of George Washington and John Adams. *The Place Names of Maryland* (Maryland Historical Society, Baltimore, 1984), p. 156.

[24]Canton House, located on the waterfront east of Fells Point, takes its name from the oriental house built by Capt. John O'Donnell, a ships master to the China trade. He brought the first cargo of Cantonese treasures to Baltimore. The area is called Canton to this day. Beirne, *Baltimoreans*, p. 37.

1856

Boyd who were at depot, & also Mr. Wils Boyd, Mrs. Boyd & Sue Jones, all on their way to Fred'ck. I had a pleasant ride to Fred'ck where I had to engage a hack to take me out home. Surprised them much.

* * * * *

Tuesday [June] 17th. Clear morning, so warm rain after a night in showers. I was in town with Father, did some shopping & was to see Mrs. Markell till I came out home.

Wednesday June 18th. Rather warm. We were busy all day picking hair[25]. Mr. Marlow called about half-past four & sat till after 8 o'clock.

Thursday [June] 19th. Still warm, very busy to-day at the hair.

Friday [June] 20th. So very warm. About two o'clock Mr. & Mrs. H. Adams & Fanny came up to spend the evening. Mr. Cox came about half-past four & sat till nine. They all had a good deal to say.

Saturday [June] 21st. Very warm. Finished the hair to-day. Marion Howard stopped awhile on her way to Mr. Ed. Howard's this evening.

* * * * *

Wednesday [June] 25th. Cloudy day. Mr. Marlow & Lewis Scholl were here to dinner. Mr. M. took the reaper to-day.

Thursday [June] 26th. Warm, with a gust of wind but not much rain in the evening. Mrs. I. Howard & Mrs. Taylor spent afternoon here & Mr. J. A. J. came with the gust and sat till after tea. I had a nice letter of Mary Sauerwein.

* * * * *

---

[25]Hair was collected in hair receptacles which were made of porcelain, silver, and even cut glass. It was worked into pencil thin lines which were applied to a selected background. White slipper satin was a particular favorite. Hair worked wreaths, bouquets, jewelry, as well as shadow box pictures were very popular in this era. Dan D'Impero, *The A.B.C.'s of Victorian Antiques* (New York, 1975), p. 75.

Saturday [June] 28th. Warm day. About five o'clock I went into town and was to see Mrs. C. Bantz, Emma Houck, Mrs. B. F. Winchester & Mrs. Markel[l]. [I] had a nice long letter of Lou Clippinger. She is very well pleased with her new home.

Sunday [June] 29th. Very warm day. I went into town and heard a very good sermon from Rev. Mr. Douglas. Went home with Derrs, went with them to Sabbath school and after tea we were going to Mr. Buck's, but were prevented by the arrival of Messrs. Eader & Sifford and very soon Ed. S. Messrs E[ader] & S[ifford] left about ten, but Ed S. did not leave till about half-past eleven.

Monday [June] 30th. Still warm. Tom took Alice & I into town. Rather [sic] I stopped at Aunt M. Artz's [and] found Mother there. We came home about twelve. About five o'clock went into town to meet Mag Derr and we went & had my daguerreotype[26] taken and to House's, Jane Ramsburg['s] & to Zacharias' to see Miss Spencer of Balt., & then to Mrs. Markel[l]'s a while, till they sent for me. Sent a note to Ella Brunner.

* * * * *

Friday [July] 4th [1856]. Quite warm. Made currant jelly & wine. Wrote Mary Sauerwein.

Saturday [July] 5th. No company. I was busy all day, and at night wrote a long letter to Lou Clippinger; had a paper from Pittsburg.

Sunday July 6th. Very pleasant day. Mother & I went into town. I went up to the City Hotel expecting to meet Maggie D. but she was not there so I went to our church and heard a very good sermon from Rev. Mr. Bechtol. He preached an hour & ten minutes, Luke 21, 23 verses.

Monday [July] 7th. Somewhat warm, with slight shower in the evening. Added a P.S. & sent my letter to Lou, also daguerreotype & ring. <u>My birthday but no presents.</u>

---

[26] Jacob Byerly, son of Charles Byerly, had an ambrotype and photography gallery on the third floor of a building on the south side of Patrick Street, the second door west of Market Street. *Williams' Directory*, p. 7.

1856

* * * * *

Thursday [July] 10th. Raining again in the morning but clear afternoon & night. Notwithstanding, I did not go to Mr. Winchester's commencement tonight.

Friday [July] 11th. Pleasant day. Aunt Shriner, Mary & Geo. S[auerwein] & James Dean were out & spent the day. I went into town after they left & was at Houcks', also Ellie B's. She came home Tuesday, so much pleased. Note from Mary E. S.

* * * * *

Sunday [July] 13th. Went into town & stopped at M. Markel[l]'s and went up to church with Mr. Markel[l] & Ella. Cousin Ed came down with us. Mr. J. A. J. came about four & staid till after eight, & Wils Boyd till 10 o'clock. Father quite sick.

Monday [July] 14th. Very warm day. Dr. was to see Father.

Tuesday [July] 15th. I went into town about half-past four and took tea at Mrs. M's with Maggie & Mary Derr, & afterwards we all took a walk.

Wednesday 16th July. Still so warm. Fannie Adams up yesterday, also old Mr. Adams. Had a letter from Mary E. Sauerwein.

* * * * *

Saturday [July] 19th. I went into town about five o'clock and stopped for Ella and we after tea did some shopping and [took a] long walk; stopped at the depot to see the cars arrive and saw Messrs. Johnson, Derr & Schaeffer there. The latter two accompanied us to Mr. M's. Ella came home & remained over night.

Sunday [July] 20th. Much cooler. Ellie & I went in early to church and heard a very good sermon, Rev. Mr. Kintz. Tom Derr came down street with us. I staid in till after evening services. Mr. J. A. J. & Cousin Ed were here after I got home.

Monday [July] 21st. Still pleasant. I was busy all day shirt-making.

1856

Tuesday [July] 22nd. Pleasant. I did not go to town as intended but wrote E. a note & had one in return. Sauerweins came tonight.

Wednesday [July] 23rd. Warmer. I went into town about ten o'clock, stopped to see Ella short time, then at Houck's. [I] saw the family, Mary & Em Sauerwein & Mrs. Jamieson & Till Jackson. [I was] there an hour or so, then came out home. I had a nice long letter from Lou Clippinger and Pa. newspapers from Mr. C. Mr. J. A. J. & Ed S. were in town last night.

* * * * *

Saturday July 26th. Very warm day. Just as we were sitting down to dinner there was a loud Rap and it proved to be cousins Fred, Lizzie & little Lizzie Koones. About four o'clock we went into town and called at Salmons' a while, though I was round [at] Houcks' most of the time. They all enjoyed the pic-nic so much. When we got home was my surprise to find Ella Brunner and Mr. Sam Hersh at our house. He had arrived at noon. He looked so handsome. Ella & Sam left about nine o'clock as E. wanted to go home.

Sunday [July] 27th. Very warm day. Nevertheless we all went into town to church. Mr. Sam Hersh joined us at the Hotel and afterwards took me out home in a buggy and staid till after dinner. Cousin Lizzie took a nap but I staid up and entertained Mr. Hersh. Mr. Jerry Cramer arrived about four o'clock and Messrs Johnson & Shriner about seven and three latter left about eleven o'clock. Mr. H & I are going to Derrs' tomorrow evening.

Monday [July] 28th. Another warm day. As the cousins are going to leave, I went into town with them. Mr. Hersh joined us at the depot. Cousin Wil Dean & Nellie went down to Balt[imore] also. After they left, Mr. Hersh & I went in the carriage to see Houcks, also to the P. O. and then down to Ella's where we sat a long time. I then came out home and assisted Mother making collars and by half-past five o'clock Mr. Hersh arrived, and after tea Mr. Sam & I went out to Derrs', tho' first we went over & gave Cousin Ed a call, and while he was fixing to accompany us we drove up to take a look at Mr. Hoke's farm; & as we came back [we] made a mistake by taking Mr. Peter Kemp for Mr. Hoke. Ed was ready and we all three went over in the buggy. Maggie & Thomas had just got home from town; [they] had hurried home from town as she heard we were coming. We spent the evening very pleasantly and left soon after nine o'clock. We had not proceeded far before Mr. Hersh renewed his suit and we were nearly two hours on the road and we were speaking of our acquaintance and progress of his love &c. I told him

1856

mine was nothing more than friendship. I bid him good bye and perhaps I did wrong by allowing him to kiss me, but we may never meet again and I take Mr. Hersh for a gentleman so I think I can have done nothing wrong. We had a long & very serious conversation and I fear he entertains an idea that I have flirted with him but he parted as tho' it were not in anger. I told him of the many ladies I had heard of his waiting on but he told me he loved none but me; if I did not marry him he would never marry; but I wished him to forget me.

Tuesday July 29th. Quite warm but several slight showers in the evening. Mr. J. A. J. stopped here to tea on his way from Mr. Michael Keefer's sale. I was in town a short time to see Ella Brunner.

* * * * *

Thursday [July] 31st. Cool breeze but sun very warm. About three o'clock I started to town, stopped for E., and we went up to Houcks' and sat awhile & then to Kunkels' a few minutes and then I did some shopping and Ella came on home. I soon came down street and went out home. Finis. So ends July, and many pleasant reminiscences of the past are connected with this Volume of my journals, and also some regrets, and the question also arises to my mind, have I acted honorable [sic] with Mr. H[ersh]. Next to the one I think I love, I'd rather marry him than any one I know. I fear he does not love me as he professes, but maybe I doubt too much, but it seems strange if he loves me now he did not at first. He says he loves me for "my good common sense" although his motives may be attributed to other causes. Could I only think he would be less fond of money, but I must say adieu and always think of him as a kind friend.

August 1st 1856. Friday. Rather pleasant day. [I] slept well last night although Father left us yesterday for Bedford Springs[27] to be away for a couple weeks. I went over early in the morning to Mr. I. Howard's and spent the day with [the] family very pleasantly. When John came from town for me in the evening, found some gentleman from Balt. had been to see me and found on arriving at home that it was Mr. Ben. Perry.

---

[27]Bedford Springs is a famous old resort in the Laurel Highlands of Pennsylvania. The springs are impregnated with sulphur, lime, magnesium, and chalybeate. Great men such as John C. Calhoun, Daniel Webster, and Henry Clay came there for periods of rest. Elsie Singmaster, *Pennsylvania's Susquehanna* (Harrisburg, PA, 1950), p. 97.

Saturday Aug. 2nd. Very much the appearance of rain but we had none during the day. I went for Ella soon after eleven o'clock and we went together to Derr's Island[28], where the Harmony Grove & Ceresville Sabbath School were holding a pic-nic, saw numerous friends who seemed to enjoy the day very much. We went to cousin Ed. S's about five o'clock and staid a couple hours & then returned home. Mr. Marlow offered to bring me home but of course I declined. I sent three papers to Mr. C. J. Clippinger.

* * * * *

Tuesday Aug. 5th. The weather early in the morning had much the appearance of rain but cleared off very pretty. Nearly twelve Mr. Houck's carriage arrived containing Lizzie Houck, Mary & Emma Sauerwein & Mary Derr. We spent the day in sewing, reading, talking and after tea took a walk, when Thomas & Maggie Derr arrived and very soon Mr. Wilson R. Boyd. They all left soon after nine o'clock.

Wednesday [August] 6th. Pleasant day. I went into town very early this morning and cut the pattern off of Ella B's skirt and endeavored to get whalebones[29] for it without succeeding. I was at Houck's a few minutes, and coming down street I had a nice long talk with E.B.

Thursday [August] 7th. Pleasant day. Early in the morning there were persons commencing to meet in Uncle Adams'[30] woods to celebrate the Democratic Barbacue[31] and about one o'clock the regular procession

---

[28] On Derr's Island, see note 20, 1854.

[29] The "whalebone" used as stiffening in ladies' garments at this time was actually baleen from the mouth of the Baleen Whales, then hunted throughout the world. Baleen is hard but flexible. *Webster's Dictionary.*

[30] See note 30, 1851.

[31] "Friends of Buchanan and Breckinridge had a mass meeting in our town -- the procession was very large. The calculations vary, (according to the different political views on the subject) was from three to five thousand -- and the length of the procession is estimated one and a half miles -- The vehicles as counted by some were 222, all sorts and sizes, male and female, parents and children, -- but there were many darkies, it so happens that the darkies are generally 'know nothings'. The barbeque was held at Valentine Adams' woods and speeches at the 'Grounds' were by Gen. Lewis Cass of Michigan and Robert Toombs of Georgia (both U. S. Senators). The procession took exactly 40 minutes to pass our door." Engelbrecht, *Diary*, II, 690.

1856

commenced coming. It was 3/4 [of] an hour entering the grove. Cousin Ed. & Jenny Adams came over about four o'clock. Mr. J. A. J. met us coming to the house and returned with us. There was a rain came up & we soon returned home. Dr. McGill & Ed S. with me. [We] found Mrs. & Miss Jamison at the house and a good many others, who all left after the shower was over. Dr. McGill, Ed S. & I went to town immediately after tea and I staid at Houcks' all night. Mr. W. R. Boyd was there to go with [us] so we did not wait longer than eight o'clock, and so Dr. McGill & cousin Ed did not come till after we left; but on the ground we were soon joined by Messrs. Eader, Schaeffer, Hobbs, Sifford, Shriner and Mr. J. A. J. and Ella B. were with us most of the time. We returned to Mrs. Houcks soon after eleven, and the gentlemen only remained a short time, and after partaking of Watermelon & Cake we retired. Mr. Wils Boyd was at our house [a] few minutes.

Friday [August] 8th. I was up early and started for home; did a little shopping and then went to M. Derr's and returned home.

Saturday [August] 9th. Very pleasant day. I intended to be in town very early but it was nearly nine till I got in; went to Houcks' and found Mary S & Lizzie just ready to go with Ginny Boyd to their house, where we had a splendid opportunity of seeing the procession, length of delegations, &c. It was much longer & nicer looking. We went up and saw the tables spread at the court house, and afterwards went to the Houcks' to dinner. After tea Mr. J. A. J. arrived and soon Geo. S. and Ed. S., Wils Boyd and Derrs arrived, and we all soon got ready and went to the court house to see Fireworks, speaking, &c. We were joined by Messrs Eader, Marlow, Schaeffer and Dr. McGill for a while. We all returned to Mrs. H's about eleven, and about half-past gents left. Derr girls slept there.

Sunday Aug. 10th. Pleasant day. Mag Derr, Mary & Em S., Em & Tilly H. and I started for church and were joined by Geo Sauerwein, Ed. S and Wils Boyd. Geo. sat with me. Mr. J. A. J. joined us and walked with Mary S. home. After dinner we attempted to take a nap but all talked too much. About three o'clock Messrs. W. Boyd, Ed S & Geo S arrived, and Mary S, Lizzie H & I went with them to Presbyterian church and heard a very good sermon from Mr. Kerr. After tea Messrs. Geo. Birely, Gus Eader, Geo. Sauerwein, Ed S., Tom D, & Wils Boyd were there. Mary Derr went home with Thomas and they had all left by eleven o'clock.

Monday [August] 11th. Cloudy all day. I came out home about six o'clock. Cousin Ed S & Geo Sauerwein came out after tea and sat all the evening. I wrote to Louise [Lou Hersh] Clip[pinger] to-day. I was in town & at Aunt M. Artz' a short time.

* * * * *

Wednesday [August] 13th. Quite pleasant day. I went in to town about five o'clock and did some shopping, and was to see Ella B awhile; and while there cousin Ed & G[eorge] S[auerwein] stopped on their way in from our house and asked [me] to go with them to Mr. Derr's and I did so. We were caught in a very heavy shower. Mr. J. A. J. was there when we arrived and [at] nearly nine o'clock Lizzie and Georgia Houck, Ginny Boyd & Dr. McGill, & Messrs. Schaeffer & Birely arrived, and all staid till after eleven o'clock. I remained over night.

Thursday Aug. 14th. Very pleasant day. We were uncertain about the picnic, so gave ourselves no trouble till ten o'clock. Mr. Wilson Boyd arrived & said they were going, and after seeing Ed &c., Mr. W. B. & Mr. G. S., Maggie D with G. S. & Em S. with Tom Derr started, all in buggies. Mr. J. A. J. and Ed. S soon came with a Spring Wagon & pair for Mary Derr & me, and we four came out home to dinner, and afterwards went down about three o'clock and staid on the ground till nearly eight, right pleasant time. All came home with me and sat nearly an hour & left.

* * * * *

Saturday [August] 16th. Busy in the morning, but after dinner I went with John to town to meet Father. Cars did not arrive till nearly five. Father looks badly.

Sunday [August] 17th. Very pleasant day. Mother & I went to church, heard a very good sermon; surprised to see Geo. S[auerwein] in church. He came down street with me; [he] is going to leave to-night for Harpers Ferry.

* * * * *

Wednesday [August] 20th. Clear cool day. Mother & I went to spend the afternoon at Mrs. I. Howard's, but I found Misses Pattie Hall, Eunice Anderson & Marion going to see Jenny Adams, so I accompanied them and spent the evening very pleasantly with them, the family, & Mrs. Wm. Reich & Miss Sophia Reich. Came home about dusk.

1856

Thursday [August] 21st. Father still feels better. Mother & I were out to Aunt M[argaret Artz]'s awhile and stopped awhile in town to do some shopping. Cool day.

Friday [August] 22nd. Pleasant day. Mother was in town awhile and as she came home Eugene Derr brought Maggie D & Mary S. out and they sat awhile & then left.

Saturday [August] 23rd. Dull morning but cleared off by noon. I was in town awhile [and] called to see Ella B & Co. The Misses Daugherty left this morning. Mother & I spent the afternoon at Lewis Fouts'.

Sunday [August] 24th. Rather cloudy early, but nevertheless I proceeded to our place of meeting and [was] joined by Mary Derr, Tom D, & Em S & Wils Boyd, & Mary S[auerwein], & Ed S[hriner], and we all proceeded to camp. There [we] were joined by Mr. Dod Santice, who remained with us all the time and brought me home at night; he remained till about half-past nine o'clock. There were a great many persons there. I saw Lina Grampton (Sarott), Lidye Johnson (Wenner) & others of old school friends and various others.

Monday August 25th. A pleasant day. Father & Mother went to camp meeting. I was home busy all day.

Tuesday [August] 26th. Quite cool. Father & I went to <u>Camp</u> to-day and heard an excellent sermon, and I was well pleased; saw numerous friends and saw Sarah Bowlus (Schaeffer) & Malinda & Soph Biser.

Wednesday [August] 27th. Somewhat warmer. Mr. Marlow was to see Father, early this morning, on business. Father and I were in town. I called to see Ella B a little and then shopped a little, and on our way out met cousin Geo. B. Burke & Mr. Ken Boyd, who had been to the house to see me, and we had quite a chat in the road. I like Geo. so much. Saw Ed. S & Mr. J. A. J. in town; [the] former invited me to tea tomorrow.

Thursday [August] 28th. Another month Lou has been married; a month ago I bid Sam good bye. I went into town about two o'clock, called for Ella but she could not go, so I went alone to Derrs', and very soon Mary D, Mary & Em S., Mrs. D., & Madam Pearson all went over to cousin Ed's to tea. Messrs. Birely & Eader were there; after tea Aunt S. was there. Mr. J. A. J. was there a short time but had to leave on account of company. I had a paper from Bedford.

Friday August 29th. Very pleasant day, with very heavy showers about noon. About ten o'clock Thomas took Madam Pearson, Mag Derr, Mary & Em S. & me over to M. Schell's to spend the day. Mr. J. A. J. & Ed S., Tommy & Mary Derr came for us and we all remained till about nine o'clock when we left for Mr. Derr's. The day passed very pleasantly. I like Lizzie very much.

Saturday August 30th. Very pleasant day. We all spent the day at Mr. Derr's. After tea Mary S., Mary D., Emma S. & I walked over to Cousin Ed's mill but did not see him. Maggie Derr was complaining with neuraligy [sic].

Sunday [August] 31st. Very pleasant day. Mary D., Emma S. & Mary S., Tom & I went to church. Ed called & took Em. All went to Sabbath school except Mary S. & I. J. A. J. returned with them, & very soon Messrs. Hobbs & Jerry Cramer, Marlow & Baker, and after tea Messrs. Joe & Dod. Gambril & Wils Boyd arrived and all spent the evening.

Monday Sept. 1st 1856. Cloudy, cool morning. Em S. & I walked over to the mill & were there sometime talking with Ed; soon after we came back Lizzie Houck came to spend the day. Cousin Ed called for me about four o'clock & brought me home. He staid to tea & till after eight o'clock.

* * * * *

Wednesday Sept. 3rd. Rather cloudy but cleared off by noon. Mr. Wils Boyd came for me about eight and by nine [we] started to town & met Mag Derr & Mr. Dod. Gambril, Em S. & Ed S., and Mary S. with Mr. J. A. J., but Mary & I exchanged gentlemen and then all started for the White Rock & had a delightful day. We returned home by night well pleased with the day. /Stopped at Mr. Markel[l]'s to see Ella but she was not home./

Thursday [Sept.] 4th. Pleasant day. I was very busy all day. [I] looked for the girls [to come] to dinner but they did not arrive till six o'clock, when Thomas Derr brought Mary D., Mary & Em S. out. T. left soon after tea and Mr. Ki. Marlow came about dusk and remained till about eleven, when we were all glad to retire. [I] had a note from Annie Schley saying they & some others would be out to-morrow evening.

Friday [Sept.] 5th. Very pretty day. Had all the girls at work. Mag Derr arrived about 7 o'clock & about eight Annie & Ellen Schley, Mary & Melie Kunkel, Cle Sifford & her friend Miss Sallie Smith and Messrs. Ed S[hriner],

1856

Jimmy Gambril & Dr. McGill. They all seemed to enjoy the evening and did not leave till after eleven o'clock.

Saturday Sept. 6th. It rained awhile in the morning but cleared off to be a very warm afternoon. Eugene Derr came for the girls about nine o'clock and by ten Mary, Em & I were ready to start to the consecration of the church[32] at Walkersville. Em & I stayed at the church and Mary, on account of her nose, went to Aunt Mary S's. After the services were over we went down too. /Annie Bentz was there also./ Mr. Marlow came to dinner and staid till we left. Thomas & Mag Derr came about four o'clock and remained till we left.

Sunday [Sept.] 7th. Warm day. Mary, Em & I were in to church and heard a very good sermon from Rev. Mr. _____. Wils & Ham Boyd came about three o'clock and Ham left about five. Wils, Mary, Em & I took a walk & just at our gate met Mr. Dod Gambril, who returned with [us] & he & Wils left about 10 o'clock.

Monday [Sept.] 8th. Rather warm. We were at home all day. I had a nice long letter from Lou Clippinger. Cousin Ed S & Ginny Boyd were out & spent the evening.

Tuesday [Sept.] 9th. Pleasant day. I was very busy about half- past ten when Mr. & Mrs. C. Steiner & Ella B. arrived and took dinner with us. About four o'clock Mary, Em and I went over to Mrs. I. Howard's. Mother went in the evening.

Wednesday Sept. 10th. Mary, Em & I went in to spend the day with Kunkels. Derrs came about four o'clock, and after tea, about eight, Annie & Ellen Schley & Cle. Sifford & friend Miss Smith & Mr. Sifford [came] and soon Tom Derr and at nine Mess. Dod & Jimmy Gambril, and afterward Ed S.... As they did not send for us we remained overnight. The company generally left about eleven.

Thursday [Sept.] 11th. Very pleasant day. About five o'clock we started into town to go take tea with Mrs. Steiner. Mag Derr, Lizzie Zack & Clara Schley

---

[32]This was the Glade German Reformed Church near Walkersville which Margaret visited August 26, 1854, when the cornerstone was laid. See note 23, 1854. The church had been founded in 1757. J. and D. Ranck, *History of the Evangelical and Reformed Church*, pp. 29, 47.

were there to tea, and after tea Mary & Thomas Derr, Ed. S. & Wils Boyd arrived and spent the evening. We left for home about ten o'clock. Wils brought Mary & Ed brought Em & I. We were some time behind them as Ed walked his horse all the way.

Friday [Sept.] 12th. Not so warm but cloudy. Took a walk after tea & Mary read aloud at night.

Saturday [Sept.] 13th. Busy all morning. Clear warm day. About four o'clock Mary, Em & I went into town and called at Houcks' [and] Siffords', [but] they were not home, and to see Kate Davis. She seemed so composed and spoke so much of her little Ada. She died Tuesday night.

Sunday Sept. 14th. Pleasant day. Mary, Em & I went to Lutheran church. [We] were placed in Mr. A. Eader's pew, and Em had him down street with her. Mother went to our church & had John Derr down street with her. He came up to the carriage and asked me to come out home with him and I did so. He staid to dinner. Wils Boyd & Thomas Derr came after tea and they all left about ten o'clock.

Monday [Sept.] 15th. Very pleasant. Busy drying corn[33] this morning. Cousin Ed. came out & spent the evening.

Tuesday [Sept.] 16th. Quite cool. Lizzie Mickley and her little daughter Sallie came out & spent the day. We walked part of the way with them.

Wednesday [Sept.] 17th. Very warm to-day. I was quite sick this morning. We were all invited to Houcks' today to tea, but I did not feel well enough to go, so Father took the girls in about five o'clock. Wrote to Lizzie Koones & Lou Clippinger. Wils Boyd and Cousin Ed brought the girls home about eleven o'clock.

Thursday [Sept.] 18th. Very pleasant day. Mary, Em & I went into town to spend the day at Aunt Jemima Scholl's. We all stopped at Ella Brunner's and then at Houses' awhile. We got to Aunt's about half-past ten. Miss Lizzie

---

[33]When corn was dried it was first husked and the silk removed. Sometimes it was blanched to set the milk. Then the kernels were cut from the ear, and it was placed in the sun or oven until it was hard. It was then stored in air tight containers. Carol Hupping Stoner, *Stocking Up* (Emmaus, Pennsylvania, 1967), pp. 115-116.

1856

Jones was there to dinner. After dinner Mary & I were up street at the P. O. & were weighed. Weighed 132. John came for us after tea & we took a ride round by [*illegible*] house.

Friday Sept. 19th. Cloudy & cool all day. We were busy sewing, etc. I made apple jelly. Messrs. Cline, Gambril & Cousin Ed were here to tea and immediately [after] tea we got ready & started to go to Schleys' to spend the evening. Kunkels, Thomas Derr, Dr. McGill, Mr. Schaeffer & Jemmy Thompson were there also. Spent a very pleasant evening and, as it rained so very hard, we remained over night and the gents all left [at] twelve o'clock. We all retired then.

Saturday [Sept.] 20th. Very bright morning. Mr. Cline according to engagement called for us about nine & brought us out home. I put some tomatoes up, and afterwards Mary & I walked over to Boyds' for a short time. Gin Boyd & Mollie Jones walked nearly home with us.

Sunday [Sept.] 21st. Cloudy nearly all day. Communion to-day, Rev. Mr. Geasy[34] preached. Mary, Em & I went to church. Cousin Ed came down street with Em. Mr. J. A. J. came [at] three o'clock, Cousin Ed & Wils Boyd about four, & Jemmy about six. All left about ten o'clock. Wrote a P. S. in Kate S.'s letter.

Monday [Sept.] 22nd. Very bright day. Lizzie & Em Houck & Kate Reynolds came about ten, & Mary Kunkel & Mag Derr about eleven, and all spent the day. Cousin Ed came about five o'clock & took Em out on horseback. Tom Derr came & took Mary K. & Mag Derr home. Ed left about nine.

Tuesday Sept. 23rd. Cloudy and rainy in showers in the afternoon. Mary, Em, & I went out to Derrs' and remained over night. Very pleasant evening with the family. Houcks left [at] 9 o'clock.

Wednesday [Sept.] 24th. Quite clear, cool day. Mary & Melie Kunkel spent the day at Mrs. Derr's. After dinner we all went to the mill & were weighed and from there took a long walk. After tea Mr. Dod Gambril came and spent the evening, and about nine o'clock Mr. J. A. J. & cousin Ed arrived just as

---

[34]Reverend Sam Geesey is mentioned in Engelbrecht, *Diary* (II, 707), as one of the ministers of the Reformed Church.

1856

we were at the table. Kunkels left about ten, Mr. G. about eleven, & Mr. J. & Ed about twelve o'clock.

Thursday [Sept.] 25th. Very pleasant day. Father came for us about ten o'clock and took us to go home. We stopped in town at House's and to do some shopping and then came out home. Derrs received invitations to Clint Johnson's[35] reception next Tuesday night, to-day. We slept part [of] the evening & read after night.

Friday [Sept.] 26th. Very pleasant day. Mary, Em & I went into town about nine o'clock. [We] stopped at Houcks' awhile [and] told them we would be back to dinner, and then went to see Mrs. C. Steiner, Cle Sifford, Mrs. Dr. Schley. [We went] back to Houcks' to dinner, and afterwards to see Houses, Kunkels, Aunt Jem[ima] Scholl & E. Brunner, but the latter was out, and then to see Lizzie Micklin awhile. Cousin Ed, Jemmy Thompson & Mr. Schaeffer spent the evening here.

Saturday Sept. 27th. Delightful day. Busy in the morning. After dinner, Mary & I started to walk, but in our lane met Miss Pattie Hall & Mrs. I. Howard, and of course we returned, as Mother could not go with Em. Mary went to town with her and brought Ginny Boyd home with her, who remained over night. John & Mag Derr soon arrived but John left soon after tea. Mr. Jemmy Gambril arrived about eight & sat till about half-past ten. He was quite entertaining.

Sunday [Sept.] 28th. Pleasant day. Mary S., Mag D. & I went in to church. Jenny Boyd went as far as Smiths' gate and went home. After church Em joined us and went out home. Mr. Boyd & Cousin Ed walked to the hotel with us. Soon after two o'clock Mr. Wils Boyd arrived and sat till about five, then went home and returned after tea & brought Jennie with him. John & Thomas Derr came about five and left after ten. Cousin Ed arrived about eight & remained over night.

Monday [Sept.] 29th. Cloudy all day. We were up early, had trunks packed, and started into town before eight o'clock. Cousin Ed took Em S. & Mag Derr into town and Mary & I went in the cart with the trunks. Messrs. Wils Boyd, Schaeffer, Jemmy Thompson, John Derr, Mary Derr & Em Houck were all in town to see the girls off. After they left I went with Mary & Mag

---

[35] See note 16, 1851.

1856

Derr shopping, and then came down street and stopped to see Ella B. awhile, and came out home on horseback. Rain tonight.

Tuesday Sept. 30th. Cloudy day. Wrote a note to Maggie Derr and sent her my breastpin to wear to-night to C. Johnson's reception. Also sent a message to Ella B.

Wednesday Oct. 1st [1856]. Pleasant. Had a message from Mag D. accompanied by pin & rosettes.

Thursday [Oct] 2nd. Lovely day. Busy cleaning parlour all day.

* * * * *

Saturday [Oct] 4th. Delightful day. Father took me into town soon after dinner and I stopped [at] Ella B['s] and after she dressed herself we took a long walk and did a little shopping & then returned home.

Sunday [Oct.] 5th. Very pleasant day. Mother & I went into church together. I stopped for Ella and we went up to church together. Mr. Cline came out about four and sat till after five. Mr. James Gambril came about five and staid till 10, Wils Boyd at seven & staid till Mr. J. G. left.

* * * * *

Tuesday [Oct] 7th. Somewhat cooler and of course more pleasant. After an early dinner I went into town, called for Ella B. and we were together to see her sister Call & family, also Cle Sifford awhile. I had a long letter from Mary Sauerwein and a note in it from George.

Wednesday [Oct.] 8th. Very pleasant day. Busy at various duties. Mr. Kline came out after tea & sat till after ten o'clock.

Thursday [Oct.] 9th. Very pleasant day. Mother & John going to [the] mountain. I [was] busy preserving & making jelly & pickles. I sent a paper to Mr. Frank Hersh relative to Cattle Show. Prof. Howard was out & made quite a long call.

Friday [Oct.] 10th. Wrote a hurried letter to Mary Sauerwein. Mother was in town in the afternoon, at P. O., returns. I had a paper from Bedford and

Father [had] two from Davenport. Messrs. Himes & Clip have moved to D. Father taken sick again tonight.

Saturday [Oct.] 11th. Pleasant day. Dr. Moran [was] out to see Father twice. Cousin Ed came about five o'clock and after tea he & I went over to see Hannah Lewis awhile. Got home about nine & Ed left then.

Sunday, Oct. 12th. Quite warm. Just as I was ready to start to church, cousin Will Dean & Mrs. Salmon arrived. I went in, stopped for Ella, and we went together to church. Mr. Tom Schaeffer came down street with me and Mr. Sam Kline with Ella, left us at the door. Found cousin W[ill] & Mrs. S. at home. They left between 3 & 4 o'clock.

Monday [Oct.] 13th. Pleasant morning, but raining slightly in the afternoon. Eclipse at [*sic*] the Moon. Sallie Miller, Isie Buckey, Misses Irene Ornedoff of Balt. & Sallie Ornedoff of Mont[gomery] Co. spent the afternoon here. Very much pleased with Miss Sallie. Had a letter from Mary H. Smith saying she & Dr. A[nnon] would be down Wednesday evening.

Tuesday [Oct.] 14th. Cloudy, damp day. I was in town awhile in the morning, did shopping and stopped to see Ella awhile.

Wednesday [Oct.] 15th. Cloudy morning. I went into town about eleven o'clock, stopped and took little Mary B. up street with me, and when I returned had an opportunity of seeing the people come from and going to the cattle show[36]. While we were at dinner Mr. Tom Kline arrived, but as E. did not know how long it would take her to dress, he left. E., Mrs. M. & I went to the cattle show together and after some goose chases were joined by Mr. Tom Kline & Cousin Ed. and had the same company to accompany us home, and very soon Mr. J. A. J. called at Mrs. Markel[l]'s and sat some time. After the gents left, E. & I took a walk and returned, and about six had a note from M[ary] H. Smith saying she had arrived. We had an engagement with Cousin E. to go through the "Fair" [and] had a very pleasant evening. Met Mary H. Smith there, also Messrs. Kline, Dod Gambril, Sam Preston & others and had a very pleasant time. [We] took Mary H. S. up to Mrs. Salmon's and then came to Mrs. M['s] and Cousin Ed sat till about eleven o'clock, and after Ella & I talking a long time we went to bed.

---

[36]Engelbrecht reports that the Fair or Cattle Show made $2,000 and a little more. Engelbrecht, *Diary*, II, 695.

1856

Thursday Oct. 16th. Delightful day. Mrs. Markel[l] & I went up to the ground soon after nine o'clock and Ella waited for Dr. Annon & Mary H. S. We all found each other, also Mag Derr, and were very soon joined by Cousin Ed and various other friends and had a very pleasant time. About one o'clock started to come out home, and waited for Dr. A., but after about an hour he returned saying his buggy was gone. We then hooked up our carriage and went out home to dinner and returned again, but Dr. A. went to see about his buggy and we went into the ground and there saw various friends and had a very pleasant time. Mr. Hobbs escorted Mary H. S. and I down to Mrs. M., & Cousin Ed., Ella, and we all sat and had a very pleasant chat for half hour or so and then left. Dr. A. came about five o'clock and about six I gave up their sending for us so I [*sic*] took off our bonnets. Dr. A. left immediately after tea and Ella & I went to the Fair and took little Mary B., and [they] had a great crowd there. Mr. Marlow & Mr. Rohrback[37] came home with us and sat till eleven o'clock; and after talking awhile E. & I retired, Mary H. having gone before.

Friday Oct. 17th. Mother came very early in carriage for us and we went to the Hotel and inquired for Dr. A. but could not find him, so after going to Mrs. Salmon's we came out home. It rained very hard all day from about nine o'clock. Dr. A. came about ten and soon after dinner Dr. A. & Mary H. S[mith] left, notwith-standing all our endeavors to prevent them.

Saturday [Oct.] 18th. Rather cloudy; however, after dinner I went into town and Ella & I took a long walk and saw a great many strangers on the street. I had a paper from Rev. John Hersh containing Mrs. McClelland's[38] death.

Sunday Oct. 19th. Delightful day. I went in with Mother to church and stopped for Ella and we went to church together. After church Mag Derr wanted me to go home with her so she went with me to Mrs. Markel[l]'s to change my shawl, and Mr. Dod Gambril also accompanied Mag & I, and Mr. Kline, Ella, and Tom Derr came down and walked up street with us. After

---

[37]Martin Newcomer Rohrback, whom Margaret mentioned on October 25, 1855, as a friend of Ellen Brunner, had moved from near Sharpsburg to Frederick (Rohrbaugh, *Rohrbach Genealogy*, p. 377). He was listed in 1859 as a merchant in *Williams' Directory* (p. 6), and in September of that year he married Ellen Brunner. See also Williams, *History*, II, 736, 910.

[38]On September 14, 1853, when Margaret visited the Hersh family in New Oxford, Pennsylvania, she met Miss Lou M. McClelland of Gettysburg, Pennsylvania.

getting [to the Derrs'] I received two notes from Mary, also a collar she had purchased for me. About three o'clock Mag Derr and I started to Cousin Ed's but did not find aunt at home, and then stopped awhile at Kemps' and from there to talk a few words to Mrs. Ford at Mrs. Buck's gate. While we were standing talking Mr. Jemmy Gambril arrived and sat till after nine o'clock. Cousin Ed came about seven o'clock & staid [until] after eleven.

Monday Oct. 20th. Delightful day. Mag, Tom, Alice Derr[39], & I all came [to town] in the buggy. Mag & I were to see Call Bantz's company, Mrs. Frank Winchester, and then to Ella's where we were to meet Tom Derr, but he did not come till two o'clock. Ella & I were out after dinner and took a long walk and I came home with Father. I had a long letter from Lou Clip[pinger].

* * * * *

Wednesday [Oct.] 22nd. Very pleasant day. About nine o'clock Ella B, Sis Ebert, Misses Ginny Entler, Ellen & Ann Brisere arrived and about half-past twelve Mother arrived with Annie Scholl. Mr. Edward Smith was here but did not come in. After dinner all ladies except Annie S. took a walk over to Jenny Adams awhile. Found Mrs. Callie Bantz here on our return and the girls had to leave very soon. <u>Had a letter and visiting card & business card from Mr. T. Jeff Himes A.M.</u>

Thursday [Oct.] 23rd. Very pleasant day but as Annie was anxious to finish her dress we did not go to Mrs. Derr's.

Friday [Oct.] 24th. Very pleasant day. Mother took Annie & I to town after dinner and we shopped and told Ella we were in town. Then Annie stopped at Boyds' while I went to Houcks' and sat and talked awhile; and after going to Dr. Jenks we went to Callie's to take tea. Cle Sifford and a Miss Burkette called. Ella came to tea, and Annie & I walked home after tea.

Saturday [Oct.] 25th. Raining in showers all day; nevertheless, I went to town and did some shopping and then stopped at Ella's awhile before coming home.

---

[39]Alice Derr, a younger sister of Margaret and Mary (see Appendix III), continued Mary Derr's diary for 1860 to 1861.

1856

Sunday Oct. 26th. Very pleasant day. Annie S. & I went to Episcopal church and were placed by sexton in Messrs. Gambril & Johnson's pew, heard a very good sermon [by] Rev. Mr. Seymour. After church came out home. After tea Annie & I took a long walk. Tom Derr & Jemmy Gambril arrived about seven o'clock and sat till after nine o'clock. A great deal of nonsense talked, etc.- - - - - -

Monday [Oct.] 27th. Cloudy day, but after dinner much appearance of clearing so Annie & I walked over to see Emma Howard, but she was not at home. So we returned and about four o'clock John William Brengle brought Jennie Brengle[40], Mary Schley & Sophia Gaither and all sat about an hour or so. Rained at night.

Tuesday [Oct.] 28th. Cleared off windy. Mother, Annie & I went down and spent afternoon with Mr. Wm. Miller's family. [We] found himself, little Evie & Willie & Miss Ann at home, and soon Mr. & Mrs. J. H. Detrick came and Isie Buckey & Sarah Miller took [tea] with us also. Got home about seven o'clock, [and] found Miss Clingan, Miss Osburn and Annie C. & Miss Welty had been here but did not remain as we were not home.

Wednesday Oct. 29th. Pleasant day. I took Annie Scholl in town to spend day & night. Cousin Ed S. was out at night expecting to see Annie. I had a nice long letter from Mary E. Sauerwein by Cousin Ed.

Thursday [Oct.] 30th. Very pleasant day. About one o'clock Annie Scholl returned with her brother Charles, who came to take her home, so our expected visits are spoiled. I went into town after Annie left and called to see Ella awhile & then came on out home. Party going to Cousin Ed's to-night.

Friday [Oct.] 31st. Cold, windy day with slight snow squall. I was busy housecleaning all morning. Mr. Schaeffer & Cousin Ed spent the evening with us. Mr. S. gave all news relative to <u>Dr. M's fixings</u>[41].

* * * * *

---

[40] On the Brengle-Scholl family relationship, see note 25, 1858.

[41] This refers to the Dr. Martin who was to marry Nellie Mering. See December 30, 1856, and January 8, 1857.

1856

Sunday [Nov.] 2nd [1856]. Lovely day. Went into town rather early, stopped at Mrs. M. and at ten Ellie & I went to church and heard an excellent discourse from Dr. Zack on Mr. Sentzbaugh's decease. The church was very much crowded to hear the funeral discourse. Cousin Ed. came down with E, & Mr. H. with me.

* * * * *

Tuesday Nov. 4th. Raining in showers during the morning. To-day will decide which of the three candidates Fillmore, Buchanan or Fremont is to fill the executive chair for the next four years.[42]

Wednesday Nov. 5th. Cold, clear day. John took me into town and we brought Ella Brunner out with us. After dinner E & I walked over to Mrs. I. Howard's and spent the evening. Mrs. Rice from town, Mrs. Clingan, Mrs. Osburn, and Miss Welty were all there. We spent a very pleasant afternoon and returned home after tea. Cousin Ed & Mr. Schaeffer spent the evening here. Mr. S told us of the Dr. etc.

Thursday [Nov.] 6th. Much warmer & very calm. E & I were home all day busy. Cousin Ed & Mag Derr came about five o'clock to tea, and afterwards Messrs. Cline & W. Boyd, and staid till after ten o'clock. Mag & E left about nine.

Friday [Nov.] 7th. Pleasant day. After an early dinner E & I went to town and were out shopping a little & to see Mrs. John Ramsburg, but she was not at home, & at Call Bantz's awhile.

* * * * *

Sunday [Nov.] 9th. Very pleasant day. I went into church and stopped for E & we went to church together. Mr. Cline was out to see me in [the] afternoon & sat about three hours.

Monday Nov. 10th. Very keen day. Father took me into town and I shopped some little, and then went to Kunkels' and sat more than an hour, and then

---

[42]In the presidential election of 1856, the candidates were James Buchanan, Democrat, John C. Fremont, Republican and Anti- Slavery, and Millard Fillmore, Whigs and Know Nothing Party. Buchanan was elected and served as President from 1857 to 1861.

1856

came out home. After dinner Mother & I went down and took tea at Mr. Grafton Fout's. Wrote to Lou Clip[pinger] to Oxford, Pa., also to Mr. H. Smith.

* * * * *

Wednesday [Nov.] 12th. Very pleasant day. Dr. McGill[43] is married to-day. Many changes among young friends. /Not very well./

* * * * *

Sunday [Nov.] 16th. Rather damp, cloudy day. I went into town, stopped for Ella and we went to church. Mr. Cline walked with Ella most of the way. Mr. Jemmy Gambrill was here at night.

* * * * *

Wednesday [Nov.] 19th. Very pleasant day. I went into town to meet Mag Derr but she did not come in, so I went with Mrs. Markel[l] & Ella to Mrs. B. F. Winchester's, but she was not in, only Mrs. Smith of Iowa. We were also at Mrs. J. G. Doll's and Ella & I at Houcks' awhile, and afterwards I went to do some shopping.

Thursday [Nov.] 20th. Thanksgiving Day. Very pleasant day. Mother went to church but I staid at home. Mr. Wils Boyd was here in the afternoon and sat an hour or so. Mr. Jemmy Gambrill arrived about seven, and about eight we started to town and stopped at the Hotel and afterwards both walked to see Sophie Gaither, and afterwards proceeded to Mr. Robert McGill's to call on the Dr. & his bride. [We] spent the time very pleasantly till about ten o'clock when we all left, and after stopping at the hotel we came out home.

* * * * *

Saturday [Nov.] 22nd. Very pretty day. Went into town in the afternoon & Ella and I did some shopping and I came out home. Cousin Ed was on the street with us. I had a nice long letter from Lou Clip[pinger] who was in Pittsburgh.

---

[43]Dr. McGill married Mary Riggs of Montgomery County. Williams, *History*, II, 1155.

1856

Sunday [Nov.] 23rd. Beautiful morning. I went into church, stopped for Ella & we went to church together. Mr. J. A. J. was out about two and sat till nearly five. I told him my opinion and my request that, while he and Clint were in partnership I did not wish him to visit me again.

Monday [Nov.] 24th. A lovely day. I slept not well, thinking how I had acted towards Mr. J. A. J. and maybe I had done wrong, for he has always been so kind to me. I went into [town] in the afternoon, stopped at Ella's and afterwards went to Worman's[44] for Mag Derr, and we went shopping and then down to [get] Ella and Mary. Ella & I went and took a walk and I came home then, & brought Mary Brunner out with me.

Tuesday [Nov.] 25th. Wrote to Lou Clip[pinger]. Mary B. seemed well amused, but as it ceased raining about three o'clock Mary & I went to town to see the Illumination, but there was none, so we spent the evening socially together.

Wednesday [Nov.] 26th. A beautiful, bright morning. Mother came in and we did shopping together & I returned home with her but, as I had promised Ella to go to the sewing society[45] with her & remained [sic] over night, E & I went to the society and did some sewing, and afterwards did some shopping and were to see Mrs. John Lynch, and then we returned to Mrs. Markel[l]'s. Cousin Ed came for us and we went down town to see the Illumination. [We] saw [the] procession pass twice. Cousin Ed left about ten o'clock. Lizzie Brengle married to Charlie Kemp to-night.

Thursday [Nov.] 27th. Pleasant day. Wrote to Nellie Mering; came home about ten, Marian Howard [came] over & spent afternoon. Em is to be married 10 Dec.

Friday Nov. 28th. Pleasant morning, but cloudy after two o'clock. I went into town with Mother, called for E and, after seeing company, went down street together. I went to Kunkels' to meet Ed but saw Mrs. McGill & Miss

---

[44] The Henry Worman house is listed on the south side of Patrick Street between Middle and Chapel Alley. *Williams' Directory*, p. 42.

[45] The Ladies Sewing Society presented a pipe organ costing $1,200 to the congregation of the Reformed Church in 1840. J. and D. Ranck, *History of the Evangelical Reformed Church*, pp. 99-100.

1856

Magruder on the street, so did not go to call. Ella & I were at Mrs. Zack['s] awhile.

* * * * *

Sunday [Nov.] 30th. Very pleasant day. I went to town and stopped at Mrs. Markel[l]'s and went to church with them. [I] came home and after eating dinner went over & sat [a] couple hours at Mrs. I. Howard's.

Monday December 1st [1856]. Very pleasant day, busy at my dress. I wrote to Mary & Kate Sauerwein.

Tuesday [Dec.] 2nd. Damp morning and raining in afternoon. [I] had a note from Mag Derr to come out to-morrow evening. I was in town to do some shopping and got home soon after two o'clock, and about three there was a rap at the front door and it proved to be Messrs. T. J. Himes & I. Silas Seaz of Rock Island, Ill. Mr. H. had a letter of introduction from Lou. They seemed to be very agreeable young men. We spent the evening talking, playing backgammon, etc. They are young men who seem to be well informed. Mr. L. [is] decidedly most pleasant on first acquaintance but Mr. H. so good-natured.

Wednesday Dec. 3rd. Raining some still. The gents & Father were looking round this morning and I was busy some little [sic]. After dinner we started into town, called for Ella and went with her, Mr. H. with me, Mr. L. with E. first through our church, then to Mrs. Zack['s] to get some sewing and afterwards to Houcks' & saw Georgia & Lizzie. Came down street and Messrs. L., H. & I all proceeded out to Mr. Derr's, where we met Mr. & Mrs. Buck, Misses Griffith & Duval & Mrs. Ford to tea; & afterwards Cousin Ed. & old Mr. Lewis called & sat the evening. Spent the evening very pleasantly till about eight o'clock, when we left for home, well pleased. So very windy to-night.

Thursday [Dec.] 4th. Still windy & cold. After dinner we went into town, stopped at E's and waited for Mag & Mary Derr, & then we all went down to Schley's and sat with Ellen & Annie; and from there [we] separated with Derrs at the corner and stopped awhile at E's, and then came out home. After tea [the] gents informed me of their determination to leave this next morning, & we spent the evening pleasantly in conversing & playing backgammon, etc. Had a letter from Mr. Samuel Thos. Heyerseck in Cedar Rapids.

1856

Friday [Dec.] 5th. Much more pleasant day. Soon after breakfast the gentlemen left for Balt., to remain I believe till Monday then go to Washington.

Saturday Dec. 6th. Pleasant day. Busy all morning house-cleaning; after dinner went into town for short time, did some shopping and returned home.

Sunday [Dec.] 7th. Father taken very sick last night with bilious cholic and still continues so. Dr. Moran was out last night, also this morning. Uncles Kemp, Lewis & Dennis Scholl were out & sat nearly all afternoon. Willie Adams was up to see how Father was. Mr. Jemmy Gambrill was over about five & sat till after eight o'clock.

Monday [Dec.] 8th. Pleasant day. Fannie Adams was up after dinner to see Father &, as I was just ready to go to town, she went with me and we stopped numerous places to shop, then came out home. Fannie left soon after. Dr. to see Father.

* * * * *

Wednesday [Dec.] 10th. Pleasant day. Mr. Haines [came] to see Father & some others sent in for a barber to shave Father. Letter of Lou Clip[pinger].

Thursday [Dec.] 11th. Rainy day. Dr. came out late and considered Father so much worse that we concluded we would like to have Dr. Tyler[46] to consult. So [we] sent in & he came immediately, but I think he thought we were needlessly alarmed. Mrs. Roderick remained with us over night.

Friday [Dec.] 12th. Pleasant day. Fannie Adams was up to see Father, also Uncle Artz & Mr. Ed. Smith. I wrote to Lou Clip[pinger] this evening.

Saturday Dec. 13th. Rather cloudy & damp. Jennie Adams was up to see Father. [I had a] note from Aunt Margaret Artz, wrote one in return. Mrs. Roderick was over this afternoon. Mrs. Clingan was up awhile also and after she left Uncle Adams was here, and then Ed. S. to tea & till after ten o'clock.

---

[46]Dr. W. Tyler was a very popular and successful practitioner for 61 years, and died in Frederick in 1872. His office and residence was on the west side of Record Street. Williams, *History*, I, 595.

1856

Sunday [Dec.] 14th. Raining in showers all day. Lewis Thomas was out to see how Father was and also Mr. R. & others. /Mrs. Howard [was here] in afternoon./

Monday [Dec.] 15th. Much more pleasant. Uncle Kemp was out in the morning. After dinner Mother went into town and very soon, Mrs. Sallie & Jennie Adams arrived, and soon Ann Keefer. All remained till about four o'clock.

Tuesday [Dec.] 16th. Pleasant day, butchering day. Dr. pronounces Father better. Aunt Mary Scholl & Randolf are here to dinner and till late in the evening.

Wednesday [Dec.] 17th. Much colder. Mother [was] busy with her lard[47]. Dr. out again. Dr. Zack & John [were] out to see Father in the evening.

Thursday [Dec.] 18th. John [was] sent for the barber, but he could [not] come.

Friday [Dec.] 19th. Damp & somewhat cloudy. Mother [in town] in the morning to tell the Dr. how Father was. I went in the evening to do some shopping & was to see Ellie B and we were up street together.

* * * * *

Sunday Dec. 21st. Quite cold. I went into town & went up to church with M. Markel[l] and afterwards came out home.

Monday [Dec.] 22nd. Sent in for Lizzie Clark and we very soon got to sewing and were very busy. Blowing hard.

Tuesday [Dec.] 23rd. Still so busy. Mr. R. here. Very windy & cold.

Wednesday [Dec.] 24th. Very cold & windy. Lizzie & I were busy all day & started to walk to town about four o'clock, found it so windy. I stopped at Mrs. Markel[l]'s and after tea Ella & I went to the Fair. Found very few persons there & seemed to be no buying at all, same way last night. Mr. Rohrback was at M. Markel[l]'s and afterwards came to the Fair for us but we had left.

---

[47]Lard is made, after the hog butchering, by heating the fat to a liquid state. This process is called "rendering."

1856

Thursday [Dec.] 25th. Christmas. All up in good time to see Christmas presents. Ella got handsome dress, pocket handker-chief, gloves, etc. Mary [got] various articles. Ella went to Mr. Val. Bruners' to dinner, Mr. Markel[l] to old Mr. Markel[l]'s. Mr. Rohrback was there & sat a long time. Various children -- Mrs. M., Mary & I enjoyed our dinner together. Ella returned about four & brought Mr. R. with her, also Ed S. at six o'clock. Dr. Delasmuth & Wils Boyd called & staid till after seven. Mr. R. went to the Fair with us. Plenty [of] people, sold [a] great deal. Mr. Gambrill came home with me. [*Five additional lines written perpendicular to this entry.*]: Jemmy Gambrill & Mr. Horace Gambrill also Jemy Craines were at our house. Frank Markel[l] & bride were at Mrs. Markel[l]'s. Dr. Sanderson & Mr. Charles Markel[l] were also at M. Markel[l]'s. Uncle Kemp & Uncle Lewis Scholl [were] at our house.

Friday [Dec.] 26th. Rather cold but clear. I came out home before breakfast. Mother was in town awhile. I went into town about four o'clock and I took Mary B. up street to do some shopping and then returned and staid over night. M. S. Birely called for Mag Derr, Cousin Ed for Ella & me, and we went to the fair and were soon followed by Mr. & Mrs. Markel[l] & Mary B & Mary Derr. At the Fair [we] were joined by Messrs. J. A. Johnson & Rohrback. Mr. J. A. J. of course left before us. Mr. R. came home with Mary Derr. The gents remained till after eleven o'clock, and we sat and talked well after one o'clock. I bought a cake.

Saturday [Dec.] 27th. Very pleasant day. Mag D. went up street with me and I called at Dr. Zack's for my cake. I left Mag D. at M. Markel[l]'s, then came out home, and as it was such a lovely day I concluded I would return to town; and after Ella had seen all the company we went together, called on Mrs. Dr. McGill, found her out, and at Houcks'; and to do some shopping. I came home unexpectedly. Ma sent for me.

Sunday [Dec.] 28th. Rather damp & cold. I went into town & E & I went to church together. I came out after church. Uncle Artz was here awhile.

Monday [Dec.] 29th. Cold day. Lizzie Clark [is] sewing for me. Messrs. Schaeffer & Sifford were out to see me [a] few minutes to have me go with them to Cousin Ed's tomorrow.

Tuesday [Dec.] 30th. Warmer. Nellie Mering was married today to Dr. Wm. A. Martin. About ten o'clock Mr. Sybly arrived. About eleven Mr. Dick Harlow and Anna Scholl arrived and all remained till about four o'clock, when I took Lizzie Clark into town, and left my regrets with E. that I could not attend the party to-night as Father has been much worse all day.

1856

Wednesday [Dec.] 31st. Pleasant morning but afternoon cloudy with every appearance of snow. Mr. Jemmy Gambrill came about half-past seven & sat a couple of hours. Thus has passed another year and perhaps I have many things to regret, but could I do them over I might not do them better; and as regards Mr. J. A. J., I may regret but I cannot think I have done wrong, and it may make me forget the love I once bore him and think of some one more worthy or maybe less so. At present, if I do not love him, best it is a friend I bid adieu, and it may be forever, on the 28th of July. I think [him] an excellent young man in many particulars and at present, if he could convince me of his love, I might marry him, but the time for my changing my name [has] not yet arrived. At present Mr. J[emmy] G[ambrill] visits me oftener but I know he does not love me.

(Photo from Scharf *History of Western Maryland)*

Edward A. Shriner "Cousin Ed,"
son of Cornelius and Rebecca Scholl Shriner

1857

"Bride & party made their appearance about six o'clock. Sat supper at ten...Dancing from about twelve till six, when people began to disperse..."

January 1st, 1857. Another year is run, another year begun, and may I improve each day and may Ella's prophesy prove true that trouble will cause my heart to be softened. Mr. I. Howard was over to see Father on business this morning. About ten o'clock I started out to Mr. Derr's, stopped for E. but she was down with little Frank Bruner, who is very ill. I went out alone. Mary & Mag D. came in with me and we all staid at Houcks' over night. Misses Julia & Mary Lyon are staying there. Mary, Mag D., Mary S., Georgia & Tilly H. & myself all went to the Fair together. We staid till about half-past nine, when we returned to the H[ouck's]. Messrs. Schaeffer & Eader were there. I had a card of invitation from Mr. & Mrs. Mering to a party Jan. 8th, given to Dr. & Mrs. Nellie Martin [sic].[1]

Friday [Jan.] 2nd. Cloudy day. Cold much worse. I wrote a note to Cousin Ed. S. relative to taking me [to Bruceville]. Came out home about ten o'clock.

* * * * *

Monday [Jan.] 5th. Cloudy. I was in town to do shopping. Saw Cousin Ed and had a nice long talk. Mrs. Hershey was here to see me & Messrs. Dill & Smith to see Father. I had a letter from Lou Clip[pinger].

Tuesday Jan. 6th. Quite cold & windy. About three o'clock Mary Derr and her father came out & sat about an hour or two, and Mary & I had a nice long talk relative to the past year.

---

[1] Nellie Mering and Dr. William A. Martin had been married on December 30, 1856.

1857

Wednesday [Jan.] 7th. Cold & very raw; John took me into town, did some shopping, saw Cousin Ed S. on the street. At Mrs. B. F. Winchester's but she was not in. Stopped at Houcks', saw family & Miss Julia Lyon. Was at Mrs. Markel[l]'s awhile, saw family all & Mrs. Charles Markell & Annie Trail. Then came out home.

BRUCEVILLE

Thursday [Jan.] 8th. Very cold. Busy till after twelve o'clock, when Cousin Ed. arrived with carriage & pair & driver to take me down to Mrs. Mering's. [We] started about half-past one and after various stoppings arrived there about five o'clock and after dressing went to the parlour, where were assembled about one hundred persons. Bride & party made their appearance about six o'clock. Sat supper at ten. Refreshment table at two [a.m.]. Dancing from about twelve till six, when people began to disperse, and we laid down to a nap till about eleven. Spent the evening very pleasantly, renewing some old acquaintances & made some new ones. Every one seemed to enjoy themselves, had a Ca[l]lithumpian Serenade[2].

Friday Jan. 9th. Not so cold. Very fashionable, breakfasted at 12 and dinner at six, and then we all fifteen got ready to go up to Mr. Delaplaine's to spend the evening. [We] went up about eight and spent a very pleasant evening and got back to Mr. Mering's about twelve. All well pleased, also sleepy. I had a very bad toothache.

Saturday [Jan.] 10th. Up & breakfasted about eight. Balt[imore] Co. folks started off about 9 o'clock, and we about ten. It began to snow before we left and snowed hard till we got home. Dixon O'Dell & Lizzie Houck came up in a buggy as we came. Just after we had finished dinner George Sauerwein arrived and sat about an hour & half. He had much to say and brought me a letter from Mary Sauerwein. I retired very early and slept well.

Sunday [Jan.] 11th. Very cold and I feared not good sleighing, so I did not go to town. Mr. James Gambrill was over after tea in his sleigh & sat the evening. He gave me an account of Maulsby party, etc.

---

[2] A Callithumpian Serenade was a noisy or boisterous performance often to honor a newly married couple. *Webster's Dictionary.*

1857

Monday [Jan.] 12th. Moderated today. Mother went down to Mr. Bushey's[3] after she heard of James' death.

Tuesday Jan. 13th. Not so cold. Mother & John went this morning to the funeral and were gone all day.

* * * * *

Thursday [Jan.] 15th. Cold day. Baked fruit cake, bound[4] it. Mag Derr walked out about twelve o'clock and I took her [home] in the carriage about three. Did some shopping and were at Mrs. Markel[l's] awhile; E. [was] not home. Paper from Ill.

* * * * *

Saturday [Jan.] 17th. I was going to town in afternoon but [it] commenced snowing about two o'clock, so [I] postponed it. I had a letter from Mr. T. Jeff Himes[5], Davenport, Iowa.

Sunday [Jan.] 18th. Commenced snowing about nine & snowed & blowed [*sic*] all day, disagreeable & cold.

* * * * *

Wednesday [Jan.] 21st. Mother [was] in town & gave us an account of how the roads were drifted. I wrote to Lou Clip[pinger] [and] got papers today. No mail since Saturday.

Thursday [Jan.] 22nd. Still no road to town & very cold.

Friday [Jan.] 23rd. Mr. R. [came] over to talk of a road through the fields.

---

[3]The Bushey place, a farm of 148 acres, was located near Limekiln on Route 85 north of Buckeystown. Williams, *History*, II, 1033.

[4]Each baked fruit cake was wrapped in several layers of cheesecloth well soaked in rum, cognac, sherry or Madeira, and placed in an airtight container. Helen Duprey Bullock, *The American Heritage Cookbook* (American Heritage Publishing Company, New York, 1964), p. 603.

[5]Mr. T. J. Himes had visited the Scholls in early December, 1856 (see December 2-5, 1856).

1857

Saturday [Jan.] 24th. Coldest day as yet. Mr. R. opened a road through fields.

Sunday [Jan.] 25th. Cold morning but [it] moderated very much. I was in town to church, [and] Communion. Stopped to see Ella after church & took dinner there.

Monday Jan. 26th. Very cold morning but moderated after while. Mother and I went into town and I went to Houcks' to meet Mag Derr and from there we went to do some shopping, and afterwards went out to their house. I had a letter from Mr. Lease enclosing three cards, one for Ella B, M. Derr & me. I helped Mag fix dress. Eugene Derr & I went in sleigh to Mr. Ogburn's to do some shopping. I enjoyed the ride. Cousin Ed spent the evening with us.

Tuesday [Jan.] 27th. Damp, disagreeable day. Company did not come. Cousin Ed [came] twice a day, and to spend the evening. Paper from Chicago.

Wednesday [Jan.] 28th. Very unpleasant day. Snowing afternoon & night.

Thursday [Jan.] 29th. Pleasant day. Cousin Ed took dinner, called in evening & spent the evening. Mr. J. Gambrill came about six o'clock, had been to our house with <u>his pair</u> & spent evening. About eight o'clock 2 Miss Houcks, 2 Miss Mains, Cle Sifford, Sue Jones, Sue Haup, Miss Delasmuth, Drs. Delasmuth & Schaeffer & Messrs. Boags, Sifford, Eader, Reich & Birely arrived & staid till half-past eleven. They all seemed to enjoy themselves very much. Cousin Ed staid till nearly one o'clock. I wrote to Mary Sauerwein for some cotton.

Friday [Jan.] 30th. Dr. Zack & Lizzie & Georgia H. came out to the Derrs' to dinner. Cousin Ed came while [we were] at dinner and took me into town, and I was at Houcks' and then came out home with Mother.

Saturday Jan. 31st. Snowed all morning. Mrs. Lewis Markell & Callie Bantz & little Mary B. came out and sat awhile. I had a letter from Lou Clip.

Sunday Feb. 1st [1857]. Mother & I went into town, stopped at Mrs. Markell['s] and Mr. Markell went to church with me. Thomas Derr came down street with me, pleasant day. Thomas & Cousin Ed were out & took tea with us. Pleasant day.

Monday [Feb.] 2nd. Colder again. I went into town to meet Mag Derr & we were at Kunkels' together and at Dr. Macgill's to make an engagement for Thursday. Mr. James Gambrill with his pair arrived about four o'clock & invited me to take a ride with him & I went to town with him and we had supper after we returned about eight o'clock. Mag Derr, Ed S., George Birely & Annie Schley arrived and after awhile, Misses Mann, Cle Sifford & Kunkels & Messrs. Jones & Sifford. They all staid till after eleven o'clock & seemed to enjoy [themselves]. Am invited to Mr. G's tomorrow night; also to go with him to Schells' Thursday night.

Tuesday [Feb.] 3rd. I went [to town] after dinner. Stopped at Mrs. Markell's and wanted Ella to come home with me. I went to Mrs. J. Houck's to see her & took tea. I did not go to Mr. Gambrill's.

Wednesday [Feb.] 4th. Quite warm. I went in & Ella & I were at Dr. Macgill's nearly all afternoon. I had [a] letter of Nellie Mering Martin.

Thursday [Feb.] 5th. Pleasant warm day. I was busy all day. Mr. Gambrill came about half-past seven o'clock & I hurried & got ready to go to Mr. Schell's. We went in a hurry, had an upset & enjoyed it. Found family all well & saw Mary & Mag Derr, Cousin Ed & Mr. J. A. J. there; spent the evening very pleasantly and all returned or started before eleven; had a pleasant ride.

Friday [Feb.] 6th. Still warm & very foggy; nevertheless, I went into town to have Dr. M. fix some of my teeth.

Saturday [Feb.] 7th. Very pleasant day. I wrote a note to Lizzie Schell to send me her slipper pat[t]ern, etc.

* * * * *

Wednesday [Feb.] 11th. Pleasant overhead. Mother & I walked into town and I soon saw Cousin Ed, who went with me to Kunkels', where we had a long talk; & from there we went shopping (Mother & I) and afterwards stopped at Houcks' till Cousin Ed called for me. Georgia H. went out to Mr. Derr's with us. We did not go [back] to Houcks'. I had letters from Mary Sauerwein & Mary Helen Smith & also a note from Lizzie Schell with pat[t]ern.

1857

Thursday 12th Feb. Right pleasant day. After dinner Cousin Ed stopped & took Georgia H., Mary Derr & me into town. We stopped awhile at Houcks' & I came then to Mrs. Markel[l]'s awhile, and afterwards walked out home.

Friday [Feb.] 13th. Mary & I entertained each other this gloomy day and succeeded well.

* * * * *

Monday [Feb.] 16th. Rained in morning, so we did not go to town till after dinner. We were at Mrs. Reese's. Lou and Ella B. joined us & from there [we went] shopping. Letter from Lou Clip[pinger] & paper from Mr. T. J. Himes. Mary Derr staid with Ellen to-night.

Tuesday [Feb.] 17th. Foggy morning, but proved a very bright afternoon. Mother & I spent the day with Aunt Mary Scholl. Stopped at Mr. Derr's a few minutes. Ella B was staying with the girls. Stopped a minute or so at Mrs. Markel[l]'s. /Found Mr. J. H. Gambrill's <u>card</u> at home when I arrived./

Wednesday [Feb.] 18th. Very pleasant day. Letter from Lou [Clippinger] saying she would be here Thursday night.

Thursday [Feb.] 19th. Busy all day. Cloudy & drizzling in the afternoon. Did not go in to meet Lou as it was so dark. Uncle Feltz Thomas died this morning.

Friday Feb. 20th. Very damp with slight rain. Mother went into town early this morning but Lou did not come last night; but near twelve o'clock there was a rap and Mr. & Mrs. Clippinger arrived. I had just sent John to town to see if they had come. We spent the day at home. All glad to see them, also to see them looking so well.

Saturday [Feb.] 21st. Foggy early but soon cleared off very prettyly [sic]. Lou, Mr. C. & I [went] into town. Went with Lou shopping, also to mantua-maker's. Saw Mr. J. A. J. in the street & had [a] short talk with him. I was at Kunkels' awhile and told them to come out to-day. When we got home, found Mag, Mary & Eugene Derr there & soon Mary & Melia Kunkel came out & spent the evening. All left after an early tea.

Sunday [Feb.] 22nd. Delightful morning. Mr. C., Lou & I went to church, stopped at City Hotel. Cousin Ed accompanied us down street. Mr.

Schaeffer came up in the parlour to see us. About three o'clock Cousin Ed & Mr. S. came out, and about 5 Mr. Gambrill arrived & all staid till about 9 o'clock.

Monday [Feb.] 23rd. Very bright pleasant day. I was busy in the morning & after dinner Mr. C., Lou & I went to town; [Lou and I] stopped to see E. awhile and then down street. Met Mr. C. when we were ready to come out.

Tuesday Feb. 24th. Very pleasant day. Lou, Mr. C. & I went out to spend the day at Mr. Derr's. Ella B, Kate Jacobs, Lizzie Houck, Martha Getzendanner, [and] Cousin Ed all took dinner at Mr. Derr's; & after dinner we all went to Cousin Ed's & were weighed. I weighed 138 lbs. I am still gaining. Soon after we came back we started for home; stopped at Aunt M. Artz's awhile & then came into town; were at Miss Reading's and also at Kunkels' awhile, and then came out home. We spent the evening pleasantly at home.

Wednesday [Feb.] 25th. Was up early, as Mr. & Mrs. C. are going to start for [New] Oxford to-day & want to get off by the seven o'clock train. I went into town with them but returned with the carriage. I found the fronts for Mr. C.'s slippers and sent them by to-day's mail. I went into town, stopped for Mary Kunkel & we started for Catechism, but Dr. Z. had none on account of Mr. Luckett's[6] funeral, so Mary & I went to Mrs. Loats[7] to see the funeral pass; and afterwards took a long walk out [to] Bentz Town[8], and I stopped awhile at Mrs. Markel[l]'s and then came out home.

Thursday [Feb.] 26th. Cooler & windy. Father & Mother have gone to Cousin Ed's to spend the day. I wrote a note to Mary D. to meet me in town

---

[6] Mountjoy B. Luckett, Jr., Esq. was a lawyer who had been the defense lawyer in several murder cases in Frederick. Engelbrecht, *Diary*, II, 634, 637.

[7] The residence of Mr. and Mrs. John Loats was near their tannery on the east side of Market Street between Patrick and All Saints streets. *Williams' Directory*, p. 24.

[8] At this time this would be thought of as a walk in the countryside as there were few houses here. Bentz Town began at the bend of Patrick Street and Carroll Creek and extended to Stephen Steiner's dwelling and tavern which stood at the west end of the town. It was included in the 1782 plat prepared for Clement Hollyday. When Frederick was incorporated in 1816, this area was included for tax purposes. Scharf, *Western Maryland*, I, 484.

1857

to-morrow afternoon. I wrote a note to Mr. T. J. Himes in answer to his of Jan. 8th.

Friday Feb. 27th. Very pleasant day. I went into town in the afternoon & Mary Derr & I went to see Mr. Wheatly, Mrs. Callie Bantz, Mrs. D. Schley & Mrs. Frank Markel[l], this latter one not being in. /Mag Derr went to Phila[delphia] to-day./ Cousin Ed joined me on the street & insisted on my staying in town & going to hear Miss Whitehouse sing; so after seeing Ellen I remained in town & I went with Cousin Ed & Ella with Mr. Rohrback, & we spent the evening very pleasantly. The gentlemen sat awhile at Mr. Markell's after we returned.

Saturday [Feb.] 28th. Quite clear & cold. Lizzie Schell & Kate Randall & George Schell spent the day here today. I was sorry I had not the materials for my slippers. They came in & brought me out home.

Sunday March 1st [1857]. Pleasant morning, but very windy at night. Mother & I were in to church. Mr. J. Gambrill came about four o'clock and remained till nearly ten.

* * * * *

Tuesday [Mar.] 3rd. Still windy. Mother & I walked out to Mr. E. Howard's and spent the afternoon. Very pleasant evening. Dr. Geo. Johnson was there.

Wednesday [Mar.] 4th. Rather cloudy & damp. I went into town with Mother and I went to Catechism and afterwards Mary Derr & I went to see Kate Bantz Davis & afterwards at Steiners' a few minutes.

Thursday March 5th. Cloudy in the morning and raining in the afternoon. Mother & I were in town at Dr. Macgill's on business; saw Mrs. Frank Markell there and also the Dr.'s lady.

Friday [Mar.] 6th. Clear & windy. I had an early dinner and went to Mrs. Graft[on] Fout's and Joan Grove & I went to Uncle Adams' and spent the afternoon. [It] passed pleasantly. Ginny & Fanny were just ready to start up to our house.

Saturday [Mar.] 7th. Rather pleasant day, considering the fall of snow last night. I went to town & stopped for Mary Kunkel and we went to Catechism together & afterwards to see Aunt Shriner awhile. I then came on down and out home. I had a note from Mary Derr wanting [me] to go home with her to-morrow, also a letter from Maggie Derr from Phil'd [Philadelphia].

Sunday [Mar.] 8th. Rather cold. I took medicine, so remained at home. Jerry Cramer & Hen Gittinger came about one o'clock & remained till about five. Mr. Gambrill came about five & remained till after ten. <u>He had much to say.</u>

Monday [Mar.] 9th. Cloudy morning and about 9 commenced snowing, but I was in town, already to go out with Eugene Derr, so I went out and spent the day very pleasantly with the family. I wrote to Maggie Derr. Cousin Ed was over at night. [It] snowed all day but cleared off about sundown.

Tuesday March 10th. Very pleasant day. After eating an early dinner Mary Derr brought me into town and I just jumped out of the buggy on [to] my horse, [and] came out home and stopped a few moments, & [then] rode down to Mr. Fout's for Joan Grove, & went to Mr. I. Howard's. Harriet, Mary & Charlotte Keefer, Sarah Miller, Mrs. Deitrick & Mrs. Jarboe, Miss Grove & Mr. Grove had all been there to dinner and remained to tea, immediately after which we started for home. I wrote to Nellie Mering Martin.

* * * * *

Thursday [Mar.] 12th. Clear day. After dinner I went down & spent the afternoon with Ellen Jarboe. Mrs. Grove, Miss Grove, Harriet & Mary Keefer were there and about four o'clock Sarah Miller & Mrs. Dietrick came & very soon Mr. Frank Grove & Miss Iris Mantz. We all left before sundown. Mother [was] at Mrs. Bushey's.

Friday [Mar.] 13th. Clear morning but cloudy afterwards. Father & Mother went up to Aunt Hedge's to dinner. I wrote to Mary Sauerwein & sent Nellie Martin's letter; had a letter from Mag Derr & paper of Mr. T. J. Himes. Snowed at night.

Saturday [Mar.] 14th. Was surprised to find the snow so deep but it [was] so warm that I went to town in the carriage after dinner. Went to Catechism & afterwards Mary Derr & I were at Houcks' and shopped some together. Ellen Brunner came out & remained over night.

1857

Sunday March 15th. A lovely day. E & I went to town about nine o'clock and stopped at Mr. M's and went to church with them. Mary Derr came out home, but there was no other company.

Monday [Mar.] 16th. Mary & I were busy this morning doing various little things and I answered Mr. J. Silas Seaz['] letter at last. Mary & I went to town about three o'clock & were to see Mrs. B. F. Winchester (not at home), and at Kunkels' sometimes.

Tuesday [Mar.] 17th. A lovely day. I was busy doing up collars, etc. all day.

Wednesday [Mar.] 18th. Pleasant day. Mary Derr was out this morning and I sent off a note to Lou Clippinger with the collar inclosed. I sent it by Mary to post.

BALTIMORE

Thursday [Mar.] 19th. Raining when I got up but ceased before eight o'clock, and I started to town to go to Balt. I had a dreary ride to Balt. A bride & groom [were] aboard the cars, Dr. Motter & lady. [It] rained very hard and [was] still raining when we got to Balt. Geo. met me and we went up to the house in a carriage, then found the family & Mag Derr all glad to welcome me. Mag D. got [there] from Phil'd. on Monday. Houcks left yesterday. Snowed hard but too warm for it today. Tom Derr spent evening. /Sam Sadtler there awhile./

Friday [Mar.] 20th. Windy day. Mag Derr & I were out shopping, stopped to see Nell Dean but she was out. Miss Fox [was] at home when we returned. Mr. Gregg called for us as by engagement, & Mag D, Kate & I went with him out on the York road to Cool Spring[9] and returned. Had a pleasant day. G. & Tilly Houck [were] here [a] short time. At night I wrote home. Mr. P. Rau and John Derr spent the evening with us. [*One line is illegible*].

Saturday March 21st. Bright, clear day. Georgie Houck & Mrs. O'Dell called about ten o'clock & sat awhile, and afterwards Mag Derr & I were out shopping, and then stopped at Mrs. Burton's where John & Thomas Derr have a room, & Mag overlooked their clothes. /Miss Sophia Banseman was

---

[9]Cool Spring is near Lutherville on the York Road (Route 45). *Rand McNally Map of Baltimore* (Chicago, IL, 1986).

here./ Mag & I returned to dinner. About four o'clock Mary S. & I started down street. Met Cousin Ed. S. on the street & he accompanied us to the Marine Bank[10], where we made a call to see the family & did some shopping as we returned. Mrs. Jim Webster was at the house when we returned & staid awhile. Cousin Ed was here at night, also Mr. A. Gregg & Thomas Derr. Retired late.

Sunday [Mar.] 22nd. Clear, delightful day. Geo. S. went with Houcks to church. Cousin Ed called for us and went [with] Mary & me, and Mag D. & Kate went along, to Dr. Irvin's. We spent the day there. Mr. Rau came in [the] afternoon. Mary S., Mag D. & I went out to hear Rev. Mr. Seiss in afternoon. When we got back found the gentlemen hat in hand ready to invite us to walk, so Mary and I went with them out Charles St. Pleasant walk. /Mr. Fulton & Cousin Nellie Dean had been [there] for me to take a walk./ After tea Cousin Ed, Mag D., Kate & I & Mr. Rau all went out to hear Rev. Mr. Lefevre preach an excellent sermon. Mr. L. came home with Kate. Found Mrs. A. Reese at home when [we] returned; had come with Mary from Dr. Irvin's.

Monday [Mar.] 23rd. Rainy morning but clear after noon. Mag Derr & I went to catechism with the girls. Miss Spilken returned & sat awhile. Mag Derr [was] out a short time. About three o'clock Cousin Ed called and sat till time to go to the cars. Mrs. Trowbridge & her sister Georgia called this afternoon. Mr. Bayfield [too], & before he left, Mr. Lefevre, also Houcks. [We were] talking all night. Mrs. Ashland [was here] but I did not see her. Was at sewing society. G. came for us. John Derr was here, also Dixon O'Dell to see <u>me</u>.

Tuesday March 24th. Pleasant morning but threatening afternoon. I went down to Neal Dean's about 9 o'clock & we were out till about 12; and when I returned [the] girls were ready & we went out to Mrs. Bayfield's, but she was not home, but afterwards [we] met her at Mrs. John Gregg's. Mrs. G. is not well, lying on her lounge. Mrs. B. wants us to spend Thursday evening with her. We were at Abells', also saw Rose & Miss Fox. Rev. Mr. Hitchcock was here while we were out. Sophie & Maria Cockrill & Nettie Kunkle were [here] to see me. Mag D., Mary S., Kate & I were all down at the boys' place, and afterwards all except Kate went out and took tea at Mag's

---

[10]The Marine Bank was located at the northeast corner of Gay and Second Streets. Scharf, *Baltimore*, p. 461.

1857

Aunt Steiner's. John Derr & Geo. S. called for us & Lewis Birely came home with Mag D.

Wednesday [Mar.] 25th. Clear & very windy. Mary S., Mag D. & I were out shopping, bought a robe. Miss Fox was here a short time. Met Annie Schley on the street & had a long talk with her. I went down & took dinner with Neal Dean, & while at dinner Mary S. called for me, as Mr. Gregg has going to call for us. Mary S., Mag D. & I went with Mr. G. out to Govanstown[11], and on our way back [they] left me at Neal's. Mary S., Mag D., Geo. S., Tom Derr came after tea, also Mr. Hinkley, Rev. Mr. Hitchcock & Mr. Firtvan, who came home with me. [We] spent a very pleasant evening.

Thursday [Mar.] 26th. Cold & windy. Houcks came up for Mag & Mary & they all went out visiting. I remained at home. Cousins Mary Bier & Sophie Mantz were up & want Mary & I to spend Saturday evening with them. Mrs. S., Mary & Kate S., Mag & I were all out shopping. Mr. Reese returned with Mary, Kate & me, & sat awhile. Geo. & Thomas Derr went with us & spent the evening at Mrs. Bayfield's very pleasantly. Mr. Gregg & Miss Fox were there.

Friday [Mar.] 27th. Clear & rather cold. While we were dressing Mrs. Brown (Mag Wolfe) was here with her child. It is a very sweet little thing. The girls were out to look at piano covers. I wrote home a short note. Mary, Mag & I were out at Mrs. John Sadtler's but found no one home. We then called at Mrs. Fanny Dix's; she would have been to see us but was prevented by sickness. Was weighed at the store. 141 lbs. After[wards] Mr. Lefevre called [and] spent the evening. Mary, Mag & I were at Abell's to spend the evening with Rose & Miss Fox. Miss Marie Bantz [was] here.

Saturday [Mar.] 28th. Clear day. Busy all morning. Mr. Gregg called for us a short time before four o'clock & took us out to Fort McHenry[12]. I never was more gratified in my life at any place. He left Mary & me at Cousin Jacob Biers['] where we spent a very pleasant evening. Two Cockrills, Nellie & George Burke were there to tea. G. called for us at ten & we left by half

---

[11]Govanstown, named for the Govan family, was then four miles from Baltimore on the York turnpike. It is now part of the city. *The Place Names of Maryland* (Maryland Historical Society, Baltimore, 1984), pp. 102, 156, 891.

[12]See note 23, 1856.

past. Margretta Nicholson & cousin had been there in afternoon & John Derr at night.

Sunday [Mar.] 29th. Cold & cloudy in morning, but clear in afternoon. Mag D., Mary S. & I went down to hear Rev. Mr. Weiner. Mr. Rau down in afternoon. He & G. walked with us down to Mr. Hitchcock's church, but we returned from church before they were back again [*sic*]. All went to church but Mary & me. G. & Mr. Rau returned to talk with us.

Monday [Mar.] 30th. Clear & pleasant day. Em & I were out on a shopping expedition, met Isie Buckey & had a talk. Mrs. Bayfield was here for a while. Mary & I went over & spent the evening at Cousin Rebecca Kink's. Mary Bier & Miss King [came] to tea, Cousin Soph & Mr. Mantz after tea. G, S, & Mr. Gregg came for us about nine & sat till we left. Cousin S. came about ten o'clock. John Derr [was] still with the girls when we got home. Thomas Derr, Lum Sadtler & Mr. Lefevre had been there.

Tuesday, March 31st. Very pleasant day. I had a letter from Mother; [she] wants me to come home. I went with Mag D. & Mary S. part-way [*sic*] & returned, found Miss Fox & Mary Abell there, & soon Houcks & Lizzie Dickey; all sat a while. Mr. Gregg called for us, and Em and Mag D. & I went with him to Canton[13]; had a pleasant ride. Mr. Webster [was] here while we were gone. All went round and spent the evening very pleasantly at Sadtlers'. [We saw] Miss Wiley, Mr. John Morris and family including Lizzie & Mr. Dickey, who is living at home. We spent the evening very pleasantly & returned about eleven.

Wednesday, April 1st, 1857. Up early and, notwithstanding it was cloudy & afterwards rained, Mary S., Mag D. & I all went out to Mount Washington under the direction of Rev. Mr. Staley and were very much gratified with the exercises. [We] saw Mrs. Sarah Bevan there and formed the acquaintance of Dr. & Mrs. Heiner at Mr. Joe. Gambrill's store. We returned by the one o'clock train.[14] Dr. Anderson was [in] to see Em to tell her of his sister's marriage. Kate & Mag [had] gone to John Derr's room. At night, first Lum Sadtler then Mr. Gregg & soon Messrs. John Derr, James Gambrill, Dixon

---

[13]See note 24, 1856.

[14]The village of Mt. Washington was situated on the Northern Central Railway five miles from Baltimore. The surroundings are hilly and romantic. Scharf, *Baltimore*, p. 839.

1857

O'Dell; glad to see them all & spent a very pleasant evening. Miss Fox came at nine.

Thursday [April] 2nd. Pleasant morning. Mr. Gregg sent his carriage for us at ten o'clock to go to his distillery[15] and spent an hour & half there very pleasantly. /Lum Sadtler there for few minutes./ We were taken in Mr. G's carriage to call at Cousin Wm. Dean's, Mrs. Steiner's, Mrs. Dr. Rau's & at Nicholson's. After noon Mag, Mary & I were at Mrs. Uhrlaub who was out, at Mrs. Bayfield [also out] but afterwards met her at Mrs. John Gregg's; & Mary & I took a walk [and] met Mr. Lefevre on the street. He had been at the house, [and] John Derr for a short time. Mag D. & I went with George to the theatre to see the "[*illegible*]" performed.

Friday, April 3rd. Pleasant day. Wrote a note home. Mag Derr left this morning. Mary Jennings (Sauerwein) was there an hour or so. Mrs. Bayfield & Houcks were there in the morning. [We] promised Mrs. B. to spend the evening with her. Afternoon, Mary & I were out shopping to see sewing machines[16], etc. Mr. Webster came home with us. Rev. Mr. Hitchcock & Misses Webb had been to see us. After tea Geo., Mary & Em & I all went up & sat the evening with Mrs. Bayfield. I spent a most delightful evening.

Saturday [April] 4th. Pleasant day. Before I was out of bed [I] had a letter from Mary Derr and a package. Soon after breakfast a letter [came] from Lou Clippinger. Mr. Gregg called for us about half-past three and Mary, Em & I went with him to Houck's pavilion. [We] had a very pleasant ride, saw Burkes. Mr. Lefevre & Emma & Fannie Harmon had been here. Mr. Gregg & Mr. & Mrs. Bayfield sat the evening with us and spent it very pleasantly.

Sunday [April] 5th. Rather cloudy. Mary & I went to Dr. Smith's church beyond the bridge on Market Street. [We] saw Burkes, [who] wanted us to dine with them. Afternoon, Lum Sadtler was there, also Mr. Rau, but Em &

---

[15]For many years Baltimore had a reputation for the manufacture of Rye Whiskeys, and at one time controlled the market in the U.S. By 1877, there were five houses engaged in its production; 450 to 500 barrels of raw material were produced daily. Fully 200 houses large and small engaged in the liquor trade. George W. Howard, *The Monumental City* (Baltimore, 1873), p. 127.

[16]These sewing machines could have been seen at the southern branch of G. Remington and Sons, No. 47 N. Charles Street. They claimed (in 1877) that their sales had increased 70% per annum for the past three years, that their machines were more elegant, made less noise and required less physical power to operate than any other machine. *Ibid*, p. 393.

I went to the Cathedral and Mr. Green walked home with us. John Derr here in the afternoon. At night all went to Dr. Morris' church.

Monday [April] 6th. Did not go to Catechism but packed my trunk while [the others were] gone. Mary & I were out awhile. Rained, snowed, hailed, etc., but notwithstanding, Mary & I went down street awhile. Wrote home. Mr. Gregg was there when we got back, who sat a couple hours. Mr. Webster [was] there awhile. Clear at night, but we did not go to sewing society.

Tuesday, April 7th. Cool, pleasant morning. Em & I were out before 9 o'clock, and after I came back Mary S. & I were out on a shopping expedition, and when I came back I ate my dinner and afterwards packed my trunk, and was ready to start. Mr. Gregg stopped in about 3 o'clock and sat nearly an hour. Mr. Cronise brought Fannie Harmon who was to go with us to the cars. I had a quiet but a pleasant ride up home. Mother & John met me in town & brought me out home, all well & pleased to see me. /Found a note from Mr. T. Jeff Himes./

* * * * *

Thursday [April] 9th. Cloudy. I went in town in [the] afternoon, was to see Ellen B. and afterwards at Mrs. Shiner's and then came out home. Mr. Ed Smith had been here. Paper from Chicago.

Friday [April] 10th. "Good Friday," pleasant morning but cloudy after dinner. I wrote to Mary Sauerwein. After dinner I went into town, stopped at Uncle Kemp's awhile and from there went out to Aunt Lizzie Brunner's awhile. Saw Annie Bentz & Ellen Kemp there. Returned home.

Saturday [April] 11th. Bright morning, busy about domestic duties. In [the] afternoon [I] went to town with Mother, went to Kunkels', then to Catechism and afterwards returned to Kunkels', and had Mary to show me about working the leaf in the undersleeves for Lou. Mary came up street with me; met Mother & John coming in for me to go home.

Easter Sunday [April] 12th. Cloudy morning. I went in, stopped for Ellen to go to church. Jimmy Gambrill [was] here in afternoon and took tea and sat till after 9 o'clock.

1857

Monday [April] 13th. Easter. /David Fout died last night.[17]/ I went into town early, had the horse shod, and then went out to Mr. Derr's and took dinner, and then started with Mary & Mag Derr with me, but it rained so hard that we all stopped at Billy Worman's an hour or so; but it still continued raining, so off we went [sic] that Mag Derr came to town with us. Col. E. Schley[18] died last night.

* * * * *

Wednesday [April] 15th. Cold, windy day. Heard of Mr. Lewis Fout's[19] death. Mother was down in the afternoon.

Thursday [April] 16th. Cold & cloudy part day, <u>sunshiny</u> rest. Mother [was] in town, morning. Afternoon, she & I went down to the funeral of Mr. Lewis Fout. He was buried on the farm. Most of the neighbors [were] there. After we got back I changed my dress somewhat and went into town, stopped at Dr. McGill's and paid him, and then went round in the carriage. Mrs. Dr. M. accompanied me. [I] attended to my business and left her at her home & came out home. Geo. Fout was here a short time.

Friday [April] 17th. Cold & very windy. Mr. W. Derr [was] here a short time. I went in town after dinner to give direction about my bonnet & post a letter to Lou Clip[pinger]. [I] sent [her] undersleeves.

* * * * *

---

[17]David Fout died at the age of 34. Holdcraft, *Names in Stone*, p. 426. The Fouts were among the early settlers who had purchased the "Rocky Creek" area which included Mt. Olivet Cemetery and most of the land between New Design Road and Ballenger Creek. Grace L. Tracey and John P. Dern, *Pioneers of Old Monocacy*, pp. 161-162. The Fout home was one-half mile south of Manchester Farm. *Bond Map*, 1858.

[18]The first Schley in Frederick was Johann Thomas who came to Frederick from Germany in 1745 and built the first house on the land where the Blue Ridge News Agency now stands at 101 East Patrick Street. Colonel Edward Schley (born 1808) was a Colonel of the Frederick Hussars. A Whig and an Episcopalian, he married Margaret Breyle with whom he had 12 children. Williams, *History*, I, 745.

[19]Louis Fout died at the age of 56 years. Holdcraft, *Names in Stone*, p. 427. See also note 17, 1857.

1857

Tuesday [April] 21st. Very changeable day. Clear part time & rain rest. I had a letter from Mary Sauerwein. Mr. J. Gambrill here to tea & till half-past ten o'clock. He seemed in an excellent humour & I loaned him a ring /he loaned me one, and/ wished I had not done it.

Wednesday [April] 22nd. Found the ground covered with snow, & [it] continued snowing till ten o'clock and then cleared away. Sent for the Dr. for Jane. [He] does not think her ill.

Thursday [April] 23rd. Pleasant day. Father started to Balt[imore]. Misses Ann & Harriet Keefer were here to tea. Plenty of talk & news.

Friday [April] 24th. Cool but clear, busy sewing all day. I'm in dreamland was happy last night. "Welcomed a friend to the house who has not trod these halls for five long months."

Saturday [April] 25th. Delightful day. Mother in town all morning. I was busy fixing [sic] in the front yard. Marion Howard came about three o'clock and remained till after tea. I went in town with John to meet Father, who came from Balt. He brought me a note from Mary S. & some patterns.

Sunday [April] 26th. So very pleasant. I stopped for Ellen B. to go to church. Heard a good sermon from Dr. Zack. Cousin L. Hedges came about two and staid till after six. Mr. J. Gambrill [came] about three & remained till after ten. He was in good humour, wouldn't give [me] my ring.

Monday, April 27th. Very windy day. I went into town with Mother and, as I stopped at Kunkels', cousin Ed. S. joined me & we paid a visit there. All [had] plenty to say & [were] very agreeable. I did some little shopping & came out home--walked out.

* * * * *

Wednesday [April] 29th. Very pleasant day. Busy sweeping, etc., early. Mag Derr arrived about eleven o'clock. About two we started and went up to Mr. Boyd's[20] and there had a chat for an hour or so with all the family & old Mr. Ball. They seemed well pleased about Ken's marriage. We started to town,

---

[20] The Boyds were close neighbors of the Scholls. They lived about one-half mile northeast of the Scholls, near the New Design Road. *Bond Map,* 1858.

1857

did some shopping, [were] out at the cemet[e]ry an hour or so, and then returned into town & made a call at Houcks', where we were very pleasantly entertained. Ada Bantz ran off last night with a Mr. Dukehart, a conductor on [the] railroad. She was but 16 last Fall.

Thursday [April] 30th. Delightful day, much like summer. Mother was in town & when she came home Mrs. L. J. Brengle & Mrs. Dr. McGill came out in Mr. B.'s carriage & sat a couple of hours, both very agreeable & great deal to say.

Friday May 1st [1857]. Pleasant morning but showery in afternoon. Mr. Wm. G. Cox was here [a] couple of hours, & [was] as agreeable as ever. Father [was] at Uncle Artz['] & found him ill with Erysipelas.

* * * * *

Sunday May 3rd. Quite warm [in the] morning and showery in the afternoon. Mr. James Gambrill came & we finished tea and sat till after ten o'clock. We did not go to church on account of the rain. We had some talk of the ring.

Monday [May] 4th. Rainy part of the day. John [is] quite sick with measles.

Tuesday [May] 5th. A lovely day & Oh! such a bright night. I was up with John all night. Dr. Moran [was here] to see Jane & John.

Wednesday [May] 6th. Pleasant day but somewhat cloudy at night. Mr. J. Gambrill was here & spent the evening.

* * * * *

Friday [May] 8th. Still attending to John.

Saturday [May] 9th. A lovely day. I was busy all day. Some person to see Mother but she was not at home. Had a letter from Lou Clippinger and Father one of Mr. Clippinger. Marion Howard took tea here.

Sunday [May] 10th. A beautiful bright day. Mother & I went to church & Mag Derr persuaded me to go home with them; Cousin Ed. S. [came] over after tea & remained till 11 1/2 o'clock. Found Mr. J. Gambrill had been at our house when I got home.

Monday [May] 11th. Much colder & cloudy. Mary & Alice Derr & I went into town. Mary & I were at the mantua maker's together and then parted, and I went to Mrs. Markell's and sat till about twelve & then walked out home. Met Mother coming in for me but would not return with her to ride back.

* * * * *

Wednesday [May] 13th. Delightful morning but cloudy towards evening. I went into town with Father. I was at Catechism, did some shopping, and then on my way to Schleys' met Annie & Mother coming into town, so [I] just went to Aunt Jem[ima] Scholl's and sat till time to come home.

* * * * *

Sunday [May] 17th. A delightful day. I went into church and, [as] we had a very long sermon from Rev. Mr. Douglas and a Communion, it was late till I got home. Cousin Ed. S. came down street with me and waited till I came home. Mr. James Gambrill came, took tea with us, and he spoke of his desires to be a beau, etc., and something of the ring. I told him there was no hope. He did not speak of his love but his desire to marry me, & also that he never would marry so long as I was single, but I let him know I did not believe him. I do not believe all gentlemen tell me & I fear his lips spoke words his heart did not feel.

Monday [May] 18th. Cold morning. I went into town & had my dress fit, & came out with Mother as she returned through town.

* * * * *

Wednesday [May] 20th. Damp, unpleasant day. I had a paper from Mr. G. L. Cline, Chicago. Ginny & Fanny Adams spent this afternoon with us. They had a great deal to say.

Thursday [May] 21st. Ascension Day. I went into town & stopped at Mrs. Markel[l]'s and talked some time and from there I took her to Mrs. Bantz['s], and went & did my shopping and returned for her, & we took a ride out the pike. I then returned home & was busy sewing. Wrote a note to Derrs to come stay while Father & Mother were gone.

* * * * *

1857

Sunday [May] 24th. I went into town and heard a long, tedious sermon from Rev. Mr. Foot. Cousin Ed came out about three o'clock & remained till after tea. I then walked over to Mr. Roderick's & sat awhile.

Monday [May] 25th. Very pleasant day. Father & Mother started to Washington and I was very busy housecleaning all day. About noon a little Jones [boy] arrived with his Grand-ma's compliments, saying the reception would not be till to-morrow night. Had a note from Mary Derr saying they would be out to-morrow. Tommy Haines staid all night. I sent a note to Coz Ed by Mother.

Tuesday [May] 26th. Another beautiful day. Busy sweeping, baking cakes and my first pies. Mr. Richard Marlow arrived about ten and sat till three, when Mag & Mary Derr arrived, and very soon Uncle Artz, who only sat a short time. Cousin Ed came to tea, and after fixing, etc., we were ready to start for Mr. Boyd's 10 minutes after nine. Bride handsomely dressed, nice table, family & company agreeable, pleasant evening, & we returned about half-past one o'clock. All staid over night. Tommy Hain[e]s kept house.

Wednesday [May] 27th. Rather cloudy. Mag & Cousin Ed left about nine, and soon Mary went to town to do some shopping for me, etc. [She] brought news we were to have company, so I was busy baking cake, etc., in [the] afternoon. We talked of Mag in connection with Pittsburgh, etc., and I began to feel very serious of her.

Thursday [May] 28th. Busy all morning [for] having a big dinner, but Mary & I were the only ones to eat it as no company came. They came for Mary D. about five o'clock and I felt lonesome, but wrote a long letter to Lou Clip[pinger]. Tommy staid here at night.

Friday [May] 29th. A lovely morning but showery in afternoon. Annie Clingan & Fannie Adams came about nine or ten, & Mrs. Kate Jacobs, Georgia Houck & Ellie Brunner, and soon Aunt Mary Scholl[21], Lewis & Annabelle. All spent the day, & Annie all night. Father & Mother came home well pleased with their visit to Washington & Baltimore & brought me handsome presents, silver forks, brushes, etc. T. Haines left after they came.

---

[21]Aunt Mary Dutrow Scholl was the second wife of Elias Scholl, Daniel's brother. *Scholl Genealogy*, p. 784.

Saturday [May] 30th. A beautiful day, but I was busy house-cleaning and had little opportunity of sewing.

Sunday [May] 31st. Cloudy morning, with quite a hailstorm in the afternoon. Mag Derr's company did not arrive.

Monday [June] 1st [1857]. Although Whit-Monday, we were white-washing, & I was exceedingly busy all day cleaning paint, etc. I am so glad we are so near done.

Tuesday [June] 2nd. Pretty all day. Busy all day laying matting. I had a letter from Mary Sauer[wein] when Mother came home.

Wednesday [June] 3rd. Bright day, shower about eight o'clock in the evening. Mother [was] in town. Annie & I [were] still busy.

Thursday [June] 4th. Pleasant morning, but cloudy after three o'clock. I went over to Mrs. Howard's & took tea. Found Annie Scholl & Mr. Clarence Hampston at home when I got back. They remained over night. [I] retired about ten.

* * * * *

Saturday [June] 6th. Bright morning. Davie Scholl came for Annabelle. I went to town [in] the afternoon & stopped for Mary Kunkel, & we went together to see Schleys; [we] met Mrs. & Miss Goldsborough there. Mrs. Henry Schley & Miss Whorl & Mary also went shopping & to see Tilly Jackson. I stopped to see Ellen B. awhile. Mag Derr /Ed Shiner/ was out after tea & sat till about half-past nine o'clock.

Sunday [June] 7th. Mother was not well but went in to church. Lovely day. Mr. J. Gambrill was here a couple of hours in the afternoon. I endeavored to cut him a bouquet but did not succeed well, but he seemed very much obliged.

Monday [June] 8th. Mother went into town & was caught in a very heavy shower; it was gusty all afternoon. Our new mirror arrived at last, very handsome. It was somewhat injured. Tommy & Mr. R. were here helping to lift awhile.

1857

Tuesday [June] 9th. I was all ready to go to town with Mother, but it rained so very hard about the time we wanted to start, I concluded to stay home.

Wednesday [June] 10th. Cloudy, but nevertheless we sent for Mr. Shroeder, & he put up the glass & fixed the castor [*sic*] on my piano, and I returned into town with him. [I] attended to some business, put my letter in the office to Mary Sauerwein & then came out home. [It] rained in torrents all night. Letter from Annie Scholl.

Thursday [June] 11th. Very warm, but clear afternoon. I went early into town, stopped for Ellen Brunner, & we went out. Spent [the] afternoon at Mrs. Derr's. Miss Stoner & Shaw of Pittsburgh arrived this morning. Over at Cousin Ed's awhile, came home about seven.

Friday 12th June. Clear morning but threatening in the afternoon. Mother & I started about 2 o'clock & went to Mrs. Lewis Kemp's, saw family [and] Misses Orendoff. Old & [*illegible*]. Mrs. K. [is] quite ill so we only sat an hour or so and then went over to Mrs. Buckey's to tea. The family [and] Messrs. William Miller & Knotly Bowers were there. Spent a pleasant evening & returned home by dusk.

Saturday [June] 13th. Clear but very warm. I went into town with Father, stopped at Mrs. Markel[l]'s till after four o'clock when Mrs. M. & I went to the Sem[inary] to see Madam Pearson & up to Mrs. Frank's to see them. When I came down street [I] found Cousin Harry Smith there, who went out home with us. [It] rained at night. I had a good old fashioned talk with Harry.

Sunday [June] 14th. Clear day. Harry & I went into town early. I stopped at Ella's while he went to the Hotel, & he called back for us & went to church. He returned to town in the evening.

* * * * *

Tuesday [June] 16th. At home all day sewing, reading, etc., disappointed not getting my bonnet. Poor Claude came home so badly hurt.

Wednesday [June] 17th. Beautiful morning but showery all afternoon. Poor Claude [was] found dead. We all miss him so much. Capt. Doub [was here] to see Father on business. About nine o'clock Mag Derr & Vic Stoner & Mattie Shaw from Pitts[burgh] arrived & spent the day & staid over night.

Thursday [June] 18th. Clear all day. They came for Derrs about three o'clock. I wanted them to stay till evening but they couldn't. Paper from Chicago.

Friday [June] 19th. Very warm. Wrote a note to Mary E. Sauerwein but did not send it, as my bonnet came, very pretty.

Saturday [June] 20th. Pretty but quite warm. Went into town & did some shopping, but stopped for Ella but she could not leave home, as her sister was not at home; she'd gone to Balt[imore]. [I had a] letter [from] Lou Clip[pinger].

* * * * *

Tuesday [June] 23rd. Pleasant morning. Mother took me over to Lizzie Schell's to spend the day. Mag Derr, Vic Stoner, & Mattie Shaw were there also; spent a pleasant day. Thomas Derr came for us about nine o'clock, & it was nearly twelve o'clock when we got to Mr. Derr's. Cousin Ed was still waiting for us. He did not leave till about one. Miss McCartney & Bob Noonan were there also.

Wednesday [June] 24th. We spent the day very pleasantly although I did not get home to-day. No company.

Thursday [June] 25th. Rather warm. Letter of Nellie Mering Martin. Eugene Derr took me into town. [I] met Mother there and came out home with her. I was busy all afternoon & retired about ten & slept soundly.

Friday [June] 26th. A lovely morning. George Birely came for me (very unexpected to me) and after having a little tea went into town, and as the rest had not come, we waited till about ten o'clock, when Cousin Ed arrived with Mag D & Vic Stoner; and Mr. Ray had Mat Shaw & Mary D with Eugene, & then she [sic] got George Shriner in with them, and we all proceeded to the mountain & spent the day very pleasantly. All seemed to enjoy it; and Oh, such a lovely spot, how could we do otherwise? Mr. B. sat about an hour or so. I retired by ten o'clock.

Saturday [June] 27th. Very warm. Cousin Ed came out about one o'clock to dinner and by three we started for Cousin H. Scholl's; and after a pleasant but very tedious route across the mountain, we arrived there about half-past

1857

seven. It is a pretty place. We spent the evening pleasantly with the family. We retired soon after ten & I slept so soundly & sweetly.

Sunday [June] 28th. A lovely, bright morning. [We] were up by seven o'clock & started for church by ten. We went to Barnesville[22] to Catholic church. Daugherty was the officiating priest. Quite a large & well dressed congregation. Was introduced to Mr. Trundle. John Cramer and Mr. Clarence Hamstead & Mother arrived about two o'clock. We started for home soon after four. Clarence & Annie came across [the] Monocacy with us, and afterwards about a mile. I like him very well. [We] found Mr. John Cramer here when I got home. He & Cousin Ed left some after ten o'clock.

* * * * *

Wednesday [July] 1st [1857]. Showery all day & cooler. I went into town in the morning and attended to Annie Scholl's commands and wrote her a note and sent her things, pat[t]erns & a pair of sleeves, & band to Miss Harding to take her. I saw Mr. A. K. Mantz in at Mr. Boyd's store. He looks well. Was at Mrs. Markel[l]'s awhile.

* * * * *

Friday [July] 3rd. Threatening to rain all day but [that] made it more pleasant than if the clouds had been out bright all day. Father took me down to the tournament[23] and I spent the evening very pleasantly in conversation and looking over at the Knights. Mr. Hobbs delivered the charge to the Knights and besides him there were several gents I knew. Mr. James Gambrill gave me his undivided attention. Mr. Dod G[ambrill] very attentive. We returned home about dusk. I was gratified but very tired.

Saturday [July] 4th. Delightful day. Disappointed [the] Derrs did not come out. I went in for Marion Eichelberger and found Mary [Eichelberger] had just arrived, so [I] brought them both out. Took Marion in [in] the evening

---

[22]Barnesville, about three miles south of Sugar Loaf Mountain, is in Montgomery County.

[23]There were many jousting tournaments. The one Engelbrecht described on August 27, 1857, had 15 Knights. He tells which Knights picked which Princesses and Queens to honor. The whole ceremony was finished with a ball at the Junior Fire Hall. Engelbrecht, *Diary*, II, 717.

but Mary returned. Met Mr. D. Gambrill & Geo. Birely at the gate, and they returned and spent the evening here, very agreeable.

Sunday [July] 5th. Very warm morning but rain in the evening, very hard gust. I went in with Mary E[ichelberger] and went to church with Mrs. W[inchester]. Heard a very good sermon from Dr. Zack.

* * * * *

Tuesday [July] 7th. My twenty-fourth birth-day. I went in by nine o'clock, called for Mary Eichelberger and we went up to the Nunnery[24] to the Distribution and saw a great many friends there. Then Mattie Shaw, Mary E. & Cousin Ed S. & I went to the Sem[inary] and remained till the exercises were over. Mattie came home with me. Cousin Ed came out and spent the evening with us.

Wednesday [July] 8th. Pleasant morning. Aunt Shriner & Miss B. Cramer came out about nine, and Mr. James Reid about half-past, & sat till nearly twelve, talking. Heavy rain about six. Cousin Ed came soon after and we all went to town. Cousin Mat & I went to the Soiree at Mr. W[inchester]'s. Mr. Geo Reilly came up street with us. Numerous friends I knew were there. Cousin Ed took Mattie out to the Derrs'. Vic, Mag & Tom Derr went out early. Mr. James Gambrill was up street awhile with us, but did not go down with me. [I] thought he would.

Thursday [July] 9th. Very warm day. [The] Derrs came in and we all went down to the Sem[inary] and were gratified by getting good seats up in front, and heard all the compositions, which were elegant. Mr. Winchester and all insisted upon my dining with them, so I concluded to accept & had [a] very pleasant time with teachers Kate Wetherson (now Mrs. Reynolds) and Mary Jane Hammond. I enjoyed all all [*sic*]. Went to Aunt S's about five o'clock & changed my dress, and went to Houcks' to go down at night. All went down and after [the] exercises went to Houcks': the girls, Houck, Derrs & Co. and myself, and gents, Joe Schell, Dixon O'Dell, Ed S., Geo. Birely, etc.,

---

[24]The nunnery was the Visitation Convent on East Second Street. In 1824 five Sisters of Charity were sent by Mother Seton from Emmitsburg to begin what is now the Visitation Convent. In 1846 they were replaced by the Visitation Sisters from Georgetown. By 1848 the present building had been built on East Second Street and Chapel Alley. Thomas R. Bevan, *The Catholic Community of the Frederick Valley* (Frederick, Maryland, 1977), pp. 30-31.

1857

& staid till nearly twelve o'clock. We went up in the wagon. I staid at Aunt S's. Thomas saw me in. I got in cautiously but she heard me.

Friday [July] 10th. Warm, with frequent showers. I went over to Mrs. Winchester's and saw Marion & Mary E of[f], and then put [my] bonnet on and went to the Houcks' &, joined by Georgia & Em, on we went to the cars, saw Mary Derr & Co. of[f] and the rest [*sic*] and then said good bye and I went up & waited at Ella B's till the[y] sent for me, which was five o'clock. So of course I was out to dinner [when] Vic[torine] Artz [was] here.

* * * * *

Sunday [July] 12th. Warm day. Mother and I went to church and heard a very good sermon of Dr. Zack. Cousin Ed came down from church with me and gave me a letter he brought from Mary S. Saw Mary Derr & Co. safe from Balt[imore], on the way to Pitts[burgh]. She is in excellent spirits. [I was] disappointed no company.

* * * * *

Sunday [July] 19th. Very warm with the appearance of rain, & I did not feel well, so did not go to town. A gust in the evening and a lovely sunset.

Monday [July] 20th. A beautiful day, very busy. Cousin Ed brought Mary Kunkel out after tea and sat the evening. Both [were] in excellent spirits.

Tuesday [July] 21st. Warm day. [I was] busy baking cake, pies, etc. Mrs. I. Howard, Marion & Miss Vic. Eaton all spent the afternoon here; [they] left about half-past seven. I walked part way with them.

Wednesday [July] 22nd. Beautiful day. I saw the Sabbath School come out[25], but I did not go over till about two o'clock and staid over till about five, when Mr. J. H. Reid and Mary Kunkel returned with me. Mr. R. remained till about ten o'clock, then [went] to town.

Thursday [July] 23rd. Shower in the morning, so Mary & I did not get to go to town till nearly ten o'clock. We were at Houcks', but [the] Sauerwein[s] were coming to-night. I then stopped at Ellen's awhile and came out home

---

[25]They were coming to a picnic in the Adams' woods.

1857

[at] nearly twelve. Mag Derr and Charlie & black Geo. came out to pick currants and I helped, and [we] were done before four o'clock. Cousin Ed brought Ella B. out to tea and sat till after nine. I had an awful headache.

Friday [July] 24th. Pretty morning. I went into town early and stopped and took Em Houck & Kate S[auerwein] out to Aunt M. Artz's with me for a ride. [The] Sauerweins just got here at six o'clock. [They were] detained all night on the road. Mr. Christ Hershey was here to dinner and till two o'clock. I was tired and wished him gone before he left.

Saturday [July] 25th. Appearance of rain early, but cleared off soon. I was in town to shop and called to see Belle Baily, but she had gone to the pic-nic.

* * * * *

Tuesday [July] 28th. Very warm with slight shower in the afternoon. I was out to Aunt M. Artz's in the morning, [and] stopped at Houcks' a few minutes, also at Ella B.'s at the door.

Wednesday [July] 29th. Pleasant morning but cloudy afternoon, and slight [sic] at night. Mrs. W. Derr & little girl were here [a] short time. I went into town in the morning and brought Ella B. out. [I] had a nice little chat with Mr. James Gambrill at the carriage while waiting for E. Ella and I went over and took tea with Jennie & Fannie Adams. Jerry Cramer & Cousin Ed came to tea & took us home, & [Ella B.] staid in town on account of Jenny B.'s illness. Mr. C[ramer], Cousin Ed & I stopped at Houcks' awhile and made arrangements for going to the tournament[26]. Mr. C. sat awhile & left by eleven. Gin Boyd & Geo. Birely were at H's also. /Mr. Belle was to see them this evening; Father & Mother saw him./

Thursday [July] 30th. Found it raining hard, so no tournament for us. Ceased about 3 or 4 o'clock.

Friday [July] 31st Very pleasant day. I went into town after dinner and did some shopping, and afterwards went to Houcks'. [I] saw the family Sauerwein & Gin Boyd.

* * * * *

---

[26]I.e., a jousting tournament. See note 23, 1857.

1857

Sunday [August] 2nd [1857]. Pleasant day. I went into church and heard a very good sermon. After tea [I] walked over to Mr. & Mrs. Isaac Howard's; saw the family, Miss Vic Eaton, Miss & Mr. Henderson & John Delashmuth. Came home about 8.

Monday [August] 3rd. [I was] at home till about four o'clock, then went to town, [and] stopped at Ella's to take some pat[t]erns off. After their tea I went up street to attend some business, stopped at Houcks' a few minutes to see the girls. Mag Derr & cousin Ed were out after I came home & sat till after nine. Letter from Mary Derr[27]. She has [sic] a very nice time.

Tuesday [August] 4th. Found it raining or rather cloudy with prospect of rain; nevertheless, Father was anxious to go to the Tournament, so we got ready & went. We stopped in town a short time at Kunkels', and then went over & [we] were soon followed by Kunkels, Ed S. & Mag Derr, Tom D. & Mary E[ichelberger]. It rained but nevertheless they had the riding. As soon as I got home Tom D. came & proposed going to Araby to see Miss Gambrill, so we hurried & had supper & went into town. [We] met Mag & Ed and went out to the mill[28], but found no one home except Mr. Horace Gambrill. He seemed very pleasant, nice voice. We talked a short time with him, then came on home; got home by 10.

Wednesday August 5th. Rainy all day. I was doing various odd jobs & then commenced working [a] pair of sleeves. [I] sent a letter off for Mrs. Nellie Martin & received a letter from cousin Harry Smith; [he had] a bust up with his northern New York friend but a new one [is] on hand.

Thursday [August] 6th. Pleasant day. Cousins Abram & Sarah Ann Adams of Covington & Fannie Adams were up to take tea. I walked part way home with them. [I was] not very well.

* * * * *

---

[27]Mary Derr came home from Tiffin, Ohio on September 16th. See below.

[28]The Araby Mill, built by Col. John McPherson in 1830, was purchased in 1856 by James Gambrill, who had moved to Frederick in 1849. It is located on the Monocacy River near Frederick Junction on Route 355. During the Civil War it was used as a hospital. Ralph Fraley Martz, *Mills on the Monocacy* (n.p., n.d.); Williams, *History*, II, 1056. The National Park Service has recently bought this property in order to include it in the Monocacy Battlefield Commemorative Park.

1857

Saturday [August] 8th. Not very well; nevertheless, was busy housecleaning when Kunkels arrived with Kate Sauerwein of Howard St., Balt. [I] was very much surprised to see her, not knowing she was up. We took a walk after dinner, and soon after we returned Mrs. John Clingan arrived & staid to tea. All left soon after. Cousin Ed brought Kate Sauerwein out & sat the evening.

Sunday [August] 9th. Mother & I went into church & heard a very good sermon from Dr. Zack & I then went up to Houcks'. Mary & I had a long talk on the bed, & Georgia said she'd never marry. Kate S., Em & Tilly H. & I went with Wils Boyd to hear Mr. Lefevre at Presbyterian church. Good plain sermon. Mr. Lefevre & came & went to church [sic]. Wils B., Em, Tilly & I took a walk & were at Uncle Lewis Scholl's to see Kate S., & at Kunkels' [a] short while, & then at Houcks'. Tom Derr came home with us. [We] also found Dr. Schaffer there. Left all by eleven & we retired.

Monday August 10th. Much the appearance of rain, but Mother soon came and we went to Shroeders & Brooks[29] to look at furniture, and very soon Tom Derr came & took Belle Baily, Sue Hunt & me out to their house, and very soon Georgia & Emma Houck, Mary & Kate S. [came,] and after awhile Dr. Zack & Mr. Michael Diffenderfer of Balt. All spent the day. Ed. S. [came] after dinner. We all spent a very pleasant day. Sue H., Belle, Mary S. and I staid over night & were sent in in the morning.

Tuesday [August] 11th. Ed S. brought me into town. I stopped at Houcks' awhile, then walked out home. I wrote a letter to Mary Derr and had a letter from Lou Clippinger. Paper from Mr. Himes.

Wednesday [August] 12th. Pleasant day. Methodist Sabbath School pic-nic [was] in the woods opposite. I sent some papers to Mr. Himes but John dropped them.

Thursday [August] 13th. Very warm. [I] sent in for the girls' trunk, [and] had a note saying Mr. Lefevre was to bring them out in the afternoon. Mr. Reed arrived about four o'clock, Mr. Lefevre with Mary & Kate about five. Mr. Reed left after tea. We had a nice long talk till nine o'clock, when Cousin Ed & Wils Boyd arrived, and then we talked of [a] mountain party, etc.

---

[29]Shroeders and Brooks were cabinet manufacturers on the west side of Market Street opposite the Market House. *Williams' Directory*, p. 6.

1857

Friday August 14th. Very warm day. [We were] busy in the morning, and had just laid [sic] down for a nap when at two o'clock there was an arrival, and Mr. H. D. Gambrill's card [was] brought [to] me, and I dressed for the parlour; and Mr. G. [was] accompanied by his sister Bettie who came to return my call. She proved quite agreeable; sat about half an hour or so. Immedi-ately after tea Mr. Geo Birely & Annie Schley arrived, and very soon Tom Derr & Belle Baily. All seemed to enjoy the evening.

Saturday [August] 15th. Still so warm, no company. Mary & Kate & I were in town to see Kate S. and Kunkels.

Sunday [August] 16th. Raining in showers during the morning. Mary, Kate & I went to church. Dod Gambrill called about six and sat till about eight o'clock.

Monday [August] 17th. Warm, sultry day. We went into town, left Kate in town and took Georgia along with us out & spent the afternoon with Sarah Ann Adams. Mrs. Henrietta Kemp was there. Left G. in & brought K. out home.

Tuesday [August] 18th. Pleasant day. Mary, Kate & I went in after early tea & was to see Sue Hunt & Mrs. Steiner's and then came out home.

Wednesday August 19th. Pleasant day. Mother & Kate went up to Boyds' to call, but staid to dinner and did not return before Mary & I went to town. We were at Misses Houses Dr's [sic] & did some shopping, then came out home. They had just got home when we returned. [They] had a peach apiece for us.

Thursday [August] 20th. Very pleasant day. Mr. Lefevre walked out about ten o'clock & soon Aunt Jem Scholl & Kate S. came. They all staid to spend the day. After dinner we took a walk & left Mr. L. & Kate in the woods when we returned. Mag Derr arrived by then & Mr. L. returned with Eugene. Cousin Ed came about five o'clock and after tea at eight Cousin E. took them home.

Friday [August] 21st. Warm day. Grand Tournament[30] day. Mary, Kate & I went in with Father, were joined on the street by Mr. Lefevre and he walked round town with [us], stopped at Houcks' awhile, then at the Dr. He sat awhile with us at Aunt Jemima's and then left us there to take dinner. After dinner two Kates, Mary & I went up to the Tournament ground accompanied by Father, had good seats and a pleasant time. Dr. McGill [was] very attentive, also [his] wife & Mrs. Delaplaine[31]. Mary & Kate staid all night with Houcks. I walked out home with Father.

Saturday August 22nd. Bright quite early, but afterwards every appearance of rain. Mr. Lefevre brought Kate & Mary out home about ten. Mr. James Reed soon arrived and both sat till about eleven o'clock. Sue Hunt, Belle Bailey & Sue Jones arrived about half-past eleven to spend the day. After tea Messrs. John Sifford & Gus Eader arrived and sat till about nine, when they left, taking Sue Hunt & Belle Baily with them. Sue Jones staid over night.

Sunday [August] 23rd. Pleasant day. Mary, Kate & I went to church and heard a sermon from Dr. Zack. Cousin Ed came down from church with us. After tea Mary & I took a long walk & met Wils Boyd coming to our house. He staid longer than we expected & Mother [was] quite uneasy about us. Wils left about half-past ten o'clock.

Monday [August] 24th. Pleasant day. Sewing, etc. After dinner [we] got ready and went out to Mr. Derr's; [we] took Kate's trunk with us. Left Kate out [there] all night as she was to go to Mt. with Mr. J. A. J.

Tuesday [August] 25th. Cool, pleasant day. Mary & I were busy till gents Messrs. W. Boyd & G. Birely arrived, [but were] soon ready & left. Mary [was] with Wils, I with Geo. to town, where we exchanged. I got in the carriage with Geo. S., & Ed. S. & Geo B. took Mag Derr, [and] Mr. Johnson, Kate. We had a very pleasant day & returned home [by] a new road, well pleased. Kate came out with us in the carriage. The gents left by ten & we

---

[30]"The Knights of Maryland and Virginia have a tournament at the Barrick Grounds. They had a Chief Marshal, William P. Maulsby, several assistants including Allen G. Quynn and Robert P. McPherson, Cornelius Staley and William Derr. Orators included Basil E. Dorsey, John Ritchie and Jame A. Lynche, Judge George R. Dennis." Engelbrecht, *Diary*, II, 716.

[31]This Mrs. Delaplaine could have been married to Theodore Crist Delaplaine or George Washington Delaplaine. C.E. Schildknecht, *Monocacy and Catoctin*, pp. 352-355.

1857

soon retired, well tired. All seemed pleased. Mr. J. A. J. looked badly, so meanly dressed.

Wednesday August 26th. Pleasant morning. About eleven Lum Sadtler & Geo. Sauerwein came & staid till after dinner. Immediately after the[y] left, we got ready and went to town to see Miss Maria Weistling and had a long chat with her & Mr. & Mrs. Rockville--pleasant visit and [for] Kate a bouquet. We then went over to Boyd[s'] and remained to tea with the family. After[wards] Messrs. Wils & Ham Boyd, Geo. Sauerwein, Lum Sadtler & Ed S. all came and sat the evening. Came home about ten, Mary & I in the wagon with Wil, & Geo & Kate in buggy with Cousin Ed, [a] pleasant evening.

Thursday [August] 27th. Cold, rainy day. At home & no company. Father went to Balt[imore] so we did not get to Kunkels', [but] wrote a note [we'll] be there tomorrow.

Friday [August] 28th. Pleasant day. Went in about eleven to Kunkels' to spend the day. Wrote Wils a note that we would accept of his kind offer to bring us home. Mrs. John Reich, Mr. & Mrs. Davis & daughter of Balt[imore] were there to spend the day. Mary & I were out part of [the] afternoon. After tea we girls went to Schleys' awhile. Ellen & Annie returned and sat awhile. Mary & Geo. Morgan stopped awhile. Wils Boyd came early & spent [the] evening, also cousin Ed. S. Geo. S. stopped at [the] porch awhile; he was here [in the] morning when we arrived. Wils B. brought Mary S. & I out home. Ham [Boyd] got in down street. Cousin Ed brought Kate S. out home, [but] did not come in.

Saturday August 29th. Very pleasant day. Mary packed her trunk & Kate her bundle, and I did various other things till about ten o'clock, when we got ready and went out to Mr. Derr's. [We] left trunk, bandbox, etc. at Derrs' and then went to the Island where the Sabbath School Festival was being held. Kunkels [and] Houcks were out in afternoon, also Mr. J. A. J. Rather dull day. Mr. J. A. J. & Ed S. went to Mr. Derr's with us. I brought Kunkels into town. Had two papers from Mr. T. Jeff Himes. Home [at] half-past seven.

Sunday [August] 30th. Pleasant day. Mother & I went to town & went to the Methodist church. Gave Mary S. letter to Ed. S., was to go to Episcopal church but girls were before me [sic].

1857

Monday [August] 31st. Very pleasant day. Home busy all day. Had Harper's Magazine[32] for Sept. from somebody.

* * * * *

Wednesday [September] 2nd [1857]. Quite pleasant, busy all day. Annie Scholl arrived about four o'clock with Mr. & Miss Hempston. Mr. H. left immediately leaving the girls here.

Thursday [September] 3rd. Delightful day. Miss Caroline Hane came out to remain [a] short time. Paper [came] from New Oxford from Frank or John Hersh. Annie Scholl [is] not well.

Friday [September] 4th. Very warm day. Annie Scholl still sick. Miss Caroline & Mother to camp.[33] Mamie Hempston & I went to town to shop. Cousin Ed brought Mary & Kate Sauerwein & Mag Derr out to tea, left about nine o'clock.

Saturday [September] 5th. Another warm day. I was very busy all day. In town a short time. Aunt Mary Scholl & Lewis came & staid over night.

Sunday [September] 6th. Appearance of rain but cleared away. Aunt Mary, Lewis, Mother, Miss Caroline, Mamie Hempston went to camp by eight. Cousin Ed came about ten, brought Mary S. & soon Wils Boyd arrived, he took Mary & I went with Ed, plenty company on the ground. Soon saw Mr. Hempston who came up & saw Annie and came back, said she was worse. Mother & Miss C. went back directly & sent for the Dr. We came home to tea about six and afterwards Mr. Boyd took Mary & Mr. Hempston took Mamie & I to camp, had a pleasant time.

Monday [September] 7th. Mr. Hempston left about nine. Mother took Miss Caroline in. Dr. was to see Annie, much better and she talked a great deal.

Tuesday [September] 8th. Warm, bright day. Annie not so well, sent for the Dr. again. Mary, Mamie, & I walked to camp after dinner. Father went with

---

[32]*Harper's Magazine* has been published from 1850 to the present time.

[33]Engelbrecht writes on this date, "The Methodist Epis Church of our town & Circuit (I recon) have a Camp meeting Now in Lane Woods 'White Oak Springs' about 2-1/2 miles South west from town - Commenced yesterday." Engelbrecht, *Diary*, II, 717.

1857

us. Saw Houcks & Mag Derr, Ed S. & Kate S. there. [We had a] right pleasant time. Mag, Ed & Kate came up to tea and sat till after eight.

Wednesday [September] 9th. At home in the morning. Afternoon Mary, Mamie & I went to camp, heard a sermon, but did not see many we knew. [We] returned soon after five. Wils Boyd came for us after eight, Brian Henderson with him in a covered spring wagon. Mamie, Mary and I went with him and we had a lively time, [and] staid till nearly one before we returned.

Thursday [September] 10th. Pleasant. According to appointment Mary Sauerwein went into town to meet Derrs. [We] received a note from Georgia H. wanting us to spend to-morrow evening with her. Invitation [came] to Mrs. P. P. Heller's reception in Philad[elphia]. [I] wrote Ed S. a note.

Friday [September] 11th. Annie [is] somewhat better. Mamie H. & I went to town, shopped a little, then went to Houcks' a short time, but did not stay in as I had no note from Ed. S. Mary & Kate S, & Mag Derr were in to tea. Pamp[h]let from Mr. T. J. Himes, Ill[inois].

Saturday 12th Sept. Pleasant day, busy most all day. No company. Dr. [called] to see Annie.

Sunday [September] 13th. Cloudy morning but clear after dinner. Mamie & I went to church, [and] found Clarence H. here when we got home. Wils Boyd [was] here after dinner. Both staid to tea but left soon after.

Monday [September] 14th. Busy all day. Cousin Ed here to tea.

Tuesday [September] 15th. Still busy, pared peaches for pre-serving. Annie S. [was] down stairs today.

Wednesday [September] 16th. Pleasant day, preserved peaches. About three o'clock Mr. C. Steiner brought Mrs. S., Mrs. B. F. W[inchester] & Miss Mollie Willis to tea. Jane was soon taken very sick. [We] sent for the Dr., old Woman, etc.[34] Every thing [was] in confusion. Jane's baby [was] dead, though. Mary Derr came home today from Tiffin O.

---

[34] Jane was one of the servants at Manchester Farm. The old woman was a midwife.

Thursday [September] 17th. Busy again. Annie Scholl and Mamie H. went to town to stay a few days. G. Sauerwein [was] here this morning.

Friday [September] 18th. Pleasant, but some appearance of rain. [I was] busy all day paring fruit. After tea Mag Derr, Ed. S., Mary S. & Wils B., George Birely & Kate S. came out & enjoyed the peaches.

Saturday [September] 19th. Rainy all day. However, I went out to Aunt M. Artz's to learn how to make currant wine, after Mother [went] in town. Kate S. left this morning.

Sunday [September] 20th. Clear again & warm. I went to church rather late, [and] saw Annie Scholl in church. She came out home with me. Mamie Hempston did not come. [I] went for her but she was going to Catholic church.

Monday [September] 21st. Rather pleasant. Father took Annie S. into town. She expected to go to Balt[imore] to-morrow, but Mother heard in town [that] they went home [in the] afternoon. Note from Derrs, also from Gin Brengle[35] were going out [*illegible*].

Tuesday [September] 22nd. Raining all morning but ceased about noon. [I] went in and took tea with Aunt S. with Mary S., Mag D. & Ed S.; were at Mrs. Winchester's awhile.

Wednesday [September] 23rd. Beautiful, clear day. Mother & Father [were] in town in afternoon. /Did not go to Boyds' as intended./ Mr. U. Hobbs [came] out & took tea. He was in excellent spirits & I tried to flatter him more.

Thursday [September] 24th. Bright day. American mass meeting[36] to-day. [I] went in town to meet Derrs as intended. Was at Ella B's awhile and then at Houcks'. They had left, so I went to Kunkels' and waited for them. We then went to Sue Hunt's, Aunt Jem Scholl's, and afterwards to Houcks' to tea.

---

[35]On the Brengle-Scholl family relationship, see note 25, 1858.

[36]"The American party (Know Nothings) had a meeting in our town and of course had Public Speaking in the afternoon. Thomas Holliday Hicks (candidate for Gov.) and many others into the night. The meeting was large and of the right 'Strype'." Engelbrecht, *Diary*, II, 719.

1857

I had a note from Annie Scholl to-day. She is home. Cousin Ed. S. & M. Birely came to take us to the court house. Mr. J. A. J. took Mary out home & Cousin Ed took Mag. Paper from Frank Hersh.

Friday [September] 25th. Home all day, busy. Charlotte Keefer & Mrs. Castle [were] here. After tea Mag D. & Geo. Birely, Mary S. & Ed. S. were out & sat the evening.

Saturday [September] 26th. Pretty day. I was busy preserving & putting up tomatoes till very late. Mr. Jerry Cramer came before I was done. And he staid over night.

Sunday [September] 27th. Pretty day. I went into town with him, stopped at Mrs. Markell's and walked from there to church by myself (prefer[r]ing [that] and telling Jerry much the same.) After church [I] went with Mag Derr to [the] hotel, got in the carriage, rode to Ellen's, got my bundle and went with Mag out home. Cousin Ed S. took Mary out. Gin Boyd at Mr. Derr's. After dinner Cousin Ed came and spent [the] afternoon. Wils B. [was] there also in afternoon, [and] took Gin home about 9. Cousin came after ten & sat till 11 1/2. All had a long talk & slept about 2 o'clock [*sic*].

Monday [September] 28th. Bright, clear morning. Mary Sauerwein goes home to-day. Cousin Ed came & took her to town. Mary & I went in the carriage; various friends [were] at [the] depot. Cousin Ed, Mag & I went to the bridge[37] and then went through Wheatley & Gambrill's distillery[38]. Then we came back to town. Mag Derr & I walked out home. Mrs. Clark was here. Cousin Ed came out after tea & took Mag home.

Tuesday [September] 29th. Father & Mother [were] in town. Note from George S. & Kate about T. Houcks coming Thursday. Schleys and Gin Brengle [here] this evening. Father arrived with Geo this morning.

Wednesday [September] 30th. Pleasant day. [I] went to town after dinner and went to Mrs. B. F. W[inchester]'s and we were out shopping together, and

---

[37] The bridge over the Monocacy on the road from Frederick to Washington (Route 355) was a covered bridge until the Civil War, during which it was ordered burned by General Lew Wallace on July 9, 1864. Glen H. Worthington, *Fighting for Time* (Shippensburg, PA, 1985), p. 112.

[38] The distillery is shown on the *Bond Map*, 1858.

afterwards went to Mrs. C. Steiner's and [she] cast a shawl on for me. I came home & Jim W. made me a needle.

Thursday Oct. 1st [1857] We had a heavy frost. [We were] busy putting up tomatoes early this morning. Georgia, Tilly Houck & Sadie Ritzell spent the day here. Nice girls. [I] sent Frank Hersh a paper.

Friday [October] 2nd. Pretty day. Busy all day on my shawl. Mrs. Killin & Duval were here.

Saturday [October] 3rd. Busy all hands [with] potatoes, I on my shawl. I had a letter from Geo [*illegible*].

Sunday [October] 4th. Mother & I were in to church. Mag Derr gave me the letter she received from Mary S. to read. I was over & took tea [at] Mrs. I. Howard's. Harriet M. Dill [was] there, also Fannie Adams.

Monday [October] 5th. [I] sent Annie Scholl's bundle into town. Cousin Ed & Mag D. out after tea.

Tuesday [October] 6th. Pleasant day. [I] wrote to George Sauerwein, [and a] note to Mary, and finished the middle of my shawl.

Wednesday [October] 7th. [I] went in early and took dinner with Mrs. Winchester. She showed me how to do the border of my shawl.

Thursday [October] 8th. [I was] busy on my shawl.

Friday [October] 9th. In town in the morning to see Ellen B. & at [the] Houcks' to see after my bonnet. [I was] busy [with my] shawl afternoon.

Saturday [October] 10th. [I was] busy, [and] finished my shawl. Mr. Ed Smith [was] down awhile. I was in town in afternoon to see Kunkels, [but they were] not home, and to see Aunt Jem[ima] Scholl & [had a] long talk with her.

Sunday [October] 11th. Mother & I went to town to church. Cousin Ed came down street with us. He had plenty to say.

1857

Monday [October] 12th. [I was] busy on my basque[39] today. [I had a] letter from Geo. Sauerwein and two papers from Mr. T. J. Himes, one a note saying he might be East in a month or 2 or might not till early spring.

Tuesday [October] 13th. Cloudy & foggy morning but clear after dinner. Mother & I were in to Cattle Show. The ladies' department is much better than ever. [We were] well pleased and saw many acquaintances.

Wednesday [October] 14th. Sultry, warm day. I wrote to Geo. Sauerwein. I went into town after dinner, called for Ellen and we went up to the Cattle Show. [The] first person to talk [with was] J. A. J. and successively Messrs. Eader, Sifford, Derr, Delasmuth, and various others. Saw many I knew. Cousin Ed accompanied me & Mr. Rohrback, Ellen to the carriage, and she had two beaux home. I came home.

Thursday [October] 15th. Found it raining when I got up, and [it] rained till about four in [the] afternoon. [I] had a nice letter of Mary Sauerwein.

Friday [October] 16th. Rather appearance of rain all day. [It] is the last day [of the] Cattle Show. [I] went into town, called for Ella, but as she had not her dinner, I stopped [at] Mrs. Smith['s] & went up with her. Balloon[40] "busted", but I soon got with Becky Trail and had a very pleasant time. Mr. Cox was with me for some time, [and] Miss Tessie Deaver & Jim Reed & Sam Preston. Mr. Reed accompanied me to the carriage.

Saturday [October] 17th. Beautiful day. Mr. James Reed was out early this morning and sat about an hour & half. [I went] down to see Harriet Keefer this afternoon. Miss Ann Miller, May Devitt & Mrs. Devrich [were] here.

* * * * *

---

[39]Basque often meant bodice or even a jacket. It often contained bone, which could be carried an inch or so below the waist, but not longer, to insure stiffness in a tight fitted blouse-like costume. Norah Waugh, *The Cut of Women's Clothes* (Theatre Arts Books, New York, 1968), pp. 273-274.

[40]Engelbrecht writes, "Prof. George Elliott intends to make a Balloon ascension and I do hope he succeed [*sic*]--this will be the 4th or 5th Ballooning in our town and always failed. About 2 o'clock p.m. when nearly inflated it 'burst its boiler' and of course a failure as usual." Engelbrecht, *Diary*, II, 722.

Tuesday [October] 20th. Very cold. Marion Howard spent [the] afternoon here. I wrote to Mary Sauerwein at night.

Wednesday [October] 21st. Still clear & cold. I went into town with Father and called at Mrs. Fout's and got a pat[t]ern of Mary. Then [I] rode out to Mr. Howard's a short time & then home. Letter from Geo. Sauerwein & [a] paper from Chicago.

Thursday [October] 22nd. /Harriet Keefer & Mr. Henry Drill married to-day./ [I was] at home all day, busy.

Friday [October] 23rd. Not so cold. When John came home [he] had papers from Geo. Sauerwein & Mr. T. J. Himes. Busy housecleaning, & put down [the] parlor carpet.

Saturday [October] 24th. Cloudy all day. Put stoves[41] up to-day. [I] went in for Father, stopped awhile at Mrs. Markel[l]'s till the cars came up, and then came out with Father. He has bought a new dressing bureau & washstand in Balt[imore].

* * * * *

Monday [October] 26th. Very cold windy day. Father went to town & brought the furniture home he had bought. We like it very much.

Tuesday [October] 27th. Still windy. I took Father to town then went to Aunt Margaret's and had quite a long talk with her; and when I came back Father gave me a nice long letter from Cousin Harry Smith. He seems affected by hard times; their house has suspended[42]. Old Mrs. Kunkel[43] is dead, died yesterday [at] 2 o'clock.

---

[41]Engelbrecht writes on September 30, 1857, "This morning we put up our stove in our shop--we have very cool mornings. We took down the stove on 1st of June past." Engelbrecht, *Diary*, II, 720.

[42]There was "a severe business panic in 1857, occasioned by speculation, over expansion of bank credits and too rapid investment" in factories and mills, but the country's economy experienced a rapid recovery. A. E. Martin, *History of the United States* (2 vols., New York, 1928), I, 657.

[43]On the Kunkle family see note 67, 1851.

1857

Wednesday [October] 28th. Cloudy, damp day. Went into town, stopped at Aunt Jem[ima] Scholl's and asked about [the] funeral, [and] then went shopping and returned for her, and we all went to old Mrs. K.'s funeral. It was quite large. Afterwards we came home.

Thursday [October] 29th. Bright but windy day. [I] went into town but found the balloon was not to ascend to-day, so [I] came home again. After dinner Mother & I went up and spent the afternoon with Mrs. E. Howard and Emily Cookson. She has a gathered breast but seems in excellent spirits. Her babe is quite a fine child but [she] advises no one to marry unless they love their husband. What I have always thought.

Friday, [October] 30th. [I was] busy all morning [until] about ten o'clock, when Mr. James Reed arrived, and about eleven, Mary & Ann Keefer, Mrs. Ellen Jarboe, Sallie Miller, Isie & Julia Buckey around to spend the day. We went to town in [the] afternoon and saw the balloon ascend, but not Prof. Elliot in it.[44] The ladies left after tea. Mr. Reid left about 11 1/2, after having told me of his intentions, etc. I could scarcely help laugh[ing].

* * * * *

Sunday Nov. 1st [1857]. Bright, pleasant day. Aunt Jem[ima] Scholl had company in church with her, so insisted upon my going home with her to dinner. Misses Maynard & brother & Miss Sue Stevenson were there. After dinner Joe Hayes came and we all went to Catholic church. I went with Mr. M. It was a lovely moonlight night & Mother came in for me. I like the ladies very well & think [them] right pleasant.

Monday [November] 2nd. Pretty morning. I went in to meet Mag Derr and we each had a tooth extracted by Dr. Schaeffer[45] and did various other shopping together. /Mag Derr & I were to see Kunkels./ I had a paper

---

[44]Engelbrecht writes, "Balloon ascension. At last Prof. George Elliot got his Balloon to ascend a few hundred feet (without him being in it), the chemicals gave out so he set her off with the basket attached. She rose gradually from Barracks Hill took a north course & there being no wind she went slowly and came down and lodged on the roof of a small log house at the S.W. corner of All Saints & Ice Alley where the boys tore the balloon to pieces--and thus ends Ballooning in our town." Engelbrecht, *Diary*, II, 724.

[45]Dr. Schaeffer and Dr. Jenks were surgeon dentists on the north side of Patrick Street. *Williams' Directory*, p. 20.

1857

from Mr. T. J. H[imes] containing a piece of poetry dedicated to M. E. S. I went out with Mag then. Lizzie Schell & Mag McCartney were there awhile in [the] afternoon. At night Cousin Ed. S. & John Derr came home also.

Tuesday [November] 3rd. Pleasant day. After dinner I came to town with John and after shopping awhile in town walked out home. /Found a letter from Mary Sauerwein./

Wednesday [November] 4th. Election day. I went in with Father, and Ellen Brunner came out with me. [We] found old Mrs. Boyd & Len Jones here when we got home, all pleasant & spent [the] day pleasantly.

Thursday [November] 5th. Drizzling part [of the] day. Mrs. Clingan, Miss Mary C. & Annie C. spent [the] day here. Ellen and I had [a] nice long talk.

Friday [November] 6th. Rather cloudy and, as Ella wanted to go home, I went in with her. Found Mrs. Markel[l] sick in bed with a cold. I sat with her till Ellen went to have her dress fit, and then came out home. I had Harper's Magazine from Mr. T. J. Himes with a program of the theatre doings at Rock Island.

Saturday [November] 7th. Very warm day. I went to town in the [sic], stopped at Aunt S's [a] few minutes, saw Mag Derr, did some shopping, called to see Sue Hunt's teeth, & then we both called at Dr. Schaeffer['s] as I wanted to make an engagement for Monday, but he was engaged. Went out home pretty soon after being at Houcks' some time.

Sunday [November] 8th. Appearance of rain. Communion Sunday. I was in church. Cousin Ed S. came down street with me.

Monday [November] 9th. Windy day. I went into town and Lizzie Houck went with me to Dr. Schaeffer['s] & he extracted another tooth for me and put the gum between two front teeth for me.

Tuesday [November] 10th. Pretty day. I went in early, stopped for Lizzie Houck and we went together to Dr. Schaeffer['s] & he plugged the 2 teeth that were separated & separated two others. Mag Derr came while I was there. Cousin Ed was in also. Mag came out home with me. Cousin Ed [came] out at night.

1857

Wednesday [November] 11th. Pretty day. Mag & I were busy in the morning and in the afternoon went in to fulfill my engagement with Dr. S. He filled 3 teeth to-day, one very small decay. Mag went out home with Cousin Ed S.

Thursday [November] 12th. Tolerably cool. After an early dinner John took me into town and I got the papers, then went out & spent the afternoon with Marion Howard, [and] returned about dusk.

Friday [November] 13th. I went [to] town, stopped at Houcks', & Georgia & Tilly went with me to Dr. S.'s, but [we] had to wait a long time and then he could only fill one tooth, as one of the others bled so profusely. It was late when he finished, so [we] went to Mrs. Houck's, had dinner and after dinner Georgia & I walked out home. Dr. S. overtook us on horseback and had a little talk. Thought he would have come out at night but [he] did not.

Saturday [November] 14th. Gloomy, dull day. Snow squall about two. G. & I got in [town] about three. We were at Dr. S.['s] but he was engaged, so we were at Mrs. Eldridge's to see her bonnets[46], & afterwards to Kunkels' & Mrs. Markel[l]'s and then I came out home. Paper from Chicago. Lychurgus Hedges came out to tea & staid over night.

Sunday [November] 15th. A lovely day. Cousin L[ychurgus] & I went [to church] in the carriage. John rode his horse. Cousin Ed came part way from church. [I] wrote a note to Dr. S. & had one in return giving me an appointment to-morrow morning, nine o'clock.

Monday [November] 16th. Raining all day. I finished my cuffs and made the sleeves and finished my morning wrapper.

Tuesday [November] 17th. Warm morning but blew up quite cool in afternoon. I was in town with Mother to shop and at Houcks' awhile. Mary

---

[46]This millinery shop was on the south side of Patrick Street west of Court Street. *Williams' Directory*, p. 12. Engelbrecht gives his views of women's fashions at this time. "Hoops, Enormously large--they cannot get into the church pew - without bending or flattening the hoop and as for going in a carriage, that is out of the Question - three ladies on a pavement take up the whole pavement--The bonnets are very Small and set on the back of the Head - the front goes up square with the Ears, so that one half of the head and all the face is exposed. Shoes with heels and as they walk alone they make a General Stamp - the Dress touches the Ground (in Length) and the Sleeves in front (at Hand) are very Large and cut Bell mouth Shape about 15 inches in front." Engelbrecht, *Diary*, II, 718.

Derr had been in yesterday to meet me & go to Dr. Schaeffer['s] but did not have the letter for me. I wrote to Mary Sauerwein to-night.

Wednesday [November] 18th. Went quite early over to Aunt Mary Scholl's to spend the day, left about 3 o'clock. [I] stopped in town a very few minutes and came out home. [I was] not very well, so did not stay in to see the torch light procession.[47]

Thursday [November] 19th. Clear, but very cold & windy. I had a nice long letter from Lou Clippinger; she has gone to house-keeping. Rels. [*sic*] out paying her a visit. I wish I was there too.

* * * * *

Monday [November] 23rd. Somewhat warmer. I went into town early, met Derrs', & we were shopping together and were caught in the rain besides. I came out home about one o'clock.

Tuesday [November] 24th. Clear, pleasant day. Mother and I went down to Mrs. Clingan's and spent the day. [We] stopped for Marion Howard, saw Mrs. Howard & Mrs. Taylor. Miss Mary Clingan leaves today.

Wednesday [November] 25th. Still cold but not windy. I went into [town], stopped for Tilly Houck and we went together to see Dr. Schaeffer, but he was not home, so I saw the carriage and came out home.

Thursday [November] 26th. Thanksgiving day. Beautiful, bright day. I staid at home with Father. Mother went to church and when she got home brought me a note from Mary Sauerwein that Mag Derr had received in her letter. Maggie Derr & Cousin Ed S. were out to tea. [They] had been to see Mrs. Wheatley.

Friday [November] 27th. Bright, pleasant day. I went down after dinner and spent [the] afternoon with Ginnie & Fannie Adams, [and] commenced crocheting a mat for [a] wash stand.

Saturday [November] 28th. Still the weather fine. Went to town soon after two o'clock, [and] stopped at Aunt Shriner's. Mrs. Dean and Annie were

---

[47]Engelbrecht did not mention this event in his diary.

1857

there. [I] was down street to shop, & Lizzie Houck & I took a long walk together. [I] made an engagement with Dr. S. for Monday. I went to Aunt S. to tea, and Cousin Ed S. came in just before tea in [the] carriage and took me out after tea to Mr. Derr's. /Saw Annie Scholl & [she] told me she was to be married on Thursday./ Cousin S. remained there till about eleven and then went home.

Sunday [November] 29th. Lovely morning. Cousin Ed came soon after nine o'clock and took Mag to Glade church, and Mary, Alice, Eugene & I went in the carriage. [We] heard a very good practical discourse from Rev. Mr. Sherford, his last, [as] he leaves there Thursday. Cousin Ed [stayed] to dinner, left before tea, but returned after tea. Also Mr. Wm. Baker the beadle [?] left soon after ten, Ed [at] 11 1/2.

Monday Nov. 30th. Very pretty morning, but cloudy by eleven o'clock. I went to town with Alice Derr when she went to school. [I] stopped for Tilly Houck and went [to] Dr. Schaeffer['s]. Mr. Lyles (friend of H's) of Conn. walked down street with us. He is a fine looking man & talks well, I should think. I was not well enough to have any thing done to my teeth. Tilly had her nerve killed. I walked out home immediately after we left there, & was in bed [the] rest of the day. Had a paper from Mr. T. J. Himes, [who] says "he will be East Christmas and after."

* * * * *

Wednesday [December] 2nd [1857]. Rather cloudy after early in the morning. Uncle Kemp came out. Father & he went down [to] the distillery[48] and afterward came to dinner, & went to town about two.

Thursday [December] 3rd. A lovely day. Cousin Ed came about one o'clock, and after eating his dinner, we started for Cousin Henry Scholl's[49]. We went by the Urbanna road. We got there by half-past five o'clock and I spent the time [until] 7 1/2, till they were married, in the bride's room, fixing, etc. They were married by Rev. Mr. Smallwood by the Episcopal service. They had two attendants, Rene Scholl & Mamie Hemstone, & Messrs. Wm. Trundle & J.

---

[48]Michael Keefer's mill and distillery were about one mile south of Manchester Farm on the New Design Road. *Bond Map*, 1858.

[49]Henry Scholl was the son of Johannes, an uncle of Daniel Scholl. He was the father of Annie Scholl, the bride. *Scholl Genealogy*, p. 784. See also note 2, 1854.

1857

Cramer. All looked well. There were [a] few young ladies, about 10, & a good many gentlemen, so [I] had a right pleasant time. I saw most of Mr. Wm. Trundle & Dr. Boulder, but lost my heart with neither. After a very handsome supper, had dancing till about 1 o'clock, when they left. Every thing passed off well. Cousin & I were invited to Mr. Hemston's to dinner tomorrow.

Friday Dec. 4th. Very bright morning, but cloudy after dinner. We had breakfast by nine o'clock. Cousin Ed, Mr. T. & Messrs Cramer came up about ten, and about twelve they all went over to Mr. Hempston's, and Renie S. & I went about 1 o'clock, [and we] had a handsome dinner. Most of the persons of the neighborhood there that were present at the marriage. We left there for Cousin Henry's about four, and then came home. We had a dark but very pleasant ride. Most of the conversation related to another marriage that is to be some time. We got home by eight o'clock and Cousin Ed sat till about nine, and left after eating brandy peaches.

Saturday [December] 5th. Damp, sultry day. We were awaken[ed] at night by Messrs. Haines & Roderick telling us Keefer's mill & distillery[50] were on fire. It was a grand spectacle but also awful.

* * * * *

Monday [December] 7th. Very pretty day. Geo. Sauerwein came out about four o'clock & took tea, [and] left soon after six. I wrote to Lou Clippinger at night.

Tuesday Dec. 8th. Very pretty morning. I was in town shopping and was out at Aunt M. Artz's but did not find her home; call[ed] to see Ellen B. as I came home. When Father came home [he] told me of Harry's passing through town and [that] he would be to see us on Friday. Mrs. I. Howard & Mrs. Taylor spent afternoon here.

Wednesday [December] 9th. Had intended going to town to have Dr. S. fill the remaining two teeth but it was too rainy.

---

[50] J. T. Scharf reports that on December 7th, Michael Keefer's mill and distillery burned. Scharf, *History of Western Maryland*, p. 564.

1857

Thursday [December] 10th. Pleasant, bright day. I went into town after dinner and went to Houcks' and Georgia went with me to Dr. S.'s rooms and I had my teeth finished.

Friday [December] 11th. Beautiful morning. Mother & I went into town early and went to Miss Sallie Vermillion's[51] and purchased my bonnet there. Met Livie Crampton & two sister-in-laws there and they got bonnets, too. I went shopping with them and Mother went down street to wait for me. Just before I was ready to come out of town, [I] met Cousin Harry on the street and, as he said business would not allow him to come out, I determined to stay in & go to the fair. He went with me to Houcks', then left. I went with Tilly to Dr. S.'s and on my return Georgia, Harry & I went to see Kunkels and Ellen B. Harry left again, and after tea we got ready and Emma, Georgia & I went to the Methodist fair. Good many there, not many acquaintants. Derrs & Ed came back with us. Harry left [at] nearly eleven o'clock.

Saturday Dec. 12th. A beautiful morning. Mother came for me about eleven and I went with her out the turnpike to meet the funeral of old Mrs. Louis Kemp[52]. Not many persons at the funeral. Harry left town this morning. I came home with Mother.

Sunday [December] 13th. Beautiful day. Mother & I were in church. Mag Derr is coming out Wednesday.

Monday [December] 14th. At home all day. Mother in town; papers from Mr. T. J. Himes.

Tuesday [December] 15th. Busy sewing. Mr. James Reid made quite a lengthy call this morning. He's going south very soon.

Wednesday [December] 16th. Dull, cloudy morning. I went in to meet Mag Derr. We shopped together and I borrowed a night gown of Mary Kunkel and we cut ours out after we came home.

Thursday [December] 17th. Still cloudy. We were busy all day. Cousin Ed came out to tea to take Mag home. After it was proposed [for us] to go to

---

[51]This millinery shop was located on the west side of Market Street opposite the Market House between Church and Second Streets. *Williams' Directory*, p. 40.

[52]Rebecca C. Kemp died December 10th. Her husband, Col. Lewis Kemp, died in 1854. They are buried in Mt. Olivet Cemetery. Holdcraft, *Names in Stone*, II, 650.

town to see the paintings on exhibition[53], so [we] went three in a buggy; [we] stopped some time in town and did not get out to Mr. Derr's till nearly ten o'clock. It rained very hard but we did not get wet. We did not go to bed till about eleven.

Friday [December] 18th. Quite a bright day with good deal of wind. Cousin Ed came about two and we started to town as soon as [we were] ready. Ed came and took Mag in, Mary & I went in wagon with Eugene. We were to see [the] pictures and I met Mother at the gallery and came out with her.

Saturday Dec. 19th. I commenced Jane's dress and was quite busy with it.

Sunday [December] 20th. Very bright day. Mother and I were in church. Cousin Ed came down to the Hotel with us. I was over at M. Roderick['s] in [the] afternoon.

Monday [December] 21st. Cloudy day, and very fast and large flakes of snow fell. Mother was in town.

Tuesday [December] 22nd. Still cloudy. About four o'clock Mr. T. J. Himes arrived.[54] He left Rock Island two weeks ago. He looks well and seems in good spirits.

Wednesday [December] 23rd. Very pretty day. Wrote a note to Mary Derr [that] I could not go to Balt[imore] [because] Mr. H. had arrived. I proposed a ride to M. Derr's but Mr. H. did not favor it. /I had a very interesting letter from Mary Sauerwein [asking me] to come [at] Christmas./ Mother saw Mary in town; said she could not go on account of [her] face.

Thursday [December] 24th. Beautiful day, quite busy today. Father [had] gone to town so Mr. Himes had to entertain himself. I wrote to Mary Sauerwein saying why I could not come, and a note for Mag Derr to come out to-morrow, and when Father came out [I] received a similar one from her; but she sent Eugene[55] out, so it was arranged.

---

[53]Engelbrecht's diary does not mention the exhibit.

[54]See November 30, 1857.

[55]Eugene, the son of John and Elizabeth Derr, was born on the old Derr homestead in 1844. Eugene studied law but became a very successful farmer. He was a county commissioner and president of the County Agriculture Society. Williams, *History*, II, 1246-1247.

1857

Friday [December] 25th. Christmas day, bright day. Mr. Himes & I went to church. Mag & Mary Derr & Ed S. came out with us to dinner, [and] left about nine o'clock.

Saturday Dec. 26th. Snowed by showers during day, but clear & windy at night. Mr. Himes and I went out & spent the day at Mr. Derr's. Cousin Ed was there to dinner. About three o'clock Cousin Ed, Mr. Himes, Mary Derr & I went over to the mill and was weighed. I weighed 134, Mr. H. 141, Mary Derr 154 & Cousin Ed 172. We were all through the mill, & Cousin Ed & I stopped and went through the house to see Miss Nancy, & the new cistern, etc. [We] met Mr. J. A. Johnson on our way to Mr. Derr's and he said, if I were going to spend the evening, he would come over. So he hurried & returned by 1/4 of 7 o'clock. He looks well and was in such excellent spirits. I fear he is my favorite still.

Sunday [December] 27th. Feared it would be cold but [it] proved to be very pleasant. Mr. H. & I were in to church. [It was] pretty full this morning. We spent the afternoon at home.

Monday [December] 28th. Cloudy, dull day. Mr. T. J. Himes left this morning for his father's in Cumberland Co. Pa. I was busy all day righting up things, etc.

Tuesday [December] 29th. At home all day, busy. Raining. I wrote to Mary S[auerwein] & Ed S[hriner].

Wednesday [December] 30th. Raining still. Wrote to Harry Smith, [and a] note to Mrs. Winchester.

Thursday [December] 31st. Bright day. I left home for Balt[imore]. Cousin Ed went with me. After dinner Mary & I were out. After tea Mr. Gregg & Em went to the panorama. Mr. Lefevre [was] here. Mary & I spent [the] evening in sewing. Ed & S. were out. We sat up till after 12 o'clock having some fun. So ended the Old year.

1858

"My 25th birthday. To think I have lived a quarter of a century and to so little purpose."

BALTIMORE

January 1st, 1858. Bright, beautiful day, so opens the new year. Lum Sadtler was here awhile in morning. Mrs. Lewis [came] to see Kate. Mary & I were down Market Street shopping about three o'clock. Mr. Gregg called in his carriage & took us out to Mrs. Tell's; Mary & I went. We had a pleasant ride. I enjoyed it much, returned by six. After tea Geo. & Ed went out. The girls and I were home together. We had a time of fun before retiring.

Saturday Jan. 2nd. Very pleasant day. We were at home all morning. After dinner Mr. Gregg sent [to ask] if we would have the carriage; so cousin Ed, Mary, Em & I accepted it and went out the Hookstown about five miles to see Vallie Weagly & Ginnie Adams[1]. We had a pleasant ride. Mr. Gregg [was] here at night & spent the evening with us all. Em & I were down street awhile. Kate Sauerwein was here in [the] afternoon. We fixed Geo. & Ed's bed and we had fun when <u>they</u> did go to bed.

Sunday [January] 3rd. Somewhat cooler. Cousin Ed, Mrs. S., Mary, Kate & I all went to Dr. Morris' church; Rev. Mr. Anspach preached. Mr. Rau [was] here afternoon & to tea. Mary & I were at Grace church in [the] afternoon. Mary & Ed, Geo & I went to hear Mr. Tiffany, Mr. Bayfield walked with us. John Derr [was] here in afternoon while we were at church; Thomas Derr when we came back at night & spent the evening.

Monday Jan. 4th. Bright day. Annie Schley, Bell[e] Bailey & Misses Mann and Mrs. Emma Spilcher & her sister-in-law were all here before <u>we</u> (Mary

---

[1]Vallie Weagly and Ginnie Adams were Margaret's cousins, daughters of Valentine Adams and his first wife Sybilla, a sister of Margaret's mother. Thomas, *Thomas Genealogy*, pp. 27-28. See also note 32, 1851.

1858

& I) went out with Ed S., and had a time hunting a ring[2], so had to order one at Mr. Gould's. Mary & I were out with Ed after dinner [a] short time. Ed left in the four o'clock train. Mary & I took a walk down Market St. After tea Mr. & Mrs. Abell & Rose, Mr. & Mrs. Bayfield, Mrs. John Gregg, Mrs. De Armitage, Misses Vondersmith & Knode & Mrs. Lafayette Hans & Thomas Derr all spent the evening here, [and] left 12 o'clock.

Tuesday [January] 5th. A mild day though cloudy. At night foggy with appearance of early rain. /I got the ring & sent it to him [Ed Shriner] by Thomas Derr. Wrote a note./ Mary & I were out shopping. Mr. Lefevre was here, saw him [a] short time. Lizzie Lefevre was here [a] short time. In afternoon Mrs. Sauerwein & Mary went with me & I got a new dress. At night John Derr & his father were here; also Mr. Gregg spent the evening.

Wednesday [January] 6th. It rained during the night and still cloudy [in the] morning. Mr. Gregg sent to know if we would [have] the carriage but [we] declined the use of it this morning. Kate & I were out shopping a little, then called to see Kate Sauerwein, & while we were gone Misses S. & H. Webb called to see me. [We] also found Mr. Gregg waiting to take Mary, Kate & I riding. We had a very pleasant ride out Franklin and in Madison Avenue. We went around to Geo's store afterwards & were weighed. I weighed 136. Mr. Gregg [was] here at night. Mary & I sewed articles awhile and then [went] in the parlour to see him. Kate & Mrs. Sauerwein [went] to church.

Thursday Jan. 7th. A clear day & much colder. This morning we sewed. Margaret Fox was here, also Mrs. Bayfield & Mrs. John Gregg. Lizzie Lefevre [was] here to see us. After I had finished my dress Mary, Kate & I called to see Neal Dean, but she was out in the country. Also [we went] to return Em Spilcher's call but she was not home, then at Mrs. Uhrlaub's and both Mr. & Mrs. [were] home. Sat & talked awhile. Em was out with Mr. Gregg. Mr. Green was here at night but the girls & I read while Em entertained.

Friday [January] 8th. Clear & cold. Mr. Lefevre here to see Kate. I read aloud to Mary. Mrs. A. Reese was here; came with Mary from Market. After dinner about 3 1/2 Mr. Gregg arrived to take Em, Mary & me down to see

---

[2]The ring was for Ed Shriner's fiancée, Maggie Derr.

the Boston Steamer[3] and then afterwards out on the York Road to Cool Spring. /Eliza McGowan was here to invite us there this evening./ Mrs. Rau was here while we were gone. Mr. John Rau [was] here at night for [a] short time. Mr. Gregg was here to spend the evening. Mrs. Cardy Kohler was here to make a call at noon. At night Mary, Kate, Geo. S. & I all went up to [the] De Armitages to spend the evening. There were about 25 persons, all very agreeable. We danced, played plays, etc. and staid till after twelve o'clock. Mr. Brooke came home with Kate.

Saturday [January] 9th. Cloudy day. Mr. Gregg called for us (Em & me) about 11 o'clock & took us to Govanstown to see Annie Mering, & then to Londontown [?] to see Mrs. Dr. Bosley but she was not home. /Mr. Lefevre [was] here this morning./ When [we] got back [we] found a note from Ed with ring to be marked. Mary & I were to see Mr. Bayfield, also Mrs. John Gregg. Mr. Fox [was] here at night.

Sunday Jan 10th. Bright morning but cloudy by afternoon. Annie Schley was here to see me before church. Mrs. S., E., K., M. & I all went to church. Dr. Morris preached. G. came to church for us. Mr. Philip Rau was here [in the] afternoon & to tea. Mary & I were at St. Paul's to church. Geo. & Philip came for us. John Derr was here awhile just before tea. All went to church but Mary & I. Lum Sadtler came home with them & staid awhile.

Monday [January] 11th. Very rainy morning. Mr. Rau called & brought me an ambrotype[4] of himself. The girls had a letter from Em Houck saying Lizzie would be down tomorrow to pay a visit. Mr. Gregg called in the afternoon & sat an hour or more. [He] came to say good-bye, but as I was not going today [he] will come again to-morrow. We spent the evening so pleasantly with all the family. I enjoyed it much; we were sewing, talking, eating, etc.

Tuesday [January] 12th. Delightful day, so much so that I regretted I had written I was coming home today. Mary & I were out shopping. [We] called at Abells' before returning, [and] found Lizzie & Emma Houck there, just come. Mrs. Dean & Mrs. Lefevre had been there. Lizzie, Em H. & Kate

---

[3]In 1856 the steamship "Joseph Whitney" of the Boston and Baltimore line began to provide passenger and freight service between the two cities. It continued, using a Light Street wharf until the Civil War. Scharf, *Baltimore*, p. 302.

[4]An ambrotype is an early type of photograph made by imaging a negative on glass backed by a dark surface. *Webster's Dictionary*.

1858

went out; also Em S. & Mrs. S. Mr. Gregg called & walked to the cars with Mary & Geo with me. They waited till [the] cars started. Ellen Kemp came up tonight, so [she] made it more pleasant. Mother met me at [the] cars. Found Father in bed but [he] is better now.

* * * * *

Thursday [January] 14th. Pleasant day. I was in town, had Annie Nihoff fit my dress, and then came out home. Mother & I went over & spent [the] afternoon at Mrs. I. Howard's. Miss Maggie Henderson was there staying.

* * * * *

Monday [January] 18th. I wrote to Mary Sauerwein. [I] was in in the morning to see Annie Nihoff & have her fit my dress, stopped to see Ellen & Mrs. Markell as I came down street, then came out home.

Tuesday [January] 19th. Beautiful, bright day. Mother went out & brought Aunt Margaret out to spend the day, [and] took her back again in the evening.

Wednesday [January] 20th. Pleasant day. [I] had a note from Mary Derr saying Mag would be out tomorrow night, & wanting me on Sunday.

Thursday [January] 21st. Appearance of rain somewhat, but cleared off by noon. Around eleven or half past Mr. & Mrs. Randolf Denton & daughter & Mrs. Peter Kemp, Aunt Mary Scholl & Lewis & Aunt Jemima S. arrived to spend the day. They all left about four o'clock. Mag & Ed S. came out after tea & sat a couple of hours.

Friday Jan. 22nd. Quite cold. I had a nice long letter from Louise Clippinger.

Saturday [January] 23rd. Clear & somewhat colder. I went out to M. Derr's after dinner, [and] John came right home. About four o'clock Lizzie & George Schell & Joe & Bob Noonan & Mag McCartney arrived and took tea & sat till about nine. We were over to Cousin Ed's before tea, and we were weighed. Cousin Ed also [came] to tea. He staid at Mr. Derr's till about <u>one</u> o'clock talking of the wedding & the fixings. Mr. Ben Perry of Wash[ington] was [there] to see me.

Sunday [January] 24th. Clear & cold. As I did not feel well no one went to church from Mr. Derr's except Mag with Cousin Ed. [They] made the

1858

engagement [the] evening before. Mr. & Mrs. Peter Kemp took tea there. Cousin Ed also [was] there to tea. After tea Mag, Mary & Alice Derr & I all went with Cousin Ed up to Hokes', [and] saw Lena & her Mother. [I] think they are very clean, common Dutch people, but if Lena had opportunities [she] would make a very smart woman. Heard Mr. Perry [was] here to see us.

Monday [January] 25th. [I] came in with Alice [Derr] when she came to school and waited at Mrs. Markel's till they sent for me. Such a lovely afternoon. Mr. Ben Perry did not come.

* * * * *

Wednesday [January] 27th. Pleasant day. I went in about four o'clock to stay all night at Mrs. Markell's. Ellen & I were down street on business before tea. Mr. Rohrback arrived about seven to see Ellen & I went with him to see a wedding in church & [we] were soon joined by Cousin Ed S. We had a place far up in church & could see. We returned to Mrs. M's & spent the evening, but left by ten o'clock.

Thursday [January] 28th. Beautiful, bright morning, but cloudy before evening. John came in for me before ten o'clock, and I went for Aunt Jemima & we went out & spent the day till about four with D. Claggett's family. They proved very pleasant. Kate is very lively, full of fun, Emma a very sensitive & sensible lady like her mother. We had a pleasant time. As we returned home saw [a] great many strangers in town, all rough in appearance.

Friday [January] 29th. Pleasant enough early, but by nine o'clock [the] weather changed & by noon, damp and cold, raw, windy. Philip Hawkin was hung today in Fred'k, [before a] great crowd, so Father said.[5] Mother & I were at home alone. I wrote to Lou Clippinger.

---

[5]"Execution just 15 minutes after 12 o'ck PM. Negro Philip Hawkins was hung, on the Barracks Ground South end of town for the murder of Negro James Diggs on the 7th of February 1857 Near Urbanna in this County. His body remained suspended for 28 minutes when he was let down and buried in a Grave near by and immediately thereafter the Gallows was taken down. I estimate the number of people at the execution about Eight thousand - I was there among the Rest. Several days later the Grave was opened in the presence of 30 persons owing to some reports that the Doctor had taken the body - but all was O.K." Engelbrecht, *Diary*, II, 733-734.

1858

Saturday [January] 30th. Pretty day. [I went] down to Uncle Adams' to see about my tenant [?], out to Aunt Margaret's after dinner, [and] stopped in town [a] short time.

* * * * *

Monday February 1st [1858]. Morning seemed as if [the] day might be pleasant, but [it] proved very unpleasant. Snowed awhile, then rained & hailed. I went down to Mr. & Mrs. Keefer['s] to spend the day. Fanny Adams & Mrs. I. Howard were there. About three o'clock Mrs. Wm. Miller, Sarah Miller & Isie Buckey arrived & staid till after tea. Fannie Adams was sent for when they arrived, & Mrs. I. Howard soon after tea but, as they [her parents] did not send for me, I remained over night. Mrs. Harriet Keefer Drill & her sister-in-law Miss Mary Drill were there.

Tuesday [February] 2nd. At home all day, busy sewing. [I] walked home from Misses K[eefer's]. [I had] missed John. Mother had sent for me.

Wednesday [February] 3rd. Pleasant day. Finishing my wrapper. I had a note from Mary Derr saying she would not be out for a week or so, [but] wants me to meet them in town on Saturday.

* * * * *

Friday [February] 5th. Cold and somewhat damp. Mrs. Jane Howard & Marion stopped for me to go see Emily Cookson and bid her "good bye" as she leaves Monday. Her baby Annie May has grown to be a pretty babe & so lively. The family [were] all home & Mrs. Taylor [was] there. We returned by four o'clock. Mr. & Mrs. H. stopped [a] short time here. Letter of Mary Sauerwein. Paper [from] Chicago.

Saturday [February] 6th. A lovely day. Annie Howard came down about eleven o'clock & spent the day. She practiced a good deal and I think could improve in music fast with a good teacher. Mrs. I. Howard & Marion came over in the afternoon and staid till after tea. [I] walked part way home with them. I wrote Mrs. L. Markel a note to tell Miss Derrs I could not meet them in town.

Sunday [February] 7th. Rather cloudy & damp. I was in church and heard a very good sermon from Dr. Zack, communion season. Cousin Ed was at the Hotel till I started, [and in] good humor.

1858

Monday [February] 8th. Clear but somewhat cooler. At home all day. Mrs. Killion [was] here before dinner. About four o'clock there was an arrival which proved to be Mr. Dod Gambrill and a cousin (a widower, I believe) of Balt[imore]. The[y] sat until nearly or after six. He talks very well. Dod looks so handsome.

Tuesday [February] 9th. Clear in the morning but very windy in afternoon. I went into town by 3 1/2, did some shopping and was to see Ginnie Brengle awhile.

Wednesday [February] 10th. Quite cold and windy. Who should arrive by four o'clock but Messrs. Gambrill & Peters again and staid to tea. They were very talkative and I suppose thought themselves very agreeable; but Mr. Peters is too old a man, is coming to see me in Balt[imore]; that is, if I cannot prevent it. I'll try, I think.

Thursday [February] 11th. Exceedingly clear but the coldest day of the winter. Mother & I were in town in the afternoon to see [the] Kunkels, Mrs. J. Schaeffer and the Misses Houses and to do some shopping. [I] was [in] to see Ellen B. a minute to make an engagement for Sunday.

Friday [February] 12th. Very cloudy and a fall of snow, an inch or so. Mr. Mullinix was here to hire Joe.

* * * * *

Monday [February] 15th. Much warmer. I wrote a note to Mag & Mary Derr to know about their coming out. I had a nice letter of Lou Clip[pinger] & a note on the Bank of Social Habits, etc.

* * * * *

Wednesday [February] 17th. Mother was in town and borrowed a tidy[6] of Aunt Shriner for me.

Thursday [February] 18th. Still cold but quite clear. I was in town, returned Mary Shriner's tidies. [I] called at Houcks & Annie Bentz's, but found them

---

[6] A tidy was a piece of fancy work, often used to protect the arms and headrest of a chair or sofa from wear or tear. *Webster's Dictionary.*

1858

out and at Mrs. McGill's. She was very pleasant & talkative, and I made an engagement to take her down to Schleys'. [I] was at Gaithers' but could get no one to answer the bell; also [at] Mrs. Markell's but she was not home, and Ellen [was] in Boonsboro.

* * * * *

Thursday [February] 20th. Cold but clear. After dinner John took me to town in the sleigh. I invited Mrs. Markell to take a ride but she declined. Ellen came home whilst I was there. As I came in [I] met Meal Kunkel going out for me to come stay all night, but [I] could not. After stopping awhile at Mrs. Markell's I went out to Aunt M. Artz's and returned her tidy, & had a little talk. [I] found cousin Ed S. at our house when I returned and he staid till about ten o'clock. [We] had quite a <u>confidence meeting</u>, [he] telling me of his arrangements & I some of my experience.

Sunday [February] 21st. Pleasant day. Mother & I went into church. Dr. Zackarias preached to the soldiers of 1812-14; he had a very appropriate discourse. After church Mag Derr insisted upon my going home with her, so I saw Mother & told her. [I] found Mary Derr in bed. Mrs. Ed Getzendanner & child there to dinner. Cousin Ed [came] over after tea & staid till after twelve o'clock.

Monday [February] 22nd. Much warmer. Thomas Derr & I took dinner with Cousin Ed. Mr. & Mrs. Randolf Dutrow & daughter Amelia & Aunt Mary Scholl were there. [We] returned to Mr. Derr's by 3 o'clock & got Mag's quilt out by 5 o'clock. Mary Derr [is] better. Cousin Ed & Jerry Cramer came soon after tea & took Mary & me out to our house. I was with Jerry. They left soon after 9 o'clock.

Tuesday [February] 23rd. Very pleasant day. John took me over to Mr. Isaac Howard's on business. Marion returned with me and staid over night. I had a Valentine today from Chicago & a paper also, [but] don't care for either.

Wednesday [February] 24th. At home all day. Sent Marion home about ten o'clock.

Thursday [February] 25th. Very pleasant day. Finished up some work. [I had a] note from Mary Kunkel to come in to-morrow or Saturday and stay over Sunday. [I] wrote to Lou Clippinger.

1858

Friday [February] 26th. Lovely day. I wrote a note to Mary Kunkel and sent it, saying I would be in Saturday to stay.

Saturday [February] 27th. Very pleasant day. The carriage went in four times but I was not ready till the last time to go in. [I] found the girls & Mrs. Kunkel well and glad to see me. After tea Meal and I were up street to shop and then took a walk; [we] returned before eight and spent the evening very pleasantly all together. Mary Kunkel cast my shawl on for me.

Sunday [February] 28th. Somewhat cooler. Mary, Meallie & I went to church. Cousin Ed & Thomas Derr came down street with us. Cousin Ed came up from Uncle Lewis' about three o'clock and took tea, and afterwards [we] went to the Episcopal church and heard an excellent sermon from Rev. Mr. Seymour. We were all so well pleased.

Monday March 1st [1858]. Cloudy, damp day. Meallie and I were up street awhile to see Sophia Gaither, but as she is so ill [we] only saw her mother. Nevins Dorsey was up from the Tan Yard and sat an hour or more. At night first Mag Derr [came,] then Miss Drucilla & Nevins Dorsey; then Nevins & Meal went down for Allen Schley, and very soon Thomas Derr arrived, and I spent a very pleasant evening, quiet of course but so pleasant.

Tuesday March 2nd. Very cold. Mother came in for me and I came out home about ten o'clock. About four Cousin Ed and George S[auerwein] came. I was surprised to see George, not knowing he was up. They sat till about nine o'clock talking of matters & things in general.

* * * * *

Saturday [March] 6th. Very cold morning but moderated after dinner. Mag, Mary & Eugene Derr [were] here to dinner. /Still neuralgia in my jaw./ After dinner we girls went up to Mr. Boyd['s] family home & Cousin Ed & Wils B. came to tea. Mary & I went home in our carriage & Cousin Ed brought Mag D. All staid over night.

Sunday March 7th. Very cold & windy. Only Maggie D. [and] Mother went to church. Mag & Cousin Ed went home about four o'clock. I had very bad pain in my face, so Mary applied hot poultice which relieved it for the time. Mary D. is such a kind, good girl, who loves so to do anything for another.

1858

Monday [March] 8th. Snowed all day, so Mary & Mother could not go in to shop. I retired very early; [I] ate no supper on account of my face. Hot poultice again.

Tuesday [March] 9th. Rather cloudy but warmer. Annie Bentz & Pete Bantz were out in the afternoon and sat a couple hours. I found this morning I had erysipelas, so of course must be particular. Mother took Mary Derr to town to go home with Cousin Ed. I shall miss her. Quite cold.

Wednesday [March] 10th. Much warmer. Mother was in town. Mary & Meallie Kunkel & their brother Jacob's children were out & sat awhile. Legislature closed its session to-day.

* * * * *

Friday [March] 12th. Very pretty day. Father & Mother were both in town to-day. I wrote a note & sent it to Mary Derr. When they returned I had a letter from Cousin Harry Smith, & a note from Mr. Rod Hobbs wanting to know if he might visit me, if only once and he would tell me all. Mr. Beall took tea here. I did not see him.

* * * * *

Monday [March] 15th. Very warm, sultry day. Mrs. I. Howard, Mrs. Charles H. & Annie H. spent [the] afternoon here. [I] had a nice letter from Lou Clip & note from G. Sauerwein in Father's letter.

Tuesday [March] 16th. Still sultry. Mrs. Taylor & Marion Howard spent [the] afternoon here, Mrs. T. talking a great deal about a widower.

Wednesday [March] 17th]. Very pleasant. Had a note from Mary Derr saying Mag would go to Balt[imore] Thursday, & perhaps she last of next week.

* * * * *

Sunday [March] 21st. Rained in morning but beautiful afternoon. Cousin Ed came out about 3 & sat till about [_____]. He was talking of bridal presents, rings, etc. Mother was down to see Mrs. Castle and sprained her knee in getting over the fence.

Monday [March] 22nd. Pleasant day but windy. Dr. Moran[7] was out to see Mother, [and] says it is only a sprain.

Tuesday [March] 23rd. Damp day. Had a note from Marion Howard saying if convenient some of their & Boyds' family would spend to-morrow afternoon with us. I wrote one in return telling them it would suit.

Wednesday March 24th. Delightful day. Father [has] gone to Uncle John Brunner's sale. After dinner Jenny & Fannie Adams [came] & very soon Mrs. I. Howard & Marion, Miss Vic Ayton, & Miss Henderson, & presently Mrs. Jones & Ginny Boyd, and about four, Cousin Ed. All left after tea except Mrs. J. & Gin, & Ed left after tea. Mollie Jones came when the wagon came, only sat a few minutes and all left. Cousin Ed about ten. /Note from Mary Derr enclosing a letter from Mag D./

* * * * *

Friday [March] 26th. Very windy day. I went to town after dinner and stopped for Ella B., and we were shopping and [went] to see Mrs. B. F. Winchester & Aunt Jem[ima] Scholl[8] and came home before six o'clock. Mrs. Geo. Birely brought Annie Schley out to spend the evening. They sat till nearly ten o'clock. [I] met Miss Lizzie Jones at Uncle Louis's.

Saturday [March] 27th. Beautiful day. I wrote a note to Mag D. & Miss S. and sent it by Cousin Ed. I sent for Miss Lizzie Jones' cap pattern.

* * * * *

Monday [March] 29th. Pretty day. [I] was in town after dinner & talked some time with Aunt Jem[ima] Scholl, then shopped a little & came out home. Did not have a letter of Mag Derr.

---

[7] Dr. J. J. Moran had his office and residence on the east side of Market Street, the second door south of Third Street. *Williams' Directory*, p. 28. Dr. Moran had attended Edgar Allen Poe during his last illness at Church Home Hospital in Baltimore in 1849. Williams, *History*, I, 592.

[8] Aunt Jemima was the wife of Margaret's Uncle Lewis [Louis] Scholl. They had a home on the south side of Patrick Street between Carroll and East Streets. *Williams' Directory*, p. 34. See note 27, 1853.

1858

Tuesday March 30th. Very pleasant day. I made butter for the first time. After dinner [I] walked over and spent the afternoon with Mrs. I. Howard's family. Vic Ayton [is] still there, [a] pleasant girl. When [I] got home found Miss Ann R. Keefer had been here.

Wednesday [March] 31st. Very pretty day. Mary Derr came about eleven o'clock and staid till four. Mag is coming home to-night. Mary [is] working her slippers. Such kind sisters to each other.

* * * * *

Friday April 2nd [1858]. Good Friday. Rather cloudy. Busy [at] home in the morning; [in] afternoon [I] went out to Mr. Derr['s]. Mag & Ed came up last night. Mr. Isaac Bond was here to dinner, [and] brought our map of Frederick Co.[9] Cousin Ed & Mag came to town as I came home. I was late [getting] home, after 10.

Saturday [April] 3rd. Beautiful day. I was busy [at] home baking in the morning, & after four o'clock went to town to meet Mag Derr. [I] was at Kunkel's, [and] Mag D. & Mary K. soon arrived. [They] had been to church. Cousin Ed soon came and after making a call Cousin E., M. & I went to Schleys' to see the girls. [I] sat awhile & then attended to some shopping & afterward came home. [I] talked to Mrs. Markell's family a while at the window.

Easter Sunday April 4th. Quite warm & very bright. I went in to church. Aunt M. Artz was in our pew and I invited her to come out home with me & she came. As Mrs. Hershey came about three o'clock, I could not go home with her, so Mother went. Mrs. H. left about five or six o'clock.

[Monday] April 5th. Cloudy in the afternoon. About three o'clock Cousin Ed brought Mary & Mag Derr out and they staid till nearly ten. We were talking of the approaching marriage arrangements, etc.

* * * * *

---

[9]This map is one of the main references in our research. It includes most of the farmers' names as well as churches, inns, towns, railroads, roads, population (including free negroes and slaves), school districts and distances, and election districts.

1858

Wednesday [April] 7th. Much colder. [I] wrote a note to Vic Ayton & had one in return, borrowed her circular, cut the pat[t]ern, etc., & returned it.

Thursday [April] 8th. [It] rained early in the morning, but as it ceased about 8 I started to town. [I] went to Mr. Houck's. Mag Derr came about 9, and we were out shopping in all the hard rain. We were at Mrs. Reese['s] about twelve and she would have us to eat. I went home with Mag Derr to cut the circular out; we succeeding in getting three out. Eugene Derr brought me to town. Mother had just come in for me in the carriage, so it just suited.

* * * * *

Saturday [April] 10th. A beautiful day. [I was] very busy so did not go to town as I had thought of doing. Lizzie Schell, Sophie Gaither & Gin Brengle were out to make a call.

* * * * *

Wednesday [April] 14th. [It] seemed so pleasant, so [I] thought not of rain. Mother & I were in town in the cart and it rained. [It] rained very hard before we came home. [I] had a long note from Mag Derr & [an] enclosed one from Mary S. to Mag Derr. [I] engaged my bonnet.

* * * * *

Saturday [April] 17th. Clear morning but rather cloudy afternoon. [I] wrote to Mary Sauerwein, [and] enclosed a note to Fannie Koones. [I] answered Rod Hobbs' note. I went to town, saw about my bonnet, then went to Houcks' to meet Mag Derr and Mary D. Georgia accompanied us. We were at Mrs. C. Steiner['s], (Mrs. C. not home), at Ella B's. Mr. Rhorback [was] there; he will not remain in Phil[adelphia].

* * * * *

Monday [April] 19th. Raining in showers all day. Mother & I [were] both busy on my travelling dress.

Tuesday April 20th. Raining in showers early and very hard. After dinner I went into town to give Cousin Ed some money to take [to] Mary Sauerwein for my dress. [I] saw Wils Boyd in town. Came home directly and was very busy all day, sewing.

1858

Wednesday [April] 21st. Cold windy day. Mary S. came up but [I] concluded [I] would not go in till morning [to get her].

Thursday [April] 22nd. Very pretty morning. I went in with Father to bring Mary S. out, but found a note instead from her in which she said she would stay at Derrs' but come out if she had an opportunity. When I came home [I] found Marion Howard, who staid till after ten. I fixed the lining in my new dress & we were very busy.

Friday [April] 23rd. Cold and with some showers towards night. About three o'clock Cousin Ed. S[hriner] brought Mary S[auerwein] out to tea. We had lots to talk of. They have decided on white kids [gloves] at last. Mother was in town & brought my bonnet home.

* * * * *

Monday [April] 26th. Clear cool day. Mother [was] in town. Mrs. Peter & Baker Fout [came] out to spend the day. I started for Derrs' about three o'clock, stopped awhile in town, and then at Aunt M. Artz's awhile. About nine o'clock Mr. Johnson arrived, Cousin Ed about eight. Mary [was] late dressing, so she and I did not get in till about half-past nine. John & Thomas Derr & Geo. Sauerwein arrived about ten and, after their <u>tea</u> and some talk, we had a rehearsal. We came in several times before we were exactly right. The gents all left after eleven, and after some talk we girls all retired. Mag slept her last single night between Mary S. & me. Letter of Fannie Koons that was.

MR. DERR'S, MAG'S WEDDING DAY

[Tuesday] April 27th. [A] bright but very windy morning, but the wind subsided a great deal till noon. We were busy serving, arranging the table, etc., all morning. The guest[s] and groomsmen arrived soon after eleven, and we proceeded to the parlour five minutes before twelve. Mr. J. A. Johnson & Mary S. [were] in front, then Geo. S. & Mary Derr, & then John Derr & I, and lastly Cousin Ed S. & Maggie D. It was a long ceremony but everything passed off well. [Neither] John Derr nor I could restrain a few tears during the ceremony and afterward [there was] a copious supply from the groom and a few tears from the bride, also Mary S. & Mary D. We proceeded to the table and from there to the Houcks' in town, and from there

to Washington, having a nice stroll around the Relay House[10]. Saw the fishing for sturgeon, etc. Mrs. Shriner[11], George Shriner, Uncle Adams, Mr. & Mrs. Dutrow, Frankie, Mr. & Mrs. Reese, Dr. Zack & Lizzie were all the guests present.

WASHINGTON

[Tuesday] April 27th [continued]. We arrived in Washington about seven o'clock and were nearly torn to pieces at the depot by the various attentive hackmen. We stopped at Brown's Hotel[12] and after some delay were assigned very pleasant rooms, Mag's very nice. The road from Relay to Washington I had not travelled for some time, [and I] saw great improvement in the country. The land has been much improved by different fertilizers. After taking our tea, we repaired to Mr. & Mrs. Shriners' room to spend the evening. The gents left soon after ten and after Mag retired we went to our rooms and very soon the gents all came to satisfy us as regards our room, the key adjoining, and after having a long talk we retired.

[Wednesday] April 28th. The gents were at our room by seven or half-past and we were ready, but it was nearly nine till Maggie & E. were ready, so we had to wait some time. Immediately after breakfast Cousin Ed and I went round to see Cousin Rebecca Koons & family. They seemed very glad to see me and insisted upon me staying with them. After we returned we all got ready and started from the patent office[13] where we spent some time, couple

---

[10]In 1858 the train from Frederick went east to Relay where connections were made to Baltimore or Washington. The Relay House there catered to passengers transferring between trains. Meals were available as well as overnight lodgings in a simple frame hotel. The Patapsco River and a very long viaduct were nearby. Herbert H. Harwood, Jr., *Impossible Challenge: The Baltimore-Ohio Railroad in Maryland* (Baltimore, MD, 1979), pp. 83, 102, 103, 218, 221.

[11]Mrs. Shriner was Ed Shriner's stepmother. She is often referred to in this diary as "Aunt Shriner." In later years, she lived in a house in Frederick. See note 18, 1860.

[12]Brown's Hotel, also known as the Indian Queen, was located on the west side of Sixth Street, just north of Pennsylvania Avenue. *Washington, City and Capital, American Guide Series* (W.P.A. Federal Writers' Project, Washington, D.C., 1937), p. 976.

[13]Now the National Portrait Gallery and the Museum of American Art, in the massive Greek Revival building which occupies the square bounded by 7th, 9th, F and G Streets, N.W. The Old Patent Office was begun in 1836, finished in 1867, and is one of the oldest public buildings in Washington. H. N. Jacobsen, *A Guide to the Architecture of Washington, D.C.* (New York, 1965), p. 53.

1858

of hours, all delighted with the variety of birds, patents, etc. and from there we proceeded to the Capitol and were in the various halls of public interest. We heard part of a speech from Henry W. Davis of Md. & reply from Stephens of Ga., and in the Senate chamber a part of speech from Peugh of Ohio. From thence we were at the green house belonging to the public grounds. It is crowded with fruits, flowers & ornamental plants of foreign climes, mostly of the tropical climes. From there a view on the river Tiber.[14] /G. S. left in afternoon train for Balt[imore]./ There was a boat on the last named river and [sic] reminds me of the picture of the ancient Tiber. From there we returned to Brown's. While [we were] fixing for dinner, Cousin Celie & Lizzie Koons arrived, and very soon Mrs. Murphy, Chic & Charley Koones. They sat half an hour or so and then left, and we went to dinner. After dinner it was late, so we did not go out again till time to go to the Capitol. When we arrived there [we were] disappointed at its dark appearance, [because] there was no night session. Therefore [we] did not see the Hall lit up. It must be magnificent. We walked around the capitol a short time, then returned to Brown's and after [a] cup of coffee, retired [to] Mr. & Mrs. S.' room for a short time, then all retired. The two Marys & I, although very tired, had a long talk about matters in general. John Derr left next morning. Mag bid him good bye.

April 29th Thursday. Very pretty morning. [We] had to wait for Mr. Johnson this morning but he was ready before eight, so after breakfast we were in the parlor awhile, [and] then after dressing we went up to the presidents' house, were in Lafayette Square to see Mill's Equestrian Statue of Jackson[15]. [We] were at the president['s] house & grounds an hour or so, then returned to the hotel to dinner, and after waiting an hour had dinner. Then after dinner [we]

---

[14]Tiber Creek flowed from its beginnings north of Capitol Hill around the foot and west along what is now Constitution Avenue to become a tidal estuary south of the White House. *Washington, City and Capital* (W.P.A. Federal Writers' Project), p. 646. By Margaret's visit in 1858, it had been lined with masonry and used as a canal for 30 years and was silted and filthy. Following the Civil War, it was arched over with brick and is now part of Washington's sewer system.

[15]The horse under Andrew Jackson has been rearing in the center of Lafayette Square since 1853. In his foundry at 15th and Pennsylvania, N.W., Clark Mills did this first casting in the United States of an equestrian statue, with the bronze from the cannon captured at the Battle of New Orleans. James H. Goode, *The Outdoor Sculpture of Washington, D.C.* (Washington, D.C., 1974), pp. 377-378; and H. N. Jacobsen, *A Guide to the Architecture of Washington, D.C.*, p. 74.

were at the Smithsonian Institute [*sic*] and at the National Monument[16], [and] afterwards returned to the Institute to a concert in the Hall. It is very spacious, capable of holding several thousand persons. There were [a] great many present. We returned to the hotel soon after eleven. We did not sit up long, [but] we girls packed our trunk to return to-morrow evening. Of course we talked some again.

WASHINGTON, MT. VERNON & FT. WASHINGTON, BALTIMORE

[Friday] April 30th. Very pleasant morning but grew very windy after twelve. We were up and had breakfast over about half-past eight. Mag broke her hoops and E. was mending them & made them so late. We started at half-past nine o'clock for Mt. Vernon. We went in the omnibus to the boat and after waiting some time went on board the steamboat. We had a pleasant ride and the scenery was very good. I enjoyed it very much. We touched at Alexandria to take off and on passengers. It looks much the same it was when I was there in Feb. '52. We arrived at Mt. Vernon soon after 11 o'clock. We walked from the boat to the domains, and first of [the] great man that once lived there was the tomb of Washington, also of his wife Martha and several other[s] of the same family. We then proceeded [to] the residence and there stood on the same threshold Washington had stood [on] and walked the same ground he had trod. It is an old house in the English style, built in a semicircle. It is wood panelled work inside & outside. There were several portraits of the family, [and] there is a lovely view of the Potomac from the piazza. I enjoyed this visit very much. We turned to the boat in time, 1:20 p.m., and then proceeded on our way to W[ashington]. We stopped at Ft. Washington for 20 minutes to look round and were very much gratified. We touched at Alexandria again on our return. We got to Brown's about half-past two o'clock. After fixing for dinner & eating, we were hurried in the Coach to go to the depot to go to Baltimore. We bid Maggie & Ed hasty farewell, no time for tears, -- it would have required very little more. M. seemed now only to realize she was married. Mary S., Mary D., Mr. J. & I were soon seated in the cars and after a short ride were at the Relay House where we parted with Mary D. & Mr. J. We concluded we saw many objects

---

[16] The National Monument is now the familiar Washington Monument. Work had begun in 1848 with the laying of the cornerstone in that year. Construction was halted in 1858 when the monument came under political and physical attack by the Know Nothing Party. Work was resumed in 1876. The Monument was finally opened to the public in 1888. *The New Columbia Encyclopedia.*

1858

we had never seen before. As G[eorge] was very busy, Mr. Phil. Rau met us at the depot; but as he lost the drayman, we walked up home by ourselves and he attended to the baggage, and we found him in Park St. when we got there. Mrs. S. welcomed us and soon Kate & Em came home, and at tea time G. came. We spent a very pleasant social evening.

[Saturday] May 1st [1858]. Very warm & sultry and showery in afternoon & at night. Miss Fox was [in] to see us; also Mrs. Gregg stopped in the carriage and invited the girls to go to the Fort in the afternoon to witness a drill. Accordingly, at 3 o'clock Mr. G[regg] called with his carriage & took Mary, Em & me down to Ft. McHenry, [a] pleasant ride. [A] large crowd [was at] the Scientific Convention. There were various exercises by both cavalry and infantry. We just got home when there was a heavy shower. Mr. Gregg there at night. Did not go in parlour till late.

Sunday May 2nd. Quite cool with some appearance of rain. In the morning Mary, Kate, Mrs. S. & I all went to church. George came for us. After dinner, Mr. Rau came at five o'clock. Mary, G., Mr. R. & I all went down to the Institute to the Union Prayer meeting held under the auspices of the Young Men's Christian Association. There were several addresses. At night George & I went to the Tiffany church, heard Rev. Mr. Chambers of Phild. preach. Mr. R. left soon after ten. Mr. Green was here & went with Em to church.

Monday [May] 3rd. At home morning. Afternoon, Mrs. S., Em & Kate & I were out shopping to look at lace shawls, etc., I wrote home. Lum Sadtler was here also awhile. At night first Mr. Fox arrived and then Mr. G. T. Kline, and about nine Mr. & Mrs. Michell, Miss Zell, Miss & Messrs Smith & _____. They all left about eleven o'clock, and after some talk we retired.

Tuesday [May] 4th. Not [a] very bright day. John Ritchie & Beth Maulsby[17] [were] married in Balt. to-day. Mary & I were out a short time but were driven home by rain. After tea Stull Deitrick came, and about eight o'clock Em & I & S. D. went round to Mr. Abell's, & Miss Fox & Cousin went with us to the Cathedral to see Miss Read & Mr. Carroll married. [There was a]

---

[17]John Ritchie, a Frederick lawyer (b. 1831), became States Attorney of Frederick County, then was elected to Congress. He became the Chief Judge of the Sixth Judical Circuit. Betty Harrison Maulsby, his bride, was raised in Frederick at Prospect Hall. Williams, *History*, II, 1328-1330.

1858

great display & [a] very great crowd. [We] came home about ten, raining quite hard. Mr. G[reen] [was] here but did not come in as Em was not home.

Wednesday May 5th. [It] rained very hard all day. Mr. Gregg again.

Thursday May 6th. [I] did not get a letter as expected, so Em & Kate & I were out shopping in the morning. [We had a] pleasant time. After dinner Mary & I were at Neal Dean's (not home), then down Market St., and afterwards out Market St. to China Hall. [We] came home tired but after tea, Mary, Em & I went round to Mr. Abell's, [and] spent evening very pleasantly with Mrs. Abell & Miss Fox. Mr. Gregg came in about nine. George came for us after ten and we returned about 1/2 after. /Had an engagement to ride with Mr. G. but rain prevented./

Friday [May] 7th. At home in morning sewing for Kate. Cloudy day. [In the] afternoon Em & I were out shopping. [We] had a very nice time, [and] enjoyed it much. I had a letter from home. [They] want[ed] me to come home yesterday but [I] did not receive it in time. [I] was weighed, weigh[ing] 139 lbs.

Saturday [May] 8th. Foggy morning but cleared off to be a lovely day. Em & I were out nearly all morning shopping, or rather pricing things. [We] met a good many acquaintances on the street & were joined by several gents. Miss Fox was [in] to see us. At half-past three [I] went to the depot & started for home; bid Mary, Em & G. goodbye. John Ritchie & bride were on the cars and several other acquaintances. /G. had a letter of Ed S. from Raleigh, [but he] never mentioned Mag, forgot he is married./ Father & John met me and I came out home immediately. [I found a] letter of Lou Clip, [and a] note from U. Hob[b]s.

Sunday May 9th. Cloudy but no rain. Mother & I were in to church. [I] saw Frank Schley at [the] hotel, [and] talked of John Ritchie's marriage. [I] told Mary Derr [that] Geo. had letter of Ed S. from Raleigh.

* * * * *

Wednesday [May] 12th. Cold, windy day. I went into town and was [in] to see E. Brunner, [at] Mrs. B. F. Winchester's, and then shopped some and stopped a while at Mrs. Dr. MacGill's. Saw Annie & Mrs. Sam Tyler there; came home about noon.

1858

Thursday [May] 13th. Ascension Day. Joe & Bill shook carpets. [I was] at Mrs. L. Fout's a short time.

Friday [May] 14th. [I] wrote to Mary Sauerwein, [and] commenced house cleaning /rain/.

* * * * *

Thursday [May] 20th. Making & putting down carpet in [the] little parlour. Letter from Mary Sauerwein.

Friday [May] 21st. Quite [a] pretty day. [We] finished carpet in [the] dining room. Mrs. I. Howard & Mrs. Taylor spent the afternoon here.

Saturday May 22nd. Pretty morning. [We] finished things in general.

Sunday [May] 23rd. Beautiful morning. I went into church. There was Communion, [it] being Easter Sunday. Mary Derr connected herself with our church, & 15 others.

Monday [May] 24th. Rained a heavy shower. I did not go to town to see the new Soldiers' parade.

Tuesday [May] 25th. [I had a] note from Mary Derr enclosing letter from Mag on boat at Selma, Ala.(??)

Wednesday [May] 26th. [I] wrote to Lou Hersh.

Thursday [May] 27th. Sent a paper to Mag S[hriner] at Tiffin.

Friday [May] 28th. [I] had a nice long letter of Mag S. from New Orleans. They were to leave there a week ago to-day.

Saturday [May] 29th. I wrote a note, [and] sent Mag's letter & returned her other to Mary. [I] also had a note from her in answer to one written [a] couple [of] weeks ago. [It] rained quite hard in afternoon.

Sunday [May] 30th. Raining so no one went to church.

Monday May 31st. Still raining. [I] had a note from Mary Derr enclosing one of her mats.

Tuesday June 1st [1858]. Father's birthday. Mother was in town. Jennie Turner to Mr. Anderson and Nan Tyler to Mr. Page were married to-day. A lovely day.

Wednesday [June] 2nd. Still clear & quite warm. I went in town early at Houcks' & shopping. Mrs. Wm. Miller & old Mrs. Detrick spent afternoon here.

Thursday June 3rd. Had the appearance of rain in the morning and rained after dinner.

Friday [June] 4th. Very much like rain all day but very little fell. Wrote to Mary Sauerwein & enclosed Kate's tape trimming.

Saturday [June] 5th. I went into [town] early. At the [post] office, letters of Lou Clip[pinger]; and [I] was at Houcks' to learn how to make the mat like there [*sic*]. Light showers of rain during the day.

Sunday [June] 6th. Beautiful morning. Mother & I were in to church.

Monday [June] 7th. Very clear but quite warm. Mother & I started a[t] six o'clock to Aunt Mary Scholl's. [We] stopped at Aunt Shriner's, little while at Aunt M. Artz's & talked, and then few minutes with Mary Derr & then up to Aunt M. Scholl's. Mrs. Biser is staying there. Annie wanted worsted, so we went to stores at Georgetown[18] & Walkersville but could get none. [We] saw Mr. Dick Marlow who soon came down and remained till after 4 o'clock. He is a very pleasant gentleman. We left soon after five and stopped a while at Mr. Derr's & had a little talk with Mary but not much. [We] want to see each other again soon to talk.

* * * * *

Thursday [June] 10th. Pleasant day. Received a Cincinnati paper, suppose from Cousin Ed. Exceedingly warm. Uncle Artz [was] here on business.

---

[18]Georgetown was an area near Walkersville. It was considered one of the prettiest villages in the Woodsboro district. *Titus Atlas*, p. 33; Scharf, *Western Maryland*, I, 618.

1858

June 11th Friday. Very warm and quite heavy gust of wind, also rain. Ma & I went over to Mrs. I. Howard's about half-past two o'clock. Jennie Adams [was] already there and later in evening Boyds' carriage arrived with Miss Lizzie Hunt, Gin Boyd, Sue & Harry James. All left after tea except I. I wrote to Lou Clippinger this morning.

Saturday [June] 12th. Still raining. John came for me early but I did not leave till after breakfast. After I got home there were very heavy showers, as much so as I ever saw. Had Alice Derr's last letter from newlyweds. /Note from Mary Keefer saying Livie Crampton [will] spend Tuesday here./

Sunday [June] 13th. So cloudy I did not go to church.

Monday [June] 14th. Showers amidst sunshine to-day. I was in town to shop and stopped at Aunt Shriner['s] who kept me talking so long it was nearly 1 o'clock when I got home. Saw several friends to talk to. Returned Alice Derr's letter to Mrs. Reese, [and] said few words to her, also to Mrs. Winchester from [a] window.

Tuesday [June] 15th. Very pleasant day. Busy all morning. Misses Mary & Ann Keefer arrived first, and soon Mrs. Ellen Jarboe with Mrs. Livie Crampton and Mrs. Grove to spend the day. Mrs. I. Howard & Clara to tea.

Wednesday [June] 16th. Quite warm. Walked into town & had Annie fit my dress, then shopped. [I] had a note from Mary Derr enclosing one from Mary Sauerwein and sat down immediately and wrote to Mary Sauerwein enclosing money for the lace shawl. [I] took dinner with Mary Kunkel and afterwards went up street on business, met Mary Derr, went shopping with her, also to see Ellen B. and then I walked out home, quite tired.

Thursday [June] 17th. Very warm. Quite busy all day sewing on my dress. I think I wrote to Lou, any way, some time this week.

Friday [June] 18th. Quite warm. As Mary S. is coming to-day, [I] thought Mother would go in to see her. [She] did so and heard she had all the things for me in her trunk. [She] also brought me letters [that] Mary had received jointly to Mary D. & me wanting me to come out to-morrow evening.

Saturday [June] 19th. Quite warm with the appearance of rain but then was none. Mother took me into town to go with Mary S. & Mary D. to meet /Eugene Derr & George S./ Cousin Ed & Maggie. We waited only a few minutes when the Western train arrived & Mr. & Mrs. S. were in, also Em Houck. We were soon in Frederick and Mr. & Mrs. Shriner and Mary Derr [and] /Eugene D. & G. S./ in Mrs. Derr's carriage. Mary S. and I walked up street to Aunt S.['s] and waited for Cousin Ed's carriage. When we went out, [we] stopped at Mr. Derr's for Mary & all went out to Cousin Ed's. Aunt Shriner's children were there, Mr. J. A. J. [came] to tea, and afterwards all Mrs. S's family. Mrs. D's and Mr. J. A. J. left about ten and we soon retired after kisses, presents and talking.

Sunday June 20th. Quite warm. Cousin Ed not well last night, so [it was] nearly nine when we breakfasted. Immediately after, Mag. S., Mary S. and I walked over to Mr. Derr's, but as Mary did not know whether we wanted to go to church, the carriage was not ready, so did not go. After dinner Mary D. went to Sunday School, and Cousin Ed, Mr. A. S., Aunt S. and children all came over to tea. Thomas Derr brought me out home soon after tea and sat an hour or so.

Monday [June] 21st. Very warm. Not very well but, busy on my cape. Father and Mother were out to Aunt Lizzie Brunner's[19].

Tuesday [June] 22nd. Quite warm. Busy till about ten o'clock on my cape, then started for Cousin Ed's. [The] girls [were] there, also Mr. & Miss Lugenbeil and very soon Mr. J. A. J. [came] to dinner. We were not dressed by three, but [were] before four o'clock, but some of the company had already arrived. We were standing most of the evening receiving company. There were a good many from town as well as from surrounding country. It is useless to particularize company, so merely say friends in general called and everything passed off well. Mr. J. A. J. left soon, about 10. I suppose it will be some time before I meet him so unofficially again.

Wednesday June 23rd. Pleasant day, and I went away to spend the day. Mag busied herself somewhat about [the] house, etc. Rev. Mr. McClain called in morning short time. Mag was not home in afternoon and I presided at tea table. After Mr. & Mrs. D. C. Johnson called and [were] very talkative. Mrs. J. said she would be happy to see Miss S "at Auburn[20]." I said "Thank you," not thinking I would call very soon. Mrs. L. Getzandanner and Mrs. L.

---

[19]Margaret was related to the Brunners through her paternal grandmother Elizabeth Brunner Scholl. *Scholl Genealogy*, p. 784. See also note 4, 1859.

[20]See note 16, 1851.

1858

Cramer were there also awhile after tea. All left by nine and as I was sleepy [I] also retired. Mag and I had a long talk in privy.

Thursday [June] 24th. Quite warm again. I busied myself somewhat about Mag's house and then sat down to talk. Aunt S. was showing Mag round this morning. Mary S. [went] over to Mr. Derr's awhile. After dinner Cousin Ed brought me out home and left Mag & Mary in town to shop. He sat [a] couple of hours and then returned for them to town.

Friday [June] 25th. So exceedingly warm, so did not go to town as intended.

Saturday [June] 26th. Quite warm, but Mother and I were in early to shop but could not decide on a dress, so she went in the evening and bought me a French muslin. I wrote a note to Maggie A. S. to give her the news.

Sunday June 27th. Very warm, nevertheless I went in to church. I walked to corner with Mary S, gave Mary my note.

Monday [June] 28th. Made the two skirts to my dress and could have done more but had no pattern; very warm.

Tuesday [June] 29th. Waited but heard nothing of [the] pattern, so [I] wrote another note to Mag Shriner. /Had my brown wrap fit Jornberg (?) Basque./

Wednesday [June] 30th. Still waiting and no note. [I went] out to Aunt M's.

Thursday July 1st [1858]. Still warm. Wrote another note but to Mary S. this time, and when Father & Mother came home [they] had the pattern and a joint note from Mary S. & Mag Shriner. They had sent it in by Houcks on Tuesday morning.

Friday [July] 2nd. Mother was in town shopping and saw the girls in town, also got a note from Mary Sauer[wein] left at Mr. Derr's store for me. I am very busy on my dress. Quite warm. Mother looked very much overheated.

Saturday [July] 3rd. Quite warm, but I had to be very busy on my dress, nearly finished the body. Father had quite a severe chill this morning, so did not go to town.

Sunday [July] 4th. Very warm. [I] was in town, walked to church with Ella & Mr. Markell from [the] hotel. Thomas Derr came down street with me.

1858

We went to the hotel with Mary S. Cousin E had gone with Mary D., and Mag was not in, as Adeline is sick since Monday. Wils B. joined Thomas D. & me and walked to the hotel with me and Wils rode out in the carriage [until we were] opposite his papa's house.

Monday July 5th. Very warm day. Busy sewing. Mother walked down to "White Oak Springs" to a "Dutch pic-nic" to see Miss Keefer about baking, and from thence to Mrs. L. Fout's to tea. Wils Boyd & Mary S. came out after tea. Mag & E. were coming along but [they] heard Dr. Nelson & lady were going to call, so did not like to leave.

Tuesday [July] 6th. Sewing and cleaning some about the house.

Wednesday [July] 7th. My 25th birthday. To think I have lived a quarter of a century and to so little purpose. I went into town but did not get in till after ten, so sat and talked awhile at Houcks', then went out with Tilly to shop, and afterwards to Seminary [a] few minutes, and then back to dinner. About four o'clock Mary S. & I started out to see Annie Bentz, Lizzie Zack, Kunkels, Schleys, Soph Gaither; and [I] wrote Lizzie Schell a note, also Anna Bell Scholl to come down Friday evening. Stopped to see Ella B. morning & evening.

Thursday July 8th [and Friday July 9th]. Rather more pleasant. I went into town rather late but nevertheless went to the Sem[inary] and got a very comfortable seat. Had a little talk with Mr. R. Hobbs. [I] told him he had changed and he said I had changed too. He is not near so handsome. I came home at noon but went in again in the evening and went up to Houcks', went with them. Wils Boyd & Dr. Schaeffer were along. Dr. Delasmuth was there also after we returned. I remained [at the Houcks'] over night but slept very little at night. Started home about 5 o'clock, Friday 9th, and soon Father and Mother went to town to bring Miss Kester out. Instead of which, Mrs. H. Fout came and we were extremely busy all day, but succeeded pretty well so somewhat atoned for the worry. Mag & Ed came out about seven, and soon Wils & Mary and then John & Lizzie Zack and aunt & cousin, Misses Hessey, 3 Schleys, G. Houck & Dr. Schaeffer, Tom Derr, Mary Derr, Ella B. & Lizzie H., Gin Boyd & Sue Jones, Ham Boyd & Mr. Brooks of Balt. & Messrs. Geo. Birely, Dod Gambrill & Lychurgus Hedges & Dr. Delasmuth. All seemed to enjoy themselves and remained till after twelve till the last left.

Saturday July 10th. Still warm. Was up early and got the dishes out of the way. Father & Mother went into town with Mrs. Fout in the morning and

1858

Jane was busy sweeping, etc., so I did not get to take my nap till after dinner, and I slept nearly all afternoon and did not feel a great deal refreshed, so went to bed early at night.

Sunday [July] 11th. Very warm, so [I] did not go to town to church. Mother walked in to church this morning, got very warm, and rode on horseback to Mrs. Bushey's this afternoon, took her some cake.

Monday [July] 12th. Picked currants to make jelly directly after breakfast. Mother & Father were in town this morning, and about four o'clock I went out to Aunt M. Artz's to return her things that had been borrowed; and I stopped a while at Kunkels' and sent a note down to Schleys that if either were going to [the] pic-nic in [the] afternoon I would take them; but Annie answered saying all were going in morning. I was caught in quite a shower coming home and it rained hard all night.

Tuesday [July] 13th. [It] rained last night & till nearly nine, so of course the pic-nic did not come off. Nice note from Lizzie Schell.

Wednesday July 14th. A slight shower in [the] morning--only a few drops--nevertheless the pic-nic party went out, so Mary Kunkel sent me word. About four o'clock there came up a very heavy shower and Cousin Ed & Maggie came just then to pick currants but too wet, so soon after seven, or maybe it was eight o'clock, they left. They had intended stopping in town but too wet.

Thursday [July] 15th. Showery all morning but still I went into town. Stopped at Houcks' awhile and came out again with Mother. Dr. Zack & lady and two Misses Ferney were here after tea to make a call.

Friday [July] 16th. Very pretty day. [I] could not get along very well with my cape so sent for Mary and had it and a note in return. Mrs. Bushey & daughter Frances were here the afternoon and after they left Annie, Mary & Ella Schley & Soph Gaither were out to make a call. Of course all very talkative & newsy.

Saturday [July] 17th. Pleasant day. Busy on my cape and finished by tea time. Lizzie & Ezra Houck were out after tea but did not get off their horses.

Sunday [July] 18th. I was in to church and Dr. Z. had very good sermon from St. Mark 8-4. [I] was asleep nearly all afternoon.

1858

Monday July 19th. It rained last night and some in this morning. I was not very well, so was lying down part of the morning.

Tuesday [July] 20th. Still raining to-day. I wrote a note to Lizzie Zack and had one in return.

Wednesday [July] 21st. Quite warm again. Mother & I were down and spent the afternoon with the Misses Keefer. Miss Charlotte only [was] home but soon Miss M. & then Miss Ann [came] and brought Ginnie Keefer from town with her. There were two quite fine showers while [we were] there.

Thursday [July] 22nd. Very pleasant morning. I went into town early, soon after nine, and after shopping some little, went to Dr. Zack's and waited for the ladies who were out; and about 10 1/2 or 11 o'clock [I] started for Mr. Derr's with Lydia Spears & Millie Z., and the rest of Dr. Z's family with the Misses Ferney soon came out. We spent the time very pleasantly till about three, when Cousin Ed came for Mag and she would have me go along. There was company over at Ceresville. Found Mr. & Mrs. Worman & children and Aunt Jem[ima] Scholl. Mr. J. A. Johnson [came] to tea, after tea we were at the mill. Mr. J. A. J. went with me to Mr. Derr's & Mag & Ed soon followed. I soon left, taking Lyd. Spear & Lizzie Z. and Millie [with] me. Lovely moonlight ride home at night.

Friday July 23rd. Had some appearance of rain but cleared off very pleasant. Mother and I went over to Mr. I. Howard['s] about eleven o'clock & spent the day. Misses Mary & Ann Keefer & Ginnie Keefer & Mrs. Ellen Jarboe were all there also. We got home soon after sundown. The Lutheran Sabbath school celebration was held to-day in Uncle Adams' woods.

Saturday [July] 24th. I was home all day. Mother and Father were in town in afternoon.

Sunday [July] 25th. Very pleasant day. Mother and I were in to church and heard Rev. Mr. Nixdorf preach. Wils Boyd over in the afternoon.

Monday [July] 26th. Home all day till after six o'clock, then went into town. [I] called at Dr. Z's, the ladies not home, [and] at Houcks'. Mary S. [was] not home, Em is to come to-night. [I was] at Ellen B's to see her company, Miss Daugherty, and then came home by [*illegible*].

1858

Tuesday [July] 27th. Very pleasant day. Mrs. John Ramsburg and James R. and little brother all walked out to spend the day. I went in with them in the evening for a ride.

Wednesday [July] 28th. Much warmer. Reformed Sabbath School pic-nic. /We were all over awhile in the afternoon./ Uncle Kemp [came] over early in the morning, & soon Mrs. Smith & Miss Kate [came] for [a] couple [of] hours, [and] Lizzie & Emma, Houcks, Mary & Em Sauerwein spent the day. Mag & Ed S. [came] to tea.

Thursday [July] 29th. Very warm. Mother and I went into town early and I went out to Aunt M. Artz's, took her some wine, [but] she was not home. I stopped in the carriage [a] few minutes to see H[ouck]'s and when I came back stopped at Uncle Kemp['s] to see Annie Bentz awhile. After finding Mother had gone down street, [I] followed on after her. So very warm. At night early Mr. Rohrback & Ellen B. & Misses Daugherty came and sat only a short time.

Friday [July] 30th. Quite warm but clear till about noon, when there was a thunder gust. I wrote a note to Mrs. B. F. Winchester and then went in for her. She helped me about my vases. Messrs. H. & F. Winchester were out to tea but left soon after. We retired early.

Saturday [July] 31st. Quite warm. Mrs. W. and I were busy at vases & other things. Mother went to town to procure paint for us. Mr. F. W. came about four o'clock for Mrs. W. and took her home.

Sunday Aug. 1st [1858]. Rained some early but nevertheless [I] went to church. Wils B. had a little to say on the corner.

Monday Aug. 2nd. Rainy early but very warm afternoon. Wils B. [was] down in morning awhile. Mountain Saturday and I with <u>Dr. Delasmutt</u>[21]. Letter of Lou Clippinger. Wils B. is going to take the girls & me to Derrs' to-morrow evening.

Tuesday Aug. 3rd. Raining and cloudy with small sprinkle of sunshine all day. Uncle Artz out in afternoon.

---

[21]Dr. V. Delasmutt boarded on the south side of Church Street opposite Record Street. *Williams' Directory*, p. 9.

Wednesday [August] 4th. Busy in the morning. Note from Mr. W. Boyd saying he would be down for me about 5 1/2 o'clock to go to Mr. Derr's. I answered it saying I would be ready and hurried and had supper [ready] but they had done [*sic*] supper when they came. We were at Mr. Derr's about 8. Soon Drs. Schaeffer & Delasmuth came and Wils & Tom Derr walked over to Cousin Ed's and he & Mag & Mr. J. A. J. came back with them and we all spent a very sociable pleasant evening till about eleven when they all left. I staid all night. Mary Derr had bites on her face.

Thursday [August] 5th. Very warm day, <u>excessively hot</u>. About 10 1/2 Eugene Derr took M. & E. Sauerwein, Alice D. & me up to Mrs. Randolf Dutrow's to spend the day. Mag & Ed, Mrs. Shriner & children were already there, also there were John Dutrow & 2 daughters, besides four gentlemen that were surveying the road. We were very warm but spent an exceeding[ly] pleasant day. We stopped at Dr. Charly Goldsborough's[22] on our way home and found [there] Dr., Mrs. & Miss G. as well as guests 2 Misses Poes, very talkative. Some neighbors also [were] there, Mrs. Jones & mother, Mrs. Eichelberger.

Friday [August] 6th. More pleasant. Came into town with Mr. Derr and walked out home. [I] wrote a note to Ella B. for her & Co. to spend tomorrow with me.

Saturday Aug. 7th. Very pleasant day. About 12 o'clock Mary, Alice, Eugene & Mary & E. Sauerwein arrived to spend the day. Mr. W. Boyd came to tea and all left about 8 o'clock.

Sunday [August] 8th. Mother and I went in to church and heard a very good sermon from Dr. Z. Somewhat cooler.

Monday [August] 9th. Very busy on a chemise band and about household duties; [and] wrote to Lou Clip at Oxford.

Tuesday [August] 10th. Busy in the afternoon preparing for the Mountain.

Wednesday [August] 11th. Clear but quite warm day. Dr. Delasmutt was here by 8 o'clock and I was soon ready, but no signs of the party at Mrs.

---

[22]Dr. Charles Henry Goldsborough lived at "Richfields" on Rt. 194, Woodsboro Pike. He practiced in Walkersville. Williams, *History*, I, 589.

1858

Reese's, so [we] rode out to Aunt M's and waited there until they came. Mary S. & Mr. W. R. Boyd, E[m] Sauerwein & Dr. Schaeffer, Mr. & Mrs. Shriner, Mary Derr & Mr. J. A. Johnson. We all enjoyed it very much and returned home by eight o'clock. Dr. D. did not come in & I soon retired.

Thursday [August] 12th. Quite warm. [I] felt exceedingly tired. Quite warm with very heavy shower in afternoon but then cleared away bright. I had lain down awhile, and between one & two o'clock Emma Cookson & Annie Howard arrived and spent the afternoon. Father & Mother were gone Blackberrying. [They] took dinner [with] Mr. Wm. C. Hoffman's.

Friday [August] 13th. Quite warm. I was in town on business and out to Aunt M. Artz's awhile. Mrs. Clarke & child to dinner.

Saturday Aug. 14th. Still warm. Mother made the Blackberry wine. I went into town in the afternoon and called at Ella B.'s and to see Jenny Brengle and at Houcks' and then returned home. Houcks told me the girls were not coming Monday.

Sunday [August] 15th. Quite warm. I did not feel very well, so was not in church. Mary Derr sent for me to come out to-morrow but it did not suit me very well, so suppose [I] shall not go.

Monday [August] 16th. Busy most of the morning. Clear nice day but did not suit me, so could not go to Mary Derr's.

Tuesday [August] 17th. Rather warm. Mary Sauerwein & baggage arrived about four o'clock. She has a sty on her eye.

* * * * *

Friday [August] 20th. Very pretty day. Emma S. & Jenny H. [were] out before breakfast. Mary & I walked to town early, were at Houcks & Houses[23], and I attended to some shopping and then [we] came out home in the cart.

---

[23]The Houses lived on the south side of Patrick Street between Market Street and Middle Alley. *Williams' Directory*, p. 20.

1858

Saturday [August] 21st. Up early and did my work. About four o'clock [we] went into town and went to see Houcks & Kunkels and had a small shower to come home in; however, it cleared again.

Sunday [August] 22nd. We were in to church. Very <u>hot</u> & dusty.

Monday [August] 23rd. About eleven o'clock Mary S. & I went over to Mr. J. Buckey's to spend the day. Mrs. Thomas and family are there. In [the] afternoon Misses Ann & Mary Keefer & Mrs. Wm. Miller were there. [We] left soon after tea.

Tuesday [August] 24th. Still warm. Mother, Mary & I were ready to start to Mrs. Ellen Jarboe's by ten o'clock but just as [we were] ready Mr. Hershey & a Mrs. Lewis arrived so detained us nearly an hour; and when we arrived found Misses M & A Keefer & Fanny Adams there and in afternoon, Mrs. Louisa Detrick. Spent a very pleasant day.

Wednesday [August] 25th. Very pleasant day. Mary went to town in the morning /to spend [the] day at H. & visit some/ and I went in after tea and brought her out, as well as Em with baggage. Em & I had so much to talk of. She gave the reasons why Wils had not been here, etc. /<u>Paper from Chicago</u>./ It was late when we retired.

Thursday [August] 26th. Pleasant day. The girls had [a] letter from home; [it] made them quite sad [that] Philip [is] so ill. We had a few tears from them at night but cheered them again with whist.

Friday [August] 27th. Rained in evening and very dark. Never-theless by eight Mr. W. R. Boyd arrived. Em's spirits were very exuberant today.

Saturday [August] 28th. Rained in morning, clear at noon but rained again, so did not get to town.

Sunday Aug. 29th. Pleasant morning after the rain. We three girls <u>in silk</u> went to church in the buggy. [We had] quite a time getting out at the hotel, but better getting in, as Dr. Schaeffer was there to help us in. He had gone & returned with E. Wils Boyd over in [the] afternoon, took E. riding again, and we enjoyed it very much. Mr. Riser also [was here] awhile. Mother only saw him, as neither E nor I were dressed for company.

1858

Monday [August] 30th. Very pleasant day. Father & Mother went to old Mrs. Worman's[24] funeral this morning. Cousins Ed & Mag S. were here to dinner. [They] left about four but [it was] too late for us for town.

Tuesday [August] 31st. Very pleasant day. We girls were up early and ready to go to town directly after breakfast. [I] wrote a note to Mary K. [that] we girls would spend Thursday with her. We stopped some /was to see Aunt Jem Scholl/ and just outside town Houcks' carriage overtook us and took Mary Sauerwein and bundles in, and Em & I walked on after them. /Lizzie Houck staid and the others called only./ At night Mr. Wils Boyd brought Gin B., Sue Jones & Miss Annie Barchus over to spend the evening, and very soon Mr. Wm. Green came to see Em. All left about or after ten.

Wednesday Sept. 1st [1858]. We girls were busy sewing, etc., Lizzie H. of course included. L. & I exchanged work, I on her shawl & she on my collar. About six o'clock Tilly & Ella H. & Miss Becky Bentz came for Lizzie and, as it had so much the appearance of rain, [they] only staid [a] short time. Also, Messrs. Boyd & Lefevre did not get out for the same cause.

Thursday Sept. 2nd. Quite warm. We three girls all went to town about eleven o'clock and went to Kunkels' to spend the day, very nice dinner. Mr. Lefevre called in [the] afternoon. After tea Mr. W. Boyd called and after partaking of cantaloupe, wine & cake all went to the court house. [We] met several friends there & Dr. Schaeffer came back with Em & Meal. We soon came out home and Wils left [at] half-past ten & as Em & I were so sleepy, so glad.

Friday [Sept.] 3rd. Sultry, warm day. Em, Mary & I all went out to Mag Shriner's and sent John back. We had fun in our wagon with springs. Mrs. Shriner, Geo. & Mary & Miss B. Cramer soon came. Mag was busy & I help[ed] her all I could. Lizzie & Tilly Houck were there to tea. I was all over the house with Mag.

Saturday [Sept.] 4th. Clear sunrise but rain in showers till about ten, gloomy prospects for the picnic. We did not go over till nearly one o'clock, and were only there about half an hour when there was a very heavy shower and we ran for the school, where we were entertained an hour or so about Liberty & its

---

[24]Margaret Worman was the wife of Moses Worman. She died on August 28, 1858. Holdcraft, *Names in Stone*, II, 1263.

precincts by some ladies of that vicinity, when Mr. Abe Shriner arrived and took us to the house. Only Mary, Mrs. S. & Miss Barbara were there, and when Mag, Mary & Alice [came they were] very draggled; [they] were on the island in a carriage. Uncle Kemp there to tea [and] took [the] other ladies home. John soon came for us. Brought letters for the girls as well as [a] note for me from Kate. Uncle P. worse, going home Monday or Tuesday.

Sunday Sept. 5th. Quite warm. As we girls wanted to wear good dresses and not be crowded we went to town in the cart. Mary Derr returned with us. Dr. Schaeffer came to the end of town with us and helped us in. Cousin Ed & Mag S. came to dinner, about three, Mr. W. Boyd, [a] little later, Drs. Delasmuth & Schaeffer. Cousin Ed & Mag & Mary Derr & Dr. D. left about five o'clock. Dr. S. [stayed] till nearly ten & Wils [left] about six. Em & I had [a] long talk after Mary was upstairs.

Monday [Sept.] 6th. As the girls would go we were up early, and had them in in time. Drs. S. & D. & W. B. & Houcks [were] at cars. We staid till they left. Met Mary Derr on her road, down too late. She went with me [to see] Misses House and then Aunt Jem Scholl, and we promised to return to dinner. We were at Mrs. Reese's awhile and went back to Uncle Lewis' to dinner. Mr. Sander there also. Mary left about two o'clock. Mr. Lefevre & W[il] B[oyd] called about two & sat more than an hour. I then went up street, met Father and came out home.

* * * * *

Thursday [Sept.] 9th. Wrote a note to the girls to send by Wils B. but he did not come, so suppose he is not going to Baltimore.

Friday [Sept.] 10th. Quite warm with the appearance of rain. /Wrote to Lou Clip at Oxford./

Saturday [Sept.] 11th. Rained in morning but cleared off in afternoon. I had a nice long letter from Mary S.

Sunday Sept. 12th. Very pretty day. Mother and I went into church. [We] found Mr. C. Hershey here when we got home. He left about 4 or five o'clock & I retired early.

1858

BRUCEVILLE & NEW OXFORD

Monday [Sept.] 13th. Lovely day. [I] wrote a letter to Mary Sauerwein and was busy most of morning getting my things ready to pack to go over to see Lou Clip. We started about one o'clock & by five or so were at Bruceville, Carroll Co., [at] Mrs. Mering's. After tea Mr. Mering & I went up to Dr. Martin's and found them away, but they returned in about 15 minutes. We sat till nearly nine o'clock and then returned to Mr. M's and staid all night.

Wednesday [Sept.] 14th. Quite cool. I was up, had breakfast & ready to start by seven or soon after and was at Oxford by 1 o'clock, where we were welcomed by Lou, [her] father & mother & brothers Frank, James & Paul & John who were then there. We had much to talk of and very much each to say to the other; they seemed very much pleased to see me, also to have Mother pay them a visit. After tea we took a walk to the depot and around town and then returned. We had watermelon after tea and then all sat in conversation till bed time. Sarah Miller & Lewis Kemp [were] married this morning.

NEW OXFORD, ADAMS CO., PA.

Wednesday Sept. 15th. Arose to find it raining very hard and [it] continued all day, so we were necessarily kept in the house all the time but spent a very pleasant day indoors. Ella McClelland arrived by the cars from Gettysburg and we had her company added to that of the family. Mr. & Mrs. John Hersh were up in the evening and staid till nearly nine. It had some prospects of clearing. We had fun about the currant wine. Frank had liquored it.

Thursday [Sept.] 16th. Raining till about six but by seven had the appearance of clearing, so we arranged to go to [a] chapel in Hanover in [the] afternoon; and accordingly by one o'clock Mr. Frank Hersh, Geo. Pittsburg [sic] & Mother in one buggy and Lou & I in one other. We got as far as [the] chapel, [and] looked through it; and on our way to Hanover then concluded, as it looked so much like rain, we would go to McSherry's town; and there [we] waited till the storm had abated and then hurried on to Oxford, not getting in[to] H[anover]. It cleared off very pretty. I forgot, Miss Ellen Himes was in [a] couple of times to see us during the morning. At night Mother, Mrs. H., Lou, Ell & I were down to Mrs. John Hersh's awhile. Mr. Alex Himes spent the evening there. [We had] fun about table games.

1858

NEW OXFORD, BRUCEVILLE, & HOME

Friday Sept. 17th. Lovely morning. We were obliged to tear ourselves away, notwithstanding all their entreaties to the contrary. We were ready, bid adieu and [were] off by half-past seven. Mr. Frank Hersh accompanied us about four miles to show us a more direct road. He is so very kind. Mrs. H. gave Mother a very pretty collar and Lou gave me a set [of] collar & cuffs & [a] handsome toothbrush and I had several little things for them. I had a very bad cold, so felt tired in travelling, but [we] arrived at Mr. Mering's about half-past twelve. Mrs. Nellie Martin & little daughter were there and soon Dr. arrived and we sat till three o'clock and [then] started home, where we arrived without any accident or stoppage of any kind by seven o'clock. [We] talked awhile with Cousin Ed on [the] pike; [he] said something about Mag wanting me to come out but don't think he knew exactly what. Mr. Wils Boyd [was] here very soon after I got home and sat only a short time. [I] suppose he only staid [a] short time as I told him [we were] just home. /Saw the comet, first tonight./ I gave him [a] package for Emma S. and 50 cts. from Mary Derr for Mag S. I unpacked my things when he left and went to bed quite tired but very thankful for a safe journey, which everyone considered [a] great undertaking. Mr. J. A. J.'s birthday.

Saturday Sept. 18th. Lovely day, not a cloud obscures the horizon. Sent a paper to Mr. F. Hersh so he may see about the Cattle Show.

Sunday [Sept.] 19th. As my cold was no better [I] did not go to church. Lovely day, so bright but quite warm at noon.

Monday [Sept.] 20th. Very pretty day. Was out to Aunt M's a short time in [the] morning. /Wrote note to Mary Derr./ Mrs. Killian [was] here to dinner.

Tuesday [Sept.] 21st. Beautiful day. Mrs. Kinney & daughter, Mrs. Kalamuse & child, & Annie Cromwell & Mrs. Edward S. were here to spend day. Mr. & Mrs. E. A. Shriner were here to tea, all left soon after tea. /Note from Mary Derr./ I made sweet pickle[d] peaches & grape jelly this morning.

Wednesday [Sept.] 22nd. Much cooler but clear. Made my grape wine, some Isabella jelly, etc. today. Mr. P. Sauerwein died today.

Thursday [Sept.] 23rd. Still quite cool & clear. Wrote a long letter to Lou Clip & enclosed [a] receipt for Mrs. H. When Mother came from town, [she

1858

brought a] note from Fannie Brengle[25] that [her] Ma & Grandma would spend the day to-morrow.

Friday [Sept.] 24th. Cloudy morning and rain in showers from ten on but sun set clear. About ten o'clock Aunt Kitty Thomas[26] and daughter Mrs. Brengle came to spend the day. I left between 4 & five to meet Mag Shriner. Robert Brengle & Mrs. Ritmore were here to tea. [I] met Mag Shriner at Kunkles'. Cousin Ed went with me to K's. After talking awhile, Mag & I were at Gaithers' but did not see Sophia, as she sent an apology to the door. We were then at Mrs. Dr. Schley's and got the news, and then [went] to Aunt Shriner's to meet Cousin Ed. We soon started out, stopped at Mr. Derr's for Mary, and we all after a bite & watermelon, cut rind for preserving. We three girls did not retire till after twelve o'clock. Old Mr. P. Sauerwein [was] buried today.

Saturday Sept. 25th. Still cloudy. Mag and I were busy all morning, I about the preserves & she baking, etc. Mary Derr left soon after breakfast. After dinner we got ready to go out visiting. About three o'clock [we] were at Mr. John Dutrow's, found ladies not home; then [we] came on down to Aunt Mary Scholl's[27] and found her home, and soon Annabelle & Miss Ella Dutrow arrived and we sat till after eight o'clock. We got home soon after nine & soon retired.

Sunday [Sept.] 26th. Lovely morning. We got ready & came to church. After, [I] was at hotel and waited till [the] girls left. Then [I] came out home on horseback in afternoon. Aunt Lizzie Brunner & daughter Mary & Annie Gittinger were here and left soon after tea. They had walked out.

Monday Sept. 27th. Very pleasant day. Went into town early and attended to some shopping. Annie Schley and George Birely [came] out after tea. I fear G. was hurt; [we] had quite a laugh about G. losing his hat.

---

[25]The Brengles were related to the Scholls and the Derrs. Gertrude Brengle (daughter of Jacob) married Johannes Scholl, the brother of Christian, Margaret's grandfather. Her sister, Ann Brengle, married Sebastian Derr the grandfather of John Derr, Jr. Grace L. Tracey and John P. Dern, *Pioneers of Old Monocacy*, p. 264.

[26]Kitty Thomas was the wife of William Thomas, a brother of Margaret's grandfather Michael Thomas. Thomas, *Thomas Genealogy*, pp. 27-29.

[27]Mary Dutrow Scholl was the widow of Margaret's uncle Elias Scholl. Their daughter was Annabelle Scholl. *Scholl Genealogy*, p. 786.

1858

Tuesday [Sept.] 28th. Very pleasant day. Mother & I were up and spent a very pleasant afternoon at Mr. Ed. Howard's.

Wednesday [Sept.] 29th. Very nice day. Busy transcribing Mr. Ulysses Hobbs' letters, all the old ones. [It] makes me think of <u>Old times</u>. His love, though I suppose has grown cold now.

Thursday [Sept.] 30th. Quite warm, like a summer's day. Annie Howard came down in the morning and remained over night. She seems so fond of music; pity she has not a piano.

Friday Oct 1st [1858]. Raining in showers during the day. Annie left about eleven between the showers. Mother was gone to town and did not return till 3 or 4 o'clock. Father [had a] letter of Frank Hersh.

Saturday [Oct.] 2nd. Very pretty day. Father answered F. H.'s letter.

Sunday [Oct.] 3rd. Quite warm again. Uncle Kemp came about 9 o'clock. I went to church; had church in lecture room. After church Mary K. & I went to the hotel to see Mag S., they agreed to go to Balt. Wednesday. Saw Mrs. Sarah Kemp there. Old Mr. Himes was at our house when I got there.

Monday [Oct.] 4th. Very warm. [I] was in town to shop & at Aunt Shriner's awhile; Mother walked to Aunt M's today. Houcks were out today, Lizzie, Tilly & Ella.

Tuesday Oct. 5th. Very pleasant, not so warm. Home all day, sewing.

Wednesday [Oct.] 6th. Rained in showers during the day, quite cool. [I received a] nice letter of Lou Clip. She is at Pittsburg[h], [and] was to leave yesterday for R[ock] I[sland].

Thursday [Oct.] 7th. Wrote to cousin J. Harry Smith.

Friday [Oct.] 8th. Was in town to shop and walked home, and commenced a worsted chair tidy.

* * * * *

Monday [Oct.] 11th. [I was] very busy all day; finished my tidy.

1858

Tuesday [Oct.] 12th. Commencement of our "Agricultural Fair." Rained all day.

Wednesday [Oct.] 13th. Cleared off quite warm. Went into town after dinner and was on the grounds all afternoon. [I] saw a great many acquaintances, amongst them John Derr & George Sauerwein and had [a] nice walk & talk with them. Came home about five o'clock. Wish Mr. F. Hersh had come. Had a nice letter from Mary Sauerwein by G. S.

Thursday [Oct.] 14th. [I] did not go in [to the fair] till after dinner, and stopped for Ella B., & Mrs. M. went with us & we had a right nice time. Saw Mr. G. S. again.

Friday [Oct.] 15th. Was in [in] the afternoon. Mr. G. S. was with me most of the time. Very pleasant day.

Saturday Oct. 16th. Very pleasant day. Mother & I were in to town early and heard the premiums, [they] had a short address from Mr. Charles B. Calvert; & at noon I went with Aunt M. & Uncle Artz to the jail and afterwards returned to the grounds to witness the tournament[28]. Fannie Adams was crowned first Maid of Honor. I was quite tired & glad to get home again.

Sunday [Oct.] 17th. I was in to church, [and] found it quite warm; & afterwards Mother & I went out to Aunt M's and sat a good long while, [and] returned home to tea.

Monday [Oct.] 18th. Pretty day. I was busy all day helping Mother to fix to go to Balt.

Tuesday [Oct.] 19th. Father & Mother started to Balt. It is [a] lovely time to be there. /Kate Sauerwein & Rev. Mr. Lefevre were married to-day./ G. Sauerwein was [here] to see me this morning & sat an hour or so & after he left Annie Howard came with music to remain with me. I was busy most of the day.

---

[28]"This afternoon there was a tournament at the Cattle Show. I counted 39 Knights including Marshalls." Engelbrecht, *Diary*, III, 4.

1858

Wednesday [Oct.] 20th. Very pretty warm day. Annie & I were busy at our respective duties. Hal came for her but I would not let her go. Letter of Mag Shriner, [from] Balt.

Thursday [Oct.] 21st. Very pretty day. Father & Mother came home to-night, so I will be no longer chief housekeeper.

Friday Oct. 22nd. Appearance of rain but cleared away before noon. I went home with Annie H., [and] found her cousin Miss Laura Getzendanner there. After dinner Annie, Laura & I went to spend the evening with Mrs. Charles Howard, was quite lite tea. William Howard accompanied me home & sat till after tea.

Saturday [Oct.] 23rd. I was home all day. Very warm. I intended going to town but staid home to see the new carpet.

Sunday [Oct.] 24th. Mother & I were in to church; & Cousins Ed & Mag S. were going to dine with Uncle Lewis Scholls' & would have me go along, so I went. This morning was the first time I have been in since Synod met. There seem to be a great many [delegates] here. We went to Baptist church in afternoon. Aunt Jem has four of the number.[29] Mother came for me about dusk & I went home.

Monday [Oct.] 25th. Very pleasant day but much cooler. I went into town early & was to see Lizzie Houck, & we went together to Synod and it was quite interesting; and I came out immediately after adjournment and went home. Rev. Mr. Dole & Aunt Jem Scholl [were] here to tea.

Tuesday Oct. 26th. Very cool day. Busy sewing on the carpet. After dinner I went in to town [and] was to see Lizzie H., and we were together in Synod and heard the role called and other business, and afterwards were shopping & I called to see Ella B. after I left Lizzie. /Saw Wm. Riley & Rev. Mr. Dole in synod today./ /Clara Hobbs [was] married to-day./ I had a letter from Rev. W. S. Hammond wanting to visit me without a formal introduction.

Wednesday [Oct.] 27th. Very pleasant fall-like day. About half-past twelve o'clock I started out to Cousin Mag Shriner's and spent the day with her, Mrs. Kate Lefevre & Mary Derr. Georgia & Em Houck were out to [see] Kate

---

[29] Families of the local church provided hospitality for the visiting Synod delegates.

1858

also. [I] came home about dusk, met Cousin E. & Mr. L. on [the] way home. [I] wrote to Mr. G. Sauerwein.

Thursday [Oct.] 28th. Very pleasant day. Up early and attending to my duties. Mr. & Mrs. J. A. Lefevre, [with] Mr. & Mrs. Shriner were out about half-past ten o'clock, and Mr. Wm. M. Riley of Gettysburg [came] soon after. Kate just came Tuesday evening. They were hurried at dinner, and left to be in town [in] time enough for [the] cars [at] half-past one o'clock. Mr. Riley & I did not go in so soon; but after two o'clock, we went to Mrs. Wilson's for him to call and then to see Annie Schley & Jane Ramsburg. Met Annie Shriner there, also Rev. Mr. Luson there; off[ice of] Dr. Ayers. After paying bill [I] came home. [I] bid Wm. Riley good-bye at Mr. R.'s. Mrs. I. Howard & Mrs. Taylor here.

Friday Oct. 29th. When I awoke found it raining and [it] rained hard all day. [We] finished sewing our parlor carpet, all we can till [we] put [it] down. Sent my letter to Lou Clippinger.

Saturday [Oct.] 30th. Very nice day. Mother [was] in town to-day. I was busy in the parlor taking up matting, etc.

Sunday [Oct.] 31st. Very pleasant. Mother & I were in to church. Prof. Gerhart preached [a] good sermon. Saw Ed & Mag S. on [the] street. After dinner Mother & I went down to Mrs. Lewis Fout's and then saw the family, Mrs. Milford & children, Mrs. Davis & children & her mother Mrs. Delasmutt. [We] came home after dusk. Olivia showed some of her wedding fixings, etc. She was to have been married Nov. 4 but put [it] off on account of him cutting his finger.

Monday Nov. 1st [1858]. A lovely day. Mother in town morning & afternoon. Mr. George Fout & Mr. C. Dutrow [came] to see Father on business.

Tuesday [Nov.] 2nd. Cloudy damp day. Mr. John Clingman [came] to see Father about renting [the] farm.

Wednesday [Nov.] 3rd. Rained in morning but pleasant afternoon. Mother & I were out to Aunt M. Artz['s] awhile. Asked over to Mrs. Shriner's soon.

1858

Thursday Nov. 4th. Cloudy, damp, rainy day. Cloudy morning, clear at noon but very damp again in afternoon late. /This should be at night the 7th./[30] I rode to town horseback, was to see Aunt Jem Scholl--Miss Lizzie Jones there--and then to see Nellie Kunkel, and most of her conversation was of Synod, etc. [I] stopped at Mrs. Markel[l]'s at the window and talked a long time; saw Georgia & Lizzie Houck there too. Walked out with Father. Mary K. is to come home Saturday.

Friday [Nov.] 5th. Raining, damp, unpleasant day. Mr. Letherly was out to paint & was done soon after noon. Paper from Mr. Frank Hersh. Mr. C. Hershey of Montgomery Co. was here & staid over night.

Saturday [Nov.] 6th. Cleared off about ten o'clock & Mr. Hershey left for home. Mr. Kemp [was] here to see Father about the place.

Sunday [Nov.] 7th. Not in town. Mother went in early and went to Uncle Kemp's a little, and stopped at [the] cemetery as she came on home, so nearly two o'clock till she came.

[*There was no entry for Monday, November 8th.*]

Tuesday [Nov.] 9th. Crossed over at fourth day of Nov.

Wednesday [Nov.] 10th. Lovely bright morning. Mr. Letherly [was] out & finished painting.

Thursday [Nov.] 11th. Went into town after dinner and was shopping. [I stopped] at Aunt Scholl's to leave an agreement & at Mrs. P. Fout's to see her little stove and then came out home.

Friday [Nov.] 12th. Pleasant appearance. John took Mother & me to town and we were stove hunting again and have been all around. [We] were at Mrs. Markel[l]'s awhile and then came out home.

Saturday [Nov.] 13th. Very pleasant day. Commenced laying the parlour carpet this afternoon. Father was in town and bought a stove of Mr. Derr for my room.

---

[30]Apparently, Margaret was writing after the days had passed which accounts for the confusion between November 4 and the 9th.

1858

Sunday [Nov.] 14th. Very pleasant day. I went into church, [and] came part way down with Mary Kunkel. Saw Nevins Dorsey at church step as I went in. He told me Mary had come, said few words to Mag Shriner.

Monday [Nov.] 15th. Still at Carpet. I was in town a while, at Mrs. Fout's to see about stove, she would want to sell. [I] had a nice letter of Mary Sauerwein & gloves & veil enclosed. Mary S. bought for me for Mrs. Lefevre a "What not"[31].

Tuesday [Nov.] 16th. Finished putting down the carpet.

Wednesday [Nov.] 17th. Cold day. Mother in town. Mr. K. here on business.

Thursday [Nov.] 18th. Very pleasant day. Stove came yesterday, [and we] made fire today.

Friday Nov. 19th. Very cold. Father & Mother [were] both in town today. [I] made fire in [the] new stove, [and] like it very much.

Saturday [Nov.] 20th. Lovely day. Butchered this morning.

Sunday [Nov.] 21st. Rained & snowed all day.

Monday [Nov.] 22nd. Apparently [it] had cleared away but afterwards [it] rained & sleeted in showers quite fast. About ten o'clock Aunt Kitty Hedges[32] & cousin Daniel & Catherine H. came & about eleven, Aunt Mary Scholl & Annabelle, and all staid till after tea. Mr. Warfield was here to rent farm.

Tuesday [Nov.] 23th. No company & [I was] busy at various pieces of sewing. [I] wrote a note to Maggie Shriner.

Wednesday [Nov.] 24th. Sent my note to town with Jane to Mag S.

---

[31]This was Margaret's wedding gift for Kate Sauerwein, now wife of the Reverend J. A. Lefevre.

[32]Aunt Kitty was Catherine Scholl Hedges. See note 28, 1851.

1858

Thursday [Nov.] 25th. Cold, windy day. Mr. Thomas O'Neal here to see Father twice today. Thanksgiving day.

Friday [Nov.] 26th. Still cold & windy. [I] finished John's coat nearly.

Saturday [Nov.] 27th. Pleasant morning but cloudy in afternoon. I went to town soon after dinner and went to Kunkels' & sat there nearly all afternoon. Mary K. did not get home till just before I left. [I] was at Ellen Brunner's a few minutes. She has been [home] from B. more than a week. /Note from Mag Shriner. Saw Ed on street./

Sunday [Nov.] 28th. Snowed nearly all day.

Monday [Nov.] 29th. Cloudy, and [I] scarcely knew what to do but however [*sic*] went in after dinner, stopped [at] Mrs. Shriner's and Mag & Ed S. & Mary Derr soon came and we went together to see Mrs. L. Hedges[33], [but] did not get in, [and] then to see Mrs. Keefer (Annie Bentz), and shopped some. Mag & I [went] back to Mrs. H's [and] found her very pleasant, ladylike, quite entertaining. And then at Houcks' for few minutes and then came out home.

Tuesday [Nov.] 30th. Did not go to town as I had some ideas [*sic*].

Wednesday Dec. 1st [1858]. Lovely day. Mr. Gallion [was] here to rent the farm for his son George.

Thursday Dec. 2nd. Snowing & rain all day.

Friday [Dec.] 3rd. Cloudy & foggy day; nevertheless, Father & Mother went to Cousin Ed's to dinner & stopped five minutes at Mr. Derr's on return.

Saturday [Dec.] 4th. Cloudy, foggy, warm day. Mother went up to Mr. Boyd's to meet Mary Derr to bring her down here to stay all night but they were not there. Mr. Gallion and his son Geo. were here all morning till after dinner & Father rented the farm to Geo. K. Gallion for one year.

---

[33]Mrs. Lycurgus Hedges lived on the north side of Third Street between Market and Court Street. *Williams' Directory*, p. 18.

1858

Sunday [Dec.] 5th. Although still such cloudy, damp day Mother went in to church.

Monday [Dec.] 6th. Lovely morning. I went into [town] to do some shopping & then was to see Call Bantz & to Miss Reading to make me a black body; and as I came down street John told me Miss Mary Derr was at Mrs. Markel[l]'s and wanted to see [me] so [I] went over and found she was coming out home with me to go to Boyds' this afternoon. After eating & changing my dress we started & went over to B's. Cousin Ed & Mag came about four o'clock & we sat till about half-past seven. Note from G. Houck today to borrow my collar & sleeve.

Tuesday [Dec.] 7th. Found it raining this morning so Mary D. did not go into town to go home. Cousin Harrie Smith came out about two o'clock & sat till after four o'clock, & wanted me to go into town with him but of course could not on account of Mary. Eugene came for Mary about five o'clock.

Wednesday [Dec.] 8th. Raining this morning but not after dinner. Mother went into town and I sent by John the collar & sleeve to G. H. & wrote her a note.

Thursday [Dec.] 9th. Clear but very cold. Walked into town, did some shopping and had my dress fit, and was at Houcks' most of the afternoon cutting the pat[t]ern off of Emma H's mantle. Mary Derr came while I was there and we were at Miss Posey's to see her patterns; none suited. Paper from Mr. F. Hersh.

Friday [Dec.] 10th. Still so cold. Went out to Cousin Ed's to dinner and came home about five o'clock. Cousin Ed. [was] not home till just before I left. Mag [has] not decided about a cloak.

Saturday [Dec.] 11th. Rather cloudy day & getting warmer. Father [has] gone to town. About eleven o'clock Emma Clagett & her mother arrived and spent the day.

Sunday [Dec.] 12th. Cloudy early but cleared & warmer. Mother went to church & Cousin Ed & Mag came home with her & sat till about four o'clock, & they left.

Monday [Dec.] 13th. We were to meet Mag in town and get the cloth for our cloaks, but as [it] rained so hard of course [we] did not go in.

1858

Tuesday [Dec.] 14th. Still raining, so no one went to town.

Wednesday [Dec.] 15th. Cloudy but not raining. Mother was in town this afternoon, heard Mag had been in both Monday & Tuesday.

Thursday [Dec.] 16th. Clear, bright day. Went into town early, was at Mr. Getzandanner's, wrote Mag Shriner a note and then had my dress fit. Went down and took dinner with Kunkels and sat till nearly three, when Mary K. & I went up street, & after a while I walked home.

Friday [Dec.] 17th. Mother went in town to meet Mag Shriner & they got material for cloaks, & she came out home with Mother to make hers here. We were laying pat[t]erns on only this morning.

Saturday Dec. 18th. Nice day. Mag & I cut our cloaks out today and commenced sewing on them. Mr. Gallion [was] here to see Father on business this evening.

Sunday [Dec.] 19th. Cold, windy day. [I was] not very well, so did not go to town. Mag & Mother went to church. Snowed at night.

Monday [Dec.] 20th. Damp day, rained some after dinner. Mag wanted to go home, so Mother went to town with her.

Tuesday [Dec.] 21st. Rainy, disagreeable day. Wrote a letter to M. E. Sauerwein & sent for my trimmings on cloak.

Wednesday [Dec.] 22nd. Very pleasant day. Cleared off. Mother was over to Mr. I. Howard['s] but did not remain long as Mrs. H. [was] not there.

Thursday [Dec.] 23rd. Busy day but clear. Mother awoke me by saying Jane was sick, so Dr. and Rache was sent for, and she had a little girl. When Father came home [I] had a letter from M. E. Sauerwein relative to price of trimmings, etc., and a note of invitation from Lizzie Schell wanting me to come out this evening to a party, but it did not suit, so I remained at home. [I had a] note of Mary Derr for Christmas.

Friday [Dec.] 24th. Bright morning. Father [was] in bed, too, & the Dr. [came] to see him, but I had to go to town. Was home by one o'clock & then baked some cakes, etc. in evening. /Wrote to Mary Sauerwein./ /Wrote Mary Derr a note./

1858

Saturday [Dec.] 25th. Christmas day, very bright. I concluded to accept Mary Derr's invitation to dine with them, so [I] went out. The family, Mr. & Mrs. E. G. Shriner & Miss Lorgenbirl were there. /Dr. Moran [came] out./

Sunday Dec. 26th. Very pleasant day but I did not go to church.

Monday [Dec.] 27th. Pleasant day. Dr. Moran [came] out to see his patient & Uncle Artz to see Father. Father seems better. Dr. M's not coming out again unless sent for.

Tuesday [Dec.] 28th. My package did not arrive as I expected by express from M. E. Sauerwein. Wrote a note [to] L. Schell acknowledging her invitation.

Wednesday [Dec.] 29th. Raining & sleeting nearly all day; no package.

Thursday [Dec.] 30th. Very disagreeable day. John walked in for the package & brought [it] as well as left a note for Mag Shriner.

Friday [Dec.] 31st. Still raining, sleeting & the trees are hung with ice. No one [went] in town, so Mag's things [were] not sent in. So ends another year. Fraught to me with much pleasures as well as some unpleasant remembrances, but none in which I think I have done decidedly wrong.

1859

"[I] found them <u>hard</u> at butchering, so I changed my dress and went at it too. We finished today or rather tonight."

Saturday January 1, 1859. Very pretty day. Mother [was] in town. [I] wrote a note & sent Mag Shriner's trimming; also wrote a note to Georgia Houck saying I would stay with them to-morrow night. [I had a] note from Mag Shriner.

Sunday [Jan.] 2nd. Very pretty day. Mother & I walked into town to church. After church [I] went up with Houcks. Mrs. Jacobs there. Some of them complaining. G. & I went to Presbyterian Church. Mr. Ross[1] preached in his own church & Rev. Dr. Vermilye of New York in ours in [the] morning. Mr. Wils R. Boyd came with us from P. church & sat awhile. At night G., Ezra, & I all went to our church to the Bible Society meeting. The address was delivered by Dr. Vermilye and very interesting. We had a nice talk after we returned.

Monday [Jan.] 3rd. Appearance of snow but [it] did not [start] till towards night. I walked out home about ten o'clock. [I] found them <u>hard</u> at butchering, so I changed my dress and went at it too. We finished today or rather tonight.

Tuesday [Jan.] 4th. Snowed in showers all day. I had such a nice long letter of Lou Clippinger. She wants me to come out badly in March; she thinks or knows of an opportunity.

---

[1] Rev. James B. Ross was installed as pastor of the Frederick Presbyterian Church in 1857. A man of great ability, he improved the church building within his first year. He was in sympathy with the South, however, and resigned in October 1862 after the Battle of Antietam. For several months after the battle, the building was used as a hospital for wounded soldiers. J. F. Minor Simpson, *Monocacy Valley Maryland Presbyterianism, A History* (Frederick, 1955), p. 17.

1859

* * * * *

[Wednesday] Jan. 19th. Very pleasant day. [I] went into town, called to see Ellen B. & Mrs. Markell and talked awhile, then went to Miss Redin's and had my dress fixed; and was at Kunkels' awhile, and when I came home found Mrs. Taylor & Marion Howard were here to tea. Walked part way home with them. Invitation [to] Mr. Fred Schley's marriage.

* * * * *

Wednesday [Jan.] 26th. Much moderated. I walked into town, stopped at Ellen's awhile, then went up to Houcks' awhile, and then came out home. Capt. Hobbs was on the street with me [a]while. Soon after [I] got home Miss Ann Keefer came to spend [the] afternoon.

* * * * *

Sunday [Jan.] 30th. Very pleasant day. Mother & I went to town to church. Dr. Zack had an excellent sermon. Cousin Mag & Ed S. would have me go home with them, so I went up street to Mrs. Reese's and went out with Mr. & Mrs. Derr and found Mag there. Cousin Ed and Billy Worman there to tea. After tea Mr. & Mrs. Kemp [were] there & sat till we went home about nine o'clock.

Monday [Jan.] 31st. Very pleasant day. Mag & I were having a nice day by ourselves till about 4 o'clock when Mary Derr came over and remained over night. Mary & I had a long talk after retiring.

Tuesday, February 1st [1859]. Lovely day, like summer. About two o'clock Mr. Geo. Sauerwein arrived and I ran to dress. Had fire in [the] parlor for him. After he left Mary went home directly, and Mag & I went with Cousin Ed to her father's, and Geo. returned with Cousin Ed to tea at Mr. Derr's. We all staid till about ten, when we went to Cousin Ed's and very soon retired.

Wednesday [Feb.] 2nd. The weather seemed very unsettled, Eugene Derr came over about eight o'clock in [the] spring wagon for Mag, George Sauerwein & me to go to town with him. Mary joined us at her father's and we had a jolly ride into town. Mary & I stopped at Annie Nihoff's and then Mrs. Reese's, to Mrs. Dr. F. Schley's, and afterwards to Mrs. R. to dinner. After dinner [it] rained, so I left my things at Mrs. Markell's and rode out [home] on horseback.

Thursday [Feb.] 3rd. Not raining but very damp. Wrote Mary Derr a note and sent recipe for curing <u>Cancer</u>.

* * * * *

Monday [Feb.] 7th. Mother [was] in town & I received a letter from Mrs. J. A. Lefevre. I wrote to Lou Clippinger at night.

Tuesday [Feb.] 8th. [*This entry & Feb. 9th transposed in text.*] Cloudy, damp day. Nevertheless [I] went in town to see Mrs. Markell, then at Houcks' for Georgia to come home with me, but she goes to Balt. tomorrow.

Wednesday [Feb.] 9th. Rained & quite damp. [I] wrote a note to Mary Derr & sent her Kate Lefevre['s] letter. Mother at Aunt Margaret's; Uncle Artz hardly will go West.

* * * * *

Thursday [Feb.] 17th. /There was a total eclipse of [the] moon this morning./ Very pretty day. Started to walk into town but Mr. Len Smith & Mary overtook me and would have me ride with them to Mr. Markell's door. I sat at Mrs. Markell['s] till after 11 o'clock, then went up to see Jane Ramsburg, and then down to Kunkels' and sat there and talked an hour or so, and Melie & I walked out home. Had a pleasant walk but most too many fences to climb.

* * * * *

Saturday [Feb.] 19th. Still some appearance of rain & rained very hard in the afternoon. I had note from Mary Derr, letter of Lou Clippinger & a letter from <u>Chicago as a Valentine</u>.

Sunday [Feb.] 20th. Raining till afternoon when it cleared off beautiful with great deal of wind. Melie & I took a long walk down in the woods to the creek.

Monday [Feb.] 21st. Very windy. Mother went into town with Meal. I wrote a note and sent [it] to Mary Derr. Dan Fout stopped to say his Mother would be up tomorrow.

1859

Tuesday, Feb. 22nd. Washington's birthday. A lovely day. About two o'clock Mrs. Lewis Fout & Lizzie came up, [and] about five Dan & Lewis Fout stopped on way from town and all [stayed] to tea & left very soon after.

Wednesday [Feb.] 23rd. Delightful, like a summer's day. [I] went in soon after dinner to see Jane Ramsburg to ask her to come out, then to Annie Schley's and sat an hour or so, and then A. & I went to see Mrs. Fred Schley, also Miss Sophia Washington; and Miss Mary Goldsborough was there, also Judge Marshall & daughter, Mrs. Dr. Geo. Johnson. We then were at Aunt Kitty Thomas' a while and from there [went] down street, stopped for Jane R.; but she had gone to the cemetery[2] and I followed on and we walked out together.

Thursday [Feb.] 24th. Another beautiful day but more wind. Jane & I started about ten o'clock for Mr. Lewis Kemp's[3] and spent the day. Isie Buckey came between 2 & 3 o'clock; we left soon after an early tea. When we got home [we] found brother Rev. Bennett here, [and] Jane & I staid in [the] parlor. I had letter from Mary E. Sauerwein. We retired abut eleven o'clock.

Feb. 25th Friday. What was our great surprise to find it snowing so hard and continue all day, with slight intermission at noon. Jemmy Thompson came out about 3 o'clock for Jane. They had an upset in starting. Brother Bennett left soon after them.

Saturday [Feb.] 26th. Very pleasant day. Too much [snow] for sleighing; the sleigh cuts through. I sent to Jane for my shawl and to know how she got in; had a note from her in return, also a paper from Mr. Frank Hersh.

Sunday [Feb.] 27th. Lovely day but afraid to venture with either sleigh or buggy, too bad the roads [sic].

* * * * *

Wednesday [Mar.] 2nd [1859]. Beautiful day. After dinner [I] started to go to Aunt M. Artz's but Bill [was] too lame, so [I] staid in town. [I] went to

---

[2]The new Mount Olivet Cemetery, not far from Manchester Farm.

[3]Mr. & Mrs. Lewis G. Kemp lived on a farm on the Ballenger Creek Road close to Ballenger Creek, about 3 miles from Manchester Farm. *Bond Map,* 1858.

Kunkels['], met Aunt Shriner & Mag there and did some shopping, and was at Jane Ramsburg's [a]while, also at Mrs. Markell's. Ellen [is] in B[altimore] to Annie Daughterty['s] funeral. Paper of Mr. Frank Hersh.

* * * * *

Friday [Mar.] 4th. Beautiful day. Thought Annie Howard & her company would come as it rained yesterday, the day they were to come. Note [came] from Mary Derr saying she would not go to Balt. till Monday; replied to it. Cloudy in afternoon.

* * * * *

Tuesday [Mar.] 8th. Very pleasant day. M. Gallion [was] here to see Father.

Wednesday [Mar.] 9th. Pleasant day. [I was] at Aunt M. Artz's awhile; note from Mag Shriner, saying when Mary D. did not go to B[altimore] but when she would. [I] also wrote her one.

* * * * *

Friday [Mar.] 11th. Some appearance of rain in morning & slight showers in afternoon. After an early dinner [I] walked over & took tea at Mr. I. Howard['s]. Kate Cockey of Urbana was there, found her very pleasant.

Saturday [Mar.] 12th. Delightful. [I] walked up to see Annie H. & Co. [*Illegible*].

* * * * *

Wednesday [Mar.] 16th. Very pretty day. I was out at Aunt Lizzie Brunner's[4] and sat awhile in the afternoon.

* * * * *

---

[4]Margaret's Aunt Lizzie Brunner and Uncle John lived on Montevue Lane, not far from David Kemp's home on Rocky Springs Road about one-half mile south of the Yellow Springs Road intersection. *Bond Map*, 1858.

1859

Friday [Mar.] 18th. Rain in showers. Jane went to town and [I] sent a note by her to Jane Ramsburg for my bandbox, & she sent a note in turn but [it] was lost.

* * * * *

Monday [Mar.] 21st. In morning somewhat appearance of rain but [it] proved a lovely day. Annie Howard came down & spent the day & night. At night Charlie, Tom & Willie Howard[5] came and sat [a] couple of hours.

Tuesday [Mar.] 22nd. Appearance of rain, then clear, & finally showers in afternoon. General movement today. Roderick left, & Gallion came.[6]

Wednesday [Mar.] 23rd. Very pleasant day. [I went] out to Aunt M. Artz['s] awhile, stopped in town to shop and to see Aunt Shriner, and awhile at E. B.'s at door. [I had a] note from Mag Shriner.

* * * * *

March 25th Friday. Warm in morning but was very windy and quite cool till evening. I walked into town after dinner, did some shopping, was at Mrs. B. F. Winchester's but did not find her in, and then at Kunkels' awhile, and afterwards at Mrs. Markell's and had a nice talk.

* * * * *

Sunday [Mar.] 27th. Appearance of rain but cleared very pretty in afternoon. I went in to church & heard an excellent sermon from Dr. Zack from Proverbs 18:24. I had not long done dinner when Mr. Hershey of Montgomery came and sat an hour or so, and soon after he left Mr. John Smith and neighbor came and sat till five o'clock. Mag Shriner & youngster [*sic*].

* * * * *

---

[5]The Howards had a tannery on the south side of Patrick Street between Carroll Street and East Street. *Williams' Directory*, p. 20.

[6]Gallion was succeeding Roderick as tenant farmer on the Scholl properties. See March 8 and April 8, 1859.

Wednesday [Mar.] 30th. Beautiful day. Wrote to Mary Sauerwein & a note to Mary Derr. I went to town after dinner, stopped at Mrs. Markels' & Ella B. went up street with me. Did some shopping & returned home. Marion Howard [had been] here but had been sent for [because] they had company.

Thursday [Mar.] 31st. Quite windy but bright. Mother was in town & heard Mag Shriner had had a baby Sunday night, and that she did not expect [it] till May.

Friday April 1st [1859]. Beautiful day. I walked into town early. [I] saw Mrs. Grafton Fout at [the] door, so stopped in a short time with her, then [went] to Mrs. Markell['s] & she went up street with me. Mary Ellen Gibson & Beccy Marky were there also. I mailed a letter for Lou Clip enclosing a collar I had made for her. Mrs. M. & I shopped & were to see Mrs. B. F. Winchester & at Mrs. Reese's but she was not in. I wanted to see her about Mag's boy.

* * * * *

Tuesday [Apr.] 5th. [I] found it [had] snowed when [I] got up but [it] did not last long or amount to more as much as a good large frost & clear the rest of day, with heavy wind in afternoon. Cousin Ed here for his honeysuckle, and told of his boy & that he thought it would live, etc.[7] [He was] prouder than [I] expected him to be.

Wednesday [Apr.] 6th. Not so windy. Mother & Father were gone to spend the day at Aunt Mary Scholl's & stopped to see Mag Shriner.

Thursday [Apr.] 7th. Pleasant very early. I went to town with Father, was to see Annie Bentz Keefer & at Houcks' & Aunt Kitty's to tell them we were coming to-morrow; & [I was] at Mrs. McGill's quite long, then came home.

Friday, April 8th. Snow squalls about noon but cleared away by two o'clock and Mother & I went in & spent afternoon at Mrs. Brengle's with the family; & Misses Mary Baer, Lizzie Seffler took tea there, and Mrs. M. Eve. Schley & Annie, Mary & Ellen were all there to call, also Mrs. Englebrecht. We came home about eight o'clock & Mr. Gallion stopped to tell Father relative to wheat.

---

[7]Mag and Ed Shriner's first born (a son) was premature and died shortly after birth.

1859

Saturday [Apr.] 9th. A lovely day. I went down to Uncle Adams' after dinner but only found Miss Sallie home; but [I] sat & talked to her till nearly five o'clock. Very pleasant afternoon.

* * * * *

Tuesday [Apr.] 12th. Rather appearance of rain, but nevertheless Mother & I went over to Cousin Dan Hedges[8] expecting to meet Aunt Mary there but she was not. We spent a very pleasant day there, were to see Aunt Kitty [a] little while. Major Baltzell & old Mr. Devilbiss were there also to tea.

Wednesday [Apr.] 13th. Damp lowering in the morning, and after dinner [I] took Father to town, & I went out to see Mag Shriner & Mary Derr & brought Georgia Houck home with me.

Thursday, April 14th. Very rainy all day. Feared it would be dull for G. but she seemed to be well content.

Friday [Apr.] 15th. Pleasant morning. G. & I were sewing. Dr. Schaeffer & brother went through to [the] other place, & Mother stopped them on way back to look at my tooth. After they left Georgia & I went over to see Miss Sallie's in reference to butter, and then took a walk out to the woods & home, and after early tea I took Georgia into town.

* * * * *

Monday [Apr.] 18th. Lovely day. I went into town after early dinner. Was at Aunt Jem Scholl's, she not at home, [and] at Mrs. John Clingham's[9] awhile; then [I went] up to Julie Derr's. Met Mary Kunkel on street & took her with me to do shopping, went down home with her & sat awhile. Saw Lizzie Zack there. John [drove me] home, found Mrs. Taylor & Annie Howard had been there to tea; also Mrs. Fred Schley, Tisher & friend & Annie Schley [came] to call but, did not get out as I was not home. Paper of Mr. F. Hersh.

---

[8]On the Hedges family, see notes 28 and 39, 1851.

[9]Mrs. John Clingham lived on the south side of Patrick Street between Carroll and East Street. *Williams' Directory*, p. 8.

1859

Tuesday, April 19th. Clear early then appearance of rain but afterwards cleared off beautifully. Down [at] Uncle Adam's to see cousin Sarah Ann.

Wednesday [Apr.] 20th. Thought it going to be lovely day, so rode to town on horseback. Was to see Mrs. B. F. Winchester and do some shopping and then to Houcks' to dinner. We were going to Dr. Schaeffer's immediately after but it was raining and continued all evening; nevertheless, we went down at four o'clock but he was not in. John came for me but I remained till after tea, then came home.

* * * * *

Sunday [Apr.] 24th. Easter day. A lovely bright day, but as buggy shafts not home did not go to church. After dinner Mother & I took a walk intending to go [to] the Misses Keefer's, but creek so high could not cross, so we went to Mrs. Lewis Fout's awhile and then came up home.

Monday, April 25th. Still pleasant. Mother in town and [saw] quite [a] crowd of darkies there. /Wrote Mag Shriner a note./

Tuesday [Apr.] 26th. Very bright morning, but I went into town after dinner & got into a very heavy shower. Waited at Mr. Derr's and dried my dress; then [went] to Mrs. Dr. Magill's and sat till the fury of shower nearly abated; then went to Kunkels' awhile but soon left and we [sic] started to walk home but soon met John with buggy.

* * * * *

Thursday [Apr.] 28th. Cloudy & very damp in morning but cleared off by noon. About ten o'clock Cousin Sarah Ann Shank & three children & Fannie Adams came up to spend the day.

* * * * *

Monday [May] 2nd [1859]. Very nice day. Mother & I were in town to take tea with Miss Keefers', and after we got home [at] 4 o'clock Miss Sallie & Mr. Gallion came over & sat till about ten.

Tuesday [May] 3rd. I went out, stopped for Mary Derr & spent day with Mag. [*Remainder of the entry is crossed out.*]

1859

[*The next entry is for May 5th.*]

Thursday [May] 5th. Early in town in morning. Down [at] Kunkels' & Meal went with me to select worsted, in afternoon to get dress, to see Jen Brengle. She not home but [I] saw her Mother. [Went to] see Aunt Jem Scholl.

[*There are no more entries until May 8th.*]

Sunday [May] 8th. Beautiful morning, and as [it was] such a lovely morning I went out to Aunt M. Artz', and she came out home while I went to church & Vic & I came home after church. I rode out when they went home.

[*There are no more entries until May 15th.*]

Sunday [May] 15th. Quite cool. We had no church so went to Houcks' and Em & I went to Methodist church and heard an excellent sermon from Mr. J. McK. Reilly.

Monday [May] 16th. Mother went in early for Lizzie Clark. Cold & clear. Kate Bantz & Lou Ebbert were out and sat an hour or two.

Tuesday [May] 17th. Rainy. Busy Sewing.

* * * * *

Thursday [May] 19th. Cleared away, so Lizzie Clark went home. I was over [at] Miss Sallie's awhile. Miss Joy sent for her honeysuckle & I wrote her a note.

May 20th Friday. Sent paper [to] Mr. F. Hersh. Still rather cloudy. I went into town, went to Kunkels', saw their friends Misses Styles & Kean, then [was] at Mrs. Bantz's, but Kate Davis gone to Balt.; so had a long talk with Mrs. Bantz & Lou Ebert.

[May] 21st Saturday. Mother & Father gone to see Uncle John Ogle[10]. Mrs. Howard & Marion here to tea. Warm, sultry.

---

[10]John Ogle died May 22, 1859, according to Holdcraft, *Names In Stone*, p. 863. He lived off Dublin Road below Devilbiss Bridge Road. *Bond Map*, 1858.

[May] 22nd Sunday. Mother gone to Uncle John O., so I did not go to church. I was over to see Miss Sallie nearly all afternoon. When Mother came home Uncle John died.

[May] 23rd Monday. Mother & Father went to funeral.

[May] 24th Tuesday. Very pretty day. In town to see Kate Bantz. She was sick but I saw her. She is coming out Thursday.

[May] 25th Wednesday. Very pretty day. Aunt Mary Scholl, Annabelle & Davis, Misses Dutrow, Mrs. Cromwell & daughter Annie, & Mrs. Dutrow spent day. /Lizzie Schell, too, & Sallie here to call short time./ Afternoon all walked over to Miss Sallie's & had Miss Sallie & Mrs. Gallion to tea. All left after tea except Mrs. Cromwell.

[May] 26th Thursday. Very pleasant morning. About ten o'clock Mrs. Kate Davis, two children & Miss Lou Ebert & Dody Bantz came and spent the day. Soon after twelve, Cousin Ed & Maggie came to dinner; again all left except Mrs. C.

[May] 27th Friday. Warm morning. Mother, Mrs. C. & children went to Mrs. Howard's to dinner & Mrs. Boyd's to tea. Mr. Boyd sent them home after tea. Invitation to Cle Sifford's reception.[11]

* * * * *

[May] 29th Sunday. Lovely day. John sick, so I did not go to church; after dinner John took Mother & me to Aunt M's. We were there some time.

[May] 30th Monday. In town in morning shopping & to see Ellen B., only Mrs. M. home. After dinner, [I went] with Father to Mary Worman's & sat till he was ready to come home. Heavy gust after we were home.

Tuesday [May] 31st. Mother & Father gone to Uncle Hedge's. Sultry & gust in afternoon.

Wednesday, June 1st [1859]. Still papering. Father right sick [at] night.

---

[11] Cle and Georgia Sifford lived on the south side of Church Street opposite Record Street. *Williams' Directory*, p. 36.

1859

Thursday [June] 2nd. Very warm. I went into town about twelve but it was nearly three till Ellen was ready to go see Cle Sifford. Hobbs met us & went to door with us. We had a very pleasant & quite lengthy call, all very pleasant. Then [we went] to see Annie Clingan's and some shopping, and afterwards Hobbs again joined me and went with me & waited till I got in at Uncle Lewis Scholl's. A very heavy gust came up & I was obliged to wait till storm abated & John came up in the buggy for me.

Friday [June] 3rd. Very warm morning. Went in, got Mrs. L. Hedges & went to Mag Shriner's to spend day. Met Mrs. Dan Hedges & Davis & Mrs. Ed Getzendanner there as to spend day. Davis Scholl [came] to tea.

June 4th Saturday. Very warm. I went into town with Father, did some shopping & to see Aunt C. Scholl[12] and at Mrs. Bantz's but could get no one to answer the bell, so came home.

* * * * *

Monday [June] 6th. Very pleasant. Mother in town & brought me a note from Mary Kunkel saying they would be out to-morrow to spend the day. I was over [at] Miss Sallie's awhile in afternoon.

Tuesday [June] 7th. Very pleasant morning. About eleven o'clock Harry Smith, Mary & Meallie Kunkel & Mary Derr here to spend the day, left about 8 o'clock.

* * * * *

Saturday [June] 11th. Very pleasant day. Uncle Artz here in morning awhile, & Miss Sallie in afternoon.

Sunday [June] 12th. Sick in bed all day till 1 o'clock.

Monday [June] 13th. Pleasant morning. Mother & I stopped for Aunt Margaret & went to see Miss Ogle; only Catherine home. Aunt Mary Scholl, Misses Dronenburg & Rinehart & Mrs. Steiner, Miss Susan S. & Mr. W. Stoner only there. Annie & Jane came home just before we left. Very heavy gust.

---

[12]See note 46, 1851.

June 14th Tuesday. Very warm, sultry day. Annie Howard came over after dinner & remained over night. We were over to see Miss Sallie a little while.

Wednesday [June] 15th. Still warm, slight showers in afternoon. Annie left about eleven o'clock. Wrote [to] Cousin A. B. Ogle, [and] Mrs. Mering.

Thursday [June] 16th. Warm day. Sent a note to Mag Shriner. Went into town after tea & was to see Kunkels & remained over night. Mary Kean [was] still there. Maria McPherson [was] there to call. Mr. E. Baugher came after tea to escort us to the court house. Had [a] pleasant time but [was] tired.

Friday [June] 17th. Up in time and soon after breakfast went out & got some worsteds. It commenced raining and rained on till nearly four o'clock. Mother sent for me about six o'clock.

Saturday [June] 18th. Very pleasant day. Went to town after dinner. Was at Mrs. Bentz's, not home, to see Annie Bentz, & at Lycurgus Hedges' & at Sophie Gaither's but did not get in. Then [I] came on out home.

Sunday [June] 19th. Very pleasant day. In to church. Came down with Kunkels and then at hotel with Mag Shriner awhile, & then came on home.

Monday, June 20th. Warmer. Wrote Annie Keeffer a note that Cousin Ed, Mag, & I would go to her mother's on Wednesday.

Tuesday [June] 21st. Very pleasant day. Soon after nine o'clock Mary Kunkel & Mary Kean arrived. After dinner, we went over to Sarah Kemp's to tea, spent afternoon very pleasantly. There was [a] shower about twilight with some thunder. Paper Mr. F. Hersh [*sic*].

Wednesday [June] 22nd. Nice morning. We girls over to see the mower & at Miss Sallie's [a] short time; saw old Mrs. Gallion & her daughter Mary on our return home. Cousin Ed Shriner here to tea. Old Mrs. Kunkel came for the girls after tea.

Thursday [June] 23rd. I started about ten o'clock for Aunt Lizzie Brunner's, stopped for Annie but she had company, so could not go. Cousin Ed & Mag Shriner, Mr. & Mrs. Herstine, little boy of Phil'd. were there. Spent very pleasant day & brought Uncle Kemp into town, who had stopped awhile at Uncle John B's; met Annie & Charlie just going out.

1859

Friday [June] 24th. Pleasant with some appearance of rain. Did not go to town. Father's back [is] worse.

Saturday [June] 25th. Pleasant day. Father worse so sent for the Dr., who was out to see him.

Sunday [June] 26th. Appearance of rain. Nevertheless went to church & heard a very long sermon from Mr. Jones.

Monday [June] 27th. Very warm. Dr. out to see Father, also Mr. Bushey. /Letter of Mary Sauerwein./ I went out to Uncle Artz's in evening and to shop in town & stopped few minutes at Kunkels' & then came home. Mr. Gallion came to see Father.

Tuesday [June] 28th. At home all day. /Small showers afternoon./ Doctor to see Father again.

Wednesday [June] 29th. Very warm. Busy making jelly & wine all day. Over [at] Miss Sallie's [a] short time. <u>Wind gust</u>.

Thursday [June] 30th. Somewhat cooler. Sent paper [to] Mr. F. Hersh, had note from Mag Shriner saying she & co. [would] spend Friday with us.

Friday, July 1st [1859]. Right pleasant. Busy all morning. About eleven o'clock Mag Shriner, Mr. & Mrs. Herstine & son of Pa., & Mary Derr & Vic Stoner of Pittsburg came to spend the day. All left soon after seven o'clock. I did not go to town as I had told the girls.

Saturday [July] 2nd. Very warm. Busy in morning. After dinner Father took me to town & left me at Kunkels'. Mr. & Mrs. Baker Kunkel there. After tea Will Brengle came & as we were going to court house met Ed Baugher coming down. We were up only short [time] to hear music as storm frightened us.

Sunday July 3rd. Very much appearance of rain, indeed had [a] few very light showers. Mary Kean & Nellie went first, afterward Mary Kunkel & I went first to Methodist [church], but hearing Mr. Riley would not preach, went to Lutheran church & heard [a] very good [sermon] from Mr. Diehl[13].

[*There are no further entries for 1859 until December 6th.*]

Dec. 6th [1859]. Little Nancy Hersh Clippinger[14] born.

---

[13]The Rev. George Diehl was the pastor of the Lutheran Church on East Church Street from 1851 to 1887. See note 11, 1856.

[14]This was the child of Lou [Hersh] Clippinger.

1859

Rev. D. Zacharias, D.D., Pastor,
Evangelical Reformed Church,
Frederick, Maryland

(Photo courtesy Evangelical Reformed Church, United Church of Christ, Frederick, Maryland)

Margaret Hood's church, the Evangelical Reformed Church, Frederick, Maryland

(Photo courtesy Evangelical Reformed Church, United Church of Christ, Frederick, Maryland)

1860

"George took me to the Hall of Maryland Institute to hear Lola Montez lecture on 'Fashions;' I was well pleased."

Sunday January 1st 1860. Very cold. Mother & I went into church and heard a very good sermon. Mary Kunkel [went] with me to the Hotel & I went down home with her to stay. Mary Derr gave me a note from Mary Sauerwein. Afternoon Mary and I went up to choir meeting. Will Ramsburg came down street with us. George & Anna Birely called Mary & me over and we sat a few minutes. Mary & I went early to the Lutheran Church to yearly Bible meeting. Lizzie Baugher had seats saved. Will & Mary Ramsburg & Baughers & we were all together. Ed Baugher came home with me & sat till after ten o'clock.

Monday January 2nd. Extremely cold but very bright. Mary & I were up street on business, but Mother did not send for me as just we sat down to dinner [*sic*]; so I waited till after dinner, then went out home. Father not so well.

* * * * *

Thursday [Jan.] 5th. Bright, cold day. Quite early Mr. Sam Clagget came, soon Miss Mary Keefer & then Fannie Adams, and remained till about four o'clock. Had a note from Mr. Ulysses Hobbs.

January 6th Friday. Very cold but moderated by noon. Annie & Catherine Ogle came to spend the day. After they left I went to town to see Mr. & Mrs. Rohrback.[1] The latter quite ill in bed.

---

[1]Ellen Brunner and Martin N. Rohrback, who had been friends since 1855 (see note 37, 1856), were married on September 3, 1859 (Rohrbaugh, *Rohrbach Genealogy*, p. 377). Their second son, Jacob, later became the diarist's lawyer and executor. Williams, *History*, p. 736; and will of Margaret Hood, January 17, 1913. There is no reference to the wedding in

1860

Saturday [Jan.] 7th. Raining & freezing all day. Wrote to M. E. Sauerwein.

* * * * *

Wednesday [Jan.] 11th. Still disagreeable. Hurrying about sewing.

BALTIMORE

Thursday [Jan.] 12th. Raining quite early but about eight appearance of clearing off, so started to town to go to Balt. Sent a paper to Mr. Frank Hersh. Mr. G. Sauerwein [met] me at depot and took me up to the house, and [I] was very kindly received by the family. After dinner Em & I were out in a shopping expedition up Eutaw & down Market St. Went to Prayer meeting.

Friday [Jan.] 13th. Cloudy this morning but cleared off before noon. M. Fox called to see us. Tillie Houck came down about eleven o'clock but thought it too late, so she remained till after dinner, when Mary, Tilly & I were out all afternoon looking for furs.

Saturday [Jan.] 14th. It hailed & rained last night & still continues through the day. Tilly & we girls did all the talking. I wrote a letter to Lou Hersh Clippinger.

Sunday [Jan.] 15th. Clear & warm, but walking very sloppy. Em, Mary, Tillie Houck, & I all went to church this morning and heard an excellent sermon from Dr. Morris. Afternoon Tillie went out to Mr. Bruce's where she is staying, and Mary & I went to Central Church to hear Mr. Mattoon, the Missionary. Kate & Mr. Lefevre[2] were there; came in and sat a while. Mary & I kept house at night.

Monday [Jan.] 16th. Very pleasant day. Kate & Mr. Lefevre took dinner here. Mrs. John Rau & little girl Adele, Mrs. James Bayfield, & Mrs. John Gregg were here. In afternoon I went with Mary to Mrs. Rau's.

Margaret's diary, since her 1859 entries are lacking between July and December.

[2]Kate Sauerwein and Mr. J. A. Lefevre were married on October 19, 1858; see also October 28, 1858.

1860

Tuesday [Jan.] 17th. A cloudy, damp morning; cleared off about noon. Mrs. Sauerwein & Mary went out shopping with me. I bought my Cape & Muff, paid $41; Miss Sallie's, & a dress for her & veil for self. After I got back to Mrs. S's I wrote home. Kate was here [a] short time in morning. /Mary & I out in afternoon./ George took me to the Hollyday [sic] Street Theater[3] to see the Banel family. Spent the time very pleasantly and enjoyed it.

Wednesday [Jan.] 18th. Alternate clouds & sunshine. I went to see about a girl for Mrs. S of a Mrs. McPherson. Mary & I then went to Kate's to spend the day. Mrs. Bayfield & Mrs. Gregg called there. Em came out after us, as she was to go down first. She said Rose Abell had sent for us to take tea there this evening. After dinner Mary & I went to see Tilly Houck, and stopped on our way home for Em at Kate's, then came home. [We] found Lou Bell, Mrs. Andrew Reese, & Miss Horn of Phil'd., Mrs. P. Sauerwein & Mary Jennings had been to see us. We got ready & went to Abell's to tea. Miss Carrie Devalin was there also. Evening passed pleasantly. George came for us.

Thursday January 19th [1860]. Clear & colder. Rev. & Mrs. Sadtler of New York called. Kate & Mr. Lefevre were here. Mrs. John P. Derr[4] & Mary Kann called. Mrs. Derr invited us to spend tomorrow with her. M. Fox [was] here for short time. Emma Davis & Lizzie Schell of Fred[eric]k here [and] Misses C & E Bayfield. Neallie Dean was here also. We intended going out, but [it] got too late, so only took short walk down Balt. St.

Friday [Jan.] 20th. A warm, clear day. Mrs. Maria Trowbridge & Sallie Green were here in the morning. About one o'clock we rode out to Kate Lefevre, had her fix our hair, then lunch; and from there [went] to Mrs. John P. Derr's to spend the day, or rather to dinner at six o'clock. We took a walk in [the] afternoon and dined at six; were at table couple of hours. George came for us about nine o'clock and, after refreshments, left. [We] reached home about 12 o'clock. Found Mr. Perry had been to see us.

Saturday [Jan.] 21st. Another delightful day. Kate was here a short time. Old Mrs. Rau was here. Mary & I dressed, went to Carter's, then out to Kate's to remain till Mr. Lefevre returned. He has gone to Harrisburg.

---

[3]See note 14, 1851.

[4]J. P. Derr, now married and a cotton merchant in Baltimore, was the son of J. Derr, Jr.

1860

Sunday [Jan.] 22nd. A real spring-like day. Kate went to her own church.[5] Mary & I went to hear Rev. Louis Kemp preach in Second English Lutheran Church. In afternoon Kate, Mary & I went to prayer meeting at Mr. Dunning's church. We went to Mr. L's church at night; Rev. M. Cross preached. Mr. Root & Mr. Arthur came home & came in & sat a while.

Monday [Jan.] 23rd. The weather continues pleasant. We left Kate's after ten, went to see Miss Tell then at Neallie Dean's, then to see Em Davis & Lizzie Schell, then to Abells', then came home. In afternoon Mary & I were out to see Mrs. Bayfield, Mrs. John Rau & Mrs. Jennings. Mrs. Urhlaub called whilst we were out. At night Mrs. S., Mary & I went to church. Rev. Mr. Anspache preached. Em went to Kate's to stay all night.

Tuesday [Jan.] 24th. Pleasant day. I was at market with Mary. Kate [was] here awhile. Mary Jennings stopped few minutes. Em, Mary & I were out at Greenmount [a] couple of hours, visited Philip Rau's grave. The girls seemed very sad. Miss Adie Spilcher & Em Brauns were here whilst we were out, also Sarah & Hester Moon. Sorry I did not get to see them. After dinner Mary & I were to see Mrs. John Gregg, then took a walk down Market Street. Was very sorry to find Mr. Frank Hersh had called and we did not get to see him.

Wednesday [Jan.] 25th. Cloudy this morning. Mr. Frank Hersh called. Glad to see him. Lou not so well. I heard of all the family. /Rev. Dr. Morris called./ Mrs. S, Em & I were out nearly all morning pricing China, etc. Afternoon Mr. Lefevre & Kate came here and we all went to Mrs. Jenning's to tea, had nice supper, etc. Kate Sauerwein[6] [was] there to tea and M. Jennings' brother [came] after tea [and] Messrs. Boehm, Pollard, Phelps, & Messrs. G. & E. Sauerwein. Spent pleasant evening, returned home by eleven o'clock.

Thursday [Jan.] 26th. Cloudy & cold. Em & I were out nearly all morning looking at plated [silver]. We had [a] nice time. After dinner Em & I were down street to buy sets of Lace. Then we got ready & went to tea at Mrs. John Rau's; Em, Mary, G., & I & Kate & Mrs. Lefevre were there; spent

---

[5]Kate's husband, Mr. Lefevre, was a Presbyterian minister.

[6]This was Kate Sauerwein of the Howard Street family. See August 8, 1857.

time very pleasantly. Letter from home. We returned home about eleven o'clock, found it raining when we came out.

Friday [Jan.] 27th. Weather variable but rather colder. Mr. F. Hersh called & sat a while. I was sick part of the day. Mary & Mrs. S. [went] to church. Mr. & Mrs. Sadtler came home for a while.

Saturday [Jan.] 28th. Bright morning but much cooler. Mr. Hersh came according to appointment at 11 o'clock & we were soon ready & went to Mt. Hope[7]; that is, Mr. H, Mary, Em & I. We had a very pleasant time, were shown through the house and then returned. Mr. H. left to meet cousin Eliza. After dinner Mary, Em & I went to see Mrs. H. Beise, not at home; then out shopping awhile; and then found we had time so we went on over to Mr. Benke's, [and] saw Mrs. Benke, Hettie Benke, Sophie Cockrill, and sat awhile and then came on home. Kate was here while we were gone. Mr. Perry invited me to go to [a] concert.

Sunday [Jan.] 29th. Very pretty day. Em, George & I went to Emmanuel Church to morning services. Heard Rev. M. Schenck. In [the] afternoon Mary & I went to hear Rev. Mr. Backus, and as we came in the house Mr. John A. Johnson was just leaving. Mr. Hersh called according to appointment at night and Mary, George, Mr. Hersh & I all went to Charles St. Church. Mr. Hersh sat awhile after church. I sent a dress to the baby & enclosed a letter for Lou.

Monday [Jan.] 30th. Very pleasant warm day. Mrs. Bayfield called in the morning and after she left Mrs. S., Mary & I were down street to shop. After dinner Mary & I went to see Misses Bayfield, and to [see] Mrs. Maria Trowbridge whom we found out, and to Mrs. John Sadtler's & Mrs. Urhlaub. I wrote home. At night Mary, Em, & George & I went up to Mrs. Bayfield's and spent the evening very pleasantly. Miss Fox [was] here in afternoon, we [were] not home.

Tuesday [Jan.] 31st. Warm, pleasant morning. Mary & I went to Market St., got in the cars & went out to Mrs. Moon's to see the girls. Sarah & Hester only were home. They had a great deal to say and we sat an hour or so.

---

[7]Mt. Hope on the Hookstown Road was purchased for a future hospital in 1858. It was surrounded by a fine estate of 300 acres and was considered one of the most complete and magnificent edifices in this county. Scharf, *Baltimore*, p. 853.

1860

From thence we went to Kate's to dinner and she fixed my hair and I came home; and about half-past seven Mr. Perry called with a carriage for me to go to a concert given to [*sic*] Mrs. M. A. Curley. /Rev. Mr. Hitchcock at Kates's./ It was raining when we went. When [the] concert [was] over found it was snowing and about an inch deep. I enjoyed it very much and [heard] quite a quantity of news. He did not come in but bid me good-bye at the door.

Wednesday Feb. 1st [1860]. Found the snow had fallen to depth of several inches. Mary & I were out [a] short time to attend to our watches, and then came home as so cold.

Thursday Feb. 2nd. Very cold. Kate here awhile this morning, [and] we were home. Mary commenced reading "Peace on Stolen Hill," and at night also.

Friday Feb. 3rd. Cold still, but not quite so much so. In morning Em & I were at prayer meeting and then shopping. [In the] afternoon Mary & I went out to Emma Davis to see her & Lizzie Schell. Mary invited them to tea for Monday. George took me to the Hall of Maryland Institute[8] to hear Lola Montez[9] lecture on "Fashions;" I was well pleased.

Saturday [Feb.] 4th. Clear & cold day. Read all morning. Kate here in the morning and wanted us to spend Monday with her. [In the] afternoon Mary & I were out to shop, then stopped at Mrs. Abell's to invite the girls for Monday evening for tea; only saw Rose, as Miss Fox was out.

Sunday Feb. 5th. Very bright day, but ugly walking. Mary, Em & I went to Dr. Morris' to church and were home all afternoon; and at night to Dr. Morris' to hear Rev. Tom Kemp. G. [went] with us then.

[*A separate entry, written at the top of the last page of the final volume of the diary, relates to this day.*] **1860, Feb. 5.** G.S. promised to tell me something next time I see him. Sunday afternoon stormy talk...

---

[8]Maryland Institute has served Maryland since 1824. A new Hall of Maryland Institute was opened in 1851 including the School of Design and a library. Scharf, *Baltimore*, II, 667-668.

[9]Lola Montez was a dancer and entertainer. She was the mistress of Louis I of Bavaria until the Revolution of 1848. Wrote *Secrets of a Ladies' Toilet with Hints to Gentlemen on the Art of Fascinating*. *Forbes Magazine*, Oct. 3, 1988, p. 19; and *The New Columbia Encyclopedia*.

1860

Monday Feb. 6th. Raining in the morning, nevertheless Em & I were out on business up to Madison and down Market St. It ceased raining about noon & cleared off. About four o'clock Tilly Houck came to tea, then Mr. & Mrs. John Rau, Louise Bowie, Miss Fox, Lizzie Schell & Em Davis, Mr. & Mrs. Lefevre, all to tea. After tea Mr. Perry came and then Messrs. Wright & Rooche. All spent the evening in talking, music, & playing "Old Maids," [&] "Euchre." I spent the evening very pleasantly. All left about or soon after eleven o'clock. Kate & Mr. L & Tilly H. remained over night.

Tuesday Feb. 7th. Very pleasant day. Mr. L. [left] immediately after breakfast. Kate L. & Tilly [left] soon and then Mary & I went to Market. After coming home Mary, Em & I got ready & went out to Kate's to spend the day. Spent time very pleasantly. Tilly Houck quite sick part of the day. Rev. Tom Kemp called & sat couple of hours in the afternoon. Tilly went to Mr. Bruce's at night. We all staid over night, & spent the day very pleasantly.

Wednesday [Feb.] 8th. We were up by 8 to breakfast. Mr. L[efevre] soon left. Lizzie Schell & Emma Davis called; [they] were going to see us too, so staid double time. We staid till about four o'clock, when we rode down Market St., did some shopping, came home, and then went out about my watch and with Mary to see Mrs. Rau. Talked and wrote at night.

Thursday [Feb.] 9th. Delightful day. Wrote a letter home and one to Mr. U. Hobbs. Kate Lefevre was down and sat nearly all morning. Mary S. & I were to see Mary Warner and then came home to dinner. About four o'clock started out, were to see Mrs. Fannie Dix, found her out, to see Miss Spilcher, who was very pleasant; Miss Brauns was there. We then went to the Marine Bank[10], saw Mrs. Mantz, Mary Bier & cousin Barbara Bier. Spent the evening reading, etc.

Friday 10th Feb. Very clear & windy. Note from Mr. Perry to know if I would go to the Opera to-night. I answered, saying I would accept his invitation. Em & I were out nearly all morning and bought butter cooler, silver plated, also silver plated waiter, a pair of butter knives I intend to give Ellen Rohrback[11] and a mustard spoon I gave to Mrs. Sauerwein. After dinner Mary & I were out to shop and then dressed for night. Mr. Perry

---

[10]The Marine Bank was established in 1810. It was located on the corner of Gay and Second Streets during the period that Margaret visited it. Scharf, *Baltimore*, p. 461.

[11]On the Rohrback wedding see note 1, 1860.

1860

came soon after seven o'clock and I was ready pretty soon, and seated in a carriage, we were driven down to Front St. Theatre[12]. We saw the Opera of "La Traviatora" [sic] performed, and Miss Annie Milner did very well but had poor support from the rest of the company. When theatre was out Mr. Perry could not find the hack, so we had a walk up home with his shawl on [sic], found the hackman waiting. [He] had missed us. Mr. Perry just left [me] at the door. Wrote a letter home again.

Saturday [Feb.] 11th. Rather cloudy. About twelve o'clock Annie Derr called, then Lizzie Schell & Em Davis, & lastly Nellie Dean. She wants us to spend Monday evening there. Annie Derr left after all. Mr. & Mrs. Lefevre were here awhile to bid me good-bye. Mary, Em & I went to Market. E. & I were there a long time.

Sunday Feb. 12th. Very pleasant morning. Mrs. S., Mary, Em and I went to church. G. came down and came home with us. Mary and I went in afternoon to Lombard St. church to hear Rev. Dr. Wm. Artz & was very well pleased. G. went with us as far as the door. At night George S. & I went to hear Rev. Dr. Cummins; & was very much pleased. I do not know that I ever enjoyed a sermon more. Mary not very well so staid at home.

Monday Feb. 13th. Bright morning, but cloudy before night. About eleven o'clock Em and I started out, had some business down Market St. then at Davis' to see Lizzie Schell and Em Davis. Lizzie not in. [We] sat awhile and then went on out to Kate's and spent the day very pleasantly with Kate & Mr. Lefevre. About five I went down to cousin Will Dean's to tea. Miss Ella Coleman there to tea. After tea Misses Crozier & Guthrie of Ken[tucky] came, also Messrs. Neal, Thayer, & Sauerwein & Dr. Knowles. Spent this evening very pleasantly. Em called by for me about half-past ten and I soon got ready to leave. When we got home found Mary not so well, so Em and I were up for some time attending to her. Miss Fox and Miss Eliza McCowan had been to see us; sorry I did not see them.

Tuesday Feb. 14th. Very beautiful morning. Em & I went to market & saw Maria Trowbridge, Annie Derr, Mary Jennings and old Mrs. Rau, then went down street, and on our road met Mr. Frank Hersh. He is not so well as he has been, looks badly. [He] was accompanied by his brother Ed of York. We

---

[12]The Front Street Theatre was located on Front and Law Streets. It housed circuses and theatrical performances. Jennie Lind performed here in 1850. Scharf, *Baltimore*, pp. 689-690.

were weighed, 142. Found Kate had been here but [had] just left, so I commenced packing my trunk and was ready by three o'clock, dinner included, to go to the cars. Mrs. Sauerwein sent Mother a can of such excellent oysters. I found Wils Boyd & George Sifford on the cars and I was glad; [we] had a pleasant ride. As our carriage was not there, Mr. Boyd was kind enough to take charge of me. I went to Mr. Derr's[13] to leave some bundles and found Mr. Markel there, who insisted on my going to his house. I went over and found Mrs. Markel very pleasant, and after the fires [were out] we retired, and I enjoyed my sleep so much. [It] look[ed] very much for rain when I left B and was very dark.

Wednesday Feb. 15th. What was my great surprise to find it snowing when I got up, so I could not walk out home. John came in soon after dinner and he returned for the carriage and brought me home. All well & glad to see me. I sent Miss Sallie's things over.

Thursday Feb. 16th. Very pretty day. Went over in the morning and explained to Miss Sallie about her dress. After dinner went to town and gave Mrs. Shriner her samples. Mary Derr came while I was there and we had quite a long talk. She expects to leave for Phil'd. Saturday morning. Aunt S. & all well.

Friday Feb. 17th. Still clear but very windy. Went over after dinner and helped Miss Sallie with her dress as I had promised her. She had a nice supper.

Saturday Feb. 18th. Snowing & blowing all day. And I have a dreadfully swollen face and great pains in my jaw, suffered all night with it. Wrote to Mary.

Sunday Feb. 19th. Still suffer a great deal with my face.

Monday Feb. 20th. Pleasant day. Father & Mother went up to Aunt Mary Scholl's. Soon after ten o'clock, who should come but James Scholl[14] &

---

[13]Mr. George Derr had a dry goods and grocery store on the northeast corner of Market and South Streets. *Williams' Directory*, pp. 10, 45, 46.

[14]James Scholl was the son of Henry Scholl, Margaret's father's cousin. He lived in the New Market District. M. T. Hitselberger, *Bridge In Time*, p. 272. See also note 49, 1857.

1860

Andrew Hedges[15]. They remained till after tea and Father & Mother came home to tea. Had a note from Aunt M. Artz saying Mr. John & Miss Mary Cooper & herself would spend tomorrow [here] if agreeable with us. I wrote one in return saying they should come.

Tuesday Feb. 21st. Very pleasant day. About ten o'clock Aunt M. Artz, Mr. J & Miss M. Cooper arrived & spent the day. All very agreeable, and my face somewhat better.

[*There are no entries for February 22nd and 23rd.*]

Friday Feb. 24th. Pretty morning. Much better. Miss Sallie came over for me to finish helping her with cutting her dress. Staid till after tea.

Saturday Feb. 25th. Very pretty day. Letter from Lou Clippinger & Father's agricultural report by State Chemist from Mr. Johnson at Annapolis.

Sunday Feb. 26th. Very pretty day. Mother in church. After noon, Mrs. I. Howard came and sat awhile; soon Wils Boyd came & she left. Mr. B told me when he expected to be married. I gave him package from Mary. He looks very well.

Monday Feb. 27th. Lovely day. Mother in town all day.

Tuesday Feb. 28th. Very bright, beautiful day. Soon after nine o'clock Mr. John Cooper came, and about twelve o'clock Mr. Ball called for him, but both remained till after three o'clock. Immediately after they left I fixed [*sic*] and went to Aunt M. Artz, and sat awhile. Father went to town & returned home with me.

* * * * *

Friday March 2nd [1860]. Lovely day. About ten o'clock Aunt Jemima Scholl, Mrs. Clingan, & Annie came & spent the day so no go to town for me.

---

[15]Andrew Augustus Hedges was son of Margaret's Aunt Catherine Scholl Hedges. Information supplied by Frank Hedges Lewis. See Appendix I.

Saturday March 3rd. Cloudy morning and raining after dinner, so I did not get to town to see the Soldiers[16].

Sunday March 4th. Pleasant morning but by ten o'clock blew up very blustery. Mother and I went to town to church. I went to hear Dr. Zack, & Mother to the new Methodist Church[17]. Heard Uncle Adams was sick.

Monday March 5th. Still windy. Mother was in town, went past Mr. Boyd's to see how Aubury Jones was. Heard Uncle Adams was so extremely ill so I went down about two o'clock, but from what the Dr. says he is not so ill. Uncle Artz, Misses Keifer, Messrs. Jarboe & Cunningham were there. Miss Sallie at our house when I got home. Mother & I went in to hear Tom Kemp's lecture--"A Visit to Jerusalem." Was very much pleased.

Tuesday March 6th. Bright morning but cloudy after dinner. Annie Howard came down this morning & staid all night. Wils Boyd & Miss Lizzie Roelke are married at 3 o'clock today.

Wednesday March 7th. Rainy in showers all morning. Mother went down to Mrs. Abe Cashel's, and when Hal came for Annie H., I then went down to Mrs. C's too. Misses Anna and Mary Kiefer were there too.

Thursday March 8th. Damp day. I went out to Aunt M. Artz' and did some shopping, and stopped at Mrs. Markel's on my return and gave Ellen the butter knives I had bought in Balt. for her for a bridal present.

Friday March 9th. Cold, windy with slight showers of snow during the day. I was over to see Miss Sallie awhile in afternoon, & when I got home felt the pain in my jaw.

Saturday March 10th. Cold, blustery day. Mr. Boyd sent us word about Aubury Jones' death and that his funeral would be to-morrow afternoon at three o'clock. Still, or rather quite, a swollen face again.

---

[16] We have not established who the soldiers were, or why they were in Frederick. They may have been on their way to Harpers Ferry, where the arsenal had been guarded after John Brown's raid of October 16, 1859. See Engelbrecht, *Diary*, III, 53, 97.

[17] The new Methodist Church on East Church Street is now the location of a city parking deck.

1860

Sunday March 11th. Clear, and afternoon very pleasant. Mother gone to church and in afternoon Father & Mother went to the funeral.

Monday March 12th. Pleasant morning but quite windy in afternoon. Nevertheless I went as far as town with Mother, stopped awhile at Aunt Shriner's[18], who had so much to say about everything, beaux included. I went to Houcks, girls not home. Letter from Mary Sauerwein.

* * * * *

Wednesday March 14th. Went down to Uncle Adams' awhile in the morning. Found him better but cousin Abram said not out of danger. Cousin H. came Sunday morning.

Thursday March 15th. Lovely day. After dinner John took me into town and I stopped awhile at Ella Rohrback's, then at Houck's & Kunkel's awhile, & afterwards to see Mrs. G. Birely but did not find her home. Uncle Adams died this evening at five o'clock, quite unexpectedly as the Dr. considered him better.

Friday March 16th. Beautiful day. I went down to see Uncle Adams' family but found I could be of no assistance, so returned & found Miss Ann R. Keefer & Mrs. Ellen Jarboe there, who dined and then left about three o'clock. I walked peice ways home with them. Father sent John for the Dr. to see Joe, and he went to the post office & brought me a letter from Mr. John Cooper of Battle Creek, Mich. I remind him so much of his wife Isabella & fell in love, etc. & wants me to correspond with him.

Saturday March 17th. St. Patrick's day but not the kind of day usually attributed to it. A lovely day. Mother in town awhile. I racked off my currant wine this morning. [They] sent word about the funeral.

Sunday March 18th. Cloudy & damp all day. Father & Mother went to the funeral in after[noon], very large, 90 carriages or over.[19]

---

[18]This was Ed Shriner's stepmother who was living on the east side of East Street between Patrick and Church Streets. *Williams' Directory*, p. 36.

[19]Valentine Adams was buried in Mt. Olivet Cemetery. "It was about the largest funeral we ever had in our town. The number of vehicles was counted by several persons. Some say 88 others 98 and one said 104 and 25 or 30 horseback." Engelbrecht, *Diary*, III, 57.

1860

Monday March 19th. Raining all day. I wrote a letter to Mary Sauerwein & a note to Mary Derr in it. Dr. Moran to see Joe.

Tuesday March 20th. Joe still sick & Dr. to see him.

Wednesday March 21st. Very windy. Dr. out to see Joe and, as there was some things wanting, I went in town with him & brought them out, also told Rache to come home to see Joe.

Thursday March 22nd. Rather pleasant day. I went into town to see the Dr. & get some things, just rode in & came out again. I sat up tonight.

Friday March 23rd. Pleasant day. Dr. to see Joe twice today. Priest here at night.

Saturday March 24th. Dr. here again twice. I sat up again tonight. I was out to cousin Ed's to get some clothes for Joe. Stopped a little while at Aunt Margaret's, saw Mrs. Keyser's likeness.

Sunday March 25th. Lovely day. Good many darkies here, also Mrs. P. Fout in afternoon, & after tea Mr. Gallion and Miss Sallie. Dr. here again twice. I think Joe [very] ill.

Monday March 26th. Pretty day. Dr. twice again. I sat up tonight.

Tuesday March 27th. Windy day. I lay down after dinner. Priest here, also Georgia & Tillie Houck for awhile. I slept tonight. Dr. [here] twice.

Wednesday March 28th. Very pretty day. Dr. thought Joe better & that he would improve, but I know this evening [I] did not think him as well. I sat up till after two o'clock.

Thursday March 29th. Pretty day. Dr. out early and pronounced Joe's disease congestion of the lungs. At night he told me there was no hope for him. His father, brother John were here. I was up till 4 o'clock.

Friday March 30th. Lovely day. Dr. out about or after nine. Told us there was no hope for him and he died just about twelve. John took me to Aunt M. Artz to tell of the funeral. At night kitchen full of darkies, spent the evening in singing & praying. Priest to see Joe in morning.

1860

Saturday March 31st. Joe was taken away for burial at about 2 o'clock. Many darkies & Mother & Mrs. Gallion went in to the funeral.

Sunday April 1st [1860]. Rache went to town to stay. Mother & I went to church & heard an excellent sermon from Rev. T. Kemp. It was pleasant in morning, but at noon when we came home very windy and disagreeable. Mr. Claggett came about four o'clock & sat till about eleven. He had lots to say; Mother entertained him a good deal as my face pained me & swelled again.

* * * * *

Wednesday April 4th. Pretty morning but showery before night; but nevertheless I was in the front yard showing John about fixing up the beds.

Thursday April 5th. Very pretty day. John helped me awhile and then went to Gallions to help with [bee] hives. I had a nice letter from Mary Derr & Mag Shriner. Mother & I went over & spent the afternoon at Mrs. I. Howard's. Mrs. H. not home but [we] staid with Marion. Mrs. H. came home before we left.

* * * * *

Saturday April 7th. Very pretty day. Father & I were in town. I shopped some & was at Houck's and Mrs. Markel's a little while. In afternoon helped Mother to finish John's coat.

* * * * *

Easter Monday [April] 9th. Showery & sunshine by turns all day. Had dinner about eleven & Mother & I started. We left Mother at Aunt Margaret's and then went to cousin Ed's and got Joe's clothes & from there to Mr. Derr's. John & Annie Derr of Balt. were there. I started home about five o'clock, stopped for Mother. Rained quite hard.

* * * * *

Thursday April 12th. Lovely day. Father & I went to town quite early. I was at Aunt Shriner's & Mrs. Reese's to meet Alice Derr, but she was in yesterday. I then was at Aunt C. Scholl's & Uncle Dennis, could not get in; and then at Ellen Rohrback's awhile; then came home in afternoon. Mother

1860

& I were at Smith's, Boyd's, Cooper's, & old Mrs. Bantz's. Mrs. Wils [B.] not home; only saw Annie Cooper, Mary MacPherson.

Friday April 13th. Quite windy; at home all day. My eyes hurt me very much.

Saturday April 14th. Quite bright but very windy day. I wrote a hurried letter to Lou Clippinger.

Sunday April 15th. Beautiful bright day but air very chilly. Mother & I were in to church, heard an excellent sermon from Dr. Zack. After church had a talk with Alice Derr. To-morrow we are to meet. Afternoon I went over to see Miss Sallie about four o'clock. Mr. Gallion came but Miss S. had told me of the dancing lessons, etc.

Monday April 16th. Showery all morning & cloudy all afternoon. Miss Sallie over awhile in afternoon. I wrote to Mag Shriner & Mary Derr in Phil'd., also to Mr. John Cooper of Michigan. Mother in town instead of me; too rainy, did not suppose Alice would be in to-day.

Tuesday April 17th. Very warm day. Father went to Mr. Dean's sale and I went with him as far as town. Went to Mrs. Reese's, found Alice Derr there but not done her dinner so went to Mrs. Winchester and sat an hour or so with Mr. & Mrs. Winchester. Then Alice and I went down to Dr. T. H. Schaeffer to have her teeth attended to. Afterwards I went to Kunkel's. Met Mrs. Jake Kunkel, Mrs. Wilson, & Mrs. Dr. Schaff there.

Wednesday April 18th. Very busy all day in Front Yard, and while we were at tea Mr. E. G. Claggett arrived and spent the evening. I beat him 5 out of 8 games of Draughts[20]. He plays well though.

Thursday April 19th. I was busy in yard till nearly noon. After dinner was at Miss Sallie's awhile. Much cooler.

Friday April 20th. Appearance of rain and some showers; never-theless Mother & I started for Aunt Mary Scholl['s], stopped awhile at Aunt M. Artz's, spent the day very pleasantly at Aunt M's. Was at Davy's store awhile in afternoon.

---

[20]Draughts is another name for checkers. *Webster's Dictionary*.

1860

Saturday April 21st. Quite, indeed very, warm. Jemmy Houck brought me the basket this morning and a letter & package from Mary Sauerwein, also a message from Lizzie about some Chrysan-themums. After dinner I went to town with Father and went to see Julia Derr & baby boy, also Aunt C[ristina] Scholl, who had burnt herself badly slaking lime[21]. [I also saw] Amanda Hedges and Houcks who had a good deal of news about Balt. & our friends.

* * * * *

Monday April 23rd. Rather cloudy all day. Mother & I went to town after dinner and shopped; then was to see Aunt C. Scholl; she seems better. When at Mrs. Markel's, [she] would have us come in, so stopped a little while, then walked home.

Tuesday April 24th. Bright but quite windy. I went to town with Father, was to see about my bonnet, also at Aunt M. Scholl's, Mrs. Salmon's, Aunt Jemima Scholl's, and then came up street to come out with Father.

Wednesday April 25th. Quite windy but clear after dinner. I was over at Miss Sallie's awhile this morning; had a letter from Lou Clippinger, speaking of a wedding I am to be invited to. Wonder who. Wrote to Mary Sauerwein, got my bonnet.

Thursday April 26th. Quite a pleasant day. John took me out to aunt M. Artz's awhile this morning. Busy sewing after dinner; got my gaiters at last.

Friday April 27th. Right pleasant day. Finished "Harriet's Hears."

Saturday April 28th. Rained in showers during the afternoon; nevertheless, Father & I were in town on business. Stopped at P. O.; letter from Mr. J. Cooper; [he had] not received my other yet. Also a note from Alice Derr to meet her yesterday.

Sunday April 29th. Quite a pleasant day. Mother & I went to church, heard an excellent sermon from Dr. Zack. Alice Derr came home with [me], had

---

[21]One of the many uses of slaked lime, made by mixing calcium oxide with water, is the manufacture of plaster and whitewash. This slaking process can produce great heat. *The New Columbia Encyclopedia*; *Webster's Dictionary.*

quite a talk in afternoon. Took a walk after tea. Cousin Ed S. gone to Phil. to see Mag S[hriner].

Monday April 30th. Much warmer and very bright. Father took Alice & me to town after breakfast. Stopped at Mrs. Lewis'[22] to have my bonnet fixed, and then at Houck's, and then to see Kate Davis awhile. Met Kate Jacobs & Tilly H. there, then came down street to meet Father & came out home.

Tuesday May 1st [1860]. Much cooler and cloudy all day. I planted my "Pot Roses" out, also a large Heart's Ease & saved flower seeds that I had. Had nice long letters from Mag Shriner & Mary Sauerwein; in the latter [a] yd. of lace enclosed for Marion Howard.

Wednesday May 2nd. Raining in showers during the day; not very well.

Thursday May 3rd. Rather gloomy morning but cleared off pretty till evening. Nearly four o'clock Annie and Jane Ogle came and staid till after early tea.

* * * * *

Sunday May 6th. Very delightful day. Mother went to church. Miss Sallie came over about eleven and remained till nearly four. I walked home with her for a walk. Mr. Claggett came about seven o'clock and remained till nine o'clock.

Monday May 7th. Lovely morning. I wrote to Lou Clip. (Much later after dinner Mother & I went over and spent the afternoon at Mrs. E[dward] Howard's. All very pleasant and very glad to see us.)

* * * * *

Wednesday May 9th. Notwithstanding the showers of rain, Father started to Balt. Mr. Gallion stopped on his way from town and asked me to accept of a little "White [*illegible*]" he had. I sent for it. Miss Sallie over awhile at night.

Thursday May 10th. Still rained in showers till evening, when there was a very heavy gust. Father walked out home, contrary to our expectations.

---

[22]Mrs. Columbia E. Lewis had a millinery shop on the west side of Market Street between Second and Third Streets. *Williams' Directory*, p. 24.

1860

Friday May 11th. Still raining, cloudy day. John in town and brought from P. O. an invitation to Hannah Lewis's marriage next Tuesday morning.

* * * * *

Sunday May 13th. Very pleasant morning, but I feared it might rain, so did not go in. I went over to see Miss Sallie & was there during the showers. She came over after tea & sat a while, brought plants.

Monday May 14th. Quite warm but sun shiny. After dinner Mother & I went over and spent the afternoon at Mrs. E Howard's. All very pleasant and very glad to see us. Marion Howard had been to our house while I was away; sent again at night for her lace.

Tuesday May 15th. Some appearance of rain but changeable all morning. Went over to see Hannah Lewis married to Mr. G. W. M. Crook. They were married about 12 o'clock; good many persons there and every thing passed off well. I had pleasant time. Saw Jem Gambrill there, first time I talked with him for about 3 years. He was very clever & attentive.

Wednesday May 16th. Very warm day. Note from Alice Derr, [saying] she would meet me anytime. Also note from G. Houck saying she would come out if I came in. Did not go to Miss Keefer's as intended. /Alice Derr here today to tea./

Thursday May 17th. Ascension Day. Cloudy all day. After dinner Mother & I walked down & spent the afternoon with Miss Keefer's very pleasantly.

Friday May 18th. Rather cloudy and appearance of rain. Kate Lefevre's baby <u>boy</u> <u>born</u> <u>today</u>.

Saturday May 19th. Warm with a heavy gust in afternoon. Notes to & from Annie Howard. Letter, nice long one, from Mary Derr yesterday. Cleaned up my room.

Sunday May 20th. Very pleasant morning. Mother & I went into town. We had no church, so I went with Mary Kunkel to Presbyterian church, and Mother with Mrs. Derr to Methodist. Mrs. D & Mother staid long time so [I] had to wait a long time at Hotel. Sent a note to G. Houck.

1860

Monday May 21st. Quite warm. I went in to fulfill my engagement with Alice Derr. Went first to Dr. Schaeffer who was engaged, so went to see Aunt Jemima Scholl awhile, and then returned and had Alice's tooth filled, and I soon came home. After dinner I went over to spend the afternoon with Fannie Adams[23]. Met Mr. & Mrs. Brown & two children. Mrs. Adams[24] was apparently very polite till after tea, when we walked in the garden and she attacked me in a very unbecoming and unladylike manner about things which she said she had heard, and farther evidenced her poor judgement & bad training by giving as her authority black Jim, or rather Fannie said that was her authority. She was very Harsh and excited, but I had to overlook it as I fear either her mind is affected or her conscience upbraids her. I feel sorry for the poor unfortunate creature whom I have so often heard speak of others' unhappiness. I fear she has no Christian's faith to support her in her real & imaginary afflictions. She had [a] great deal to say of me & my Mother, and her family, which I suppose is nothing to brag of.

Tuesday [May] 22nd. Appearance of rain all day, but nevertheless, accepted Mrs. I. Howard's invitation for this afternoon and went over to her house and took [tea] with the family and Miss A. & M. Keefer. Mr. John Lewis was here when we returned, and sat till about ten o'clock.

Wednesday [May] 23rd. Quite warm. Home all day. Old Mr. Cline here after tea.

Thursday [May] 24th. Quite a pleasant morning. I went into town, was at Houcks' awhile. Georgia, Lizzie & Mrs. Jacobs & Mrs. Houck [have] gone to Washington. Sue Hunt [was] there and I walked part way down street with Em & her. Was at Ellen Brunner's awhile. Letter of 8 pages of Mr. John Cooper. Mr. & Mrs. Wils Boyd & Sue Jones here.

Friday May 25th. Rather cloudy, & I was uncertain whether I should go to Mr. Winchester's May party, but finally decided to go. Stopped for Mrs. B. F. Winchester but she was gone. Left Mother to spend day at Aunt M. Artz's.

---

[23]Fannie Adams was the youngest daughter of Valentine Adams (see note 32, 1851). She lived until 1904. Adams-Nelson Family Bible.

[24]Mrs. Sarah Adams was the second wife of Valentine Adams (see note 30, 1851). Holdcraft (*Names in Stone*, p. 65) states that she was not buried with her husband and his first wife Sybilla in Mt. Olivet Cemetery. In the Adams-Nelson Family Bible is an entry: "Sarah Elizabeth Adams died Nov. 10th, 1898, aged 89 years, 2 months and 29 days."

1860

I stopped for Alice Derr, & Eugene accompanied us over. Spent the day pleasantly enough; came home about Sundown.

Saturday [May] 26th. Pleasant morning but about [sic] a <u>Gust</u> seemed to be rising, which gave vent in torrents of rain about two o'clock & severe thunder & lightning. Father & I had gone to town & I went no farther up street than Mrs. Markel's, as it rained so hard & was too damp. Letter from Lou Clippinger. Wrote note to Mary Derr & Mag S.

Sunday May 27th. Clear morning but cloudy in afternoon. I went into town to church, had communion today; five joined by confirmation today.

Monday May 28th. Quite a pleasant day. In afternoon I was awakened from my nap by the arrival of Mr. James Cooper, Miss Mary H. Cooper & Miss Cooper [sic], who made quite a call and were very pleasant.

* * * * *

Thursday May 31st. Weather quite warm & changeable. I wrote to Mary Sauerwein and went in and gave it & the daguerreotype of Philip to cousin Ed to take to Mary. Also wrote to Lou Clippinger and sent a paper to Mr. Frank Hersh. I did some shopping and was to see Kunkels, had a long talk there with the girls. Stopped few minutes with Ellen Rohrback and then rode out home. Hail storm this afternoon and at night.

Friday June 1st [1860]. Father's birthday.

Saturday June 2nd. Busy all morning and part of afternoon. Mrs. Taylor & Mrs. I. Howard & Clara H. here to tea; heard of Mrs. John Markel's death.

Sunday June 3rd. Not very clear & showers in afternoon. Ellen & Mr. Rohrback came out with me from church, remained till after tea, when I took them into town again.

Monday June 4th. Quite warm. I had a very nice letter of Mag Shriner and was busy in afternoon.

Tuesday June 5th. Very much appearance of rain. Ellen Kemp & Joe Noonan married this A.M.

Wednesday June 6th. Quite pleasant. John took me into town after dinner and I was to see Annie Bentz Keefer, & Aunt C. Scholl, and then stopped to tea at M. Houck's and Georgia & I walked out together. Cousin Harry Smith here today.

* * * * *

Friday June 8th. Very delightful day. John took Georgia & I up to spend the day at Dr. Claggett's[25]. Everything passed off pleasantly. Quite a storm of wind in evening but little or no rain. Rob Claggett came to town with us. When I got home found a letter from Mr. Frank Hersh awaiting me, apprising me of his approaching marriage and his desire that I should be present. Quite gratifying.

Saturday June 9th. Very much cooler. G[eorgie] & I were most of the day in the house. I went in with her about five o'clock, did some shopping and returned, found Mr. Tom Claggett here, who sat till nearly nine o'clock. /Mag Shriner & Mary Derr came home today./

Sunday June 10th. Quite pleasant day. Mother & I were in to church. Dr. Zack preached from Matthew 22nd, 42. "What think ye of Christ." In afternoon was over to see Miss Sallie awhile; and Lychurgus Hedges & John E. Gittinger were here but did not get in. Mr. Andrew Gregg & Miss Rose Morris of Balt. married today.

Monday June 11th. Somewhat warmer in afternoon. I went in for Kate Davis & Sue Ebert, & we went out to call to see Lizzie Schell. Lizzie very pleasant. I then came and brought Father out home.

Tuesday June 12th. Warmer again. I rode into town on horseback and stopped at Ellen Rohrback's awhile, then shopped some, and afterwards was at Mrs. Lewis Markel's for an hour or so, and then rode out home, rather warm & fatiguing.

Wednesday June 13th. Very pretty day. Father & Mother gone to spend the day at Mrs. Duderar's. Mr. Abe Shriner sent me some cherries by them.

---

[25]Dr. Claggett lived near Petersville. Hitselberger, *Bridge in Time*, p. 396.

1860

Thursday June 14th. Kate Davis, Lou Ebert, Mr. & Mrs. Steins, Mrs. Schley and children [were] out.

Friday June 15th. Note from Mrs. I. Howard & wrote one in return. Aunt Liz Brunner, Charlie and Annie Keefer & baby John & Mary spent the day here.

Saturday June 16th. [I] wrote & sent Mr. F. Hersh pair of slippers.

Sunday June 17th. Very pleasant. Mother & I were in to church and heard a sermon from Dr. Luich on Observance of the Sabbath Day. In afternoon went out to Aunt M. Artz['s] and sat an hour or two.

Monday June 18th. Soon after breakfast Father said if we wanted [he] had better go & get the vinegar [*illegible*]. Mother & I went over to Miss Ogle's and spent the day. Called for Aunt M. Artz but she could not well go along. All very pleasant and the day passed off pleasantly.

Tuesday June 19th. Quite warm with showers in afternoon. After an early dinner John took me out to see Mary Derr & she went with me and took tea with Mag Shriner. Houcks came out just before we left but only made a call. I stopped at Aunt M. Artz', brought Miss Mary H. Cooper into town with me. And Father came out home with me.

Wednesday June 20th. Bright day. Mr. Frank Hersh and Miss Eliza A. McClelland were married today in Emmanuel Church. Shower & sunshine together. I went into town late, called to see Mrs. Kate Davis & L. Eberts and then went out to call on Mrs. Hannah Crook, caught in the showers. Sent John to Aunt C. Scholl for the flowers & she sent them.

* * * * *

Friday June 22nd. Mother in town morning & about four o'clock I went to Aunt M. Artz' to get cherries, and also brought Vic[torine] home with me.

Saturday June 23rd. Very pretty day. Whitewashed the Parlor & put up the curtains, etc.

Sunday June 24th. Pretty day. I staid home with Vic. Mother went to church. After church Mother & Vic went to [see] Miss Sallie [a] little while.

1860

Monday June 25th. Bright day. Mother took Vic home in afternoon & got some cherries.

Tuesday June 26th. Quite warm; indeed, very. I went into town about ten o'clock and did some shopping, then went up and spent the day very pleasantly with Ellen Rohrback. After tea we went to see Madam Pearson & Miss Wright at the Seminary and also to see Sue Hunt. [I] had cards of <u>Mr. & Mrs. Frank Hersh & Eliza A. McClelland</u>. After I came down street John came for me, & Ellen & Mr. R. rode as far as the cemetery on my ride home. Mr. Lewis and his daughter Mrs. Hannah Crook were here & sat couple hours; and of all the talk Old Lewis heads all.

* * * * *

Thursday June 28th. Exceedingly warm. Father took me into town. shopped a little, then at Houck's long time, then to see Miss Mary Kunkle. Called at Bantz' but could make no one hear. Found Jean Ogle here when I got home. Picked currants in evening.

Friday June 29th. Sent Jane into town with some currants for Kate Bantz. When Mother came home had letter from Mary Sauerwein.

Saturday June 30th. Made currant jelly before breakfast. Rained little but cleared off warm. Father & I went to town. I shopped a little, then went to Kunkle's for couple of hours.

* * * * *

Monday [July 2, 1860]. Cloudy early, then clear. Mother & I were in town to shop and then home. <u>Our Bell</u> [is] hung at last. Showery all afternoon from 2 1/2 o'clock. Note from Hannah Crook today. [I was] surprised.

* * * * *

Thursday [July] 5th. Quite cool day. I rode to town on horseback, was to see Lou Ebert and then at Houcks', and then Georgia, Emma, Mag Shriner, & I went to Mr. Winchester's Commencement and returned to Houcks' to dinner. Emma Claggett there also to dine. After tea Georgia and I walked down with Mag Shriner to Uncle Lewis Scholl's. Stopped at Kunkel's awhile at night. George & Georgia H. & myself went to the Seminary to exercises. Pleasant time.

1860

Friday July 6th. Very pleasant day, indeed quite cool. Soon after breakfast G. Houck went with me to Kunkle's & Mary & I walked out home. We were in the house till evening.

Saturday July 7th. My birthday. Not very well. About five o'clock, Mary & I walked over to see the Reaper, and were in to see Miss Sallie a little while. Mary Brunner sent me <u>nice pears</u> by Father & Mother. Cards from [New] Oxford of Mr. & Mrs. F. Hersh.

Sunday July 8th. Very pleasant day. I went [to town] early on account of Mary K., who went home. Went to church with the girls and then came home after.

Monday July 9th. Pleasant day. I was busy all day. About 6 1/2 o'clock cousin Harry Smith came and we started for a ride; and I thought of staying, so returned to change my dress, and we went into town. I staid with Kunkel's. Cousin H. came down about 9 o'clock, we all went to Houcks' to make a call. Cousin H. sat till about 11 o'clock.

Tuesday July 10th. Quite warm. Nellie & I were up street in the morning. Cousin H. came about noon &, according to appointment, we went to the Distribution of Premiums at Catholic School[26]. Harry staid to dinner & left for Phil. I was down at Clingans' for couple of hours in afternoon. Mother came and I walked home with her after tea.

Wednesday July 11th. Quite warm. Cousin Ed & Mag Shriner were here to tea.

Thursday July 12th. Quite warm morning. After dinner cooler. I saw old Mrs. Gallion go through the yard, so went over and saw her & her daughter Mary; and as it rained had to stay to tea, and Mr. George brought me home in his buggy and it still rained.

Friday July 13th. Pretty morning. About ten o'clock John took me to town and I called to see Jane Ramsburg & Ginny Brengle, had very pleasant visit; after shopping some came out home.

---

[26]Classes at St. John's Literary Institute began in 1829 in a building on East Second Street almost where the present school continues to exist. Scharf, *Western Maryland*, I, 521.

1860

* * * * *

Monday July 16th. Very warm day. I [was] in town to shop and was to see Lou Ebert about going up to Piedmont[27]. She is to let me know.

Tuesday July 17th. Still quite [warm]. Father & Mother took [an] early ride. Mr. G. Harry Davis out to see [me] awhile about coming to Piedmont. [He] was very anxious I should go & will do all for me to enjoy myself. In afternoon, Mother & I went over and spent the afternoon at Mrs. I. Howard's; enjoyed it.

Wednesday July 18th. Very warm. Wrote a note yesterday and had one today in reply from Cousin Ed. Sewing when not too warm. After tea Mr. & Mrs. Geo. Birely were out & sat short time; had little Carrie Hane with them. Wrote to Mary Sauerwein.

* * * * *

Friday July 20th. Warmest day of the season. A very bright Meteor visible between 9 and 10 o'clock.[28] Mr. Perry out a short time about dusk to pay a call. He was very agreeable and will take tea here on Sunday.

* * * * *

Sunday July 22nd. Much cooler. I went into church and heard Rev. Tom Kemp preach an excellent sermon. After church Mary & Alice Derr went with me a little while to old Mrs. Bantz'. Sis Ebert not very well. Slight shower & stormy about 3 o'clock but cleared off before five, when Mr. Ben Perry made his appearance and remained to tea. [He] left soon after. Very much the appearance of rain and did rain after night. Mr. P leaves to-morrow for Pied[mont].

---

[27]Margaret was planning to visit her friend Kate Bantz Davis at her home in Piedmont which was then in Virginia (now West Virginia). It is located in the mountains, on the north branch of the Potomac across the river from Western Port, Maryland. It was a station on the B&O Railroad.

[28]Engelbrecht saw the meteor at about 1/2 past 9 o'clock. He said it passed over New York to the southeast and was very brilliant and large. Engelbrecht, *Diary*, III, 69.

1860

Monday July 23rd. Raining in showers till about 9 o'clock. Immediately after dinner shopped a little in town & was to see Rev. Mr. & Mrs. Lefevre but they had not arrived at their boarding house as yet. Had such a nice letter of Mary Sauerwein.

Tuesday July 24th. Still so cool of nights. Old Mrs. Bantz & Lou Ebert were out this morning and sat an hour or so. When Mother came [she] brought me a very nice letter from Mr. Geo. Sauerwein, on business, of course; also a circular from Mr. H. Winchester. Wrote a letter to Lou Clippinger did not owe her one but felt like writing to her.

PIEDMONT

Wednesday July 25th. Quite a warm day. Was busy; about ten o'clock, Mag Shriner & Rev. Mr. & Mrs. J. A. LeFevre, nurse & child came, and remained till about three o'clock. Mr. LeFevre took me into town to do some shopping. After they left I commenced to pack & was ready & into town till quarter of 6 o'clock. Mrs. Ebert was at the cars. Met Mr. Davis at Bridge[29] and proceeded with him to Piedmont, had very pleasant ride. Met Miss Hoffman of Harpers Ferry on the cars & had a long talk with her about her sister Mrs. A. Hersh. We arrived at P. about 10 o'clock and all the family up to see us and a very hearty welcome we received.

Thursday July 26th, 1860. I woke to breakfast about 7 1/2 o'clock. Lovely morning & scenery so grand. Was introduced to Mr. Vance, so pleasant but [I] thought him quite bashful. Kate sick with headache. Was at store couple of times. Mr. D[avis] & Kate took a ride on horseback in evening. We felt too tired. Mr. Davis gone to Parkersburg in the Express train. We slept in afternoon. Mrs. Wm. Davis & Miss Mattie Tillson were [in] to see us. Kate better & down to tea. I forgot to speak of Mr. John T. Vance, the gentleman who takes his meals at Kate's.

Friday July 27th. Pleasant day. Missed Mr. Davis. [I] took a walk this morning. Was at Mrs. Wm. Davis'. Mrs. Anderson here a little while. [We were] at Mr. Vance's store and from there to the depot to meet old Mrs.

---

[29]This bridge was over the Monocacy River at Frederick Junction, where connections were made with the main line of the B&O Railroad. Mr. Davis, Kate's husband, worked for the railroad. (See July 26 and 29, *et passim*.) The Frederick travelers were Margaret Scholl and Lou ("Sis") Ebert.

Davis. Kate D., Mrs. Wm. Davis, and I were together. Mr. V. gone to Hudson. Mr. Davis returned tonight.

Saturday July 28th. Nice day. Took a walk before breakfast over into Westernport[30]. Were up at Mrs. Davis' awhile. Mr. Vance came up for us to tell us he was home and asked us to go through the machine shops. Lost my Cameo pin but found it again. Sis[31] shopped some, I with her. [We] did some blackberries for Kate. Wrote a letter home. Mr. Davis and I took a ride before tea; after tea Kate, Sis & Mrs. D. took a ride, and while they were gone I took charge. Mr. Davis returned at night. Mrs. Wm. Davis, Miss Rogers, Mattie Tillson, and children of neighborhood there. Mr. Vance in after tea an hour.

Sunday July 29th. Appearance of rain but cleared off. Messrs. Davis & Vance went to church with us, but Mr. D. after leaving us went to Westernport. Brother Forest preached. Mr. V. came back in afternoon for us to walk, also old Mrs. Davis, but we did not care to go. Dr. & Mrs. Gerstelle[32] & daughter Josey to see us for an hour or so. At night, Mr. Vance invited us to go to church in Westernport, but it had so much the appearance of rain we concluded not to go. Messrs. D. & V. went.

Monday July 30th. Quite warm. About six o'clock Kate, Mr. Vance & I started to take a ride on horseback and went about five miles going & returning on the New Creek road; enjoyed it very much. Mr. Davis & Sis went after tea by moonlight till 9 o'clock. Kate & I went to Mrs. Wm. Davis[']. Several of the young ladies were on the pavement jumping the rope and I enjoyed it too, but Mr. Vance came up suddenly and joined me so I had no further opportunity of jumping the rope. Nice letter of Frank H.

---

[30]Westernport, Maryland got its name as it was the westernmost depot for portage across the Potomac River from the Cumberland River Railroad to the B&O. Hazel Groves Hansrote, *Allegany County Scrapbook* and *Rail Track in Alleghany County, MD*, Book I (Preservation Society of Allegheny County, Cumberland, MD, 1980), pp. 3, 68.

[31]During most of her trip account, the diarist refers to Lou Ebert as "Sis." The latter continued her Piedmont visit after Margaret went home. See August 25, 1860.

[32]Dr. Gerstell was the first resident physician in the Westernport District. James W. Thomas and T. J. C. Williams, *History of Allegany County, MD* (Baltimore, MD, 1969 reprint), p. 487.

1860

PIEDMONT/LANACONING

Tuesday July 31st. Bright early in the morning. [I] took a walk. Mrs. Anderson & Mrs. Miller were to see us, and it rained slightly while they were here, so sat some time. Clear in afternoon. Old Mrs. Davis down; also Mr. G. N. Smith (a cousin of Mr. D.'s from Elkridge, Md.); and very soon Mr. & Mrs. Davis, Kate & Hallie, Messrs. Vance & Smith, Sis & myself got on the car and went to Lanaconing Mines. The scenery on the road is very fine but at the village it is grand, and oh! I enjoyed it so much. The Superintend[ents] have fine houses and the miners very pretty neat cottages, and they ought all to be happy. They have a very pretty church and George's Creek runs around and through it, & they have a bridge to make it still more romantic. I felt so happy. We walked all around & then took a seat to wait till all were ready to return. We came down in a car but at great speed <u>without steam</u>. Mr. Smith remained to tea and sat the evening, also Mr. Carl Getty. Do not know whether Mr. Vance there or not.[33] Wrote a letter to Mary E. Sauerwein.

PIEDMONT

Wednesday August 1st [1860]. Pretty day. Sis & I walked before breakfast. [I was] not very well till after dinner. After tea, Mr. Vance brought me a letter from Lou Clippinger, such a nice long one, 8 pages. And according to previous engagement Mr. Vance came in accompanied by Mr. Smith, and according to engagement, Mr. Vance & I, Mr. S. & Sis walked over to the Chalybeate Spring[34] in Westernport, nice walk, then went up street, and Mrs. Anderson would have us stop there awhile. Mr. & Mrs. Randall were there. We sat about an hour and then had a glorious walk home by moonlight. Gentlemen sat till after ten o'clock. Kate & Mr. Davis took a ride on horseback.

Thursday August 2nd. Bright, pleasant morning. Sis & I went over to the Spring before breakfast. Old Mrs. Davis, Mrs. Wm. Davis, Kate, Randall, & Miss Lizzie McMahon all here this morning. Messrs. Vance & Smith here at night. Letter from Mother.

---

[33]Here is an indication that Margaret was writing some of her diary notes later than the actual date. See August 28, 1860.

[34]Chalybeate Spring is a mineral spring containing iron. *Webster's Dictionary*.

PIEDMONT/GRAFTON

Friday August 3rd. Appearance of rain. Nevertheless, Mr. Davis & Hallie, Sis & I started for Grafton[35] on the Cars. [We] took the last seat and enjoyed the ride & Scenery very much. Cheat River is grand. Messrs. Davis & Smith saw us off, & Mr. Tommy Davis met us at Grafton, we went into the Hotel, and after being in our room we went to dinner. After dinner awhile we went up to Davis & Co.'s store and spent most of the afternoon there. I wrote a letter to Mag Shriner. Was introduced to Mr. Joel White, formerly from Piedmont. I liked him very much, but [he] has almost too much of a smile. Mr. Tommy Davis seems very pleasant but no pretensions to good looks, but what matters that? Mr. Tommy D. took a long walk with us across the bridge and we had a fine view of Grafton, and I enjoyed it so much. We were all round the town, too. Started home about 20 min. of 10 o'clock; both of the gents were to see us off. Had a pleasant ride home; came down with Capt. Dukehart, who was very pleasant. I wrote a letter to Mag Shriner up there, and when I got home found one waiting me from Mary E. S., wanting me to come on & go and see the "Great Eastern"[36] next week.

PIEDMONT

Saturday August 4th. Very warm. [I was] not at all well to-day. Wrote a letter to Mary E. S. saying I would not be down to go see the "Great Eastern." Old Mrs. Davis down to see us. Mr. Smith to see us. Mr. Davis & Sis took a ride on horseback. Rained at night. We were up at Mrs. Davis' in the evening. I have been learning to play chess and am fond of it.

---

[35]Grafton, west of Piedmont, sprang up as a village when the B&O Railroad was completed in 1856. It was named as a "graftin on point" for the many branch lines to the mines, etc., that joined the main line. *West Virginia, A Guide to the Mountain State* (NY, 1941), p. 510.

[36]The "Great Eastern," one of the earliest of the iron steamships built for the trans-Atlantic trade, had a screw propeller rather than a paddlewheel. It was launched in Great Britain in 1858. *The New Columbia Encyclopedia*, "Steamships."

1860

Sunday August 5th, 1860. Rained in showers, but about ten o'clock thought it would clear, so Sis, Mr. Vance & I started for Catholic Church and were soon joined by Mr. Smith, who took Sis. We soon all were turned back and at eleven we started to Presbyterian Church and, the Minister not being there, Mr. Moore made a few remarks, prayed & sang and we were home soon after eleven o'clock. It is a very pretty neat little church, so clean & nice. Mr. Vance, nice fellow, Mr. Smith, remained to dinner and some time after, and were to return to walk but they were too late. Mr. & Mrs. Davis, Katie & Hallie, Sis & I all went over to Westernport for a walk, and talked awhile with Mrs. Miller & then went to Mrs. Anderson's and stopped awhile. Mrs. Templeson there. Returned about sundown. Appearance of rain but there was none. Mr. & Mrs. Wm. Davis down awhile. Mr. Smith went with me to church, Kate & Mrs. Davis also. Mr. D. & Sis remained at home. I don't know, but think we all took a walk late at night. Mr. D. gone again.

Monday August 6th. Quite warm. I do not remember today, but am sure Mr. Smith was here at night and that he remained very late and closed the shutters for us. He is a nice, clean fellow. Mr. D. returned tonight.

Tuesday August 7th. Very warm. Mr. Smith called so early. We of course were at Mrs. D['s] and they [were] at our house and no doubt at the store, as it was usual to do so. Mr. Vance asked one of us to ride this evening, so Sis accepted. After tea Kate, Sis & I went over to Westernport to pay some visits (I remember Mr. V. & I had a game of something), and were at Mrs. Miller's, found no one in, and then went on to Mrs. Dr. Gerstelle's and sat the evening. Mrs. Anderson there. Messrs. Anderson & Davis & Vance soon came, and about half-past nine o'clock we started home. Mr. Vance with me. He sat till half-past ten, then left us to sleep, he said; but about twelve o'clock he & Mr. Smith & 10 others returned and gave us a serenade. They sang "Hard times no more," "Blue Bells of Scotland," and another, and played several instrumental pieces. I bumped my mouth and eye dreadfully, but by applying the Arnica [was] soon well, and we retired again about 1 o'clock. It was very kind of our friends. We expected to have gone to the mines but heard there was a man killed, so did not go. Mr. D. wanted me to ride on horseback with him but [I] did not feel well enough.

PIEDMONT/FRANKLIN MINES

Wednesday August 8th. Bright very early, but cloudy afterwards. About 9 o'clock Messrs. Vance & Smith, Kate Davis & I started for Kerr's Franklin

Mines[37]. Kate & I walked the bridge, Messrs. Davis & Vance accompanying us. On the opposite side we had Messrs. Smith & Bice & Dr. Gerstelle as assistants in mounting our horses. Mr. V. with me, and I rode <u>Harmerson's race horse</u> but don't think it will beat. Mr. Kerr met us when we arrived at the mouth of the mines, and the Gents & I dismounted and Mr. Kerr accompanied us through the mines, and I felt very grateful for their kind attention. I never had a correct idea of a mine. I got my dress very much soiled, but how could it be other ways among so much stove, coal and slough [*sic*] some times. When we came [out] Mr. V.'s lamp gave out. It had rained some, and Mr. Kerr would have us [go] to the house short distance off. Were introduced to his wife, a nice, pleasant lady. We were treated to lemonade & cake & think the gents enjoyed something stronger. Mr. K. [has an] excellent Piano. I tried to play but could finish nothing or "something of the sort." About five o'clock Mr. Davis received a dispatch from Dr. Hammond saying he & Mary Jane & two children would be down in evening train. So Kate fixed up and we went over to the depot to meet them. Mr. Vance went with us, and from there to P. O. After tea we were over at Store and were joined by Mr. Vance and Dr. Gerstelle, who came home with us, and had watermelon, and after <u>that</u> all left and we prepared for bed.

Thursday August 9th. Pretty day. Were up early for breakfast so Company could start in the early train. We went over to the depot with them, and ate our breakfast after our return. I wrote a letter to Lou Clippinger in the morning. Afternoon busy in some way. [I] think Mr. S. Smith there; he is, very often in the day. At night Mr. & Mrs. Davis, Sis & Mr. Vance & Mr. Smith & myself went over to the Woodside House to hear Mr. Bennett of Hagerstown speak, and Mr. McDonald replied. We had quite a pleasant time, but tore my dress coming home.

Friday August 10th. Quite warm. Kate, Sis & I were out shopping, and at Mr. Vance['s]. Met Mr. Smith, who came home with us. Stopped at Mr. Davis' store; & Mrs. Anderson there and we sat and talked a long time. [She] invited us to tea that evening. Mr. Smith & I were up in the Piedmont Savings Institution and Mr. Getty [was] very pleasant. We soon returned home. Mr. Smith, I think, played a <u>Game of Chess</u> with me and said I was improving. I wrote a letter to Mother this evening, before starting. Kate & children went

---

[37]The Franklin Mine with its four openings was one mile west of Westernport, Maryland. *Maryland, Its Sources, Industries and Institutions*, by Members of Johns Hopkins University and others (Baltimore, 1893), p. 97.

1860

first; as there was so much appearance of rain, she stopped awhile at Mrs. Miller's but we went straight to Mrs. Anderson's. And soon after tea there was a very heavy rain and lasted till after eight o'clock; and we intended starting through all, but by the time we were ready, it had ceased, and it was not such very unpleasant walking. I was with Mr. Smith & kept behind, & [we] had a lamp to ourselves & got home splendidly, but Sis slipped on the bridge, but no damage. Gents staid till late, and I think I had a game of chess, & was near beating Mr. Vance.

Saturday August 11th. Very warm. Mr. Tommy Davis here to breakfast; had come from Grafton last night. He sat awhile after breakfast. <u>Had a talk at dinner table</u>. Mr. T. Davis here just before dinner & little while before tea. After tea Mr. T. Davis & Sis, & Mr. Vance & I walked over to Westernport to get her fan, & to tell me the Blue Ribbon Story and this Tale in which I was the Heroine. We had to hurry back as Mr. V. had an engagement. He left soon but returned again, and Mr. Smith & Mr. Davis both, & we had a game of Whist, and Sis & Mr. V. [a] game of backgammon. Gents of course left Saturday night before 12 o'clock.

Sunday August 12th. Very pretty morning but warm again. /Mr. & Mrs. D., Mr. V. & I went over to the Station for [*illegible*]./ Mr. T. Davis spent day here. Sis [was] sick, so she did not go, Kate, neither. Kate & I were at Mrs. Wm. Davis and Mr. Davis came in and wanted me to go to church, so I went home and hurried and was ready by 10 minutes, and Messrs. Davis & Smith accompanied me to church and heard Mr. Cleaver preach. Mr. S. & Mr. T. D. both to dinner. Mr. S. remained and talked till about 4 o'clock, then went to take a nap, and was to return in an hour and half to take a walk, but he staid too long, so old Mrs. D. came down, and Mr. & Mrs. D. & family & Sis & self started to walk, & were soon joined by Messrs. Vance & T. Davis. Mr. V. & I walked twice around by the church on the river and enjoyed it. Mr. Smith came just as we returned and wanted me to walk with him on the mountain, but [I] concluded it was too late. After tea the gentlemen spent the evening with us. We had cake and watermelon. /Mr. Davis left for Zanesville tonight./ Mr. Smith staid after the others left.

Monday August 13th. Rained today. Mr. Vance sent us *Professor at the Breakfast Table*[38], some [passages] marked. Mr. Tom Davis was at the

---

[38]*The Professor at the Breakfast Table*, by Oliver Wendell Holmes, was published in 1860. W. R. Benét, *The Reader's Encyclopedia* (NY, 1948).

house, but we were not up to see him. At night, Messrs. Smith & Vance [were] there, and had a game of Whist, or I think I played "seven up"[39] with Mr. Smith, & Sis checkers with Mr. Vance.

Tuesday August 14th. Very pretty day, and I was to see Mrs. Wm. D. & C., & old Mrs. D. [came] to see us. I had a letter from Mag Shriner. At the store Mr. Smith joined [me] and we started for a walk and went on Railroad track as far as "Hampshire Mines" and back. [I] believe it was three miles, enjoyed it very much. Mr. Smith staid till 11 o'clock, and Mr. V. said he could have come then, as he just returned from the "Lodge" as some one came head foremost out of the door. Mr. Davis came home tonight.

PIEDMONT/SWANTON & FRANKVILLE

Wednesday August 15th. Pretty day. Sis & I were over to Mr. Vance's store to shop and he invited us to go to the concert to-night, had been [*illegible*] invited. Took a nice walk with Mr. Davis to the Road. Sis & I, before we accepted, were over again to exchange some worsted and Mr. Smith came home with us. Mrs. Anderson there awhile in evening. Messrs. Vance & Smith came after tea for us to go [to] the concert, & Kate & Mr. Davis went with us and I was glad they did, for it looked a pretty hard crowd, but we had chairs removed from the mass. The gents staid and we had a game of whist. [They] invited us to go to Swanton[40].

Thursday August 16th. Quite cool. The gents came for us at breakfast & we got ready and went over and took the train and rode as far as Frankville which is named after old Gov. F. Thomas of Md.[41]; and there were invited

---

[39]The game of "Seven Up" is a form of "All Fours" card game played by two or three players. The first player to reach a total of seven points wins. C. H. Goren, *Goren's Hoyle, Encyclopedia of Games* (NY, 1961), pp. 229-231.

[40]Swanton, Maryland, is west of Piedmont, not far from Deep Creek Lake. It is on a spur of the B&O Railroad. *Maryland: Official Highway Map* (published by the Maryland Department of Transportation).

[41]Gov. Francis Thomas was a colorful character. A Frederick native, after being delegate in Annapolis and a representative in Congress, he was elected Governor in 1841. He fought a duel with a Mr. William Price. He married Sally McDowell, daughter of the Governor of Virginia, she being 20 years of age while he was 42. Thomas became extremely jealous and suspicious. He published a pamphlet of his version of his family problems, which he distributed to the members of Congress. He was granted a divorce by the legislature in 1848. Thomas and Williams, *History of Allegany County, Maryland*, I, 277, 287.

1860

on Mr. Perkins' private Car and went on it as far as Swanton and stopped awhile; and then the gentlemen prepared the Hand Car and we started for Piedmont, Messrs. Perkins, Smith & Vance and Mrs. Davis, Sis & I. We stopped to gather berries several times and still got home by about twelve. Mr. Smith staid & talked some time and then walked over to the store with us & weighed us. I weighed 131 lbs., and [he] even sat awhile after he came back. Saw old Mrs. D. today. I wrote a letter home.[42] Miss Holt had been to see us. Mrs. Anderson and Alice came over before our tea and sat till about nine o'clock and Mr. A. came for her. Kate went as far as Mrs. Wm. D.'s and when she returned we waited, but she forgot & went to sleep. So when Mr. D. came [we] had our game of whist, and then a game of euchre with Mr. S., & Sis & Mr. V. with the backgammon board. The gents staid pretty late. Mr. Davis left for Balt. to-night.

PIEDMONT/NEW CREEK

Friday August 17th. Very pretty day. Mr. Smith came this morning & played a game of Chess, and I was so glad he did for really I think I must have had the "blues awfully" but it dispelled them all. At dinner Mr. Vance asked us to go to the concert; so did Mr. S. this morning. Mr. V. asked one of us to go to New Creek with him this evening and I accepted the invitation. Mrs. Davis both [were] down, and when he came [I] had to hurry to be ready. We were gone 2 hrs. 5 min. and had a delightful ride. He went on business but did not detain me long at the store and I did not dismount. Dr. Gerstelle was at our house while we were gone. I commenced to dress for concert before tea and was soon ready after, but Kate D. & Hallie not so quick. Mr. Smith took me & Hallie, Kate with Sis & Mr. V. Much nicer looking audience than Wednesday and we were well pleased, and beside [I] was between the two Gents, and also Mr. White of Grafton on other side of Mr. Smith. Prof. Johnston quite a wit, though Mr. V. and I concluded there was a little <u>sand</u> in our eyes. After we went home [we] had a game & some cake. Mr. V. got awake & staid pretty late. /Mrs. Anderson [was] here a little at night./

Saturday August 18th. I think a lovely morning. Mr. Vance came home in good time to dinner so we had a game of chess before & after dinner. They sent for him to go to the Bank to meet Col. Hemsberg. He came too early for tea and I was so sleepy, had only time to hurry [to] dress and go see him

---

[42]After the word <u>home</u>, the following words were written and then crossed out: "We waited for Kate to play whist but instead of course ...."

and play our game of chess. He is so clever, was not over after tea on account of having company. We have several books of Mr. Vance's to read: Marble Faun[43], Professor at the Breakfast Table. He is so kind. Mr. Smith staid till nearly twelve. When we were playing spoke of the grand aspect of the sky, but too much engaged to leave for it. Mr. Davis comes to-night. Sis let him in, I did not hear.

PIEDMONT/WALK TO BLOOMINGTON

Sunday August 19th. Very pretty morning. Messrs. Vance and Smith came for us to go to church, & Mr. V. asked me and we had a right warm walk and so many steps to ascend. Church was in, so stopped awhile to rest before we heard the sermon about parents' duty to their children. Mr. Smith staid to dinner, and when the gents were leaving Kate told them of the walk we wanted, and Mr. Vance staid and talked till he saw Miss Lizzie McMahon coming & then suddenly left; but returned before five when, according to engagement, I walked with Mr. V. & Sis with Mr. S. We had a delightful walk; and when near Bloomington sat down to rest & talk; & presume [we] sat nearly an hour; and then how to return was the question, and as Mr. V. said not any farther by railroad, of course I wanted to go a different way. So we went and had a very delightful walk and was surprised to find it six miles. When we had got to Piedmont they were uneasy about us. and I think it was unnecessary though. We fixed supper. Gents cut bread & ham and we really did enjoy our supper very much. Everything tasted so good. Mr. D. soon came home and said he was glad to see us. Mr. & Mrs. Wm. Davis soon came down to eat Watermelon, and we went up after old Mrs. Davis; and [she] seemed very much gratified, told us what a handsome couple we were, Mr. V. & I. We ate the Watermelon, then I retired to write the letter to Em Sauerwein; and such a time I had writing, all talking & Mr. Smith by me. Well, what must they do but add a P. S., both Mr. V. & Mr. S., and would not let me see it. So I put a piece in Capitals and Mr. V. wrote on back of it. Well, after having the letter to seal and direct, they left, taking it with them, but really I believe Mr. V. staid later than Mr. Smith. Took a walk late at night and had fun with papers.

---

[43]*The Marble Faun* by Nathaniel Hawthorne was published in 1860.

1860

PIEDMONT/BOGUS DISPATCH

Monday August 20th. Very pretty day. Sis & I were out shopping, and at Mr. Vance's met Mr. Smith, also Mrs. Anderson & Miss Miriam Hudson, & Mr. Smith came home with [us], and [we] found the two ladies there when we got home. All sat some time, Mr. Smith much longer than the ladies. In afternoon Kate, Sis & I all went over to Westernport to pay some visits; was to see Mrs. Miller and then to Mrs. Anderson's, met Mrs. Gerstelle, Miss Holt, & Miss Miriam Hudson & the D.'s there. Kate invited all the foregoing there to tea. When we left, there was some appearance of rain; nevertheless we waited at store for the mail, but learned Mr. Vance had my letter from Mother, so went home and [I] demanded it of him and was surprised he gave me such peaceable possession of it; and while I was reading it at Parlour door Rev. Mr. Woodworth arrived and sat the evening. Quite pleasant. Mr. Smith came while we were at tea. Mr. D. not home to tea. Mr. Vance came in after nine with a "<u>Bogus Dispatch</u>" from George, and I tell I was frightened, but after finding it was from George & to wait till Saturday, I was perfectly satisfied. I could not wait but wanted to reply, [and he] said he would tell me in morning. Mr. Davis left unexpectedly for Grafton to-night. The gents and us girls took a walk about eleven and were afraid of disturbing the neighbors. Mr. Vance wants me to take ride in morning. Mr. Smith is a great tease, so is Mr. Vance.

PIEDMONT/RIDE TO BLOOMINGTON
& WHITE SULPHUR [SPRINGS]

Tuesday August 21st. Bright morning. /Sis & I took a walk before breakfast to the Spring in Westernport./ Mr. Vance asked me at breakfast table if I would be ready in half an hour to ride to the White Sulphur Springs across the Mountain and I said yes, but was half-past nine till we started, and Flora so gentle, we had an elegant ride, loped through Westernport, but afterwards rode in a walk to the Spring and back. Enjoyed the scenery very much and drank from a tumbler Mr. Vance had hid last spring there. He seems so thoughtful and I think so considerate. When we reached Westernport [he] wanted to know if I would go to Bloomington with him, and as we had time I consented. He had to go on business at the Magistrate's Office and I rode up and waited for him. We then were stopped to take some money to the Bank. Well, when we got home [I told] them of the elegant ride, but kept quiet till evening about Bloomington till [I] thought they would find us out. Mr. Vance home couple hours at dinner; he looked so nice. We enjoyed the views we missed on Sunday; stopped to see it & [I] wonder what we were talking about. Mr. Vance confessed the hoax about [the] dispatch. All [was] told what he had [done], [*illegible*]. Well, about five o'clock Mrs. Anderson arrived, and notwithstanding the rain, Mrs. Anderson & Misses Holton & Hudson arrived and after awhile Mr. Anderson came to tea. Mr. Davis came too in accommodation train, and Mr. Vance to tea, so we all enjoyed it very much. After [he] found Mr. Davis [was] going off at night, so [*sic*] Mr. Smith offered his company and as it did not cost him anything [he] concluded to accept his kind offer. Messrs. Davis, Anderson & Vance went to the "Lodge", and when they returned went home with the ladies, then came back and sat till nearly twelve, and it was one o'clock when I was ready to retire. My last night at Piedmont.

PIEDMONT & HOME

Wednesday August 22nd. Rained very hard. Mr. Smith called us at half-past five o'clock. Dressed in a hurry, fastened my trunk and then went out to breakfast. Mr. Smith came and took breakfast with me, also Sis, but no one else. I was up to bid old Mrs. Davis "Good-bye." Mrs. Wm. Davis in bed yet, so did not see her. Mr. Vance came to escort me to the depot. Mr. Smith met us on the way and we three had a nice talk at the station. I told Mr. V. what perhaps I should not, that I had heard he was a flirt, and I know I don't believe it. I believe I was sort of pleased, or something of the sort, or it would not have given me so much pain & sorrow to see he felt it so. Well, the train soon came and was leaving, and Mr. Vance bid me good-bye and I was left to Mr. Smith, and I enjoyed the ride home very much; he pointed out all the places of interest to me. Em Sauerwein & Miss Butler of Cumberland were at the depot in Cumberland to see me and I had a short talk with her. At Martinsburg the cars stopped for dinner, and were there some time. At Harpers Ferry [we stopped] to have the other train pass, so had some time there. Mr. Smith generally [gets] out there. Soon arrived at Monocacy junction, and got in the omnibus car[44], [and] there saw Caroline McCleary and Annie Pettit who had got on at Dirffields; also Mr. Eader of Fred'k. At Fred'k Father met me, also John with him, so J. drove us up to old Mrs. Bantz's to see them, but they were not home but [we] left the contents of the basket there. Then got the baggage and came out home. Old Mrs. Rohrback

---

[44]Monocacy or Frederick Junction was the connection for the ride to Frederick from the B&O Railroad. The "Cars" were backed from the junction into the Frederick Station, by now at All Saints and Market Streets. H. H. Harwood Jr., *Impossible Challenge: The Baltimore & Ohio Railroad in Maryland* (Baltimore, 1979), pp. 144, 165.

1860

& Ellen R[ohrback] & her mother, Mrs. Brunner, were here spending the day. Well, I gathered what flowers I could and made two bouquets, one for Mr. Smith, the other for Mr. V., but Mr. S. said he would only give Mr. V. one bud. I gave Mr. S. his tea at five o'clock, and the others ate afterwards, and they left about sundown. John said Mr. S. just [had] time to get on Cars. Well, as soon as possible I got to bed as so tired & sleepy.

Thursday August 23rd. Carpenters here. Showery all day. Busy unpacking and finding a place for everything and everything to that place. Took a nap in Afternoon but still ready for sleep at night again; so I think I can make up for some lost time. Several showers during the day.

Friday August 24th. Was up early and rode to town expecting to see Mr. & Mrs. Lefevre, but got to town more than half hour after the cars left. I did not know the time. Just returned home again and as I was going in the house, a wagon drove up and old Mrs. Sims and two grandchildren came to spend the day. I was very busy all day, as I wanted to help Jane so she could get done her washing.

Saturday August 25th. Bright day. I was very busy all day house cleaning as Carpenters finished yesterday. About six o'clock I went into town, called to see Mrs. Bantz and Mrs. Ebert and talked there a long time. [Mrs. Ebert] says she has heard from Sis and [she has] not been well. Sorry to hear it.

Sunday August 26th. Bright, clear day. Mother & I went to church & Mary Derr would have me go home with her. Mr. & Mrs. John Derr[45] there, Annie been up about 12 days, looks very well. Took dinner & tea there, and went over to Mag's and staid with Mary Sauerwein over night. We had a long talk after retiring. John & Annie Derr, Mary & Alice sat till about ten o'clock, then returned to Mr. Derr's. Had watermelon.

Monday August 27th. Bright morning. Immediately after breakfast Mary Sauerwein & I went over to Mr. Derr's but John & Annie had gone, so we sat awhile & then returned to Mag's to dinner. After dinner Cousin Ed took me into town. I stopped at P. O. & had a note from Mr. Smith, then walked on out to the Cemetery, when I thought there was a heavy rain coming up, so stopped in there till it was over. Sent word home to send for me, and John

---

[45]On John Derr and his wife Ann, who now lived in Baltimore, see note 4, 1860. See also Appendix III.

met me at the Mud hole. Found Mrs. Bushey & Annie Mary here to tea. Rained after I came home but they left after it was over.

Tuesday August 28th. Clear, but soon clouded over and rained nearly all day. So I had fine opportunity of writing up my journals[46] and couple of letters. Wrote to Kate Davis and Lou Ebert in one letter of 8 pages.

Wednesday August 29th. Clear this morning. I finished off the letter to Kate & Lou and wrote one hurriedly to Geo. Sauerwein, and Mother took them in to mail. Over [to] Miss Sallie to give [her] her collar.

Thursday August 30th. Pleasant day. Was in town to see Aunt C. Scholl[47], saw Miss B. Bentz there, and at Annie Bentz's but did not get in, also at Ellen Rohrback but could not get in there. Told Wils B. [I] was coming over on Friday, Aug 31.

Friday August 31st. Warm and with appearance of rain, so did not go to Boyds'; also Mother staid too long in town.

Saturday September 1st [1860]. Lovely day. Father said he would take me out, so got ready and went to cousin Ed Shriner's and went with Mag & Mary Sauerwein over to the pic-nic; very pleasant time. Houcks & I do not know who all [were] there. We went over to cousin Ed['s] about three o'clock to meet Em Sauerwein, who was [in] from Cumberland where she had been spending some time, and after fixing her up we went back to the pic-nic & remained till after sundown and went home. Very well pleased with the day's proceedings and quite tired. Mary Derr staid all night with us.

Sunday September 2nd. Cooler but clear. Mary Derr went home before breakfast and at church time sent the carriage over for one of us, and Mary D. went with them. I went home from church with Mother and read most of the afternoon.

Monday September 3rd. Appearance of rain. Nevertheless, I went to town with Father and went to see Lou Ebert and sat with her couple of hours and then came out home; and in afternoon Mother & I went up to old Mrs.

---

[46]See note 33, 1860, and Introduction.

[47]See note 46, 1851.

1860

Boyd's and spent the afternoon. Old Mrs. Preston and Mrs. J. Wesley Veitch of Washington, D.C. were there but, after hearing old Mrs. P. talk awhile, she left. Miss Lewis & brothers there after tea. We spent the afternoon very pleasantly and returned home about half-past seven o'clock.

Tuesday September 4th. Still cloudy but no rain. Busy all day.

Wednesday September 5th. Very pretty day. Busy in the morning but was obliged to go to town awhile in the afternoon. Called to see Ellen Rohrback and her two sisters-in-law, and from there went up street and saw Hon. S[tephen] A. Douglas[48] arrive, and also saw him on the stand when speaking. Came out home soon, thinking Lou Ebert might be here.

Thursday September 6th. Cloudy morning but appearance of clearing. Father & I went into town early and I went to Mrs. Bantz's, and Lou & I went to Mrs. F. A. Schley's[49] and saw the family all, & saw the procession[50] pass, which was very long & quite imposing. We had a nice time, then stopped few minutes at Uncle Kemp's[51], then went & took dinner with Annie Bantz Keifer, all pleasant. [We went] then to Houcks' [and] Derrs'. Sauerweins & Mag Shriner [were] there. From there we went to the Hotel to see Mrs. Appold and Miss Downey. We then went up for Lou E. and took a walk, and then went back and got ready to walk out home; but Rev. & Dr. Jno. Zack met us, and Rev. got out and Dr. Jno. brought us out home, and we had a very pleasant ride home. We soon thought of bed and found we were not at P[iedmont].

---

[48]Douglas, Senator from Illinois, was the presidential candidate for the northern wing of the Democratic party in the 1860 election. Martin, *History of the United States*, I, 778-779. Engelbrecht stated, "There was a large assembly present," when Douglas spoke at the Court House. Engelbrecht, *Diary*, III, 75.

[49]Dr. F. A. Schley had a pharmacy and dry goods store and residence on the south side of Patrick Street between Market and Court Streets. *Williams' Directory*, p. 34.

[50]Engelbrecht wrote, "The Friends of Bell and Everett (candidates of the Constitutional Union Party) have a County Meeting today in our City--they had a procession this forenoon-- there were 3 Bands of Music to 142 vehicles and many horsemen. It was 16 1/2 minutes in passing at the corner of Market and Church Streets where I was standing." Engelbrecht, *Diary*, III, 76.

[51]See note 11, 1853.

1860

Friday September 7th. Very warm day with appearance of rain [in the] afternoon. Mrs. Castle & Miss Ann Kiefer came up & spent the afternoon, and Lou & I took a walk part-way with them; & as soon as we returned, Cousin Ed Shriner, Alice Derr, & Mary Sauerwein arrived; Alice & Cousin Ed only sat little while but of course Mary S. staid.

* * * * *

Monday September 10th. Pretty day. Mary & I walked to town, at Houcks' and, then at Kunkel's, who would make us stay to tea, and we came up to Derr's to meet the carriage after.

Tuesday September 11th. Pretty day. Mary & I [had a] long talk and about twelve o'clock Mr. John Derr, Mary, Alice, Willie, & Emma Sauerwein arrived, about three o'clock Mrs. Boyd & Sue Jones, & afterwards cousin Ed & Mag Shriner; and when tea [was] nearly ready Miss Appold & Miss Downey & Lily Appold arrived and staid till after tea, & very soon all left. Mary Derr remained. Gin Boyd & Charlie Jones came for Boyds.

Wednesday September 12th. We were at home all day talking, reading, etc. /Afternoon Em & I walked to town to see Aunt S. Scholl./

Thursday September 13th. Quite pleasant day. Mrs. I. Howard & Claire here to tea. Mary Derr not well & frightened us. Note from Lou Ebert.

Friday September 14th. Very beautiful day. Willie came for Mary about noon, and they left soon after two o'clock; and we had early tea & went to town afterwards. /Em & I rode on horseback./ Saw Mr. J. A. Johnson on the street; has been suffering with his feet for 3 weeks. [We were] at Mrs. Bantz' to see her & Lou Ebert, both very agreeable.

* * * * *

Monday September 17th. Not very bright, but after dinner John took us over to Mr. Boyd's to call, also to Lizzie Schell's. We expected to see Em Davis, but [she had] gone home Saturday. Had a note from Mary Kunkel for us to come in Thursday & stay [a] few days. Lizzie Houck came out home with us. I wrote a note to Mag Shriner saying she must meet us at Aunt Mary Scholl's on Thursday.

1860

Tuesday September 18th. Bright, beautiful morning. Mother gone to market, and after breakfast Em & I took the horse and went to Mrs. Bushey's to return the tumbler, and [we] sat awhile & were treated to grapes, and then went to Miss Kiefer's and talked awhile to Miss Charlotte, then came out home. [We] found Lou Ebert & Dodie Bantz had been here & just gone. Some rain in afternoon. At night I wrote a long letter to Kate Bantz Davis.

* * * * *

Thursday September 20th. Quite cloudy, but as we had sent word, determined we would go. Lizzie Houck stopped at home. We stopped a few minutes at M. Derr's. Em was in, & said Mary Derr [was] in bed. We spent the day very pleasantly at aunt Mary Scholl's and enjoyed the peaches & cream very much. When we started home it was lovely, but [it] soon changed to very threatening, and we had quite a variety, till we reached home, from sunshine to showers. Old Mrs. Gallion died this morning.

Friday September 21st. Lovely day. Mary & Em S. went in early to go to Kunkels' to spend the day. I went in late in evening & we staid over night. We were over to Mrs. Wilson's little at night. Nice letter of Lou Hersh Clippinger.

Saturday September 22nd. Beautiful day. I was [in] to see Lou Ebert and sat an hour or so, then shopped some, & remained at Mr. Kunkel's till about four o'clock in the evening, when we walked out home.

* * * * *

Wednesday September 26th. Very pretty day. All home all day expecting Ed Shriner & Mag but they did not come. Miss Sallie [came] over to tea, also Salleyann Meyers. We walked with them part-way home.

Thursday September 27th. Cloudy with appearance of rain. Never-theless, we started & would not be turned back by little rain. So [we] went on. Rained very hard after we were out but cleared some before we started home. Stopped a little while to see Mary Derr.

Friday September 28th. Beautiful day. Cousin Ed & Mag here to dinner & left about three o'clock. After tea took the girls into town to stay at Houcks'. They wrote to George & I put in a P.S. Father not well enough to be up today.

* * * * *

Monday October 1st [1860]. Rainy most all day. Wrote a note to Marion H. to send my wooden needles home. Mr. Gallion [came] to see Father after tea & sat till ten o'clock.

Tuesday October 2nd. Warm, sultry with showers most all day. Dr. Worman[52] here to see Father on business and took dinner. /Had [the] stoves fixed./

Wednesday October 3rd. Pleasant morning, but rain before night. I was in town; called at Houcks' and Em Sauerwein went shopping with me. I took her back to Mrs. H's and then came out home. Letter from G. Sauerwein.

* * * * *

Friday October 12th. Quite cool, & heavy frost. I went into town early, was at Houck's awhile, then at Mrs. Bantz', who had gone to Piedmont, [and] then to sit couple of hours with Ella B. Came home then, and was in town again in afternoon to shop some.

* * * * *

Monday October 15th. Beautiful day. After dinner went into town and stopped at Houcks' and got Mary Sauerwein, and we all went over to deposit the things. I was at Markel[l]'s awhile to wait for Mother. Letter of Sis Ebert.

Tuesday October 16th. Quite [a] pleasant day. [I] went into the Fair in evening and soon met Meallie Markel[l][53] and remained with her till I met Houcks & Sauerweins, and remained with them till just before the close, when

---

[52]Dr. A.D. Worman (1812-1898) was a homeopathic doctor in Frederick. Williams, *History*, I, 596.

[53]Meallie Markell was the daughter of Amelia and Samuel Markell. She lived at a house on the west side of South Market Street, the second door south of South Street. *Williams' Directory*, p. 26.

1860

I was joined by Lt. Col. Hobbs, who came out to the carriage with me. There was a fine Balloon Ascension by Professor Light[54] about five o'clock.

Wednesday October 17th. Much cooler. I went into town after dinner, & before we entered the [fair] gates I joined Annie Howard & Dr. Veitch and remained with them till I saw the girls. I saw various friends, Mag Shriner, Isie Buckey and others. Mr. Marlow saw me out, & Em up street, in his two-horse buggy. Cousin Henry Scholl wife & daughter here over night.

Thursday October 18th. Pretty morning after rain last night. Cousin Henry went into town early & I went with them. Thought I [would meet] Mr. G. W. Smith on [the] way, and so it proved. I went direct to Mr. H's and then took walk with Em, then [was] at Misses Houses', & at depot to see ministers come[55], and after an early dinner up to the Fair where I saw numerous friends; and after awhile [I met] Mr. Smith; and we walked and talked and he went up with me, [and] we took a walk before returning. At night Mr. & Mrs. Sam Stans of Balt. arrived and soon went to church; and Lizzie, Mrs. S. and I went to hear Ex-Gov. Thomas[56] speak; and when we returned found Luke Jones and Tom Barche there. All left by 10 1/2 o'clock and we soon retired.

Friday October 19th. Cold, raw day. But was out early & up to see Mrs. B. F. Winchester and Mrs. Mering, who is staying there; then at Synod awhile, and soon saw the Military[57] pass, and afterwards [went] up on the Fair Ground, where we walked, talked, etc. till nearly 4 o'clock, when there was a general leaving. And we, after seeing Mr. Houcks, etc., came out home, Mr. Smith with us. Rained hard at night.

---

[54]Engelbrecht writes, "Mr. John A. Light (almost a play on names) made a beautiful assension from the Barracks in a NE by N direction & came down in the Roman Catholic Graveyard lot between 3 & 4th Street. The above John A. Light fell from a balloon in December 1860 and was killed with a broken neck. So Say the Newspapers." Engelbrecht, *Diary*, III, 80.

[55]The ministers were coming to the Synod the next day.

[56]Ex. Gov. Francis Thomas addressed a meeting of political parties for three hours, resulting in a vote of 314 for Union, 201 against. Engelbrecht, *Diary*, III, 89.

[57]The military parade which marched through town included many bands and companies of mounted guards. This was the 79th anniversary of the Surrender of Lord Cornwallis at Yorktown. Engelbrecht, *Diary*, III, 80-81.

1860

Saturday October 20th. Still raining in showers nearly all day. Mr. Smith rendered himself quite agreeable, and went into town to leave at 1/4 before 6 o'clock for P[iedmont]. I went up and got Mrs. Mering & brought her out home with me.

Sunday October 21st. Unpleasant morning, but cleared off by noon. I went in early with Mrs. Mering, up to Mrs. M[arkell's] and sat a few minutes before church, and then heard an excellent sermon from Rev. Dr. Morris of Balt. I went up to Mr. H's after church for some things, and then Tilly came home with me and we spent the afternoon in talk and etc. Miss Sallie over at night.

Monday October 22nd. Foggy but cleared off to be beautiful day. I took Tilly home & went according to promise to sing with Mrs. Winchester; and about four o'clock, left, and on way home [I] met Mr. Davis, who had been out here and had a long talk. [He] said Mr. S[mith] had got home and Mr. Vance was coming soon. Letter of Lou Clippinger.

* * * * *

Thursday October 25th. Lovely day. Mother in town and when she came home, brought me a letter from Mr. G. W. Smith <u>offering me his "Hand and Heart" as a husband, and asked if I would accept Hallie's cousin G. W. S. [It was] prettily done, but I never can.</u>

Friday October 26th. Foggy morning. [I was] in town awhile in morning to shop, and afternoon to see Mrs. Bantz & Kunkels. Meal talked [a] heap. Letters of Geo. & Mary Sauerwein.

Saturday October 27th. Lovely day. Aunt Margaret came out about noon and staid till after early tea, when [I] took her home and brought Father home from town.

* * * * *

Monday October 29th. Rather cloudy but warm. Mother & I went out to spend the day at Mrs. Derr's. Mary looks badly, so thin. I wrote a reply to Mr. G. W. Smith of Piedmont and told him I could only feel friendship for him, and a note to Kate Davis to send with Anderson's Air Pistol.

1860

Tuesday October 30th. Rainy in morning but ceased by ten o'clock but still damp. [I] was in town on business & to see Mrs. Markell a little while. Wrote to Lou Ebert at night.

Wednesday October 31st. Rainy in showers all day. Mr. Gallion here a little while. I wrote to Lou Clip., also a long letter to Mary Sauerwein.

* * * * *

Monday November 5th. Lovely day, so balmy. I went into town in afternoon and was persuaded to stay over night with Kunkels. Was at Houcks' awhile and at Mrs. Markel's. Lizzie Kunkel was in town also. We had a pleasant evening and fine view of both processions[58]. I had a nice long letter of Mary S. saying George would not be up tomorrow night.

Tuesday November 6th. Quite bright but windy. Lizzie, Meallie and I were up street, and I then walked out home & was busy.

* * * * *

Monday November 12th. Very pretty day. Mother & I were in town this afternoon.

Tuesday November 13th. Mother and I intended to go to town, but Aunt Mary Scholl & Annabelle[59], came & prevented.

Wednesday November 14th. Very pleasant, indeed quite warm day. Nice letters of Kate Bantz Davis & G. Sauerwein. I went in town with Father, was at Houcks' awhile & at Mrs. Dr. Schley's, not home, and at Kunkels' awhile, then came home. Wrote [to] Lou Clippinger.

---

[58] This was the day before the 1860 election. Engelbrecht writes, "Last night both Bell and Everett (Union Party) Breckenridge and Lane (Southern Democrat Party) had torch processions--both parties turned out well but it was supposed that the Bell party was the largest (were counted) they both marched at the same time but regulated their march. So that they did not interfere with each other--after the procession the Bell men had speaking at the Court House Yard & the Breckenridge party spoke at the Market House lot." Engelbrecht, *Diary*, III, 83.

[59] Annabelle was Margaret's cousin, the daughter of her father's brother Elias and wife Mary. *Scholl Genealogy*, p. 784. See also May 29, 1857.

1860

Thursday November 15th. Lovely day. Mother & I were going to town in afternoon but Annie H. came, & spent the day. Mr. Cox here to tea.

Friday November 16th. Lovely day. Annie H. left about 10 o'clock, & we butchered & afterwards I went in [town] on horseback & brought Meallie K. out.

Saturday November 17th. Rained today, so made it dreary for Meal, as had to be in house all day.

Sunday November 18th. Rainy morning but cleared off beautifully, & about four o'clock Meal & I walked to town & I staid over night with her. We went to church. Mr. Bake Kunkel [was] there over night. Mr. Meals preached. Saw Mrs. Dr. Schley.

Monday November 19th. I went up early to see & found the package & a letter of <u>Lou Ebert</u>, at Derrs' Tavern instead of Derrs' store[60]. Mrs. S. brought [it] up two weeks ago. [I was] at Aunt M. Artz' with Mother. Wrote Mag S. a note to meet us on Thursday at Aunt J. Scholl's.

Tuesday November 20th. Quite cool. Walked over to Annie Howard's, [and] spent day and night. Wrote to Lou Ebert.

Wednesday November 21st. Cold, with snow squalls. Annie & I went over and took dinner with Ginny Smith. I had a nice letter of Nellie Mering Martin, quite unexpected.

Thursday November 22nd. Lovely day. Mother & I went in to spend the day at Aunt Jem[ima] Scholl's. Cousin Ed & Mag Shriner in to tea. Miss Stevenson Hammond of Liberty there, [and] also Mrs. Clingan, awhile in afternoon.

Friday November 23rd. Great change. Had been snow last night & snowed off and on till afternoon. Lizzie Baugher and Mr. Baker of Winchester [were] married to-night.

* * * * *

---

[60]See note 13, 1860. Derr's Tavern was Derr's Hotel on North Market Street, William R. Derr, proprietor. *Williams' Directory*, p. 10.

1860

Wednesday November 28th. Warm, and cleared off about noon, beautifully. I was in town about an hour to shop. About three o'clock Mr. Wm. Cox of Carroll Borders walked out & sat till after eight o'clock.

Thursday November 29th. Lovely day for Thanksgiving. Mild and balmy as Spring.

* * * * *

Sunday December 2nd [1860]. Quite cold and windy. Mother & I went to church and Meallie Kunkel told me cousin J. Harry Smith was here and wanted me to stay in, so went home with her. He joined us at [the] corner & went down home with us, [but] only sat little while, as [he] had partial engagement for dinner. He came down about three or four and sat till after ten.

Monday December 3rd. Had moderated much, [so I] early left Mr. Kunkel's, went to Mrs. Dr. Schley's & sat awhile. Then [I went] to Aunt C. Scholl's and afterwards to Annie Bentz Keefer's to dinner, after dinner [to] old Mrs. Bantz' & she not home. Also [I went] to Ellen Rohrback's & she [went] with me to Mrs. Millie Markel's for tea, and walked out home.

Tuesday December 4th. Thought [I] would go to town again but too unpleasant. Snowed till about 2 o'clock. Had a letter from Lou Ebert, also wrote to Geo. & Mary Sauerwein.

Wednesday December 5th. Quite nice day. Expected Mrs. Drietrick & Kemp but they did not arrive. Note from Annabelle Scholl saying she was to be married & wanted me to wait on her; also one from Davis wanting me to meet him in town next Tuesday. I wrote one in return & took it into town & left it.

* * * * *

Friday December 7th. Beautiful day. Snowed some last night. Was busy in the morning. Annabelle Scholl & Miss Florence Steiner arrived soon after 11 o'clock & wanted me to go to town with them. I went with them shopping & was done by 2 1/2 o'clock. Then at Mrs. Rohrback['s] & Mrs. Markell's & neither home; then at Mrs. Fout's & Mrs. Derr's awhile, & then, walked out

1860

with Father. Mr. Claggett & Dr. Bruce Thomas[61] were here and sat the evening. Dr. Thomas quite nice looking & very agreeable.

Saturday December 8th. Rained today. Nice letter of Lou Clippinger. Mr. C. returned Tuesday, & little Geo. Hersh died yesterday morning.

* * * * *

Tuesday December 11th. Cold and clear. Mother & I went into town to meet Aunt Mary & Annabelle. I was at Houcks' & Aunt Shriner's awhile; then saw them, & we all went home & took dinner [at] Uncle Lewis Scholl's. Then I went out home with them, and after tea went over to Rev. Mr. Steiner's, and Florence came home with us and staid all night.

Wednesday December 12th. So pleasant but cold. We started to town about eleven o'clock and I stopped to see Mary Derr [a] little while. With A. & F. went to Kemps' & Davis to cousin Ed's. I shopped with [the] girls, then went to see Mrs. Bantz couple hours.

* * * * *

Monday December 17th. Butchering day, & a lovely day it was. Mag & Ed Shriner out awhile.

* * * * *

BALTIMORE

Wednesday December 19th. Rained about seven & continued all day. I went into town and had a pleasant ride to Balt. Messrs. Derr & Sifford were on the cars and very pleasant. Mr. Sauerwein met me at depot & took me up home. All well, & I had a very bad headache & took nap in afternoon. Kate & Mr. LeFevre [were] here awhile.

Thursday December 20th. Rained in morning but cleared off by noon. Mary & I were out this morning & shopped some. Miss Reifsnider here to dinner

---

[61]Dr. Bruce Thomas (b. 6/20/33; d. 3/14/13) married Evelyn Virginia Cunningham and was pension examiner and physician to Monteview (Alms House) and the jail for several years. G. L. Thomas, *Thomas Genealogy* (Adamstown, MD, 1954), p. 31.

1860

& left in Fred'k. train. Em, G, & I went to [the] cars with her. Afterwards [we] took a walk down Market Street, & then called at Miss Ebert's awhile. Rev. Mr. Stark [was] here.

Friday December 21st. Very pretty day. Kate and Walter came about eleven o'clock & soon Mr. LeFevre & Rev. Mr. Galt came. Kate & I were out for [a] couple [of] hours. In afternoon Em & I were out to walk and shop. Mrs. Fannie Dix here awhile.

Saturday December 22nd. Found it raining when we got up but cleared off by noon. Mrs. S., Mary & I were out awhile in [the] afternoon & had a pleasant time.

Sunday December 23rd. Quite pleasant. Em, Mary, Mrs. S., & I went to church & heard Rev. M. Stark preach. [We] met Mr. F. Hersh here on street, will call at night. Mrs. S., Mary & I went to church. Em & I [came] home. Mr. Plumber [was] here.

Monday December 24th. Dodie Bantz here awhile this morning. Heard of Tom Derr's death[62] & [it] made us all so sad. Died at Port au Prince [on] Dec. 3rd. Mr. Frank Hersh [was] here awhile. We girls were out in afternoon.

Tuesday December 25th. Christmas day. Snowing in morning but cleared off by noon. Kate, Mr. LeFevre & Walter here to spend the day. Mrs. Urhlaub & Mr. Heidel here to call. /Mr. & Mrs. LeFevre staid all night./ Mrs. S. gave me a book.

Wednesday December 26th. Quite cold. Mr. & Mrs. LeFevre & Em & I were down street & bought Kate a coffee pot for Christmas gift. In afternoon Mary, Em & I were out to Mrs. Rau's and sat awhile, then took [a] walk down Market Street.

Thursday December 27th. Lovely day. Mary & I were round to see Sis Ebert & sat a long time, & Mr. G. W. Smith of Piedmont came just as we were

---

[62]Tom Derr, the second son of John and Elizabeth Derr, died of yellow fever in Port au Prince, Haiti on December 3, 1860. He was in charge of the cargo (supercargo) of the Brig Bohio out of New York. Newspaper clippings in the leaves of Margaret's diary provide further details.

leaving; sat little while & talked; then [we went to] Mrs. Urhlaub's, she not home, then [to the] dentist, & afterwards home. Mrs. Wm. Sadtler here to dinner & tea. Mary & I were out awhile in afternoon. I felt very sad meeting Mr. Smith, & I suppose more than he did. I hope I did no wrong.

Friday December 28th. Rather cloudy. Kate came from Market & we, Mary, Kate & I went up to Mr. Gregg's to see Mrs. Gregg laid out; but they were just fixing her so [we] did not see her but saw her husband, Mr. James Gregg & Mrs. Andrew Gregg. Met Neallie [Dean] on street & had a little talk. Kate went home, and Mary, Em & I got ready & went out & took dinner with her. Mrs. Urhlaub [was] there. [We] came home to tea, found a gentleman had been to see me; and [I] suppose it was Paul Hersh, as I had a letter from Lou Clip wanting me to come up with him tomorrow morning if I did not fear the diphtheria. Mrs. & Miss Harmon of Richmond were here also. At night George took Mary & me to a concert at New Assembly rooms[63] by Madame Pauline Colson, Perri Brignoli, Sersine & Musical Piano. I suppose it was very fine but operatic music does not suit me, so I enjoyed the "Laughing Song," by Colson and "Serenade" by Brignoli. [We have an] invitation to Mrs. Gregg's funeral.

Saturday December 29th. Cloudy, damp day. In the house till after dinner. Rev. M. LeFevre & Kate came soon after dinner & George, Mary & Em & I went to Mrs. John Gregg's funeral. Dr. Backus & Rohers & Mr. Israel conducted the funeral services. George & I were in the carriage with Mr. & Mrs. Balderson & they had lots to talk [about]. Found Paul Hersh had been here, and he came again soon after 8 o'clock; & about nine George, Mary, Em, Paul & I went down and sat an hour or so with Mrs. & Miss Harmon of Richmond.

Sunday December 30th. Found it raining when we got up. Mary, Em & I went to Mr. Foulk's to church. At home [the] rest of the day.

Monday December 31st. Found it had snowed, but nevertheless Em & I went to market. Expected Mrs. & Miss Harmon to dinner.

---

[63]The New Assembly Rooms at the northeast corner of Hanover and Lombard Streets, finished in 1851 for Col. John Howard, were noted for the concerts given there. Scharf, *Baltimore*, p. 680.

1860

(Photo by C. Kurt Holter)

Manchester Farm, Margaret Scholl Hood's home,
New Design Road, Frederick, Maryland

1861

"Battles at Bull's run."

January 7th [1861].[1] Came home from Balt.

January 15th. Annabelle Scholl[2] & John D. Cramer married.

January 16th. Mrs. Barrick dinner party for old Folks & party at night for young ones.

January 17th. Dinner party at Mr. Cramer's, large, about 500.

January 18th. Dined at our house.

January 27th. Church service & dinner & supper at Rev. Mr. Steiner's, night; Mr. Cramer's home next morning.

January 28th. Wrote to M. E. S.

February 6th [1861]. Letters to Lou Clip & from M. E. Sauerwein.

---

[1] The diary entries for 1861 show a very different pattern from that of previous years. Incomplete and extending only to July 19, they are closely written, often with two or three dates on a single line, and covering slightly more than one page. Notes about events of political importance, with no comments on them, are interspersed among terse records of social occasions and Margaret's correspondence. The nature of these notes may indicate something of the diarist's perturbation about events of this time.

[2] Annabelle, Margaret's cousin, married John David Cramer. He was a descendent of the immigrant Johann Georg Cramer who arrived in Philadelphia from Germany in 1705. John David was a very successful farmer in Walkersville. Annabelle Scholl was his second wife. Williams, *History*, II, 1267-1269; Holdcraft, *Names In Stone*, p. 273.

1861

February 10th. Letter of Lou Clip, baby picture.

February 13th. Letter to Lou Ebert.

February 21st. Letter to Lou Clip.

February 20th. Married, Marion B. Howard & Mr. John Lenseny of Carroll County, Md.

February 20th. Married, John Cooper Esq. & Miss Marie E. Trimper, both near Battle Creek, Mich.

February 28th. Letter to Mary E. Sauerwein.

March 18th [1861]. Letter of Lou Ebert.

March 28th, 29th, 30th. Kate Davis & family out the three days.

April 3rd, 1861. Letter of Lou Clip.

April 5th. Letter to Mary E. Sauerwein.

April 10th. Letter of M. E. S.

April 12th & 13th. Bombardment of Ft. Sumpter [sic].[3]

April 19th. Not in Balt.[4]

---

[3] The Bombardment of Fort Sumter at Charleston, S.C., signals the beginning of the Civil War.

[4] This entry may reflect Margaret's decision against visiting the Sauerweins at this time. President Lincoln, after the firing on Ft. Sumter, had summoned all militiamen from the states that had not seceded to come to Washington, but trouble broke out at Baltimore. "The Massachusetts and Connecticut troops on their way to Washington, D.C. were attacked by some of the rabble throwing Stones into the Cars and breaking nearly all the windows in the Cars & reports says 9 persons were killed. Martial law was declared by Gov. Hicks (who was there at the time) everything there is in commotion -- today the Telegraph says that all the Bridges on the Rail Road leading to the City were destroyed. Hail Columbia, Happy Land." Engelbrecht, *Diary*, III, 97.

April 26th. Extra session Legislature.[5]

May 4th [1861]. Wrote to Lou Clip.

May 10th. Mr. Vance of Piedmont & Davis of Grafton here today, glad to see them. Mother married 29 years.

May 13th. Legislature adjourned to June 4th.[6]

May 18th. Letter to Lou Clippinger.

May 18th. Wrote to Mary Sauerwein.

May 22nd. Wrote to Mary S. *[May] 23*, wrote to Geo. Sauerwein.

May 29th. Letters of Mr. G. Sauerwein & sister Mary E. S.

June 4th [1861]. Legislature reassembled.[7]

June 6th. Wrote to Mary Sauerwein.

June 13th. Wrote to Lou Ebert.

---

[5] A special session of the Maryland legislature, called by the governor to decide whether Maryland should secede from the Union, was by his special order moved to Frederick from Annapolis. "The Legislature of Maryland Met in our City yesterday at the Court House at 12 ock. About 2 ock they adjourned to meet again at 5 ock p.m. They will meet this morning at the new Hall of the Reformed Parsonage Property corner of Market and Church Street, [Kemp Hall]. [Gov.] Thomas Holliday Hicks is also here staying at the Dill House." Engelbrecht, *Diary*, III, 97. At this time Annapolis had been occupied by General Butler's Union Troops who were keeping a watch on things to be sure that Maryland did not secede from the Union. Nathan Miller, "Assembly Visits Frederick, Surrenders to Union Flag," *Baltimore Sun*, Feb. 16, 1961. See also Daniel Carroll Toomey, *The Civil War In Maryland* (Baltimore, MD, 1983), p. 16.

[6] The legislature adjourned because resolutions sympathizing with the South were passed and the House (meeting on the third floor of Kemp Hall) refused to accept a Senate resolution (they were meeting on another floor of Kemp Hall) to raise the national flag over the meeting place.

[7] The legislature reassembled at this time and a committee was appointed to visit President Lincoln to report to him that they had not been able to meet with President Jefferson Davis to find out if "the Confederacy was willing to entertain any proposition from the United States for a peaceful settlement." Williams, *History*, I, 370.

1861

June 29th. Received a letter of Mary Sauerwein.

July 1st [1861]. Wrote to Lou Clip.

July 15th. Letter of Lou Clippinger.

July 18th. Wrote to Mary Sauerwein.

July 22nd. Wrote to <u>Mrs. J. Hays Carson</u> (Mary Keen that was).

July 19, 21st. Battles at Bull's Run.

[and thus the diary ends]

1861

Margaret "Mag" Derr Shriner, daughter of John Derr, Sr.

(Photo courtesy Hood College Archives)

John Derr, Sr.

(Photo from Williams, *History of Frederick County, Maryland)*

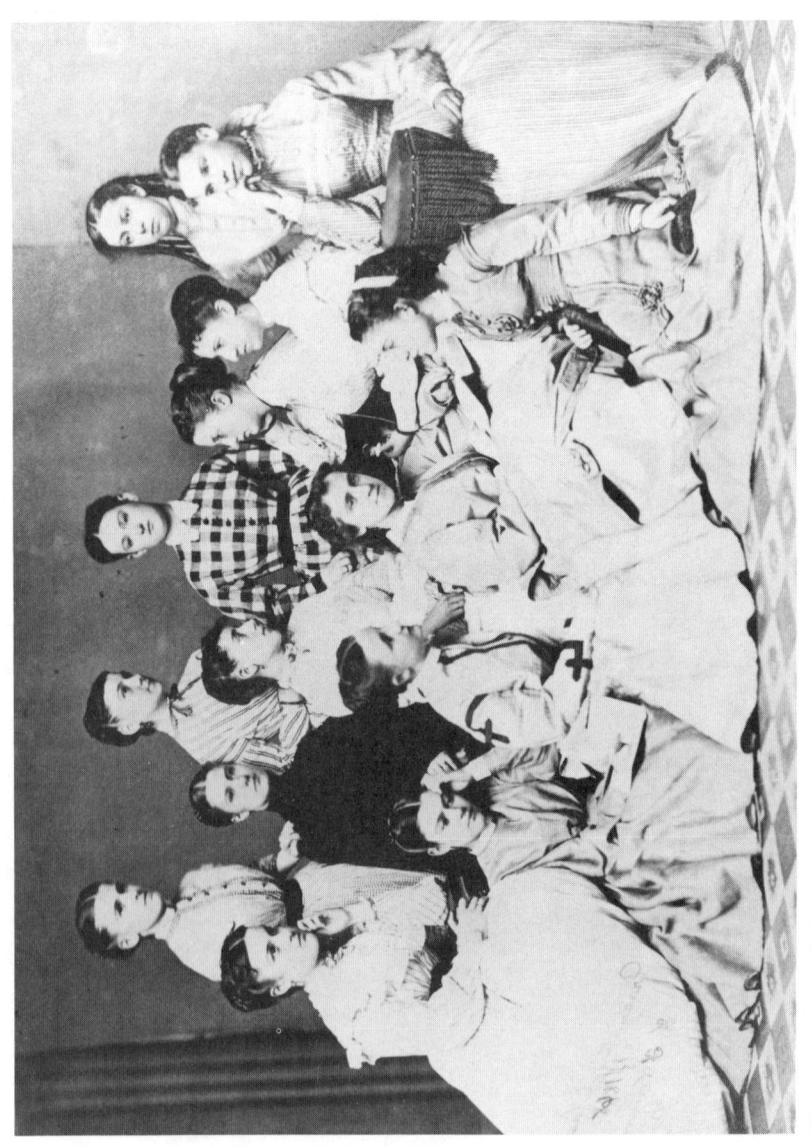

(Photo courtesy Hood College Archives)

Graduating Class of 1868
The Frederick Female Seminary, Frederick, Maryland

(From an unsigned print, courtesy the Maryland Historical Society)
The city of Frederick in about 1850

BIBLIOGRAPHY

A. Manuscript Sources

Adams-Nelson Family Bible, printed 1859, with family data entered by Jeannette Adams Nelson and her descendents (1859-1936).

Diary of Margaret Scholl, 1851, 1853-1861, in the collections of The Historical Society of Frederick County, Inc., Frederick, MD.

Diary of Mary Derr and Alice Derr, 1853-1861, owned by Melinda Derr Cecil of Frederick, MD.

Selections from the genealogy of the Hedges family, provided by Frank Hedges Lewis of Frederick, MD.

B. Printed Sources

Engelbrecht, Jacob, *The Diary of Jacob Engelbrecht, 1818-1878*. Edited by William R. Quynn. 3 vols., published by The Historical Society of Frederick County, Inc., Frederick, MD, 1976.

Hitselberger, Mary Fitzhugh and John Philip Dern, *Bridge in Time: The Complete 1850 Census of Frederick County, Maryland*. Monocacy Book Co., Redwood City, CA, 1978.

Holdcraft, Jacob Mehrling, *Names in Stone, 75,000 Cemetery Inscriptions from Frederick County, Maryland*. N.P., Ann Arbor, MI, 1966.

Rohrbaugh, Lewis Bunker, *Rohrbach Genealogy*. Philadelphia, PA, 1970.

Schildknecht, C. E. S., *Monocacy and Catoctin*. N.P., 1985.

Scholl, John Jacob, *The Colonial Branches, Scholl, Sholl, Shull Genealogy*. Grafton Press, New York, 1930.

Thomas, G. L., *Thomas Genealogy*. Adamstown, MD, 1954.

Wampler, Roy H., *The Derr Family 1750-1986*. Gateway Press, Baltimore, 1981.

Williams, C. S., *Williams' Frederick Directory, City Guide & Business Mirror*. Vol. I (1859-1860). Reprinted Silver Spring, MD, 1985.

C. Maps and Illustrations

Baltimore: A Picture History 1858-1968. Compiled by the Maryland Historical Society, Baltimore, 1968.

BIBLIOGRAPHY

Baltimore in Old Engravings, 1873-1880. Baltimore, 1985.

Beirne, Francis F., *Baltimore, A Picture History*. Published by the Maryland Historical Society, Hastings House, New York, 1957.

Bond, Isaac, *Map of Frederick County, MD, from Correct Instrumental Surveys by Isaac Bond, C.E.* Baltimore, 1858.

Cantor, Jay E., *Winterthur Portfolio*. New York, 1985.

Goode, James M., *The Outdoor Sculpture of Washington*. Smithsonian Institution Press, Washington, D.C., 1974.

Jacobsen, Hugh Newell, *A Guide to the Architecture of Washington, D.C.* Published for American Institute of Architects, New York, 1965.

Kouwenhoven, John, *The Columbia Historical Portrait of New York*. New York, n.d.

Lake, D. J., C.E., *Titus Atlas of Frederick County Maryland*. Published by C.O. Titus Co., Philadelphia, 1873.

Maryland: Official Highway Map. Published by Maryland Department of Transportation, Baltimore, n.d.

McCauley, Lois B., *Maryland Historical Prints, 1752-1889*. Maryland Historical Society, 1975.

Rand McNally Map of Baltimore. Rand McNally and Co., Chicago, IL, 1986.

D. Secondary Works

Andrews, Mathew Page, *History of Maryland: Province and State*. New York, 1929.

Baker, Jean H., *Ambivalent Americans, The Know-Nothing Party in Maryland*. Baltimore, 1977.

Baym, Nina, *Women's Fiction, A Guide to Women in America, 1820-1870*. Ithaca and London, 1978.

Beeton, S. S., *Beeton's Book of Household Management*. First edition facsimile, London, 1859.

Beirne, Francis F., *The Amiable Baltimoreans*. New York, 1951.

Benét, William Rose, ed., *The Reader's Encyclopedia*. New York, 1948.

Bevan, Thomas R., *220 Years, A History of the Catholic Community of the Frederick Valley*. Frederick, MD, 1977.

Bode, Carl, *American Life in the 1840's*. Berkeley, CA, 1959.

Budden, Julian, *The Operas of Verdi*. New York, 1973.

Bullock, Helen Dupre, *American Heritage Cookbook*. New York, 1964.

Calasbetta, Charlotte, *Fairchild's Dictionary of Fashion*. New York, 1975.

Cummins, Maria Susanna, *The Lamplighter*. Privately published, 1854.

BIBLIOGRAPHY

Decker, Harry, "Bantz Fortune Influenced History," *The Frederick News*, November 28, 1990.
Dictionary of American Biography. (n.p., n.d.)
D'Impero, Dan, *The A.B.C.'s of Victorian Antiques*. New York, 1875.
Dorsey, Leslie and Janice Devine, *Fare Thee Well*. New York, 1964.
Dubb, J. D., D.D., *The Reformed Church in the United States*. Lancaster, PA, 1885.
Dunn, David, et al., *History of the Evangelical and Reformed Church*. Christian Education Press, Philadelphia, 1961.
Finley, Ruth, *The Lady of Godey's, Sarah Josepha Hale*. Philadelphia, 1931.
Franklin, John Hope, *A Southern Odyssey*. Baton Rouge, 1976.
Frederick News Post.
Freeman, John W., *Stories of Great Operas*. New York, 1984.
Goren, C. H., *Goren's Hoyle, Encyclopedia of Games*. New York, 1961.
Grove, William Jarboe, *History of Carroll Manor, Frederick County, Maryland*. Lime Kiln, MD, 1928.
Hall, Clayton Colman, *Baltimore, Its History and Its People*. Lewis Historical Publishing Co., New York, 1912.
Hansrote, Hazel Groves, *Allegany County Scrapbook*. Preservation Society of Allegany County, Cumberland, MD, 1980.
Harbaugh, Linn, *The Life of Rev. Henry Harbaugh, D.D.* Reading, PA, 1900.
Harris, William H. and Judith S. Levey, *The New Columbia Encyclopedia*. Columbia University Press, New York and London, 1975.
Harwood, Herbert H., Jr., *Impossible Challenge: The Baltimore-Ohio Railroad in Maryland*. Baltimore, 1979.
The Heidelberg Catechism. Publication Board of the Reformed Church, St. Louis, 1902.
Hein, David, *A Student's View of the College of St. James on the Eve of the Civil War: The Letters of W. Wilkens Davis (1842-1866). Studies in American Religion*, The Edwin Mellen Press, Vol. 30. Lewistown, NY, 1988.
Helfenstein, Ernest, *History of All Saint's Parish*. Frederick, MD, 1932.
Historical Society of Carroll County, *The First 150 Years, A Pictorial History of Carroll County, MD, 1837-1987*. Westminster, MD, 1987.
Howard, George W., *The Monumental City, Its Past History and Present Resources*. Baltimore, 1873.
Keeler, Mary Frear and Barbara Batdorf, *The Frederick United Presbyterian Church: Chapters In Its History 1780-1980*. Frederick, MD, 1980.
Kidwell, Claudia B., *Suiting Everyone*. Smithsonian Institution Press, Washington, D.C., 1974.

BIBLIOGRAPHY

Kieffer, Elizabeth Clark, *The Life of Henry Harbaugh*. Pennsylvania German Society, Vol. I, Reading, PA, 1945.

Kohler, Carl, *A History of Costume*. New York, 1863.

Lesbian Herald. Published by the Lesbian Literary Society of the Woman's College of Frederick, Oct. 1896-1922. Name changed to *Hood College Herald*, 1922; *The Herald*, 1938.

Little, Glen L., *A Brief History of Rose Hill Manor*. Frederick County Parks and Recreation, Frederick, MD, 1971.

Markell, C. Sue, *Short Stories of Life in Frederick in 1830*. The Historical Society of Frederick County, Inc., Attic Treasures, Frederick, MD, 1948.

Martin, A. E., *History of The United States*. 2 vols. New York, 1928.

Martz, Ralph F., *Mills on the Monocacy*. Privately printed. (n.d.)

Maryland, Its Sources, Industries, and Institutions. Johns Hopkins University Press, Baltimore, 1893.

Miller, Nathan, "Assembly Visits Frederick, Surrenders to Union Flag," *Baltimore Sun*, February 16, 1961.

National Union Catalog. Library of Congress, 1956. London: Mansell, 1966-1980.

Oberholtzer, Ellis P., *Philadelphia, A History of the City and Its People*. Philadelphia, 1912.

Olson, Sherry H., *Baltimore, The Building of an American City*. Baltimore, 1980.

Papenfuse, Edwin C., *A New Guide to The Old Line State*. Baltimore, 1976.

Pennsylvania. Pennsylvania Writers' Project, New York, 1940.

The Place Names of Maryland. Maryland Historical Society, Baltimore, 1984.

Profile of American Colleges. 15th ed. New York, 1984.

Rail Tracks in Allegany County, Maryland. Published by The Preservation Society of Allegany County, MD, 1980.

Ranck, James and Dorothy, *"Unto Us," A History of the Evangelical Reformed Church*. Frederick, MD, 1964.

Ross, Isabel, *Taste in America*. New York, 1967.

Scharf, John Thomas, *The Chronicles of Baltimore, being the Complete History of "Baltimore Town" and Baltimore City*. Baltimore, 1874; reprint by Kennikat Press, Port Washington, NY, 1972.

_____, *History of Western Maryland*. 2 vols. Philadelphia, 1882; reprinted, Baltimore, 1968.

Simpson, J. F. Minor, *Monocacy Valley Maryland Presbyterianism, A History*. Frederick, MD, 1955.

Singmaster, Elsie, *Pennsylvania's Susquehanna*. Harrisburg, PA, 1950.

Stevens, Sylvester K., *Pennsylvania, Birthplace of a Nation*. New York, 1964.

BIBLIOGRAPHY

Stoner, Carol Hupping, *Stocking Up*. Emmaus, PA, 1967.

Thomas, James W. and T.J.C. Williams, *History of Allegany County, Maryland*. Reprinted, Baltimore, 1969.

Toomey, Daniel Carroll, *The Civil War in Maryland*. Baltimore, 1983.

Tracey, Grace L. and John P. Dern, *Pioneers of Old Monocacy: The Early Settlements of Frederick County, MD, 1721-1743*. Genealogical Publishing Co., Inc., Baltimore, 1987.

Trail, Florence, *In Memorial of Ariana McElfrish Trail*. Richard G. Badger, Boston, 1929.

Wampler, Roy H., *The Derr Family 1750-1986*. Baltimore, 1987.

Warner, Sam Bass, Jr., *The Private City, Philadelphia in Three Periods of Its Growth*. Philadelphia, 1968.

Warren, Mary and Mame, *Baltimore, When She Was What She Used To Be*. Baltimore, 1983.

Warren, Nancy M., *Carroll County, Maryland*. Published by the Bicentennial Committee of Carroll County, Westminster, MD, 1976.

Washington, City and Capital, American Guide Series. Works Progress Administration, Federal Writers' Project, Washington, D.C., 1937.

Waugh, Norah, *The Cut of Women's Clothes*. Theatre Arts Books, New York, 1968.

The Way to Play. The Diagram Group, Bantam Books, New York, 1975.

Weagley, Russel S. and Nicholas S. Wainwright, *Philadelphia, A 300 Year History*. (n.p., n.d.)

Webster's International Dictionary. Springfield, MA, 1984, 1986.

Wentz, Abdel Ross, *History of the Evangelical Lutheran Synod of Maryland, 1820-1920*. Harrisburg, PA, 1920.

_____, *The Lutheran Church of Frederick, Maryland, 1738-1938*. Harrisburg, PA, 1938.

West Virginia, A Guide to the Mountain State. Works Progress Administration, West Virginia Writers' Project. New York, 1941.

Williams, Thomas John Chew, *History of Frederick County Maryland From The Earliest Settlements to The Beginning of The War Between the States. Continued From the Beginning of the Year 1861 Down to the Present Time* by Folger McKinsey. 2 vols. Frederick, MD, 1910; reprinted with Index, Baltimore, 1967.

Willson, Everett B., *America's Vanishing Folkways*. South Brunswick, NJ, 1965.

Woman's College of Frederick, Maryland, Catalogue 1897-98. Frederick, MD, 1898.

Worthington, Glen H., *Fighting for Time*. Shippensburg, PA, 1985.

APPENDIX I

Scholl Genealogy — Appendix I

Christian Scholl   m. Elizabeth Brunner
b. 1770 d. 1826   b. 1775 d. 1821

1. Daniel   m. Maria Thomas
   b. 1798 d. 1873   b. 1806 d. 1873
   1. Margaret   m. James Mifflin Hood
      b. 1833 d. 1913   b. 1821 d. 1894
2. Catherine   m. Andrew Hedges
   b. 1799 d. 1878   b. 1800 d. 1875
   1. Daniel   3. Julia   5. Andrew A.
   2. Lycurgus   4. Lewis Valentine   6. Lewis Abraham
3. Charlotta   m. George Gittinger
   b. 1801 d. 1851   b. 1798 d. 1886
   1. Anna   2. Margaret
4. Elias   m. Susan Shearer
   b. 1804 d. 1851   b. 1812 d. 1834
        m. Mary Dutrow
              d. 1894
   1. Annabelle   2. David   3. Lewis
5. Rebecca   m. Cornelius Shriner
   b. 1807 d. 1838   b. 1800 d. 1854
   1. Edward   m. Margaret Derr
      b. 1807 d. 1901   b. 1832 d. 1862
   2. Cornelia
6. Lewis   m. Jemima Maynard
   b. 1809 d. 1881   b. 1822 d. 1902
   1. Mary
7. Dennis   m. Margaret Bartgis
   b. 1812 d. 1884   b. 1816 d. 1884
   1. Margaret   3. Mathias
   2. Fanny   4. Helen
8. Mary Elizabeth   m. Daniel Bentz
   b. 1816 d. 1903   b. 1803 d. 1842
        m. John H. Brunner
          b. 1813 d. 1903
   1. Daniel Bentz
   2. Infant (unnamed) Bentz
   3. Mary Elizabeth Brunner
9. Christianna
   b. (?) d. 1862

APPENDIX II

Thomas Genealogy — Appendix II

Michael Thomas m. **Margaret Ogle**
b. 1774 d. 1842 — b. 1776 d. 1854

1. Sybilla m. Valentine Adams
   b. 1803 d. 1847 b. 1800 d. 1860
   1. Eleanore
   2. Sarah
   3. Valietta
   4. Abraham
   5. Jeannette
   6. David
   7. Caroline
   8. Fanny
   9. William
   10. Robert
2. Maria m. Daniel Scholl
   b. 1806 d. 1876 b. 1793 d. 1873
   1. Margaret m. James M. Hood
      b. 1833 d. 1913 b. 1821 d. 1894
3. Christian
   b. 1807 d. 1834
4. Joseph T.
   b. 1812 d. 1876
5. David m. Elizabeth Stouffer
   b. 1812 d. 1876 b. 1817 d. 1894
   1. Lewis C.
   2. Margaret C.
   3. Alfred
   4. Sarah
   5. Laura
   6. Joseph P.
   7. Jeannette
6. Margaret m. C. Burr Artz
   b. 1815 d. 1887 b. 1801 d. 1878
   1. Victorine
7. Lewis M. m. Susan Snively
   b. 1819 d. 1882 b. 1820 d. 1882
   1. Clayonia
   2. Fanny
   3. Christian
   4. Alice
   5. Margaret
   6. Anna
   7. Caroline

APPENDIX III

Derr Genealogy — Appendix III

Sebastian Derr m. Elizabeth Loy
m. Catherine Brengle

1. Maria   m. Casper Devilbiss
   b. 1767 d. 1850   3. George   b. 1773 d. 1793
2. John Sr.   m. Catherine Steiner
   b. 1774 d. 1838   4. Thomas m. Anna Steiner
                             b. 1780 d. 1845

1. Catherine   m. Jacob Reese   3. Ann m. John Getzendanner
   b. 1797 d. 1884   b. 1801 d. 1883
2. John D. Jr. m. Elizabeth Lugenbeel
   b. 1798 d. 1866   4. MaryAnn m. Daniel Getzendanner
                     b. 1802 d. 1861   5. Frederick d 1823

  1. Catherine
     b. 1837 d. 1840
  2. Margaret   m. Edward Shriner
     b. 1832 d. 1862
  3. Mary
     b. 1834 d. 1906
  4. John P.   m. Ann Warner
     b. 1835 d. 1869
  5. Thomas
     b. 1837 d. 1860
  6. William H.
     b. 1839 d. 1839
  7. Son
     b. 1841 d. 1841
  8. Alice
     b. 1842 d. 1926
  9. Eugene   m. Frances Groverman
     b. 1844 d. 1921
  10. William R. m. Frances Gittinger
      b. 1846 d. 1915
  11. Charles
      b. 1849 d. 1883
  12. Ezra   m. Julia Latham
      b. 1851 d. 1935

APPENDIX IV

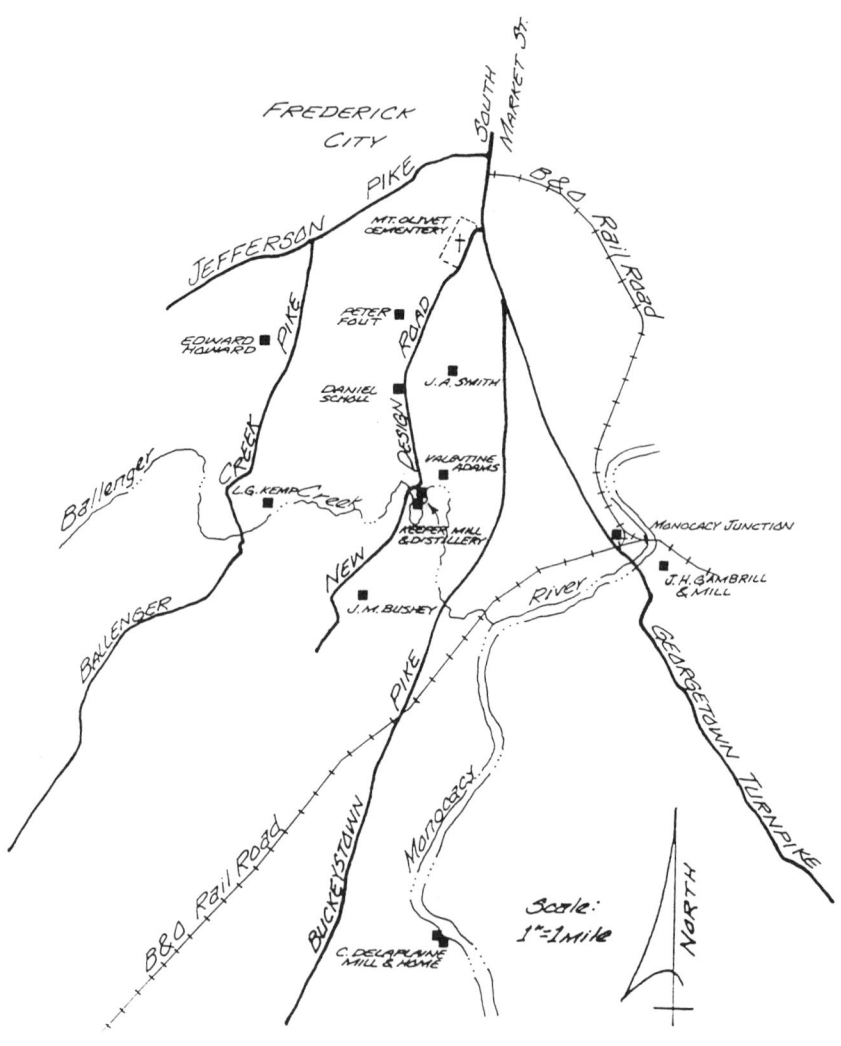

South of Frederick in 1858

APPENDIX V

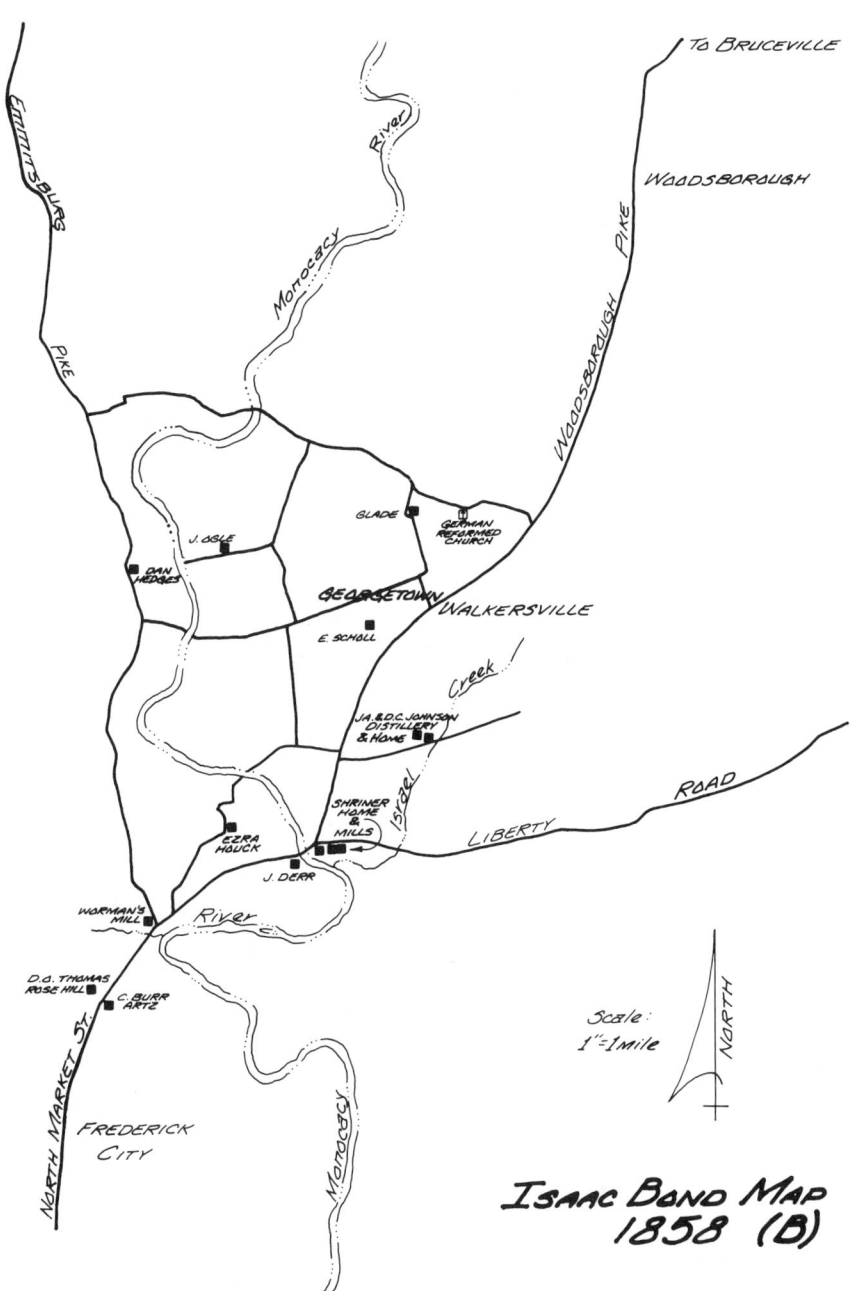

North of Frederick in 1858

APPENDIX VI

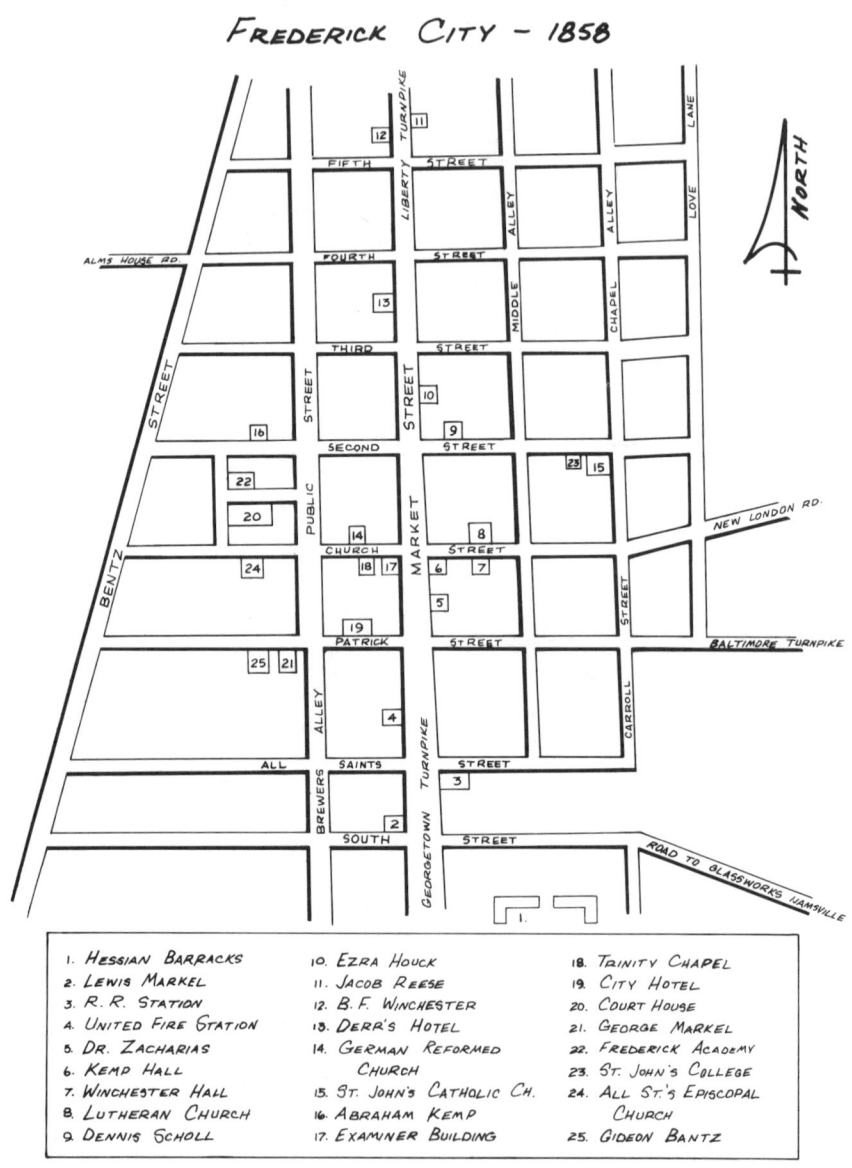

The city of Frederick in 1858

INDEX OF PLACES

The following Index of Places is designed to help the reader locate, and understand more about, the places mentioned by Margaret Scholl Hood in her diary entries. All places are in Maryland unless otherwise noted. The index reference "425, n. 5, 1861" means that the place cited will be found on page 425 in footnote 5 for the year 1861. The other references are to page numbers of this book.

Alexandria, Virginia, 11, 41, 47, 84, 132
Amboy, New Jersey, 104
Annapolis, Maryland, 123; 380; 425, n. 5, 1861
Anne Arundel County, Maryland, 49, 138
Auburn. See Frederick County, places in
Baltimore, places in or near, *et passim*
   Canton House, 233, n. 24, 1856; 273
   Charles Street Theatre, 174
   Cool Spring, 270, n. 9, 1857
   Emmanuel Church, 175, n. 12, 1855
   Fells Point, 2, n. 7, 1851
   Fort McHenry, 233, n. 23, 1856; 272; 326
   Franklintown, 231, n. 22, 1856
   Front Street Theatre, 378, n. 12, 1860
   Gilmore House, 229, n. 21, 1856
   Govanstown, 272, n. 11, 1857
   Greenmount, 6, n. 12, 1851; 174; 374
   Holiday Street Theater, 10, n. 14, 1851; 373
   Madison Avenue Temple, 6, n. 11, 1851
   Marine Bank, 271, n. 10, 1857
   Maryland Institute (Hall), 376, n. 8, 1860
   Mt. Hope, 375, n. 7, 1860
   Mount Washington, 273, n. 14, 1857
   New Assembly Rooms, 421, n. 63, 1860
   Sauerwein family homes, 1, n. 1, 1851; 172, n. 9, 1855; 173; *et passim*
   Wharf, the, 173
Baltimore, visitors from Frederick in. See *especially* John P. Derr, Margaret Derr, Margaret Scholl, Edward Shriner
Baltimore and Ohio Railroad, 12, n. 17, 1851; *et passim*
Barnesville, Maryland, 284, n. 22, 1857
Battle Creek, Michigan, 424
Bedford, Pennsylvania, 242, 248
Bedford Springs, Pennsylvania, 238, n. 27, 1856
Bloomington, Maryland, 405, 406
Boonsboro, Maryland, 316
Bruceville, Carroll County, Maryland, 12, n. 20, 1851; *et passim*. See also Margaret Scholl, travels of
Bull Run, Virginia, 426
Camden, New Jersey, 104
Carroll Borders, 418
Carroll County, Maryland, 101, 424
Cedar Rapids, Iowa, 191, 256
Ceresville, Maryland
   Mill at, 1, n. 1 and 3, 1851; 49, n. 73, 1851; 88; 335
   Shriner residence at, 1, n. 3, 1851; 335
   Singing Association at, 212, n. 1, 1856
Chambersburg, Pennsylvania, 93
Charleston, South Carolina, 144
Chicago, Illinois, 62, 275, 299, 316, 339, 357
Cleveland, Ohio, 93
Conewago Chapel, Pennsylvania, 94, n. 37, 1853; 228
Covington, 288
Cumberland, Maryland, 59, 407, 409
Cumberland County, Pennsylvania, 308
Davenport, Iowa, 249, 263
Elkridge, Maryland, 398
Ellicott Mills, Maryland, 12, n. 18, 1851
Emmitsburg, Maryland, 40, 67
   Colleges at (Mt. St. Mary's; St. Joseph's), 83, n. 28, 1853

441

INDEX OF PLACES

Fort Sumter, South Carolina, 424, n. 3, 1861
Franklin Mine, 400; 401, n. 37, 1860
Frankville, Maryland, 403
Frederick, events in
   "American" mass meeting, 295, n. 36, 1857
   Art exhibit at gallery in Frederick, 307
   Balloon ascensions, 181, n. 14, 1855; 298, n. 40, 1857; 300, n. 44, 1857; 414, n. 54, 1860
   Barnum's Menagerie, 139, n. 18, 1854
   Camp meetings, 43, n. 70, 1851; 242; 293, n. 33, 1857
   Cattle show. See Fairs (in Frederick), Frederick, events in
   Democratic barbecue, 239, n. 31, 1856
   Execution of Philip Hawkins, 313, n. 5, 1858
   Fairs (in Frederick)
      Agricultural fair, 100, n. 42, 1853; 102, n. 44, 1853; 202; 203; 346; 414
      Barracks (Barricks) Hill (Grounds), 148, n. 28, 1854; 181, n. 14, 1855; 291, n. 30, 1857; 300, n. 44, 1857
      "Cattle fairs" (shows), 148, n. 28, 1854; 201; 202, n. 25, 1855; 248; 249, n. 36, 1856; 250; 298; 343
      Church fair, 258, 259
      Fireman's fair, 101
      Jefferson, fair at, 179
   Fireworks, 187, n. 20, 1855; 190, n. 22, 1855; 240
   Irving Association, 155, n. 31, 1854; 161, n. 2, 1855; 218, n. 7, 1856
   Jousting, 284, n. 23, 1857; 287, n. 26, 1857
   Know-Nothing barbecue, 187, n. 20, 1855; 204, n. 27, 1855; 206
   Lafayette's visit, 101, n. 43, 1853
   Maryland legislature, meetings at, 425, n. 5-7, 1861
   Parades, 51, n. 75, 1851
   Political parades and speeches, 202, n. 25, 1855; 240; 410, n. 50, 1860; 414, n. 56 and 57, 1860; 416, n. 58, 1860
   Thanksgiving, 113, n. 58, 1853
   Tournaments, 284, n. 23, 1857; 287; 288; 291, n. 30, 1857
Frederick, places in
   Barracks (Barricks) Hill (Grounds). See Fairs (in Frederick), Frederick, events in
   Bentz Town, 267, n. 8, 1857
   Bridge, 296, n. 37, 1857; 396, n. 29, 1860. See also Frederick Junction and Monocacy Junction, Frederick, places in
   Churches
      Baptist, 347
      Catholic, 32; 44; 85, n. 29, 1853; 295; 300
      Episcopal, 210; 218, n. 9, 1856; 252; 292; 317
      Lutheran, 45; 129; 220, n. 11, 1856; 369, n. 13, 1859; 371
      Methodist, 186, n. 19, 1855; 197; 292; 369; 381, n. 17, 1860; 388
      Presbyterian, 178; 217, n. 5, 1856; 240; 289; 355, n. 1, 1859; 388
      Reformed, the church of Margaret Scholl, 13-15, n. 27, 1851; 253; 350; *et passim*. See also Rev. Daniel Zacharias
   Court House, 187
   Fair grounds. See Fairs (in Frederick), Frederick, events in
   Frederick Female Seminary, ix; 14, n. 26, 1851; 16; 23; 25; 38; 39, n. 65, 1851; 86, n. 31, 1853; 137; 179; 285; 333; 393
   Frederick Junction, 12, n. 17, 1851; 396, n. 29, 1860; 407, n. 44, 1860
   Frederick Market House, 156, n. 32, 1854
   Herald Buildings, 17, n. 36, 1851
   Hotels
      Central Hotel, 2, n. 4, 1851
      City Hotel, 53, n. 2, 1853; 87; 120; 191; *et passim*
      Derr's Hotel and Tavern, 417, n. 60, 1860
      Talbott's Hotel, 125, n. 3, 1854
   Independent Fire Company, 56, n. 8, 1853

INDEX OF PLACES

Frederick, places in, continued:
Jail, 346
Junior Fire Company, 219, n. 10, 1856
Manchester Farm. *See* Daniel Scholl
Monocacy Junction. *See* Frederick Junction
Mt. Olivet Cemetery, 113; 129, n. 7, 1854; 358, n. 2, 1859
Picnic grounds near, 33; 43; 46, n. 71, 1851; 48; 182; 192, n. 23, 1855; 195; 239; 243; 283; 333; 336
Railroad, 12, n. 17, 1851
Richfields, 337, n. 22, 1858
Reservoir, 31, n. 55, 1851; 41; 46; 85
Rose Hill Manor, 64, n. 16, 1853; 79
Schools
    Frederick Academy of the Visitation (the Nunnery), 285, n. 24, 1857
    Frederick Female Seminary. *See* Frederick Female Seminary, Frederick, places in
    Harmony Grove and Ceresville Sabbath School (Sabbath School), 140, n. 20, 1854; 239
    Mt. St. Mary's College, 83, n. 28, 1853
    Prospect Hall. *See* St. John's Literary Institution
    St. John's Literary Institution (Catholic School, St. John's Academy, St. John's College), 40, n. 66, 1851; 85, n. 29, 1853; 394, n. 26, 1860
    St. Joseph's Academy, 83, n. 28, 1853
Stores
    Bayfield's, 11
    Derr's, 178; 192; 332; 379, n. 13, 1860; 417
    Eldridge's millinery, 302, n. 46, 1857
    Gambrill's, 273
    Lewis' millinery, 387, n. 22, 1860
    Markel's, 185, n. 16, 1855; 218
    McEldowney's, 176
    Miller's, 186
    Rau's, 11
    Sadtler's, 176
    Schley's Dry Goods, 218, n. 8, 1856; 410, n. 49, 1860
    Shroeders & Brooks, 289, n. 29, 1857
    Thomas's, 18, n. 37, 1851
    Vermillion's millinery, 306, n. 51, 1857
United Fire Company, 14, n. 25, 1851
Winchester Hall, 14, n. 26, 1851.
See also Frederick Female Seminary, Frederick, places in

Frederick County, places in
Araby Mill, 288, n. 28, 1857
Auburn, 10, n. 16, 1851; 331
Bond Map of, 206, n. 29, 1855; 320, n. 9, 1858
Churches
    Dunkard (Church of the Brethren), 72, n. 23, 1853
    Glade German Reformed, 244, n. 32, 1856
    Haugh's German Reformed, 35, n. 61, 1851
    Israel's Creek, 226, n. 16, 1856
    Pipe Creek Friends' Meeting House, 74, n. 25, 1853
Copper Mines, 80, n. 26, 1851
Dearbought, 1, n. 2, 1851
Derrs' Island, 140, n. 20, 1854; 239, n. 28, 1856; 292
Derrs' Woods, 191
Distilleries
    Johnson's, 10, n. 16, 1851
    Keefer's mill and distillery, 304, n. 48, 1857; 305, n. 50, 1857
    Wheatley & Gambrill's, 296, n. 38, 1857
Jefferson, 179
Johnsville, 221
Linganore, 195
Linganore Mills, 168
Manchester Farm. *See* Daniel Scholl
Middletown, 91, 217
White Rock, 46, n. 71, 1851; 192, n. 23, 1855
Winebrenner's woods, 195
Frostburg, Maryland, 103
Georgetown (Washington, D.C.), 11, 67, 80, 142

INDEX OF PLACES

Georgetown, Frederick County, Maryland, 80, n. 26, 1853; 329, n. 18, 1858
Gettysburg, Pennsylvania, 30, 47, 93, 95, 97, 227, 348
  Gettysburg College, 97, n. 39, 1853; 98
  Gettysburg Seminary, 97, n. 39, 1853; 98
Grafton, West Virginia, 399, n. 35, 1860; 402; 404; 406; 425
Hagerstown, Maryland, 84, 185, 401
Hanover, Pennsylvania, 95, n. 38, 1853; 96; 97; 228; 229; 342
Harpers Ferry, West Virginia, 31, n. 56, 1851; 32, n. 57, 1851; 113; 241; 396; 407
Harrisburg, Pennsylvania, 373
Howard County, Maryland, 213
Hunterstown, Pennsylvania, 96
Illinois, 135
Kentucky, 378
Lancaster, Pennsylvania, 19, 59
Lancaster County, Pennsylvania, 97
Liberty, Maryland, 50, 89
Lisbon, Maryland, 84
Littlestown, Pennsylvania, 92
Lutherville, Maryland, 173
Manchester, Maryland, 103, 112
Martinsburg, West Virginia, 38, 57, 65, 116, 118, 134, 179, 407
McSherrystown, Pennsylvania, 228, 342
Mercersburg, Pennsylvania, 91
  Mercersburg College, 39, n. 65, 1851
Michigan, 382, 385
Middleburg, Carroll County, Maryland, 34; 69, n. 20, 1853; 74; 135
Monrovia, Maryland, 142, n. 22, 1854
Montgomery County, Maryland, 88, 105, 349
New Creek, Maryland, 404
New Market, Maryland, 79, 88, 89
New Orleans, 328
New Oxford, Pennsylvania, 93, n. 35, 1853; 213; 293; 337. *See also* Margaret Scholl, travels of
New Windsor, Maryland, 35, n. 62, 1851; 50. *See also* Margaret Scholl, travels of
  Calvert College, 50, n. 74, 1851
  New Windsor College, 35, n. 62, 1851
New York, 104-106, 355, 373

New York World's Fair, 103, n. 46, 1853
Parkersburg, West Virginia, 396
Philadelphia, 6, 19, 27, 82, 88, 103-109, 113, 115, 153, 268, 321, 326, 373, 379, 385, 387, 394. *See also* Margaret Scholl, travels of
Piedmont, West Virginia, 61, n. 13, 1853; 134, n. 14, 1854; 395, n. 27, 1860; 396-407; 410; 413; 415; 420. *See also* Margaret Scholl, travels of
Pittsburg[h], Pennsylvania, 92, 95, 97, 227, 235, 254, 280, 282, 286, 345, 368
Port au Prince, Haiti, 420, n. 62, 1860
Prince George's County, Maryland, 85
Raleigh, North Carolina, 327
Relay, Maryland, 323, n. 10, 1858
Richmond, Virginia, 56, 421
Rock Island, Illinois, 256, 307
Rockville, Maryland, 151
St. Louis, Missouri, 9
Selma, Alabama, 328
Somerset County, Pennsylvania, 52
Swanton, Maryland, 403, n. 40, 1860
Sykesville, Maryland, 76
Sylvan Retreat, 53, 77. *See also* Manchester Farm, Frederick County, places in
Taneytown, Maryland, 34, 35, 69, 72
Thorndale, Carroll County, Maryland, 35, n. 60, 1851; 71
Tiffin, Ohio, 125, 294, 328
Union Bridge, Maryland, 74, n. 25, 1853
Uniontown, Maryland, 71, 73, 75
Urbana, Maryland, 143, 359
Virginia, 79, 99
Walkersville, Maryland, 204, 329
Washington County, Maryland, 91
Washington, D.C., 11, 19, 41, 49, 62, 79, 95, 122, 123, 191, 257, 280, 312, 323-325, 389
Westernport, Maryland, 397, n. 30, 1860; 398; 401, n. 37, 1860; 402; 406
Westminster, Maryland, 70
Winchester, Virginia, 417
Woodsboro, Maryland, 79
York, Pennsylvania, 59, 95, 96, 126, 227, 378
Zanesville, Ohio, 402

INTRODUCTION TO INDEX OF PERSONS

For the convenience of readers, genealogists, and family historians, the *Diaries of Margaret Scholl Hood* includes both an Index of Places (which begins on page 441) and an Index of Persons, which follows directly below. There are nearly two thousand names listed, with many variations in spelling. Because these diaries were intended for Margaret's use only, she often abbreviated names or used initials; she also was careless in her spelling.

In the Index of Persons, the editors attempted to cite the first appearance of every name; however, the individual may be referred to earlier in the text. If the individual is cited many times, page numbers were chosen from various years to indicate that the person is mentioned throughout the diaries. Because of space limitations, the citations are listed three to five times, with the note *et passim* indicating that this name appears elsewhere in the text. Those individuals closely connected to Margaret by ties of family or friendship are indicated as such by using her initials M.S. Additional information about some of these individuals, considered important by the editors, also has been cited where appropriate. The citation "114, n. 59, 1853" means that the name will be found on page 114 in footnote 59 for the year 1853. The other references are simply to page numbers where the name will be found.

As to Margaret Scholl, a thorough reading of the diaries will enable the reader to discover her many activities, with both the Index of Places and the Index of Persons providing references that reveal some of the more important aspects of the life of this young woman.

Note to Genealogists: For those interested in further research, the source materials for the diaries are available in the Hood College Archives, as are the computer disks containing the entire volume. Additional information may be found by referring to the Thomas, Derr, and Scholl genealogies, or by contacting the Historical Society of Frederick County, Inc., or the C. Burr Artz Library Maryland Room. Please note that where surnames are unknown, individuals have been listed under their first names.

Aaron,
   servant of Mrs. I.
      Howard, 102, n. 45,
      1853
Abbott, the Miss, 142

Abell(s), 131, 171, 271, 311,
   373, *et passim*
   Mary, 273
   Messrs., 175
   Mr., 310, 326, 327

   Mrs., 310, 327, 376
   Rose (Rosa), 130, 173,
      271, 310, 373, *et*
      passim
Abrahams, Miss, 171

INDEX OF PERSONS

Adams
Abraham F. (A., Abram, Coz. A.F.), cousin of M.S., first son of Valentine, 13, 20, 32, 44; family of, 15, n. 32, 1851; marriage of, 114, n. 59, 1853; 116; *et passim*. Appendix II
Caroline, cousin of M.S., fifth daughter of Valentine. Appendix II
David, cousin of M.S., second son of Valentine. Appendix II
Eleanore, cousin of M.S., first daughter of Valentine. *See* Cooper
Fanny (Cousin F., Fannie), cousin of M.S., sixth daughter of Valentine, 19, 27, 44, 144, 196; family of, 15, n. 32, 1851; 389, n. 23, 1860; *et passim*. Appendix II
H., 20
Jeannette (Ginnie, Jeanette, Jennie, Jenny), cousin of M.S., fourth daughter of Valentine, 19, 88, 113, 144, 258; family of, 15, n. 32, 1851; 309, n. 1, 1858; *et passim*. Appendix II
Messrs., 22
Robert, cousin of M.S., fourth son of Valentine. Appendix II
Sarah A., cousin of M.S., second daughter of Valentine. *See* Shank
Sarah A., née Kemp, wife of Abraham, 85; 114, n. 59, 1853; 116; 367
Sarah E. (Mrs. Sallie, Sallie, Sally), née Mehrling, second wife of Valentine, 15, n. 30, 1851; 38; 258; 389, n. 24, 1860; *et passim*
Sybilla, née Thomas, first wife of Valentine, 15, n. 32, 1851; 309, n. 1, 1858. Appendix II
Valentine (Uncle A., Uncle Adams), 15, n. 30, 1851; 239, n. 31, 1856; 309, n. 1, 1858; 314; 362; *et passim*
children of: *see* Abraham, Caroline, David, Eleanore, Fanny, Jeannette, Robert, Sarah, Valietta, and William
death of, 382, n. 19, 1860
Appendix II
Valietta, cousin of M.S., third daughter of Valentine. *See* Weagly
William (Willie), cousin of M.S., third son of Valentine, 33, 183. Appendix II
Albaugh, Mrs., 21
Anderson
Dr., 233, 273
Dr. Mort, 105
Eunice, 241
Isaac (Judge), 121
Jennie, née Turner, 329
Mr., 329, 400, 407
Mrs., 396, 398, 400, 403, 406, *et passim*
Rev. Mr., 228
Angle, J., 89
Annon, Dr., 250
Anspach (Anspache), Rev. Mr., 309, 374
Appold
Lily, 411
Miss(es), 198, 411
Mrs., 410
Arnold, Lew, actor, 82
Arthur, Mr., 374
Artz
C. Burr (Uncle, Uncle Artz), 23, n. 44, 1851; 222; 329; 357; 368; *et passim*
child of: *see* Victorine
Appendix II
Margaret (Aunt Artz, Aunt M.), née Thomas, wife of C. Burr, 13, n. 23, 1851; 23, n. 44, 1851; 162; 222; 316; *et passim*.
Appendix II
Rev. Dr. William, 378
Victorine (V., Vic), cousin of M.S., daughter of C. Burr, 23, n. 44, 1851; 29, n. 52, 1851; 166; 167; 392; *et passim*.
Appendix II
Ashland, Mrs., 271
Autobinen, Rt. Rev. John, 50
Ayers, Dr., 348
Ayton, Vic, 319-321
B., Callie, 48
Backus, Rev. Mr. (Dr.), 375, 421
Baer, Mary, 361
Bailey (Baily), Belle, 171, 173, 291, 309
Baker
Mr., 50, 417
Rev. Mr., 4
William (Wm.), 304
Balderson
Mr., 421
Mrs., 421
Ball
Lewis, 142
Mary, 142
Mr., 147, 380
old Mr., 277
Baltzell, Major, 362
Bane, Mr., 146
Banel family, actors, 373
Bantz
Ada, 278
Callie (Call, Cally), née Brunner, 17, 28, 77, 264, 268, *et passim*
Dody (Dodie), 365, 412, 420
Gideon, 2, n. 4, 1851
Gideon, Sr., death of, 148
Kate. *See* Davis

INDEX OF PERSONS 447

Bantz, continued:
  Marie, 272
  Mary, 264
  Pete, 318
  Sophie, 175
  Mr., 37, 43
  Mr. T., 5
  Mrs., 29, 279, 367
  Mrs. T., 5, 8
  Mrs. William (Mrs. Wm., Mrs. Wm. L.), 79, 159, 164
  old Mrs., 407, 418
  William (Mr. Wm.), 44
Barche, Tom, 414
Barchus, Annie, 340
Barnum, P. T., 8, n. 13, 1851; 139, n. 18, 1854
Barr, Mr., suitor of M.S., 147-150, 153-155, 159-165
Bartgis, Margaret. See Scholl
Barthelow, Mary. See Buckingham
Bassemer, Mr., 44
Baugher
  Ed (E., Mr. E.), 367, 368, 371
  Lizzie, 115, 371, 417
Bausman
  Miss, 2, 4, 6, 9, 172, et passim
  Mr., 7, 11, 172, 174
  Sophia (Miss S.), 7, 175
Bayfield
  Miss, 110
  Miss C., 373
  Miss E., 373
  Misses, 130, 172, 175, 375
  Mr., 6, 11, 271, 309-311
  Mrs., 6, 11, 176, 310, 375, et passim
  Mrs. J., 7
  Mrs. James (Mrs. James H.), 5, 133, 232, 372, 375
  Mrs. John, 3
Bealle, J., 146
  Mr., 144
Beam, George (Geo.), 130, 131
Beard, Mr., 3, 4, 7
Beatson, E. See Jones
Beauman, Henrietta, 121

Bechtol, Rev. Mr., 235
Beer, M., 16
Beise, Mrs. H., 375
Bell
  Lou, 373
  Mr., suitor of M.S., 147; 148; 152; 155; 410, n. 50, 1860
Belvin
  Missouri, 128
  Mrs., 88
Benke
  Hettie, 375
  Mr., 375
  Mrs., 375
Bennett
  brother Rev. (Brother), 358
  Mr., 401
Bentz
  Annie. See Keefer
  Becky (B.), 340, 409
  Cal, 220
  Daniel, first husband of Mary Elizabeth Scholl child of: see Daniel Appendix I
  Daniel, cousin of M.S., son of Daniel. Appendix I
  Lewis, 71
  Lizzie. See Jamison
  Mary Elizabeth, née Scholl. See Brunner
  Mrs. J., 71
Bevan, Mrs. Sarah, 273
Bier, 232
  Barbara, 377
  I., 174
  Jacob, 231, 232, 272
  Mary, 175, 232, 233, 272, 377, et passim
Bierley (Bireley, Birely, Byerly)
  Anna, 371
  Charles, 15, n. 31, 1851
  Ed, 212
  George (G., Geo., Mr. G., Mr. Geo.), 47, 240, 290, 344, 395, et passim
  Jacob, 15, n. 31, 1851; 235, n. 26, 1856
  L., 3
  Lewis, 272
  M., 9, 296

M. S., 259
Mary, 51, 79, 80, 103, 114, et passim
Miss, 3
Mr., 4, 48, 242, 264
Mrs. George (Mrs. G., Mrs. Geo.), 319, 382, 395
Bireley, Birely. See Bierley
Birnie
  Ellen, 69
  Fannie, 69
  Hester, 69
  Miss(es), 34, 71
  Mrs. Roger (Mrs. R.), 35, 71
  Roger, 69
  Rose, 69
Biser
  Malinda, 242
  Mrs., 204, 329
  Sophia (Soph), 242
Bladen, Mr., 45
Boags, Mr., 264
Bolles, Mrs., 93-97
Bond, Isaac, surveyor for map of Frederick County, 206, n. 29, 1855; 320
Borsley, Mrs., 222
Bosely
  Mary, 2
  Mrs. Dr., 311
Boulder, Dr., 305
Bowers, Knotly, 282
Bowie, Louisa (Louise), 232, 377
Bowlus, Sarah, née Schaeffer, 242
Boyd, 186, 190, 246, 290, 295, et passim
  Dan, 190
  Ginny (Gin, Jenny), 88, 162, 247, 296, 333, et passim
  Hamilton (H., Ham), 53, n. 3, 1853; 137; 215; 292; 333; et passim
  Ken (K), 86, 109, 140, 162, 234, et passim
  L., 55
  Lizzie (Mrs. W., Mrs. Wils), née Roelke, wife of Wilson, 381, 385, 389

INDEX OF PERSONS

Boyd, continued:
M., 109
Miss, 87
Mr., 85, 152, 177, 293, 351, *et passim*
Mrs., 197, 234, 365, 411
old Mrs., 301, 409-410
Wilson (W., W.R., Wils), 139, 162, 209, 253, 292, 381, *et passim*
Boyle, Charlie, 70
Brady
Gregg, 38
Jack, 132
K., 14, 16
Brauns, Em (Miss), 374, 377
Brengle
Catherine. *See* Derr
Fannie, 344, n. 25, 1858
Ginnie (Ginny, Jen, Jennie, Jenny), 43, 252, 315, 338, 364, *et passim*
John W., 252
Lizzie. *See* Kemp
Mrs., 344, 361
Mrs. L. J., 278
Mrs. S., 14
Robert, 344
Will, 368
Brewer
Elizabeth (Eliz, Eliza, Liza, Liza J.), 79, 124, 156
L., 64
Lucretia, 14, 79
Breyle, Margaret. *See* Schley
Brignoli, Perri, singer, 421
Brinkley, Miss, 214, n. 2, 1856
Brisere
Ann, 251
Ellen, 251
Brooke (Brooks), Mr., 85, 311, 333
Brown
Emily B. (Em), née Pearce, wife of William, 47, 63
Mag, née Wolf(e), 119, 132, 272
Misses, 2
Mr. (Mr. B.), 17, 20, 61

Mrs. B., 61
Mrs. Mary, 54
William A. (Wm. A.), 63
Bruce, Mr., 372, 377
Brunner (Bruner)
Ann M. *See* Kemp
Callie. *See* Bantz
Ed, 165
Elizabeth. *See* Scholl
Ellen. *See* Rohrback
Frank, 261
Jacob, 13, n. 24, 1851
John (J. H., Uncle), 68; 319; 359, n. 4, 1859; child of: *see* Mary
Lucretia, 26, 30, 37
Mag M., née Pypher, wife of Val, 63, 65
Mary, cousin of M.S., daughter of John, 344. Appendix I
Mary Elizabeth (Aunt Lizzie), née Scholl, wife of John, 344; 359, n. 4, 1859; 367. Appendix I
Mr. M., 62, 82
Mrs., 212, 408
P., 17
Val (V.), 62, 63, 82, 259
Buchanan, President, 253, n. 42, 1856
Buck
Beverly, 173, 203
Mr., 235, 256
Mrs., 251, 256
Buckey, 189
Annie, 32, 206
Isa (I., Isie, Isy), 26, 42, 112, 169, 358, *et passim*
Juliet (Julia), 42
Mary. *See* Miller
Miss, 42, 205
Mr. J., 18, 339
Mrs. Jacob (Mrs. J.), 18, 26, 63, 206
Buckingham
Mary, née Barthelow, 54, 119
Mr., 119
Burke
Belle, 232
George (Geo. B.), 233, 242

Natta, 232
Burkette, Miss, 251
Burrier, Fannie, 29
Burton, Mrs., 31, 270
Busey, Rev. Mr., 216
Bushey
Annie M., 409
Frances, 334
Mr., 122, 368
Mrs. (Mrs. B.), 20, 122, 139, 334, 409, *et passim*
Butler
General, 425, n. 5, 1861
Miss, 407
Byerly. *See* Bierley
Byre (Byer), Mary, 48, 140
Byrne, Mr., 85
Calvert, Charles B., 346
Camel, Mr., 103
Campbell
Annie (A.), 17, 193
Lottie A., 39
Carmack
Miss, 35
Miss E., 35
Carroll
Mr., 326
Mrs., née Read, 326
Carson, Mary, née Kean, wife of J. Hays, 364, 367, 368, 426
Carter
Miss, 7
Mrs., 9
Cashel, Mrs. Abe, 381
Castle, Mrs., 296, 318, 411
Chambers, Rev. Mr., 326
Chandler, Mrs., 25, 37, 101
Chapman, Mary, 101
Chatard, Dr., 130, 233
Choate, Miss, 101
Ciders
C., 95
Miss, 93
Clabaugh (Claybaugh)
Mr. A., 76
Mrs. Ada, 76
Mrs. M. C., 19
Mrs. Margaret, 24
Claggett (Clagett, Clagget)
D., 313
Dr., 391, n. 25, 1860
E. G. (Mr.), 384, 385, 387, 419
Emma, 313, 352, 393

INDEX OF PERSONS 449

Claggett, continued:
  Kate, 313
  Rob, 391
  Sam, 371
  Tom, 391
Clark (Clarke)
  Lizzie, 258, 259, 364
  Mr., 40
  Mrs., 296, 338
Claude, 282
Claybaugh. *See* Clabaugh
Cleaver, Mr., 402
Cline (Kline)
  Mr., 246, 248, 253, 254
  old Mr., 389
  Sam, 249
  Tom, 249
Clingan (Clingham)
  Annie, 120, 177, 280, 366, 380, *et passim*
  Frank, 117
  John, 348
  Lewis, 161, 164
  Miss, 15
  Miss Mary, 20, 150
  Mr., 136, 150
  Mrs., 19, 20, 120, 197, 289, *et passim*
  Mrs. John, 289; 362, n. 9, 1859
Clippinger
  Louise (Lou, Mrs. C. L.), née Hersh, friend of M.S., wife of C. L., 29, n. 53, 1851; 30; 36; 121; 125; *et passim*
  birth of her daughter Nancy, 369, n. 14, 1859
  in Frederick, 30-34, 224, 225
  letters to M.S. from Pittsburgh, 254
  M.S.'s visit with in New Oxford, 92-98
  marriage to C.L., 229, 266, 327, 355, 372, *et passim*
  visits at Manchester Farm, 116, 213, 214, 266, 267, *et passim*
  wedding trip to Baltimore, 229, 230
  writes M.S. about wedding plans, 220
  Nancy Hersh, 369, n. 14,

1859
  Mr. C. L., 213; 226, n. 17, 1856; 227-230; 266; 267; *et passim*
Clity
  Mr., 182
  Mrs., 182
Coblentz, Miss A. (Annie), 24, 29
Cockey
  Dr., 198
  G., 20
  Mrs., 198
Cockrill (Cockrel)
  Maria, 232, 271, 272
  Sophie, 232, 271
Coleman, Ella, 25
Colson, Pauline (Madame), singer, 421
Cookson
  Annie M., 314
  Emily, 300, 314
  Mr., 90
Cooper
  Annie, 385
  David, 21, n. 41, 1851
  Eleanore (Nellie), née Adams, wife of David, 19; 21, n. 41, 1851. Appendix II
  James, 390
  John, of Michigan, 382, 385, 386, 389, 424, *et passim*
  Judge, 21, n. 41, 1851; 60
  Marie E., née Trimper, wife of John, of Michigan, 424
  Mary H. (M), 196, 390, 392
  Minnie (little, M.), 71, 196
  Miss, 390
  Mrs. John, 196
Cover
  John, 73
  Lou, 72
  Miss Lizzie, 72
  Mrs. Milton, 35
  T. F., 35, 69, 74
  Tom, 71, 72, 75, 76
  Wilt, 72
Cox
  Miss, 35
  Mr., 148, 191, 210, 221,

234, *et passim*
  Mrs. William (Mrs. Wm.), 195
  William, 217
Craines, Jemy, 259
Cramer
  Annabelle (Annabell, Annabella), née Scholl, wife of John D., 65; 344, n. 27, 1858; 416, n. 59, 1860; 418; 423, n. 2, 1861. Appendix I
  Jeremiah, 201, 212
  Jerry, 196, 316
  John, 284
  John D., 423, n. 2, 1861
  John G., 423, n. 2, 1861
  Mary Ann. *See* Hammond
  Miss, 212
  Miss B., 285
  Mr., 177, 305
  Mrs. L., 332
Crampton, Livie, 306
Creager
  Mr., 46, 48
  Mr. E., 33, 37
  Old Mr., 136
Cromwell
  Annie, 343, 365
  Dick, 33, 40
  Lizzie, 81
  Mr. R., 18
  Mrs., 365
Cronise
  Kate, 142
  Old Mr., 142, 179
Crook (Crooks)
  G. W. M., 388
  Hannah, née Lewis, wife of G. W. M., 187, 197, 217, 249, 388, *et passim*
  Mary, 73
  May (Miss M.), 74
Cross, Rev. M., 374
Crumbaugh, Miss, 80
Cummins, Rev. Dr., 378
Cunningham
  Evelyn V., 419, n. 61, 1860
  Mr., 381
Curley, Mrs. M. A., 376
D., Ophelia, 38
Daniels, Mary, 115

INDEX OF PERSONS

Darling, Grace, 229
Daugherty
  Annie, 359
  H., 143
  Miss(es), 44, 242
  priest, 284
Davis, 425
  Emma (Em, Miss E.), 55, 373, 376-378, *et passim*
  G. Harry, 395
  Hallie, 398, 400, 404
  Ham, 223
  Henry G. (Capt., Capt. Davis, Capt. H., Harry, Mr. Davis), B&O railroad man, 55; 396, n. 29, 1860; marriage to Kate Bantz, 61, n. 13, 1853; residence and work at Piedmont, West Virginia, 134, n. 14, 1854; 396; *et passim*
  Henry W., 324
  Jefferson, 425, n. 7, 1861
  Kate (K., K.B., Katie, Katie B.), née Bantz, friend of M.S., wife of Henry G., 2, n. 4, 1851; 16; 24; 28; 32; *et passim*
    death of daughter Ada, 245
    first daughter of, 120, 121
    marriage to Henry G., 2, n. 4, 1851; 61, n. 13, 1853; 268
    moves to Piedmont, 134, n. 14, 1854
    two children of, 365
    visit of M.S. to Piedmont, 396-407
    visits in Frederick, 245, 364, 387, 391
    visits to Manchester Farm, 365, 424
  Mollie, 170
  Mr., 396-407, 425
  Mr., of Baltimore, 292
  Mrs., 397, 400
  Mrs., of Baltimore, 292
  Mrs. William, 400, 401, 405
  old Mrs., 396-399, 403- 405, 407, *et passim*
  Rev. Mr., 170
  Tommy, 399, 402
  William, 400, 401, 405
Dawney (Dorney, Downey)
  Eliza, 7, 110, 171
  Kate, 7, 110, 171
  Miss, 410, 411
Dealman, Dr., 98
Dean
  James, 236
  Mr., 132, 232, 385
  Mrs., 232, 303, 311
  Nellie (Neal, Neallie, Nell), née Gordon, 231-233, 270, 310, 327, 378, *et passim*
  William A. (Wil, Will, Wm., Wm. A.), of Baltimore, 11, 84, 132, 172, 378, *et passim*
DeArmitage, Mrs., 310, 311
Deatrick (Deitrick, Detrick, Dietrick)
  J. H., 252
  Mrs., 42, 269
  Mrs. J. H., 252
  Stull, 326
Deaver, Tessie, 298
Deffenderfer (Diffenderfer)
  Dr., 174
  Michael, 289
DeFord, Mr., 43
Deihl (Diehl), George (Mr., Rev. Dr.), 220, n. 11, 1856; 369, n. 13, 1859
Deitrick. *See* Deatrick
Delaplaine
  Cally, 86
  Caroline, of Carroll County, 74
  George Washington, 291, n. 31, 1857
  Kate, of Carroll County, 74
  Mr., of Carroll County, 74, 262
  Mrs., of Carroll County, 74
  Mrs., of Frederick County, 25; 291, n. 31, 1857
  Theodore Crist, 291, n. 31, 1857
Delasmouth (Delasmuth, Delasmutt)
  Dr. V., 193; 196; 264; 336, n. 21, 1858; 337; *et passim*
  Francis, 32
  John, 288
  Miss, 264
  Mr., 298
  Mrs., 348
Denison, Miss, 233
Denniston, John, 95
Denton
  Mrs. Randolf, 312
  Randolf, 312
Derr
  Alice, fourth daughter of John D., Jr., friend of M.S., 251, n. 39, 1856; 313; 341; 385; 408; *et passim.* Appendix III
  Ann, second daughter of John, Sr. *See* Getzendanner
  Ann (Annie, Mrs. John P.), née Warner, wife of John P., 373; 384; 408, n. 45, 1860. Appendix III
  Anna, née Steiner, wife of Thomas. Appendix III
  Catherine, first daughter of John D., Jr. Appendix III
  Catherine, first daughter of John, Sr. *See* Reese
  Catherine, née Brengle, second wife of Sebastian, 344, n. 25, 1858. Appendix III
  Catherine (old Mrs., old Mrs. D.), née Steiner, wife of John, Sr., 49. Appendix III
  Charles, seventh son of John D., Jr. Appendix III
  Elizabeth, née Loy, first wife of Sebastian. Appendix III
  Elizabeth, née Lugenbeel, wife of John D., Jr., 307, n. 55, 1857. Appendix III

INDEX OF PERSONS   451

Derr, continued:
  Eugene, fifth son of
    John D., Jr., 1, n. 2,
    1851; 189; 244; 307, n.
    55, 1857; 390; *et
    passim*. Appendix III
  Ezra, eighth son of John
    D., Jr. Appendix III
  Frances (Mrs. William),
    née Gittinger, wife of
    William R. Appendix
    III
  Frances, née
    Groverman, wife of
    Eugene. Appendix III
  Frederick, second son of
    John, Sr. Appendix
    III
  George, second son of
    Sebastian. Appendix
    III
  George (Mr. Derr),
    proprietor of Derr's
    store, 349; 379, n. 13,
    1860
  John, Sr. (Old Mr.),
    first son of Sebastian,
    1, n. 2, 1851.
    Appendix III
  John D., Jr. (J.D., Mr.),
    first son of John, Sr.,
    1, n. 2, 1851; 49; 307,
    n. 55, 1857; 320; 384;
    et passim. Appendix
    III
  John P. (J., John), first
    son of John D., Jr., 6;
    7; 49; 65; *et passim*
    at Mag Derr's
    wedding, 322
    husband of Ann
      Warner, 384, 408
    working in Baltimore,
      121; 170, n. 7, 1855;
      193; 273; 373, n. 4,
      1860
    Appendix III
  Julia (Julie), née
    Latham, wife of Ezra,
    362, 386
  Margaret, friend of
    M.S., second daughter
    of John D., Jr. *See*
    Shriner
  Maria, daughter of
    Sebastian. *See*

Devilbiss
  Mary (M. Derr), friend
    of M.S., third
    daughter of John D.,
    Jr., 23; 58, n. 10, 1853;
    140; 322; 357; *et
    passim*
    diary of, xi; 14, n. 26,
      1851
    visit to Tiffin, Ohio,
      288, n. 27, 1857
    Appendix III
  Mary Ann, third
    daughter of John, Sr.
    See Getzendanner
  Sebastian, father of
    John, Sr. Appendix
    III
  Thomas, third son of
    Sebastian. Appendix
    III
  Thomas (T., Tom,
    Tommie, Tommy),
    second son of John
    D., Jr., 23; 32; 45; 50;
    140, n. 19, 1854; death
    of, 420, n. 62, 1860; *et
    passim*. Appendix III
  William H., third son of
    John D., Jr.
    Appendix III
  William R., proprietor
    of Derr's Hotel, sixth
    son of John D., Jr.,
    291, n. 30, 1857; 417,
    n. 60, 1860. Appendix
    III
Detrick. *See* Deatrick
Devalin, Carrie, 373
Devilbiss
  Casper (C.), 50.
    Appendix III
  D., 20, 50
  Maria, née Derr, wife of
    Casper. Appendix III
  Mrs. D., 20, 50
  old Mr., 362
Devitt, May, 298
Devrich, Mrs., 298
Dickey, 273
  Lizzie, 171, 273
  Mr., 273
Dietrick. *See* Deatrick
Diehl. *See* Deihl
Diffenderfer. *See*
  Deffenderfer

Diggs, James, 313, n. 5,
  1858
Dihoff, Miss, 81
Dill
  Harriet M., 297
  Mr., 261
Disney
  Mr., 132
  Mrs., 132
Dix, Fanny (Fannie), 132,
  171, 172, 377
Dixon, Miss, 80
Dole, Rev. Mr., 347
Doll
  C., 38
  Lottie, 39
  Miss, 15, n. 33, 1851
  Mrs., 152
  Mrs. J. G., 254
Donohue, Miss, 48
Dorney. *See* Dawney
Dorsey
  Basil, 291, n. 30, 1857
  D., 193
  Dennis, 218
  Drucilla, 317
  Lloyd (Dr., Dr. D.),
    193; 205; 221, n. 12,
    1856
  Miss, 10, n. 16, 1851
  Mr., 213
  Nevins, 193, 317, 350
Doub
  Capt., 119, 282
  Ellen, 186, n. 19, 1855
  Mr., 28
  Mrs., 28
Doud, Jane. *See* McCleary
Douglas
  Rev. Mr., 235, 279
  Stephen A. (Hon.), 410,
    n. 48, 1860
Downey. *See* Dawney
Drakely, Mrs., 5
Drill
  Harriet (Miss H.), née
    Keefer, wife of Henry,
    15, 99, 299, 314
  Henry, 299
  Mary, 314
Dronenburg, Miss, 366
DuBois, Father John, 83, n.
  28, 1853
Duderar, Mrs., 391
Dukehart
  Capt., 399

INDEX OF PERSONS

Dukehart, continued:
Mr., 278
Duncan
Mr., 104
Dunham
Fanny, 36
Ginnie (G.), 6, 11, 15
Mr., 56
Mrs., 6, 38, 200
Dunning, Mr., 374
Dutrow
Amelia, 316
Ella, 344
Francina, 21
Ham, 191
John, 337, 344
Julia, 80
Mary. *See* Scholl
Misses, 182, 365
Mr., 44, 323
Mr. C., 348
Mr. J., 21, 80
Mrs., 44, 198, 323, 365
Mrs. J., 21
Mrs. Randolf, 195, 316, 337
Randolf, 195, 316
Duval
Miss, 256
Mrs., 297
Eader
Gus, 291
Mr., 85, 195, 407
Eagle
Frances, 19
Mr., 32
Eaton, Miss Vic, 286, 288
Ebert (Ebbert, Eberts)
Lucretia (Lou, Lou E., Sis), friend of M.S., 29; 160; 251; 364; 397, n. 31, 1860; *et passim*
Miss, 420
Mrs., 160, 396, 408
O., 6
Sue, 391
Eichelberger
Marion, 284
Mary, 119, 284, 285
Mr., 133
Mrs., 337
Eldridge, Mrs., 302
Ellicott Brothers, 12, n. 18, 1851
Elliot, Prof., 298, n. 40, 1857; 300, n. 44, 1857

Ellis
Lucy, 227, 228
Mr., 229
Mrs., 95, 96, 227, 228, 229
Endsor (Endsors), Mr. J., storekeeper, 5, 20
Engelbrecht
Jacob, 14, 100, 102, 239, 313, *et passim*. *See* Bibliography
Mrs., 361
Entler
Fanny, 220
Ginny, 251
Miss, 218
Erner, Miss, 195
Everett, 410, n. 50, 1860
Feller, Mrs. A., 16
Ferney, Miss, 334, 335
Fessler, old Mrs., 16
Fillmore, Millard, President, 62; 253, n. 42, 1856
Finckel, Lou, 34
Finney (Finey)
Mary E., 63
Mr., 54, n. 5, 1853
Mrs., 102
Firtvan, Mr., 272
Fisher
Dr., 228
Jane, 228
Fite, Lizzie, 134
Fitzgerald, Mrs., 6
Fleming
Dr., 85, 86, 91
Harriet (Hariet), 208
Foot, Rev. Mr., 280
Ford, Mrs., 251, 256
Forest, Brother, 397
Foulk, Mr., 421
Fout
B., 27, n. 51, 1851; 29; 36; 65; 111; *et passim*
Baker, 322
Dan, 358
David, death of, 276, n. 17, 1857
George, 276, 348
Grafton, 254
Lewis (Louis), 242; 358; death of, 276, n. 19, 1857
Mary, 112
Mrs., 20, 30, 299, 350

Mrs. Grafton (Mrs. Graft), 268, 361
Mrs. Greenberry, 22
Mrs. Lewis, 222, 333, 348, 358, 363, *et passim*
Mrs. Peter (Mrs. P.), 112, 124, 147, 322, 349, *et passim*
Mrs. William, 33
Olivia (Lizzie), 124, 348, 358
William, 33
Fox
M., 372, 373
Margaret, 310
Miss, 130, 230, 326, 327, 375, *et passim*
Mr., 311, 326
Mrs., 231
Franks, Mrs., 282
Fremont, John C., candidate, 253, n. 42, 1856
French
Lottie, née Hauer, 128, 146
Mr., 26, 128
Mrs., 32, 140, 149
Fries, Mrs., 50
Fritchey, Mr., 69
Fulton
John, 20
Mr., 271
Gaither, Sophia (Sophie), 161, 317, 321, 333, 367, *et passim*
Gallagher, Misses, 48
Gallian (Gallion), 384
George K., 351
Mary, 367
Mr., tenant of Daniel Scholl, 351; 353; 359; 360, n. 6, 1859; 363; *et passim*
Mrs., 365
old Mrs., 367, 394, 412
Galt
John, 135
Rev. Mr., 420
Gambrill (Gambrel, Gambril)
Bettie, 290
Dod (D., Dod G.), 207, 246, 284, 290, 333, *et passim*

INDEX OF PERSONS 453

Gambrill, continued:
　Ginny, 189
　Horace (H. D.), 288, 290
　James (J., Jemmy, Jimmy), suitor of M.S., 225; 260; 273; 278; 288, n. 28, 1857; *et passim*
　Joe, 273
　Miss, 288
Gardiner (Gardner)
　Lucy, 228
　M., 25
　Marianne, 172
Garrott
　Ginnie, 52
　Lenie (L.), 20, 21
　Louise (Lou), 45, 85
　Mr. H., of Baltimore, 45
　Mr. J., 45
　Mr. R., of Baltimore, 45
　Olivia (Livie, O.), 20, 50, 61, 139
Geesey,
　Sam (Rev. Mr.), 246, n. 34, 1856
George (Geo.), 287
Gerhart
　Emmanuel V. (Dr.), 229, n. 19, 1856
　Isaac (Rev. Mr.), 229, n. 19, 1856
　Prof., 348
Gerstelle (Gerstell)
　Dr., 397, n. 32, 1860
　Josey, 397
　Mrs. (Mrs. Dr.), 397, 400
Getty, Carl, 398
Getzendanner (Getz, Getzandanner)
　Ann. *See* Derr
　Daniel (Dan), 60; 139, 140, n. 19, 1854; 167. Appendix III
　John. Appendix III
　Laura, 347
　Mary Ann, née Derr, wife of Daniel. Appendix III
　Martha, 267
　Miss, 117
　Mr., 353
　Mrs., 117
　Mrs. Dan (Mrs. D.), 167, 169
　Mrs. Ed., 316, 366
　Mrs. L., 331
Geyer, Dr., 142
Gibson
　Mary Ellen, 361
　Rev. Mr., 164, 166, 220
Giddings (Gidings)
　Miss, 139
　Prissy, 160
Gifford. *See* Sifford
Gilbert, Miss, 2
Gillen, Nellie, 227
Gittinger
　Anna (Ann, Annie), cousin of M.S., first daughter of George, 125, 344. Appendix I
　Charlotta (Aunt C.), née Scholl, wife of George, 14, n. 29, 1851. Appendix I
　Ellen, 188
　Frances. *See* Derr
　George, 14, n. 29, 1851; children of: *see* Anna and Margaret. Appendix I
　Hen, 269
　John E., 391
　Margaret, cousin of M.S., second daughter of George, 125. Appendix I
Gittings, Miss, 147
Glaize, Mr., 54
Godey, Louis A., 68, n. 19, 1853
Goldsborough (Goldsboro)
　Charles H. (Dr. C., Dr. Charly), 337, n. 22, 1858
　Edward Y., 128, n. 5, 1854
　Mary (Miss), 128, 281, 337, 358
　Mrs., 128, n. 5, 1854; 281; 337
Gordon (Gorden)
　Charles, 232
　David, 133
　Nellie. *See* Dean
Gould, Mr., 310
Govan, 272, n. 11, 1857
Gowen, Eliza M., 172
Graham
　John, 64, n. 16, 1853
　Mrs. John, 64, n. 16, 1853
Grampton, Lina, née Sarott, 242
Grandmother. *See* Margaret Ogle Thomas
Green
　Sallie, 373
　Mr., 310, 326
　William, 340
Gregg
　Andrew (A.), 231, 271, 391
　James, 421
　Mr., 5, 230, 274, 308-311, 326, *et passim*
　Mrs., 326, 421
　Mrs. G., 271
　Mrs. John, 271, 310, 372, 374, 421, *et passim*
　Rose, née Morris, wife of Andrew, 391, 421
Griffith, Miss, 256
Grove
　Frank, 269
　Joan (Miss J.), 220, 268, 269
　Mr., 269
　Mrs., 269
Groverman, Frances. *See* Derr
Guthrie, Miss, 378
Gwynn, Annie, 84
Hagge, Lizzie, 119
Haines
　Caroline, 35
　Hannah, 181, 186, 189, 205
　Miss, 9
　Mr., 35, 180
　Tommy, 170, 280
Halbert, H., 25
Hale, Sarah Josepha, 68, n. 19, 1853
Hall
　Ann, 138, 144
　Isaac (Uncle), of Washington City, 41
　Jenine, 138
　Joe, 144
　Julie, 144
　Misses, 42, 51
　Mr., 233
　Mr. A., 19
　Mrs. A., 19

INDEX OF PERSONS

Hall, continued:
  Patty (Pattie), 144, 145, 147, 241
Hamm, Carey, 30
Hammond
  Dr., 401
  J., 14
  Mary Ann, née Cramer, wife of Richard, 61, n. 15, 1853
  Mary Jane (Mary J.), 25, 285, 401
  Mollie J. (M.J.), 29, 61
  Mr., 8
  Mrs. J., 64
  Richard, 61, n. 15, 1853
  Stevenson (Miss), 417
  William S. (Rev. Mr., Rev. W. S.), 130, n. 8, 1854; 347
Hampston (Hamstead), Clarence, 281, 284
Hand, Mr., 136
Hane, Caroline (Carrie), 293, 395
Hans, Mrs. Lafayette, 310
Harbaugh (Harbough), George (Geo.), 168
Harding, Miss, 284
Hardy
  Dr., 45
  Miss, 45
Harlow, Dick, 259
Harmon
  Dr., 201
  Emma, 175, 274
  Fannie, 274, 275
  John, 231
  Miss, 421
  Mr., 231
  Mr. E., 174
  Mrs., 60, 231, 421
  Mrs. E., 175
  Mrs. John, 231
Hart, Amelia (Meallie, Melia), née Kunkel, 113, 142, 191, 357, 366, *et passim*
Hartman
  D., 61
  Mary E. (Mary Lizzie), née Wood, 41, 55, 56, 60, 61, *et passim*
Harvey, J., 10
Harwood
  Annie, 5, 8

  Mrs., 181
Haskins, Sis, 211
Haslet, Emma, 108
Hauer (Haver), Lottie. *See* French
Haup, Sue, 264
Hausey, Mrs. Charles, 133
Hawkin, Philip, hanged, 313, n. 5, 1858
Hay, Dr., 229
Hayes, Joe, 300
Hayne, Rev. Mr., 175
Hearne, Miss, 132
Hedges
  Amanda, 386
  Andrew A., cousin of M.S., fourth son of Andrew E., 380, n. 15, 1860. Appendix I
  Andrew E. (Uncle), 14, n. 28, 1851; 195; 196; 365; children of: *see* Andrew A., Daniel, Julia, Lewis A., Lewis V., and Lycurgus. Appendix I
  Catherine (Aunt Kitty, Mrs. Andrew, Mrs. H.), née Scholl, wife of Andrew E., 14, n. 28, 1851; 350, n. 32, 1858; son of, 380, n. 15, 1860. Appendix I
  Daniel (Cousin, D., Dan), cousin of M.S., first son of Andrew E., 20, n. 39, 1851; 350. Appendix I
  Julia, cousin of M.S., daughter of Andrew E. Appendix I
  Lewis A., cousin of M.S., fifth son of Andrew E. Appendix I
  Lewis V., cousin of M.S., third son of Andrew E. Appendix I
  Lycurgus (Cousin L., Lychurgus), cousin of M.S., second son of Andrew E., 14, n. 28, 1851; 54; 333; 367; *et passim*. Appendix I
  Mrs. Dan, 366

  Mrs. Lycurgus (Mrs. L.), 351, n. 33, 1858; 366
Heidel, Mr., 420
Heims (Hiems, Himes)
  Alex (Al), 95, 96, 101, 342
  Ellen, 342
  Mrs. A., 112
  Mrs. Cornelia, 95
  old Miss, 93
  Old Mr., 345
  T. J. (T. Jeff.), 256; 263, n. 5, 1857; 275; 292; 298, n. 5, 1857; *et passim*
Heiner
  Dr., 273
  Mr., 179
  Mrs., 273
Heller, Mrs. P. P., 294
Hempston
  Mamie (Miss), 293-295
  Mr., 293, 305
Hemsberg, Col., 404
Henderson
  A., 10
  Brian, 294
  Maggie, 312
  Miss, 288
  Mr., 197, 288
Henry, E., 72
Herman
  Miss, 131
  Mr., 131
Hersh
  Allen, 92, 98, 227, 227
  Charles (C., Charley, Mr., Mr. C.), 30, 94, 97, 98
  Edward (Ed, Mr. Ed., Ned), 95, 378
  Ellen, 227
  Frank (Mr. F.), 92, 116, 224, 228, 296, *et passim*
  George (Geo. E.) 92, 227
  Georgie and nurse, 95
  James, 92, 97, 98, 228, 342, *et passim*
  John, 92, 95, 227-229, 293, 342, *et passim*
  Ledda, 227
  little George, 419
  Louise. *See* Clippinger

INDEX OF PERSONS 455

Hersh, continued:
Mr., 30, 94, 229
Mrs. (Mrs. H.), 92, 98, 227-229
Mrs. A., 396
Mrs. C., 97-98
Mrs. Frank, 227, 393
Mrs. George, 92
Mrs. John, 95, 97, 227-229, 342
Mrs. Nelson (Mrs. Nels), 227
Mrs. William, 92, 96
Nelson (Nels), 227-229
Paul, 33, 92, 229, 342, 421, *et passim*
Samuel (Sam, S.), suitor of M.S., 33, n. 58, 1851; 36; 93; 228; 231; *et passim*
correspondence with M.S., 116, 121, 125, 134, 231, *et passim*
his first courtship of M.S., 96
papers sent to M.S., 115, 129
renewed proposal in Baltimore, 230
renewed proposal in Frederick, 237, 238
visits at Manchester Farm, 33, 34, 125, 213
written proposal is rejected, 146, 148
William, 92, 95
Hershey
Christ (C., Mr.), 190, 287, 341, 349
Mrs., 261, 320
Herstine
Mr., 367
Mrs., 367
Hessey, Miss, 333
Hester, Miss, 69
Heyerseck, Samuel Thomas, 256
Hickley, Bob, 116
Hicks, Thomas Holliday, 295, n. 36, 1857; 425, n. 5, 1861
Hiems. *See* Heims
Higgins
Dr., 149
James, 190
Himes. *See* Heims

Hines, P. H. (Mr. P. H.), 27
Hinkel, Mr., 189
Hinkley, Mr., 272
Hinson, Mr., 163
Hitchcock, Rev. Mr., 232, 233, 271-274, *et passim*
Hobbs
Capt., 356
Clara, 89, 103, 347
Lt. Col., 414
Mr., 148, 152, 161, 163, 366, *et passim*
Rod, 89, 98, 142, 318, 321, *et passim*
Ulysses (Mr. U., Mr. U. H.), suitor of M.S., 154, 157, 170, 345, 377, *et passim*
William (Wm.), 80
Hoffman
Ada, 119
Betsy, 129, 149
J., 55
Melia, 47
Miss, 115
Miss, of Harpers Ferry, 396
Mr., 161
William C., 338
Hoffmeyer, Rev. Mr., 22
Hoke
Hal, 91
Lena, 313
Mr., 237
Holland, Sue, 226
Holton, Miss, 174, 407
Hood
James, xii. Appendix I and Appendix II
Margaret E., née Scholl, wife of James
biographical sketch of, xi
birthday of, 38, 84, 137, 185, 235, *et passim*
diary of, ix; xi; 398, n. 33, 1860; 409
local activities of: *see* Frederick, events in, and places in
special friends of: *see* Kate Bantz, Ellen Brunner, the Derr family, Louise

Hersh, Penelope Mering, the Sauerweins
suitors and proposals: *see especially* Mr. Barr, Mr. Bell, James Gambrill, Sam Hersh, Ulysses Hobbs, J. A. Johnson, Dr. MacGill, G. W. Smith
travels of,
to Baltimore (B, Bal. Balt.), 1, 103, 130, 170, 229, *et passim*
to Bruceville, 34-36, 69-77, 134, 262, 342, *et passim*
to Harpers Ferry, 31, 32
to New Oxford, 92, n. 34, 1853; 227; 342
to New Windsor, 35, n. 62, 1851; 50
to Philadelphia/New York, 104-109
to Piedmont, 395, n. 27, 1860; 396-407
to Washington, D.C., 323-325
views on marriage, 57, 77, 157, 158, 220, *et passim*
Appendix I and Appendix II
Horman, Laura, 136
Horn
Miss, 373
Mr. J., 10
Horns, Misses, 7
Horsey, O., 149
Houck (Houcks)
Amelia (Melie, Mely), née Sauerwein, 3, 175
Charlie, 117
Ella, 340
Emily (Em, Emma), 287, 289, 311, 331, 352, *et passim*
Ezra, 21, n. 42, 1851
Georgia (G., Georgianne), 21, n.

INDEX OF PERSONS

Houck, Georgia, continued: 42, 1851; 47; 103; 153; 264; *et passim*
  Jemmy (Jimmy), 153, 386
  Kate. *See* Jacobs
  Lizzie, 103, 262, 264, 301, 340, *et passim*
  Misses, 139
  Mr., 142
  Mrs., 17, 103, 302
  Mrs. J., 265
  Tillie (Tilly), 140, 270, 297, 372, 373, *et passim*
  William, 117
House
  Chrissy, 131
  Miss(es), 170, 179, 315
Howard
  Annie, 29; 338; 345; 346; 360, n. 5, 1859; *et passim*
  Charles (Charles H., Charlie), 145; 179; 360, n. 5, 1859
  Claire (Clara), 178, 390
  Cordelia, actress, 174, n. 11, 1855
  E., 51, 122
  Edward (Ed), 129; 160, n. 6, 1854; 345
  Emily (Em), 33, 125, 177
  Emma, 170, 171
  Hildah (H, Huldah), 40, 125, 126, 129, 150, *et passim*
  John (Col.), 421, n. 63, 1860
  Linden, 99
  Marion. *See* Lenseny
  Mr., 125
  Mr., actor, 174
  Mr. E., 45
  Mr. Isaac, 16, n. 34, 1851; 125
  Mrs., actress, 174
  Mrs. Charles, 33, 347
  Mrs. Edward (Mrs. E.), 44, 65, 68, 145, 147, *et passim*
  Mrs. H., 145
  Mrs. Isaac (Mrs., Mrs. I., Mrs. I.H., Mrs. J., Mrs. Jane), neighbor of the Scholls, 16, n. 34, 1851; 31; 51; 125; 314; *et passim*
  Prof., 213, 214, 248
  Tom, 360, n. 5, 1859
  Virginia (Ginnie, Ginny, V.), 33, 44, 51, 138
  William (Willie), 117; 347; 360, n. 5, 1859
Hudson, Miriam, 406, 407
Huff, Mr., 182
Hughes, Mrs., 6, 7
Hunt
  Lizzie, 330
  Mr., 87
  Mr. D., 38
  Mrs., 8
  Sue, 289-291, 295, 389
Hurst, Rev. Mr., 4
Irvin, Dr., 271
Irving, Mr., 46
Isaac, Miss, 139
Israel, Mr., 421
Jackson, Tilly (Tilly J.), 17, 20-22, 28, *et passim*
Jacobs
  B. L., 116
  Kate (K., Kate H.), née Houck, wife of B. L., 17; 21, n. 42, 1851; 116; 129; 146; *et passim*
  Mrs., 355, 389
James
  Harry, 330
  Miss, 15
Jamets, Dr., 230
Jamison (Jameson)
  Eliza, 2
  Lizzie (Mrs. S. B.), née Bentz, wife of S.B., 57, 58, 85, 132, 175, *et passim*
  Mary, 2
  Mr., 16
  Mr. S. B. (S. B. J.), 19-21, 24, 57, 58, *et passim*
  Mrs. I., 15, 173
Jane, servant of Daniel Scholl, 57, n. 9, 1853; 294, n. 34, 1857; 334; 350; 353; *et passim*
Jarboe
  Fanny, 35
  Mr., 381
  Mrs., 269
  Mrs. Ellen, 159, 269, 300, 330
Jarrett, Mr., 134
Jenkins, Miss, 37
Jenks
  Dr., 217, n. 6, 1856; 251; 300, n. 45, 1857
  Fanny, 2, 12
Jennings
  Mary (M., M.S.), née Sauerwein, 1, n. 1, 1851; 172, n. 9, 1855; 274; 373; 378; *et passim*
  Mrs., 374
Joe, servant of Daniel Scholl, 13, n. 21, 1851; 22; 162; 184; 315; *et passim*
John, servant of Daniel Scholl, 13, n. 21, 1851; 22; 341; 349; 351; *et passim*
Johns, Dr., 175
Johnson
  Bettie L., 27
  D. C. (Clinton, Clint), brother of J. A. Johnson, 196; hosts parties, 157, 247; residence at Auburn, 10, n. 16, 1851; 331
  Dr., 153, 170
  Dr. A. J., of Baltimore, 177
  Dr. George (Geo.), 268
  Henry, 127
  Huldah, 170, 188
  John A. (J. A., J.A.J., Mr. J.A.J.), suitor of M.S.
    associations with M.S., 18, 58, 112, 127, 170, *et passim*
    his distillery, 59, 63, 67, 77
    M.S. breaks off relations with, 255, 260
    residence at Auburn, 10, n. 16, 1851
  Lidye, née Wenner, 242
  Maria, 99, 221
  Mr., 217
  Mrs., 153

INDEX OF PERSONS 457

Johnson, continued:
Mrs. D. C., 331
Mrs. I. H., 57
Mrs. Ross, 119, 128
Mrs. Dr. B. P., 119
Mrs. Dr. George, 358
old Mrs., 128
Ross, 119; 128, n. 5, 1854
Thomas (doctor), 10, n. 16, 1851
Thomas, Governor, 64, n. 16, 1853
Worthington, 53, n. 4, 1853
Johnston
C., 85, 86
Prof., 404
Jones
Aubury, 381
Charlie, 411
E., née Beatson, 8, 9, 57
Len, 301
Lizzie, 246, 319
Luke, 414
Miss, 191
Mollie, 246, 319
Mr., 17, 57, 265, 368
Mrs., 17, 319
Rev. Mr., 102, 126
Sue, 264, 291, 411
Joy, Miss, 364
Kalamuse, Mrs., 343
Kann, Mary, 373
Karl, Miss L., 95
Kay, Mr., 142
Kean (Keen), Mary. *See* Carson
Keefer (Keifer)
Ann R. (Miss A. R.), 37, 102, 320, 335
Annie, née Bentz, wife of Charlie, 32, 139, 194, 207, 392, *et passim*
Baby John, 392
Charlie, 392
Charlotte (C., Miss C.), 38, 68, 117, 335, 412, *et passim*
Ellen (E.), 16, 32, 40, 42, 47, *et passim*
Ginnie, 335
Harriet. *See* Drill
Jacob (J., Mr. J.), 16, n. 34, 1851; 33; 195

Mary (Miss M.), 32, 42, 99, 335, 392, *et passim*
Michael, 238; 304, n. 48, 1857; 305, n. 50, 1857
Miss R., 23, 25
Misses, 81
Mr., 26
Mrs., 42
Mrs. J., 16
Mrs. Michael, 102
Nellie, 55
Keen. *See* Kean
Keller
Charles, 15, n. 32, 1851
Lizzie, 32, 44
Paul, 108
Kemp
Abraham (A., Uncle), 58, n. 11, 1853; 139; 188, n. 21, 1855; 275; 336; *et passim*
Ann M. (Aunt Kemp, Aunty Kemp), née Brunner, wife of Abraham, 22; 47; 58, n. 11, 1853; 120; 188, n. 21, 1855
Charles (Charlie), 255
David, 114, n. 59, 1853
Ellen. *See* Noonan
H., 141
Lewis (Col.), 306, n. 52, 1857
Lewis G., 358, n. 3, 1859
Lizzie, née Brengle, wife of Charles, 221, 227, 255
Louis (Rev.), 374
Mr., 140, 356
Mrs., 42, 127, 356
Mrs. Henrietta, 290
Mrs. Lewis, Jr., 41
Mrs. Louis, 18
Mrs. Peter, 312
Peter, 127, n. 4, 1854; 237
Peter (Rev.), 127, n. 4, 1854
Rebecca C. (Mrs. L., old Mrs. Louis), wife of Col. Lewis, 42; 306, n. 52, 1857
Sarah (Mrs. Lewis G.), née Miller, wife of Lewis G., 63; 269; 314; 342; 358, n. 3,

1859; *et passim*
Sarah A. *See* Adams
Tom (Rev.), 376, 377, 381
Tommy, 42
Kephart
Eugenia (Eugenie, G., G.K., Gene, Genie), 19; 23; 32; 37, n. 63, 1851; 113; *et passim*
Kerchner
Dr., 91
Mr., 10
Kern, Kate, 82
Kerr, Mr., 401
Kerr, Rev. Jacob W. B. (Mr.), 217, n. 5, 1856; 240
Kester, Miss, 333
Keyser, Mrs., 383
Kiel, Bill, 102
Killian (Kilion, Killin, Killion)
Maggie, 225
Mrs., 17, 24, 297, 343
King
Miss, 273
Mr., 228
Sally, 185, 190
Kink, Rebecca, 273
Kinneman, Dr., 170
Kinney, Mrs., 343
Kintz, Rev. Mr., 236
Kline. *See* Cline
Knifroof. *See* Nihoff
Knowles, Dr., 378
Kohler, Mrs. Cardy, 311
Koones (Koons)
Celia (C.), 60, 324
Charley, 324
Chic, 324
E., 47
Fannie (Fannie R., Fanny), 55, n. 6, 1853; 57; 126; 153; 164; *et passim*
Fred, 191, 232
Lizzie, 57, 68, 115, 237, 324, *et passim*
Mr., 132
Mrs. Fred, 191
Rebecca, 323
Koontz,
Miss H., 35, 36
Krantz, Miss, 34
Kretzer, Mr., 9

INDEX OF PERSONS

Kunkle (Kunkel)
  Amelia. *See* Hart
  Baker, 368
  Jacob, 182
  John, 41, n. 67, 1851; 191
  Kate (K.), friend of M.S., 41, n. 67, 1851; 103
  Lizzie, 416
  Lucy, 49
  Mary, 44, 51, 123, 147, 267, *et passim*
  Misses, 89
  Mr., 48
  Mr. C., 31
  Mrs. Baker (Mrs. B.), 66, 368
  Mrs. Jake, 385
  Mrs. P., 66, 159
  Nettie (Nellie), 271, 368
  old Mrs. (old Mrs. K.), 299, 367
  Phillip (Mr. P., P., Phil), 15, 66, 80, 147, 368, *et passim*
Kuster, Mrs., 225, 230
Lafayette, 101, n. 43, 1853
Lail, Allen, 215
Landis
  Mr., 34, 35
  Mr. D., 34
  Mrs. D., 35
Langenbeil. *See* Lugenbeel
Late
  A. (A.R.), 17, 33
  B., 58
Latham, Julia. *See* Derr
Lease, Mr., 264
Lee
  Miss, 197
  Mr., 197
Lefevre (Lefever)
  James (Mr., Mr. J.A., Rev., Rev. Mr.), of Baltimore
    in Frederick, 193, 231-233, 289, 348, 396, *et passim*
    marriage to Kate Sauerwein, 346; 372, n. 2, 1860
  Kate (K.S., Kate S., Mrs. J.A.), née Sauerwein, wife of James, 1, n. 1, 1851; 25; 289; 350, n. 31, 1858; 374, n. 5, 1860; *et passim*
    marriage to James, 346; 372, n. 2, 1860
    visits in Frederick, 45, 47, 140, 188, 287, *et passim*
  Lizzie, 193, 310
  Miss, 179, 230, 231
Lehman, Mrs., 84
Leiby
  Col., 93-95
  old Mrs., 95, 97
Leigh
  Lottie, 25
  Mrs., 44, 48
Lenseny
  John, 424
  Marion (M., Marion H., M. Howard), née Howard, friend of M.S., wife of John, 18, 40, 356, 361, 424, *et passim*
Lentman, Mrs., 72
Letherly, Mr., 349
Levening
  Mr., 110
  Mrs., 110
Lewis
  Aunt L., 66
  G., 66
  Hannah. *See* Crook
  John, 197, 206
  Miss, 177-179, 197
  Mr., 177
  Mrs., 309, 339
  Mrs. Columbia E., 387, n. 22, 1860
  old Mr., 197, 206, 211, 256
  Uncle L., 66
Light, Professor, 414, n. 54, 1860
Ligon, Mr., 148, n. 28, 1854
Lincoln, Abraham, 424, n. 4, 1861; 425, n. 7, 1861
Lindsay, Miss, 45
Loats
  Call, 89
  John, 84; 267, n. 8, 1857
  Miss, 124
  Mrs. Cal., 173
  Mrs. John, 14; 84; 267, n. 7, 1857

Locke, Mr., 104
Lorgenbirl. *See* Lugenbeel
Lowes, Emma, 133
Loy, Elizabeth. *See* Derr
Luckett
  Mountjoy B., Jr., 267, n. 6, 1857
  Mr., 267
Lugenbeel (Langenbeil, Lorgenbirl, Lugenbeil)
  Elizabeth. *See* Derr
  Miss, 331, 354
  Mr., 331
Luich, Dr., 392
Lumans, Mrs., 187
Luson, Rev. Mr., 348
Lyles, Mr., 304
Lynch (Lynche)
  Jame A., 291, n. 30, 1857
  Mr., 161
  Mrs. John, 255
Lyon (Lynn)
  Julia, 261, 262
  Mary, 261
MacGill (Macgill, McGill)
  Dr. (Dr. Mc, Dr. McG), suitor of M.S., 39, n. 64, 1851; 85; 193; 203; 204; *et passim*
    marriage to Mary Riggs, 254, n. 43, 1856
    proposal rejected, 223
  Mary, née Riggs, wife of Dr. MacGill, 191; 254, n. 43, 1856
  Mrs., 196, 255, 316, 361
  Mrs. Dr., 259, 327
  Mrs. R., 14
  Robert, 254
Mackley (Machly, Mickley), Lizzie, 102, 245
Mackey, Mary E., 193
Magruder
  Dr., 125
  Miss, 256
Mahon, Rev. Mr., 228
Mains, Miss, 264
Mainster,
  Laura, 48
Mann, Miss, 265, 309
Mantz
  A. K., 284
  Iris, 269
  Mr., 273

INDEX OF PERSONS 459

Mantz, continued:
  Sophie, 232, 233, 272, 273
Markell (Markel)
  Amelia (Mealie, Meallie), daughter of Samuel, 188; 413, n. 53, 1860
  Amelia, wife of Samuel, 413, n. 53, 1860
  Charles (C.), 62, 259
  Charlotte, née Trail, wife of Charles, 8, 62
  Frank (F.), 33, 129, 220, 259
  Lewis (Mr. L.), storekeeper, 21, 64
  M., 218, 236, 258, 259
  Mr., 63, 176, 236, 259, 332, *et passim*
  Mrs., 58, 176, 259, 265, 361, *et passim*
  Mrs. Charles (Mrs. C.), 30, 262
  Mrs. Frank, 268
  Mrs. John, 390
  Mrs. Lewis (Mrs. L.), friend of M.S., 13, n. 24, 1851; 33; 61; 65; 264; *et passim*
  old Mr. Markel, 259
  Samuel, 413, n. 53, 1860
Markey
  Mary, 181
  Mr. D., 17
  Mrs. D., 17
Marky, Beccy, 361
Marlow
  Mr., 182, 234, 239, 244, 250, *et passim*
  Mr. B. C., 195
  Mr. Ki., 243
  Mrs. B. C., 194, 205
  Richard (Dick), 182, 280, 329
Marmaduke, Miss, 84
Marsh
  Mary, 135
  Mr., 135, 136, 145, 155, 156, *et passim*
Marshall, Judge, 358
Martin
  Penelope (Mrs. Nellie, Nellie, P., Pench), née Mering, wife of William, 12, n. 20,

1851; 29; 134, n. 13, 1854; 259; 265; *et passim*
  daughter of, 343
  M.S. visits Bruceville for post-wedding celebration, 262
  M.S. visits the Martins, 342, 343
  M.S. visits with, at Bruceville and Carroll County, 34-36, 69-77
  marriage to William, 261, n. 1, 1857
  visit to M.S., 154
  William A. (Dr., Dr. M., Dr. Wm. A.), of Carroll County, 36; 71; 73-76; marriage to Penelope Mering, 252, 259, n. 41, 1856; 342; *et passim*
Mason, Mrs., 172
Mattoon, Mr., 372
Maulsby
  Betty. *See* Ritchie
  William P., 291, n. 30, 1857
Maynard
  Howard, 89
  Jemima. *See* Scholl
  Misses, 300
  Mrs., 89
  Nathan, 88, 89
  old Mrs., 80, n. 27, 1853
  Tom, 89
McCann, Miss, 56
McCannon, Mrs., 198
McCartney
  Mag, 301, 312
  Miss, 198, 283
McClain, Rev. Mr., 331
McCleary
  B., 198
  Caroline, 407
  Jane, née Doud, wife of Perry, 56
  Perry B., 56
McCleery, Henry, 218, n. 9, 1856
McClelland
  Eliza A., 392
  Ella (Ella McC), 97, 342
  Lou M., 97; 250, n. 38, 1856

Mag, 93, 97, 115
  Maria, 95, 228, 229
  Mrs., death of, 250
  Mrs. John, 98
McCowan. *See* McGowan
McDowell, Sally. *See* Thomas
McGill. *See* MacGill
McGowan (McCowan, McGowen)
  Eliza, 311, 378
  Miss(es), 131, 174
McMahon, Lizzie, 398, 405
McPherson
  Col. John, 288, n. 28, 1857
  Maria, 367
  Mrs., 373
  Robert P., 291, n. 30, 1857
Meals, Mr., 417
Mering (Mehring, Mehrling)
  Annie, 35, 74, 311
  Clay, 76
  Dixon (D.), 35, 135
  Grannie, 34
  Joan (Joanna, Joanne), 34, 35, 69, 75
  Mr., 35, 70, 74, 261, 262, *et passim*
  Mrs., 72, 84, 261, 262
  Mrs. William, 34
  Penelope, friend of M.S. *See* Martin
  Roy George, 70
  Sarah E. *See* Adams
  Thomas, 74
  uncle W. M., 36
  William (Wm.), 76
Metzger
  Miss, 2, 4, 170
  Miss B., 5, 8
  Miss R., 43
  Miss S., 4-6, 8
  Misses, 5, 7, 9, 11
Meyers, Salleyann, 412
Michell
  Mr., 326
  Mrs., 326
Mickley. *See* Mackley
Middleton, Annie (A.), née Zacharias, 115
Miley, Mrs., 93
Milford,
  Mrs., 348

460 INDEX OF PERSONS

Miller
  Ann, 252, 298
  Evie, 252
  J., 26
  Lou, 81
  Mary (Mrs. Wm.), née Buckey, wife of William, 18, 30, 206, 314, 339, *et passim*
  Mrs., 206, 398, 400, 402
  Sallie, 169, 249, 300
  Sarah. *See* Kemp
  William (Wm.), 252, 282
  Willie, 252
Millet, Caroline, 110
Milner, Annie, singer, 378
Milton, Mr., 34
Mines, Mrs., 81
Mochis, Maria, 132
Moffat, Miss, 137, 140, 141
Monroe, Elder, 226
Montez, Lola, 376, n. 9, 1860
Moon, 175
  Hester, 8, 175, 132, 374, 375, *et passim*
  Sarah (Sallie), 3, 8, 374, 375
  Mrs., 375
Moore
  Lydia, 40
  Mr., 400
Moran, Dr. J. J., 249; 257; 319, n. 7, 1858; 383
Morgan
  George (Geo.), 292
  Mary, 292
  Rev. Mr., 109
  Tom, 198
Morris
  Charles, of York, 131
  Dr. John, 9
  John, 2, 273
  Maria, 125
  Miss, 2
  Rev. Mr. (Dr., Rev. Dr.), of Baltimore, 7, 97, 131, 230, 372, *et passim*
  Rose. *See* Gregg
  Willian Lee (Wm. Lee), 149
Mort, S., 47
Motter
  Dr., 270
  Taylor, 67

Mound, Dr., 2
Mouss, Mrs., actress, 8
Mullinix, Mr., 315
Munder
  Mr., 4
  Mrs., 4
Myers
  Gates, 93
  Kitty, 24
  Miss, 169
  Mr., 228
  Mrs., 17, 89
Nash, Mrs., 171
Nauss, Mr., 50
Neal, Mr., 378
Nelson
  Dr., 20, 333
  Henry, 181
Nicholson
  Ike, 172
  Lizzie, 231
  Margrette (Margretta, Marguerite, Miss M.), 132, 172, 174, 231
  Miss, 131, 132, 172
  Mr., 131, 132
Nicodemus
  Eveline (Evie), née Smith, wife of J. L., 44; 55, n. 7, 1853; 114
  J. L., 114
  Mary, 24, n. 49, 1851
Nihoff (Knifroof, Nixdorf, Nixdorff)
  Annie, a seamstress, 176, 224, 312, 356
  Rev. Mr., 335
Noonan, 197
  Bob, 283, 312
  Ellen, née Kemp, wife of Joe, 275, 312, 390
  Joe, 312, 390
  Mr., 198
  Mrs., 198
Norris
  Mr., 195
  Rachel, 195
Nussbaum, 47
O'Brien, Mr., 198
O'Dell
  Annie, 134
  Dixon, 262, 271
  Mrs., 270
O'Donnell, Capt. John, 233, n. 24, 1856
O'Neal, Thomas, 351

Ogburn, Mr., 134, n. 15, 1854; 264
Ogle
  Aaron (A.B., Coz.), 8, 110, 125, 367
  Annie, 24, 37, 366, 371, 387, *et passim*
  Catherine, 366, 371
  Jane, 366, 387
  John (uncle, Uncle John O.), 364, n. 10, 1859; 365
  Margaret. *See* Thomas
  Oliver (O., O. G.), 24, 37, 80
Orndorf (Orendoff, Ornedoff, Ornedorff)
  Irene, 42, 249
  John, 42
  Misses, 282
  Sallie, 249
Osborne, Sophia, 120
Osburn, Miss, 252
Owings, Jack, 108
Page
  Mr., 101; 119; marriage to Nan Tyler, 329
  Mr. C., 17
  Mrs. (Mrs. P.), 101, 119, 124, 156
  Mrs. Calvin, 79
  Nan, née Tyler, 329
Passivant, Rev. Mr., 97
Pavel, Mr., 20
Peale
  Raphael, 8, n. 13, 1851
  Remrandt, 8, n. 13, 1851
Pearce, Emily B. *See* Brown
Pearson
  Madam (Mad.), 88, 218, 242, 243, 393, *et passim*
  Mrs., 25
Peiper, Mr. M. S., 113
Perkins, Mr., 404
Perry
  Benjamin (Ben, Mr.), 103, 175, 238, 377, 395, *et passim*
  Miss, 182
Peters, Mr., 315
Pettit,
  Annie, 407
Peugh, 324
Phelps, Mr., 374

INDEX OF PERSONS 461

Philips
  Mrs., actress, 82
  Rev. Mr., 191
Phleeger, Mrs., 147, n. 27, 1854
Pierce, Gen. Franklin (Frank), President, 62; 103, n. 46, 1853
Pifer
  Dr. William (Wm.), 75
  Miss A., 101
Pillbury, Len, 176
Plumber, Mr., 420
Plummer
  Dr., 4
  Miss, 181
  Miss M., 219
  Mr., 420
Poe, Misses, 337
Pollard, Mr., 374
Pool (Poole)
  Kate, 36
  Lucretia, 36
  Maggie, 36
  Miss, 214
  Mr., 36, 90
  Mr. E., 89
Posey, Miss, 352
Potts, Mary, 128
Powell
  Alice, 131
  Lillian, 131
  Mr., 13
Powers, Miss, 127
Preston
  Mr., 128
  Old Mrs., 410
  Sam, 91, 190
Price
  Billy, 161
  Mr., 85
Pugenet, Mrs., 31, 32, 37
Pusey, Professor, 181, n. 14, 1855
Pypher, Mag M. *See* Brunner
Quynn, Allen G., 291, n. 30, 1857
Ramsburg
  Jane, 83, 184, 235, 348, 394, *et passim*
  Mary, 371
  Mrs. John, 253, 336
  Mrs. L., 161
  Will, 371
Randall

Kate, 268
Miss, 173
Mr., 398
Mrs., 398
Rau
  Adele, 372
  Dr., 127
  John, 4, 131, 173, 311, 377, *et passim*
  Johnny, 131
  Mr., 4, 130, 176, 309
  Mrs., 131, 132, 372, 377, 420, *et passim*
  Mrs. Dr., 274
  Mrs. John, 3, 230, 232, 372, 377, *et passim*
  old Mr. P., 4, 132
  old Mrs., 131, 170, 232, 373, 378
  Philip (Mr. P., P. B., Phil), 2, 131, 173, 326, 374, *et passim*
Ray, Mr., 283
Raymond, 17
Read, Miss. *See* Carroll
Reading (Redin, Reding), Miss, 224, 267, 352, 356
Reed (Reid), James (J. H., Jim, Mr.), 136, 289, 291, 298, 300, *et passim*
Reese
  Catherine (Mrs. Jacob), née Derr, wife of Jacob, 24, n. 47, 1851; 110, n. 57, 1853; 323. Appendix III
  Jacob, 24, n. 47, 1851; 323. Appendix III
  Mr., 28, 88, 272, 323
  Mrs., 28, 88, 266
  Mrs. Andrew (Mrs. A.), 271, 310, 373
Reich, 209
  Messrs., 183
  Miss H., 182
  Miss L., 182
  Miss S., 14
  Mr., 264
  Mr. P., 17
  Mr. W., 17
  Mrs. John, 292
  Mrs. P., 17
  Mrs. William (Mrs. Wm.), 241
  Sallie, 28
  Sophia, 241

Reifsnider, Miss, 419
Reilly (Reily, Riley)
  George (Geo.), 285
  J. McK., 364
  Mr., 369
  Mrs., 227-229
  William (Wm.), 229
  William M., 348, 369
Reisman, Sallie, 35
Reynolds
  Kate, née Wetherson, 246, 285
  Miss, 155
  Mr., 176
Rhoderick (Roderick)
  Mr., tenant of Daniel Scholl, 139; 167, n. 6, 1855; 201; 209; 360, n. 6, 1859; *et passim*
  Mrs., 148, 189, 194, 196, 201, *et passim*
Rhorback. *See* Rohrback
Rice
  Martha, 117, 214
  Mr., 22, 26
  Mrs., 180, 253
  William (Wm.), 137
Richardson, Mr., 63, 131
Riddlemoser, J. E., 15, n. 31, 1851
Riggs, Mary. *See* MacGill
Riley. *See* Reilly
Rinehart, Miss, 182
Riser (Rizer)
  Mr., 177, 180, 201, 225, 339, *et passim*
  William (Wm.), 184
Ritchie
  B. F., 168
  Bert, 91, 163
  Betty (Beth), née Maulsby, wife of John, 326, n. 17, 1858
  Dr. Albert, 221, n. 14, 1856
  John, 291, n. 30, 1857; 326, n. 17, 1858
Ritman, Mrs., 150
Ritmore, Mrs., 344
Ritzell, Sadie, 297
Rizer. *See* Riser
Roach, Gorman I. (G.), 3
Robbins, Lou, 173
Roberts, Dr., 73
Robinson,
  Mr., 156, 232

INDEX OF PERSONS

Rockville
  Mr., 292
  Mrs., 292
Roderick. *See* Rhoderick
Roelke, Lizzie. *See* Boyd
Roen, Hoffman, 218
Rogers, Miss, 397
Rohers, Dr., 421
Rohrback (Rhorback, Rohrbach)
  Ellen (E., E.B., Ella, Ellen R., Nellie), née Brunner, wife of Martin,
    friend and relative of M.S., 15, n. 33, 1851; 54; 119; 124; 235; *et passim*
    marriage to Martin (1859), 371, n. 1, 1860; 377; 382; 393; 409; *et passim*
  Jacob, son of Martin, 371, n. 1, 1860
  Martin N., friend of M.S., 202; 250, n. 37, 1856; 258; marriage to Ellen Brunner, 371, n. 1, 1860; *et passim*
  Mr., 268, 313, 336, 390
  Mrs., 418
  old Mrs., 407
Roman, P., 61
Root, Mr., 374
Rosenmiller, Miss, 96
Ross, Rev. James B. (Mr.), 355, n. 1, 1859
Rowe
  Dr., 148, 151
  Mrs., 151
Sadtler, 176, 273
  Catherine, 231
  Charlie (Charley), 1-4, 7-9, 130, 131, *et passim*
  George (Geo.), 176
  John (J.), 103, 176
  Kate, née Sadtler, wife of I., 62
  Lizzie, 2, 5, 8, 9, 12, *et passim*
  Lum (Lem), 9, 130, 172, 273, 326, *et passim*
  Miss C., 5
  Miss K., 5
  Misses, 11
  Mr., 2, 5, 176
  Mr. I., of Chicago, 62
  Mr. J., 11
  Mr. J. P., 9, 11
  Mrs., 2, 373
  Mrs. J., 5, 6
  Mrs. J. P., 9
  Mrs. John, 176, 272
  Mrs. Louisa, 174
  Mrs. Thomas, 171
  Mrs. William (Mrs. Wm.), 7, 9, 232
  old Mrs. P. B., 7
  Rev., 373
  Sam, 270
Sallie, Miss, 362-366, *et passim*
Salmon, 237
  Mrs., 249, 250, 386
Sanders, Mr., 163
Sanderson, Dr., 162, 259
Santice, Dod, 242
Sarott, Lina. *See* Grampton
Sauerwein
  Amelia, of Howard Street family, Baltimore. *See* Houck
  Edward (Ed, Mr. E.), of Howard Street family, Baltimore, 2, 10, 374
  Eliza, 7
  Emma (E., Em), of Park Street family, Baltimore, 7
    at Park Street, 326, 372, 373, 420
    visits in Frederick, 90, 243, 337, 340, 411, *et passim*
  George (G., G.S., Geo., Geo. S., George S.), of Park Street family, Baltimore, 2, 3, 170, 326, 374, *et passim*
    business associate of Daniel Scholl and Edward Shriner, 1, n. 1, 1851; 7; 10; 25; 327; *et passim*
    conversation with M.S., 376
    visits in Frederick, 47, 65, 163, 191, 330, *et passim*
  Kate I, of Park Street family, Baltimore, friend of M.S. *See* Lefevre
  Kate II, of Howard Street family, Baltimore, friend of M.S., 1, n. 1, 1851; 172, n. 9, 1855; 175; 289; 374, n. 6, 1860; *et passim*
  Mary (M.E., M.S., Mary S.) I, of Park Street family, Baltimore, friend of M.S., 1, n. 1, 1851; 2; 25; 165; 170; *et passim*
    visits in Frederick, 45, 143, 188, 408
  Mary II, of Howard Street family, Baltimore, friend of M.S. *See* Jennings
  Mrs., of Park Street family, Baltimore, mother of Em, George, Kate I, and Mary I, 1, n. 1, 1851; 5; 132; 171; 373; *et passim*
  Mrs. P., Jr., of Howard Street family, Baltimore, 10
  Mrs. P., Sr., of Howard Street family, Baltimore, 5, 10, 11, 230, 373, *et passim*
  Peter, Jr. (Mr. P., Jr.), of Howard Street family, Baltimore, 1, n. 1, 1851; 10
  Peter, Sr. (Mr., Mr. P., Mr. P.S., old Mr. P.), of Howard Street family, Baltimore, 1, n. 1, 1851; 9; 10; 11; 230; death of, 343, 344; *et passim*
Saunders, Haze, 182, 184, 187
Savage, Martha, 231
Schaeffer (Schaffer, Shafer)
  Billy, 174
  Melinda, 91
  Mr., 44, 132, 186, 212, 217, *et passim*

INDEX OF PERSONS

Schaeffer, continued:
  Mrs. D., 17
  Mrs. J., 315
  Mrs. Luther, 64
  Mrs. W., 46
  Sarah. *See* Bowlus
  T. H. (Dr.), 289; 300, n. 45, 1857
  Tom, 109
Schaff (Shaff)
  Dr., 30
  Mrs. Dr., 385
Schaffer. *See* Schaeffer
Schell
  George, 268, 312
  Joe, 285
  Lizzie, 170, 312, 321, 333, 378, *et passim*
  M., 243
  Mr., 197, 265
Schenck, Rev. Mr., 375
Schley
  Allen, 317
  Annie, 58, 86, 161, 214, 243, *et passim*
  Clara, 244
  Dr. F. (Dr. F. A.), 218, n. 8, 1856; 410, n. 49, 1860
  Edward (Capt. Ed, Col. E.), 103; 276, n. 18, 1857
  Ellen (Ella), 214, 243, 334, 361
  Frank, 327
  Fred, 356
  John T., 276, n. 18, 1857
  Margaret (Mrs. M. Eve.), née Breyle, wife of Edward, 276, n. 18, 1857; 361
  Mary, 181, 214, 334, 361
  May, 86
  Miss C. Olney. *See* Wilson
  Mrs., 392
  Mrs. D., 161, 212
  Mrs. F. A. (Mrs. Dr.), 247, 344, 356, 410, 416, *et passim*
  Mrs. Fairfax, 189
  Mrs. Fred, 358, 362
  Mrs. Henry, 281
  Mrs. Max, 88
Scholl
  Annabelle, cousin of M.S., daughter of Elias. *See* Cramer
  Annie Serena (Miss Scholl), seamstress, 41; 122, n. 2, 1854; 135; 251; marriage of, 304, n. 49, 1857
  Catherine, first daughter of Christian. *See* Hedges
  Charles, 252
  Charlotta, second daughter of Christian. *See* Gittinger
  Christian, father of Daniel. Appendix I
  Christianna (Aunt C., Christina), fifth daughter of Christian, 24, n. 46, 1851; 135; 409; 418. Appendix I
  Daniel (Father, Pa), of Manchester Farm, father of M.S., first son of Christian, 13, 54, 120, 162, 214, *et passim*
    gives up farming, 165, n. 5, 1855; 167, n. 6, 1855
    his birthday, 32
    household servants of: *see* Jane, Joe, and John
    illness of, 257, 353
    purchases and uses reaper, 134, n. 15, 1854; 136; 185, n. 17, 1855
    tenants of: *see* Gallian and Roderick
    trip to Baltimore, 103
    trip to Philadelphia/New York, 104-109
    wife of: *see* Maria Thomas Scholl
    Appendix I and Appendix II
  David (Davie), cousin of M.S., first son of Elias, 165. Appendix I
  Dennis, fourth son of Christian, 384
    children of: *see* Fanny, Helen, Margaret J., and Mathias
    Appendix I
  Elias (Uncle E.), second son of Christian, 21, n. 40, 1851; 65; 80; 162; 213; *et passim*
    children of: *see* Annabelle, David, and Lewis
    death of, 216
    wife of: *see* Mary Dutrow Scholl
    Appendix I
  Elizabeth, née Brunner, wife of Christian, 331, n. 19, 1858. Appendix I
  Elizabeth (Aunt Betsy), née Stroup, second wife of Johannes, 102; her death, 179; 180, n. 13, 1855
  Fanny, cousin of M.S., second daughter of Dennis. Appendix I
  George (Uncle Jake), 133, n. 12, 1854; death of, 180, n. 13, 1855
  Helen, cousin of M.S., third daughter of Dennis. Appendix I
  Henry (Cousin H.), 44; 304, n. 49, 1857; 379, n. 14, 1860
  James, 379, n. 14, 1860
  Jemima (Aunt J., Aunt Jemima), née Maynard, wife of Lewis, 79; 80, n. 26 and 27, 1853; 180; 245; 291; *et passim*. Appendix I
  Johannes, 180, n. 13, 1855; 304, n. 49, 1857
  John, 41
  Lewis (Uncle L., Uncle Lewis), third son of Christian, 43; 65; 79; 80, n. 26, 1853; 289; et passim
    child of: *see* Mary Appendix I

INDEX OF PERSONS

Scholl, continued:
  Lewis (Louis), cousin of M.S., second son of Elias, 65. Appendix I
  Margaret, née Bartgis, wife of Dennis. Appendix I
  Margaret E., daughter of Daniel, the diarist. *See* Hood
  Margaret J., cousin of M.S., first daughter of Dennis. Appendix I
  Maria (Ma, Mother), née Thomas, mother of M.S., wife of Daniel, 13, 54, 120, 160, 213, *et passim*
    her sprained knee, 318
    her wedding anniversary, 425
    illness of, 221
    Appendix I and Appendix II
  Mary (Aunt Mary, M.), née Dutrow, second wife of Elias, 47; 65; 280, n. 21, 1857; 344, n. 27, 1858; *et passim*. Appendix I
  Mary, cousin of M.S., daughter of Lewis. Appendix I
  Mary Elizabeth, fourth daughter of Christian. *See* Bentz and Brunner
  Mathias, cousin of M.S., son of Dennis. Appendix I
  Rebecca, third daughter of Christian. *See* Shriner
  Susan, née Shearer, first wife of Elias. Appendix I
Schoolfield, Till, 196, 223
Scott
  Annie, 71
  Charles (Charlie), 34, 70, 72, 73
  Eugenia (Gene, Genie), 34, 35, 69, 71-76, *et passim*
  Mr., 34
  old Mrs., 71
Seabrook, Mr., 218, n. 7, 1856
Seaz, I. Silas, 256, 270
Seffler, Lizzie, 361
Seiss, Rev. Mr., 271
Semmes, B. F., 168
Sentzbaugh, Mr., 253
Sering, Mr., 49
Seton, Mother Elizabeth, 83, n. 28, 1853
Seville, Miss, 131
Seymour, Rev. Mr., 252, 317
Shafer. *See* Schaeffer
Shaff. *See* Schaff
Shank, Sarah A., née Adams, 23, 363. Appendix II
Shanks, J., 23
Sharp, Ally, 19
Sharpstein, Mrs., 60
Shaw
  Mattie, 282, 283, 285
  Miss, 282
  Mr., 179
Shearer
  Osburn, 161
  Susan. *See* Scholl
Sheares, Susan, 164
Sheilds (Shields)
  Harriet, 170
  John (doctor), 120, 126, 137; death of, 146
  Mrs., 57
  Mrs. Dr., 24, 51, 123, 126
Sherford, Rev. Mr., 304
Sherman, Mrs., 228
Shields. *See* Sheilds
Shipley
  Mr., 5, 132, 172
  Mrs., 5
Shope, Mary, 38
Shriner
  Abe, 191
  Annie, 22, 32, 39
  Blanche, 134
  Cornelia, cousin of M.S., daughter of Cornelius. Appendix I
  Cornelius (Uncle S., Uncle Shriner), mill owner, 1, n. 1 and 3, 1851; 33; 49, n. 73, 1851; 142, n. 24, 1854; 145
    children of: *see* Cornelia and Edward
    Appendix I
  Edward (Cousin Edward, Coz E.S., Coz Ed., E.S., E. Shriner, Ed, Ed S.), cousin of M.S., mill owner, son of Cornelius, 1, n. 1 and 3, 1851; 33; 45; 142; 168; *et passim*
    marriage to Margaret Derr and wedding trip, 322, 323-330
    premature son, 361, n. 7, 1859
    wedding plans, 310, n. 2, 1858; 312; 316; 318; 320
    with Mag Derr, 1, 253, 280, 295, 296, *et passim*
    Appendix I and Appendix III
  George, 323
  Lew E., 72
  Margaret (Mag, Maggie), née Derr, wife of Edward, 1, n. 2, 1851; 3; 43
    in Baltimore, 1, 23, 33, 100, 170
    in Philadelphia, 268, 269
    marriage to Edward and wedding trip, 322, 323
    return to Frederick after wedding trip, 330
    son of, 361, n. 7, 1861
    Appendix I and III
  Mrs. Cornelius (Aunt S, Aunt Shriner), second wife of Cornelius, 9; 11; 12; 323, n. 11, 1858; 382, n. 18, 1860; *et passim*
  Rebecca, née Scholl, first wife of Cornelius, 1, n. 3, 1851. Appendix I

INDEX OF PERSONS

Shriver
  Augustus, 70
  Caroline, 70
  Keener, 70
Shroeder, Mr., 282
Sifford (Gifford)
  Cle, 243; 244; 248; 264;
    365, n. 11, 1859; et
    passim
  Georgia (Georgie), 365,
    n. 11, 1859; 379
  John, 142, 190, 218, 291
  Mr., 235, 240, 244, 259
Silk, Mrs., 8
Simmons, Mr., 72, 73, 85
Sims, old Mrs., 408
Slagle
  Edward, 96
  Mrs. Edward, 97
Slick, Mrs. Abington, 34,
  72
Slingluff, Mr., 101
Smallwood
  Rev. Mr., 304
  William, 15, n. 31, 1851
Smith
  Caroline (C., Miss C.),
    31, 33, 38
  Dr., 274
  Edward (Ed), 165, 192,
    275, 297
  Eveline. See Nicodemus
  F. (doctor), 165
  G. N., 398
  G. W. (Mr., Mr. S.),
    suitor of M.S., B&O
    railroad man
    correspondence to
    M.S., 408
    in Baltimore, 420
    in Piedmont, 398-408
    marriage proposal
      received and
      declined, 415
  Harrison (Cousin
    Harrie, Cousin Harry,
    Cousin J. Harrie, H.,
    Harrie, Harry S., J.
    Harry)
    business problems of,
      299, n. 42, 1857
    letter to M.S., 299
    M.S. makes a gift for,
      112
    meets M.S. in
      Philadelphia/New
      York, 104, 106-109
    visits at Manchester
      Farm, 38-40, 78,
      152, 282, et passim
  Jennie (Ginny), 417
  John (J.), 161, 162, 192
  John A., 165
  Kate, 162, 192, 336
  Len, 357
  Lewis Motter, 59
  Mary H., 59, 137, 265,
    357
  Messrs., 326
  Miss(es), 169, 326
  Mrs., 298, 336
  Mrs., of Iowa, 254
  Mrs. William, 117
  William (Wm.), 55, 117
Snively, Susan. See
  Thomas
Spear, Mrs., 79
Spears, Lydia, 335
Spencer, Miss, 235
Spilcher
  Adie, 374
  Emma (Em), 309, 310
  Miss, 377
Staley
  Cornelius, 291, n. 30,
    1857
  Rev. Mr., 273
Stans
  Mrs. Sam, 414
  Sam, 414
Stark, Rev. Mr., 420
Steiner (Stiener)
  Anna. See Derr
  Aunt, of Mag Derr, 272
  Capt., 3, 7
  Catherine. See Derr
  Christian (Mr. C.), 3,
    100, 149, 189, 244, et
    passim
  Florence, 418, 419
  Frank, 141
  Lizzie. See Stern
  Mr., 3
  Mrs., 3, 175, 244
  Mrs., on Lombard
    Street, Baltimore, 3
  Mrs. Christian (Mrs.
    C.), 7, 88, 189, 244
  Mrs. Fred, 175
  old Mrs., 175
  Rev. Mr., 419, 423
Steins
  Mr., 392
  Mrs., 392
Stern
  Mr., 83
  Mrs. (Lizzie), née
    Steiner, 83
Stevenson
  Miss H., 89
  Mr., 97, 98
  Sue, 300
Stiener. See Steiner
Stipes, Mrs., 134
Stockton, Rev. Mr., 7
Stone, Mr., 23
Stonebraker
  (Stonebreaker)
  Alice (Miss A.), 86-88
  Almira, 115
  M., 91
  Mrs., 175
Stoner
  Mr. W., 366
  Susan, 282, 366
  Vic, 282, 283, 368
Story, Miss, 87
Stouffer, Elizabeth. See
  Thomas
Stover, Mrs., 6
Stowe, Harriet Beecher,
  107; 174, n. 11, 1855
Strohn, Mrs., 4
Stroup, Elizabeth. See
  Scholl
Styles, Miss, 151, 364
Swope, David, 98
Sybly, Mr., 259
Tanent, Rev. Mr. M., 228
Taneyhills, Misses, 47
Taylor
  A., 68
  Barney, 99
  C., 9, 40
  Chett (C.), 42, 82, 101;
    death of, 109
  Miss E. I., 175
  Mr., 38
  Mrs., 82, 86, 110, 144,
    314, et passim
  Mrs. Griffin (Mrs. G.),
    25, 26, 153
  Mrs. Harry, 139
  Mrs. J. A. (Mrs. J.), 18,
    19, 29
  Mrs. Col., 110
  old Mr., 183

INDEX OF PERSONS

Tell
  Louisa, 132
  Mrs., 309
Tembleson, Mrs., 400
Thayer, Mr., 378
Thomas
  Alfred, cousin of M.S., second son of David, 222. Appendix II
  Alice, cousin of M.S., third daughter of Lewis. Appendix II
  Anna, cousin of M.S., fifth daughter of Lewis. Appendix II
  Caroline (Carrie), cousin of M.S., sixth daughter of Lewis. Appendix II
  Christian, cousin of M.S., son of Lewis. Appendix II
  Christian, first son of Michael. Appendix II
  Clayonia, cousin of M.S., first daughter of Lewis. Appendix II
  David (Uncle D., Uncle D.O.), third son of Michael, 24, n. 45, 1851; 222; purchases Rose Hill, 64, n. 16, 1853; 79; *et passim*
    children of: see Alfred, Jeannette, Joseph, Laura, Lewis, Margaret, and Sarah
    Appendix II
  Dr. Bruce, 419, n. 61, 1860
  Elizabeth (Aunt Liz, Aunt Lizzie), née Stouffer, wife of David, 140, 142. Appendix II
  Fanny, cousin of M.S., second daughter of Lewis. Appendix II
  Felty (Uncle, Uncle F.), 184, 185
  Francis (Ex-Gov., Gov. F.), 403, n. 41, 1860; 414, n. 56, 1860
  Henry (Uncle H.), 18, 61, n. 37, 1851; 193
  Jeannette, cousin of M.S., fourth daughter of David. Appendix II
  Joseph P., cousin of M.S., third son of David. Appendix II
  Joseph T., second son of Michael. Appendix II
  Kitty, wife of William, 344, n. 26, 1858; 358
  Laura (Laura T.), cousin of M.S., third daughter of David, 24. Appendix II
  Lewis C., cousin of M.S., first son of David. Appendix II
  Lewis M., fourth son of Michael, 258
    children of: *see* Alice, Anna, Carrie, Christian, Clayonia, Fanny, and Margaret
    Appendix II
  Margaret, third daughter of Michael. *See* Artz
  Margaret (Grandma, Grandmother), née Ogle, wife of Michael, 13, n. 23, 1851; 17; 23; death of, 152, n. 30, 1854; *et passim*. Appendix II
  Margaret, cousin of M.S., first daughter of David. Appendix II
  Margaret, cousin of M.S., fourth daughter of Lewis. Appendix II
  Maria, second daughter of Michael, mother of M.S. *See* Scholl
  Michael, father of Maria, 344, n. 26, 1858. Appendix II
  Sally, née McDowell, wife of Francis, 403, n. 41, 1860
  Sarah, cousin of M.S., second daughter of David. Appendix II
  Susan, née Snively, wife of Lewis M. Appendix II
  Sybilla, first daughter of Michael. *See* Adams
  William, 344, n. 26, 1858
Thompson, Jemmy, 358
Tiffany, Mr., 309
Tillson, Mattie, 396
Tilyard (Tylard), Alice, 8, 9, 42
Todd, Mr., 91
Trail
  Annie, 193, 262
  Becky, 298
  Charlotte. *See* Markell
  Lewis, 85, 86, 101
  R., 10
Travers, Kate, 134
Trimper, Marie E. *See* Cooper
Trowbridge
  Maria, 373, 375, 378
  Mrs., 271
Troxel (Troxell)
  Jenny, 84, 92
  Kate, 72, 73
  Mr., 69-72
  Mr. F., 69
  Mr. F. J., 73
  Mrs. F., 69
Trump, Mrs., 8, 11
Trundle, William (Mr., Mr. Wm.) 284, 304, 305
Tucker, Mrs., 8, 9, 133
Turner, Jennie. *See* Anderson
Tylard. *See* Tilyard
Tyler
  Annie, 327
  Mrs. G., 17
  Mrs. Sam, 327
  Nan. *See* Page
  William (Dr.), 39, n. 64, 1851; 257, n. 46, 1856
Urhlaub (Uhrlaub)
  Helena, 174
  Mrs., 132, 231, 274, 232, 310, *et passim*
Vance,
  John T. (Mr. V.), 396-398, 400-407, 425
Veitch
  Dr., 414
  Mrs. J. Wesley, 410
Verdi, G., 10

INDEX OF PERSONS

Vermillion, Sallie, 306, n. 51, 1857
Vermilye, Rev. Dr., 355
Vernon
  G., 25
  Mrs., 128
Vondersmith, Miss, 310
W.
  Mrs. William (Mrs. Wm.), 181
  William (Wm.), 181
Wagner, Dr. (Mr.), 134, 135
Waight, Mr., 132
Wallace, General Lew, 296, n. 37, 1857
Wappiler, Father William, 94, n. 37, 1852
Ware, Eveline, 3
Warfield
  Basil, 89
  Kitty, 102
Warner
  Ann. *See* Derr
  Mary, 377
  Miss, 171
Washington, Sophia, 358
Waske
  Mr., 184
  Mrs., 184
Waters
  Dr., 56
  Nannie, 35
Weagly (Weagley)
  Annie, 124
  James (Mr. W.), 15, n. 32, 1851; 53; 181
  Valietta (Mrs. James, Vallie), *née* Adams, wife of James, 15, n. 32, 1851; 68; 117; 181; 309, n. 1, 1858; *et passim*. Appendix II
Weaver, Mr., 101
Webb
  Gussie, 86
  Miss, of Baltimore, 85
  Miss H., 310
  Miss S., 310
  Misses, 274
Webster
  Ellen, 147
  F., 17
  Mr., 7, 230, 273, 274
  Mrs. Jim, 271
Wechebeger, Miss, 5
Weiner, Rev. Mr., 273
Weistling, Maria, 292
Welles, Clinton, 233
Welty, Miss, 252, 253
Wenner, Lidye. *See* Johnson
Wetherson, Kate. *See* Reynolds
Wheatly (Wheatley)
  Mr., 268
  Mrs., 303
White
  Becky, 73
  Dr., 73
  Joel, 399
Whitehouse, Miss, 268
Whorl, Miss, 281
Wiley, Miss, 273
Wilhelm, Miss G., 150
Willard, Mr. E., 45
Williams
  General, 49, n. 73, 1851
  Miss, 174
Williamson, Rev. Mr., 69
Willis
  Mollie, 294
  W. D., 218, n. 7, 1856
Wilson
  Ann Matilda, 129
  C. Olney, née Schley, wife of F. R., 124
  Dr., 130
  F. R., 124
  John, 105
  Mr., 2
  Mrs., 348, 385, 412
  Sam, 151
Winchester
  B. F., 12, n. 19, 1851; 88
  Eva K. (Evie), 25; 47; 58, n. 12, 1853
  F., 336
  Hiram (H.), 14, n. 26, 1851; 58, n. 12, 1853; 156; 336; 393; *et passim*
  Martin (M.), 84
  Mr., 101, 385
  Mrs., 101, 385
  Mrs. B. F., 12, n. 19, 1851; 36; 39; 88; 336; *et passim*
  Mrs. Frank (Mrs. F.) 25, 68, 82
Winebrenner, Mr., 195
Wolfdale, Lottie, 132
Wolf (Wolfe) Dr., 9
  Lewis, 142
  Mag. *See* Brown
  Mr., 142
  Mrs., 171, 175
Wolse, Miss, 34
Wood
  Bob, 41
  Mary E. *See* Hartman
Woodworth,
  Rev. Mr., 406
Worman
  Billy, 276, 356
  Dr. A. D., 413, n. 52, 1860
  Margaret (old Mrs.), 340, n. 24, 1858
  Mary, 167, 365
  Moses, 340, n. 24, 1858
  Mr., 49, 335
  Mrs., 49, 335
Wright
  Miss C., 25, 393
  Mr., 377
Wyatt,
  Rev. Mr., 74
Zacharias
  Annie. *See* Middleton
  Dr. Daniel (Dr. Z., Dr. Zack, Rev. Dr.), pastor of the Frederick Reformed Church, 14, n. 27, 1851; 114; 166; 267; 356; *et passim*
  John (Dr.), 323, 333, 335, 410
  Kate, 37
  Lizzie, 244, 323, 333, 335, 362, *et passim*
  Millie, 335
  Mr., 69
  Mrs., 69, 256
Zell, Miss, 326

Conewago Chapel 1787

Sept 10th Wednesday. Mary, Em. & I went in to spend the day with Kunkels. Lewis came about four o'clock and after tea about eight Annie & Ellen Schley & Ole Sifford & friend Miss Small & Mr. Sifford and son Tom Sen and at nine Mess. Sod & Jimmy Gambril and afterward Ed S. As they did not send for us we remained over night. They company generally left about eleven.

Thursday 11th Very pleasant day. About five o'clock we started into town to go take tea with Mrs. Steiner. Mag Sen Lizzie Jack & Clara Schley were there to tea and after tea Mary & Thomas Sens, Ed S. & Milo Boyd arrived and spent the evening. We left for home about ten o'clock Milo brought Mary & Ed. brought Em & I. We were some time behind them as Ed. walked his horse all the way

Friday 12th Not so warm but cloudy. took a walk after tea & Mary read aloud at night.

Saturday 13th Busy all morning Clear warm day. About four o'clock. Mary Em & I went into town and called at Hincks, Siffords they were not home and to see Kate Hans. She seemed so composed and spoke so much of her little Ada. She died Tuesday night

Sunday Sept 14th Pleasant day. Mary, Em & I went to Lutheran church. Were placed in Mr. B. Eader's Pew and Em had him down street with her. Mother went to our church & had John Sen down street with her. He came up to the spring and asked me to come out home with him and I did so. He staid to dinner Milo Boyd & Thomas Sen came and after tea and they all left about ten o'clock